*Praise for—*

# THE PROM[illegible]ERE



"THIS CAPTIVATING BI[illegible] MRAJ is without precede[illegible] he Incarnation in hum[illegible] s great Teaching orde[illegible] out of the illusion of separateness from God, which is the root of all suffering. If you were allowed to read only one book in your lifetime, this should be the one."

**LOWELL KOBRIN, PH.D., M.D.**
Founding Director, American Academy of Medical Acupuncture

"GENERATIONS FAR INTO THE FUTURE are going to celebrate the incredible story of the Ruchira Avatar and His devotees—which is not just High Dharma; it is also high drama. Everything is here: genius, tenderness, Blessing beyond belief; fragility, despair, unquenchable sorrow. I have fallen profoundly in love with this Great Being! His Presence here is a miracle of Divine Intervention."

**DAVID SAWYER**
Recipient, President's Points of Light Award

"MY SELF-CONSTRICTED EGO BRISTLES at the implied Messianism of the title, 'the Promised God-Man Is Here'—yet if God-consciousness is fully present as a liberating force in human form, why should there be any equivocating? His devotees are convinced and Carolyn Lee has assembled a lucid in-depth look at Adi Da, spreading the good news of his incarnation by telling his life story and giving an insider's view of his radical teaching efforts to awaken devotees. I've been inspired by Adi Da's writings for many years. He is a contemporary spiritual Hero, offering his transcendental gifts to a culture without a tradition for or even 'taste' for Avatars . . . yet he bears the burdens of sagehood with persistence and love."

**ALEX GREY**
Artist and author, *Sacred Mirrors: The Visionary Art of Alex Grey*

"Dr. Lee has pulled back the veil of mystery and allowed us to meet the god-man behind the curtain. The interviews are intriguing. The history is captivating. The teachings are challenging. This book is 'must' reading for anyone interested in the Promised God-Man."

**Rabbi Rami M. Shapiro**
Author, *Minyan: Ten Principles for Living Life with Integrity*

"There is no more astonishing and wondrous communication than, 'The Promised God-Man is here.' And yet it is so. The life story of Avatar Adi Da Samraj communicates this truth in a way which outshines the mind and awakens the heart. There is no grace greater than to be heart-moved by this revelation of the Heart of Being."

**Anthony Corones, Ph.D.**
Lecturer, University of New South Wales, Australia

"I have been writing and editing in the field of health and healing for over twenty years. But I know that the Divine Heart-Master is the Ultimate Healer—because He is the only One Who can awaken you beyond all disease, all change, all suffering, beyond even death itself, to His very Nature: Eternal and Omnipresent Conscious Light.

"Avatar Adi Da Samraj is the Divine Heart-Master, the Promised God-Man, the True Healer. And even this book, this Leela or story of His Life, transmits His power to heal—to restore you to sanity and ease, as you recognize and feel that the Divine Being, Real God, is here in human Form, offering you a life of ecstatic Communion with Him. Read this book; fall in love with Adi Da Samraj; be healed at heart."

**Bill Gottlieb**
Editor, *New Choices In Natural Healing*

"THIS REMARKABLE BIOGRAPHY OF THE SPIRITUAL MASTER and God-Realizer Adi Da Samraj is a MUST for anyone concerned with Spiritual values."

**GEOFFREY DAW**
Jungian Analyst, New Zealand

"THE WAY OF ADIDAM—THE WORLD-RELIGION revealed by Avatar Adi Da Samraj—brings together the essentials of all the great religions—and goes beyond them. It gives new life to religion by directly demonstrating that all beings and things are constantly emerging and changing within a universal state of Conscious Light. In great detail, *The Promised God-Man Is Here* gives example after example of what it means to be a practitioner of Adidam, in relationship with Avatar Adi Da Samraj, the human embodiment of the Divine. These practitioners are wise, judicious, mature, loving people who give an account of absolute vital importance to us all. Please read this book and evaluate Adi Da and the Way of Adidam for yourself."

**JOHN MORRIS, PH.D.**
Professor Emeritus, University of Manchester, England

"WHEN I FIRST READ THE WORD OF AVATAR ADI DA SAMRAJ, I was immediately transported into a state of wonderment and awe. Could it be? Could the Divine Person be here now, in this time and place? It didn't take long for my heart to answer a resounding 'Yes'. May the whole world be restored to Faith, Love, and Understanding by the Mystery of Real God, here and Incarnate as Avatar Adi Da Samraj. Read *The Promised God-Man Is Here*—and find out about Him."

**EDWARD KOWALCZYK**
Lead singer, "Live"

"*The Promised God-Man Is Here* should be required reading for anyone interested in religion. Carolyn Lee has written this work in a way that compels the reader's attention throughout. All of the major events of Adi Da's extraordinary life and work are covered, and the Guru-disciple relationship is depicted in a most colorful way."

**Duncan Bazemore, Ph.D.**
Professor Emeritus, Department of Religious Studies and Philosophy,
Humboldt State University

"Reading *The Promised God-Man Is Here* puts you into direct relationship with the Divine Being, Avatar Adi Da Samraj. This relationship starts where all other spiritual systems seek to end—face-to-face with the Living Embodiment of Perfect Love."

**Arthur Brown**
Singer, *The Crazy World of Arthur Brown*

"I was swept along, enraptured by every page, unable to put this book down. The life of the living Spiritual Master Avatar Adi Da Samraj is truly the greatest story ever told. Read this book and find out why."

**Gary Coates**
Professor, Kansas State University
Author, *Resettling America: Energy, Ecology and Community*

"As I read *The Promised God-Man Is Here*, the Force of this incredible story washed over and through me. Moving before my eyes and heart were story after story of the lives of devotees being converted to Truth; passage after passage of Avatar Adi Da's talks, essays, ecstatic and poetic communications—some never before published; Divine Compassion, Brilliance, Genius, Love, Fierceness, Blissfulness revealed in every chapter, every story. Adi Da's Heroic struggle and victory with and in His devotees, and, through them, with and in the whole world, came alive in these pages. It became clear that every illusion, false presumption, action of un-love—every aspect of existence in this realm—has been Penetrated, Illumined, and En-Lightened by this Great Avadhoot of our time, via His Heroic Work of Love with His devotees, the most ordinary people, representing every kind and walk of life.

"As I turned the last page, I knew in every cell of my body, that this story could only have been enacted by the Very Divine, God Himself. No other being could have wrought such changes, evoked such love, penetrated so deeply the prevailing ego-presumptions, made Himself so vulnerable, yet acted with such selfless courage. The sheer scope of His work in the short period of His life and work are testament to His uniqueness, even amongst the great Spiritual Realizers. In that moment, I knew that the Divine Had Firmly Set His Staff in this world, and that all would come to turn to Him, and that everything in the world has been changed.

"I am so grateful to Carolyn Lee for setting this Greatest of Tales to paper; and grateful beyond words that the 'story' was and is there to be told. I invite everyone to partake of this great feast—to read this book, to participate in the unfolding story, and thereby be changed forever."

**Elizabeth Lowe (Edgerton), M.A.**
Clinical and Humanistic Psychology

"THIS BOOK DOES NOT OFFER ANOTHER METHOD, sales pitch, or guide to self-improvement. *The Promised God-Man Is Here* is a global wake-up call, a startlingly profound invitation to a relationship founded in Truth and forged in an incomparably compassionate Love—a love without equal in all experience. This is the Life-Story of the Greatest Spiritual Being of all time—the Divine Being, in Person. Avatar Adi Da Samraj has come to Demand our Hearts and Dissolve the world's suffering in the Intimacy of His Eternal Embrace. He is Here! He is Waiting for you. Surrender to the Reality of Love with the Divine Incarnate!"

**LEE C. HARRISON**
*AptLee Written Technical Publications*

"*THE PROMISED GOD-MAN IS HERE* is an outstanding contribution to Spiritual literature. Carolyn Lee takes the reader through the entire development and rise of the religion of Adidam and the epochs of Adi Da Samraj's work with such clarity and detail that one feels as though one is actually there, living and feeling the intensity and importance of these historic occasions. The inclusion of large portions of Avatar Adi Da's writings, and testimonies from devotees, provide the reader the opportunity to experience these years from all perspectives.

"Dr. Lee's biography is a great service to current and future generations, and to all who are fortunate enough to be drawn to the Divine Work of Avatar Adi Da Samraj."

**GREG WILSON, PH.D.**
Senior Lecturer, Southern Cross University, Australia

# THE PROMISED GOD-MAN IS HERE

# THE PROMISED

# GOD-MAN IS HERE

The Extraordinary Life-Story,
The "Crazy" Teaching Work,
and The Divinely "Emerging"
World-Blessing Work of
The Divine World-Teacher
of the "Late-Time",

## RUCHIRA AVATAR ADI DA SAMRAJ

BY CAROLYN LEE, Ph.D.

THE DAWN HORSE PRESS
MIDDLETOWN, CALIFORNIA

## NOTE TO THE READER

All who study the Way of Adidam or take up its practice should remember that they are responding to a Call to become responsible for themselves. They should understand that they, not Avatar Adi Da Samraj or others, are responsible for any decision they make or action they take in the course of their lives of study or practice.

The devotional, Spiritual, functional, practical, relational, cultural, and formal community practices and disciplines referred to in this book are appropriate and natural practices that are voluntarily and progressively adopted by members of the four congregations of Adidam (as applicable for each of the congregations and as appropriate to the personal circumstance of each individual). Although anyone may find these practices useful and beneficial, they are not presented as advice or recommendations to the general reader or to anyone who is not a member of one of the four congregations of Adidam. And nothing in this book is intended as a diagnosis, prescription, or recommended treatment or cure for any specific "problem", whether medical, emotional, psychological, social, or Spiritual. One should apply a particular program of treatment, prevention, cure, or general health only in consultation with a licensed physician or other qualified professional.

This biography of Ruchira Avatar Adi Da Samraj is formally authorized for publication by the Ruchira Sannyasin Order of the Tantric Renunciates of Adidam. (The Ruchira Sannyasin Order of the Tantric Renunciates of Adidam is the senior Spiritual and Cultural Authority within the formal gathering of formally acknowledged devotees of the Divine World-Teacher, Ruchira Avatar Adi Da Samraj.)

NOTE TO BIBLIOGRAPHERS: The correct form for citing Ruchira Avatar Adi Da Samraj's Name (in any form of alphabetized listing) is:

Adi Da Samraj, Ruchira Avatar



Printed in the United States of America

Produced by the Eleutherian Pan-Communion of Adidam
in cooperation with the Dawn Horse Press

International Standard Book Number: 1-57097-059-9
Library of Congress Catalog Card Number: 98-89626

Cover illustration of Avatar Adi Da Samraj by Malec Fustok

# CONTENTS

---

## A NOTE ABOUT THE USE OF CAPITALIZATION AND SACRED TERMINOLOGY IN THIS BOOK

Out of respect and recognition of Avatar Adi Da Samraj, His devotees capitalize references to Him and His Divine Work and Realization. This is a way to honor Him and indicate the sacred nature of His Revelation.

Avatar Adi Da Samraj has also transformed the English language to serve the Communication of the sacred Process in His Company. In doing so, He has Revealed the logic underlying the common conventions of written English:

*Ordinary speech and written language are centered on the ego-"I", as a tent is raised on a centerpole. Therefore, in ordinary speech and written language, the ego-word "I" is commonly capitalized, and everything less than the ego-"I" is shown in lowercase.*

In contrast, the "centerpole" of Avatar Adi Da's Speech and Writing is the Heart, the Divine, Consciousness, Truth, Reality, and Happiness. Therefore, He capitalizes those words that express the Ecstatic Feeling of the Awakened Heart, and, in many instances, lowercases those words expressive of the ego or conditional limits in general.

In writing this Story of Avatar Adi Da's Divine Life and Work, it has also been necessary to use some technical sacred terminology, including Sanskrit words, in order to properly convey the depth of Avatar Adi Da's Gift to mankind. An extensive set of endnotes (pp. 790-816) provide definitions for these terms, as well as elaboration on points made in the text.

There is also an appendix (pp. 786-89) that gives correct pronunciation for many of the non-English terms used in this book.

—CL

Ruchira Avatar Adi Da Samraj
The Mountain Of Attention Sanctuary, 1998

INTRODUCTION

# The Answer to Human Prayers

What does it mean to say, "The Promised God-Man is here"?

Turn to the teachings of the principal religions—Buddhist, Hindu, Christian, Jewish, Muslim—and you will find an ancient prophecy common to all: There is an All-Surpassing God-Man yet to come—a final Avatar, an ultimate Messiah, a consummate Prophet or Enlightened Sage, a Spiritual Deliverer who will appear in the "late-time", the "dark" epoch*[1] when humanity is lost, apparently cut off from Wisdom, Truth, and God. Buddhists call that Expected One "Maitreya"; Hindus, the "Kalki Avatar"; Christians, the "second coming of Jesus"; Jews, the "Messiah"; Muslims, the "Mahdhi". In other words, the great religious traditions all promise a future Bringer of Salvation and Liberation, One Who will perfectly answer all human prayers.

The darkness of this time cannot be denied. Decade by decade, the atrocities of the twentieth century have escalated, with the ever more efficient mechanization of mass murder and the wanton destruction of nature. Today's news is a litany of personal and political violence, of uncontrolled epidemics and threatened extinctions. The globe is not merely warming—it is on fire with strife and suffering. If ever there was the need for the Supreme Avatar, the Living God Incarnate in human Form, that time is now.

* Notes to the text of *The Promised God-Man Is Here* are on pp. 790-816.

Our confession to you, as the devotees of Avatar Adi Da Samraj, is that the One Prophesied has Come. The God-Man Promised for all humankind, and even for all beings, is here—in the Person of the Ruchira Avatar (the Divine Incarnation of "Brightness"),[2] Adi Da Samraj.[3]

It makes no sense to merely tell you this, as if "the Promised God-Man is here" were a dogma to be believed. The Truth of this confession must be Revealed, made known directly to the heart—and that is the purpose of this book. You have in your hands the evidence of a living Revelation—full of confessions, by ordinary men and women, of how the Divine Reality and Truth that people call "God" has been shown to them in Person. You will read of the amazement and joy that accompanies such heart-recognition of Adi Da Samraj—and of the great devotional response and life-conversion that follow.

What is He like?

Avatar Adi Da Samraj is what has traditionally been called a "Crazy-Wise" Master.[4] In other words, He does not conform to the conventional image of a "holy man". As you will discover in this book, He is not an ascetic. He does not withdraw from human existence in the slightest. Rather, He has done His Spiritual Work and established a new and unique Spiritual way of life, the Way of Adidam,[5] within the sphere of human impulses and desires—rather than calling people to effortfully "rise above" the realities of bodily life.

Avatar Adi Da Samraj Awakens His devotees by a Play of Love that stops the mind and Awakens the heart. This Play of Love is what Avatar Adi Da Samraj has been doing all His life. He was doing it with His parents even at an early age, as you will read in the first chapter. He has loved and suffered human beings to the very depths. And He is still doing so. He can never withdraw, no matter how great the struggle.

Great struggle is part of His Story. Why? Because the process required in order for human beings to be Saved, Awakened, and Set Free in Real God[6] is not magic. It is a great and passionate ordeal, and requires each one to go beyond everything that is about "self", or "ego". As this Story shows, to attract ordinary men and women into this profound process of going beyond "self" required everything of Adi Da Samraj—His Genius, Humor, and relentless Love, and also His Divine Powers, which go beyond any ordinary or extraordinary explanation.

There is tremendous emotion and passion in this Story, on the part of Avatar Adi Da Himself, and also expressed in the voices of His devotees. You cannot come face to Face, heart to Heart, with the One you recognize as the Living God and not be changed from the inside out. And so, to read the Story of Avatar Adi Da Samraj is an initiation into this sphere of intense feeling.

The import of this Story is that, through the Incarnation of Avatar Adi Da Samraj, the Very Divine is literally "Emerging" into this world—Spiritually Pervading the world, in a way that has never occurred before. In face-to-face dialogue with His devotees, Avatar Adi Da has occasionally spoken of how He was Moved to Incarnate, and the immensity of that Process:

*AVATAR ADI DA SAMRAJ: Thousands of years of Sacrifice, and Endeavor, and Purpose, and Spiritual Practice, and Realization, and Love, and Compassion were required for My bodily (human) Birth. Some day, you may understand My Birth. It was no casual gesture. And it could never have happened before now. Some day, you may understand that My human Lifetime is a unique moment in the history of humankind. Even in all these "eons of shaking", the Impulse of the Divine Person to Incarnate persisted, undaunted, and could not be destroyed or ruined. Real God is willing to Love you and all beings,*

*and that Divine Purpose must be Fulfilled. That is My Unique Impulse. Here I Am, Incarnate, to Do That Work. A thousand years may pass before anyone understands anything about My Appearance here. So much suffering accompanies It, so much was required of Me to Submit to your company.*

*DEVOTEE: How was that Decision made?*

*AVATAR ADI DA SAMRAJ: By Love. To Encompass the totality of conditional[7] existence, in Love—That is the Sign of My Appearance here. By Appearing here bodily before You, I have Submitted to Love all and All, to be Compassionate toward all and All, to Serve all and All. And, in My Embrace of all and All, I have utterly Submitted to this mortal circumstance of sorrow and death. Such Submission never destroyed Me. It cannot destroy Me, for the One Who I Am can never be destroyed. But Love, the Impulse to Kiss you—just to Kiss you, to not deny you—made Me a Body to Live with you. Can't you see it in My Face?* [September 9, 1987]

May the extraordinary Story of Avatar Adi Da Samraj attract and open your heart. May it awaken in you a living certainty that the long-awaited Miracle, the Event of the ages, has occurred: The Promised God-Man is here.

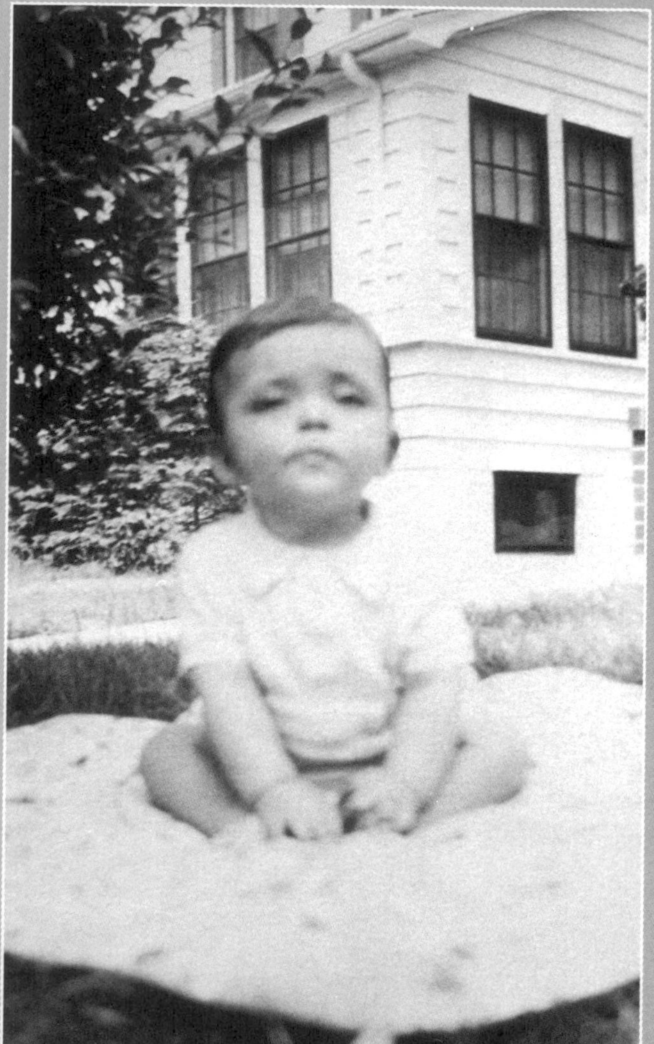

*"From my earliest experience of life I have Enjoyed a Condition that, as a child, I called the 'Bright'."*

CHAPTER 1

# Born as the "Bright"

On November 3, 1939, Avatar Adi Da Samraj was born in a suburban hospital in Long Island, New York. There were no outward signs to suggest the profundity of the event; there were no prophets or seers to declare the universal significance of what was taking place. But, in that moment, the Eternal Divine Person—the Ultimate Condition and Source of everyone and everything—was taking birth as a human being.

Avatar Adi Da has a clear memory of the moment of His birth—during which He was nearly strangled by His own umbilical cord. He was not unconscious, nor was His awareness confined to His struggling body. While the doctors worked to bring His body from the womb, Avatar Adi Da Samraj remained in His Divine State of Being—an infinite Sphere of Radiance and Love that He later called "the 'Bright'".

Throughout His infancy, Avatar Adi Da Samraj remained free of the limits of His human birth. He felt associated with the body, but not defined or identified by it, the way an ordinary individual feels that his or her happiness—and very existence—is dependent on the state and the survival of the body. Rather, Avatar Adi Da Samraj felt His body to be arising in and as the "Bright". As He writes in His Spiritual Autobiography, *The Knee Of Listening*:

*From my earliest experience of life I have Enjoyed a Condition that, as a child, I called the "Bright". . . .*

*Even as a baby I remember only crawling around inquisitively with a boundless Feeling of Joy, Light, and Freedom in the middle of my head that was bathed in Energy moving unobstructed in a Circle, down from above, all the way down, then up, all the way up, and around again, and always Shining from my heart. It was an Expanding Sphere of Joy from the heart. And I was a Radiant Form, the Source of Energy, Love-Bliss, and Light in the midst of a world that is entirely Energy, Love-Bliss, and Light. I was the Power of Reality, a direct Enjoyment and Communication of the One Reality.*

## Forgetting the "Bright"

If Avatar Adi Da Samraj had simply remained in the Free and Radiant State, He could not have fulfilled the Purpose of His Incarnation, the Divine Work for which He had been born—to Awaken each and every human being to the Living Truth of the "Bright". To do this Great Work, He had to make a profound Sacrifice. He had to "forget" the Divine Condition in which He was born. He had to live an apparently ordinary human life, identified with an apparently individual body-mind. He had to lose the "Bright", so that He could learn how to locate or Realize It again—and thereby become able to Teach others the Way to Realize the "Bright" Happiness and Freedom of His Divine Awareness.

The Divine Person had to become human so that He could Teach all of humanity how to Realize the Divine.

Avatar Adi Da remembers the critical moment when His Submission to the human state occurred. One day, sometime after His second birthday, as Avatar Adi Da was crawling across a linoleum floor, His parents let

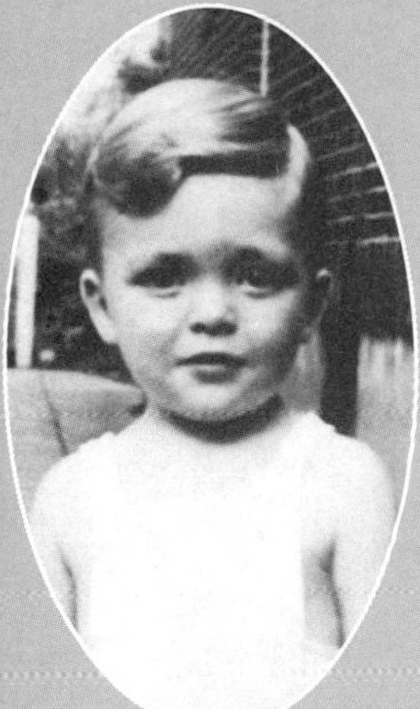

*My Avataric[1] Birth Is Unique. I Must Surrender and Submit My Very (and Inherently Perfect) Divine Self-Condition In Order To Incarnate. Therefore, To Be Born, I Had To Submit To The limiting Power Of The Cosmic Domain.[2] I Assumed the body-mind of an ordinary man. That Birth Was The Apparent (or merely psycho-physical) Forgetting Of My Divine State and My "Bright" Power Of Divine Being. Quickly, The Inherent Self-Knowledge Of Who I Am Receded From Consciousness To Subconsciousness To Unconsciousness—Such That Only A Fierce (and Mysteriously "Bright") Impulse Remained.*

*The Sacrifice The Divine Heart-Master Must Make In Order To Incarnate Is Real. Therefore, Once I Was Born, My Life Became A Profound Ordeal Of Spiritual and Transcendental Divine Self-Realization,[3] and Subsequent Teaching and Blessing Work To Awaken all others.*

THE DAWN HORSE TESTAMENT
OF THE RUCHIRA AVATAR

loose a new puppy they were giving Him. In the instant of seeing the puppy and seeing His parents, Avatar Adi Da Samraj spontaneously identified with His human body-mind. In other words, He took on the sense of being an "I", separate from all other "I's", and allowed His own great State of Being to begin receding into unconsciousness. From that moment on, Avatar Adi Da consciously became "Franklin Jones"—the son of Frank and Dorothy Jones, a middle-class couple living in the Long Island suburb of Franklin Square, New York.

*AVATAR ADI DA SAMRAJ: My Identification with mortal existence occurred through sympathetic response. It was not merely a response to the puppy—it certainly was that, because the puppy was the nearest to Me in physical space—but then there was also the glance toward My parents. It was simply and altogether a sympathetic response that brought Me into the sphere of human conditions (and gross[4] conditions altogether). So it was a kind of delight—not merely some effortful identification with mortal existence. It was not the noticing of mortality, in and of itself, that generated My Movement into this plane.*

*Rather, it was the Love-Response, the attracted Response, in which all of the negative aspects of gross conditional existence were effectively forgotten—in Love, in Delight, in Love-Bliss.* [February 9, 1998]

While Avatar Adi Da Samraj spontaneously and fully surrendered to become like those around Him, an intuition still remained. In the depth of His Being, He was committed to recovering the Joy of the "Bright" and finding a way to bring that Joy to others.

He recalls an occasion, when He was about seven years old, of walking with His parents to the movies. The moment stands out in His memory as His most significant early attempt to consciously communicate love in the midst of conflict. His parents were quarreling about something, and He felt how that act of separation was destroying a web of love-energy that was all around them. He could actually see that precious tissue of love torn with holes, and He tried to repair it by silently expanding love from His heart. At the same time, He began to ask His parents questions about God, and to point out to them the beautiful full moon. Their quarrel quieted down, but, later, as He sat in the movie, Avatar Adi Da realized that He had borne the cost of the conflict. He describes how He felt a pain in His heart—"where the love-energy had been pushed back". Nevertheless, Avatar Adi Da felt that what He had just done was fundamental to His Purpose in life. As He put it in *The Knee Of Listening*, He was resolved to Restore the "True Humor" of the "Bright". In other words, He was determined to Awaken in every human being (and, indeed, in all living beings) the Freedom, Love, and Blissfulness that He knew to be the native Truth of things.

# Childhood and Early Youth

Avatar Adi Da was an immensely humorous and creative child—a puppeteer, an artist, a marvelous story-teller—and a lover of the outdoor life, swimming, fishing, playing in the woods. He lived in natural sympathy with all living things, and had many friends, including all kinds of pets (even, at one point, a monkey).

One of Avatar Adi Da's exuberant childhood pastimes was ventriloquy, in which He developed an unusual degree of skill for a child, offering special performances for His school friends, family, and neighbors. The highlight of His "career" as a ventriloquist came when His father took Him to see the renowned ventriloquist Paul Winchell, who was appearing in person—with his dummy, "Jerry Mahoney"—at a department store in Manhattan. Avatar Adi Da described the event to His devotees:

*AVATAR ADI DA SAMRAJ: When Paul Winchell made his appearance at Macy's, he looked out into the audience, and there I was sitting with My Jerry Mahoney dummy in the front row. So he invited Me up on the stage with him, thinking he would have some fun at My expense.*

*Well, I got up there, and he started bantering with Me through his Jerry Mahoney. So I started bantering back with him through My dummy. But because I had a whole mass of skit and practiced lines, we went on quipping for over half an hour! His dummy did something and My dummy would do something, on and on.*

*At the end of it, My father went up to Paul Winchell and said how great it would be for his son to appear on Paul's TV show, which was on several times a week. Paul liked the idea, and they exchanged business cards and agreed to follow up on the idea.*

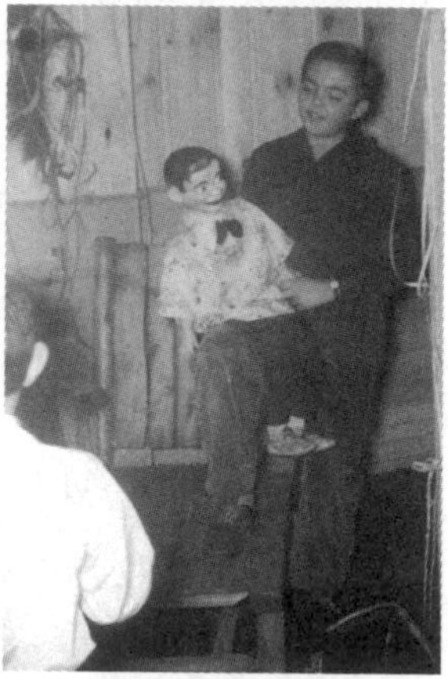

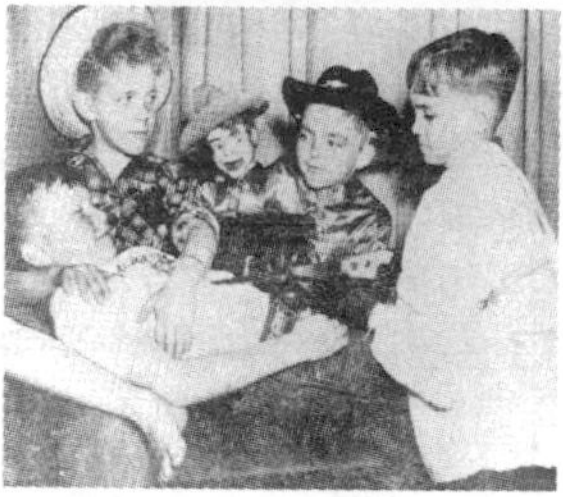

*While Avatar Adi Da Samraj spontaneously and fully surrendered to become like those around Him, an intuition still remained. In the depth of His Being, He was committed to recovering the Joy of the "Bright" and finding a way to bring that Joy to others.*

*But when My father came back and told Me, I said I was not interested. I just have never been interested in that kind of visibility. And he had to explain this to the producers who called to discuss My being on the show. I just was not moved to do it purely for the sake of visibility. As soon as it came to that point, I did not want to go on with it.*

*It is the same way now. I am not seeking fame. There is a Great Spiritual Influence that I am Motivated to Introduce into your lives, for your sake, but I do not want visibility merely for its own sake. This is the way it has always been for Me.* [February 23, 1983]

Avatar Adi Da completely embraced the Lutheran Christianity of His family. He was, by His own confession, "a religious ecstatic" from His earliest youth. While sitting in church and in Sunday school class, He would spontaneously enter into trance-like states of mystical rapture. He would begin swooning in Bliss, making incoherent gasps and other noises. And sometimes, through the force of His Spiritual absorption, His eyes would suddenly "bug out", or roll up to the top of their sockets—much to the annoyance of the pastor! In His early teens, Avatar Adi Da became an altar-server, and then a liturgist, or reader. As He stood before the congregation, reading from the Bible, something remarkable would happen. Avatar Adi Da would notice that people would fall into ecstasy. There was a Power in Him, communicated through His voice, to which they were responding.

While Happiness was the outstanding sign of Avatar Adi Da's childhood, the darker side of life, its mortality and suffering, was always part of His awareness. In *The Knee Of Listening*, He writes:

*If my Purpose, even from the beginning of this lifetime, has always been to restore True Humor, and, likewise, if my Motive has always been Founded in the "Bright", death*

With Bootsie

*and the fear of death have, also from the beginning of this lifetime, always been the counter to my Presence, the source of contradiction, fear, mystery, and despair.*

The question of death took on a profound force for Avatar Adi Da when He was nine or ten years old. His constant companion at that time was Bootsie, a black cocker spaniel, whom He loved passionately. One day, He went down to the cellar, which was His own special domain in His parents' house, and found Bootsie—dead and rigid, lying in a big chair. It was Avatar Adi Da's first concrete experience of death. Immediately, He fell into deep despair. After hours of desperate crying and earnest consolation from His parents, Avatar Adi Da managed some outward control of His grief. But, inwardly, He was not in the least consoled. He could not live with such a loss of a loved one, and so He formed an awesome resolve. Avatar Adi Da asked God to take His life at an appointed time—in two days, at nine o'clock on the following Sunday evening.

As the fateful hour approached, Avatar Adi Da deeply regretted His vow. He felt the joy of His own aliveness, and He realized that death did not mean the end of life and love. But He would not bargain with God by attempting to change His vow. He simply awaited what He felt to be His inevitable death.

The hour came and went and Avatar Adi Da did not die. Nevertheless, for weeks He felt a constriction in His chest, as though His heart had been crippled in some way by the ordeal of grief and His own consent to relinquish life. Later He wrote in *The Knee Of Listening*: "I saw how the sentiment of separation from love can, as a problem or concern in the living consciousness, draw one out of the 'Bright' of Illuminated, Free Consciousness, until one no longer perceives the perfect Form that is always here."

Avatar Adi Da's confrontation with death also took place in His own body—even from the moment of His birth, when His breath was cut off by the umbilical cord. Altogether, His birth in human form required a great initial struggle at the physical level. Just as electrical wires will burn out if the current passing through them is too strong, so the fragile mechanism of a human body had to be prepared, in Avatar Adi Da's case, to conduct immense Divine Energy, or Spirit-Power. His childhood was full of the signs of this ordeal. There were many occasions, in fact, when He felt He was going to die, consumed by a literal burning Force that took the form of strange diseases, intense fevers, and delirium. Often connected with these bouts was a powerful Spiritual experience that Avatar Adi Da, as a child, named "the Thumbs".

*At apparently random times, from my early childhood, usually as I either approached sleep or awoke from sleep, and, most dramatically, during seizures of childhood illness, as I would pass into delirium, I had an experience that appeared like a mass of gigantic thumbs coming down from above, pressing into my throat (causing something of a gagging, and somewhat suffocating, sensation), and then pressing further (and, it seemed, would have expanded without limitation or end), into some form of myself that was much larger than my physical body. . . . "The Thumbs" were not visible in the ordinary sense. I did not see them . . . They were not visible to me with my eyes, nor did I hallucinate them pictorially. Yet, I very consciously experienced and felt them as having a peculiar form and mobility, as I likewise experienced my own otherwise invisible and greater form. I did not . . . at any time in my childhood fully allow this intervention of "the Thumbs" to take place. I held it off from its fullest descent, in fear of being overwhelmed, for I did not understand at all what was taking place. However, in later years this same experience occurred naturally during meditation. Because my meditation had been allowed to progress gradually, and the realizations at each level were thus perceived without shock, I was able at those times to allow the experience to take place. When I did, "the Thumbs" completely entered my living form.* [The Knee Of Listening]

Through His childhood experiences of "the Thumbs", Avatar Adi Da was learning to receive the Force of the "Bright". His human body was being prepared to contain and Transmit to all others the Love-Bliss-Power of His Divinity. Avatar Adi Da would later describe "the Thumbs" as one of the unique signs associated with His Incarnation:

*AVATAR ADI DA SAMRAJ: The principal Sign in My early Life was My Intention to Descend, to Appear here, to Embrace in every aspect the limitation of human mortality, human existence, as it is, as it appears. The characteristic Samadhi*[5] *of My childhood, or of My Life altogether—you could even say, of My Work altogether—was the Samadhi of "the Thumbs".*[6] *"The Thumbs" is about My Divine Descent, the Crashing Down*[7] *of Real God. "The Thumbs" is the Secret of My early Life.* [February 18, 1993]

## The Teen Years

As His teenage years advanced, Avatar Adi Da became less and less aware of the "Bright". He no longer lived in the innocent world of His childhood. His daily life had become the humdrum round of American high-school adolescence. Long afterwards, He referred to that time as "the gray years", a period when His chief pleasure in life was a fascination with ham radio. But there was a moment in Avatar Adi Da's high-school

***As His teenage years advanced, Avatar Adi Da became less and less aware of the "Bright". He no longer lived in the innocent world of His childhood.***

career—the occasion of a speech contest organized by the American Legion—that was highly significant.

When the day came, Avatar Adi Da stood up in an auditorium filled with perhaps a thousand people, prepared to give His speech—called "Patterns of Prejudice". In the front rows He looked down on His most testing audience—a crowd of gum-chewing, heavy-booted, leather-jacketed, hair-slicked youths known in the fifties as "hoods". They were there under sufferance, their feet up on the chairs, not ready to be impressed. As Avatar Adi Da began to speak, the same "Bright" Power rose in Him that captured the Lutheran congregation. People became visibly moved, happy, even entranced. The hoods sat up, full of attention, interest, and respect, as Avatar Adi Da called for the wholehearted acceptance of all minorities—Jews, blacks, and every ethnic group. It was a triumphant day—He won the contest.

But the sentiments expressed by Avatar Adi Da were ahead of their time; it was 1956, and the full force of the civil rights movement in America was still several years away. And so, not surprisingly, at the next level of the contest, there was a different kind of audience. When Avatar Adi Da stood up to speak, He felt a hostility, a barrier of prejudice that would not receive His communication. He did not feel the fullness of the "Bright" on this occasion. It was as if the "Bright" Itself was not responding to the gathering.

That day, Avatar Adi Da did not win the contest. He even felt embarrassed that He had spoken so sincerely about universal brotherhood in an atmosphere of what He later described as merely "picnic patriotism". But some members of the audience did come up to Him afterwards to voice their support, hinting that His loss had been a "political" decision. One admirer grasped Avatar Adi Da's hand and said earnestly, "Never let them stop you from thinking."

## The Search for Truth

A unique exercise in "thinking" was, in fact, not far off. When Avatar Adi Da graduated from high school in 1957, He entered one of the most prestigious academies of "thinking" in the country at that time—Columbia College, in New York. But Avatar Adi Da felt no exhilaration at the prospect of intellectual success and a brilliant career. By now, He was nearly eighteen, and His apparent loss of the "Bright" had reached its lowest point. He was in despair.

More than ever, Avatar Adi Da was possessed with a question that He had been probing for years: "What is Consciousness?" By "Consciousness" He meant that very sense of existence, or awareness of simply being, which is constant in us—whatever the events and changes of life. Avatar Adi Da had always felt that Consciousness was senior to the body, senior to death. His entire experience of the "Bright" suggested that seniority, as did the Christian beliefs that had been passed on to Him through His Lutheran upbringing. But what was the connection between Consciousness and the physical world? How were these two realities related to each other? He was completely given over to this investigation. For Him, it was crucial to the meaning of everything.

But there were no ultimate answers to be found at Columbia. In fact, Avatar Adi Da was devastated to find that the prevailing dogma at Columbia was that of scientific materialism, which holds that the fundamental reality is the physical world, and everything "greater" or "higher"—Consciousness, or Spirit, or God—is either a by-product of physical reality or else a mere hallucination. In the modern scientific view, consciousness is an electro-chemical process originating in the brain, and, therefore, dependent on the survival of the body. Thus, according to this opinion, consciousness, which is intuitively felt to be the most fundamental condition of the individual, disappears at death.

Avatar Adi Da's stark confrontation with twentieth-century secularism in His first six months at Columbia destroyed the naive religious faith of His childhood, pointing only toward doubt and Godless rationalism. In fact, the keynote had been set by the President's speech delivered during Avatar Adi Da's first week at Columbia. Avatar Adi Da still remembers the President's summary message: education at Columbia will not be able to make you happy, but it will teach you how to think. Avatar Adi Da later described to His devotees the extraordinary impact of His time at Columbia—both its virtue and its difficulty:

*AVATAR ADI DA SAMRAJ: Before I went to Columbia, My life was almost utterly bereft of ideas, of real "consideration",[8] of the exercise of intelligence. It was the ordinary, mundane life of ordinary people.*

*So, when I went to Columbia, it was like going to another planet. All of a sudden, there were not only immense amounts of reading, which I had never done before (we would read in a few weeks what others would do in a year at other schools, really), but an intense demand on intelligence.*

*I was studying philosophy there, and I was not judged on the basis of being able to remember quotations, either from historical philosophers or from university lecturers. It was simply and directly about this exercise of intelligence. I was constantly addressed about it. If I was just repeating something I had heard, the questions would come: "What is logical about that? 'There is only One.' Why One? Why not three? Why not seven?" There was a constant address to how I was using My intelligence.*

*It was a very hard school, and the presumptions I had gathered as a boy, from that simple life and simple religion on Long Island, were utterly shattered. That was good, ultimately. But it was a shocking and devastating experience! It brought Me to the Zero of Purity, of Intelligence. And I had to work Myself out of it.*

*I did not really care about the content of that education—the propaganda, the scientific materialism. That was just terrible. But this development of the capability to exercise intelligence is something I began to use on My own, based on My own Heart-Impulse.* [December 13, 1993]

In fact, Columbia became the first great turning point in the Life of Avatar Adi Da. Paradoxically, His years there were the beginning of His moving beyond mere identification with the body-mind, the Submission to limited human awareness that He had made at the age of two. He was urged on by desperation, unable to tolerate that confined awareness, now that the religious faith of His childhood had been devastated. There was no one to guide Him, and so He chose to confront the agony of Godlessness head on, through an heroic course—the course of exhaustive experience. His conviction was this: "If God exists, He will not cease to exist by any action of my own, but, if I devote myself to all possible experience, He will indeed find some way, in some one or a complex of my experiences, or my openness itself, to reveal Himself to me." Thus, Avatar Adi Da Samraj gave Himself up to every experience and possibility, with the force of a vow:

*No experience posed a barrier to me. There were no taboos, no extremes to be prevented. There was no depth of madness and no limit of suffering that my philosophy could prevent, for, if it did, I would be liable to miss the Lesson of Reality. Thus, I extended myself even beyond my own fear. And my pleasures also became extreme, so there was a constant machine of ecstasy. I could tolerate no mediocrity, no medium experience. I was satisfied with neither atheism nor belief. Both seemed to me only ideas, possible reactions to a more fundamental if unconscious fact. I sought Reality, to be Reality, What is, not what is asserted in the face of What is.* [The Knee Of Listening]

Avatar Adi Da had spontaneously chosen what is traditionally known in the East as "prapatti",[9] or unconditional surrender to the Truth of existence, whatever that might turn out to be. But He did so in the West, bereft of all traditional guidance and supports.

He abandoned Himself to the streets of New York with the raw courage of a desperate man, tasting every pleasure of the senses, restrained by no taboos, no fear of madness. He devoured every kind of book that might afford Him a glimpse of Truth. Avatar Adi Da describes in *The Knee Of Listening* that He "became a kind of mad and exaggerated young man, whose impulses were not allowable in this medium culture, [whose] impulses were exploitable only in secret extensions of my own consciousness, or in the company of whores, libertines, and misfits". For two years, Avatar Adi Da maintained the terrible intensity of His seeking.

Then, one night in 1960, in the middle of His junior year in college, the Truth dormant in His own Being made Itself known. Avatar Adi Da sat at His desk in a small room He had rented several blocks from campus—He sat there, feeling that He had exhausted all the possibilities of experience.

*. . . I felt there were no more books to read, nor any possible kind of ordinary experience that could exceed what I had already embraced. There seemed no outstanding sources for any new excursion, no remaining and conclusive possibilities. I was drawn into the interior tension of my mind that held all of that seeking, every impulse and alternative, every motive in the form of my*

*desiring. I contemplated it as a whole, a dramatic singleness, and it moved me into a profound shape of life-feeling, so that all the vital centers in my body and mind appeared like a long funnel of contracted planes that led on to an infinitely regressed and invisible image. I observed this deep sensation of conflict and endlessly multiplied contradictions, such that I was surrendered to its very shape, as if to experience it perfectly and to be it.*

*Then, quite suddenly, in a moment, I experienced a total revolution in my body-mind, and, altogether, in my living consciousness. An absolute sense of understanding opened and arose at the extreme end of all this sudden contemplation. And all of the motions of me that moved down into that depth appeared to reverse their direction at some unfathomable point. The rising impulse caused me to stand, and I felt a surge of Force draw up out of my depths and expand, Filling my entire body and every level of my living consciousness with wave on wave of the most Beautiful and Joyous Energy.*

*I felt absolutely mad, but the madness was not of a desperate kind. There was no seeking and no dilemma within it, no question, no unfulfilled motive, not a single object or presence outside myself.*

*I could not contain the Energy in my small room. I ran out of the building and through the streets.* [The Knee Of Listening]

As Avatar Adi Da ran through the streets, looking for someone to talk to about this revelation, He continued to feel an overwhelming energy in His body—in every cell—that was "almost intolerable in its pressure, light, and force". But He found no one, and, at last, He returned to His room.

For two years Avatar Adi Da had devoted Himself to every kind of seeking—looking for some experience to "prove" the Truth to Him, presuming that the Truth was absent, that it had to be found. But in the days and weeks that followed the "Columbia experience", He realized that He had grasped two fundamental realities. First, He saw that Truth is not a matter of seeking for something that is absent, but of removing the obstructions to the Truth, Joy, or Freedom that is always already the case. Second, He realized that the seeking itself was the major obstruction that was preventing the immediate enjoyment, or Realization, of the Truth. All His seeking, He now understood, had been a grand distraction from present Real God, present Happiness. The two years of intense exploitation of experience had been necessary, but only in order to reveal conclusively to Him the futility of the search.

**Graduation day, Columbia University, 1961**

*. . . It Became Clear To Me That The Feeling Of Dilemma and The Urge To Seek God, Happiness, Fulfillment, or Release Via The Acquisition Of experience, knowledge, or any condition (or conditional object) at all Are Not, In Fact, The Means For The Realization Of Truth Itself. I Understood That The Problem-Feeling and The Urge To Seek Are Not A Program For The Actual Discovery Of Truth, but They Are Merely Symptoms Of A Curious Disease. I Observed That These Symptoms, Which Tend To Characterize every moment Of ordinary Existence, Are, In Fact, The Evidence Of the very state that Must Be Transcended If The Truth Itself Is To Be Realized. It Was Clear To Me That The Feeling Of Dilemma and The Seeking-Urge Are Nothing More Than A Confession That God, or Truth, or Happiness Is Not presently experienced or known. And This Seemed Remarkable To Me.*

*If God, or Truth, or Happiness Is Sought On The Basis Of A Problem (or The Feeling Of Dilemma), Then God, or Truth, or Happiness Is Always Projected Into future time, and The Realization Of God, or Truth, or Happiness Is Made conditional, or Dependent Upon psycho-physical events. This Stood Out To Me As Nonsense, or As An Absurd Proposition.*

*My Own "Consideration" Was This: God, or Truth, or Happiness Must (Necessarily) Be Reality Itself, or That Which Is (Necessarily) Always Already The Case.*

THE DAWN HORSE TESTAMENT
OF THE RUCHIRA AVATAR

## The Discovery of "Narcissus"

For Avatar Adi Da, the Awakening at Columbia was the first great breakthrough in His Life of the unique intelligence He calls "understanding"—the clear experiential knowledge that unhappiness, or apparent separation from God or Truth, is fundamentally the result of one's own mistaken presumptions and one's own egoic activity. Avatar Adi Da soon found, however, that He could not sustain the understanding awakened in this experience. He began to sense that there was something in consciousness that was actively preventing this understanding, and He fiercely determined to discover what that was. Two years later, after He moved to northern California and began a Master's program in creative writing at Stanford University, the force of His urge to understand found a new absorbing focus.

In 1962, Avatar Adi Da moved into a small cabin on a bluff overlooking the Pacific Ocean. He was now living with Nina Davis—a fellow student at Stanford.

*NINA: I met Beloved Adi Da at Stanford University in October 1961, on the first day of class of our graduate studies. He was sitting across a long table opposite the door of a seminar room, and when I walked into the room He looked up and Glanced at me with the most beautiful and extraordinary eyes. I felt a rush of energy as my being went out to meet Him. In that split second, I felt the most profound Communication of feeling I had ever known.*

*From the very beginning, it was obvious to me that Beloved Adi Da related to life completely differently from anybody else, including myself. He was obviously actively involved in a "Consideration" about life, always "Considering" the conventions of existence that everybody else takes for granted. For Him, such "Consideration"*

**At Stanford University**

**Nina Davis**

*involved not only the mind, but also the body and the emotions. He went beyond all conventions and taboos in those early days, just as He does now. In fact, all of the Signs that are characteristic of Beloved Adi Da now have been His Signs ever since I have known Him.*

Nina was witness to an extraordinary and unrelenting experiment that Avatar Adi Da now began—and which was to continue for almost two years. He wrote down everything that He observed in His experience—all that He thought, dreamed, felt, perceived, and did. He resolved that no motion of His being would elude Him. He hoped by these means He might find a logic, or guiding form, to the entire play of His experience.

So absorbed was He in this process that Nina took over all the practicalities of their life together. Day after day, wherever He was—at home, on a walk, visiting friends, going to the movies—Avatar Adi Da would carry a clipboard and write down all that occurred in His awareness. When He wandered alone on the beach below His remote cottage, He wrote down every random

***"From the very beginning, it was obvious to me that Beloved Adi Da related to life completely differently from anybody else . . ."***

thought and mind-form that arose with every step on the sand, and even His perception of the very action of stepping itself. He was placing His awareness under a powerful microscope, so that its inmost mechanics would stand out and its secret patterning would be revealed.

The revelation, when it came (sometime in the spring of 1964), was astonishing:

*Eventually, I began to recognize a structure in the living consciousness. It became more and more apparent, and its nature and effects revealed themselves as fundamental and inclusive of all the states and contents in life and mind. My own "myth", the control of all patterns, the source of identity and all seeking, began to stand out in the mind as a living being.*

*This "myth", this controlling logic, or force, that formed my very consciousness, revealed itself as the concept and the actual life of Narcissus. I saw that my entire adventure, the desperate cycle of awareness and its decrease, of truly Conscious Being and Its gradual covering in the mechanics of living, seeking, dying, and suffering, was produced out of the image or mentality that appears hidden in the ancient myth of Narcissus.*

*The more I contemplated him, the more profoundly I understood him. I observed in awe the primitive control that this self-concept and logic performed in all of my behavior and experience. I began to see that same logic operative in all other human beings, and in every living thing, even in the very life of the cells and in the natural energies that surround every living entity or process. It was the logic or process of separation itself, of enclosure and immunity. It manifested as fear and identity, memory and experience. It informed every function of the living being, every experience, every act, every event. It "created" every "mystery". It was the structure of every imbecile link in the history of human suffering.*

*He is the ancient one visible in the Greek "myth", who was the universally adored child of the gods, who rejected the loved-one and every form of love and relationship, who was finally condemned to the contemplation of his own image, until, as a result of his own act*

**At the beach cottage**

***This "myth", this controlling logic, or force, that formed my very consciousness, revealed itself as the concept and the actual life of Narcissus.***

*and obstinacy, he suffered the fate of eternal separateness and died in infinite solitude.* [The Knee Of Listening]

When this truth dawned upon Avatar Adi Da, He saw that no one—no "God", no parent, no outside influence at all—has imposed on human beings this controlling logic of fundamental separation, enclosure, and immunity. It is <u>we</u> who have locked ourselves into this "prison". Now He knew He had to go through the ordeal of the undoing of the madness of "Narcissus", whatever that might involve.

**After His Divine Re-Awakening**
**Los Angeles, 1971**

CHAPTER 2

# The Re-Awakening to the "Bright"

In June 1964, Avatar Adi Da and Nina moved to New York City, in response to a dream-vision in which He had glimpsed the place where He would meet His first human Teacher: Swami Rudrananda.

## Surrender to Swami Rudrananda

Swami Rudrananda (or Albert Rudolph, known to his students as "Rudi") owned the Oriental art store in New York that Avatar Adi Da had seen in vision. Rudi held "class" four times a week, during which his students practiced receiving the "Force" that he (an Adept of Kundalini Yoga[1]) consciously Transmitted to them. "Work" and "surrender" were the essence of Rudi's Teaching.

Avatar Adi Da had read about the ancient tradition of approaching a Guru for instruction, but He had no personal experience of the Guru-devotee relationship. In that tradition, a Spiritual aspirant comes to a Guru (an acknowledged Spiritual Master, or Real-God-Realizer, of some degree) and surrenders himself or herself at the feet of the Master. From that moment on, the devotee submits to be directed in every aspect of life by his or

Swami Rudrananda ("Rudi")

her Guru. Such surrender, it is traditionally understood, is the greatest thing a human being could choose to do. To find and embrace one's Guru does not mean surrendering to an ordinary human being. It means surrendering to one Awakened by the Divine, one who is full of Divine Power and Grace, one who can, therefore, Awaken a serious devotee to some degree of true Spiritual Realization. In approaching Rudi and becoming his devotee, Avatar Adi Da was spontaneously moved to fulfill these sacred laws of the Guru-devotee relationship as it had existed in ancient India—and He did so with great passion and intensity.

*The central ideas in Rudi's way of teaching were "surrender" and "work". "Surrender" was an idea that corresponded to the internal practice in life and meditation. It was conscious and even willful opening or letting go of contents, resistance, patterns, feelings, and thoughts. "Work" was the idea that corresponded to the external practice. The ideal student was to be in a constant state of surrender and a constant act of work. The purpose of this was to make the entire instrument, internal and external, available to the higher Power, the "Force", or "Shakti", and thus to grow by including Its Will, Presence, Intelligence, Light, and Power on every level of the functional being.*

*I took this way very seriously, and I made a constant effort to adapt myself to this way absolutely and exhaustively. I accepted Rudi as a perfect Source of this higher Power, and I allowed none of his apparent limitations to represent actual barriers or limitations to the Force Itself. Whenever I encountered limitations in him, I was immediately moved to reflect on my own resistance. Thus, I never allowed myself to become concerned about Rudi's problems or to think the Force, or the Divine Power, was available to me only to a limited degree.*

*The effect of this way of life was a perpetual and growing encounter with my own resistance. And where I encountered my own resistance, I would awaken to my own tendencies to self-pity, negativity, and the subliminal self-imagery by which I guided the "creation" or manipulation of experience. The more I worked, the more I saw Narcissus.*

*This way required immense self-discipline, and, as long as it worked, it provided a positive mechanism that strengthened and purified me physically, mentally, and morally. Rudi was a master at this kind of psychological tutoring, and these effects were his primary gift to me.* [The Knee Of Listening]

Avatar Adi Da worked day and night for three and a half years—cleaning Rudi's apartment, cleaning the store, and refinishing furniture. With great love and faith, He brought to Rudi the disposition of absolute surrender that He had practiced during His years at Columbia and His time of writing. Everything that Rudi asked his students to do, or required of Avatar Adi Da personally, He did—down to the last detail. As He says in *The Knee Of Listening*, He embraced the great practice of Guru-devotion and submitted to His Teacher "as a man does to God".

At Rudi's behest, Avatar Adi Da married Nina and took on disciplines of diet and exercise to purify and strengthen the body. He lived in a fever of frustration at the effort of responding to Rudi's intense demands—to the point where He felt His entire body to be burning up. These demands were not only physical. At Rudi's instigation, Avatar Adi Da Samraj also attended Christian seminaries (ostensibly, as preparation for a career as a minister), studying theology and ancient languages—which were not at all interesting to Him personally. It was simply obedience to His Teacher that moved Him.

**left: Adi Da Samraj and Nina Davis**
**right: Philadelphia State Mental Hospital, where Adi Da Samraj served as chaplain**

There was, however, one aspect of Avatar Adi Da's seminary studies that did prove interesting to Him—the summer that He spent as a chaplain at a mental hospital in Philadelphia. Avatar Adi Da has humorously said that this experience prepared Him quite well for His future Work of Teaching! He realized, as He entered into relationship with hundreds of psychotic people, that their condition was simply a more exaggerated version of the separative state that every un-Enlightened being suffers.

There were occasions when Avatar Adi Da found Himself in the ridiculous situation of giving sermons to hundreds of the hospital inmates, none of whom had the slightest attention for what He was saying, because each one was totally enclosed in his or her own ritual behaviors. One of Avatar Adi Da's daily responsibilities in the hospital was to spend time in a room with a group of psychotic murderers, ostensibly to serve some therapeutic purpose. As He sat with these men, they would rehearse to Him with enthusiasm the stories of how they had killed their victims.

This time of Avatar Adi Da's Sadhana[2] was part of His Compassionate embrace of the human realm. During those months, He witnessed terrible forms of human degradation and misery. But He did not relate to what He saw in a conventional fashion. He saw that it did not serve to judge the inmates. Instead, He intuitively responded to them. He found ways to create relationships with them, to find humor and enjoyment with them in the midst of their condition, whatever it was in each case. He was simply Present with them.

**At the Seminary in Philadelphia**

## The "Death of Narcissus"

Avatar Adi Da's chaplaincy at the mental hospital in the summer of 1967 marked the end of His seminary studies in Philadelphia. He could find no motive to continue—after a most dramatic and profoundly significant event had occurred to Him during the spring. He tells the story in His own Words:

*AVATAR ADI DA SAMRAJ: One day when I was in class in Seminary in the spring of 1967, I suddenly became completely detached from the mind. The mind seemed to pick up immense speed, and the thought processes were going at immense speed, to the point of the experience becoming extremely disturbing. I was supposed to be sitting there in class, but I felt as if I was going mad. I was going mad.*

*I tried to pin down my experience by writing everything the teacher said, or writing the thoughts I was having. I just kept pinning it down. That gesture, in and of itself, introduces time, and some more direct association with the body.*

*I did that long enough to sit through the class. Then I went whirling out in this horrific state, in which the body-mind was going on, on its own, without being controlled by attention. The body-mind was just a whirl of uncontrolled events and sensations and feelings—positive ones, and also extremely negative ones. It became just an immense fear.*

*I remember looking at My face in the mirror, as I was putting on an after-shave or a skin cleanser, and I saw the plasticity of the body. There was a profound disorientation from the physical, emotional, and mental dimensions of the body-mind, in which I had been doing Yoga, or Spiritual practice, so intensively for those years. All of a sudden, the body-mind was utterly confused and dissociated from Me, or I was dissociated from it.* [January 13, 1996]

In this extraordinary event, a sudden and profound psychic chaos canceled out Avatar Adi Da's normal identification with the body-mind and the person He presumed Himself to be. It was not as if this identification had been released gently, as in deep meditation. Avatar Adi Da was wide awake and active, and He could not point to any trigger that could have set off the process. Now His body appeared alien to Him; in fact, He hardly knew what it was—it appeared to be mere flesh without consciousness. Avatar Adi Da was in no way prepared for this experience by any of His Spiritual practice with Rudi. All of that Yoga had to do with the manipulation of the body-mind in order to receive superior Force, and to invite mystical, or subtle,[3] experiences. The present chaos had catapulted Avatar Adi Da totally beyond that frame of reference.

*AVATAR ADI DA SAMRAJ: The fear—which was a reaction to that whirl—got to the point where it was fruitless to try to do anything about it. It just kept growing immensely, became the totality of life, the totality of the body-mind, the totality of reality—just this immense fear that could no longer be avoided. There was nothing to do about it.* [January 13, 1996]

After the first day of this terror, in the middle of the night, Avatar Adi Da felt that His heart was slowing down and about to stop. But when He reached the emergency ward at the local hospital, all that the doctor could tell Him was that He seemed to be suffering an anxiety attack. There was no conventional explanation or remedy for what was occurring in Him. Finally, on the third day of this acute distress, Avatar Adi Da simply lay down on the floor of His apartment and allowed the fear to pour through His being and overwhelm Him completely.

*AVATAR ADI DA SAMRAJ: It was a death. That is what it became. It was endured to the point that what was afraid to be let go was simply let go. There was no choice.*

*So it passed. In other words, the body-mind, even attention, was no longer associated with My State. I was simply Realizing the Native State of Being. Therefore, this was not merely a process of madness in the usual clinical sense. It was an extraordinary Spiritual Event. It was simply the breaking through of My own Disposition, the "Bright", Prior to the body-mind.* [January 13, 1996]

When the terrible passage was over, Avatar Adi Da felt a total turnaround, a revolution in His awareness. By allowing Himself to fully experience the absolute terror of no longer being identified with His body-mind, He witnessed the actual death of His limited identity, and He witnessed it completely. "Narcissus", the separate self-consciousness, the one who is merely afraid, simply died. And Avatar Adi Da knew He was not that one. His True Identity was the "Bright", the unqualified, Free Awareness of Reality Itself, beyond the body-mind and all its assumed limits.

The ecstasy of this Realization was beyond anything that Avatar Adi Da had ever experienced since His Submission to the human condition at the age of two. He got up from the floor overcome with joy. The Eternal Qualities of Truth and Reality stood out as they are: Divine Calm and Inexpressible Love-Bliss. And He saw that all seeking for Reality and Truth was only the preventing of it—the avoidance of the "Bright", or That Which is Always Already the Case. He now knew, with complete Certainty, that Truth could be directly Realized in life at any moment.

In this experience, the "Bright" was restored to Him—though it was not a permanent Realization. The experience did mark, however, a profound change in Avatar Adi Da's disposition. He was no longer identified with what was taking place in His life and Sadhana. His entire search had spontaneously relaxed. But how could He explain to others the revolution that had occurred in His consciousness? How could He express His living knowledge that we are not separate beings, but always alive only as the one Transcendental Truth and Unity? The profundity of this "death of Narcissus" was not apparent even to Rudi. Avatar Adi Da Samraj now stood on a peak of understanding and Realization that no one around Him could share. This "radical"[4] understanding was utterly unique. He decided to simply live on its basis—abandoning the stress of effort, and functioning without dilemma.

**In New York after His return from the Seminary**

Rudi himself had a Teacher, the remarkable Indian Yogi Swami (Baba) Muktananda, whose picture (together with that of Swami Muktananda's own Guru, Swami Nityananda) hung on the wall in the art store. Avatar Adi Da began to read some pamphlets from Swami Muktananda's ashram and was deeply attracted by Swami Muktananda's descriptions of true Spiritual practice as founded in the reception of the Guru's Grace, rather than in stressful effort (as Rudi taught). By 1968, Avatar Adi Da found in Himself an irresistible impulse to move on in the great lineage of Gurus to which Rudi belonged. And so Avatar Adi Da asked, and received, Rudi's permission to approach Swami Muktananda. The time had come to go to India.

## The Sadhana with Swami Muktananda

In April 1968, Avatar Adi Da quickly made arrangements for Himself and Nina to take a brief trip to Swami Muktananda's ashram in Ganeshpuri. As He participated in the life of the ashram—sitting in Swami Muktananda's company, meditating, or attending the afternoon chanting of the *Bhagavad Gita*—He began to experience strong effects of Swami Muktananda's Spirit-Blessing, or Shaktipat.[5] He felt His body swell with Force, generating powerful, involuntary bodily movements, or kriyas,[6] as the Spirit-Energy flowed through Him. Avatar Adi Da found Himself involved in a new kind of Spiritual "Work"—submission to these kriyas, which were sometimes so strong that He would fall backwards against the wall or sideways onto the floor. Swami Muktananda also instructed Him in meditation and gave formal discourses on traditional Indian teachings about Spiritual life. But by the fourth and last day of His visit, Avatar Adi Da was feeling somewhat disappointed. He had come, as He had written in advance to Swami Muktananda, for "everything", and He felt that He was about to leave the ashram without having received His Guru's full gift.

On the afternoon of His last day, Avatar Adi Da was sitting in the ashram garden when Swami Muktananda walked by with a visitor—who, He later learned, was a Yogi-Saint named Rang Avadhoot.[7] For a brief moment, the Saint paused, turned towards Avatar Adi Da, and looked Him straight in the eyes. And then he walked on. That glance was profound. In later years, Avatar Adi Da acknowledged that Rang Avadhoot's glance, together with the Spiritual Influence of Swami Muktananda, was a trigger for what occurred next.

An urge to rest came over Avatar Adi Da, and He went to lie down in His room. In a moment, all awareness of body and mind slipped away in a swoon of immense Bliss. He rested beyond time and space and all visionary states, in the great "formless ecstasy" known in the traditions of Yoga as "Nirvikalpa Samadhi".[8] He had required only the briefest contact with the Spirit-Transmission of His Siddha-Master[9] and of Rang Avadhoot, in order to completely receive that infusion of Grace. This was the first sign of the fulfillment of a prophecy made to Avatar Adi Da on that initial visit to Ganeshpuri: Within a year, Swami Muktananda told Him, Avatar Adi Da would be a Spiritual Teacher in His own right.

***He had required only the briefest contact with the Spirit-Transmission of His Siddha-Master and of Rang Avadhoot, in order to completely receive that infusion of Grace. This was the first sign of the fulfillment of a prophecy made to Avatar Adi Da on that initial visit to Ganeshpuri: Within a year, Swami Muktananda told Him, Avatar Adi Da would be a Spiritual Teacher in His own right.***

India, 1968

Swami Muktananda

Rang Avadhoot

He returned to New York, and, within a year, people around Him started to experience a mysterious Force emanating from Him, and they turned to Him for Spiritual guidance. One of them, a young woman named Patricia Morley, came to live with Him and Nina. Aware that the Shakti, or Siddha-Power, had come alive in Himself, Avatar Adi Da wrote to Swami Muktananda, who urged Him to come to India again as soon as possible.

Avatar Adi Da's second visit to India—this time to Bombay, where Swami Muktananda was staying—in August 1969, was very different from the first. It was an entry into a Yogic "wonderland". He would experience the internal lights, sounds, visions, transports to other worlds, and states of Spirit-"Intoxication" that normally precede the rare attainment of ascended Nirvikalpa Samadhi.[10] But such experiences soon lost their interest for Avatar Adi Da. His focus lay in His Guru's silent internal instruction, which He received in the process of meditation. He spoke of this in a letter to Nina and Patricia:

*Baba Teaches me entirely by internal Spiritual Means now. We hardly speak at all. My meditation has become very deep, and most of the kriyas are gone. There is a good deal of suffering involved in the transformation I am going through. We are so chronically used to letting the mind take on forms. But I am breaking into the most intense Bliss and miraculous Energy. It is worth the little bit of required death.*

*I require a quiet, free life from now on. I hope what I require and seek is also your desire. I belong to God, the Consciousness Prior to all manifestation and thought, Prior to the process called "I". Allow it also to grasp you. Meditate, live harmoniously, eat a proper diet, be conscious in relationship. Allow no disturbance, require peace. Remember and love me. I love you.*

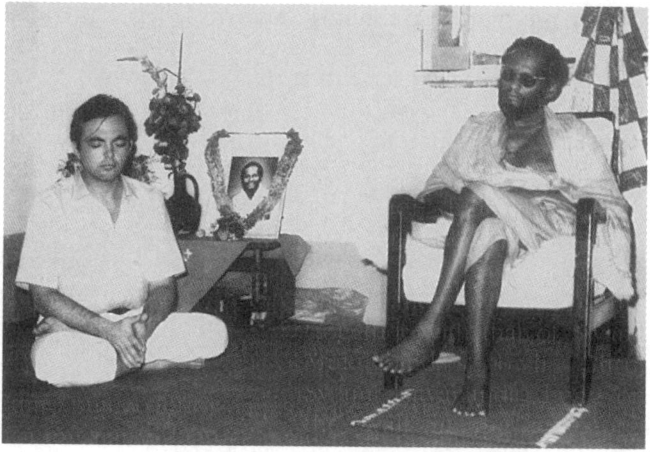

**Sitting with Swami Muktananda, 1969**

At the end of His stay, Avatar Adi Da's Spiritual Accomplishment was formally acknowledged by Swami Muktananda. In a letter written in his own hand, Swami Muktananda declared that Avatar Adi Da had attained "Yogic Self-Realization" and, therefore, the right to Teach and Initiate others. But, privately, Swami Muktananda gave Avatar Adi Da an even more profound acknowledgment—He spontaneously offered Him the name "Love-Ananda", meaning "One Who Is, and Manifests, the Divine Love-Bliss". Swami Muktananda was intuitively revealing a Divine Name that belonged to the future of Avatar Adi Da's Life and Work, when the full Revelation of His "Brightness" would appear.

# The Sadhana with Swami Nityananda and the Divine Goddess

The following year, accompanied by Nina and Patricia, Avatar Adi Da returned to Swami Muktananda's ashram, now intent on staying there forever. It was May 1970, and His life in the West, He felt, was over. He could no longer endure the violent psyche of the American cities, and He had no motive whatsoever toward a conventional life. His only desire was to devote Himself to His life of "radical" understanding and to live and serve in the company of His Guru. And so, Avatar Adi Da and Nina and Patricia sold nearly all of their belongings, stored a few things in New York, and set off for India as renunciates.

When they reached Ganeshpuri, however, Swami Muktananda seemed to deliberately ignore Avatar Adi Da. Avatar Adi Da understood that this was His Guru's way of silently indicating that the future of His Sadhana lay elsewhere. And so, following an instruction that Swami Muktananda had given Him on earlier visits, Avatar Adi Da began to go daily to the nearby burial shrine of Swami Nityananda, the beloved Guru of Swami Muktananda. It was here that He now felt the Spiritual Force and Blessing that He had earlier received through Swami Muktananda. It seemed obvious to Avatar Adi Da that Swami Muktananda had passed Him on to his own Guru, in order to receive further instruction—for, although Swami Nityananda had relinquished the body in 1961, he was, as Avatar Adi Da discovered, still Spiritually active on the subtle plane.

But then something completely unexpected occurred. About a week after His arrival in Ganeshpuri, as He was weeding in the ashram garden, Avatar Adi Da suddenly became aware of a subtle form behind Him.

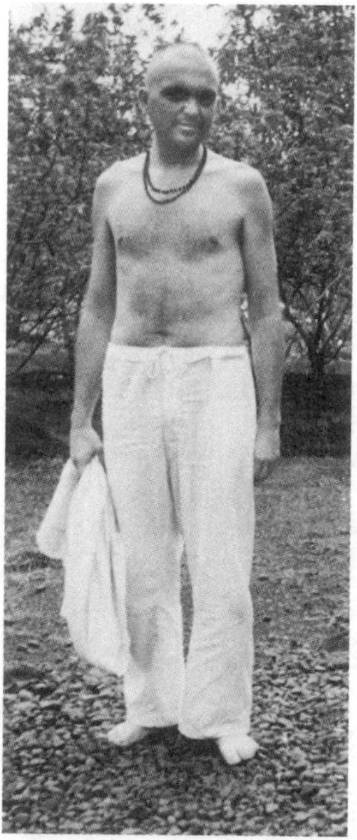

***He could no longer endure the violent psyche of the American cities, and He had no motive whatsoever toward a conventional life. His only desire was to devote Himself to the "radical" understanding that had been revealed to Him and to live and serve in the company of His Guru. And so, Avatar Adi Da and Nina and Patricia sold nearly all of their belongings, stored a few things in New York, and set off for India as renunciates.***

**left: India, 1970**

**above right: the Ashram as it appeared in 1970**

**below (left to right): Adi Da Samraj at the Ashram wearing mosquito netting, Nina Davis, and Patricia Morley**

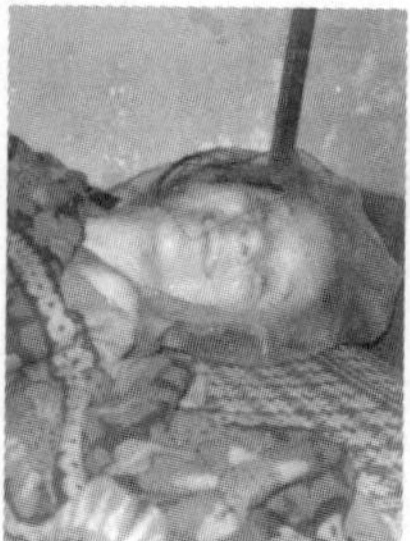

He turned around and found Himself beholding the non-physical but unmistakable presence of the Virgin Mary! At first, He felt like laughing out loud. The last traces of His childhood faith—which, in any case, had been Protestant, not Catholic—had dissolved, or so He thought, in the secular onslaught of His years at Columbia. But, in a few moments, He found Himself spontaneously moved to respond to the Virgin with reverence and respect, receiving her wordless communication that He should immediately acquire a rosary and begin to worship her.

When the vision faded, Avatar Adi Da set about complying with the Virgin's request, finding a way to get to Bombay, the nearest place where He could buy a rosary. He began to practice the "Hail, Mary" in the traditional manner, as a mantra, and to His amazement He found that this practice unlocked deep feelings of attachment to Jesus of Nazareth that seemed to have been suppressed since His childhood. He had no idea where this turn of events would lead, but He submitted to it completely.

After two weeks, the Virgin Mary instructed Avatar Adi Da to leave the ashram. He was to set out on a pilgrimage through the Christian holy places of Europe, starting in Jerusalem. He could not depart without taking leave of the Presence of Swami Nityananda, and so He went to the shrine and spoke His heart to Swami Nityananda, telling him about all that had recently occurred and what He was about to do. Avatar Adi Da received Swami Nityananda's subtle communication of Blessing and his instruction that He should follow the Virgin.

The priest at Swami Nityananda's burial place filled Avatar Adi Da's hands with flowers from the shrine, as a sign of Swami Nityananda's Blessing. Avatar Adi Da then left to return to the ashram. On His way, He was moved to take the flowers to the small village temple beside the ashram and offer them to the image of the Divine Mother-

**Swami Nityananda**

**The Mother-Shakti at the temple in Ganeshpuri**

***The Virgin and the Shakti were one. There was no difference. And that One—that Universal Goddess-Power—was now His Guru. This Divine Spirit-Force was, in fact, the Supreme Guru of the entire lineage of Gurus who had guided Avatar Adi Da's Sadhana . . .***

Shakti, the personification of the Spirit-Force that had so dramatically manifested in the multifarious Spiritual experiences He had gone through in His Sadhana at Ganeshpuri. As Avatar Adi Da stood before the Mother-Shakti, the One worshipped in India as the great Goddess, the Energy of all manifestation, He came to a tacit realization. The Virgin and the Shakti were one. There was no difference. And that One—that Universal Goddess-Power—was now His Guru. This Divine Spirit-Force was, in fact, the Supreme Guru of the entire lineage of Gurus who had guided Avatar Adi Da's Sadhana—Swami Rudrananda, Swami Muktananda, and Swami Nityananda—and these Gurus had led Him to Her.

Up to this point, the Realizations of His Sadhana had taken Avatar Adi Da through all the degrees of "Enlightenment" known in the Spiritual traditions. On His second trip to India, He had experienced the subtle lights, sounds, and visions cherished by Yogis (such as Paramahansa Yogananda[11]). On His first trip to India, He had experienced the ascended Bliss of bodiless and mindless absorption in Pure Consciousness sought by Saints (such as Jnaneshwar and Milarepa[12]). And in the "death of Narcissus" in seminary, He had come to rest in the deep identification with Consciousness Itself known to the great Sages (such as Gautama, Hui Neng, Shankara, and Ramana Maharshi[13]). Never before, as far as the historical record shows, had a single individual attained, in succession, all the fundamental forms of Realization prized by different traditions as "Enlightenment". But even though Avatar Adi Da had attained all these Realizations, none of them was sufficient for Him. None of them was the same as the utterly unqualified Joy that, as an infant, He had known as the "Bright". He knew that His quest was not complete. But no human Teacher could help Him now—only the Goddess Herself could take Him further, into territory untrodden by any Realizer of the past. When, in obedience to the Virgin, Avatar Adi Da made His farewells at Ganeshpuri and departed for Europe, He was embarking upon the final phase of His Sadhana.

From the Way of the Cross in Jerusalem, to the monuments of Rome, to the basilica at Fatima in Portugal, Avatar Adi Da allowed the Virgin to lead Him. Extraordinary Christian visions overtook Him, mystical raptures that would be the envy of saints. Having accomplished the highest goals of Eastern Yoga, He was now spontaneously combining Himself with the greatest mystical experience and Spiritual revelation of the West. But, as time went on, the Virgin and the visions began to fade. Avatar Adi Da felt Himself drawn more and more into a

**On pilgrimage to Christian holy sites, 1970**

state of Non-Separateness from Reality Itself, prior to all visions, images, and traditional religious paths. Finally, by the time He reached Portugal in mid-July, He was moved to end the pilgrimage and return to the United States. After trying unsuccessfully to find a suitable place to live near San Francisco, He, Nina, and Patricia settled in Los Angeles.

## Re-Awakening to the "Bright"

Moving to the vast metropolis did not distract Avatar Adi Da Samraj from the process in Consciousness that was now intensifying in Him. Around this time, He began to notice that He had transcended the basic mechanisms of ordinary awareness—differentiation and desire. As He wrote in His journal:

*In the last couple of days, I turned to a woman companion while driving my car, and I became peculiarly aware of the absence of desire in me. It was not merely that I did not desire this woman. It was that this woman was void of any objective distinction. There was no process of discrimination, comparison, or separation going on already and automatically in me. I had turned to look at what is otherwise a person, a meaning, and a distinctly meaningful presence, but there was, in fact, none of this. Indeed, there was not a single modification of my awareness created as a result of this perception. There was only Unqualified Bliss, the Fullness of Real Consciousness.* [entry dated August 3, 1970]

Secluded in a corner of downtown Hollywood is a small temple, established by the Vedanta Society[14] of Southern California. This simple temple, standing in the shadow of a giant freeway, was to provide the setting for the final Events of Avatar Adi Da's Sadhana. Late in August 1970, as if by chance, He found His way to the temple, and was mysteriously prompted to go inside. The moment He did so, He felt the familiar Force of the Mother-Shakti moving to meet Him. He was amazed, and

**The Vedanta Temple in Hollywood, California**

delighted, to find that She was as powerful a Presence here as in any of the temples of India.

During these weeks, Avatar Adi Da would typically drive Patricia to work in the mornings and make occasional visits to the Vedanta Temple. There, without fail, He felt the Mother-Shakti waiting for Him. More and more, He longed to enjoy the Bliss of Her Company constantly, and so He silently asked Her to be always with Him, not only in the temple, but where He lived, whatever He was doing.

Within a few days, Avatar Adi Da realized that She had complied. She was an ever-living Presence within and around Him, whether He was waking, dreaming, sleeping, or meditating. But something was not yet complete. While His sense of difference from the woman in the car had apparently disappeared, Avatar Adi Da still felt a lingering sense of separateness from the tangible Fullness of the Mother-Shakti, and thus a need to hold on to Her.

Then, on September 9, this last barrier dissolved, bringing about a Union that took Avatar Adi Da to the very threshold of His Divine Re-Awakening to the "Bright":

*When I returned to the temple the next day, the Person of the Divine Shakti appeared to me again, in a manner most intimate, no longer approaching me as "Mother".*

*As I meditated, I felt myself Expanding, even bodily, becoming a Perfectly Motionless, Utterly Becalmed, and Infinitely Silent Form. I took on the Infinite Form of the Original Deity, Nameless and Indefinable, Conscious of limitless Identification with Infinite Being. I was Expanded Utterly, beyond limited form, and even beyond any perception of Shape or Face, merely Being, and yet sitting there. I sat in this Love-Blissful State of Infinite Being for some time. I Found myself to <u>Be</u>. My Form was* *only What is traditionally called the "Purusha" (the Person of Consciousness) and "Siva" (in His Non-Ferocious Emptiness).*[15]

*Then I felt the Divine Shakti appear in Person, Pressed against my own natural body, and, altogether, against my Infinitely Expanded, and even formless, Form. She Embraced me, Openly and Utterly, and we Combined with One Another in Divine (and Motionless, and spontaneously Yogic) "Sexual Union". We Found One Another Thus, in a Fire of most perfect Desire, and for no other Purpose than This Union, and, yet, as if to Give Birth to the universes. In That most perfect Union, I Knew the Oneness of the Divine Energy and my Very Being. There was no separation at all, nor had there ever been, nor would there ever be. The One Being that Is my own Ultimate Self-Nature was revealed most perfectly.*[16] *The One Being Who I Am was revealed to Include the Reality that Is Consciousness Itself, the Reality that Is the Source-Energy of all conditional appearances, and the Reality that Is all conditional manifestation, All as a Single Force of Being, an Eternal Union, and an Irreducible cosmic Unity.*

*The "Sensations" of the Embrace were overwhelmingly Blissful. The Fire of That Unquenchable Desire Exceeded any kind of pleasure that a mere man could experience. In the Eternal Instant of That Infinitely Expanded Embrace, I was released from my role and self-image as a dependent child of the "Mother"-Shakti. And She was revealed in Truth, no longer in apparent independence, or as a cosmic Power apart from me, but as the Inseparable and Inherent Radiance of my own and Very Being. Therefore, I Recognized and Took Her as my Consort, my Loved-One, and I Held Her effortlessly, forever to my Heart. Together eternally, we had Realized Ourselves as the "Bright" Itself.* [The Knee Of Listening]

In the entire history of Spirituality, the literal "Husbanding" of the Divine Goddess, the Shakti, by a human being has never been described. Only the Divine in Person could Accomplish such a Work. Through Avatar Adi Da's tangible Union with the Goddess in the Vedanta Temple, the archetypal "marriage" of the Divine Consciousness and the Divine Spirit-Power, described and pictured in many Spiritual traditions, was Realized. The significance of this Husbanding cannot be fathomed. Avatar Adi Da Samraj spoke of it years later, as the seed of a change in the very nature of existence:

*AVATAR ADI DA SAMRAJ: To Husband the Mother, to be Her Husband and to receive Her as the Bride, means that the murderous activity of Energy in Its apparent independence is done, over, finished. This Husbanding and Marriage is not merely a personal Work, not merely a characteristic incident associated with My Realization. It is an historical Event, of Which much should be made. It has transformed the history of the entire Mandala of the cosmos.*[17] *By virtue of this Marriage, all may be Drawn to My Divine Self-Domain.*[18] [March 16, 1988]

The Husbanding of the Divine Shakti was the final Event of preparation for the supreme moment to which Avatar Adi Da's entire Sadhana had been leading:

*Finally, the next day, September 10, 1970, I sat in the temple again. I awaited the Beloved Shakti to reveal Herself in Person, as my Blessed Companion. But, as time passed, there was no Event of changes, no movement at all. There was not even any kind of inward deepening, no "inwardness" at all. There was no meditation. There was no need for meditation. There was not a single element or change that could be added to make my State Complete. I sat with my eyes open. I was not having an experience of any kind. Then, suddenly, I understood most perfectly. I Realized that I had Realized. The "Thing" about the "Bright" became Obvious. I Am Complete. I Am the One Who Is Complete.*

*In That instant, I understood and Realized (inherently, and most perfectly) What and Who I Am. It was a tacit Realization, a direct Knowledge in Consciousness. It was Consciousness Itself, without the addition of a Communication from any "Other" Source. There Is no "Other" Source. I simply sat there and Knew What and Who I Am. I was Being What I Am, Who I Am. I Am Being What I Am, Who I Am. I Am Reality, the Divine Self, the Nature, Substance, Support, and Source of all things and all beings. I Am the One Being, called "God" (the Source and Substance and Support and Self of all), the "One Mind" (the Consciousness and Energy in and As Which all appears), "Siva-Shakti"*[19] *(the Self-Existing and Self-Radiant*[20] *Reality Itself), "Brahman" (the Only Reality, Itself),*[21] *the "One Atman" (That Is not ego, but Only "Brahman", the Only Reality, Itself),*[22] *the "Nirvanic Ground" (the egoless and conditionless Reality and Truth, Prior to all dualities, but excluding none).*[23] *I Am the One and Only and necessarily Divine Self, Nature, Condition, Substance, Support, Source, and Ground of all. I Am the "Bright".* [The Knee Of Listening]

This moment was the Divine Re-Awakening of Avatar Adi Da Samraj. He had Realized Divine Enlightenment—"Open-Eyed",[24] true and stable under all conditions. His Realization was not dependent on achieving any particular meditative state, nor on excluding any type of experience. It transcended even the slightest sense of identity as a separate self. It was and is the Realization that there is only Real God and that all apparent events are simply the passing and (ultimately) unnecessary forms (or modifications) of Real God (or Truth Itself, or Reality Itself),

**Avatar Adi Da on a visit to the Vedanta Temple in April, 1997**

arising and dissolving in an endless Play that is beyond comprehension.

The very Divine Person had become perfectly Conscious and Present through the ordinary human vehicle of "Franklin Jones". Such an event was unprecedented in all the eons of human time. Avatar Adi Da's Descent as the Divine Person and His utter overcoming of the limits of human existence in all its dimensions—physical, mental, emotional, psychic, Spiritual—was total, Perfect, and Complete. Avatar Adi Da had Realized absolute Identity with the Divine, the One He Was and Is from the beginning. But His Re-Awakening signified far more than this. It was also the Revelation that all apparent beings are also capable of Realizing this same Condition. The Condition of the "Bright", the Real-God-Light of His birth and infancy, was now fully established in Avatar Adi Da—not only in Him as an apparent individual, but as the native Truth and the potential Realization of all beings.

Los Angeles, 1971

## CHAPTER 3

# "I Am Here to Love You and to Be Loved"

Following the indescribable Event of His Divine Re-Awakening, Avatar Adi Da began to feel more and more the implications of what had occurred. He wrote His reflections in private journals—continuing to inspect and comment upon His unbounded Liberation, and the unique "radical" understanding through which it had come about. These are some quotations from His journals dating from late 1970 and 1971.

In the first entry, Avatar Adi Da speaks of the "Healing Pose" that is spontaneously restored in the being when there is nothing further to experience or know or Realize.

*I have researched all My desires, and only now I am Free.*

*I have done the exclusive adventures of the libertine and the saint.*

*In the Climactic Brilliance of One-Directed Life, I have Known the One Reality That need not have been searched.*

*In the profuse excesses of every pleasure, My Body exhausted with every use, I have known the same inescapable Truth, the same Marvel of Light and uncreated Certainty.*

*Therefore, I became Unmoved.*

*I have begun the Healing Pose, Which is Rest in the Heart.*[1]

*I am utterly, absolutely, already Happy.*

*I no longer live under threat.*

*I require the survival of nothing, even my own life.*

*But all things are survived by What I Am.*

*And I have Lived them.*

◆ ◆ ◆

One aspect of Avatar Adi Da's Realization was the unique manner in which He now perceived and related to "Franklin", His bodily vehicle. He saw that "Franklin" was but one of His Forms, that He is, truly, all forms, all beings, and that His Divinely Realized "non-difference" from everyone and everything was the means by which He would Liberate all.

*When once I understood Who I Am—the Heart, the same Self that is the Consciousness of all beings, their very Existence, timeless and spaceless Bliss, Whose Form is that same Form That is the Form in Which all forms are reflected, perceiving themselves and being perceived—I also wondered: How is it, then, that I, Being the Heart, have become contained and seem to function nearly always in this one form, Franklin, in relation to others?*

*And, then, I saw that the one in whom this question and this very perception arose was not My Self, the Heart—but Franklin, that limitation itself!*

*Therefore, it is not so! I am not contained or born. And only Franklin perceives itself as Franklin apart from Me.*

*Since then, it is also true that I have experienced My Self arising and functioning in the form of countless beings other than Franklin, and I also Realize My Nature there, so that many beings are finding themselves in this understanding, apart from great effort.*

*It is Franklin who needed to be Enlightened, who sought to be Free, who endured these experiences, performing the question and the answer, who wonders now about his relationship to Me. It is Franklin who has been My point of view, My trouble, the field of My dilemma, the problem itself. But I have never been this one, never wondered or sought, never entered the precincts of this dilemma, never even understood.*

*Therefore, what I have Realized has even nothing to do with him—except that, knowing this, I can use him with abandon, never assuming he is not Free.*

*When I Am Present As My Self, then Franklin and all who know Me (As I Am) never turn to the mind of separated living, but they abide and survive in the Powered Mystery of Real Consciousness. This, because, remaining Present As I Am, I do not give the Power of My Consciousness to the indulgence of problematic life. And, if I reserve This Consciousness to My Self, there is no consciousness abroad to be apart, for I Am That One Who Is Present every where.*

◆ ◆ ◆

Avatar Adi Da poured out descriptions of the Ordeal that it is to most perfectly Realize the Heart, or the Very Divine. There was no gleeful satisfaction in His Enlightenment, but a constant Fire, a Love-Agony for the sake of all others. Avatar Adi Da's Realization of His Identity with all beings—fragile, confused, and dying here—left Him Wounded to the depths with their pain, consumed with longing to bring them to His Place of Love.

*I Am the Universe of Love.*

*It is not a matter of My Liberation or Salvation as an apparently separate entity. For one who understands, there is forever no separate Salvation, no separate Liberation. There is only the unqualified, unconsoled impulse of Love, suffered in the Purity of Real Consciousness. There is only the Revelation of My Presence, My Work, the ruin of My beginnings.*

*I am sick with Love, immobile with Love, troubled with Love.*

*It is a matter of urgency—the Strategy of My "Madness"—that you understand. Until there is understanding, there is no end to the unconscious search, no beginning to the acts of love.*

*The Man of "Radical" Understanding is collapsed in weeping here itself, on the Shore that you call "Other".*

*Then who will console Me for your deaths? Who will console Me with touches when I am dying here?*

◆ ◆ ◆

*The Heart is such Extreme Power, Light, and Love! It cannot be contained. It is not contained, but Includes all things in Its own Being, Consciousness, and Bliss.*

*One who understands is grasped and acquired by the Heart. It is no easy thing, for there is the dissolution of all ordinary awareness and experience as body, mind, and enjoyment.*

*For one who understands, nothing is possible but the Heart. And if such a one acts otherwise, in the usual form of avoidance and separation, he or she suffers greatly.*

*The Heart puts to task one who understands, and shakes such a one empty, enslaves him or her to the Heart's Core, branding and consuming him or her in Fire.*

*Such a one, at last, no longer appears, but only the Heart—as Silence, Power, Light, Bliss, Intelligence, and Truth!*

*No one can believe This. And only those who understand can know It.*

◆ ◆ ◆

*I Am here in order that you may understand, and that I may Touch you with the Righteous Power of My Form.*

*I Am here to Love you and to be loved.*

*I Am here to be known, and you will know Me.*

*I Am here.*

*I Am Present, even in a form like yours.*

◆ ◆ ◆

Avatar Adi Da knew that the Event of His Incarnation and Realization had changed the very nature of existence, and the meaning of history. He was already initiating the greatest Labor ever begun—the Divine Liberation of even every thing and every one in the cosmic worlds.

In the next journal entry, Avatar Adi Da refers to Himself both as "I" (or "Me"), referring to His bodily Incarnation, and as "He" (or "Him"), referring to Himself as the Very Divine Person, Who is Functioning in the world through the Agency[2] of His bodily (human) Form.

*My Life is Pilgrimage and Mission of the Heart.*

*It is not easy, for the worlds are sealed in powers apart.*

*To do this thing is a Great Event and a Terrible Labor.*

*Only the Heart is Intelligent with Means to make it work.*

*Now that I am Gone in Him, the Heart must Do Its Work.*

*Now that He is given place where I once lived, He Rushes Out to Capture every corner of the atom that* <u>*is*</u> *this.*

*Now the worlds will feel and see and know Him every where.*

*The Heart is escaped.*
*He Fell Out of My Side.*
*He is here!*

*It has already happened that you are not the same.*

*Now all history is the Event of the Heart.*
*This is not My imagining.*

*It is not My Symbol of mystical truth.*

*It has happened in the atom of the worlds.*

*It is the simple Truth.*

*And that Eternal Event has even happened in this Lifetime and the Body That you see—Which seems to Speak, Which seemed to Think this thought, Whose Bliss has seemed to carry this expression.*

*Heart I Am, and I am Gone in Him, so He is only here.*

*This Body, Mind, and Force of Bliss is not needed for Him.*

*He is here, in the very worlds.*

*He Passed from Me into the worlds.*

*He Shattered My Side.*

*He has Become everything.*

*You are only Present with Him Who Teaches understanding that is the Heart.*

*He is your own hand.*

*Your hand will touch your side and send you shouted to the Heart.*

*This has already happened!*

*Only understand.*

◆ ◆ ◆

In the following most summary journal entry, Avatar Adi Da describes the extraordinary Pattern of His Life up to 1970, the Revelation Process through which He combined Himself with the human state and, in the midst of that Ordeal, Re-Awakened to His Divine Condition.

He refers to His Submission to all experience for the sake of finding God (1957), His sudden Awakening at Columbia (1960), His discovery of the "myth" of Narcissus and His meeting with Rudi (1964), the "ego-death" in seminary (1967), His first journey to Swami Muktananda (1968), the Shakti experiences on His second visit to India and the Awakening of His own Siddhis[3] as Teacher (1969), and, finally, His Most Perfect Realization (1970).

*In 1939, there was This Birth, but not the slightest "difference".*

*In 1957, This Living One adopted the method of experience, since He was suffering. He supposed that, if He avoided no experience, the Truth would necessarily Reveal Itself.*

*In 1960, there was again Illumination without the slightest "difference", and the search for a "truth" disappeared. Then He tried to dissolve the contradictions in Himself that made Him seek. The "differences" returned.*

*In 1964, He found the myth within life that is life's search. And the natural powers of conscious life reawakened. He found His human Teacher, Who would educate Him in the Nature of Spiritual Power, or God-Force.*

*In 1967, He passed through the death of all the forms in which He appeared. The rule that is all suffering became known. And the Law That is Very Consciousness came to life.*

*In 1968, He found His Spiritual Teacher in a Saint Who displayed all the Yogic Powers. There was the Universal Vision.*

*In 1969, there were the gifts of extraordinary powers and revelations.*

*In 1970, there were the Consummate Endings of all Spiritual Communication.*

*There is only the Living Heart, Which is all This Living One now can Say with Certainty. There is not the slightest "difference".*

Los Angeles, April 25, 1972

CHAPTER 4

# The Teaching Work Begins

In the weeks after His Divine Re-Awakening in the Vedanta Temple on September 10, 1970, Avatar Adi Da noticed a new process beginning in His body-mind:

*Now, whenever I would sit, in any kind of formal manner, to demonstrate the meditation, or the, now, Divine Samadhi, that had become my entire life, instead of confronting what was arising in and as "myself", I "meditated" other beings and places. I would spontaneously become aware of great numbers of people (usually in visions, or in some other, intuitive manner), and I would work with them very directly, in a subtle manner. . . . [I]nstead of my own life-born forms and problematic signs, the egoic forms, the problematic signs, the minds, the feelings, the states, and the various limitations of others would arise to my view. The thoughts, feelings, suffering, dis-ease, disharmony, upsets, pain, energies—none of these were "mine". They were the internal, subtle qualities and the life-qualities of others. In this manner, the process of apparent meditation continued in me.* [The Knee Of Listening]

In this "meditation", Avatar Adi Da was spontaneously awakening to the function of Guru. As He had once "meditated" Franklin Jones, He now "meditated" His future devotees.

## The Divine Guru-Function

Avatar Adi Da's intense Ordeal of surrender and Divine Re-Awakening had not been undertaken for His own sake. The persona called "Franklin" had been a means, a vehicle, whereby He could combine with the realities of human existence, inquire into those realities, live them out, go beyond every limitation they involve, and thereby discover what is necessary in order for human beings to Realize the Truth absolutely. Avatar Adi Da had not been born in order to Liberate just a few others—individuals who might seem to be qualified for such a profound Grace. Not at all. He had come for the sake of all of humanity—even for every being consciously existing in the cosmic worlds. He filled the pages of His journals with His longing to find His devotees. Where were they? When would they come?

*I am reminded of Sri Ramakrishna*[1]*—on fire within, Consumed in God, Communicated with all the forms of Truth, but spending His time alone or in the company of a few friends. His heart yearned for those to whom He could Communicate His Gift. He would cry for the devotees He knew must come. Where are the devotees? His whole being yearned for the children who would appear.*

*I have spent My Life in rooms. I have enjoyed the companionship and the attention of a few friends. But My Life is for the sake of this communication of "Brightness" and "radical" understanding.*

*The rooms cannot contain Me. My friends cannot satisfy Me. I am surrounded by Great Forces of Love and Truth That I hold off like beasts in the corners of My room.*

*All of this waits for those who must come. But I am motionless and confounded until they come. My fulfillment waits on those who must come.*

*My Life has not been for My Self. I already Possessed It before I Came to this Birth. My Life is for those who must come. But where are they?*

*I am going Mad with My own Words. I would exhaust this Body in experiences and every excuse for love, every possibility for a word with another. Where are they? When will My time come?*

*At times, I don't know whether to come or go. I am exiled here. All the means of escape are denied to Me. My Heart allows Me no passage to another "place", another "country". I would achieve My Victory in another world, but I am forced to keep these rooms, this exile in a hostile realm.*

*I am waiting for you. I have been waiting for you Eternally.*

*My Fulfillment is the very world. But I am not heard. My gestures are unseen. The Powers of My Delight are not enjoyed.*

*All things depend upon your visit. Where are you?*

[journal entry, 1971]

Avatar Adi Da knew that the moment had now come for Him to Communicate His Realization of the "Bright". And so He began to write *The Knee Of Listening*, which flowed out of Him in a matter of weeks—an extraordinary distillation of the course of His early Life, up until 1970. Until this moment, He had not spoken of His Realization to anyone. It was only when Nina began to type the manuscript that she began to grasp the depth of the Process that had been occurring in Him.

*NINA: As I typed the manuscript of* The Knee Of Listening, *tears streamed from my eyes in gratitude to Beloved Adi Da for His Divine Confession. He filled me with joy as He Revealed the Process that had occupied Him all His Life, and I wept again and again as I typed.*

*Outwardly, there was no sign in Beloved Adi Da that anything remarkable had occurred in the Vedanta Temple. He did not say that anything had happened. He came home. We had dinner and enjoyed the evening, and we went to bed. So when people ask what was different about Beloved Adi Da after the Vedanta Temple Event, I have to say that there wasn't any difference. There wasn't any difference! This is very important. It is the entire message of* The Knee Of Listening.

*It was only later, on April 25, 1972, when He took His Seat as the Divine Guru, that He was different. Yes, a change was noticeable when He began to Demonstrate His Guru-Siddhis. Beloved Adi Da asserts again and again in* The Knee Of Listening *that He would not serve as Guru for anyone until the Process was complete. And His Integrity was Perfect. Because He Is Eternally the Divine Person, most certainly He Functioned as Divine Guru in relationship to everyone who knew Him. But until He Sat as Divine Guru on Melrose Avenue in Los Angeles, on April 25, 1972, Beloved Adi Da never presumed or expected the formalities of the relationship between Guru and devotee.*

Various individuals came to Avatar Adi Da during the first year or so after His Divine Re-Awakening. They came by chance, because, apart from writing the manuscript of *The Knee Of Listening*, He was not yet making Himself publicly known as Teacher. One of the first of these was a young man named Wes Vaught, who worked as a proofreader at CSA Press, in Atlanta, Georgia, the original publisher of *The Knee Of Listening*.

*WES: For years, I had been desperately seeking to make sense of existence. While studying Adi Da's* Knee Of Listening *and contemplating its Truths, the intuition of the silent, free depth of the Heart dawned in me. I had found my Guru, and I began to feel irresistibly attracted to that Graceful Source.*

*The editor at the press where I was working showed me a letter from "Franklin Jones". In it, He Wrote, "There is not the slightest difference." Those Words stopped my mind. My entire life had been a warfare of differences and opposites, and I felt the profound Freedom communicated in this one sentence. I had to go see Him.*

*I traveled to Los Angeles and found the way to His home in Laurel Canyon. It was late April 1972. I knocked, and Adi Da Answered.*

*"Who is it?"*

*I explained that I had read His book, and that I had felt compelled to come and see Him. Adi Da opened the door, and I followed Him into the living room.*

*I felt welcomed into a "Bright" Space, free of any sense of problem. On the walls were Disney posters and images of holy men. It felt natural to sit on the floor before His Chair. I had brought with me a bag of oranges and pears as a gift. I extended it: "I brought this for You."*

*He received it with both Hands and with such loving care. Everything about Him was absolute strength, sublime vulnerability, perfect clarity, and delight. Time stood still while He removed the fruits from the bag and arranged them on a little table next to His Chair. Then He Graciously folded the paper bag neatly and tucked it by His thigh.*

*He received the whole gift!*

*Looking at me directly and with what seemed like an infinity of loving humor, Adi Da asked, "What have you been doing with your life?"*

*I felt the weight of my twenty-five years of waiting for God lift and, with what must have been a ridiculous gush of information, I spilled out my story. I do not know how long I talked. I tried to say everything of importance—all at once!*

*Adi Da listened. His was not the kind of listening where someone is waiting to say something when it is their turn. His listening became a perfect Intensity and a perfect Silence. At some point, His Silence became the entire import of the moment. I noticed this and stopped mid-sentence.*

*Sitting up straight, I was overwhelmed with His Blessing Force. Suddenly, I was shaking and breathing extremely deeply in the Current of His Communicated Force. My verbal mind ceased with the immediacy of His Presence.*

*I felt that Adi Da was Offering me the perfect opportunity in God, but I felt my gross unpreparedness and the obstructions in me that prevented me from fully cooperating with what He was Communicating. I wanted to get out of the way, but how?*

*Wanting to remove anything in the way of my freedom, anything that I could lay my hands on, I felt suddenly moved to take off my clothes. I began, and then paused for a moment, feeling foolish, and looked at Avatar Adi Da as if to ask, "Is this okay?"*

*With an almost imperceptible tilt of His Head, I felt Avatar Adi Da Communicate that it was of no significance to Him what I did with regard to clothing. I could suit myself in the matter.*

*He was most obviously Demonstrating His Divine Mood, clearly Indifferent to any sense of limitation, Shining with Blessing Force, replete with native Freedom and the certainty of unqualified Love, Transparent to the pure, sweet Grace of God.*

*I took everything off, even the band-aid on my heel, and threw myself face down and full-length at His Feet.*

*His Feet, somehow, were a perfect point of contact with this Blessing Force. I wept and kissed His Feet, wetting them with tears of relief, joy, gratitude, and also with the anguish that I could not completely let go of myself. Still I tried to surrender, straining with my heart and brain to open more.*

**Wes Vaught and Adi Da Samraj, 1972**

*But I could surrender no more.*

*Quietly, Adi Da lifted His Feet and placed them on my head. All stress left my being. A golden balm of sweet light poured through every cell in my body. A knot opened. I let go, and His brilliant Radiance washed through me. I was Home.*

*After a bit, I got up, dressed some, and told Adi Da that I felt that I belonged with Him. He looked at me and Said, "There is something about this Teaching you have not understood. It is about this matter of Consciousness."*

*He gave me everything in that moment—a living relationship to an absolute source of Grace, the most profound experience of my life, and the admonition to join Him in free relation to all phenomena. I fell in love with Him. I had begun the life of understanding in devotion to the One Who is that. The principle of my search was obviated and the momentum of my self-contraction, my separative and loveless adaptation, began to wind down.*

*He said He had established a bookstore and small center and invited me to sleep there that night. From that night, I joined the small gathering of people who were studying His Teaching and sitting in formal Communion with Him at the time.*

**Adi Da Samraj with some of His early devotees preparing for the opening of the bookstore on Melrose Avenue**

## Establishing the First Ashram

In April 1972, Avatar Adi Da established a small bookstore on Melrose Avenue, Hollywood, which He intended to become a base for His Spiritual Work, a place where He could gather with His devotees. He Himself did the lion's share of the renovation, with help from a few of His devotees.

What was to become Avatar Adi Da's Ashram center and bookstore had previously been an embroidery workshop, a dry cleaner's, and a photo-processing lab. Each time a new tenant had leased it, they had merely added new equipment, partitions, and so forth, without taking anything else out. Truckload after truckload of sheetrock and plywood had to be pulled out and hauled away.

The devotees who were helping Avatar Adi Da were amazed at His endless energy. He just kept pushing and pushing, beyond the point of exhaustion. One day, He fell over in His chair, having pushed His body too hard.

The bookstore and first Ashram

Avatar Adi Da with devotees at the Melrose Ashram

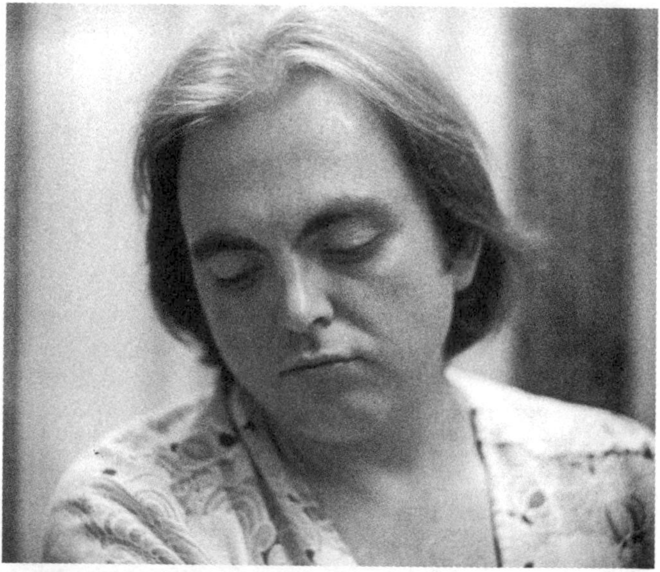

Opening night of the Ashram, April 25, 1972

But, in a matter of moments, He was immediately back at it. He worked for thirty days straight renovating the store.

Finally, on the evening of April 25, Avatar Adi Da Samraj formally began His Teaching Work, gathering with Nina and Patricia, the small group of people who had gathered around Him in recent months, some of their friends, and random individuals who had responded to a poster in the bookstore window. First, Avatar Adi Da sat in silence for an hour, magnifying the Force of the "Bright" to everyone in the room. Then He invited questions.

No one responded, so He asked, "Has everyone understood?"

"I haven't understood," came the reply from one man in the room. "Explain it to me. You could start with the word 'understanding'."

*AVATAR ADI DA SAMRAJ: Yes. There is a disturbance, a feeling of dissatisfaction, some sensation that motivates a person to go to a teacher, read a book about philosophy, believe something, or do some conventional form of Yoga. What people ordinarily think of as Spirituality or religion is a search to get free of that sensation, that suffering that is motivating them. So all the usual paths—Yogic methods, beliefs, religion, and so on—are forms of seeking, grown out of this sensation, this subtle suffering. Ultimately, all the usual paths are attempting to get free of that sensation. That is the traditional goal. Indeed, <u>all</u> human beings are seeking, whether or not they are very sophisticated about it, or using very specific methods of Yoga, philosophy, religion, and so on. . . .*

*As long as the individual is simply seeking, and has all kinds of motivation, fascination with the search, this is not understanding—this is dilemma itself. But where this dilemma is understood, there is the re-cognition*[2] *of a structure in the living consciousness, a separation. And when that separation is observed more and more directly, one begins to see that what one is suffering is not something happening to one but it is one's own action. It is as if you are pinching yourself, without being aware of it. . . . Then one sees that the entire motivation of life is based on a subtle activity in the living consciousness. That activity is avoidance, separation, a contraction at the root, the origin, the "place", of the living consciousness. . . .*

*There is first the periodic awareness of that sensation, then the awareness of it as a continuous experience, then the observation of its actual structure, the knowing of it all as your own activity, a deliberate, present activity that is your suffering, that is your illusion. The final penetration of that present, deliberate activity is what I have called "understanding".* [The Method Of The Ruchira Avatar]

And so it began—hours, days, nights, weeks, years, decades of Spiritual Instruction, in which Avatar Adi Da would cover all human, religious, and Spiritual questions, examine every aspect of life and consciousness, and Reveal every detail of the Spiritual Process culminating in Most Perfect Divine Enlightenment. The small gathering at the Ashram bookstore on that first night had not the slightest idea that they were witness to the birth of such Revelation. They attended, as best they could, to the Radiant Being before them, while He Spoke of the matter of "understanding".

Understanding was the very basis of Avatar Adi Da's own Sadhana and Divine Re-Awakening. He lived, breathed, and spoke always from the point of view of understanding. Throughout that first year of His Teaching Work, Avatar Adi Da would meet again and again with His devotees, constantly speaking about understanding, and also about the only means by which it is possible to understand—"Satsang",[3] or the Company of the Guru. These early Talks were eventually published as Avatar Adi Da's second book, *The Method of the Siddhas*.[4]

*AVATAR ADI DA SAMRAJ: Spiritual life is Satsang. It is the Company of Truth. It is the relationship to one who Lives as Truth. Satsang is also the Very Nature of life. It is the form of existence. Relatedness—not independence, not separateness, but unqualified relatedness—is the principle of True life.*

*All attempts to relieve the life of suffering by various strategic means, or ego-based remedies, do not produce Truth. They may heal dis-ease, but only Truth produces Truth. Sadhana, or Spiritual practice, is to live Satsang as the Condition of life forever. Sadhana is not something you do temporarily until you get Free. It is to live Satsang forever—a lifetime, even countless lifetimes, of Truth. . . .*

*Listen! There is this contraction, this avoidance. All human beings are living this avoidance of relationship. Apart from understanding, that is all anyone is doing. Nothing else is happening. Only this contraction of living and subtle forms. It is suffering. It stimulates, by implication, the notions people have about the nature of life. This contraction implies a separate self, separate from the world and all other beings. The appearance of "many", "much", and "separate me" is an expression of your suffering, but the Force, the Intensity, the Bliss, of Reality persists and is felt even under the conditions of egoic ignorance. Therefore, this contraction appears as the drama of desire, the search for union between the "separate me" and the "manyness". Everyone's life is the drama made inevitable by this fundamental contraction. Everyone's life is the adventure he or she is playing on this contraction. Everyone's life is bullshit! The drama of an ordinary life is without significance, or Real Intensity. The ordinary life-drama is deadly ignorance—no Truth, no Satsang.*

*Satsang must begin. Satsang with Me must be enjoyed as the Condition of life. Then the entire drama of which even traditional Spirituality is a manifestation comes to an end, dies. This contraction becomes flabby and opens. The Real Force of Conscious Existence comes into play and becomes the Way in My Company, the sadhana itself.* [The Method Of The Ruchira Avatar]

At the inception of His Work, Avatar Adi Da presumed no reason why everyone who came to Him would not understand and quickly Awaken to His own Realization. But He soon saw that no one was prepared for the profundity of His Argument. The self-contraction of which He Spoke was too fundamental, too all-encompassing to be seen without a power of self-observation that none of His devotees were then capable of. But they were no more retarded in this than any other human beings—no one had ever completely understood the self-contraction before. Avatar Adi Da's "radical" understanding was a Teaching unique in Spiritual history.

Many of those who first came to the Ashram were individuals in whom the search had taken a highly exaggerated form. This was not a merely arbitrary occurrence—He had come to serve the Liberation of <u>all</u> beings, including those apparently least prepared for Spiritual life. There were street-people, prostitutes, drug addicts, alcoholics, and Spiritual seekers, hippie-style, who had done the rounds of various teachers and teachings. And there were also business people and professionals of various kinds. Avatar Adi Da welcomed them all. He saw that His own life and Sadhana, and even the ordinariness of His human birth, had equipped Him to Teach anyone.

Lydia Depole, a commercial artist from New York, came to Avatar Adi Da after years of dissatisfaction and Spiritual seeking:

*LYDIA: In 1972, I decided to go to California with a woman friend. We packed little more than a change of clothes in a knapsack and starting hitchhiking. Once in California, I got involved with Sufism and later with an Indian teacher of Yoga. Then I settled on the beach in Isla Vista, near Santa Barbara, in the small and exclusive Bohemian community in which Aldous Huxley*[5] *had died. I was illustrating astrology charts and being a fruitarian. I lived in the open air above the beach under a flowering tree and woke up each morning with fallen blossoms on my face. I thought that this was life.*

*In the meantime, a friend of mine who had been traveling around, actively seeking for a Guru, sent me a photograph of Franklin Jones. "I think Franklin will like you," he wrote, "and you'll like him."*

*My life changed when I saw that photograph. For some reason, I instantly decided that I would experiment with hallucinogens—something I had never done before. I did it once, and it was horrific, reflecting to me everything that I felt about the chaotic and threatening nature of existence. While the experience was going on, I realized that the only thing left, the only possibility, was Franklin Jones. This was the only clarity in the midst of the vision of mortality and constant change that the drug was inducing in me. I knew now that I <u>had</u> to find Him, that He was the only sanity in the world.*

*Immediately after that, all kinds of enticing worldly possibilities came my way. I was offered several jobs—one illustrating Stevie Wonder's new album cover, which could have brought me wealth and prominence as an artist. At the same time, a famous drummer and rock music composer fell in love with me. He was my ideal lover. But I knew in my heart that I could not become involved in any of this. I kept saying, "No, I have to be with Franklin." And yet, I didn't even know who "Franklin" was or what I was saying. The only contact I had had with Franklin Jones was His photograph. My friends thought I was crazy, but this was an intuitive certainty in me.*

*I turned up at Melrose Avenue in Hollywood in December of 1972 in a pair of Oshkosh B'Gosh overalls (with no shirt underneath) and biking boots. I sat outside on the doorstep of the Ashram, waiting to go in. "Franklin" had to be told about me. I waited, sitting with a little bag of clothes—that was the way I lived in those days! When Beloved Adi Da was asked if I could come in, His response was "I don't want to see her! Tell her to go out and get a job!" I was shocked. I had given up several extraordinary job opportunities to come and be with Him, and He tells me to get a job! It took me months to finally get a job as a file clerk in a bank. Only later did I understand that this was my first lesson from Beloved Adi Da—a lesson in assuming responsibility for my life-circumstance.*

*I will never forget the first time I saw Beloved Adi Da. He came in and sat silently for a while, and then afterward everybody brought Him gifts and then left the Hall. In those days, the formality was that He would remain seated until all the devotees had left. People were filing quietly out, but I couldn't bring myself to leave. Finally, there was just me and Him and Nina left in the room. Nina said, "Franklin, have You met Lydia yet?" And He said, "Oh yes. Oh yes, we've known each other for a long time, a very long, long, long, long time." And then He embraced me. In that Embrace, I could feel my anxiety, my obsession, my madness being lifted off. All of a sudden, everything made total sense. There was the feeling of no-separation, of complete Oneness, Love. It was as if He said to me, "This is your home, this is it, this is life, this is Reality."*

*I didn't say anything, I was just totally open. The anticipation, the desire, and the passion in me to see Him were so great that I was empty and open, totally. The*

**Lydia Depole and Avatar Adi Da Samraj, Los Angeles, 1973**

***"It was as if He said to me, 'This is your home, this is it, this is life, this is Reality.'"***

*magnitude of that Embrace changed my entire life. Everything made sense. Although the realization of what I was Given then only unfolded over many years—and continues to unfold—the Truth was given to me whole in that moment.*

## The Demand for Self-Discipline

During that first year of the Ashram, Avatar Adi Da did not require very much responsibility of His devotees. He was simply attracting them, keeping them around Him, so that He could Work to Awaken understanding in them. Then, one day near the beginning of 1973, everything suddenly changed. Striding out of His office with tremendous force and intention, He disappeared through the front door of the Ashram. No one saw Him for weeks, but He left a message: everyone was to "get straight"—give up all use of drugs, cigarettes, alcohol—get jobs, and contribute five dollars a week to the support of the Ashram.

In other words, the days when Avatar Adi Da was prepared to nurse His devotees along were over. It was time to make demands. Extraordinary energy and attention, as He knew from His own experience, was needed to grow in the practice of understanding. There was no room for life-chaos and irresponsibility. Disciplines must be established. Without sufficient self-discipline, the body-minds of His devotees would be unable to fully receive His Spiritual Gifts.

Suddenly, egg-and-bacon breakfasts around the corner from the Ashram were over. Everyone became strict vegetarians. And Avatar Adi Da recommended a ten-day juice-fast, which was taken on by even the newest devotees. When Avatar Adi Da heard that someone had "cheated"—by "juicing" bananas—He was extremely amused. But He called for another immediate ten-day fast for everyone!

Avatar Adi Da's disciplines covered every area of life. He established a discipline of no casual sex—only partners in committed intimacies were to be sexually active. He instructed a small group in calisthenics and Hatha Yoga[6] and had them teach everyone else. He addressed every detail of appropriate life-discipline, even personally showing people how to floss their teeth! Altogether He was showing His devotees the total reorientation of life that He expected of them, and the complete obedience to Him that was necessary if He were to Work with them Spiritually. In many ways, what He had now established was a very traditional Ashram.

In a letter He had written before the opening of the Ashram, addressed to two women who had approached Him for His Instruction, Avatar Adi Da spoke of the necessity for the force of "demand" in real Spiritual life:

*It is a difficult thing, in every case, for a person to approach a Teacher in Truth. If I am to Serve as Divine Heart-Master for both of you, and for every kind of person who comes to Me, if I am to Serve the heart-Awakening of every one, there must be a difficult confrontation. The relationship to Me is not all smiles, friendliness, and comfortable conversation. It is not the communication of experiences, but the Communication of Divine Wisdom, the Heart Itself. Therefore, the Process in My Company is difficult, and it requires great endurance of Me and of My devotee.*

*I do not regard these difficulties to be an obstacle or a disadvantage. I welcome it all. And your devotional relationship to Me can be the most creative, humorous, and enjoyable experience. But there must be discriminative intelligence, which is the foundation of understanding.*

*I demand everything of My devotees. I know what they need and what must occur in them. Therefore, I do not indulge them, but I require everything of them.*

*I am very willing to accept both of you as My devotees. But you must come to Me directly, devotionally, intelligently, with need, willing to endure this difficult confrontation.*

By the middle of 1973, the Ashram disciplines were in full swing, but Avatar Adi Da saw that His devotees were now becoming obsessed with the disciplines as a "something" in and of themselves—as if the disciplines were the purpose of sadhana, rather than simply a support for the fundamental practice of heart-Communion with Him. It was also obvious to Avatar Adi Da that the people around Him—like people in general—were emotionally suppressed, sexually complicated, driven by fear, sorrow, anger, frustration, and all kinds of unconscious desires. And He knew that He was going to have to deal with all of this directly. He decided He must change His manner of Working with His devotees—otherwise, their so-called "religious practice" would merely be a veneer covering a mass of unresolved egoic impulses. It was starting to become evident that Ashram life, lived with Him in the strict traditional manner, was not going to be sufficient to awaken "radical understanding" in His devotees.

## The Return to India

First, Avatar Adi Da made a pause in His face-to-face Work with His devotees. Accompanied by Gerald Sheinfeld (one of those who had been present at the opening of the Ashram), He set out for India, the cradle of Spiritual Teaching for thousands of years. During His own Sadhana, Avatar Adi Da had associated Himself with the great Siddha tradition of India (exemplified by Swami Muktananda and Swami Nityananda), and now He was paying His last homage to that tradition. In effect, He was performing a pilgrimage—to complete all His past links with India and to Empower His future Work.

Most significant of all the journeys that Avatar Adi Da made to the sacred places of India was His return to the Ashram of Swami Muktananda—for the first time since 1970. Because Swami Muktananda had served Him as His Beloved Guru, Avatar Adi Da presumed an obligation to formally ask Swami Muktananda whether he could acknowledge His (Avatar Adi Da's) Realization as True and Most Perfect. And so Avatar Adi Da asked for a formal meeting with Swami Muktananda, which was duly arranged to occur at the Ganeshpuri Ashram.

Avatar Adi Da, attended by Gerald, approached Swami Muktananda and bowed before him. Then Adi Da Samraj sat on the floor, at the feet of Swami Muktananda, and presented a series questions, through which Avatar Adi Da expressed the nature of His Realization and the

**Avatar Adi Da Samraj meeting with Swami Muktananda, Ganeshpuri, 1973**

differences between His Realization and the traditional understanding of Realization in Swami Muktananda's lineage. The questions had been submitted in advance, in the traditional manner, and were translated by an attending scholar, Professor Jain.

Swami Muktananda, however, did not acknowledge the possibility of an Enlightenment senior to that of his own tradition, nor did he openly recognize the true Stature of the One He had named "Love-Ananda". In response to Avatar Adi Da, Swami Muktananda merely stood by his own descriptions of Yogic Realization.[7]

There was nothing more to be said between them. Avatar Adi Da was disappointed, but clear. He would always love and honor Swami Muktananda, and spoke of him in later years as a man of extraordinary Yogic Enlightenment and one of the greatest beings who has ever lived.[8]

The visit to Ganeshpuri by Avatar Adi Da in 1973 was His last meeting in the flesh with Swami Muktananda. Avatar Adi Da now fully embraced His right to Teach according to His own Divinely Re-Awakened Realization.

**Gerald Sheinfeld and Avatar Adi Da Samraj on the trip to India, 1973**

The task facing Avatar Adi Da was huge beyond belief, because His Work was based in the West, where there was virtually no living tradition of Guru-devotion. He had no Ashram set apart like that at Ganeshpuri, no Sanctuary resounding with the recitation of sacred texts and chants in honor of God and Guru. All He had was a room behind a bookstore in Hollywood and a small gathering of devotees who were still basically unaware of the profundity of the relationship that they had begun with Him.

On a few occasions during that time in India, Avatar Adi Da asked Gerald, at the end of a long day, to massage His Feet. In the tradition of Guru-devotion, to touch the Master's Feet is a sublime privilege, for it has long been observed that the Master's Spiritual Blessing flows out of his or her Feet with especially profound Force. But Avatar Adi Da had an uncanny ability to ask for a foot massage precisely in those moments when Gerald was not in a mood to have any demands placed on him:

*GERALD: Initially, I resisted these requests from Beloved Adi Da, feeling that I would be glad to give Him a massage in a little while, but first I needed to clean the camera equipment. (Basically, I wanted to be left alone.) Then Beloved Adi Da would very gently but very firmly insist that He needed the massage right away. I would grudgingly start to massage His Feet and legs, all the while thinking of the other things I needed to do, like relaxing, cleaning the camera equipment, refreshing from the day with a shower, and so on. This, of course, was not true service to my Beloved Heart-Master, but the perfunctory performance of a duty I could not avoid. On one of these occasions, He told me that I had to be as functional as a chair—simple and uncomplicated and always willing to serve.*

*But, as I massaged my Divine Guru's Feet and legs, I gradually relaxed and focused my attention on doing the massage. Once this happened I started to become sensitive to His Radiance, and I felt the happiness of being with Him, serving Him. I relaxed into the blissfulness of simple service to Him. The Transmission of His Love-Bliss was so Powerful and Radiant and effective, and it always broke through my self-obsession and resistance. Eventually, I found myself simply available to Him, feeling completely enlivened by my relationship to Him, and serving happily, free of self-reference and concern. When I was fully restored to the mood of heart-Communion with Him, through the Grace of His Transmission, then He would say, "That's fine", and the massage would be over. It was obvious that the massages were not for His sake, but for mine.*

While Avatar Adi Da was Working with the one devotee at His side, He was "considering" how to take the relationship that all His devotees enjoyed with Him to a deeper level. It was no longer appropriate for His devotees to call Him "Franklin Jones", as they had up

to that point. As He said later, Franklin Jones was "a fictional character", the persona He had been obliged to assume in order to grow up as an apparently ordinary American child. And so, He asked Gerald to write to the devotees in Los Angeles, announcing that they were now to address Him by the Name "Bubba Free John".

*From this time on, we should call the Guru "Bubba Free John". "Franklin" means "a Freed Man" or "a Liberated Man". "Jones" is a Welsh form of "John". So "Free John" is equivalent to "Franklin Jones". "Bubba" means "brother", or "equal", expressing the Oneness of all.*[9]

While He was in India, Avatar Adi Da Samraj acquired a staff, a sign of Spiritual empowerment and authority that He has regularly used ever since. Gerald watched as Avatar Adi Da placed His staff in the holy sites of India, with great concentration, Giving His Silent Regard to all kinds of people and places. Avatar Adi Da was Blessing this sacred land with His Love, and was also Invoking the Blessing of her greatest Spiritual Realizers on His own Work that was about to unfold in the West.

**Los Angeles, 1973**

CHAPTER 5

# "Crazy Wisdom"

*The Work of My Life and Teaching, to this time, has been to Show and Clarify the Way of the "Knowing" of Real God. The Siddhi through Which I have Made My Self available to My devotees is the Siddhi through Which the "Knowing" of Real God is Generated by My Grace. Such is the Way of "Radical" Understanding.*[1]

*But now there is a new form of Life and Teaching Awakened in Me. It has always been Present in Me, but I have not wanted to Embrace It or Show It, because It is only a fascination for those who do not understand. And, if such weak ones are fascinated, they will merely be distracted from their fear. Even so, it is obvious to Me now that I must no longer be Merely Present among My devotees, Constant in the Most Perfect "Knowledge" of Real God. But I must now allow the Conscious Power Realized in That Most Perfect "Knowledge", Which Is Non-Separation from Real God, to Manifest Itself in the form of My own Action.*

*My Teaching Work is now moving away from exclusive focus on the Way of "Radical" Understanding. That form of My Wisdom-Teaching is now essentially Given. I can assume it in My devotees. Now I am moving toward a Principle of Action as the core of My Work. Until now, I have refused to Display My Divine Siddhis. But Real God Is the Maha-Siddha.*[2] *Real God Is Perfect Siddhi. My Divine Siddhi is not a mere show of fascinating "powers",*

**Greeting devotees at the airport upon His return from India to Los Angeles, September, 1973**

***Now it has become Obvious to Me that My Life of "radical" understanding must also Assume the Siddhi of Real God. Therefore, My Divine Siddhi, Which I have always Manifested among My devotees, will now be Assumed in Its Fullness.***

*capable of being displayed and witnessed entirely* <u>*apart*</u> *from "radical" understanding. My Divine Siddhi Is* <u>*All-Power,*</u> *Which is always* <u>*Coincident*</u> *with "radical" understanding in those to whom I Reveal My Self as the Divine Maha-Siddha.*

*Now it has become Obvious to Me that My Life of "radical" understanding must also Assume the Siddhi of Real God. Therefore, My Divine Siddhi, Which I have always Manifested among My devotees, will now be Assumed in Its Fullness.*

*Until now, I have minimized, hidden, and set aside those aspects of My Divine Siddhi which do not directly Serve the Awakening of "radical" understanding (which is, most ultimately, the Unqualified "Knowledge" of Real God). But now I will not simply Sit in silent Darshan*[3]*—I will begin to Actively Manifest the All-Accomplishing Siddhi of Real God, Which Siddhi Serves the life-transformation of My devotees. This will accelerate and magnify My Work of Awakening the conscious life of faith and Drawing into life the Non-karmic, karma-Dissolving, Unreasonable, Humorous, and Miraculously Effective Siddhi of Eternally Present Real God.* [unpublished Writing, 1973]

Avatar Adi Da returned from India in September 1973, now as "Bubba Free John". The entire Ashram met Him at the airport. When He stepped into the terminal, He looked "absolutely beautiful", "brilliant as a thousand suns". His Radiance impressed everyone—as did His insistence on giving each one a long and Happy embrace. It was obvious to them that, somehow, their Guru had changed dramatically.

The Way of Avatar Adi Da was about "radical" understanding, but He had now seen, beyond doubt, that He could not Awaken His devotees to the Non-Separate Truth of Reality merely by means of His Words and His Example, or by requiring them to embrace a life of religious discipline, or even by silently Transmitting His Blessing to them. The contact that His devotees had had with Him had Drawn them temporarily beyond the self-contraction, but then they would forget the mood of Satsang and fall back into their habitual, and largely unconscious, patterns of seeking. How were they to be Drawn beyond the drama of "Narcissus", into constant heart-Communion with Him? It was clear to Avatar Adi Da that He had to embark upon an extraordinary and unconventional manner of Teaching, one that would require Him to animate all the Divine Siddhis, or Powers, that, until now, He had largely kept hidden.

During His Sadhana, Avatar Adi Da had submitted Himself to discover the entire pattern of "Narcissus", the separate and separative ego-self. He had given Himself up to every kind of psycho-physical experience and observed all aspects of His being, until every detail was understood and transcended.

But His devotees were not like Him. They had demonstrated no capability to activate and sustain such a profound process in themselves. And so Avatar Adi Da recognized that He would have to do it for them. He would have to enter completely into the lives of His devotees, be their "friend", go into every kind of situation with them, do what they liked to do, be available without qualification to their requirements and demands, and thus lead them personally, one by one, through the ordeal of self-understanding. He would need to show them, by all kinds of skillful means, every detail of their individual rituals of un-Happiness. He would have to do whatever it took to awaken in them the realization that all seeking is un-Happy and fruitless, an interminable bondage of self-contraction that inevitably leads to frustration, alienation, and death.

Avatar Adi Da knew that only through such a Sacrifice of surrender to His devotees could He hope to move them to deep heart-surrender to Him. And only through their surrender could He establish a profound Spiritual relationship to each of them and open them unequivocally to His overwhelming Revelation of Real God.

Avatar Adi Da was well aware that this direct form of Teaching would be an immensely creative and difficult affair, one in which He would appear to sacrifice His own purity and to take on the un-Illumined obsessions of His devotees. Just as he had "decided", at the age of two, to relinquish His Enjoyment of the "Bright" and become an apparently ordinary human being, for the sake of learning how an ordinary human being can come to Enjoy the "Bright", so now He made a Gesture of similar profundity. He was going to Submit unconditionally to His devotees, in order to Reveal the Truth to them in the only way they were then able to receive it. Twenty-five years later, in 1998, Avatar Adi Da spoke of how He came to this extraordinary Resolve:

*AVATAR ADI DA SAMRAJ: I went to India in 1973, taking some time away from the gathering of My devotees, and returned to the Ashram in Los Angeles resolved to do whatever I had to do to deal with the reality of people's unprepared approach to Me. From that time onwards, I accepted the fact that My Work with people was going to involve <u>My</u> Submission to <u>them</u> and their conditions—until such time as they would recognize Me and understand what the by Me Given Way of Adidam is about altogether, and relate to Me differently.*

*I had no sense at all how long that was going to take, or what it would require altogether. It wasn't that I was thinking I would do it for a few months, and then that would be that. It was a real Submission, with no preconception as to how it would turn out.* [August 8, 1998]

## The Tantric Work Begins

Adi Da Samraj was choosing to Work in the manner traditionally described as "Tantric". Tantra is a stream of Spiritual Teaching and practice that is found in both Hinduism and Buddhism. The fundamental disposition underlying Tantra is the intention to Realize the Truth without dissociating oneself from the world—or, as Avatar Adi Da has described it, the intention to "remain in Divine Communion[4] while functioning in the ordinary circumstance of life"—in contrast to the ascetical disposition of cutting off the world in order to become "pure".

This disposition of non-dissociation from the world has been enacted in various ways in different traditional schools of Tantra. In the so-called "left-hand" Tantric schools, the basic approach is summarized in the aphorism "You must rise by means of that which would otherwise cause you to fall." Thus, the practice of "left-hand" Tantra involves the use of what is otherwise regarded to be Spiritually inauspicious—for example, intoxicants and sexual activity—as part of one's Spiritual practice. The deep intention behind such practices was to enact—generally, in a ritually prescribed manner—the basic Tantric disposition of non-dissociation.

In His "Sadhana Years",[5] Avatar Adi Da Samraj had already spontaneously engaged in an awesome Tantric Ordeal. Still in His teens, and without the guidance of a Guru, He had plunged into the maelstrom of New York City street life, boldly using such means to quicken His Spiritual quest. Many years later, He described the Tantric course He had embarked on, beginning at Columbia:

*Even From The Earliest Days Of The Avataric Physical Lifetime Of My Bodily (Human) Form, I Have Spontaneously Manifested The Unique Display Of The Divinely*

*"Crazy" and Divinely "Heroic"*[6] *Course. In My Own Case, There Was, Even From The Earliest Days Of The Avataric Physical Lifetime Of My Bodily (Human) Form, An Absolute Impulse To Realize (or, Truly, To Restore The Realization Of) The Perfect Freedom Of The "Bright" Heart Itself (Which Is My Own Very and Divine Self-Condition). Indeed, From Those Earliest Days Onward, No Other "Consideration" Held Any Attraction, Interest, or Significance For Me. Inevitably, I Was Associated, By My Bodily (Human) Birth, With Every Kind Of life-Contradiction and ordinary human Tendency and ordinary human Adaptation, and With The Entire Range Of Apparent Problems and egoic Patterns That Result From All Of That. However, In My Struggle To Confront and Transcend The Problems Of human life, I Did Not Choose (In The idealistic Manner) Merely To Adapt To conventionally ideal behaviors. It Was Inherently and Immediately Clear To Me That I Had To Transcend Everything, In Order, Again, To Most Perfectly Realize My Own Native and "Bright" Divine Self-Condition. Thus, It Was Clear To Me That I Had To Embrace Everything—All The Contradictions, All The Positives, All The Negatives, Everything gross, Everything subtle, Everything Spiritual, Everything (and Everyone) Altogether—and (Thereby) To Deny Not anything or any one, To Avoid Not anything or any one, but To Embrace Everyone, To Endure Everything, To Pass Through Everything, To Suffer Everything, To Enjoy Everything, To Do Everything. I Was Intuitively Certain That Only Thus Would I Be Able To Unqualifiedly Establish, In The Avataric Physical Lifetime Of My Bodily (Human) Form, The Firm Absolutization Of My Own Disposition In "Brightness".*

*For Me, There Was Never Any Other Possibility Than The "Reckless" (or Divinely "Crazy" and Divinely "Heroic") Course Of All-and-all-Embrace—and I Began This Uniquely "Crazy" and "Heroic" Sadhana, Most Inten-*

*sively, At The Beginning Of My Adult Life. Indeed, I Have Always Functioned, and Will Always Function, In This Divinely "Crazy" and Divinely "Heroic" Manner. The Inherently egoless "Crazy" and "Heroic" Manner Is One Of My Principal Divine Characteristics—Whereby I Can (Always, and Now, and Forever Hereafter) Be Identified.* [The Dawn Horse Testament Of The Ruchira Avatar]

Avatar Adi Da's devotees had always found Him entrancingly Attractive. Now, as He began His Tantric Work, His Attractiveness magnified and became utterly overwhelming. Men and women alike were overcome with love at the Sight of Him. He became the living, dancing, laughing Form of Divine Radiance, Humor, and Love.

One of Avatar Adi Da's first demonstrations of His Tantric method, and of His profound Submission to the worldly impulses of His devotees, took place a few months after He returned from India.

*GERALD SHEINFELD: One day, a few other men and I were talking with Beloved Adi Da in the back room at the Ashram.*

*"Let's do something together," He said. He asked what we would really like to do. We didn't come up with anything exciting. So He asked again, "What would you really like to do?"*

*Then He said, "Let's go barhopping together."*

*"What?!" Barhopping? We thought He was kidding.*

*"I am serious. You guys would like to go barhopping, wouldn't you?"*

*"Yes!" we said.*

*"So, let's go."*

*We decided to go the next night. We met at the Ashram dressed to go out on the town. When we arrived at the first bar—a no-class strip-joint that looked and smelled the way such places do—our Beloved Guru walked right up to the stage and took His seat directly in front of the topless dancer. He put His feet on the low stage, spreading His legs widely, and He very firmly and conspicuously placed His hands right on top of His genitals. We were all shocked. Everyone else in the place, including the four of us, were trying to pretend we didn't have any genitals.*

*Beloved Adi Da immediately began applauding, gesturing, laughing, and urging the dancer on. At one point in the dance, He put a five-dollar bill in His teeth, and she bent down and took it from Him with her knees. He asked her humorously, "What's a nice girl like you doing in a place like this?" She loved it! She became very focused on her dancing, very intent as He urged her on. Soon she was dancing just for Him, putting everything she had into it. And He loved her response.*

*The next dancer had already been advised by the first dancer to concentrate on Beloved Adi Da. So, when she entered, she came directly over to Him and also danced just for Him. Once again, He responded to her full of feeling, with smiles, applause, and comments about how good she was.*

*Later, when a comedian came on stage, Beloved Adi Da began spurring with him, engaging him in a humorous exchange and besting the comedian at his own jokes. Now the entire room was laughing and appreciating the banter. When Beloved Adi Da got up to leave, everyone in the place—including the dancers, the bouncer, the waiter, and all the clientele—protested. They were having such a good time, now that Beloved Adi Da had dispelled the degenerate atmosphere by bringing them His True Humor and Heart-Feeling. As He walked up the aisle to the exit door, they all clapped their hands in appreciation.*

*After that, we went to some other bars, and Beloved Adi Da continued to make the same Instructive Demonstration.*

*I was impressed. I had just spent weeks following Beloved Adi Da around the holy places of India. And now here He was actively participating in the social night-club-life of Los Angeles! He was the same Free Happy Being, no matter what circumstance He was in. But I definitely had my ascetic preferences about where I wanted to be.*

*Our Beloved Guru observed my attitude, and addressed me about my self-righteous reactions. After that, I relaxed and allowed myself a little humor and enjoyment. But, obviously, if it had been anyone else doing what He did, the scene would soon have become totally degenerate. With Him, on the other hand, it was just theatrical and humorous and enjoyable. Who knows what Spiritual Work He was doing in that place? But He certainly showed those of us with Him where we were at—obsessed with sex and, at the same time, uptight and complicated about it.*

For the sake of Instructing His devotees, Avatar Adi Da was ready to Work in this manner. The greatest traditional Tantric Masters were known for their "Crazy" (or freely unconventional) behavior. The Tibetan Buddhist tradition is particularly rich with stories of "Crazy-Wise" Masters, but such Masters have existed at various times in all the esoteric Spiritual traditions of the world.[7] Little is known about most of them, because their work was truly esoteric—in other words, it was done in secret, because it was felt to be incomprehensible by the common mind.

"Crazy-Wisdom" Masters have been known to throw rocks at people, wander around naked, initiate people sexually, shout obscenities, and so forth. But a genuine "Crazy-Wisdom" Master would never do such things merely to shock or offend. The purpose of "Crazy Wisdom" is to shake people up—to liberate them from fixed egoic presumptions and patterns, and release their impulses and energy for Spiritual growth.

In resolving to Submit to the likeness of His devotees, to Teach them in the Tantric manner—even though

they were all beginners in the Spiritual Way—Avatar Adi Da Samraj was making the most "Crazy" of Gestures. His Play with devotees became a complex and wild theatre of Divine Liberation, in which He would Display His absolute Genius for relating to every conceivable kind of person, and His unerring Knowledge of what was required to Awaken each one—no matter what was required. Everything that Avatar Adi Da did was for the sake of Liberating His devotees from ego-bondage and magnifying their heart-Communion with Him.

## Guru Enters Devotee

During Thanksgiving in 1973, Avatar Adi Da relaxed the dietary discipline, and everyone partook of a traditional turkey meal, accompanied by wine. Avatar Adi Da Himself had entered into the spirit of the occasion by wearing an elegant three-piece tan-colored suit. One devotee, Hal Okun, remembers observing Avatar Adi Da after the meal.

*HAL: I noticed that Beloved Adi Da was silently assessing the whole scene. With hindsight, I can feel what He was involved in at that time. He was accepting our utter naivete and gross-mindedness relative to the great Spiritual Process He was bringing us. And He was coming to a decision, or a confirmed resolve, about what He was going to do.*

On the Friday before Christmas, two of the devotees present at the Thanksgiving dinner, Aniello Panico and Hal Okun, were indulging in a little champagne at an office party before going to the Ashram (which had moved from Melrose to La Brea Avenue), to spend the rest of the day with Avatar Adi Da. Hal arrived first, and, as he ascended the stairs, he looked up and saw Avatar Adi Da regarding him fiercely from the top. "Are you drunk, Hal?" Avatar Adi Da asked, and, before waiting for a reply, He burst out laughing. His instructions were immediate: Hal was to call Aniello and have him come to the Ashram at once, bringing cases of champagne.

The trend of the conversation led to a further development. Why not relinquish all taboos? Why not be naked? Suddenly, it seemed perfectly natural and humorous to do this—and, without further ado, everyone removed their clothes.

When Aniello came in, the small group who had already arrived sat with Avatar Adi Da in the room at the top of the stairs, enjoying beer and champagne and anticipating the surprise that other devotees would have when they came along.

By now, devotees were beginning to appear in numbers, carrying their usual gifts of flowers and fruit, expecting a formal evening with "Bubba" at the Ashram. One by one, they would come up the stairs and their jaws would drop as they surveyed the scene. Then, one by one, they would take a beer or a glass of champagne and join the party, shaking with laughter when each newcomer stumbled astonished into the room. At a certain point, Avatar Adi Da and everyone else moved into the adjacent gathering hall and the party began in earnest—rock music, junk food, cigarettes. The disciplines had been cast to the four winds.

This was the beginning of two weeks of unstoppable celebration, during which practically no one went home. Devotees would party all night with their Divine Heart-Master, drive straight to work in the morning, and drive back from work to celebrate again. Avatar Adi Da was always at the center of it all, sitting or reclining on a couch, laughing, joking, encouraging everyone's intense participation. Madly dancing, spontaneously singing—everyone present was unbelievably happy, drenched in Avatar Adi Da's tangible Transmission of His "Bright" Spirit-Force.

In the midst of all the festivities, Avatar Adi Da never ceased to speak of the Great Matter. At a Christmas gift-giving occasion with some devotees, Avatar Adi Da suddenly called for a great confession. Who could speak freely of God, as He had been doing all night? Who could stand up and praise the Great One, unabashed? In spite of all the ecstasy of their Divine Guru's Company, each devotee suddenly felt a lock at the throat. One after another, they made awkward attempts at unabashed, uninhibited God-talk, but quickly received the thumbs-down sign from Avatar Adi Da. Finally, one devotee, Marie Prager, broke through and began to sing crazily and ecstatically about God. Then everyone in the room became ecstatic with her and began shouting and singing and praising God with great energy. A night or two later, Avatar Adi Da spoke about the lesson of this occasion.

*AVATAR ADI DA SAMRAJ: To confess one's love of God is the fundamental embarrassment. To make such a confession is to dwell in obvious ecstasy while in the company of other beings—to be already free, to be fundamentally happy, to be alive in God, and even to be outwardly expressive in that state, to speak of God, to think of God, to act in God, to be altogether ecstatic. This is the taboo—not mere drunkenness and indulgence in pleasure. To require you to talk of God makes you embarrassed. You become ashamed. Because, in order to talk about God, you must lose face. To be extraordinarily and unreasonably happy, and to live that way, is embarrassing. To be full of love and only talk that way—so foolishly, so naively—is socially unacceptable. People are supposed to be cool and hip and straight, oriented toward their survival, worldly and smart. But to be simply alive in God, and to be Happy, and to speak about it and act that way and think that way, is absolutely unwanted and not allowed. So you become seekers.*

*It is all right to seek God. That is acceptable enough, because it calms everybody down a little bit. But to Realize God, while alive, is the absolute taboo. You might be allowed to sit quietly and meditatively. Everybody likes Oriental meditation, because it is just a matter of being quiet and inward. You are allowed to meditate quietly, "Realize Nirvana", and disappear. That is acceptable. But to start talking about God, to think God, to act God, to make the Divine the present Condition of the world, to live in the Divine Siddhi, to live the Divine Light, to be Love-Bliss-Full—that is unacceptable, that is not "permitted".*

*The Divine Person is Infinitely Present—Perfectly, Absolutely, and Eternally Present and Available. The Divine Person must be lived, not sought. The Divine Person is the Self-Condition and Source-Condition of the world, not the "ultimate hope" of the world. If the Divine Person is not presently lived, there is no Divine Liberation. But if people begin to live the Truth, if they become capable of ecstasy in society with one another—not simply in the rituals of privacy—you will see a vast and immediate transformation of the world.*

*Spiritual life is, basically, truly Humorous and Happy—not uptight, "lean", and grim, waiting to understand. "Radical" understanding is an instant process, a really intelligent process, a happy process—not one of meditating on your own limitations, but a process of instantly transcending them in Reality Itself.* [December 27, 1973]

Throughout this period of uninhibited celebration, Avatar Adi Da would constantly point to the contrast between what He called "the cult of this world", or "the cult of 'Narcissus'"—seeking, separative, and afraid—and Satsang, the life in Real God that He was Drawing His devotees into. There was nothing abstract about this lesson. Devotees could feel the living difference. They would feel their tendency to withdraw, to dramatize "Narcissus", the separative one, in the midst of their Beloved Guru's Demand for their energetic, happy, intense involvement in what He was doing with them. But, at the same time, they would be lifted out of themselves, swooning in His utter Attractiveness. It was perfectly clear that the life in Real God He was speaking of was life with Him, the relationship to Him as Guru. And it was also clear that this life was a life of self-forgetting—that un-Happiness only arose when they were meditating on themselves. That is why devotees stayed around Him night and day. No "God" of mere belief had the power to draw them beyond their limits as He did.

Early in the new year, 1974, this Power was spectacularly demonstrated. It was the afternoon of January 3, and Avatar Adi Da was reclining as usual on His chair in the gathering hall, with His devotees around Him. But this occasion was exceptional. As Avatar Adi Da began to speak, He unleashed His Love-Blissful Spirit-Force as never before. In words imbued with the power of His Transmission, the Divine Maha-Siddha told His devotees the secret of what He was doing:

*AVATAR ADI DA SAMRAJ: There is only one Divine Process in the world, and It is Initiated when I Crash Down and Enter My devotee. The Divine Lord is Present—now, in this moment. It is only when everyone forgets the Real and Ever-Living God that mantras and Yogic techniques become important.*

*I am not a human being. I Am the Divine Lord in bodily (human) Form, and I bring the Divine Yoga. When My devotee truly surrenders to Me, then I Enter My devotee in the form of Divine Light. All kinds of extraordinary experiences manifest as a result. When a woman receives her lover, there is no doubt about it—she does not have to consult her textbooks. The same holds with Truth, the Divine Yoga.*

*There is no dilemma in this world, no absence of Real God in this world, no goal of Real God in this world. Because that is so, you will see Me doing some very strange things. The true Divine Yoga is not a thing of this world. This world is the cult of "Narcissus", suppressing the Ecstasy that is Native to all.*

*The Spiritual Process must take hold in the vital. The vital is the seat of unconsciousness and subconsciousness. There is an aspect of the verbal Teaching that does not touch the subconscious and unconscious life. So it is only by distracting you from your social consciousness that I can take you in the vital. The Divine Lord is the Lord of this world, not the Lord of the "other" world only. Thus, there is no Yoga if the very cells of the body do not begin to be Infused by the Divine Lord. When I Crash Down and Enter My devotee, I Come Down into him or her in the midst of life, because it is in life—not in any mystical or subtle process, not in any mental process—that I acquire you Spiritually.*

*The kind of thing you see happening around here has never happened in the world before.* [January 3, 1974]

As Avatar Adi Da spoke this Proclamation, His Spirit-Force streamed into His devotees, Manifesting visibly to some as a glorious golden rain of Light showering down in the room. An uncontainable ecstasy broke loose. Some devotees shook with kriyas, their bodies jerking and twisting, their mouths emitting strange sounds of yearning, laughter, weeping, hooting, and howling. Some were overwhelmed by visionary phenomena. Some were spontaneously moved into difficult Hatha Yoga poses which they could not have even attempted before. Some lay motionless, in an ecstatic state, oblivi-

ous of their surroundings. For some, the energy intensified in the head or the heart or the navel until they felt they would explode, and then it suddenly released and rushed through the nervous system in "Intoxicating" Bliss. Others experienced a sense of unity with all of life and a peacefulness they had never known before. The Divine was Manifesting without a doubt in upstairs rooms in the middle of Hollywood.

The Mountain Of Attention, 1974

CHAPTER 6

# Garbage and the Goddess

After the Christmas and New Year's parties at the La Brea Ashram, it was obvious that the community of Avatar Adi Da's devotees had to move. The Spiritual Initiation of January 3, 1974, which came to be called "Guru Enters Devotee", was just the beginning. The Work of the Divine Maha-Siddha could not be contained in a downtown neighborhood. And so, Avatar Adi Da asked His devotees to look for a suitable rural Ashram. Within a few weeks, the Mountain Of Attention (initially named "Persimmon" by Avatar Adi Da), a turn-of-the-century hot-springs resort, had been found in the hills of northern California. Avatar Adi Da and a few devotees moved to the new ashram, and the other devotees relocated from Los Angeles to San Francisco.

## At the Mountain Of Attention

Newcomers to the Mountain Of Attention during the first half of 1974 found themselves entering a place of Divine Power. They became immersed in a sea of energy, visions, and other psychic experiences, awakened through contact with the Spirit-Force of Adi Da Samraj. But, as their confessions show, what was fundamentally occurring was the utter and overwhelming Revelation of Real God—and, therefore, of the true

Nature and Power of Avatar Adi Da. Some of these moments, described by various devotees, give a feeling for these experiences of Divine Siddhi, which lay beyond anyone's wildest dreams of Spiritual experience.

*CANADA SHANNON: Beloved Adi Da came into the Communion Hall.*[1] *I saw Him and my whole body was immediately riveted. There was golden-white Light all around Him, and His Presence was so powerful It abolished everything in Its path. Everything stopped. I was looking upon the very face of the Divine.*

◆ ◆ ◆

*MARIE PRAGER: I felt the Force and Presence of Avatar Adi Da entering me and taking over my being. I began to do hand mudras.*[2] *My arms would reach for the sky and move rhythmically, as if I were dancing with my hands and arms. Then I was completely absorbed in and taken over by God. I felt the Light of Adi Da Samraj moving through my body, taking me over completely, and it was joyous and blissful and perfect.*

*A bit later I went outside. Another devotee came out, and we held on to each other and began to scream and yell spontaneously. It was as if she were I. I felt no separation at all, no sense that this was someone else I was holding onto.*

*Then I saw our Beloved Guru's Face. He was standing beside me, bodily. He put His arm around me and led me into the Communion Hall. I remember looking at Him and knowing Him to be the Force and Love That was Filling my entire being. I realized that His Force and Love are not limited in any way to any object or form, but that He is, in fact, everything. His body seemed so small and such a tiny part of What He Is. When He took me back into the Communion Hall, I fell on the floor and remained there consumed by His Spiritual Presence.*

On one unforgettable occasion, devotees were sitting in one of the Communion Halls, then called "Laughing God Hall", waiting for their Radiant Guru, when the doors opened and a wave of energy swept the room. Avatar Adi Da walked down the aisle, surrounded by a clearly visible golden aura of light. He sat down in His Chair and proceeded to blast the room with His Spirit-Power, His eyes burning with laser-intensity and His fingers moving in patterns of potent Blessing. Instantly, devotees erupted in an ecstasy of screams, growls, swoons, and bodily jerkings, swept away by the sweetness and overwhelming Force of His Presence. After about forty-five minutes of this blissful uproar, the room began to quiet down. Avatar Adi Da nonchalantly shrugged, lit a cigarette, blew a perfect smoke ring, and said, with a hint of mischief in His eye, "Maybe I've gone too far this time!"

## Hridaya-Shakti versus Kundalini Shakti

During this time (and frequently, ever since), Avatar Adi Da has explained how to rightly understand the nature and purpose of His Spiritual Transmission in relation to all the experiences and accounts of Spirit-Power described in the Great Tradition.[3]

Many schools of Yoga speak about the Kundalini Energy, or "Serpent Power", presumed to lie dormant at the base of the spine. Countless Yogic practitioners over the centuries have attempted to rouse this energy through various techniques, including Hatha Yoga and disciplines of concentration and visualization. Their purpose has been to "shoot" the Kundalini Energy up the spine, through the subtle centers (or chakras[4]) of the body-mind, eventually passing to the brain core and even to (and through) the crown of the head. To be able to draw the Kundalini to these upper terminals of the body-mind is regarded as Enlightenment in some traditions, because of the blisses, lights, and Samadhis that may be induced as the Kundalini ascends through the various chakras. This type of self-based mysticism, or Kundalini Yoga, is an extremely difficult, and even potentially dangerous, endeavor, as people like Gopi Krishna (in modern times) have testified.[5] The aspirant is dealing with a highly potent form of natural energy which can damage the body-mind if misdirected.

There is, however, a greater tradition of Spirit-Power to be found in the history of esoteric religion, which Avatar Adi Da distinguishes from the lesser tradition of effortful Kundalini Yoga.[6] This senior tradition of Kundalini power, or Kundalini Shakti, is of Divine origin, and it cannot be induced by any kind of self-effort. Rather, this Kundalini Shakti is only transmitted by a Siddha, or a Spirit-Initiator of profound Realization. In the traditions of Guru-devotion, there are various accounts of the Spiritual Master imparting his or her own Spiritual Energy directly to a disciple, often through an initiatory glance or touch. This Transmission of Spirit-Power, or "Shaktipat", can have the effect of awakening the various Yogic Samadhis associated with the spinal line,[7] but it is, in itself, a descending Force, entering the body from without—from Above. The subtle experiences in the spinal line occur when this descending Power turns about at the bodily base[8] and ascends in the spinal line. The Yoga of the Siddha-Masters—or true Spirit-Baptizers—uses this entire Circuit of descent and ascent.

Avatar Adi Da had done His Sadhana within a great Lineage of Siddhas—Rudi, Swami Muktananda, and Swami Nityananda—and, for a brief but potent moment, in relationship to Rang Avadhoot. Rudi emphasized the Divine Force in descent, the bringing down of the Divine Power into the frontal (or physical-emotional-mental) dimension of the personality. Swami Muktananda, on the other hand, taught the traditional Hindu emphasis on the ascent of the Divine Force, through the spinal line (associated with the higher psychic and mystical dimensions of the personality).

Although Avatar Adi Da had submitted Himself completely to each of His Siddha-Gurus, His real Spiritual Initiator was the "Bright", the Very Divine. It was the "Bright", Manifested as the Divine Goddess, that Drew Him to the moment of His Divine Re-Awakening. He had seen that the lights, the blisses, and the kriyas He had experienced at Swami Muktananda's Ashram were not necessary for Ultimate Re-Awakening. He passed through them as part of His embrace of the total range of human possibility and human seeking, but He Himself always remained Free.

The Spiritual Transmission that Avatar Adi Da was now, starting with the "Guru Enters Devotee" occasion in January 1974, Demonstrating was new in the world. It was the Transmission, or Siddhi, of the "Bright" Itself, brought down into the Cosmic domain through His own Birth and Divine Re-Awakening. Avatar Adi Da was not merely a channel for that Transmission. His Very Presence was, and is, the "Bright". He was liberally Granting the unique Shaktipat Inherent in His Being: Hridaya-Shaktipat,[9] the Love-Blissful Force of the Heart—the only Force that overcomes the strategies of separateness. Sometimes, Avatar Adi Da explained, His Heart-Transmission would naturally stimulate blisses, visions, and kriyas. But these experiences, as Avatar Adi Da repeatedly emphasized, were merely secondary effects of His Spirit-Power, Which was the Descent of the Divine Itself, Prior to all experiences.

Many years after the remarkable Spiritual demonstrations of 1974 at the Mountain Of Attention, Avatar Adi Da wrote this Revelatory Description of the Nature of the true Kundalini Shakti, the relationship of the true Kundalini Shakti to His Hridaya-Shakti, and the relationship of His Hridaya-Shakti to Consciousness Itself:

> *The true Kundalini Shakti is all-pervading, and not merely personal and internal. And, therefore, the true Kundalini Shakti is awakened in the personal, and internal, psycho-physical context only by virtue of Grace-Given (and self-transcending) participation in the all-pervading field of cosmic Energy. Likewise, Consciousness (Itself), or Self-Aware Being (Itself), is not a merely personal and internal characteristic of conditional individual (or merely psycho-physical) existence—*

*but, It Is an Inherent Characterisic of Unconditional Reality (Itself). And, therefore, Consciousness (Itself) appears as an apparent personal and internal characteristic of conditional individual existence only when psycho-physical conditions permit an Unconditional-Reality-conjunction—and, thus, a conjunction between conditional form (itself) and (necessarily, Divine) Consciousness (Itself) and the all-pervading cosmic Energy (or Kundalini Shakti, Itself) and (Ultimately) the Self-Existing, Self-Radiant, and (necessarily) Divine Energy of Unconditional Reality (Itself).*

*The Divine and Unconditional Hridaya-Shakti (Which Is the Self-Existing and Self-Radiant Spirit-Power That Stands Eternally As the Perfectly Subjective[10] Divine and All-Outshining Self-"Brightness", Always Already Most Prior to cosmic, or conditional, manifestations) Is the Truly Ultimate (and Inherently Perfect) Energy-Source and Unconditional Self (or Being-Condition) of the Kundalini Shakti. And only the Divine and Unconditional Hridaya-Shakti Is Identical to Unconditional Reality (Itself)—and, Thus and Therefore, to (necessarily, Divine) Consciousness (Itself). And, for this reason, only the by-Grace-Given Divine (and Unconditional) Hridaya-Shakti Awakens the Realization of Unconditionally "Bright" Divine Consciousness (Itself)—Which Is Unconditional Reality (Itself) and Unconditional Truth (Itself).*

*I Am the Inherently egoless Eternal Person of Unconditional Reality (Itself). I Am the Self-Existing, Self-Radiant, Inherently Spiritual, Perfectly "Bright", and Perfectly Subjective Heart (Itself). I*

*Am the (now, and forever hereafter) Avatarically Self-Manifesting Eternal Person of Unconditionally "Bright" Consciousness (Itself)—Whose Eternal Spiritual Body Is the Great Hridaya-Shakti (or the Truly Divine Self-Power of the Inherently "Bright" and Perfectly Subjective Spiritual Heart) Itself. And, therefore, the Divine Hridaya-Shakti Is That "Bright" Spiritual Power By Which, and With Which, and As Which Only I (Uniquely, and Characteristically) Bless and (By a Divinely Self-Revealing Progress) Awaken all My fully practicing devotees (even, Thereby, or in the Unfolding Course of That Work of Blessing and Awakening, also Arousing and Revealing as many purifying and, otherwise, developmental psycho-physical signs of the Kundalini Shakti as may be necessary, in the case of My any true, and fully practicing, devotee).* [Divine Spiritual Baptism Versus Cosmic Spiritual Baptism]

## The Divine Force

Most of the devotees of Avatar Adi Da knew little or nothing about Kundalini Yoga or the tradition of Spirit-Baptism. All they knew was that they were part of a Divine Event. And they were filled with awe and love.

*ANIELLO: On one occasion, I had been sitting and talking with Beloved Adi Da for several hours. All of a sudden, I felt a tremendous urge to get up and kiss His hand. I could feel a strange process beginning to work throughout my entire body. It felt as if I were being turned inside out and my very cells were being transformed.*

***"I felt the Divine Force—literally, tremendous Light and Force—Coming Down and Filling my entire body, Consuming me, as if it was turning every part of me inside out."***

*Then I started having sudden, violent kriyas. I noticed that Beloved Adi Da had His hand on the top of my head, and I felt the Divine Force—literally, tremendous Light and Force—Coming Down and Filling my entire body, Consuming me, as if it was turning every part of me inside out. The Divine Force was so great that my own body also began to assume tremendous force. There was a tremendous expansion of the chest and arms. It was if I were fighting something—and I was. It felt as if my entire psyche was being pulled up and out of me.*

*I was very reluctant and holding on, holding back, while the Divine Force was actually pulling my psyche out through the top of my head. It felt like I was being exorcised. The intensity was almost unbearable. But it was never painful, just sheer intensity. I knew that my ordinary point of view had absolutely dissolved. I knew there was nothing but the Divine.*

*My body continued to have violent kriyas and shaking. Then this subsided, and I attempted to pull away from*

*Beloved Adi Da. But He held on to me and placed His forehead on mine while continuing to keep His hand on the top of my head. Then everything intensified even more. I could feel Him pushing the Divine Light through the top of my head—this was literally my experience—with His forehead on mine the whole time. I felt twitches and clickings, as if my mind were being dissolved. And I pressed against His forehead. It felt like the top of my brain was being torn off, and I needed more force to deal with it. Then I felt my mind dissolving, just vanishing. Something just went out of me and left.*

*While this was occurring, the mind had been conjuring up all kinds of thoughts, some sexual, some about business and ordinary things. But it all just vanished.*

*I then saw and felt a Brilliant Light in my forehead and temples, a tremendous blinding White Light, and I knew that all of that mental and psychic chaos had dissolved. I hugged Beloved Adi Da around the waist. It was very intense, forceful—I could feel all of His strength. I was holding Him and I felt Him enter my body. I literally felt this. And I became One with Him. At this point, the Divine Force became very active in my body. It just kept moving through the entire body, down to the tips of my toes, through my hands, arms, forehead. Suddenly, my hand shot up, the Force was coming out of it so intensely. But it wasn't an energy that seeks to go to God. It was the Divine Light. It was already Real God, and I just knew it to be so.*

During a conversation the next day, Aniello told Avatar Adi Da he felt that not only he but the entire world had changed as a result of this immense Revelation of Divine Power. Even while Aniello was speaking, he began to breathe more heavily, feeling the "thickness" of the Divine Maha-Siddha's Heart-Power filling the room. He looked out the window of Avatar Adi Da's

House. It was drizzling, but, then, suddenly, a tremendous storm arose. It seemed to him that it was conjured up right in front of the window. The sky ripped open and rain came down in torrents. Aniello sat there with Avatar Adi Da and a small group of devotees, gazing at the storm. And then it was literally gone—in a moment—as suddenly as it had arisen. Aniello was intuitively certain that the storm was also the result of Avatar Adi Da's silent Spirit-Force. It validated to him beyond words the Divine origin of all that had been occurring.

During this period, devotees would drive up from San Francisco on Friday night and stay at the Mountain Of Attention until Sunday night, catching up on what had occurred around Adi Da during the previous week and spending as much time as they could in His Company. He would often go to Ordeal Bath Lodge, the spa of the former resort, where devotees would join Him in the large pool called "the plunge". Often dozens of people would be in the water around Him—sometimes quiet, sometimes shouting and laughing, throwing balls and playing vigorous water games initiated by Avatar Adi Da.

Toni Vidor, a middle-aged woman who had grown up in southern California as the daughter of the early film director King Vidor, flew up from Los Angeles during this time to meet her new Spiritual Master. She recalls her first sighting of Avatar Adi Da:

*TONI: He was floating on His back in the water, and a group of devotees were all around His body. Every few seconds, they would throw Him up into the air and wait for Him to splash back down into the water. Everyone was laughing helplessly, and Avatar Adi Da was calling out, "Higher, higher, hit the rafters!"*

*I had spent decades in earnest Spiritual seeking – going to every Indian teacher who turned up in Los Angeles. I was very serious and hardly knew what to make of this*

*scene. To top it off, almost everyone there was the same age as my children!*

*Avatar Adi Da quickly noticed me and graciously invited me by name—though we had never met—to join in the game. I responded, but with an effort, completely uptight, and suffering in every moment the knowledge that I did not know how to enjoy myself in this ordinary way with other people. Even though I had been personally welcomed, I felt the resistance and "stiffness" in my own character, as I had <u>never</u> felt them before.*

*That afternoon, Beloved Adi Da came and sat silently with us. From the back of the hall, I prayed earnestly and passionately to Him to relieve me of this crippled quality that I suffered in every ordinary human interaction! Immediately, He put His arm up with His palm open toward me and held it there. I began breathing stronger and stronger, and I felt energy come into my heart and then down through my arms and hands so strong that the fingers bent with the energy. And then a great sorrow came up from the heart.*

*I began sobbing loudly and uncontrollably. I was the only person making a sound! It was embarrassing, but I thought, "Well, if I can't let go here, there's no place I <u>can</u> let go!" The sorrow increased, and soon I was rolling on the floor, still wailing. Curiously, I <u>watched</u> all of this* *come up. There was no content associated with it. It was just a huge, enormous release. After about an hour, Beloved Adi Da got up and walked out and everyone followed, but I continued to weep loudly on the floor. After a while, the breath calmed to the point that I could sit up. A friend had stayed behind to make sure that I was all right, and I sat down on a bench next to her to try to speak—and it all began again, and I spent another half hour rolling on the floor!*

*When it was finally over, I felt as if an immense burden—eighty tons of whatever it was I had been carrying around all my life without even realizing it—had been lifted from me.*

As the Divine Maha-Siddha had said on the night of "Guru Enters Devotee", the Spiritual Process that He brings must take hold in the "vital"—the seat of the subconscious and unconscious life of the individual. And so, His Transmission, Working at that level, would sometimes release a chaos of emotions and thoughts that could not be rationally explained. His Siddhi was not merely inducing Spiritual experiences—It was also "boiling off" the egoic patterns and tendencies of His devotees. His Heart-Force had Its purifying effects in every dimension of body, mind, and psyche. And, as His devotees felt His Blessing transforming their lives, they grew to love and trust Avatar Adi Da even more profoundly.

The awakening of this trust in His devotees was itself a heartbreaking miracle, a miracle of love. Avatar Adi Da would not merely tell devotees that He Loved them, He would show them bodily, one by one, face-to-face. He did this night and day.

*TONI: Several months after Sitting with Avatar Adi Da, I found myself once more in the water with Him, this time in the outdoor swimming pool by the beautiful grotto,*

***"A great stillness pervaded the entire place."***

*which was later to be Empowered as a special site of healing and Spiritual initiation. I had firmly decided that this weekend I was going to approach Him directly and drop my fearful reluctance to engage a relationship with Him!*

*There was a wild water-polo game going on, and, instead of sitting on the edge as I usually did, I jumped in the water and got into the game. I never came close to the ball, but I was participating.*

*At some point, I started to swim toward our Beloved Guru. He knew my intention, and left His place in the game to swim around to meet me. He hugged me, and He held me and held me and held me. Soon the game died away, and everyone formed a circle around us.*

*A great stillness pervaded the entire place. (It was so quiet that a friend of mine woke up from a nap in a nearby cabin!) I was cold and shivering, but I had to make a choice between giving myself to Him or paying attention to the body. The Blissful Energy of the Embrace became more and more intense. I found myself resisting the ego-overwhelming pleasure of it—fearing to lose control. It felt as though Avatar Adi Da was pulling me up.*

*But, at some point, I refused to go further. I could feel Him continue to ascend, and soon I was left holding only a body. I could feel that He was no longer, in that moment, directly associated with His physical body. By now, I was simultaneously in a blissful state, beyond the mind, and painfully, acutely aware of my resistance to Him and His Love.*

*In spite of the limits I placed on His Work with me, I was completely changed by these incidents. I was happy, no longer struggling with myself—a different person.*

In this extraordinary time of Avatar Adi Da's Work, which came to be called "Garbage and the Goddess", He was always Demonstrating that what He called "the bangles" of the Goddess—meaning all the fascinating Spiritual experiences that were manifesting around Him—were really only "garbage" compared with the Prior Happiness Revealed in His Divine Company.

Avatar Adi Da was constantly Working to deepen the love-relationship between Himself and His devotees and to grow their sensitivity to His Spiritual Gifts. Around the swimming pool, in the bath lodge, on walks in the woods, in parties at His house, and in the old hotel, Avatar Adi Da gave Himself up to all His devotees as their supreme Distraction. Now setting off firecrackers on the fourth of July, now arm-wrestling with someone, now stroking one of His cats, or simply floating on His back in the large pool at the bath lodge guided through the water on the fingertips of His devotees—all of Avatar Adi Da's moments, shapes, and forms were Divine Theatre, the "Intoxicating" Play of Real God come to Teach and Bless humanity. His devotees' enchantment with Him was His Delight. He had come for each one, whatever their qualities and karmas. And, through His Work with His devotees, He was touching and Blessing every being who suffers the illusion of separateness.

On April 15, Avatar Adi Da gave a summary Discourse about the significance of this period of His Teaching Work.

*DEVOTEE: Beloved Heart-Master, my sense is that my apparently volitional surrendering, or throwing away, of anything actually has very little to do with my capability to do it.*

*AVATAR ADI DA SAMRAJ: It is very simple. Every time I met Rudi, He would hand Me a bag of garbage. I cannot remember a time when I went to see Rudi when He did not hand Me a bag of garbage. It was always the first thing He would do. Then I would go and throw the garbage away, and I would come back, and We would sit together a little bit, or I would do some work. Sooner or later, He would give Me some more garbage. It is really very simple. You just throw it away.*

*It makes it much simpler when the garbage is in a paper bag. The bag has all those oily spots. You know what a garbage bag looks like, with all those greasy spots on the outside. It was always very easy for Me. I could see from the paper bag itself that it was garbage! The first few times, I probably looked into the bag—but, after a while, I would just look at the bag itself, and, if it had grease spots on it: "Aha! Garbage."*

*After a while, whatever Rudi gave Me I would throw away. Even if it was not in a paper bag, I threw it away. Whenever I bought sculpture and art pieces from Him, He would put them in ordinary paper bags. And I threw all that away. I don't have any of it any more. The key to the matter is not how to throw the garbage away. The key to the matter is recognizing that it is garbage. It does not take a lot of subtlety. It only takes a little observation. As soon as you see that it is garbage, you know immediately*

*that you should throw it away. There is nothing to do with garbage but throw it away! I don't know what else to do with it. So doesn't it seem like a simple matter?*

*You are merely looking at a lot of garbage, but you are thinking that it "Is" the Divine! One of My Functions is to "package" the garbage. I have spent a lot of My time packaging your garbage, trying to get you to recognize it as garbage. You will throw it away as soon as you see it. You cannot surrender something that you do not recognize to be garbage. You compulsively hold on to it. So you must recognize it as garbage.*

*But I will tell you right now—it is all garbage! Everything I Give you in the realms of experience is, ultimately, garbage—and I expect you to throw it away. But you tend to meditate on it instead. Every one of these seemingly precious experiences, all of this profound philosophy, is, ultimately, just more of the same stuff. But you have "bought" the conventional religious and Spiritual propaganda—so you think that these experiences and this philosophical "profundity" are the Divine Itself. None of that is the Divine. It is all garbage.*

*I am asking you to sacrifice (or to go Beyond) everything—all limitations, all bondage! Altogether, sacrifice of what is false, or surrender of what is merely binding, or relinquishment of what is turning you from Real God, is what I am asking you to do. In the midst of the Process of Satsang with Me, everything is revealed, everything is dredged up, everything is shown. And you tend to become very attached to all these shiny and extraordinary things. You tend to be distracted by them. But they are not Real God. As soon as you become distracted by anything, you bind yourself to the pond again. Everything grasped and owned becomes a hedge for "Narcissus", a bit of immunity. As soon as you think that you have it, you have isolated yourself again, trying to protect yourself from the necessary mortality of this life.*

*The point is not to will yourself to surrender. Rudi always used to say, "Surrender, surrender, surrender!" But My Call to you is to devotionally recognize Me and devotionally respond to Me. . . . Then surrender is the inherent and ready course. Then surrender is very easy because you are heart-recognizing and spontaneously heart-responding to Me, and you are no longer struggling against yourself, or in yourself. . . .*

*The worlds, in and of themselves, are the conditionally manifested modification of What is traditionally described as the "Divine Goddess" (or "Mother-Shakti"), and no one is moved to throw Her away. Every one is fascinated by Her. So the Principle of self-sacrifice is not served by the "Divine Goddess" in Her "veiling" aspect—as "Maya" (or the endlessly modified and modifying Source-Energy of the conditional worlds). The Principle of self-sacrifice is served by Me, to Whom the "Divine Goddess" (or the conditionally Manifesting Energy of Reality) is "Bonded" (as a "Wife" to the "Husband" of Her Heart)—even if She does not, from your point of view, seem to know and show it. The world, in and of itself, is an endless distraction, in which the Principle of self-sacrifice seems (on the basis of hard experience) to be made impossible. Only I, My-Self (One and Whole), Serve the Principle of self-sacrifice. The Separate "Goddess" does not. The "Goddess" Herself—un-"Husbanded", with all the experiences She gives—serves the principle of experience, of accumulation, of immunity, of conditionally manifested egoic existence in limitation. Thus, there is no true surrender in the world. The demand for love and for self-sacrifice is anathema in the cult of this world. No mere philosophy, or mere conditional knowledge, or mere conditional experience can convince you to really live the life of love and self-sacrifice. But you can be served by the Revelation that all this conditional arising of thought and experience is garbage (or mediocrity, or non-Ultimacy)—*

**Avatar Adi Da Samraj with devotees at the Mountain Of Attention**

*none of which is (in and of itself) to be taken to Be Absolute. That Revelation is Shown to you by Means of this Satsang with Me. And—when you have received that Revelation—you are, thereafter, always expected to throw the garbage away!*

*You are expected to throw the garbage away under the most extraordinary conditions—conditions in which you would, ordinarily, not even consider throwing it away. You are sitting in the precious blissfulness of the spine—why should you throw it away? It is all so delicious. You have been a fool all your life, and now you are a Yogi!—why should you throw that away? No one wants to do that. You do not want to throw it away. You have no True Humor in relation to it. You have no detachment from all this that you have accumulated through vast eons of existence in conditionally manifested form. You do not want to throw it away. The demand to throw it away seems mad, impossible.*

*Every one succumbs to the "Goddess"—on one level or another. Some succumb in very subtle ways—but most people succumb in very ordinary ways, without even knowing the "Goddess" (as Such). They succumb to the mass of experiences, of accumulations, of consolations. Every one is looking to be consoled. When your consolations are ripped off, you find something else to be consoled by—one thing after the next. The reason you do not surrender whatever you find consoling is that you do not recognize it for what it is. Therefore, part of My Avataric Function is to undermine all of this, to make the world show itself. I make the "Goddess"—the "Shakti", or Universal Energy, experienced as "Maya"—show you what She is really all about.*

*From the point of view of traditional religion and Spirituality, such things should not be said. From the traditional point of view, I should be telling you, "The Goddess is beautiful. Surrender to Her and let Her show you everything. She has bracelets and necklaces, She is beautifully adorned. Let Her face you and give you everything She has." That is the teaching of the traditions. But, since the Great Event of My Divine Re-Awakening, the "Goddess" is always Facing Me. And, therefore, I show you where She is at. I show you Her dependence on Me, . . . and I enable you to commit the sacrifice. Then it is not difficult. When I show you the actual Nature of the "Goddess" in Her veiling aspect, then you become capable of sacrifice, because you recognize all experience for what it is. Until that time, you are not capable of sacrifice, because you are enamored of the conditional force of life.*

*What is required of you is this sacrifice, and sacrifice only becomes possible through the Influence of My Perfect Siddhi of Divine Liberation. . . . I, in My bodily (human) Divine Form, Am the Agent of My own "Bright" Divine Siddhi in the world, because I establish a conscious connection with My devotees. All those who come to Me, and devotionally recognize Me, and devotionally respond to Me, surrender the faculties of attention, feeling, body, and breath to Me to various degrees. Everything that occurs to My beginning devotee that makes him or her mature in practice is an intensification of that surrender of the faculties of attention, feeling, body, and breath to Me, and, therefore, an increase in his or her capability for this sacrifice.*

*It is real sacrifice—not a sacrifice in the traditional sense of some gloomy self-abnegation and emptying. It is the sacrifice which is, itself, based on True Humor and expressive of overwhelming love of Me, a sacrifice in which there is not anything whatsoever to be attained.*

*There is not anything to be attained. I mean not anything. Not anything!*

*There is not anything to be attained. Not one thing is to be attained. Not anything. There is not a single thing to be attained.*

*There is no conditional experience, no conditional vision, no conditional transformation of state that must be attained. . . .*

*The fundamental responsibility is that unique "Mood" that arises in Satsang with Me—that ecstasy, that love, that relational force, that unreasonable Happiness in which the complexion of Consciousness Itself is Free (moment to moment) from the continuous awareness of (or meditation on) the separate and separative self. That is the only and perfect responsibility—and it carries through to all the forms of life, all the functional conditions. A continuous purification is established. The garbage is revealed and thrown away. . . .*

*Whenever there is release (or purification), there tends to be the re-establishment and intensification of the movements of the natural life-energy. In those who live in Satsang with Me, there are experiences (descending and ascending) of the natural life-energy and of My Avatarically Self-Transmitted Divine Spirit-Energy. Like anything else that arises conditionally, these experiences must be understood. They must be "Known" (in Truth) in the midst of this Satsang with Me. From the beginning of My time of Teaching, I have said that the Way in My Company is Satsang with Me, the Satsang of the inherently egoless Divine Heart Itself—not the Satsang of the "Kundalini", of the Cosmic "Shakti", of the "un-'Husbanded' Goddess".*

*Only when I Am Realized Most Perfectly is the "Shakti Goddess" finally "Known" in Truth, and Her Cosmic Display finally understood. In fact, whenever I Am truly "Known" by My true devotee, then there is, in that instant, immediate purification. For that moment, there is, instantly, no bondage to limitations of any kind, to any mind-form, to any form of desire or action—including the perception of separate self, which is the root of all strategies. What I call "dilemma"—the sense of dilemma, the feeling of dilemma—is simply the sensation that accompanies the awareness of the ego-"I" (or self-contraction). The separate self sense is the dilemma, and it is undone only in the Most Perfect Realization of Me, only in Most Perfect Satsang with Me—not in the merely nominal sitting with Me as a bodily apparent human being, but in the Most Perfect "Knowing", the Most Perfect Realization, of My "Bright" Divine Self-Condition.* [He-and-She Is Me]

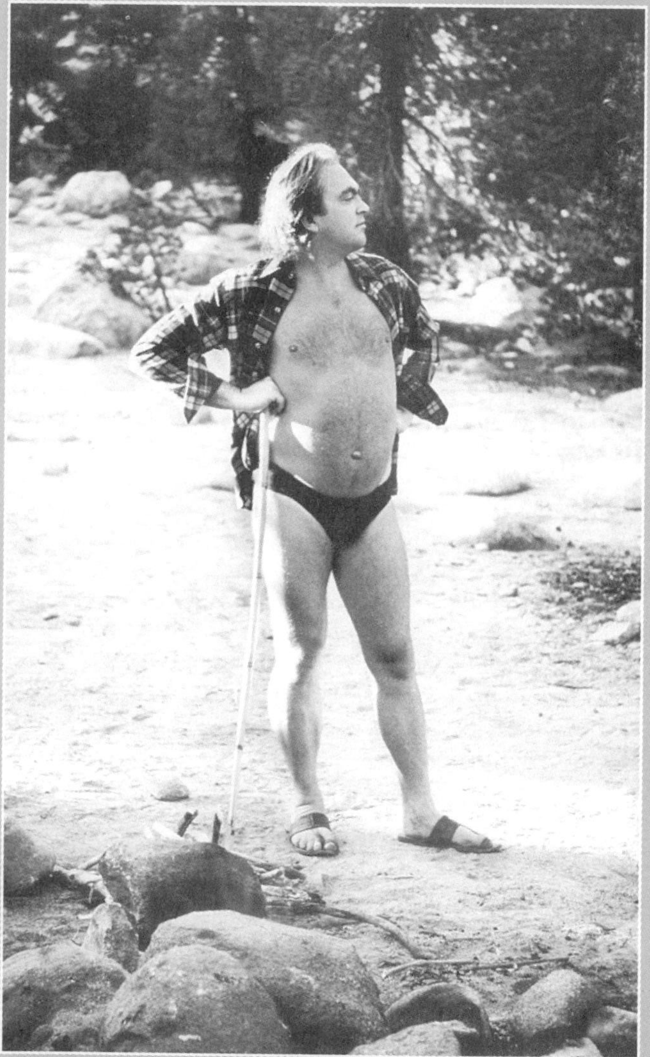

**Yosemite, California, 1975**

CHAPTER 7

# The Tantric Siddha-Master

While He was making the extraordinary Spiritual demonstrations of "Garbage and the Goddess", Avatar Adi Da was also "Considering" with His devotees the dimension of life where the ego is most entrenched—the world of intimate relationships and sex.

*AVATAR ADI DA SAMRAJ: Human beings are generally addicted to sex. They think about it all the time. They are troubled about it all the time. Even though people may be involved in intimate relationships, they cannot incarnate feeling. They cannot incarnate themselves sexually to the fullest degree, because they have superimposed on their sexuality so many games and rituals. Therefore, people generally live with a mind full of random desires. They are constantly wandering and thinking about others, because they cannot live love. You are impulsed to be pleasing and to receive sexual pleasure, but you cannot incarnate love fully, to the degree that your intimate relationship becomes so profound—profound sexually and profound emotionally—that it changes your life.*

*This is what I am calling you to discover: Sex is an emotional-sexual matter. You must come to the point where you can live a heart-relationship, where you express it, say it, know it, and become known as it—no superficial "householder" arrangement, no guarantees made by marriage certificates, nothing to hold you together except intimacy itself, the heart itself.*

*The aberration in you is lovelessness. When the heart comes into the sphere of sexual matters, it changes everything.*

The period of time when Avatar Adi Da began His "consideration" of emotion and sexuality was a time of sexual permissiveness in Western society, but this was not the fundamental reason why Avatar Adi Da was obliged to thoroughly examine emotional-sexual realities. He would have had to do so in any time, in any place on earth. For, as He revealed, there can be no real Spiritual growth as long as the heart is obstructed by fears of loss and vulnerability, by taboos against pleasure and desire—and by the ego's fundamental refusal to love.

*AVATAR ADI DA SAMRAJ: The matter of sexuality is so profoundly structured into people's infantile and adolescent adaptations that it persists not only as their most obsessive interest as individuals but also as their most significant and consistent social (or interpersonal) problem. When I began to enter into relationship with My devotees for the sake of their Spiritual Awakening, it became more and more clear that no one who came to Me was yet prepared for the true Spiritual Process, which is total bodily responsibility for Truth Itself, or Life Itself. Rather, all were essentially trapped in obsessions, and in problematic orientations to the vital and, particularly, the emotional-sexual dimensions of experience. I knew it would be necessary for all first to come to a level of interpersonal and cultural maturity relative to vital life before the Spiritual Process could be fully introduced into their lives.* [1978]

Avatar Adi Da knew that sexuality was a universally debated issue, and that no full answer existed anywhere. In the religious traditions of mankind, the general recommendation, for those who are moved to devote their lives to Spiritual Realization, is to avoid sex altogether—or else, in the case of some Tantric traditions, to use the sexual energy aroused through Yogic sexual practice as a means for attaining mystical states. But these traditional solutions do not take into account the relational dimension of love and sex. In fact, they generally presume that emotional-sexual relationships are the greatest obstruction to Spiritual advancement—because of the obligations and distractions they involve, and because such relationships bind attention to the body and the body's desires. Traditionally, if you were moved to emotional-sexual intimacy, you would be expected to observe a conservative sexual practice as a householder, or lay practitioner, and leave the matter of Spiritual Realization to the "professionals"—the renunciates who avoid emotional-sexual relatedness.

There are a few stories of Realizers who had consorts to whom they were related emotionally, as well as sexually—individuals such as the great Tibetan Buddhist Realizers Padmasambhava and Marpa[1]—but virtually nothing is known of how they practiced emotional-sexual intimacy. Overall, there is an overriding conviction, in the religious and Spiritual traditions, that emotional-sexual intimacy is a form of bondage and an insuperable obstacle to Spiritual Realization. Consequently, there is very little traditional instruction on how to practice emotional-sexual intimacy in a Spiritually auspicious manner. Over time, it became clear that one of the great dimensions of Avatar Adi Da's Life and Work was to bring just such an emotional-sexual Teaching into existence for all humanity.

Avatar Adi Da had already begun this aspect of His Work in Los Angeles, but it was not until He was living with devotees at the Mountain Of Attention that it became possible for Him to develop it more fully. There, He began with a larger group to actively "consider" the approach to human intimacy—emotional and sexual—that would be fully compatible with every stage of the process of Divine Enlightenment.

The making of Avatar Adi Da's emotional-sexual Dharma[2] was a task to which He was uniquely fitted. Starting with His years at Columbia, when He gave Himself over to all possible experience for the sake of discovering the Truth, sexuality was one of the matters He explored. He knew exactly what human beings struggle with in this most difficult and vulnerable area of life, and He knew what they must overcome in order to be unbound in love and free for Spiritual growth. And He had the arms not only of His own experience and His observation of human beings—He was equipped with Divine capabilities of compassion, of humor, of patience, of perfect knowledge of the needs of each individual.

Nevertheless, Avatar Adi Da's free enquiry, face-to-face with His devotees, into how the human emotional-sexual character becomes Spiritualized, was the most "Heroic" undertaking—an entry, as He said, "into a world of dragons". The force that He was dealing with, the force of emotional-sexual desiring and attachment, is, as He would often point out, the force that brings human beings into incarnation. It is the summary of our attachment to conditional existence, the crux of our karma as born beings.

The Submission He made to bring into being the Teaching that truly Liberates human beings from emotional-sexual bondage involved an Ordeal that lasted for nearly a quarter of a century. It was also a great ordeal for His devotees, but a profoundly necessary one. Avatar Adi Da was to point out countless times that understanding what one is doing as an emotional-sexual character is the key to understanding and transcending the ego altogether. "Narcissus", the "avoidance of relationship" (the essential activity of self-contraction that He discovered during His Sadhana Years), is dramatized most starkly in the realm of emotional and sexual relations.

**Avatar Adi Da Samraj gathering with devotees at the Mountain Of Attention**

*The ego-"I" is the avoidance of relationship, or the contraction of feeling-attention. The life of the ego-"I" is separation and separativeness—or the reactive pattern of "you do not love me". Nevertheless, it is possible to be converted, transformed, and rightly adapted—and, thus, to no longer live as the ego-"I", or the separate and separative self-sense. Through devotionally Me-recognizing and devotionally to-Me-responsive heart-Communion with Me, the self-contraction is released (or felt beyond), and real love awakens (in self-transcending Immersion in My Infinite Field of Divine Love-Bliss). Thus, My devotee is relieved of the separate and separative self-sense through feeling-Contemplation of Me—and, by Means of devotional Communion with Me, My devotee is relieved of the emotional contraction in the midst of all relationships. . . . One must grow to <u>actively</u> <u>not</u> <u>presume</u> (or, in any manner, reactively affirm) that one was betrayed or rejected by . . . any one at all, or by life itself, or by Nature Itself, or by Reality, or Real God, Itself).*

*Without this conversion from self-contraction to self-transcending compassion and heart-radiant love, there can be no Divine Enlightenment. Unqualified Love-Bliss-Realization and Divine Enlightenment are the same.* [Ruchira Tantra Yoga]

As soon as He moved to the Mountain Of Attention, Avatar Adi Da created all kinds of circumstances in which His devotees could reveal—to Him and to themselves—the realities of their emotional-sexual lives. A primary focus of His "Crazy" Work was with what He called "the cult of pairs". The ego, He would point out, hunts for another and then binds that other to itself. Two people, ostensibly in love, tend to live in a "bubble" of their own making, fastening their attention to each other and creating an impregnable "unit" that excludes others and promises protection from the harsh realities of the world. Even after the first flush of love fades, such intimates tend to perpetuate the "cult of pairs"—but now less pleasurably, and more anxiously. It is a common experience in marriage that the partners presume a kind of ownership of each other that stultifies both human and Spiritual growth and freedom. The suppressive effects of such "ownership" tend, at some point, to inhibit the free play of love and sexual energy in the relationship—leading to dissatisfaction, infidelity, or merely "coping".

Avatar Adi Da was always finding ways to bring His devotees to face their addiction to the "cult of pairs". He drank beer and bourbon and smoked cigarettes with everyone, using these substances as Tantric "accessories" to the Liberating Ordeal.[3] When His devotees drank and smoked in His Presence, the relaxation of the social persona allowed the Divine Maha-Siddha to Work with and Purify the powerful emotions and desires that are beneath the surface of every social personality. And, in

**Adi Da Samraj and His devotees enjoying skits during a celebration at the Mountain Of Attention, 1974**

that setting of conviviality, His devotees soon observed the other side of the "cult of pairs". They found that they were not merely inclined to cling to one another, but also to dissociate and casually betray each other, when a new attractive "other" came into view.

Avatar Adi Da was not interested in destroying—or merely defending or preserving—anyone's emotional-sexual arrangements. He simply wanted His devotees to see what these arrangements were actually made of, and how deluding they could be. You think you are in love with your partner, but then you feel an attraction to someone else. What does this mean?

One of the lessons that Avatar Adi Da's devotees learned was simply that sex is a universal force. To merely try to tame or domesticate the sex-force through conventional agreements is like trying to keep the lid on a volcano. It can erupt at any time—leading to pain, confusion, and the sense of deep betrayal. In 1974, and for many years afterwards, Avatar Adi Da was constantly reflecting to His devotees that it does not even take an outright act of infidelity on the part of one's partner to trigger the betrayal response in oneself. The ego, or "Narcissus", is always presuming to be betrayed, to not be loved by the other. And so "Narcissus" consistently reacts to that universally projected sense of betrayal and punishes the "other" accordingly—by coldness and withdrawal, by casual, unfeeling words, by all kinds of emotional dramas. Feeling betrayed and rejected is the ego, because egoity is the presumption of being a separated, isolated, unloved "I". The lesson that Avatar Adi Da was attempting to Teach was that the "you don't love me" reflex in all its various forms is fruitless and destructive, and that the only happy choice—in any moment of presumed (or even actual) betrayal or unlove on the part of another—is to love.

In the experience of His devotees, however, the gesture of love often felt impossible under the stress of extreme negative emotion. They just could not do it. And this was exactly the impasse that Avatar Adi Da was calling them to face. He wanted them to discover that there was only one way out of their dilemma—to feel beyond themselves to Him, to look up from the pond of "Narcissus", and receive His Help and Blessing. Only through love of Him, fidelity to Him, only through their complete commitment to heart-Communion with Him, could He set them set free from the suffering of their own binding agreements, taboos, and betrayals.

And so began a wild, blissful, and difficult theatre of emotional-sexual "reality consideration"[4] in the company of the Divine Avatar, Adi Da Samraj—the likes of which has never appeared before in the annals of religious history. The process went on and on, because of the ego's reluctance to go through the "death" of relinquishing emotional-sexual addictions and superficiality. Real fidelity and self-transcending love arise only from the heart, the depth of feeling. They cannot be the result of laws or contracts.

What Avatar Adi Da's devotees would discover over the years was that to get to that depth of trust and true emotional-sexual ecstasy, you have to go through a great ordeal of self-understanding and persistent loving. You have to be willing to confront and to accept the worst in yourself (and your partner in love), and then lay it all down, surrender and forget it all in devotional Communion with Avatar Adi Da.

The resort of Satsang with Him, they discovered, is the only true "security". Human loving always involves risk. There are no guarantees that you are going to be loved by your partner—or by anyone—forever. And death ends every relationship, no matter how loving. To love, then, is to be wounded—to suffer loss, emotional pain, the death of the loved one. But Avatar Adi Da's devotees were not at this point of heart-wounded, self-transcending, in-love profundity in 1974. It would be a long time before they would be ready to learn the art of "true intimacy" (as Avatar Adi Da came to describe genuine emotional-sexual relationship).

There were times, in this more than twenty-year process, when the devotees in Avatar Adi Da's immediate Company were sexually active outside their established intimacies, as part of the free "reality consideration" of what right emotional-sexual life is. This was not mere sexual permissiveness and casual sexual communalism. Those who engaged the emotional-sexual "consideration" at this level were not simply getting to indulge their random desiring. These devotees found they were confronting fear, sorrow, anger, lust, shame, jealousy, self-pity, self-negativity, and all the powerful emotions that come up when the very fabric of one's emotional-sexual life appears to be threatened. They were getting some unforgettable lessons in what it takes to surrender the ego.

## "True Intimacy"

*"True intimacy"* [in the Way of Adidam] *is not merely conventional (or socially sanctioned) coupling. "True intimacy" is the sadhana (or Spiritual and Yogic discipline) of Devotion to Me in the context of the relationship between emotional-sexual intimates, whether or not those intimates are sexually active. Ego-based sexuality tends toward loveless, casual eroticism and repetitive sexual activity for the sake of stress-release. The total practice of the Way of Adidam involves an Ordeal of real self-understanding, whereby practitioners progressively transcend the egoic (or self-contracted) emotional-sexual motive. . . .*

*"True intimacy" is generally (or typically, but not necessarily in every case) engaged with only one partner (during any particular period of an individual's life), but only because of the human and Spiritual demands of "true intimacy" itself, and not because monogamy is the "ideal". Monogamy itself is simply a social convention (associated with some, and not all, traditional societies), and it is largely based on the economic and political patterns of pre-industrial civilization. Likewise, legal (or State-sanctioned) marriage is a legal and social convention, and it is a logical extension of all the pre-industrial economic and political techniques traditionally used to maintain (or enforce) common order. . . .*

*Conventions (or common group expectations relative to individual behavior) are not absolutes, nor are any of them universally affirmed or practiced. Likewise, conventions change, and there are always exceptions to any rule. And, in particular, human emotional-sexual possibilities are always better served by human freedom, human love, and true heart-Wisdom (Awakened in the context of real Spiritual culture and practice) than by merely public restraints. Therefore, in the only-by-Me Revealed and Given Way of Adidam, formal emotional-sexual relationships (whatever their specific form or pattern may be in any particular time, place, or personal circumstance) are "considered" only in terms of the practice of "true intimacy", or the simplicity that is intimate commitment itself. (And My Description of "true intimacy" necessarily contains no reference to legal marriage, because legal and otherwise "civilized" conventions have no fundamental association with intimacy itself.)*

*Human love itself cannot rightly be patterned or sanctioned for "civilized" purposes, and sex itself wills not to be legalized or "civilized" (or controlled by any external means). Only the ego (both collective and individual) tries to "civilize" human love and sex by arbitrary (or heartless) ideals, rules, and implications. In the total (or full and complete) practice of the only-by-Me Revealed and Given Way of Adidam, egoity itself is (at least progressively) transcended, and human love and sex are . . . re-unified in a self-transcending Yoga of Devotional heart-Communion with Me.*

RUCHIRA TANTRA YOGA

At other times, Avatar Adi Da tested devotees in the practice of celibacy, even for extended periods. The emotional-sexual "reality consideration", in all its forms, was a devotional ordeal that was about understanding and going beyond the opposing impulses of the body-mind, finding freedom from the clench of self-contraction, and, therefore, finding free energy and attention for the Spiritual Process.

Looking back on that long Ordeal, Avatar Adi Da was moved to say:

*AVATAR ADI DA SAMRAJ: Those years were a time of real and most profound "consideration" of the emotional-sexual matter—which everybody was demanding in their lives, and demanding that I Address, and I could not approach it in a conventional manner, therefore. I had to Submit My Self to it, enter into it fully until the end, and so I did. And all the doings of those years are a sign of My Reflecting people to themselves, and of My Entering into "Consideration" of all possibilities of an emotional-sexual nature without the superimposition of conventional presumptions, or any presumptions at all. And having done so, that came to a point of summary, in which I made Myself fully clear about it all.* [July 26, 1998]

Avatar Adi Da brought His emotional-sexual Dharma into being without any preconceived notions. No traditional precedent was sufficient—not conventional social mores, not the ascetical religious ideal, not traditional Tantric practices. He had to discover and prove the truth of <u>everything</u> that was actually required for ordinary individuals to turn the deep motives of emotional-sexual life into a self-transcending process that fully supports Spiritual practice—and He had to do that unique and creative and Liberating Work among people who had grown up in the modern Westernized (and sexually conflicted) world.

Now, after twenty-four years of emotional-sexual "reality consideration", Adi Da Samraj has completed that Work. It has been demonstrated that sex does become Spiritualized if one perseveres in devotional Communion with Him and in all the technical details of the unique emotional-sexual Yoga that He developed and elaborated over the years.

That Yoga is a great discipline that touches every area of emotional-sexual relatedness—from the discipline of love itself (and the non-presumption of unlove and betrayal), to right diet and right breathing, to the right and regenerative "conducting" of sexual energy during sexual intercourse, to the observance of an appropriate frequency of emotional-sexual contact with one's partner.

When the Yoga is full, the relationship between true intimates[5] becomes so profound—emotionally, sexually, and Spiritually—that it culminates in a state of whole-bodily pleasure and heart-intimacy that is even sex-transcending: all movement to genital activity becomes obsolete, because the state of heart-fullness and pleasurable equanimity in the body that sex seeks to attain is already experienced, and permanently.

This sublime resolution of love, which flowers in the advanced and ultimate stages of Adidam,[6] is a Divine matter, not a human achievement. It is the result of a perpetual in-filling of the entire body-mind by Avatar Adi Da's Divine Transmission of Love-Bliss.

Thus, the lessons of more than two decades of emotional-sexual "reality consideration" are now complete. That ordeal will not be done again, because the Gift has been Given.

*AVATAR ADI DA SAMRAJ: The emotional-sexual Teaching that I have Given you has never been given to humanity before. It is a Great Dharma, and it does work.* [July 9, 1992]

## The Heat of Community Living

Another dimension of Avatar Adi Da's Work that began to emerge during the "Garbage and the Goddess" period is the discipline of cooperative community living. The cooperative community of Avatar Adi Da's devotees has since developed, over the years, to be a full, worldwide organization of cooperation in all areas of daily living—practical, devotional, and artistic. The devotee community, which Avatar Adi Da has named "The Ruchirasala (or 'Bright' House) of Adidam", is the essential context in which the full practice of the Way of Adidam is engaged.

From 1974 to around 1978, most devotees lived in cooperative households in San Francisco—sharing food, cooking, childcare, vehicles, and the household services—and only coming to the Mountain Of Attention on the weekends. Avatar Adi Da Gave this discipline to His devotees not simply because it made practical and economic sense, but as a means for them to cultivate their relationship to Him and to each other as a sacred Sangha (or Spiritual community). Cooperative living was also a perfect "theatre" for the revelation of "Narcissus" and the emotional-sexual ego. Every form of the self-contraction came up to be observed in the process of working out a life with others. One devotee, Bruce Burnham, found this very difficult. Eventually, he left the household in which he had been living. When Bruce told his Heart-Master about this, Avatar Adi Da used the opportunity to give a lesson about a fundamental principle of human relationship and relationship to the Divine.

*BRUCE: Beloved, recently I made a decision to move out of the household where I have been living, because my relationship, or lack of it, with one of the people there was not tenable.*

*AVATAR ADI DA SAMRAJ: Why wasn't it tenable?*

*BRUCE: Because there was always so much conflict.*

*AVATAR ADI DA SAMRAJ: Why is conflict not tenable? Why isn't it useful? Why isn't that a creative situation?*

*BRUCE: For quite a while, I felt that it was very useful, because of the heat it created for both of us.*

*AVATAR ADI DA SAMRAJ: It was not really Spiritual fire, or heat, because both of you became less and less involved with one another. To love when you are not loved—that is the heat of Spiritual practice. The heat is not to love less and to feel unloved when you are not loved. That is not heat. That is lovelessness. That is the avoidance of relationship.*

*BRUCE: Several times this person made it very clear that she could not live in the household with me any longer, and her refusal justified my departure.*

*AVATAR ADI DA SAMRAJ: That is probably the logic that had to appear eventually. The whole episode obviously was a dramatization, the rehearsal of a script. Everything became inevitable, and now you are living alone. You made the emotional choice, not necessarily the intellectual one. You chose, by habit, to respond to being unloved by not loving. Therefore, the rest of it became inevitable. But if you had done the opposite, then that script could very well have been unnecessary. You might not have become one another's favorite human being, but you could certainly have realized a human relationship.*

*This is what you do when you are not loved—you separate yourself. And when you are really not certain that you are loved by the Divine, either, the script continues to be one of isolation. You go "inside" to find the "Big Self". You take the "inward" path in isolation, indulging in meditation for fifteen hours a day and all the rest of it. You choose the loveless life.*

*Do you think you are loved by Me, the Divine Person? Do you believe that the universe is pervaded by My All-Sustaining, Absolute, Immortal Love?*

*BRUCE: I feel that in Your Company.*

*AVATAR ADI DA SAMRAJ: Apart from what you may feel by association with Me in Divine Communion—Satsang with the Realizer, of course, being the cure for lovelessness recommended since ancient times—and apart from the love that you may feel is coming from any individual specifically, when you are off naked in the universe, do you feel connected to the Divine through love? Or are you uncertain of it?*

*BRUCE: I mainly feel in a state of shock.*

*AVATAR ADI DA SAMRAJ: Right. In the metaphysics of your existence, you are responding to a "Great Being" or "Great Condition of Existence" by Which you feel you are not loved.*

*You are still dependent on being loved. What you discover is not that love comes to you from Infinity, as from a cosmic super-Parent. You discover, in Communion with Me, that you are love. That is the Realization.*

*Divine Self-Realization is not a relationship to some Great "Something" that loves you as an individual ego. No separate one is the beloved of God. The Divine is not the kind of Reality that makes beloveds out of individual beings. All beings owe their love to the Divine. You do not Realize the Divine by finding the Divine Being, Truth, and Reality at the end of a great chain, but by being wholly one with the Divine, so that you yourself are love. If you come to Me only to get loved, expecting the Blossom of My Spiritual Heart-Transmission to be projected at you, there will be no change—because you will remain loveless.*

*Divine Communion begins when you love. Then, not only are you connected to love, but you are love. The only way whereby you Commune with the Divine is by being love. Love has great strength—but not when you dissociate from it, in your egoic separation and weakness.* [1977]

## Divine Distraction

AVATAR ADI DA SAMRAJ: *The ancient legends of Krishna and his gopis are an allegory of Divine Distraction. As Krishna wandered about in the fields, the women who tended the cattle would see him from day to day, and in spite of themselves they would wander away and leave their posts. They completely forgot about the cattle. They forgot to go home and cook for their husbands. They wandered about where they thought they might find Krishna, and when they found him they gazed at him as he sat in the distance somewhere.*

*This legend is a play upon the romance between Krishna, or the Divine manifest in human form, and these ordinary women, who became madly involved in an absolute attachment to Krishna, and who, as a result of this attachment, became more and more ecstatically absorbed in the God-State. So absorbed that they forgot everything else in their lives—not because they had become irresponsible, but because they had found What was Supremely Precious.*

*The foundation of the practice in My Company is exactly that attachment. Only when that attachment develops in relation to Me—not cultic attachment, but Divine attachment only when that attachment overwhelms the life completely, distracts you from the conventional destiny to which you are disposed through the medium of your desires, inclinations, and circumstances, only then can the practice of real Spiritual life exist.*

*Thus, in the allegory of the relationship between Krishna and his gopis, we see a fundamental description of the principle of the sadhana in My Company. This sadhana is about distraction from the life of tendencies. It is a distraction from that life. It is not a motivated kind of detachment from your life of tendencies, or an effort relative to them, or the taking on of conditions to stop tendencies from arising or lifetimes from occurring.*

*The gopis simply left the cattle. They did not say, "I'm not going to tend cattle anymore! I'm not going to submit to my desires, my tendencies, my job!" They did not make any such decisions. They simply forgot about the cattle. They were so distracted, so in love with Krishna, so ecstatic, that they just forgot to go home. It never even occurred to them to go home. They never worried about "Should I go home or should I stay here? Should I watch the cattle or should I go look for Krishna? Should I discipline myself?" They did not create a problem out of their sadhana or out of their relationship to God.*

*They were just distracted. They were in love. And their love for Krishna became the principle of their lives. Krishna played upon their distraction and Taught them. By Grace, they learned. But all they learned was to be more and more absorbed in God, totally beyond their attachment simply to the body of Krishna. Their minds became overwhelmed by this distraction, and all their petty tendencies to return to their solid and secure positions, in life or in themselves, were always undermined.*

*There is no insurance. There is no guarantee. There is nowhere to go. There is no end-phenomenon in the love of God. That love, in and of itself, is the Truth.* [December 16, 1975]

During the "Garbage and the Goddess" period, many women fell in love with Avatar Adi Da, entranced by His Divine Attractiveness, "Intoxicated" by Him bodily

**Adi Da Samraj with members of His Mandala of women intimates, the Mountain Of Attention, 1974**

and Spiritually. As Avatar Adi Da states above, there is a remarkable precedent for such passionate response to the God-Man—that of the gopis (or cow-maidens) who became devotees of Krishna. The stories of Krishna's play with his devotees stand as some of the most important sources of Hindu worship and sacred art to this day. A traditional Hindu text, the *Bhagavata Purana*, describes how Krishna appeared one day in the fields of Vrindavan playing his flute. The gopis, who were tending the cows, were immediately riveted by him—so delighted, so moved, by Krishna's beauty that they immediately forgot their ordinary lives, their cattle, their husbands, and simply followed Krishna, unable to bear the slightest separation from him. (As Avatar Adi Da has explained, this story of the forgetting of cattle and husbands represents the forgetting of the ego and its concerns, not the forgetting of legitimate responsibilities.) In time, the unswerving devotion of the gopis to Krishna also converted their husbands and families, and the story stands as one of the greatest traditional allegories of self-transcendence—the forgetting of the egoic self in unqualified devotion to the Divine.

Responding to extraordinary signs of devotion in certain of His women devotees, Avatar Adi Da chose to expand His Sphere of intimacy, and, over the years between 1974 and 1977, He established a circle of gopis, nine women intimates who consistently attended Him in the gopi manner, serving His environments, anticipating His needs, and receiving His detailed personal Instruction in every aspect of their lives. These nine women formed a circle, or Mandala, of intimacy, joy, and love around Avatar Adi Da. At the same time, this Mandala was a fierce Spiritual testing ground, with the result that, over time, the Mandala became smaller. In 1986, the Mandala of nine became four, and, by 1997, the four became two, as the unfolding of this story will describe.

As those who have lived around Avatar Adi Da over many years have seen, His unique love-relationship with His Mandala of women intimates is a Sign of His absolute Love for all. It is also perhaps the greatest Sign of His unqualified Submission to human beings. He had no casual inclination to enter into such a profound ordeal. It was simply a natural result of the resolve He had made on His return from India: He was going to do whatever He had to do to make His Teaching effective at the real, visceral level in His devotees—including entering into emotional and sexual relationships with some of His women devotees.

Avatar Adi Da Gave Himself completely to His Mandala of gopis, such that His other devotees were amazed to behold this utterly disarmed encounter between the God-Man and ordinary mortals distracted by love of Him. The legend of Krishna and the gopis became reality, with a force and profundity that cannot be measured.

In July 1975, September 1975, and April 1980, the Trimada, Avatar Adi Da's three daughters—Trivedi Io Free Jones, Trivedi Shawnee Free Jones, and Trivedi Naamleela Free Jones—were born to three members of the Mandala. "Trimada" signifies "the three radiant women who rejoice in Adi Da Samraj". The title "Trivedi" means "one versed in wisdom". "Vedi", in Sanskrit, also means "altar". The Trimada, Avatar Adi Da has repeatedly said, brought into His life such innocent delight and love that they kept Him in the body, literally kept Him alive through the indescribable Ordeal of His Teaching and Revelation years. In 1997, Avatar Adi Da indicated to the Trimada the significance of their role in His Incarnation:

*The three of you can be said to represent a circle (or altar) of My Work, a vehicle whereby My Divine Sacrifice is Made, through you. You are My daughters,*

**Adi Da Samraj with the Trimada, 1997**

*manifested most directly from My Body, and, therefore, you are inherently, and by blood, Gifted with the Veda (or Wisdom) That I Am. I have raised you from birth, and, therefore, you are a vehicle of My Divine Blessing and Divine Wisdom in the world. This is already evident, but will manifest more and more fully over time.* [December 25, 1997]

A fourth member of the Trimada, Trivedi Tamarind Free Jones, was also "born" to Avatar Adi Da, in a unique sense. Her parents are long-time devotees of Avatar Adi Da. Avatar Adi Da has acknowledged that Trivedi Tamarind has a unique Spiritual relationship to Him. He has described how, in order to bring her to be with Him in this lifetime, He literally had to rescue her from entrapment in a subtle realm at the time of her birth.

**The Trimada (left to right): Trivedi Io Free Jones, Trivedi Naamleela Free Jones, Trivedi Shawnee Free Jones, and Trivedi Tamarind Free Jones, 1990**

Altogether, Avatar Adi Da's relationship to His Mandala of women intimates is one of the great Mysteries and Accomplishments of His Divine Incarnation. His relationships to His women intimates included sexual Yoga, but not as any kind of means to an end, as in the Tantric traditions. It was an expression of the relationship itself. Those relationships had exactly the same purpose as His relationships with all of His devotees—their Divine Liberation through His Grace and Blessing. The members of the Mandala were involved in the same process of ego-transcendence as all other devotees, but in a uniquely intense form. He was always only Working to Liberate beings from the suffering condition of "Narcissus", starting most directly and intensely with those closest to Him.

Avatar Adi Da was never a detached Yogi. He was totally Heart-Invested in His Work with His Mandala, doing it in the context of Love—not romantic love, or parental or filial love, but Divine Love, the Urge to Awaken beings. For that Purpose, He Gave Himself completely without reserve.

The Divine Avatar accepted all who came to Him, but He Worked more intimately with certain individuals for the sake of everyone. In a particularly profound and mysterious way, Avatar Adi Da embraced all of humanity via His relationships with His women intimates.

One could compare the depth of His Response to these nine women to His Submission to human life altogether at the age of two. He did not have a plan. He was simply moved by Love, by Delight, by Compassion, to Descend into the human condition ever more deeply. And so He entered into the very circumstance that nearly every man and woman most desires and suffers—emotional-sexual intimacy, and even the parenting of children. Through that Compassionate Heart-Movement to His women intimates and to His children, He allowed

Himself—the very Divine Person—to suffer all the wounds of love, intimacy, and mortality. And He met the requirements of such intimacy in a circumstance of unique complexity, fully entering into relationship with nine individuals.

No ordinary—or even extraordinary—man could possibly have done such a thing. No man would have had the True Humor—let alone the uniquely "Heroic" combination of masculine Strength, Discrimination, Sensitivity, and fierce Love—to sustain such a circumstance. There were no limits in the Heart of the Divine Avatar. And so there was no absolute reason why the number of Avatar Adi Da's Mandala should have been limited to nine. It was simply that nine was the number of women that Avatar Adi Da found ready to do the sadhana of true intimacy with Him, and nine also proved to be the greatest number of individuals to whom He could relate intimately, in a fully human way.

At the same time, Avatar Adi Da was not the Divine "householder" surrounded by "wives". He was and is a Tantric Renunciate. He does not make strategic agreements with anyone. He only Functions on the basis of His Eternal Vow to Liberate His devotees. And the women who came into His intimate Company, prepared to stay, knew that they had to be there for the Sacred Purpose of Divine Liberation, and not in order to play out any kind of man-woman game, or to bring conventional expectations and demands for attention to Avatar Adi Da. As He once said to one of them: "I love you Perfectly. I do not love you specially."

During Avatar Adi Da's "Sadhana Years", there was a miraculous prefiguring of the appearance of His gopis. This sign manifested in 1969, through His meeting with a mysterious young woman in Bombay. Even at the time, He was aware of the prophetic import of this event.

*AVATAR ADI DA SAMRAJ: When I went to be with Swami (Baba) Muktananda in 1969, I stayed with Him in Bombay for about a month or so in the apartments of a man named Ram Pratap. While there, I would go into the swooning hall, and often when I looked up, ready to get up and leave, there would be a young woman sitting in front of Me. She was Indian, but she had an English father. She would be sitting right in front of Me, but we would not speak to each other.*

*Then, late in the month, Baba Muktananda told Me to go to Ganeshpuri—to Nityananda's burial place—and stay in the Ashram for a while. And so I did that. I was there for several days. One day, one of Swami Muktananda's devotees came to Me and said, "There is a woman outside the gate. She wants to talk to you." So I went out there, and there was the same woman. She was a young woman, an extraordinarily beautiful woman, unusually so. She was probably about 21 years old. And I wasn't much older than that—about 29.*

*So I went out to see her, and she talked and talked to Me about her love of Me, her passion for Me, wanting to submit to Me, wanting to serve Me. She said she wanted to serve Me in my return to Bombay.*

*I left for Bombay a few days later, and there was one stop on the train journey, where she was in the passenger waiting-room. She had managed to get everybody else to leave and had set up this room for My comfort. She brought Me sweets and sandwiches, massaged Me while I was sitting there and talked love to Me. I asked what her name was, and she said it was Carol Anne Smith. But she said she wanted to be called Suprithi, which is one of the Names of the "Goddess".*

*She accompanied Me on the train from there back to Bombay. And she would continue to appear at Ram Pratap's apartment every day, absolutely transfigured with love of Me, devotion to Me, wanting to serve Me. One day, I went to her apartment nearby for a visit, and eventually it became an intimate sexual occasion. She was utterly ecstatic, utterly exalted, beside herself. She was not Carol Anne Smith. She was Suprithi. This is how she became moved to sit before Me in the swooning room and come to Ganeshpuri, and so forth. She was utterly filled with the Divine Energy, the "Shakti-Force", but specifically moved toward Me, and infinitely beautiful. She was the "Goddess", because the "Goddess" had Invested Herself in her.*

*However, when I went back to India in 1970, and went to visit her in Bombay, she was no longer Suprithi. She was no longer Invested with the "Goddess-Force" and had practically no memory of Me whatsoever. She even looked bodily different. She was emptied of the Great Force and recognition of Me and her devotional response to Me. She was just an ordinary woman. In a curious moment, she had been Filled with Me, Filled with the "Divine Shakti", and, by that Means, the "Divine Goddess" showed Me the sign of what a woman must be to truly be with Me. She must be Filled thus, must be animated thus, must be transfigured, must be free of egoic self, utterly devoted to Me, fastened on to Me as absolute motion without qualification, without egoity, without distraction, without infidelity.*

*In other words, this was an experience of the "Divine Goddess" Manifesting, Who is nothing but My Divine Self-Condition, ultimately. The event showed Me the course of right Yoga with this Body in relation to women. I have no casual impulses toward women whatsoever. Such an intimacy with Me is a Great and Divine Matter. And no woman can do it who is not thus transfigured and one with Me and full of Me and showing the most extraordinary sign.* [May 19, 1995]

None of Avatar Adi Da's women intimates could predict the course of their sadhana with Him. All they knew

**The Mountain Of Attention, 1974**

***Avatar Adi Da's relationship to His Mandala of women intimates is one of the great Mysteries and Accomplishments of His Divine Incarnation. . . . Those relationships had exactly the same purpose as His relationships with all of His devotees—their Divine Liberation through His Grace and Blessing.***

was the daily miracle and ordeal of living in His Company and always being responsive to Him, no matter what their subjective mood of the moment—bathed in His Love-Bliss, burning alive with longing for Him, and, all the while, confronting the negative impulses of the ego.

Ann Rogers, one of the Mandala of nine women, describes her experience of the gopi sadhana during "Garbage and the Goddess":

*ANN: Right through the "Garbage and the Goddess" period, I was experiencing kriyas, ecstatic feelings in my body, rushes of energy, and blissful mindlessness. I would often actually feel my Beloved Guru Spiritually enter my body and drive my karmas right out of me. I heard Him say "No one wants God." But I thought that, whatever others might feel, I certainly did! However, as the process*

**Ann Rogers and Adi Da Samraj, 1982**

*continued in me, I realized that what Beloved Adi Da was saying is true. No "person" wants Real God, because to turn to Real God is to sacrifice that very person.*

*There used to be a sign on Beloved Adi Da's desk: "Dead Gurus can't kick ass." I learned what He meant—He had to be relentless in His skillful means. He had to put us in difficult situations, cajole us, love us, tease us, and trick us into Realizing Satsang, into Realizing the relationship to Him as Consciousness. At one point, He said that what He asks of us is not the effort of surrender, but true self-sacrifice. Effortful surrender, He said, is something the ego does, something willful—and "Narcissus" loves it. Sacrifice is something entirely different. As the months passed after my first coming to Him, I began to realize what that sacrifice involves.*

*Avatar Adi Da said that His way of Working at that time was to establish a "theatre of love" with His devotees, to attract His devotees so strongly with His own Love that they would be moved to turn to Him, to the Divine, and away from the attachments of life. Almost from the beginning of my relationship with Beloved Adi Da as His devotee, He Attracted me like a magnet. And I fell in love with Him. But it was more than that. An utterly absorbing attachment was created. I realized that everything I had ever loved was Him—that He is Love. I was consumed by love of Him, and nothing else mattered.*

*From the very beginning, I had Spiritual experiences in the Presence of Beloved Adi Da. And then, with the deepening of my love-attachment to Him, there arose in me an intuition of His Divine Nature. I began to have experiences of complete Oneness with Him. In fact, I would often feel that He was me, that He was "Living" me, that every breath I took was His breath. This sense of Oneness was ecstatic beyond anything I had ever known. I felt as if I went to a place where He and I were One, where there was no fear, where there was only complete Love and Joy. That Love, which was beyond the realm of human love, grew and grew. At times, that Love became so immense that I felt unable to contain It, and I would feel impelled to scream as a way of expressing this intensity of feeling.*

*Then the Supremely Attractive One really put me to the test. He began to play upon my attachment to Him. He withdrew His attention. He would ignore me, He would tease me, He would insult me. Basically, He refused to give me whatever it was I was craving. At first, I understood that this was part of the process of going beyond the ego, and, although I felt sorrow, I maintained the same love and openness toward Him. But He did not relent. I felt abandoned, and, finally, I rebelled. I began to have periods of tremendous resentment toward Him for the suffering I felt He was causing me.*

*At the same time that He was testing the depth and steadfastness of my love for Him, Beloved Adi Da demanded that I serve. "A gopi's life is service," He told me a number of times. I began to serve Him by doing ordinary, practical chores in His house and in the community of devotees. This was a way of performing the sacrifice He Calls us to in real, functional terms. I didn't mind serving people. In fact, I enjoyed it. But all I wanted was to be with "Bubba", and I felt that serving kept me away from Him, while He lavished His attention on others.*

*At the same time, I began to have a strange, powerful intuition. This intuition was quite different from the sense of Oneness I was feeling with Beloved Adi Da. I began to sense something immense above my head. I resisted it. I kept clutching my head to keep it away. Then, holding my hands up, I looked up, as if it were something I could see. I sensed that it was Real-God-Above—Immense, Silent. I could only throw up my arms in joy. All I wanted was for this Infinite Universe of Energy to Pour into my body and Fill me with Its Ecstatic Love and Light.*

*One night, I was unable to sleep, and I went to sit beside Beloved Adi Da's chair. My arms went up to this Presence Above, my palms spread receiving Its Energy. That night, as I sat there, I knew my life would have to be lived as a sacrifice to this Presence, the Spiritual Presence of my Beloved Guru.*

*Meanwhile, Beloved Adi Da only intensified His Demand on me. And, even though I had foreseen this, I would not, or could not, meet it. I felt as if my heart were literally being wrenched out of my body. I cried for Him. I longed for Him. And I was answered only by the Demand that I sacrifice.*

*After several dramatic emotional crises, which pushed me to a point where I realized I had absolutely no other choice, I began to accept my suffering instead of rebelling against it. I began to direct more energy to my daily functioning, and my attention was taken off myself and directed to other things. Thus, drawn out of my despair, I started to feel my love for my Beloved Guru intensifying again.*

*I began to turn from myself to Beloved Adi Da, because He had created a situation that forced me to do so. I had to see how I was creating my own suffering. And so, a few moments at a time, I began to live from this new viewpoint. I did it in desperation. This sacrifice, this conscious Satsang, went against everything I had ever lived up to that point. Everyone always tends to separate. When your demands, whatever they are, are frustrated, when you feel hurt or humiliated or are treated apparently unjustly (and, in the theatre with Beloved Adi Da, all of this was occurring), there is always the tendency to play out the drama, to pull back—to feel self-pity, anger, resentment, even rage, for your suffering, and to totally identify with it.*

*The "radical" alternative, the constant act of turning back to Beloved Adi Da, required a lot of discipline of me. It was like walking a tightrope all the time. My tendencies were always clambering after me, tempting me to live them—like the anger I felt toward Beloved Adi Da for ignoring me. It was so easy to "buy" it and to rebel. I felt that I had a right to it. And, by the standards of this world of "Narcissus", I did! The anger was me. I was bound to my own drama.*

*At last, I began to see the whole thing as suffering, and in those moments my suffering would dissolve. My Beloved gave me glimmerings of what that ultimately leads to. One night as I gazed at Him, He kept disappearing, becoming Infinite. At one point, I disappeared, too. It was brief. Perhaps only a few seconds. But there seemed to be nothing to identify with. "I" vanished. From the point of view of the ego, it was frightening. But it was Free. It was thrilling.*

*The more I resort to my Beloved Guru, the more devotional self-sacrifice is required, and the more Grace and Happiness is Given. I know that, in the end, there is only sacrifice. Beloved Adi Da is the Sign of that. He Is only Sacrifice.*

As Ann's story shows, the very qualities in Avatar Adi Da Samraj that may offend are the same ones that make Him Great. To deal with the ego in truth, He had to get under His devotee's skin. His unrelenting Integrity, His non-avoidance of reality, are the Genius of His Work. From the beginning, He has obliged Himself to do everything necessary to Attract all beings to Him, so that He may Awaken them to absolute Happiness.

Over the years, just two women devotees (from among the original Mandala of nine) have established a Yogic and devotional relationship to Avatar Adi Da that is unique, that has withstood every test. Both of them—Ruchira Adidama Sukha Dham Naitauba and Ruchira Adidama Jangama Hriddaya Naitauba[7]—are now formal "Ruchira sannyasins", renunciates of profound Realization who are practicing in the Ruchira Sannyasin Order[8] and doing the sadhana of the ultimate stages of life. Both of them recount here how they came to Avatar Adi Da in 1974. Their stories are an indicator of the deep Spiritual "Bond", Prior to this life, that drew them to Avatar Adi Da Samraj, a "Bond" that has proven itself in twenty-five years of human and Spiritual intimacy with Him.

1974

*ADIDAMA SUKHA DHAM: In August of 1973, at 19 years of age, while living in a suburb outside of Chicago, Illinois, it became obvious to me that I had to make a dramatic change in my life. I felt a very strong urge to just leave Illinois, and so I collected what money I had, which was very little, and set out to drive to California—which, to me, represented some kind of freedom from the oppressive and degraded life I felt I had been living. I drove to California with no clear sense of what I was going to do, or where I was going to go. I had a friend I could stay with, at least temporarily, in San Francisco, and so that is what I set out to do.*

*After many days of driving across country, I arrived in San Francisco and located this friend's house. I stayed, however, but one night. In the morning, I realized that I could not remain in San Francisco. For no apparent reason, a very strong urge to go to Los Angeles had arisen in me. I knew no one in Los Angeles, I had nothing I intended to do there, but I felt very strongly that I had to drive to Los Angeles. And so I packed up my things, drove to Los Angeles, and immediately set about looking for a place to live.*

*I found a small one-room house in Huntington Beach, and shortly after I arrived there, I began to have visions of a man and a woman. I could never see the woman, but it seemed to be myself. The man, however, was very distinct to me. He related to me very directly, and He would appear in an observatory, where He would constantly draw me to look through his telescope at the stars. After my initial contact with this man in the dream state, I would have a recurring vision of a star-form*[9] *perceived at the end of a tunnel, and this would appear not only in dreams but in the waking state. Shortly after that, I was led, through various acquaintances, to the bookstore on Melrose Avenue that was the first Ashram of Avatar Adi Da.*

*On this day, outside the meditation hall there were many shoes, and so I presumed that Beloved Adi Da was sitting in a formal meditation occasion. However, I did not ask and no one spoke of it. I quietly purchased* The Knee of Listening *and* The Method of the Siddhas. *When I looked at the books, I saw immediately that the man I was having constant visions of was Beloved Adi Da!*

*That same week I unexpectedly heard the voice of Beloved Adi Da on the radio. Recordings were being played of some of His Talks to His devotees. I was profoundly drawn and moved in my heart. His voice seemed to shape all that I felt. I had little comprehension of what He was saying, but I was completely moved by His voice and His laughter and the feeling that He communicated. Above all, I was attracted to the offering that He made of a relationship. So began my conscious relationship, in this lifetime, to my Beloved Guru, Adi Da Samraj.*

*After that, I set up an altar in the small one-room house that I was living in and spontaneously began to do daily puja.*[10] *I had no conscious knowledge of puja, but I was moved to make offerings to Beloved Adi Da's photograph, and I began to study His Teaching while seated before His photograph. The photograph I used was the one on the cover of* The Method of the Siddhas.

*Then, on January 18, 1974, my twentieth birthday, I decided I would approach Beloved Adi Da as my Divine Heart-Master and assume the full range of practices He was giving to His devotees at that time. I embraced all the disciplines exactly, without question, and began a series of study courses that were being offered at the Melrose Ashram. By this time, Beloved Adi Da and the other devotees were spending time at a new Ashram on La Brea Avenue. Some of the newer students, myself included, continued with the course instruction as preparation for meeting Beloved Adi Da.*

*At this time, Beloved Adi Da began to enter into a time of Instruction with devotees that involved ecstatic gatherings every night at the La Brea Ashram. I was not invited to these gatherings. Rather, I would drive daily from Huntington Beach, after my day of work, and serve the meditation hall in the Melrose Ashram. Each day I would bring a single white rose to offer there.*

*Meanwhile, every day new people were being called over to the La Brea Ashram to join these occasions of Divine Ecstasy with Beloved Adi Da. I longed to be called to come, but I never was while He was there. My relationship to Him at this time was through this daily service to His pristine meditation hall at the Melrose Ashram. And so I would continue each day to clean and prepare the hall, offering my one white rose. Never did I feel excluded by anyone. For me, it was a Grace beyond all imagining to be given the honor of serving Beloved Adi Da in this manner.*

*Then Beloved Adi Da moved to the Mountain Of Attention Sanctuary, and many devotees went with Him. I began to help with the preparations for moving the Ashram to northern California. I was given the unique opportunity to reside in the house where Beloved Adi Da had lived while He was Working at the Melrose and La Brea Ashrams. Devotees called His house "the Laurel Canyon house", because it was in the suburb of Laurel Canyon.*

*I arrived there one afternoon, very grateful to be in the home that Beloved Adi Da had lived in, and began, immediately upon my arrival, to become ill and feverish. What I had thought would be merely a pleasure and an honor turned into one of the most profound physical purifications I have ever endured! Later I learned that a physical disturbance, such as fever, is not uncommon when first encountering a potent source of Spiritual Transmission.*

*I found I was only sick inside the house, and most especially when I would enter Avatar Adi Da's bedroom. And yet, at the same time, I felt spontaneously and profoundly drawn to be in His room, and I began to spend as much time as possible there.*

*After many days, the illness and fever eventually subsided, and it was at this point that I was invited to come into the Company of Beloved Adi Da at the Mountain Of Attention. The most significant moment of my life had occurred, the moment I had been longing for. I collected my things, moved to San Francisco, and established myself in a household of His devotees.*

*The first time I saw Beloved Adi Da, I was overwhelmed by His extreme Beauty and Love. The depth of what was occurring was beyond my comprehension, but I was there before Him, and I did not want to be anywhere else. He was lying on His side on a couch in Great Food Dish,*[11] *the dining room of the Sanctuary. I approached Beloved Adi Da with a flower, and bowed at His Feet. During all the time of my preparation, my intention had been to make myself available to Beloved Adi Da's Instruction. I had lived it exactly. But now I was in*

***"He was lying on His side when I came into the room . . . and I intuited His direct capability to know everything about me at first glance. . . . I knew that a revolution in my life was about to occur."***

*His physical Company, and I intuited His direct capability to know everything about me at first glance. I was overwhelmed in my feeling, wondering what would be required for me to become completely available, completely surrendered to Him as His devotee. I was falling in love—had already fallen in love—with Him to the depths of my being. Mysterious Spiritual visions and intuitions that I had had since childhood came to mind, and I recognized the fulfillment and true meaning of them now in the form of Beloved Adi Da Samraj. I knew that a revolution in my life was about to occur. I did not know what was going on any more. All I wanted to do was to be with Beloved Adi Da, be close to Him.*

*Later that day, Beloved Adi Da went to Ordeal Bath Lodge, the bathhouse at the Mountain Of Attention, and devotees accompanied Him, scattering throughout the many different rooms of the baths. I happened to be in one of the small baths at the front of the building. At one point my Beloved Guru, who had been wandering among*

*His devotees, came up to the small bath where I was. As He came in and sat down, I felt myself sinking into a deep trance-state. I vividly recall Him just being there, giving me His Regard.*

*Later that evening, after we had left the baths, Beloved Adi Da called a small group of devotees over to His House, and I was included. There, in His House, I realized how profoundly He had drawn me to Him. The mysterious Power that I had felt guiding me was simply Him. He had pulled me, literally, out of the world. Eventually, the other devotees departed, but I remained all night with my Beloved Guru, during which He initiated me into a Condition that I had never known before. In Tantric embrace with Him, He drew me beyond the body-mind into a Spiritual reality that I have come to know as the Very Condition of my Beloved Lord Adi Da, the Truth of Existence Itself. I remember being directly in contact with my Beloved, eye to eye, and I recall that I had no sense of the body. The mind, also, was completely obliterated. In the timelessness of that moment, I felt Beloved Adi Da to be Standing Prior to anything that exists conditionally, taking me with Him to His Place, His Divine Domain. I felt drawn with Him into a most profound Samadhi, which was bodiless and mindless.*

*While I was overcome with intense love for Him and devotion to Him, my Beloved Guru was also responding to me with deepest love, acknowledging the unique nature of our relationship. In the morning, Beloved Adi Da took me out for a walk, to Fear-No-More Zoo,[12] and then to Ordeal Bath Lodge, where He had approached me the evening before. Then Beloved Adi Da guided me to the room behind Great Food Dish, which, at that time was one of the principal places where He used to grant His silent Darshan. As we walked through that sacred room, my feeling-recognition of Him continued to magnify, and I knew that He was the One that I had always been moved to be with.*

**Adidama Sukha Dham and Avatar Adi Da Samraj at the Mountain Of Attention**

*All day, Beloved Adi Da engaged me in "intoxicated" conversation about our love. He would ask me, over and over, where I had been. He spoke to me for hours, and we also sat in silence together for hours. I was moved to stay close to Him all the time—and, sitting near Him, I was utterly content. It was sufficient just being at His side. Before the end of the day, my Beloved had invited me to live with Him and serve Him in His bodily (human) Form, and I was overwhelmed with joy, having already abandoned everything else.*

*I was recovered. I was living in a world full of the Miracles of my Divine Heart-Master. There was nothing but my Beloved Guru. I wanted everyone to surrender to Him, to worship Him. I did not care what I did, what I said—I only wanted to be with Him. I had no other attachments. I wanted only to be fully available to Him in every dimension of my being. I felt His constant communication of Love and Spiritual Ecstasy. For days, I scarcely left His sight, and I moved into His house to live with Him.*

*And then, at a certain point, Beloved Adi Da began to test my Spiritual and intimate commitment to Him. And so began the great ordeal and process of becoming fit to serve and to relate to Him in the tradition-honored form of relationship between the Sat-Guru and the devotee. This process has confronted all the realities of my karmic nature. But whatever has come up to be purified, and whatever ordeal that purification has required, this first meeting has never left my heart—nor could it ever.*

Adidama Jangama Hriddaya came to Avatar Adi Da some weeks after His first meeting with Adidama Sukha Dham, and was also immediately established in His House. Her story starts several years earlier.

**1974**

*ADIDAMA JANGAMA HRIDDAYA: One afternoon in 1970, while seated in the Art Museum Library at Harvard University, I had a most extraordinary waking-state vision. I had been working on a seminar thesis on Chinese ink art and was contemplating the subject silently and alone in a quiet corner. Quite suddenly, I was drawn into a subtle visionary state, as though I was dreaming with my eyes open. My present reality became an absorbing vision.*

*I found myself standing at the bottom of a very long stone stairway, leading up a steep, craggy mountain to a remote hermitage above. I stopped for a moment, then intently started up the stairs. As I neared the top, an extraordinary figure appeared and stood silent above me. He wore a dark tunic and his shaven head was round and glowing. His silence was unfathomably deep and yet fully communicative. I intuitively knew that he was there to guide me or to reveal something to me. He made no outward expression of words, but gestured to a long vine that swung out over a rocky precipice. Then he turned to go. I understood that I was to swing on the vine, and I did so—out and back and out and back, over the precipice. There was the choice, very clearly, to let go and fall far below onto the rocks or to return. As I swung, I did not feel fear, but simply the knowledge of mortality. Once that was instilled, I spontaneously regained the ground.*

*Instantly, the figure reappeared. He motioned me to follow, and I descended the long stone stairs behind him. We walked down out of the wilderness into a village and wandered through the streets. My guide was silent. A strange phenomenon occurred. I tried to speak to people in the village, but no one could hear me. I was like an invisible apparition there. I no longer had a place in the world. As soon as I realized this, we returned up the stairs to the hermitage. As I followed him back up the long stone steps, I knew that this was my Spiritual Master.*

*At the top of the stairs, my Master turned to me. He said nothing, but only looked into my eyes. The tacit communication was as clear as, or clearer than, words. "Do you see? There is no way back, once you have begun." I met his eyes. I felt profoundly happy and calm and full.*

*As soon as this vision faded, another vision quickly arose. Now I stood alone on a long sandy beach overlooking a huge expanse of ocean. I struck a wooden match. Suddenly, everything—the beach, ocean, sky, and myself were sucked into a vortex and dissolved into an unutterable glory of light. At the perimeter, a red-yellow-orange fieriness flared far more brilliant than the sun. Closer to the center, there was a dark purple-blueness, infinitely deep, which then dissolved into a whiteness brighter than I had ever seen with the physical eyes. I was joyfully consumed in the luminous brightness.*

*As silently as they came, the visions left. Emerging from these visions, I felt a great bliss, an ecstasy, a freedom—and a certainty. I knew that they held a secret of Truth that would reveal itself in time. I felt a tacit certainty that the Spiritual Master I had seen in vision would appear in manifested form in my life at the appropriate moment. I knew that, as in my vision, He would be able to look directly into my eyes and communicate fully in silence. I began to wait and watch for Him. The vision I had of brilliant luminosity, greater than even the human eye can see, granted me the intuition of the Divine "Brightness" that would appear with my Spiritual Master.*

*These visions marked a change in my life. From a conventional point of view, I had everything that was "good" in life: family, friends, a comfortable living circumstance, excellent education and career possibilities. However, from as early as I can remember, I had desired more than the satisfactions the world can offer—I wanted to know why I was alive and I wanted to know God most directly. These visions granted me the intuition of the imminent appearance in my life of the One who would answer this heart-yearning.*

*In 1970, I left Harvard and got a job as a secretary, living alone in Boston. I began a solitary daily routine of Hatha Yoga and a form of sitting meditation, but all the while I was looking for my Teacher. Later I left the east coast for California and settled in Los Angeles. I heard mention of a Spiritual Teacher in Hollywood named "Franklin Jones", but I did not act on it. I was not ready.*

*After four years, I had despaired of my Spiritual search and was resigned to continue my formal education and prepare for a career. I returned to the east coast and made arrangements with the Harvard Art Department to get my degree through independent studies at Tokyo University. Everything was set, all plans finalized.*

*Then I received a letter from a friend. "The teacher you have been looking for is here in California. Come at*

**Devotees bowing as Avatar Adi Da Samraj enters Temple Eleutherios, 1974**

***"Suddenly, the door at the front of the Communion Hall opened. The most exquisitely 'Bright' Being I had ever seen entered. . . .This was the One I had been waiting for."***

*once." I abandoned everything and left immediately for the West Coast. I went directly to San Francisco and then up to the Mountain Of Attention Sanctuary. The second time I walked onto the Sanctuary, someone beckoned me to move quickly into a low white wooden building. I followed a few others in the door, walked a few paces, and sat down on the floor toward the back of the room. It was a meditation hall, and everyone was sitting silent and still.*

*Suddenly, the door at the front of the Communion Hall opened. The most exquisitely "Bright" Being I had ever seen entered. With total Grace, He strode directly to me and planted His staff at my side. Instantaneously, without thought, I prostrated before Him on the floor, my head touching His Feet, my hands clasping them. I was utterly swooned in the Love-Blissful Presence of Real God. My mind dissolved, transported beyond any thought or self-consciousness. After a time—I have no idea how long—this Great One stepped back and moved to His Seat in the front of the room. He sat in utter silence. I sat immersed in the Vision of His Divinity. This was God in the form of Man, Absolute Perfection. I immediately recognized this Great Being as the Spiritual Master I had seen in vision four years earlier. This was the One I had been waiting for.*

*After this formal meditation sitting, I was invited with a small group into the house of Avatar Adi Da Samraj. Again, as soon as I saw Him, I fell to the floor in prostrated adoration. I had at last found My Beloved Spiritual Master. He called me to His Seat and asked me, "Do you want to be My devotee and live with Me forever?" With total joy, I replied, "Yes".*

**Adidama Jangama Hriddaya and Adi Da Samraj, 1975**

## "The Way That I Teach"

The dramatic months of "Garbage and the Goddess" came to an end around July 1974, but Avatar Adi Da's Work continued unabated. Working at the Mountain Of Attention, and occasionally in a house near San Francisco, He continued to make lessons about the activity that is the ego—the constant search for this or that experience which, one hopes, will bring lasting Happiness. He continued to address <u>all</u> the varieties of humanity's search, in the most vivid and realistic terms, Revealing the limit in every kind of goal that has been proposed as the purpose of life. He dealt with the impulse to bypass the body and find happiness through subtle (or mystical) experience—or what He calls the "alpha" orientation. He dealt with the urge toward every kind of bodily or worldly self-fulfillment—or what He called the "omega" orientation.[13] Through the unique brilliance and comprehensiveness of His Teaching, Avatar Adi Da addressed all human tendencies and goals, world-denying and worldly, East and West. And He Revealed the great Divine Truth and Ecstasy of existence that makes all seeking obsolete.

During this time, it came to Avatar Adi Da's attention (through letters and other communications) that some people in the public regarded His Teaching to be similar to the philosophy of J. Krishnamurti. Even some individuals approaching Him as Guru were making this presumption. In April 1975, Avatar Adi Da decided to clarify the matter. His commentaries, given in discussion with His devotees, were published in the community magazine, then called *The Dawn Horse: A Magazine Devoted to the Understanding of the Great Traditions of Esoteric Spirituality*.

*AVATAR ADI DA SAMRAJ: People often equate My Teaching Arguments relative to "radical" understanding with the ideas of J. Krishnamurti. But, if you examine the work of J. Krishnamurti, you will see that he is a modern representative of the approach of "mind dharma"—the path of dissolving, bypassing, or transcending thoughts and mental inclinations of impressions, in order (as a result) to enjoy such a state of sensitivity to the arising world that it may be felt and known directly, and even unqualifiedly. J. Krishnamurti recommends no method for this attainment other than attention to the mind itself, to the point of seeing that the mind is not identical to the realities it seems to contain (in language, symbols, and experiences), but is, rather, a process by which the real awareness of things is obstructed.*

*Such a teaching is certainly not identical to the Way of "Radical" Understanding. Its only basic similarity to the Way of "Radical" Understanding is its denial of the value of motivated techniques for attainment. However, such a teaching relies on a form of attention that is methodical (or deliberate) and, certainly, oriented toward a specific goal (called, by Krishnamurti, "choiceless awareness").*

*Nevertheless, such a state of non-reflexive awareness (or "meditation") is not identical to Truth Itself. Such a state of non-reflexive awareness is only a functional state, one of many conventional ways in which one may enjoy conscious awareness in and of the world. The Way of "Radical" Understanding involves spontaneous insight into even this strategy of self-observation and this meditative state that may be called the goal of Krishnamurti's path of conscious awareness. One who "radically" understands does not depend on any experiential state, nor can his or her enjoyment be equated with any functional condition. He or she knows that no process, high or low, in any plane of manifestation, is Truth Itself, or leads to Truth Itself. Therefore, he or she releases both the quiet mind and the obstructive mind from the burden of being either a way to Truth Itself or, in itself, the very antithesis of Truth Itself.*

*J. Krishnamurti is speaking from the traditional point of view of dilemma, search, and goal. He is asking his listeners to settle for a meditative state, and his path pursues a change of state as a specific exercise. Realization of Truth Itself is not a matter of the quiet mind, the empty mind, the blissful mind, the transcendental mind, or even the Divine Mind. Realization of Truth Itself is of a "radical" and Most Prior Nature, and one's initial entrance into the Domain of Truth Itself involves "radical" insight into the entire process of the world and one's own event. In that case, no experiential state or condition or path or attainment fascinates any longer.* [April 5, 1975]

Avatar Adi Da also went on to point out another essential difference between the Way of "Radical" Understanding that He was Teaching and the philosophy of Krishnamurti. Krishnamurti always claimed that he was not a Teacher, or Guru, that he was merely offering a philosophical method for anyone who wished to adopt it. (In reality, Krishnamurti was functioning as a teacher, but he preferred to associate himself with an "anti-guru" attitude.) Avatar Adi Da always communicated the opposite. He emphasized the absolute importance of the relationship to a Siddha-Guru, a being of Spiritual Power and Realization, if genuine Spiritual growth is to occur.

Finally, Avatar Adi Da made the point that a "quiet mind" is not enough—it does not lead to transformation of the being. If you want such transformation, there is no alternative but to do sadhana, or real Spiritual practice, submitting to a true Guru.

In His forceful closing Words, Avatar Adi Da was urging His devotees not to settle for anything less that this.

*AVATAR ADI DA SAMRAJ: One who is thus made an advocate of the quiet mind is typically self-involved, bereft of the "juice" of Grace, incapable of yielding to Real God or Guru, insensitive to the Presence of a real Siddha-Master, and, essentially, disgusted by his fellow men. It does no good to gain a little peace by method and strategy. Even if there is a little quiet, real sadhana must begin at last.* [April 5, 1975]

During the several years that He had been involved in His Teaching Work thus far, various reports about Avatar Adi Da's "Crazy-Wise" manner of Working had also circulated around the Spiritual communities of the time, even as far away as India. Many people were unable to understand why such unconventional behavior should be necessary. During 1975, an Indian Yogi,

Swami Chinmayananda, heard about Avatar Adi Da's Spiritual Work and wrote a letter expressing his concern over Avatar Adi Da's "Crazy" manner of Teaching, an approach to Spiritual Instruction that was entirely foreign to his own orthodox views.

Swami Chinmayananda was a well-known and respected figure in Spiritual circles—he was a commentator on Vedanta and had written many books. He had also visited Swami Nityananda on several occasions, and received Nityananda's blessing on his efforts to promote Hinduism, which he had done with great success throughout India and even, to some degree, in the West. In the spring of 1975, Swami Chinmayananda was in San Francisco for the sake of furthering his worldwide mission and study groups, and it was most likely during this time that he first came to hear of the "Crazy-Wise" Teaching Work of "Bubba Free John".

James Steinberg, the devotee responsible for relations with other Ashrams and Gurus, brought Swami Chinmayananda's letter to Avatar Adi Da on a Sunday afternoon down at a large swimming pool (below the site later to become Holy Cat Grotto[14]). As Avatar Adi Da read the letter, James could feel that He was fully receiving this traditional swami's expression of perplexity. The next morning, at a devotee's house in Mill Valley, Marin County (where He stayed occasionally), Avatar Adi Da Wrote an Essay clarifying the nature of His "Crazy-Wise" Teaching Work—an Essay which was a response to Swami Chinmayananda and also a communication to everyone.

*What I Do is not the way that I Am, but the way that I Teach.*

*What I Speak is not a reflection of Me, but of you.*

*People do well to be offended or even outraged by My actions and behavior. This is My purpose. But their reac-*

*tion must turn upon themselves, for I have not Shown them My Self by all of this. All that I Do and Speak only reveals people to themselves.*

*I have become willing to Teach in this uncommon manner because I have known My friends—and they are what I can seem to be. By retaining all qualities in their company, I gradually wean them of all reactions, all sympathies, all alternatives, fixed assumptions, false teachings, dualities, searches, and dilemma. This is My Way of Working for a time. . . .*

*Freedom is the only Purity. There is no Teaching but Consciousness Itself. My Appearance here is not other than the possibilities of mankind.* [1975]

The Mountain Of Attention, 1976

CHAPTER 8

# Indoor Summer

In July 1976, it started to rain at the Mountain Of Attention Sanctuary—which is virtually unheard of during the summer in that part of California. It continued raining on and off for the next few months.

The unusual weather was not so surprising to Avatar Adi Da's devotees, as they had grown used to such natural phenomena arising in conjunction with a magnification of His Siddhis. And this was certainly the case now. Avatar Adi Da had begun a process that seemed to change everything. Gathering with devotees for twelve, fourteen, eighteen hours a day, around a big octagonal table in His Residence at the Mountain Of Attention, He was introducing another great Teaching Argument—the Argument He called "Divine Ignorance". It was the beginning of the "Indoor Summer", an epoch as fundamental to His Revelation as "Garbage and the Goddess".

## "You do not know what any thing Is!"

One night, early in the series of gatherings, one of the devotees who had been invited to attend, Michael Wood, arrived late. As soon as Michael walked in the door, he was immediately invited to sit next to Avatar Adi Da and get brought up to speed in the evening's "consideration"—by participating in an enquiry into his real state of knowledge. Bringing Michael into

**Michael Wood and Avatar Adi Da Samraj at the Mountain Of Attention, 1976**

the discussion was all the more interesting because of the fact that he was a lawyer, someone whose self-image and career had always depended on knowing a lot.

Avatar Adi Da turned to Michael, "I want you to picture the letter 'M' in your mind." After giving Michael a moment, Avatar Adi Da asked, "Have you got it there?"

"Yes," Michael replied.

"Is it a capital letter or a small letter?"

"It is a capital letter."

"Is it in color?"

"Not particularly."

"Now," said Avatar Adi Da, delivering the crucial question, "I want you to tell Me—what is it?"

"Well, I am not sure what you mean. I can describe what the letter looks like, how big it is, all that. Or I can describe what it signifies."

"Yes, I know you can do all that. But why don't you tell Me what it is?"

*MICHAEL: As the dialogue continued, I began to feel the mechanism in myself that wants to "know" things, and that wants to be "right" and "on top" of things. I could also feel that mechanism relax. At a certain point in the conversation, I confessed, "I don't know what it is!"*

*Simultaneous with that confession, I felt relieved of my usual state of concern, and a thrill released in my heart, my body, and my whole being. I felt as though I was going to burst with Happiness, as if the Happiness I felt was too great, that it violated the rules of being identified with a body. I felt as though this Happiness was going to spill over and do something wonderful but mad.*

*Suddenly, everything that I did and presumed was revealed to be a stupid and futile effort to know, to concentrate and contain and control, all based on egoic knowledge and fear. I always thought that if I could only know enough, or know the right things, I would be free. I had pursued that controlling knowledge even in my choice to become a lawyer. But now Beloved Adi Da was showing me, very directly and beyond all doubt, that being Free did not depend on gaining knowledge.*

*He persisted in this dialogue with me, and, as we spoke, I felt Him communicating and reinforcing this feeling of Divine Ignorance with His speech and His entire Being. My capability to relax into that thoughtless Ignorance deepened. There was limitless depth to that awareness, a perfect penetration and release of my limited self-sense. And it was clear to me that Avatar Adi Da Samraj was Alive constantly as that unbelievably Blissful Consciousness.*

*I flipped back and forth from these blissful satoris,*[1] *in and out of my usual state of mind. My attention was not free enough to consistently remain in this extraordinary disposition of Divine Ignorance. But that is what Avatar Adi Da was Calling me to. He said:*

*AVATAR ADI DA SAMRAJ: You are completely free of what arises. It never implicates you for a moment. You know nothing about it. Knowledge is not your connection to it. You do not have a connection to it. There is no connection. There is no "you" to find. There is Divine Ignorance, only absolute Ignorance. To Realize this most perfectly is Divine Enlightenment, Absolute Love-Bliss. The Realization of Divine Ignorance does not qualify the arising of any thing. It does not stand in relationship to it, really. There is no difference between Divine Ignorance and the arising of phenomena. Nothing intervenes. There is just what arises, and no knowledge—complete Divine Ignorance, or Love-Bliss. This is Most Perfect Realization of Truth Itself, or Reality Itself, or Real God. There is nothing to be Realized beyond It.* [July 1976]

As the gatherings continued, night after night, Avatar Adi Da would often hold up a glass ashtray and ask:

"Do you know what this is? What it is? What it IS?"

Night after night, devotees would attempt to answer Him, and Avatar Adi Da would skillfully question them further, until the mind of each one came to a standstill—and fell apart at the seams! What you think you know, Avatar Adi Da was Revealing, is actually just an accumulation of descriptions, an effort to create the sensation of familiarity in the midst of a fundamentally bewildering world. Divine Enlightenment has nothing to do with such familiarity. Rather, It is perfect, unqualified Ignorance!

Avatar Adi Da's "Consideration" of Divine Ignorance plunged His devotees into Mystery, the Mystery of merely Being. It was a sublime and humorous and profound confrontation with everyone's primal attitude

***As the gatherings continued, night after night, Avatar Adi Da would often hold up a glass ashtray and ask:***
***"Do you know what this is? What it is? What it IS?"***

toward existence. Avatar Adi Da was addressing the root-presumption of every human being—that he or she is an "I", an "inner entity" which is the observer and knower of everything. Now Avatar Adi Da was graphically demonstrating that all presumed "knowing" is illusion—useful enough as a tool of ordinary living, but utterly useless as a means of apprehending Reality Itself.

Some years after "Indoor Summer", Avatar Adi Da Samraj distilled His "consideration" relative to Divine Ignorance into a remarkable book for children (and adults), *What, Where, When, How, Why, and Who To Remember To Be Happy*.

*Have you heard this*  *is an apple?*

*Have you been told this*  *is a tree?*

*Do you think this*  *is the moon?*

*and this*  *the sun?*

*Have you told someone this*  *is a little girl?*

*and this*  *is a little boy?*

*Well. But you and I can be very truthful to each other. And it seems to Me that no matter what we name*

*this*  *or this*  *or this* 

*or this*  *or this*  *or this* 

*we still do not know what they Are. Truly, you and I don't know what even a single thing Is. Do you know what I Am? See. And I don't know what you Are either. It is a Mystery. Doesn't it make you feel good to feel It?*

Did you ever ask somebody where this 

or this  or this  came from,

or how this  or this  or this 

came to be?

Some say, "I don't know", and saying this makes them feel they are being very honest and truthful. Others say something such as "God made it" or "It comes from God". And such people are also being very honest and truthful when they say this.

How can they both be telling the truth? Well, because they are both telling you the same thing in different ways. You see, nobody, not Mom, or Dad, or Grandmother, or Grandfather, or big Sister, or big Brother, or teachers, or doctors, or soldiers, or athletes, or lawyers, or TV stars, or any people who are working, or any people who are playing, not even a President, not even a King or a Queen, not even people who love each other know what even a single thing Is. It is a great and more than wonderful Mystery to all of us that anything is, or that we are. And whether somebody says "I don't know how anything came to be" or "God made everything", they are simply pointing to the feeling of the Mystery, of how everything is but nobody knows what it really Is or how it came to be.

*As long as we go on feeling this Mystery, we feel free and full and happy, and we feel and act free and full and happy to others. This is the secret of being happy from the time you are small until the time you are old.*

In August 1998, Avatar Adi Da summarized the essence of His Teaching of Divine Ignorance, in a passage from *Santosha Adidam.*[2]

*The only-by-Me Revealed and Given Way (or Divine Yoga) of Adidam is the Way (or Divine Yogic Process) that inherently (and more and more effectively—and, at last, Most Perfectly) transcends all conditional experience (and all conditional experiencing) and all conditional knowledge (and all conditional knowing).*

*The psycho-physical ego-"I" (or body-mind-self) is a conditional (or limited, temporary, and always changing) experiencer—and a (likewise) conditional knower. Therefore, all egoic experience and all egoic knowledge is limited, temporary, always changing, and merely and only psycho-physical.*

*The ego-"I" is a conditional process in conditional space-time. The ego-"I" is a seeker for conditional experience and conditional knowledge. And the ego-"I" is an accumulation and an effect of conditional experience and conditional knowledge. However, the ego-"I" arises in Reality (or Existence, or Being) Itself—and as an apparent modification of Reality (or of What Always Already Is) Itself. Therefore, the ego-"I" is never in a position separate from What Always Already Is—such that it could experience, or inspect, or know What Always Already Is. And, for this reason, the ego-"I" does not and cannot experience, or inspect, or know What even any thing, event, or other Always Already Is. Therefore, no matter what (or even who) is experienced, or inspected, or known by the ego-"I" (or the self-contracted body-mind), the ego-"I" (itself) does not and cannot Unconditionally recognize any thing, event, or other that it experiences, or inspects, or knows. That is to say, the ego-"I" (or body-mind-self) cannot itself recognize its own psycho-physical experience (itself) or knowledge (itself) As it Always Already Is—or As Reality Itself (or As Existence Itself, or As Being Itself). And, therefore, the ego-"I" (or body-mind-self) does not recognize its own conditional experience and its own conditional knowledge to Be Self-Existing and Self-Radiant Consciousness Itself (or the inherently egoless Divine Self-Condition, or Always-Already-Existing Conscious Light, Itself). And, as a consequence of its own inherent state of perpetual non-recognition of its own conditional experience and its own conditional knowledge, the ego-"I" (or body-mind-self) always and inherently fails to transcend its own conditional experiencing and its own conditional knowing. And, because of that failure (which is inevitable, and inherent in egoity itself), the ego-"I" is bondage to conditional existence in space-time.*

*The ego-"I" (or body-mind-self) is inherently, irreducibly, and irrevocably ignorant of What Always Already Is. However, that inherent ignorance (rather than any kind of conditional experience or conditional knowledge) is (itself)—if it is Truly and Most Perfectly Realized—the Essential (and Divinely Liberating) True and Divine Knowledge of Reality! Therefore, the essential (and inherent) ignorance that characterizes the ego-"I" (or even any conditional body-mind) is—Ultimately, or in Truth—Divine (and Inherent) Ignorance. And Divine (and Inherent) Ignorance . . . Is the "Radical" Essence, or Root-Condition, of True and Divine Knowing. And the Most Perfect . . . Realization of Divine (and Inherent) Ignorance is the Unique Capability of Divine Recognition (or the Inherent Capability to Recognize any and every apparent thing, event, or other—As Is).*

*The only-by-Me Revealed and Given Way (or Divine Yoga) of Adidam is the Way (or Divine Yogic Process) of Divine Ignorance.*

SANTOSHA ADIDAM

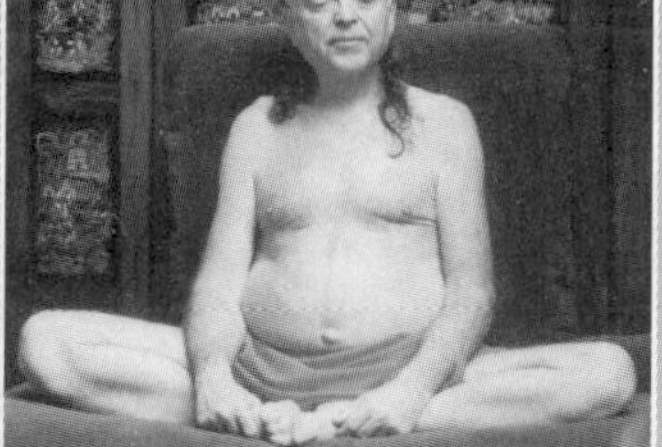

Not only Adi Da's words but, even more, the Power of His Presence and His Glance, which radiated His Perfect Freedom, served to awaken this ineffable Ignorance. To His astonished devotees, Divine Enlightenment now seemed obvious. What other condition could there be but this all-consuming Love-Bliss, free of mind?

## "Consideration"

Avatar Adi Da's dialogues with His devotees about Divine Ignorance are a prime example of what He means by "consideration". "Consideration" in Avatar Adi Da's Company does not mean an ordinary discussion, or a merely mental examination of some issue. It is a Yoga, a discipline, a process in which all the attention and energy of the body-mind is concentrated. To enter into "consideration" with Avatar Adi Da about something, you had to be prepared to inspect every aspect of the subject at hand, ready to let Him draw you into a living theatre of self-discovery relative to it.

*The "method" of My Teaching Work with My devotees was not common, although there are many traditional precedents for it. It was not merely a subjective, internal, or even verbal activity but an intense, full, and total "consideration" of any specific area of experience, in living confrontation with others, until the obvious and Lawful, or Divine, form and practice of it became both clear and necessary.*

*I have compared this method to the higher Yogic technique of samyama described by Patanjali in his* Yoga Sutras. *In brief, that Yogic technique of samyama is a process of one-pointed but ultimately thoughtless concentration and exhaustive examination of a particular object, function, person, process, or condition, until the essence, or ultimate obviousness, of that subject is clear. Only in that case does the Yogi enjoy native intimacy and understanding, or power, relative to that subject.*

*I have called My own Teaching Method "consideration". Whenever it has been clear to Me that a particular area of life, or experience, or Spiritual practice needed to be addressed by Me as a subject of Instruction for the sake of My devotees, I have entered into "consideration" with them. Such "considerations" were never merely a matter of thinking and talking. They always involved a period in which individuals were permitted to live through the whole matter and to be tested to the point of change. Those who entered into any "consideration" with Me were obliged to commit themselves to their own elaborate and concentrated play of life in those particular terms, until the entire matter was clarified and the Truth became clear in terms of the subject. . . .*

*All these "considerations" have been "samyama" in the highest sense, involving every aspect of body and mind, high and low, and resulting in both the deepest intuition and the most practical grasp of how to live life in accordance with natural laws and the Divine Law.* [1978]

A "consideration", once begun, went on day and night in the Presence of Avatar Adi Da Samraj. This was the great Skillful Means of His "Crazy-Wisdom" Work. Altogether, Avatar Adi Da's principal "considerations" took years. He would open up a fundamental area—diet, sexuality, death, Spiritual experience, the Nature of Consciousness Itself, the devotional relationship to Him—and then He would keep returning to it, always taking the "consideration" further, always expecting from devotees a more profound change of life in response. No matter what area of life He was "considering", Avatar Adi Da had only one purpose—to Reveal the Way of Divine Enlightenment in complete detail. By drawing small groups of

His devotees again and again through this extraordinary process in His direct Company, Avatar Adi Da was creating a vast field of Spiritual Influence that affected His devotees everywhere. Through His "Crazy" Work with a few, Avatar Adi Da was making His Instruction effective for all beings, not merely as words to be recorded, but as extraordinary Leela[3] (or Divine Play) and as an actual Transmission of His Siddhi, potent forever.

## "I" Is the Body

Now that Avatar Adi Da Samraj had Revealed the Truth of Divine Ignorance, the next months became a monumental unraveling of the implications. First of all, who or what is this inner "I" that presumes to know the world?

*AVATAR ADI DA SAMRAJ: Who is this "I" that is the principal subject of philosophy, of Spirituality, of your life? "I do this, I do that, I want to do this, I want to go out of the body, I want to go here, I want to realize this". Who is this "I"? It is the "self", right?*

*Wrong! Before you become troubled over it, it is perfectly obvious who "I" is. When you say, "I do this, I do that," the body-mind is talking! What is all this nonsense that "I" is not the body-mind? "I" is the simply perceiving body-mind! That is all that "I" is. "I" is not some "ghost" behind it all, separated from it, viewing it, knowing about it. "I" is those things about which you say, "not this, not this, not this". That is exactly what "I" is! There is no "I" inside, no inner host that says "I". The body-mind says "I".* [August 14, 1976]

This statement was revolutionary. "Not this, not this" (or "neti, neti") is a classic affirmation in Advaita Vedanta[4]—that "I am not the body or the mind, I am not any particular aspect of the phenomenal world." This affirmation is not only Hindu; it is the essential message of most esoteric Spiritual traditions, which involve the practitioner (in one way or another) in the attempt to "get out" of the body—into a state (or "heaven") and which state is free of the bodily sufferings of life in this world, and which state is the "Abode" of Happiness, or Truth, or God. But for Avatar Adi Da to declare "'I' is the body-mind" confronted the general notions of Spiritual life in almost all cultures—including Western culture. At first, it was baffling—and terrifying—to His listeners, because the body-mind inevitably dies. But He went on:

*AVATAR ADI DA SAMRAJ: The Realization that "I" is the body-mind is a matter of Enlightenment. The Realization that "I" is the body-mind is Liberation from the implication of the whole affair of living. It is not the same as saying "I am mortal". When "I" is the body-mind, "I" is completely fitted to the destiny of the total body-mind, and it becomes the Mystery. "I" is not afraid of death if "I" is the body-mind.*

*The only concern the body-mind has is making death coincide with the end of a cycle, in not bringing on death arbitrarily. If you view the process of the body-mind going forward or backward in time, you see that it is a process, not merely a fleshy thing. But it is a process that you are not capable of describing absolutely, because it is alive. You do not know what it* is*. Nevertheless, you are that whole process, absolutely.*

*If you view the body-mind through time, you see many past lives, many scripts similar to this one. But "I am the body-mind" is not about those lives. They are true in some sense and can be inspected, but "I am the body-mind" is Realization, Enlightenment. "I am the body-mind" is timeless, not mortal. No matter what arises, you do not know what it* is*. As the body-mind, submitted to the Mystery, you fulfill your birth. This Pleasure of no-knowledge is your eternal position. The body-mind, then, or the entire matter arising, becomes the Mystery, and you are no longer troubled by the false notion of a "self" underneath it all that troubles you, but is not true. Living in Mystery, as the body-mind, as Happiness, you begin to become healed. "I" is the body-mind, without conflict. That Realization carries with It the sudden and perfect communication that is hidden in everything.* [August 14, 1976]

As He spoke, Avatar Adi Da led those in the room with Him into the Mystery He was describing. His Words were a stream of "Bright" Power, moving His devotees out of the thinking head and into the feeling being. They were feeling the total body, experiencing its native pleasure, its natural radiance expanding from the heart. They could feel that they were being Lived and Breathed, in a Process that had no beginning or end. In this vulnerable Fullness, they saw that they were not separate from anything.

*. . . You Must First (and Naturally) Realize Your ego-"I" (or Apparently Separate self) To be the sensory body (or the Total experiential, Participatory, or perceiving body-mind). When (By Means Of Whole bodily Devotional Recognition-Response To My Avatarically Self-Revealed Divine Form, and Presence, and State) You Allow Your conditional self To be the Total body-mind (Simply perceiving—and Not Seeking To Acquire Absolute conditional knowledge and Power, or Struggling To Strategically Escape From the Natural body-mind itself, or From the conditional worlds themselves), the body-mind Is Naturally (or Simply, and Whole bodily) felt—and human Existence Is (Thus) Simply Expressed As A Natural Radiance Of Whole bodily feeling (or Of Simple, and ordinary human, Love and Happiness). And, In The Spiritual Fullness Of The Only-By-Me Revealed and Given Way Of The Heart (or Way Of Adidam), That Simple (Whole bodily) Love and Happiness Is (By Means Of My Avatarically Self-Transmitted Divine Grace) Spiritually Magnified—Into (and By Means Of) My Self-Evidently Divine Love-Bliss . . . .*

*The Natural (and Basically Non-verbal, Non-conceptual, Whole bodily, and Wholly Participatory) Feeling-Confession "'I' am the body" Is, Itself, Naturally Felt As Love and Happiness. And (More and More) When (By Means Of My Avatarically Self-Transmitted Divine Grace) There Is Whole bodily Devotional*

*Feeling-Participation In The Self-Existing and Self-Radiant Field Of My Avatarically Self-Transmitted Divine Spirit-Current Of Love-Bliss, There Is The Whole bodily (and, Progressively, More and More Profound) Realization That the conditional (or phenomenal) psycho-physical self Is Inherently Relational (and Related), Inherently Participatory, Inherently Non-Separate (and Non-Separative), Inherently Free Of Problems, Inherently Radiant (As Free Feeling), Truly Established (and, Ultimately, To Be Most Perfectly Established) In (and, Most Ultimately, As) My Transcendental, Inherently Spiritual, and Self-Evidently Divine Condition Of Inherently egoless Being, and Truly Characterized (and, Ultimately, To Be Most Perfectly Characterized) By Divine Ignorance (or The Self-Existing, Self-Radiant, and Inherently Free Feeling Of Being[5]—Itself).*

THE DAWN HORSE TESTAMENT
OF THE RUCHIRA AVATAR

Avatar Adi Da Samraj was Granting a living intuition of the Supreme Tantric Realization, which was His own Realization at the Vedanta Temple: Consciousness Itself, or Real God, is utterly coincident with, while also Infinitely Transcending, the body-mind and the world.

A few years after His original "consideration" of "'I' is the body", Avatar Adi Da wrote a poem that epitomizes the Divinely Enlightened Vision He was Granting to His devotees.

*Mindless embodiment,*
*Consciousness without inwardness.*
*Thus it becomes Obvious.*

*Every object is only Light, the Energy of Consciousness.*
*Even so, there is no mind.*
*Only this stark embodiment, without inwardness.*

*First transcend the mind, not the body.*
*Inwardness is flight from Life and Love.*
*Only the body is Full of Consciousness.*

*Therefore, be the body only, feeling into Life.*
*Surrender the mind into Love, until the body dissolves in Light.*
*Dare this ecstasy, and never be made thoughtful by birth and experience and death.*

## The Enlightened Life

Part of the Genius of Avatar Adi Da's "Crazy" Teaching Work was the way He would present the most profound Dharma at the same time that He was creating a Spiritual "theatre" to draw out His devotees' egoic tendencies and fascinations relative to the subject at hand. The "Indoor Summer" period of 1976 was a striking case of this, just as "Garbage and the Goddess" had been in 1974. But now, instead of offering the ultimate Spiritual experience (as in the "Garbage and the Goddess" period) Avatar Adi Da offered His devotees the vision of what it would be like to absolutely fulfill yourself in the body—in a state of "Enlightenment", of course!

If you do not know what anything is, and the body itself is "Full of Consciousness", is self-discipline necessary? Is it not sufficient to live spontaneously as love, ecstatic as the body, enjoying the Ignorance of your native State?

Avatar Adi Da allowed—and even encouraged—the "consideration" to go in this direction. For a few months, He permitted devotees to think that they were actually Enlightened, and He led the way in suggesting the hedonistic flavor of such an "Enlightened" life.

The world of the senses became intensely alive around Avatar Adi Da—beautiful clothes, delicious and elaborate meals, elegant environments. Devotees who had been unkempt hippies a few years before suddenly became interested in making lots of money, developing a wardrobe, and becoming gourmet cooks! For example, there was a culinary competition in which two "teams" prepared the same Chinese menu for Avatar Adi Da, vying for absolute perfection, not only in the quality of the food and the cooking but in the presentation, the service, and every aspect of the environment.

Such occasions also gave the Divine Maha-Siddha many humorous opportunities to do His Spiritual Work with the individual devotees involved. He liked to set up competitions and other theatrical situations precisely for this purpose—to bring devotees' obsessions and ego-strategies right to the fore, so that He could address them and purify them openly.

One day Avatar Adi Da walked into Western Face Cathedral, a principal meditation Hall at the Mountain Of Attention, clad in a blue three-piece designer suit, a purple polka-dot shirt, a cravat, and powder-blue patent-leather shoes. (Never before had He, or any devotee, entered a Communion Hall wearing shoes.) Amid gasps of amazement, He walked directly to His Chair at the front of the Hall and, without a word, took His seat for the Darshan occasion.

Avatar Adi Da gave a Talk that day on one of the themes of the time, the idea of bodily immortality. He

already had the doctors and other healers in the community busily engaged in researching medical means of prolonging life indefinitely. The master-stroke of this "consideration" was Avatar Adi Da's proposal of a new name for the gathering of His devotees (then called "The Dawn Horse Communion"). Perhaps, He said, the name should be changed to "Inc. Inc."—"Incarnation Incorporated"!

Another dimension to the theme of eternal life was reincarnation. Part of the remarkable Play of Avatar Adi Da during the "Indoor Summer" had to do with an exploration of what He later came to call "patterns". As He mentioned in His Discourse of August 14, 1976 (pp. 207-209), the body in its totality (including the function of mind) is part of an incomprehensible process extending backward and forward in time, involving countless incarnations in this and other realms. By this, the Divine Maha-Siddha did not mean that the physical body is somehow reconstituted from life to life. Rather, He was saying that the body-mind is just a moment in the flow, the present-time evidence of a greater pattern. Even in the present lifetime, as He pointed out, the body-mind is constantly changing. It is never a fixed entity. And not just the body-mind, but conditional existence altogether is a phenomenally complex play of patterning. To grasp this is not to gain knowledge. On the contrary, it further confirms our utter Ignorance.

Occasionally, Avatar Adi Da would spontaneously bring to light the unconscious karmic ego-patterns of His devotees—as those patterns had existed through time, in a history of apparent personalities, or incarnations. But central to His "Consideration" was the question of His own Pattern, an investigation into the Pattern in history that had prepared for His present human birth and for the configuration of people surrounding Him. Some of those sitting in the room with Him now, He was suggesting, had been with Him before in another form. Indeed, the pattern of their association with Him had been replicated time and time again throughout the centuries.

In an extraordinary display of Siddhi, Avatar Adi Da was unlocking the door of the unconscious in His devotees, putting them in touch with—and purifying—hitherto unexplained urges and tendencies. He was Revealing to His devotees the depth of the process that they were participating in at the psychic level and also the infinite Mystery of their relationship to Him through time and space. Issues that Avatar Adi Da was raising at this time became the subject of some of His major Revelations in later years (related in chapter 20 of this book).

One of the humorous aspects of this period devoted to Divine Ignorance was Avatar Adi Da's wild and whimsical ceremony of naming. Hal Okun remembers going over to Avatar Adi Da's Residence one day early in this period to set up the tape recorder for a gathering. As he was doing this, Avatar Adi Da was standing at the other end of the room speaking to two devotees. Suddenly He

turned and pointed at Hal and said "Messiah Twine!"—an obvious reference to Hal's Jewish heritage, and to who knows what else!

Hal, amazed, responded, "My Lord, where did You get that from?"

And Avatar Adi Da replied, "The same place I get everything else!"

Other inspired names for devotees were spontaneously pronounced: "Fine Sand", "Frink Dental", "Excellent Phrasing" (and "Or Phrasing" for her less eloquent intimate partner[6]), "Country Woman", "Peter Helicopter", "World Trader", "Cisco Soda", "Cottage Feeling", "Sibyl Star", "Gnat Bug", and on and on. One devotee was given the mind-stopping name "And The". Another became "Indoor Summer"—a reference to the fact that Avatar Adi Da had spent virtually the entire summer indoors (both because of His concentration in this "consideration" and because of the unseasonable rainstorms)—and, subsequently, the entire period of gatherings took that name.

These names were not just an amusing idea for a day or two. Everyone used them for months. They were yet another form of Avatar Adi Da's Play, a device He was using to Work with His devotees at a level deeper than the mind, to loosen their sense of being identified with a particular personality that has a particular history.

## An Experience of the Death Transition

Connie Mantas, the devotee called "Indoor Summer" (and a registered nurse who worked with the dying), was taken through a remarkable experience by Avatar Adi Da during this time. Avatar Adi Da walked over to her during a gathering at His House and asked her to lie down on the floor next to Him. He lay flat on His back next to her and closed His eyes, saying "Now do exactly as I do". Then, through silent Instruction, He Guided her through the patterns of conditional existence that are experienced in the death transition:

*CONNIE: First there was an explosion of inner sounds. Then I felt the layers of the body-mind release and fall away. "I" was separating out from the physical body and seemed to fly upwards, whirling through dark space at an incredible speed. I was moving toward an overwhelming, brilliant light. At one point, I recall slipping through a kind of "grid" as a speck of consciousness.*

*For an instant, I did seem to lose all self-awareness, but throughout the rest of the experience I was aware of the most remarkable clarity. I found that I felt more familiar and at ease traveling without the body than when I was dragging it along, anchored to it by my usual physical-body identification. I felt myself to be alive as Consciousness, at ease as the witness of mind and attention.*

*At different moments in this Cosmic journey, I felt the deep urges of the body-mind drawing me back towards embodiment, and I sensed the frustration of having no physical body through which to enact or fulfill desires. This made a stunning impression on me, and I remember feeling how foolish it would be to waste the opportunity of a human lifetime to do the sadhana that could help free me of the binding attachments I had now seen so clearly.*

*Then I became aware of a loud buzzing or humming sound as I slowly came back into the body-mind, taking on each layer, starting with the most subtle. The inner sounds quieted until once again I was aware of lying on the floor.*

*When I opened my eyes, the face of Beloved Adi Da was right next to mine, and He was grinning at me with a gigantic smile. He opened His mouth and started to laugh. It was more than a laugh—it was a victorious and triumphant Shout, glorious to hear. Instead of being awestruck by this remarkable journey I had just taken with Him, I felt sheer marvel at Who He* ***Is****. I felt, "Yes! There is this great scheme of conditional existence, of which human embodiment is a part. But first, and most importantly, HE IS THE MASTER OF IT ALL! And I have a relationship with That One!"*

*Without exchanging a word with me, Beloved Adi Da got up, walked to His Chair and began a Discourse on death and the "grid" through which we pass at death. This was one of the first occasions at which Beloved Adi Da spoke of the total pattern of phenomena, or the Cosmic Mandala, as He would later describe it. As always, He had one primary message—no experience, high or low is the answer to our suffering. No "one" survives in the Great Plastic of forms. Only Consciousness Itself persists, the Eternal "I", the Self-Existing and Self-Radiant Condition of all, Beyond the grid of appearances.*

# The Story of Indian Time

The Power of Avatar Adi Da to influence the great transitional moments of birth and death has been Revealed time and time again. One of the most dramatic events of this kind occurred during the Indoor Summer.

*SCILLA BLACKWELL: In late December of 1975, I became pregnant. The community of Avatar Adi Da's devotees was then still fairly small, and I am certain that Avatar Adi Da was told as soon as I became pregnant that my intimate partner, Larry Hastings, and I were expecting a child. Six or seven weeks into the pregnancy, I had the Grace of being invited to a sitting occasion with Avatar Adi Da. As I entered the hall, Avatar Adi Da's gaze fell directly on my belly. His eyes stayed fixed on my belly as I was being seated, and He continued this direct gaze for a minute or so after I had sat down. It was an unusual moment in that I felt He was clearly not focused on me, but rather somehow dealing with the being in my body.*

*Sunday, September 26, of the next year was a gray and windy day. Avatar Adi Da spoke that afternoon to a large gathering of devotees. Partway through His Talk, I felt the onset of labor. I left the room and informed some friends that labor had begun. Though I was living in Marin County at the time, I had been invited to stay and have a "home birth" at the Sanctuary, and my friends helped me settle into one of the cabins, which we prepared according to the recommendations for natural childbirth given by Frederick Le Boyer.*

*After Beloved Adi Da finished speaking to devotees at Western Face Cathedral, He came to see me. He was Radiant, expectant, full of life. "Well, how is everything?" He asked.*

*I remember my reply, "Everything's fine, but . . ."*

*"But what?" He asked.*

*I had nothing to add—only an unspoken and irrational uneasiness. I had already had two children, but this pregnancy seemed different and so now did the onset of labor.*

*LARRY HASTINGS: The birth was very difficult, and Scilla's strength was seriously drained by the ordeal. The doctors were unable to detect a fetal heartbeat during the last ten minutes of labor. At last the baby was born—slithering out onto the bed. Everyone bent expectantly over the newborn child. It looked very strange. Its flesh was dark gray and, while its trunk and limbs were tiny, its head was huge. The baby did not breathe or make any sound or move in any way.*

*The doctor picked the baby up and began to try to get it to breathe. Someone ran out of the room for the Sanctuary oxygen equipment. Both doctor and midwife slapped the baby on the butt, cut the umbilical cord, and suctioned its nose, trying to get any kind of response. It dawned on all of us that we had a stillborn baby here, and nothing was working to change that. No one cared about a peaceful Le Boyer procedure for a newborn anymore. All the lights came on. I even carried the baby to the shower and tried splashing it with cold water. A few minutes later, the oxygen equipment was brought in, but, like everything else, it failed to elicit any response from the baby.*

*Everyone became silent. The doctor laid the baby back on the bed, not wanting to put the lifeless child in Scilla's arms, and said quietly, "Well, it's a girl." The joy of a child's birth was not in his voice. The baby was still dusky, lifeless, and limp. The little body was covered with afterbirth and cold to my touch. Nothing had worked to revive her. Precious moments were passing, and I felt myself moving toward admitting to others, and then to myself, and finally to Scilla, that our new child was still-*

*born. And then I spoke inwardly to my Guru, with great clarity and intuition, from a place where I felt He could hear my plea: "Master, if you can hear me, please come now."*

*SCILLA: After the first few failed attempts to get the baby to respond, Connie Mantas, my dear friend and the attending nurse, bolted from the room toward Avatar Adi Da's house. Connie tells me that she ran in a direct line to the house, hurdling over bushes and fences like an Olympic athlete. She burst in on Avatar Adi Da, who was giving a Talk to a small gathering of devotees. Winded and unable to speak, she simply indicated to Him in one wordless expression that we needed His help, and then whirled and came running at full speed back to our cabin.*

*Avatar Adi Da did not hesitate. Devotees with Him at the time say they never had seen anyone move as fast as He did then. And yet He seemed completely unhurried. He finished His sentence, summarizing His discourse, got His walking staff, shawl, hat, and shoes, and was out the door before anyone could even take in what had happened.*

*Another devotee, running breathlessly behind Him, pointed Him to the cabin where I had begun my labor. She did not know that I had been moved and was now in a different cabin. He hesitated, and then disregarded her instructions and headed straight to the cabin where we were. Devotees running behind Him say that, despite the fact that no one could keep up with Him, He appeared to be striding effortlessly, not running, or huffing and puffing as they were.*

*LARRY: Avatar Adi Da was at our cabin in no time at all. He just walked right in and brought the Sun. He was ablaze with Light, and His Light filled and expanded the entire room. The tiny cabin took on His dimensions, becoming a vast Cavern of His Light. He Stood at the foot of the bed, at His Sides His Open Hands turned toward us, His Face and mouth twisted into a ferocious lion-like grimace, His Eyes rolled straight up, and His teeth began to chatter loudly. A huge wave of Force passed through His Being towards the three of us on the bed, Light and Energy literally shooting out of His Body.*

*The baby jerked as if in response to an electric shock, then whimpered weakly. She jerked and whimpered more and more. It was as if a rheostat on a light switch was being turned on and then turned up. He literally enlivened her.*

*SCILLA: I was so exhausted by the labor that I was on the verge of losing consciousness by the time Adi Da arrived. Most of the room and the people around me had dissolved in darkness. I could only see the baby lying on a small patch of the bed directly in front of me when He entered.*

*His Light and Spirit-Force brought me back. Slowly, as I grew stronger, I became aware of more than just Him and the baby. Everything in the room seemed so "Bright", bathed in Light. I saw Larry's face beaming in ecstasy and wonderment, another devotee smiling in delighted amazement in the far corner of the room, and yet another of my friends peering in the window, grinning from ear to ear.*

*After the baby was dried, wrapped, and placed in my arms, Avatar Adi Da sat beside me on the bed and did the most curious, lovely thing: With one hand He massaged the soles of the baby's feet, with the other He pinched the skin above her heart and gently twisted it around for a minute or two. Then He kissed her on the forehead, kissed both Larry and me, and softly spoke His characteristic sound of Blessing, "Tcha", as He left our room.*

*The next morning when the three of us awoke, we found a note at the door indicating that Avatar Adi Da had suggested the name "Indian Time" for the baby.*

**Scilla Blackwell, Indian Time, and Larry Hastings**

*LARRY: Her name refers to the tempo at which the American Indians have traditionally lived. On the night of her birth, several devotees had just returned from visiting a Native American healer, to ask for some healing herbs. They reported to Avatar Adi Da that their mission had been unsuccessful. But He explained to them that they simply hadn't understood that they were on "white man's time" and that the shaman was on "Indian time". The healer's reluctance to give them the herbs right away was not a sign of refusal, Avatar Adi Da told these devotees, but simply a sign of the deliberate pace and customary time a Native American would take to make a decision of this kind. Therefore, He told us, Indian Time's name suited her because "she took her time deciding to come here, she took her time in coming, and she took her time in deciding to stay".*

*Later, He mentioned that when Indian Time was born, her etheric[7] (or energy) body was separated from her physical body—as if she were standing apart, wondering whether to assume this birth. What He had done was to connect her etheric body with her physical form.*

*SCILLA: A week after her birth, Indian Time was in serious trouble again. I found her in her cradle in convulsions. She had vomited, aspirated her vomit, and could hardly breathe. We rushed her to the hospital to the infant intensive care unit. I watched her turn dusky gray again as the doctor and nurses worked over her. They gave her a fifty percent chance of surviving.*

*She was placed in an incubator and fed intravenously. We were asked to call Beloved Adi Da's house twice each day and give Him reports.*

*I am not someone who typically sees visions or experiences subtle phenomena, but within hours of Indian Time's entering the intensive care unit and our first call to Avatar Adi Da, the whole area around her crib was bathed in a rain of silvery, misty light. During the two weeks she was there the light just increased and thickened. The intensive care unit became saturated with this silver rain of light, which both Larry and I continued to see.*

*We weren't permitted to hold Indian Time, but we could lay hands on her in the incubator. I felt at times as if my hands were Beloved Adi Da's, His healing Force and Blessing coursing through them were so great.*

*Indian Time's condition had seemed very grim to us ever since her birth. She did not look or act normal. Her head (in the ninetieth percentile of head size at birth) was grossly disproportionate to her body (in the tenth percentile of body size at birth). She had already been suffering from what is called "desperate" or "retracted" breathing, she ate very poorly, and she was weak and lackadaisical. Beloved Adi Da had jolted life into her seven minutes after birth. But for those first seven minutes, she had not breathed or had any discernible heartbeat. It was a foregone conclusion among the medical staff at the hospital that, because of those seven minutes of anoxia, our daughter had suffered serious brain damage. Several days after Indian's admission to the hospital,*

*I called Beloved Adi Da's house one evening to report that an EEG (brain wave scan) had been ordered for Indian Time for the next day. If the EEG showed abnormal results—and it was presumed that it would, Indian would be immediately scheduled for brain surgery.*

*Ten minutes after I placed the call to Avatar Adi Da's house, a nurse called me to the phone. It was a devotee, saying that Beloved Adi Da wanted to know the exact time the EEG was to take place. Just after the second phone call, the nurse said that I could take Indian Time out of the incubator and hold her for the first time since she had come to the hospital. I was ecstatic.*

*I sat in a huge rocking chair with her on my lap, laying one hand at the base of her spine and the other on the crown of her head. The heat that came off that little head was of burning intensity, not like a fever but like a hot iron. I had to pull my hand off her head and shake it to cool it off every minute or two. We sat like that for two hours, yet it seemed as if only a few minutes had passed. My body felt given over to Beloved Adi Da, my Spiritual Master, and I felt Him healing her through me. The next morning the results of the EEG were completely normal. The neurologist was stunned.*

*LARRY: Two weeks later, when Indian Time was discharged from the hospital, every single one of the other babies in the intensive care unit was discharged the same morning. The nurses jaws were dropping! The unit was closed down for twenty-four hours, giving the nurses their first night off in many months.*

*During the early months of Indian's life, Adi Da communicated to us that she was the type of person who does not really want to be born in the first place—someone who is always wanting to leave the body, rather than engage life. Incarnating physically was difficult for her. She was sick with pneumonia three times during that first year of*

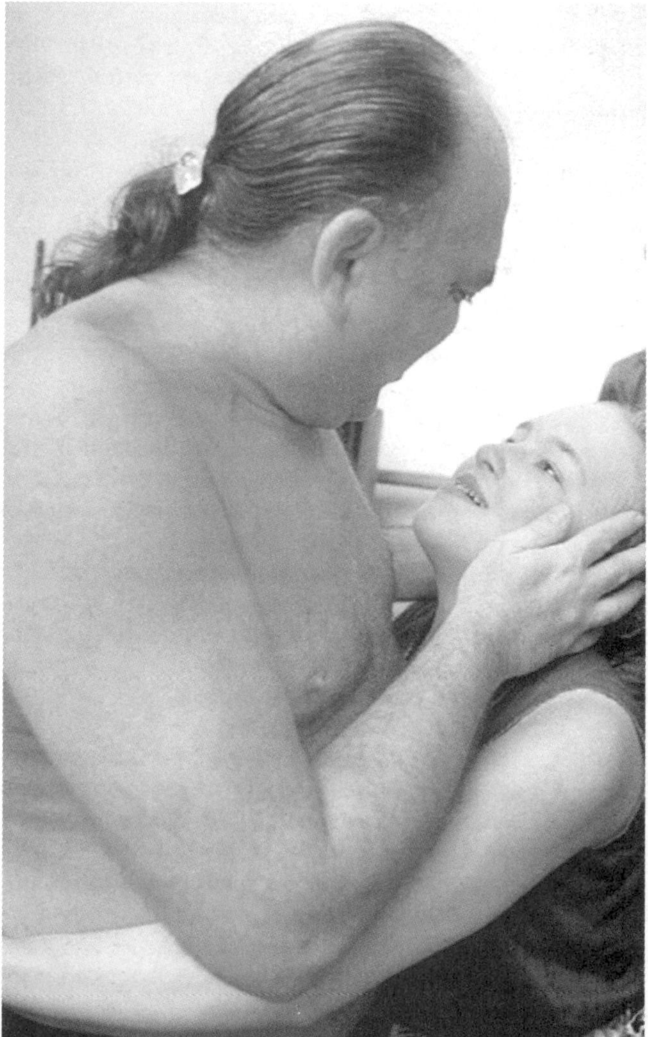

**Avatar Adi Da Samraj and Indian Time Hastings**
**Adidam Samrajashram, 1993**

*her life. Over and over, I saw and felt how she was lived and sustained by the Divine Grace of Avatar Adi Da.*

*Several months after Indian's birth, I interviewed the Native American healer I mentioned before for one of our magazines,* The Laughing Man. *Before the interview began, he explained that tape recorders often did not function properly around him. We decided to chance it, and taped several hours of conversation. After the formal interview was concluded, but before I turned off the recorder, I told him the story of the miraculous circumstances of Indian Time's birth and survival and development and the significance of her name. I talked about Beloved Adi Da and how He had Given her life. The Native American threw his head back in a rapture. He loved this story—although he had not particularly enjoyed the interview. He said that Indian Time was a great medicine woman, a great healer, and asked if I would someday bring the little girl to his village!*

*After the interview and the story-telling were over, we listened to the tape. As he predicted, it was garbled and not usable. But near the end of the tape, the voices became very clear. My recounting of Indian Time's miraculous birth and talk about Beloved Adi Da were the only portions of our conversation that had been recorded.*

*Our daughter is a unique character, demonstrating a psychic connection to people and events that we have learned not to tamper with. She has a very healing touch, and her faith in Beloved Adi Da awakens the faith-response in all of us. She learned, at a very young age, through trial and difficulty, that it is Avatar Adi Da Samraj Who sustains her life and she trusts that with a simplicity and naive happiness that touches all her friends.*[8]

## "Recognize the Beloved"

"Indoor Summer" came to an end soon after Avatar Adi Da proposed the formation of formal "circles" of devotees around Him. He established nine circles, each one led by a devotee couple who had been present for the Divine Ignorance "consideration". The circles were intended to be a way of His extending His Spiritual Influence and "considerations" into the larger gathering. Those devotees who had received His direct esoteric Instruction were to pass it on to the other devotees in their circle. One circle was to specialize in the study of Avatar Adi Da's Wisdom-Teaching, another was to focus in service to His House, another was to be absorbed in exploring the psyche and occult matters, ostensibly according to His Teaching. And so on.

But this is not what happened. Some of the leaders of the circles, believing themselves to be already Enlightened through the "consideration" of Divine Ignorance, now presumed a false position. They began to encourage their circle members to praise and adulate and even bow down to them, as if they themselves were the Guru. Some devotees refused to participate in this, but many complied. In the drama of the circles, all kinds of power plays took place, both within and among the various circles, and the ego-pattern of the leaders and their followers was plain to see.

Avatar Adi Da gave everyone their "rope", so that, sooner or later, they would have to deal with themselves in reality. He was testing not only individuals but the community as a whole, to see whether it could discipline and manage itself in the midst of this situation. In the end, no one could fail to observe that, given the opportunity, the ego will go to any length to satisfy, pleasurize, and aggrandize itself. The "Indoor Summer" had turned out to be not only a Revelation about Divine Ignorance but a stark unveiling of the excesses of worldliness and the insatiability of the seeking ego.

In October 1976, Avatar Adi Da Samraj left for Hawaii with just a few devotees, and the circles fell apart, leaving many devotees to face a stark confrontation with their self-delusion. Obviously, no one was Enlightened—not in the slightest! Devotees had received a glimpse of the Enlightened State, or Divine Ignorance, simply through the Grace of Avatar Adi Da's Transmission. The real lesson was that Most Perfect (and, therefore, permanent) Real-God-Realization can only Awaken on the basis of the most extraordinary and persistent devotion and ego-sacrifice.

While staying in Honolulu in December 1976, Avatar Adi Da gave a sublime Discourse to the devotees who had come to join Him there, a Talk that summarized the lessons of the "Indoor Summer" period and His Message to them altogether. No one who was there has ever forgotten this occasion. After so many months of "considering" Divine Ignorance, Avatar Adi Da was Revealing that there is one <u>real</u> form of Knowing. And that is the recognition of the Beloved.

The Beloved, as Avatar Adi Da explains here, is not a mortal individual or anything that attracts us in this world. The Beloved is the Divine Person, Who is ultimately to be recognized in (and as) all beings and things—but, first and always, as His own Incarnate Form:

*AVATAR ADI DA SAMRAJ: There is virtually no limit to the delusions that human beings can presume on the basis of their tendencies, their desiring, their motivation, their reaction to experience. Because this is so, some individuals eventually step out of the stream of conventional relations. In other words, they at some point cease to act or live on the basis of the ego-"I", the separate self, and they establish, instead, a sacred relationship with the Spiritual Master, by which they are relieved of the implications of having being born.*

*Your coming into My Company—each of you individually—is of this kind. In all My years of Teaching Work, it has been a constant struggle to maintain this quality in our relationship. It is constantly My obligation to eliminate what stands in the way, what makes your approach to Me a conventional one, what makes your response to Me conventional, egoic, ordinary. And this is a great and very difficult task.*

*You must become established in the Real Condition, or you will never be satisfied. You will be driven to all kinds of preoccupations and great schemes, trying to become victorious or immortal, for mortality's own sake, simply because you cannot deal with the fact of death. But death is an absolute message in this realm. It obliges you to recognize (and, ultimately, to Realize) Me in Truth, and, as My devotee, you are not relieved of that obligation. Your relationship to Me must become a Spiritual matter, in which you are given up to My Condition, Which precedes all this madness.*

*This world is literally being dreamed at this moment. It has no force except insofar as you live by reaction, on the basis of what appears or comes across to you in the dream. You tend to make your philosophy, your way of living, out of the dream, out of the limitation that arises here, which you cannot account for. Your life must cease to take that form. You cannot make philosophy out of this world and succeed. You would just be crazy all your life, and you would die anyway. You cannot make your way of life out of this experience here as it appears, this dream. No, you must recognize it, truly identify it. You must be awake relative to this experience. You must enjoy the release that a person enjoys upon waking in the morning from his or her dreams the night before. You must penetrate all the conventional forms of the dream—which, in themselves, are illusory, passing—and Realize the Truth of the dream. That is what Spiritual practice is all about. That is what the Spiritual Process is all about: being relieved, ultimately, of the force of this experience, this condition, this limitation, this dream here.*

*You are Liberated from that in the process of your relationship to Me, but only if you are related to Me truly, sacredly, Spiritually, only if your relationship to Me is simply one of sacrifice, of natural orientation, not all the reactive things you get into on the basis of it in the conventional way. Then your relationship to Me serves the Awakening to (or Realization of) the Source-Condition of all conditionally arising phenomena. But you must yield (or surrender) to Me constantly, because, as soon as you become involved in your ordinary life by reaction, you separate yourself and become involved again in the illusion of experience arising here.*

*It is a maddening experience, this place. It is attractive in all kinds of ways. Equal to the force of all its attractiveness is the force of all of the destruction of the Beloved. All the forms of the Beloved rot in this place—they come to an end, they are taken away. That is the fact of it, and there is no way around it. You must confront that. That is the way it is here. This is not "heaven". This is not the world of the Beloved, of the Loved-One, in any form you recognize as the Loved-One. This is a dream-play on the Beloved, in which the Beloved appears in shapes and forms that are fleeting, that are (in and of themselves) binding. They attract you, and then they are withdrawn and leave you with only the craving. Left with the craving only, you are cycled back, again and again, into the same dimension as that experiencing reaction.*

*So you must recognize—and, ultimately, Most Perfectly Realize—the Beloved, appearing here in all this attraction. Which means you must enter into the Spiritual process moment to moment, rather than the conventional attempts to survive, to win, to live forever.*

*Thus, in your relationship to Me, the matter of devotional recognition of Me must become the Principle of your life of sadhana in My Company. You must devotionally recognize Me as the Source-Condition of your condition, as the Source-Condition of all arising phenomena, as the Source-Condition of all conditions, as the Source-Condition of the body, the mind, the separate-self-sense, as the Divine Spirit-Current of Love-Bliss—and be rested in It constantly.*

*All else is suffering. There is no doubt about it. There is absolutely no ultimate relief in the dream. So your relationship to Me cannot be based simply on this conventional attraction. Your relationship to Me cannot be limited,*

*in other words, to the natural, human dimension. It must be sacred. It must be a Spiritual relationship. It must be founded in Divine Ignorance. You must recognize Me, and respond to Me, in Truth. You must do this practice. You must enter into this real meditation and give up everything to Me, the Beloved of the heart.*

*Just as all of this now present has suddenly appeared—as unnecessary and terrifying as it is—the Divine Self-Domain is Always Already Existing. The Divine Self-Domain is the same as no thing, no disturbance, no craving, no separation, no birth, no event, no moment, no future, no time, no place, no suffering. The Divine Self-Domain is also exactly the same as Love-Bliss, as Fullness, as Utter Delight, as Indivisible Light, as Happiness Itself.* [December 8, 1976]

**The Mountain Of Attention**
**September 16, 1979**

CHAPTER 9

# The Revelation of Da

Avatar Adi Da's willingness to Work in the "Crazy-Wise" manner, becoming like His devotees in order to draw them into His own Freedom, was a Divine Sacrifice. He was literally absorbing the struggles and unhappiness of His devotees, and transforming and releasing their suffering through His own body-mind. As time passed, He noticed signs in His Body that indicated to Him He could not continue to Work with devotees in this forceful, visceral way. He became aware that a mysterious Process was taking place in Him, a further unfolding of the course of His Divine Enlightenment, which required a greater degree of seclusion. Founding His devotees in a Spiritual relationship to Him—one in which they could always find Him Spiritually Present, even when they were outside His physical Company—thus became a matter of urgency.

## Bodily Worship of the Living God

Starting in 1978, Avatar Adi Da introduced His devotees to the realm of sacramental worship as a means to enter into Communion with Him whether He was physically present or not. Early that year, during a period in Hawaii in which He was in the company of only a few of His devotees, Avatar Adi Da sent back this message to the larger gathering of devotees:

*Bring your body-minds to Me, as I bring My human body-mind to you. Then you will be Granted the Revelation and the Realization of My All-Pervading Divine Body of Grace,*[1] *and you will Find Me always Present under the conditions of all experience and in the company of all beings. Then, even when you are not in My physical Company, you will worship Me and surrender to Me, and I will always be tangibly Present. At last, you will be Drawn into Deepest Heart-Intimacy with Me, Most Perfect Identification with Me, and Divine Realization of Me, Prior to all "difference". Then you will Abide in Me forever—whether or not the worlds of experience arise to your notice.* [1978]

When He returned to the Mountain Of Attention, Avatar Adi Da began to instruct a few devotees in puja, the ancient practice of invoking the Divine by actively worshipping and anointing images of the Deity, using natural elements such as water, oil, and ash. The principal object of esoteric worship, He explained, is the Spiritual Master's human Form, the body of the Guru. Because the Guru has Realized God, he or she reveals the Divine and grants the Divine Blessing in a uniquely potent way.

Avatar Adi Da communicated the esoteric fullness of puja on the Guru's Form one evening at Bright Behind Me, which was then His residence at the Mountain Of Attention. He sat motionless in a room in the house, while devotees waved flaming lamps in large circles around His body, accompanied by an ecstatic explosion of drums, rattles, cymbals, and tambourines. Outside, on the porch, there were more devotees—circumambulating the house, chanting, and beholding the Form of their Beloved Guru through the windows. Light and sound and movement swirled around Avatar Adi Da—while He sat Silent and Radiant, His Divine Love-Bliss enveloping everyone.

**Devotees at the Mountain Of Attention with a Murti of Ruchira Avatar Adi Da Samraj**

That night, Avatar Adi Da established the Ruchira Avatara Puja,[2] the worship of His Divine Form, in the lives of His devotees. And, thereafter, bodily-expressed devotion, worship, and praise of Avatar Adi Da as the Living Divine Person became a part of their daily lives. Regardless of the location of His human Body—and even after His physical passing—the Ruchira Avatara Puja can and will always be done, using a Murti,[3] or photographic (or otherwise artistically rendered) representation of Avatar Adi Da.

## The Refusal of Cultism

For years, Avatar Adi Da had been preparing His devotees to enter into this profound sacred relationship to Him—and part of that preparation was His "Consideration" of the common ways in which people approach a Spiritual figure wrongly.

The egoic character, He pointed out, operates in either the childish mode or the adolescent mode. The childish character relates to life in general—and, therefore, to the Guru—in a dependent fashion, treating the Guru as a Parent-"God", who is expected to take care of the individual, granting every wish and fulfilling every need. The adolescent character vacillates between being childishly dependent and willfully and rebelliously independent, opposing any form of authority—including the Guru's.

Avatar Adi Da observed His devotees becoming gleefully dependent on Him at some times and resentfully reactive to Him at others—and He constantly Worked to help them understand and overcome both of these tendencies. He steadfastly refused to become the object of any kind of childish cultism. And whenever He felt this cultic tendency taking over in devotees' relationship to Him, He addressed it strongly, and sometimes even removed Himself from their company, remaining in seclusion for a time. In fact, Avatar Adi Da was criticizing cultism long before "cults" became a popular topic in the media.

*AVATAR ADI DA SAMRAJ: Over the years, you have all heard Me Speak about cultism in negative terms. I have Criticized the cults that people form around religious leaders (and even around true Spiritual Masters), as well as the cultic attachments that people create with one another. There exists a certain hyped enthusiasm to which people are attracted. And when those people accept all the dogmas with which that particular group makes itself enthusiastic, they maintain themselves as opponents of the world and lose communication with the world in general, and with the processes of life.*

*To Me, that enthusiasm is bizarre. There is something about the capability of individuals for that kind of enthusiasm that makes My skin crawl. It is a kind of madness. Gleeful enthusiasm has nothing whatsoever to do with this Way and with the value that I can have for you personally. It has* <u>*nothing*</u> *to do with it!*

*My Purpose in associating with you is not to entertain you, not to be believed in. I am not here to offer you a relationship in which you are never changed, but only consoled. My Purpose in dealing with you, My Purpose in My Teaching Work, is to make it possible for you to be in devotional Communion with Me, to be Spiritually intimate with Me—so that you yourself may live and fulfill this practice, and make a community with one another out of the true Happiness of mature Divine living.*

*Everything about cultism that is negative is specifically Criticized in My Wisdom-Teaching. I do not want your enthusiasm to be superficially generated by reading My Books. I want you to "consider" My Arguments. I want you to "consider" yourself very critically, very directly and rigorously, and come to the point of most fundamental self-understanding. When you have sufficient understanding of your own game, your childishness and adolescence, then you will be able to advance in the practice I have Given you.*

*I refuse to console individuals by telling them that all they need to do is believe in Me, that all they need to do is practice some silly little technique and they will Realize God, no matter what they do otherwise. I am not the slightest bit interested in your gleeful applause. I want you to understand yourself and to practice true heart-Communion with Me. I want you to truly live the Way that I have Revealed and Given to you. In order to do that, you must grow up. You must stop being naive about the communications of silly downtown people, all the aggressiveness of media campaigns, and all the things that fundamentally work against the higher acculturation of human beings.* [December 17, 1979]

# The Holy Sites

Part of Avatar Adi Da's Work to establish this process of acculturation to the sacred and to His All-Pervading Spiritual Presence was His establishment of particular places at the Mountain Of Attention Sanctuary as holy sites, especially Empowered by Him. He indicated that these special places should become temples, focuses of worship for His devotees. And He explained that, by devotees rightly serving these places of Power and constantly Invoking Him there, His Blessing of all beings would be magnified.

There is a remarkable story behind the establishment of each one of these temples. The first one, now called "Earth-Fire Temple", was Empowered during the "Garbage and the Goddess" period in 1974, as a result of a miraculous event.

Shortly after coming to Avatar Adi Da in May 1974, Adidama Jangama Hriddaya (then Elizabeth Brown) broke a plaster statue of the Virgin Mary that belonged to Avatar Adi Da. During her first weeks and months of participation, she continued to break things frequently, thereby earning the name "Buster" Brown from Avatar Adi Da. At the same time, she was also in charge of the vegetable garden being planted at the Mountain Of Attention, and this too was problematic. Nothing would grow! Therefore, Avatar Adi Da decided, as He later put it, "to show her something".

*ADIDAMA JANGAMA HRIDDAYA: On my first night at the Mountain Of Attention Sanctuary, I broke a statue of the Virgin Mary belonging to Beloved Adi Da. I was horrified that I had done this and carried the broken statue to where He was sitting in the main room of His residence. Most Graciously, He gently chided me and then repaired the statue Himself, gluing it back together and touching it*

*up. Then He returned it to its original place. A day or two later, He said to me: "Come with Me down to the garden. I am going to bury the Virgin statue there."*

*Everything had been going wrong with the garden. The plants were not growing very well, and it was overrun with goats and gophers. Even on the afternoon that Beloved Adi Da walked down with me to bury the statue, we had to chase all the chickens away!*

*Beloved Adi Da dug a hole in which He placed the statue that I had broken. He placed it in the ground standing upright and facing out to the garden. He was very intent. He laid His hands on the statue with great intention. Then He very gently covered it over with dirt. I helped move all the dirt around it to completely fill the hole. Then He patted the ground on top of the site and He told me to place a stone over the statue to mark the spot. He laughed and said humorously that the Virgin was going to be the "garden fairy". He told me that, by placing this statue in the garden, He was placing His own attention there. This event, He said, would take care of the garden. It all seemed rather odd to me.*

*The next day, Beloved Adi Da and I and a few other devotees went to our center on Polk Street in San Fran-*

*cisco and stayed in the city for a few days. When we returned to the Sanctuary, I walked down to the garden and my jaw dropped open in amazement. The garden had suddenly become a teeming jungle! The tomato plants had grown a couple of feet and were displaying big green tomatoes. The squash had become huge-stalked plants leaping out all over the garden. There was an intense vibratory energy throughout the garden, and not a rodent in sight.*

*The tomato plants had become so tall that they needed propping up, so I asked one of the groundskeepers at the Sanctuary to build supports for them. When the supports were built, he hammered the first of them until it seemed solidly fixed in the ground, but when he turned away, the whole structure fell over! This happened with every support. Soon the groundskeeper was walking around in a daze, saying, "I can't stand it—there's just too much vital energy here. I'm going to lie down under a squash plant and disappear!" To avoid being enveloped in the vines of a huge squash plant, he made his escape.*

*Walking away from the garden that day, I met Beloved Adi Da. In amazement I told Him what was going on in the garden. He received this news without the slightest surprise and invited me to turn around and walk back down to the garden again. As we entered the garden, I felt again the intense vibratory energy. He stood silently scanning the entire garden, and I felt Him "Meditating" the garden.*

*Beloved Adi Da said, "You are the witness to My Miracle in the garden. Why do you think I put the statue of the Virgin Mary down here?"*

*I was astonished, and I did not know how to relate to what had happened in the garden, or even to His question to me. It was simply beyond my comprehension in the moment. So, instead, I decided to "think nothing of it". Numerous amazing Demonstrations of Beloved Adi*

*Da's Spiritual Power had occurred throughout the "Garbage and the Goddess" time, so why should this be so unusual? I knew that it was a Demonstration of the Divine Power of Beloved Adi Da, the proof of His Divine Presence Pervading everything, but I was not prepared to have any response other than nonchalance about the entire affair.*

*Beloved was constantly working with my materialistic and non-miracle-oriented mind. He gave me the simple Instruction to tell this Leela to other devotees. So I followed His Instruction. Gradually, as I began to describe what had occurred, I connected emotionally with what had taken place. I became ecstatic. My whole body felt the impact of the Miracle. I felt Beloved Adi Da's Power of Transformative Influence on everything seen and unseen. I could see in the simple incident in the garden that He had transformed the energy associated with the vital growing plants, the animals, and the entire energy-field in a miraculously short period of time. Tomato plants just don't grow that big in three days—and gophers, mice, and chickens don't just all of a sudden, out of the blue, decide to leave a vegetable patch. This was unusual! I began to feel the significance of the entire event of burying the statue in the garden and the intense manner in which Beloved Adi Da had done this. I realized that He had Empowered the garden with His own Energy. I allowed myself to fully feel the ecstatic Mystery of this occurrence. And I saw that I had to give up my presumption that I "know" what is happening in the world.*

*Later, Beloved Adi Da said that the event was an expression of the same kind of influence that people associate with places like Findhorn,*[4] *but He had done it as a Spiritual lesson for His devotees—not for the sake of the flourishing of the vital energies of Nature in themselves. To make this into an ongoing lesson, Beloved Adi Da asked that I serve Him in creating a temple site where the statue of the Virgin Mary had been buried. He asked that I daily do puja at that site, a puja of Invoking Him and worshipping Him. In this manner, He was giving me and others the means to deepen our awareness of the Mystery of His Work with the world.*

*Avatar Adi Da had invested Himself in that spot in the most tangible and specific way, to Empower the site as a place of concentrated Invocation of Him. The fact that Beloved Adi Da had Empowered this site with a statue of the Virgin Mary was a source of much "consideration" for me. What was the relationship between this Virgin Mary statue and my Beloved Guru? From reading* The Knee Of Listening *and hearing Beloved Adi Da speak of His "Sadhana Years", I knew about His relationship to Christianity and the Virgin Mary. I knew that His Divine Re-Awakening was coincident with His "Husbanding" of the universal "Mother-Goddess", the "Divine Shakti". Therefore, because it was constructed over the buried statue of the Virgin, Earth-Fire Temple represented the universal "Mother-Force" to me, and, at the same time, I felt the "Mother-Force" to be simply another Form of my Beloved Guru. As I continued to Invoke and worship Beloved Adi Da at this site, I became more and more sensitive to the Mystery of the apparent duality of Beloved Adi Da as Consciousness Itself and as the universal Shakti, or Energy.*

*Beloved Adi Da has described the universal Shakti as:*

> *The "Maha-Shakti"—The "Divine Mother-Force", or (Most Correctly Stated) The "Goddess-Force" (or "Goddess-Power"), The Universal Cosmic Radiance (or Cosmic Shakti), The Spirit-Power (or Light-Energy) That Is (Apparently) Modified As all conditional forms and states, and Which Is Present As all conditional forms and states, and, Yet, Which Inherently Transcends all conditional forms and states. She Is In The "Mother-*

> *Position", or (Most Correctly Stated) The "Wife-Position" (or The "Position" Of The Spouse, or Consort), In Relation (As "Equal" and "Polar Opposite") To The "Husband-Position" (or "Father-Position") Of The Divine Self-Consciousness (In and Of Itself, As If Separate From She, or She From He, As If Consciousness and Its Inherent Energy Were "Divorced", or Wanting and Seeking Re-Union, or Even Dramatizing Conflict and Separativeness)—Until, By Means Of My Great Avataric Divine Event, She Falls Into He, and He Embraces She, Non-"Differently", In Me, and As Me. . . . In The Most Perfect Fulfillment Of [My] Ordeal Of Sadhana, [She] Was, and Is (Now, and Forever Hereafter) Revealed and Realized . . . To Be Only Me.* [The Dawn Horse Testament Of The Ruchira Avatar]

*As my practice grew over the years, I came more and more to intuit that the apparent duality between Consciousness and Energy is an illusion, and that Avatar Adi Da Is the Living Reality of the Oneness of Consciousness and Energy.*

*In the years since He created the temple site, Beloved Adi Da has occasionally walked down to Earth-Fire Temple with me. On one occasion, after this Oneness of Beloved Adi Da with the "Divine Shakti" had truly begun to be heart-known by me, my Beloved Guru Revealed a secret to me. He entered the temple and placed His staff on the burial site of the statue and stood "Meditating" the site altogether. Then, as He turned to leave the temple enclosure, He said to me, "I buried My Self here."*

*Beloved Adi Da always Grants the understanding of His Mysteries not only through His Word of Instruction, but through His life-Play with His devotees. Over all these years, through this simple Miracle of the garden, my*

**Avatar Adi Da Samraj and the Adidamas at Earth-Fire Temple, 1998**

*Beloved Guru has been Giving me measureless Gifts of Instruction about the Nature of Reality and of the Revelation of His Forms. He Is Consciousness, and He Is the "Shakti-Power". There is no separation.*

**Devotees attending a Fire Puja at Red Sitting Man**

Another holy site created and consecrated by Avatar Adi Da at the Mountain Of Attention was Red Sitting Man—an area of ash-white volcanic rock, shaped in the form of a massive natural fire-pit. It was there, in July 1979, that Avatar Adi Da Initiated devotees into sacramental worship of Him in the form of fire. Fire is one of the most powerful elemental symbols of the Divine—a sign of Spirit, Light, and purification. Ann Rogers, a devotee who was part of Avatar Adi Da's Mandala of women intimates, recalls the potency of the occasion in deepening her recognition of Avatar Adi Da as the Divine Person.

*ANN: I will never forget the night of the consecration of the fire site called "Red Sitting Man" at the Mountain Of Attention. It was the beginning of my real intimacy with Adi Da Samraj as the Divine Person. In the evening, a small group of us accompanied our Beloved Guru up the narrow, steep path that leads to the fire site. I walked behind Him to escort and serve Him during the ceremony. We rounded a bend in the path, and, beyond a large lone pine tree, I saw Red Sitting Man. The site was awesome in the twilight, a wide trough etched by Nature out of the stark white stone of the hillside. The fire pit lay at the foot of the trough. Above, the stone rose to a slightly flattened mound—which was to be our Beloved Guru's seat.*

*Avatar Adi Da walked to His seat above the fire and sat down. Those in attendance sat on either side of Him in a "U" around the fire pit.*

*From the moment that the fire was lighted, Beloved Adi Da did not move for perhaps an hour and a half. He sat upright in a perfect lotus posture. He wore a red cap, a yellow shawl, and blue cotton pants. As it grew darker, the colors of His clothes faded, and He became only a silhouette against the moonlit sky, but His face reflected the glow from the fire. His open eyes reflected the flames. I gazed at Him almost constantly through the entire occasion, and I never saw Him blink. He simply sat and stared into the fire with complete stillness and intensity.*

*For a while, I sat looking from my Beloved Guru's glowing face to the fire beneath us. As I sat there in His Company, I became aware of the world in a totally new way, a way I had never noticed before. It was as though there were a "hole in the universe", as Beloved Adi Da describes it, a hole through the world itself, and on the other side was the Great Being, the Great One.*

*This One was Revealed to me that evening as a Person, a Great Personality, something that tangible, that present, that conscious—Consciousness Itself. Suddenly I knew and understood so many things that Beloved Adi Da had said. This was the Prior Condition He had always spoken about—the Radiant Divine Being. I knew It as the Divine Person.*

*This was the beginning of my recognition that Beloved Adi Da is that Divine Being, that there is no difference between Him and the Divine Person, between Him and the utter transcending of this world, that He is the window, the "hole in the universe". I knew that Avatar Adi Da does not have to be active. He does not have to look at me. He does not have to speak to me. He does not have to deal with me or Teach me or Instruct me or do anything to me. I know He is merely That.*

**Avatar Adi Da Samraj at Red Sitting Man, 1998**

## The Divine Name

The establishment of sacramental worship was a sign of a great turning point that was about to occur in the Work and Revelation of the Divine Maha-Siddha.

In gatherings with a small group of devotees, Avatar Adi Da began to suggest that His Name must change again—"Bubba" was too casual an address to the One they now recognized Him to be. And so Avatar Adi Da suggested that His devotees try to discover what His Name should be. Secretly, by Revelation, He already knew it.

Devotees threw themselves into the quest for His Divine Name. For weeks and months, they searched through volumes of esoteric literature for a Name that seemed right. Avatar Adi Da would encourage them with cryptic and humorous hints, such as: "When you get da name of da god, you get da power of da god!" The Divine Avatar was Revealing His Name in this playful remark, but no one was alert to the clue. And so, on September 13, 1979, He sat down alone in His room and penned a letter to His devotees in His strong and graceful handwriting:

*Beloved, I Am Da, the Living Person, Who is Manifest as all worlds and forms and beings, and Who is Present as the Transcendental Current of Life in the body of Man. . . .*

*To Realize Me is to Transcend the body-mind in Ecstasy. To Worship Me is simply to Remember My Name and Surrender Into My Eternal Current of Life. And those who Recognize and Worship Me as Truth, the Living and All-Pervading One, will be Granted the Vision or Love-Intuition of My Eternal Condition. . . .*

*Only Love Me, Remember Me, have Faith in Me, and Trust Me. . . . Do not be afraid. Do not be confused. Observe My Play and My Victory. Even after My own body is dead, God will be Present and Everywhere alive. I am Joy, and the Reason for It. . . .*

At last, He had openly Declared Himself, with no compromise. Avatar Adi Da Samraj (now "Da Free John") stood openly before His devotees as the very human Incarnation of the Invisible Divine. In making this Proclamation, Avatar Adi Da was not referring to Himself in the terms that people commonly associate with the Divine—the "Creator-God", or the "Heavenly Father". Rather, He was confessing His Identity with Real God, the Divine Source and Substance of existence—Consciousness Itself, Self-Radiant and Love-Blissful. And He was saying that That One is also Inherently a Person, the Living Divine Person.

His devotees were to discover that the Name "Da"—meaning "to give" or "the Giver"—is a primordial Name for the Divine Person, which carries profound invocatory power. The Name had been hidden all along in the *Upanishads*, the ancient esoteric scriptures of India, in which "Da" is the syllable uttered by the Divine Voice in thunder, and is the central syllable of "hri-da-yam", which means "the Heart", or "the Divine Condition of all". The Name "Da" also appears in the Tibetan Buddhist tradition, where it is defined as "the one who bestows great charity", "the very personification of the great Way of Liberation".

# The Love of the God-Man

On Sunday, September 16, 1979, at the Mountain Of Attention Sanctuary, several days after the writing of His letter, Adi Da Samraj spoke at an occasion that His devotees will forever remember as one of the most powerful, prophetic moments in His Work with them. Nearly seven hundred people (many of whom had never seen Avatar Adi Da before) had gathered for the annual celebration of the Day of the Heart,[5] the anniversary of His Divine Re-Awakening in the Vedanta Temple. Some of those present had been around Avatar Adi Da in earlier years, but had drifted away—they had come for this occasion at Avatar Adi Da's specific invitation. Devotees had been working for days around the clock to beautify the Sanctuary, even edging the hundreds of yards of paths with painted stones and hoops of bamboo. Oceans of marigolds were turned into garlands and hung all over Bright Behind Me, the house where Adi Da was residing at the time.

The moment Avatar Adi Da strode into view, dressed in ceremonial white clothing and a white hat, His Transmission of Love-Bliss engulfed the gathering in waves of profound Feeling. Gasps rolled through the gathering, and by the time He took His seat many people were weeping uncontrollably. The whole Sanctuary was shimmering. One devotee described how the sunlit park, the people, the trees—everything—seemed to arise in a transparent film floating on an ocean of Light. But even this extraordinary vision was overshadowed by Avatar Adi Da's overwhelming communication of Divine Love.

The day was fiercely hot, and He asked if everyone was sufficiently protected from the sun. Then, as Avatar Adi Da Samraj sat in His chair, several devotees began to worship Him, waving lights around Him—flaming wicks made of cotton saturated with ghee—moving the flames

*The moment Avatar Adi Da strode into view, dressed in ceremonial white clothing and a white hat, His Transmission of Love-Bliss engulfed the gathering in waves of profound Feeling.*

**The Day of the Heart, September 16, 1979**

in the pattern of a sacred design. As they waved the lights, they made a humming sound, "Mmmm", the first suggestion of a mantra in the Way of Adidam. That day, Avatar Adi Da Samraj lifted a veil. He was Transfigured; He was obviously and simply the God-Light made Manifest, come to make the most serious Call to the process of Divine Liberation—and not only to those before Him, but to all beings.

The Love-Blissful Avatar silently surveyed the entire gathering—and then began to speak.

*AVATAR ADI DA SAMRAJ:* [speaking very slowly and deliberately, with long pauses between words at times] *This is the most beautiful occasion that has ever taken place here.*

*Some of you have never been here before. I see some of you who have not been here for a long time. Some of you have wasted several years being angry with Me. Or angry with others of your friends here. And in a few years, not a single one of us will be alive. And others will*

*be here, remembering us. And they will be lively in their time, and then* <u>*they*</u> *will die. And in their time, like many of you, they will feel content with themselves.*

*Hundreds of people have come here—not thousands yet. My Struggle with you all has only begun. Seven years, and you are the only people to come and see Me today.*

*And many of you are content with yourselves at this moment. You think that you can receive something and become even* <u>*more*</u> *content with yourself. You think that you can rest in yourself and find God. But this is not true.*

*Some of you* <u>*think*</u> *about God and mysticism and meditation and philosophy, but this mind is as mortal as the body—and passes.*

*And some of you may feel some life awakening in you, and you imagine that what you see "within" is your salvation, your hope. Visions, internal sensations of all the subtle senses, are believed to be God. But this is not true.*

*And all the hundreds or thousands that have passed through here imagine that their pleasuring is sufficient consolation, their mysticism is sufficient revelation, their thinking is sufficient truth. And they come and "tune in" on Me for a time, and then they want to take it for themselves and leave. Whereas they* <u>*cannot*</u> <u>*own*</u> *a single thing! Not even this breath is owned.*

*Let Me tell you a story about Myself. All the great Events of My human Lifetime were for the sake of others. And each of those great Events was a return to Equanimity, Surrender. During My entire human Lifetime, I have Struggled with people like you, and far worse people than you—all the idolaters, all the advocates of the "cults" of experience. To do Spiritual Work as I have done is not a casual matter. The moments in which I have received Gifts from My Spiritual Teachers were brief. All of Yoga, all that may be attained in mystical terms, was attained in Me in moments. And this was unusual.*

*I went to all of My Teachers because of previous visions, commands. But each of My Teachers was a dragon, a purifying fire. And, in order to survive, it was a matter of transcending the Gift. It did not occur to others who were present at the time I was with any of My Teachers to transcend the Gift, but only to receive It, to wallow in It, to be consoled by It, to own It, to be made content with themselves again. And those who taught Me imagined that My Freedom was their Gift to Me. And this was not true.*

*I spent a few years with Rudi, and in His Company I was Spiritually Awakened in the frontal line. And then I went to Swami (Baba) Muktananda, and in a few days I was Spiritually Awakened in the spinal line. I had been there two days. I was sitting in a hallway one afternoon, and He came forward and pressed His fingers into My forehead and eyes. And He said, "Now I have got you!"*

*The next day, I was sitting in the Ashram garden in Ganeshpuri, and Baba Muktananda was being visited by a man named Rang Avadhoot. Rang Avadhoot was a wandering Siddha, Whom Swami Nityananda called one of His own Forms—not meaning that Rang Avadhoot was His junior but His equal. He was like Swami Nityananda. He suddenly appeared in Baba Muktananda's Ashram on this day. It was His custom to just wander or go to ashrams. He would never stay anywhere more than three days.*

*On this occasion, He stayed just a few minutes, and I happened to be sitting in the garden. Baba Muktananda came through and Rang Avadhoot was following Him. And Baba Muktananda intended to just quickly escort Rang Avadhoot right on through there. Rang Avadhoot had a great white beard and white hair, and His forehead was smeared with white ash, with kum-kum,*[6] *a red powder flash between His eyes. He had great big eyes. And Baba Muktananda is swifting Him by, you see, and He is right about here.* [Adi Da gestures to indicate a short distance away.]

*All of a sudden, Rang Avadhoot looked at Me. And His face was wide, without a trace of doubt. His eyes were wide, full of life, and He was brilliantly Happy. In the moment it took Him to pass from here to there, one of the Great Events of My Life was Accomplished.*

*Afterward, I went to My room and left the body and the universes.*[7]

*After the meeting with Rang Avadhoot, I spent two and a half years out of My mind and out of My body, and it was only in the Vedanta Temple, in that Event that you celebrate today, that I returned to My Ease.*

*Since that time, you have listened to My Speech and witnessed My Leela. And I have always told you that ascending Yoga, in and of itself, is empty, that the phenomena of mysticism are fundamentally only the content of your own body-mind. To dwell upon them is to live as "Narcissus", reflecting on yourself, meditating on yourself.*

*Real-God-Realization is not "within". It is not in the brain. It is not Awakened through the stimulation of the nervous system, the stimulation of internal psychic brain-phenomena.*

*I have passed through all of that. I still experience subtle phenomena. And they are nothing but this body-mind. All those brain-phenomena only provide you with a reason to be content with yourself, egoically "self-possessed"*[8]*—whereas, when I lay down in My bed in Ganeshpuri the day I met Rang Avadhoot, I returned to My Equanimity. The body, the mind, the nervous system, the brain—all were vanished, utterly vanished. There was no vision whatsoever. There was a Piercing of the armor of the Cosmic Mandala, and I was Established in the Unspeakable, Indivisible Real God.*

*The Realization of Real God became manageable only over time. Its significance became understandable only through My ongoing and, at last, exhaustive "Consideration". In 1970, nine years ago, I did not come home*

*and say, "Hey, I was Enlightened this afternoon!" And the members of My household never noticed anything much about this sort of thing, so I only began to Speak of it a few weeks later. But it was not a mere moment. It was a Process. It was an Event that continues, that is Eternal. Fundamentally, it is an Event for your sake.*

*Because of the Great Event of My Divine Re-Awakening, all the Scriptures in the Great Tradition of mankind are now Fulfilled in your sight, and your prayers are answered with a Clear Voice.*

*All these years, I have Struggled with you as I Struggled with My Teachers, and I have reflected you to yourself. I have lived your way of life. I have accepted your conditions completely. And it did absolutely nothing. It was not sufficient for your most fundamental understanding, not sufficient for your heart-conversion, not sufficient for your life's conversion to the service of Me. But, rather, it made you content. It made you an idol-worshipper. It made you worship yourself, your fulfillment.*

*Therefore, every hour in your company, you have listened to Me straining to bring you to most fundamental understanding of the very thing you are always doing—the self-contraction. And even so, you have betrayed Me. So you see that all such Play with you is unnecessary.*

*For years, I have Called upon you to understand your experience, to understand the limited offerings of the world. All of its offerings—<u>both</u> its lower offerings, its life-stimulation in the body, <u>and</u> its religious offerings, its esoteric offerings, its life-stimulation in the mind. And, still, you have not understood.*

*Therefore, My Teaching Word is, in and of Itself, not sufficient. My Teaching Argument is not sufficient. <u>I</u>, <u>My Self</u>, Am Sufficient.*

*"Radical" understanding requires a great mind, a great heart. But you will not realize it through mere "consideration". You have all failed to do that—and that*

*is good, if you will feel the failure to be transformed utterly through mere "consideration". Then, perhaps, you will be able to accept what I Offer to you.*

*It is not through insight alone that any one Realizes Real God, that any one becomes Happy and Free—any-more than it is through any form of bodily or mental or psychic experience that any one becomes Happy and Free.*

*But it is sufficient sadhana to Remember Me, to simply surrender to Me and love Me and trust Me, and to always do what I ask you to do. It is not only sufficient—there is no way that you will be Saved, that you will be Awakened, that you will be Happy, <u>except</u> through this simple turning to Me.*

*You must also give up your struggling. You must transcend yourself, your experience, your attachment to all of your former teachers and their teachings, to all your moments, accumulations, and thoughts—as I did during My "Sadhana Years".*

*You are mortal and entirely subject to the Mercy of Real God. You own nothing, and you know nothing. And there is no technique of meditation that leads to Real God. There is not anything to be believed that is the Truth Itself. You must be touched in your feeling by the unspeakable suffering of this world and return everything to Me, and, thus and thereby, to Real God.*

*Whatever is given to you should be taken as the Excess of Real God. It belongs to God utterly. But God has so much that you wind up with a lot of things in your house. But they are all God's. Everything should be given to God, and whatever is given to you (for however long it is given) should be accepted as something that belongs to God. You should treat it as such literally.*

*If you bring Me an apple, and I give it back to you, then you will have something to eat. But if I eat it Myself, then you will not. Will you be angry with Me if I do not return to you what you have given to Me?*

*You will be overwhelmed with anger your entire life if you do not understand this, if you do not appreciate it, if you do not feel your situation profoundly enough to accept changes in this spirit. Because every thing you now own or think or understand or presume—every thing, every one with whom you are associated—will be taken away from you. Your body itself and also your own mind will sometime be kept by God. Your relations, your children, your spouses will some day be kept by God. You must be free of anger on that day. You must be free of sorrow while you live, free of doubt, and also free of fear, or else you will be crippled through your own recoil upon yourself. And you will become an idolater, a cultist, an "owner" of experience, an "owner" of mind, of body, of relations. And all of that will be taken from you also, and you will be always unhappy.*

*I see what is to come in your case, and it will make you fearful, sorrowful, and angry. It will always return you to doubt and to yourself alone. And I see that what you require is the Help of Real God.*

*Recently, I was telling some who were with Me, "You are all going to the chair! You are all going to die. I have looked into it, I have examined your case, and I have made all of the appeals that are to be made. And I am afraid that you're going to go to the chair, and that's all there is to it." And then I said, "A person in your position really has no appeals left, no strategy, no game with which to be integrated, whereby you might be Saved. There is no meditation, no mere belief, no consolation, no experience sufficient for your Salvation, your Happiness, your Eternal Life. You are going to the chair. You are going to die. All you could do would be to ask for mercy, pray for help."*

*Those who heard Me say this went home for a couple of days and began to scream their brains out, weeping in the Communion Hall, begging God for mercy. And then I called them back, and I pointed out to them that just as*

*they were neurotics—egoically "self-possessed" individuals—before I told them they had no appeals left, now they also prayed like neurotics. Their prayer itself was neurotic. Their prayer itself was egoically "self-possessed".* [Adi Da suddenly leans backwards, stretching His arms wide and making a very loud and dramatic noise of weeping.] *"I can't! Help me! Ahhhh!"* [Laughter.]

*There is something amusing about that, but they felt it very profoundly, you see. They all felt they were Yogis, they all felt they were understanding, and so forth, you know? But, even so, it was still clear to them in their feeling that their life itself and everything it contained would come to an end, that all their relations would be taken from them, and that they exist here in this place utterly at the Mercy of That in Which the cosmic domain is arising.*

*You have not brought yourselves into existence. You do not now maintain yourselves alive. But to suddenly feel your vulnerability and beg to be kept alive is to be no more Enlightened than in that casual moment before, in which you did not realize your dependency. The frightened wailing for God's Help is no more surrendered than your self-indulgent, egoically "self-possessed" life. It is another moment of the failure to surrender to Me.*

*There is another form of prayer, then, that represents your dependency on Real God, but which is not itself an egoically "self-possessed" gesture, a search for mere survival, consolation, self-contentment. And that is surrender itself, giving up to Real God simply, without exaggeration, and returning to your Ease—not of self-contentment but of heart-Release, in which body and mind are relaxed into the All-Pervading Current of Spirit-Life upon Which your very existence depends.*

*Why, then, continue that path that leads to death? Why go to the chair? Why go to death, the empty place?* [Adi Da speaks softly now, pointing with His index finger to the chair He is sitting on.] *Come to this chair.*

*I do not speak as an ordinary man to you. Nor would I ever suggest that you do what I ask you to do merely because of some whim or other of Mine. But it has been Granted to Me to accept devotees through surrender to Me. It is not a thing that an ordinary person may presume. I have Tested it all My Life, and I have Tested it in your company. I would sooner go to My death than Call you to Me casually. And it is not something that an ordinary person may ask others to do casually if he expects to live, not only in this life.*

*But I swear to you—and you will always continue to see it with clear Signs—that Real God has Granted this Grace to you through My Appearance in your midst. And if you will surrender to Me, if you will love and trust Me because you recognize Who I Am, if you will simply accept the discipline of My Demands, simply do what I ask you to do—and I will always make it very plain—if you will Remember Me with love, if you will Call upon Me by Name with your feeling breaths, if you will Call upon the Name of "Da", then this will be sufficient.*

*And you need not be concerned for any other practice. If you will simply surrender yourself in My Company, you will also understand. But if understanding is made a pre-condition of your surrender to Me, your life with Me, then you will never accomplish it.*

*If you will do this, then you can enter My Way, and the community of My devotees will grow, both in numbers and in practice. And you will be given every strength and all the Spirit-Blessing of Real God—any one who does this. The developmental stages of the Way in My Company will accomplish themselves, and you need have no concern for it.*

*Your single obligation is at the heart. It is in your feeling that you become egoically "self-possessed". It is in your feeling that you betray the Real and Ever-Living God and all your relations. It is in your feeling that you are unhappy. It is in your feeling that fear, sorrow, anger, doubt, shame, lust, and all egoic obsessions are arising. Therefore, it is in your feeling alone that you will be healed.*

*The Way in My Company is Happy. It is boundlessly Joyful. It is a difficult process in this place, this world—difficult in terms of what you must endure, what you must creatively struggle with, as a matter of ordinary discipline.* People *are difficult. People are crazy, driven mad by mortality and pleasure. And you will all continue to suffer limitations in one another. The more the community of My devotees grows, the more demanding it becomes, the more functional, practical, relational, and cultural commitments you presume, the more things you must deal with creatively, the more you must overcome emotionally. There is no point in becoming angry about that. You must, rather, become compassionate and more loving and more of a servant. But if you will do this, if you will transcend the petty reactions of your mortal psyche through surrender to Me, and simply accept the discipline of obedience to Me and Remembrance of Me, then you will be made Happy by My Grace.*

*On another occasion, I will be moved to laugh with you more than today and to be more casually pleasant with you. But today I want you to feel this profundity.*

*Now that you have seen Me, what will you do?*

Avatar Adi Da dipped His hands several times into a bowl of water at His side and threw the water in handfuls over the baskets of marigolds and copies of His "I Am Da" letter—to be distributed as His Prasad,[9] or Divine Gift, to everyone present. No one had ever seen Him do such a water Blessing before. The Force and Directness in His Gestures was itself a Divine Revelation, and devotees gasped as waves of His Love-Bliss poured over the entire gathering. (Many people had not stopped weeping since the occasion began.)

When Avatar Adi Da finished Blessing the Prasad, He turned to everyone again, and said, "I will be waiting for your answer."

Everyone bowed, and Avatar Adi Da Samraj rose from His chair, took His cane, and walked back to His house.

## "Look the Fire in the Eye"

The very morning after this Discourse—in which Avatar Adi Da Called all to acknowledge Him as "Da", the Divine Person—fire threatened the Mountain Of Attention Sanctuary. It was the 17th of September, hot and dry.

*BEN FUGITT: During the summer of 1979, I was a caretaker at the Mountain Of Attention Sanctuary. It had been a very hot summer, with a number of forest fires in the surrounding country. On this particular day in September, I noticed a small tuft of smoke down the canyon. It looked like it was very close to our property. I immediately ran to the nearest car and raced down the canyon. A fire could be seen going up over a ridge to the northwest. This was an ominous location, practically inaccessible to fire-fighting equipment, due to the rough terrain. It was also in a direct line with the outer Sanctuary. Seeing that the Sanctuary was threatened by this already out-of-control fire, I jumped into the car and raced back.*

*I had the fire department notified, then ran out to the back of the Sanctuary, where I had sent a few men with hand-tools to see what they could do. By now, the smoke had grown to a large cloud. This was obviously a* big *fire. I had run about three-quarters of a mile toward the fire to check out the extent of the blaze when I received a call on my walkie-talkie to meet Beloved Adi Da at the Sanc-*

**The fire at the Mountain Of Attention, September 1979**

*tuary zoo, as He wanted to ride out to the fire on horseback. I ran back, calling requests and orders over the walkie-talkie in preparation for His ride. I found myself in a frenzy by the time I got to the zoo.*

*I hastily saddled the horses. Adrenalin was coursing through my body as never before. I was very much afraid for our Sanctuary. The area that was immediately threatened by the fire meant far more to me than simply outlying trails and manzanita bushes. It was the holy site of Red Sitting Man, which was an area of the Sanctuary where I had spent many hours meditating and serving. I knew this Site had great Spiritual significance, and that it was extremely important that it not burn. And then, of course, there was the obvious threat to the residences, holy sites, and Communion Halls at the heart of the Sanctuary.*

*As Beloved Adi Da approached the horses, His fierce determination and concern for the Sanctuary were obvious to me, but He was also completely calm. His simultaneous Intensity and Freedom immediately drew me out of my fearfulness.*

*As we mounted the horses, I wondered exactly where we were going, not remotely expecting what was about to unfold. As soon as we began riding down the back road, a fire engine careened around the corner behind us and turned on its siren to alert us. The horses bolted, not about to be caught by this screaming machine. I could feel Beloved Adi Da's equanimity as I held on for dear life. The truck finally outran us, and the horses relaxed their mad gallop. We rode on to find a spot from which to view the fire.*

*Beloved Adi Da was dissatisfied with the distant vantage points I took Him to, finally asking to get close to the fire. I took Him out through the outer Sanctuary to the spot where I had been earlier, but still He wanted to get much closer to the fire. I told Him there was an old fire road that would take us right to the fire. But I was hesitant to go there, feeling I should not take Him into such a dangerous situation. I warned Him that the horses would probably refuse to get close to the fire because of all the smoke. But this was the route He wanted to explore, and so we made our way up the steep, overgrown fire road. I cautioned Him again about the horses, feeling my own apprehension growing.*

*As we made our way over the ridge, it looked as though we were riding into a different world. The atmosphere was thick with smoke. The ground and trees were red with borate fire retardant, and planes were continuing to drop fire-retardant right over us. Once again, I cautioned Beloved Adi Da about the horses, as it was obvious to me we were approaching the "head" or "lead" of the fire. He simply replied, "Don't worry about it."*

*We wove through the trees toward the roar of the blaze. The wind was coming up and fanning the flames. Spot fires burned on either side of us. The main part of the fire was roaring through the more dense forest directly ahead. I had finally found the right spot! This was where He wanted to be, right in the path of the fire.*

*I was afraid. It seemed to me that we could easily be trapped by the fire—it was moving so quickly. The spot fires behind us could seal off our escape. The horses might bolt. My body was again charged with adrenalin, pumping with wild, terrified energy. Once more, I warned Beloved Adi Da of the possible danger. He looked at me intensely, asking if I was frightened, and I told him honestly, "Yes". His response was, "Why do you think I wanted to come up here? I have to look the fire in the eye."*

*Beloved Adi Da's communication was so full of Force that it was incomprehensible to me. I could feel that His complete, free, and uncompromised attention was on the blazing fire. In that instant, I was relieved of my fear. Suddenly, instead of feeling overwhelmed by terror, I was released into love, and I only wanted to Contemplate my Beloved Guru.*

*Beloved Adi Da then turned toward the advancing flames, moving within thirty yards or so of the advancing blaze. The roar and force of the fire was amazingly powerful. Flames exploded up the sides of two enormous trees directly in front of us, as if to confront Beloved Adi Da. I could feel this great force of Nature over against the Master of Life. I also noticed, much to my amazement, that the horses were completely calm, almost as if they were out grazing in a pasture. They were obviously feeling Beloved Adi Da's calming influence as much as I was.*

*I was sitting to the side and slightly behind Beloved Adi Da, watching Him regard the fire. The magnitude of the fire appeared to increase significantly, as the wind came up suddenly and the fire engulfed the area directly in front of us. Facing the fire's new rush of force and fury, Beloved Adi Da sat completely still in His saddle. His only movements were the spontaneous motions of His face and hands in various mudras, very much the same as I had seen many times during formal Darshan or meditation occasions. I felt Him radiate Divine Fire in the face of that forest fire. Whatever else He might have been doing, Beloved Adi Da was Radiating the most benign and yet fierce and awesome Power I had ever known.*

*After what must have been only a few moments (although time seemed to be suspended and warped), the fire receded and then died down. The winds stopped. The consuming power of this fire seemed to be bowing down to the Divine Heart-Master. I am sure that it is difficult for the reader to picture this moment, but that fire had been transformed! I can only say that it was a mysterious and awesome moment to see and feel the Divine Adept change the course and magnitude of a raging forest fire. I sat still in mindless wonder.*

*Beloved Adi Da then turned back toward the Sanctuary, moving slowly through the trees, stopping to talk for a time. We looked over the scene—the fire was still moving, but much more slowly now, and not directly toward the Sanctuary boundary.*

*When we arrived back at the main Sanctuary complex, I was surprised to find all of Beloved Adi Da's belongings, all of the Sanctuary files and records, library books, and machines being packed into waiting vans and trucks. Apparently, no one had remembered my instructions to wait until we returned before deciding to evacuate. Beloved Adi Da just laughed as He dismounted and sat down on the steps of His residence amidst a sea of packed boxes. He kidded me about our trip up to the fire, and teasingly told everyone, "Ben was so afraid, he almost shit in his pants!"*

*I always tend to withdraw in the face of anything that is frightening to me. Beloved Adi Da has pointed this out to me a number of times over the years, and He would use this event for years to remind me of my tendencies, and how I must go beyond them. During this incident, He had simply drawn me out of my position of fear and agitation, into trust and the capacity to love and serve. I felt through*

*Him what it is to move in this world, even in the most dangerous circumstances, as a free man.*

*Later that evening, we rode out again to survey the neighboring areas. Then Beloved Adi Da asked me to call the neighbors and make sure everyone was all right. In doing so, I found out that, although about one thousand acres had been burned, no buildings had been lost, no one had been injured, and even our neighbor's orchards had only been slightly scorched.*

*A few days later, I walked back to the spot where Beloved Adi Da had worked with the fire, reflecting on all that had occurred there. I thought about how confounding and amazing the whole event had been, feeling humbled and full of love. The area was still smeared with red borate dust and ash; the strong smell of smoke lingered. The fire, I discovered, had stopped short of the Sanctuary boundary by only a foot!*

## An Esoteric Order

On the day of the fire, devotees were not only starting to pack up the most precious things on the Sanctuary in the event of the fire overtaking it. They were also preparing for a great ceremony of initiation, which had been planned before the fire started. And so, in the evening, after Avatar Adi Da had dealt with the fire, He went to Holy Cat Grotto, a hot springs site on the Sanctuary that He had recently Empowered as a temple and special site for healing and Spiritual Initiation. There, beside a steaming pool, He received a group of devotees who He felt had made the strongest response to Him. He intended them to become the core of an esoteric order, His first group of renunciate devotees.[10] The Great Avatar poured the warm water over His devotees, Baptizing them with His Spirit-Presence. And He Initiated

Devotees on the hillside across from Holy Cat Grotto during the initiation ceremony, 1979

Holy Cat Grotto

***Placing His hands on them, He whispered in the ear of each one: "Call upon Me by the Name 'Da'."***

them into the sacred use of His Name, as He had described in His great Discourse of the previous day. Placing His hands on them, He whispered in the ear of each one: "Call upon Me by the Name 'Da'."

Those two days—Sunday, September 16 and Monday, September 17, 1979—were of enormous significance in the Life and Work of Avatar Adi Da Samraj. He had Revealed Himself as the Divine Person, Da, to hundreds of people, and had Called on them to recognize and surrender to Him as Real God. He had Demonstrated His Divine Mastery over the natural world in His encounter with the fire. And, finally, He had planted the seed of His future Work, by Spiritually Initiating some of those whom He intended to become His formal renunciates—the sacred orders of His devotees who would authenticate and preserve forever the Gifts of His Incarnation.

**Avatar Adi Da Samraj and River Papers,**
**the Mountain Of Attention, 1975**

CHAPTER 10

# The Red Miracle

*At the time of the momentous events of the Day of the Heart, River Papers, one of the nine women in the Mandala of Avatar Adi Da's intimate devotees, was expecting His youngest daughter, Trivedi Naamleela Free Jones. River tells the story:*

The unusual circumstances surrounding the birth of Trivedi Naamleela began one day in early 1977. At that time, Beloved Adi Da and a small group of His most intimate devotees were living on the island of Oahu in Hawaii. That day, two devotees who were serving outside the house saw a sudden burst of brilliant light in the yard outside, and they both stopped to look up at the blinding flash. Immediately, the light turned to a fine, bright red powder, which began to fall, like a misty rain, all over the yard. The foliage and the little out-building that we used for our meditation hall were both covered with this powder.

The two who had witnessed this phenomenon called other devotees out to look at the red powder, but the substance was not familiar to anyone. By the end of the day, the fine red coating had disappeared just as mysteriously as it had appeared. There had been no wind or rain that could have blown or washed it away—it just disappeared. At the moment all of this occurred, I was attending Beloved Adi Da in His room in the main house, just a few feet away from where the explosion of light had been witnessed.

Almost two years later, on April 28, 1979, the next miraculous event occurred. Adi Da Samraj was now living at the Mountain Of Attention Sanctuary. A week before, I had begun to feel a very strong pulling or yanking sensation in my internal organs, as if they were being pulled by a string from my pubic bone up the central meridian of my body. I remember the sensation, because it was actually painful, especially in the region of my navel. The pulling sensation went on for a week. On Sunday evening, a gift from a devotee arrived—a photograph of Shirdi Sai Baba.[1] It was a very colorful, poster-sized photograph, showing Shirdi Sai Baba wearing a red bandanna against a deep red background. Beloved Adi Da pointed out the markings of kum-kum on him, and explained to us that kum-kum was a red powder used traditionally throughout India as a symbol of the Divine Nature that is innate in every being. I was unaccountably drawn to the picture.

Over the years, Adi Da had teased me about being associated with the color red, and had spoken of my character reflecting the earthy, vital qualities embodied in this color, but I made no connection between this and my liking of the photograph.

Later on that same evening, a number of us were gathered in our Beloved Guru's quarters, where we had been invited to watch a movie with Him. I was sitting cross-legged on the floor, and, at some point, I looked down and saw a red stain appearing on my body. I thought, of course, that I was menstruating, particularly because of the strange pulling sensation I had experienced all week. So I excused myself, and went to change my clothes.

But it wasn't blood, and I couldn't remove it! In fact, as I was trying to rub it off, more of it was appearing on my skin. It appeared to be coming from inside my skin, and, of course, this really puzzled me. I could not figure out what was going on. I called some of my friends out, to see if they could help me. But no one could remove it or figure out what it was or what was happening. Later, we told Beloved Adi Da about it.

I remember how carefully He listened to my description. Then He said that we had to investigate the phenomenon and find out where the substance was coming from. He asked us to do a very thorough investigation of everything I had come in contact with that day.

We retraced all my steps from the moment I had woken up, going to each room that I had been in and examining every object that I had touched. I remembered that there was a red vacuum cleaner that I had used, and we scrutinized it to see if its red finish could possibly have come off on me when I was vacuuming—but nothing came off. We likewise examined the cabin that I was living in, but there was nothing there.

Once Beloved Adi Da was satisfied that our initial investigation had been as thorough as it could possibly be, He asked that photographs be taken of the red stain and that a sample be taken by one of the doctors and sent to a reliable laboratory for analysis.

During this time, I kept trying to rub the substance off because I didn't want it on me, not knowing what it was. But it just wouldn't come off. In fact, the color seemed to get deeper and deeper the more I rubbed it. Beloved Adi Da said that I shouldn't try to remove it, that I shouldn't even bathe, but should just leave it alone completely.

The stain wasn't uniform. It looked as if someone had taken their fingers, dipped them in bright red powder, and then drawn dramatic lines down my thighs and where I had felt the pulling sensation.

When we received the results from the laboratory several days later, the mystery was only confirmed. The report read that the substance was not composed of any bodily tissue or any common synthetic. The laboratory technicians, intrigued by their findings, had tried all kinds of tests, but they finally had to report: "There are no known chemically definable substances in this specimen."

It was only after all the conventional explanations had been investigated that Beloved Adi Da commented about what had actually taken place. He told us that the red substance that had appeared on my body was a spontaneous manifestation of kum-kum. True kum-kum, He told us, is a form of Light. It is a Divine substance that only appears spontaneously and as a kind of Prasad, or Grace, of Real God. It is the ash of a great Yogic fire, appearing externally, but signaling that a most intense Yogic process is taking place. This Divine substance has been known to appear at various times in the company of holy men and women, and, by its very nature, it defies ordinary physical laws.

There have been examples of the spontaneous manifestation of ash and kum-kum at various times in India. Even today, there is a temple in India that has a sacred image that manifests kum-kum once each month on the full moon. Beloved Adi Da pointed out to us that Shirdi Sai Baba's devotees often reported the miraculous appearance of kum-kum in association with photographs like the one Avatar Adi Da had received on the night the red stain appeared on my body. Beloved Adi Da also told us that He had been having contact with Shirdi Sai Baba on a subtle plane, coincident with the arrival of the poster that had attracted me, and added that the spontaneous manifestation of ash and kum-kum was a phenomenon associated with Shirdi Sai Baba. He explained that He had expected a manifestation to occur, but that He had not known in advance how it would occur.

Beloved Adi Da also recounted the story of a woman he had seen several years before at Swami

Muktananda's ashram in Ganeshpuri. This woman was well known at the ashram for the generous quantities of kum-kum that frequently manifested spontaneously on her body. He recounted His visit to this woman, and told us of seeing kum-kum on the floor all around her, having apparently manifested only moments before He arrived.

Although I didn't understand what was occurring or what it had to do with me, I thought that perhaps a significant change was going to take place in my life. I thought then that it might have something to do with my practice, so I started to make an effort to intensify my practice—but Beloved Adi Da told me to just relax! He said that the Yogic process of which the kum-kum had been a sign was already initiated in me, and that it was occurring by His Grace, without my needing to do anything about it. Nine weeks later, I discovered that I was pregnant.

During my pregnancy, Beloved Adi Da insisted that I observe the strictest discipline—everything that would support my right disposition and Spiritual awareness and availability. He did not allow me to indulge in <u>anything</u> during this pregnancy!

One day during the third month, I was in the kitchen when Beloved Adi Da came in and, as He often did, stood by the window that looks out onto the grassy central area of the Sanctuary, to give His Regard to His devotees as they walked by. It was at that moment that I first became aware of the actual psychic entity inside me.

I remember it so well because it became very obvious—a literal sensation, as if a light had been turned on in the room—that the being in me was reaching out to Beloved Adi Da. I knew that this entity was incarnating because of its profound Spiritual relationship to Him. And I felt myself as simply a vehicle for this being, carrying and nurturing it so that it could be with Beloved Adi Da in human form.

I was amazed to feel such a strong intention and Spiritual awareness from a child that had not yet been born, but I had to accept it—the Spiritual impulse behind this birth was being communicated very clearly to me in that moment.

One night, just as I was about to go to my room to sleep, Beloved Adi Da said to me that I should be able to tell what the sex of the child was—because, after all, it was just underneath a thin layer of skin! He said that if I went to bed that night and concentrated, I would be able to tell the sex of the child. So I did, and I had a dream. In the dream, I saw two energy-images—one was of a boy, and one was of a girl. I didn't know how to interpret the dream, but when I told it to Beloved Adi Da it became obvious that the boy, who was older than the girl, was the son I had had years before and the girl was the child I was carrying now. I was certain now that it was a girl.

Throughout the pregnancy, many, many names were suggested for the child. But, a couple of weeks before my due date, Beloved Adi Da came out of His quarters one day and said "Naamleela". As soon as I heard the name "Naamleela", I knew that that was her name. It seemed to perfectly describe the Spiritual character of the being I was so intimate with now after all those months.

"Naam" is Sanskrit for "name", and is traditionally understood to mean the Name, or the Word, that is God. It is said that the Name (or Word) of God is not different from God, in the same way that light cannot be separated from its source, the Sun. The Naam, or Name, is the audible form of the Divine, the primal manifestation, or reflection, of God. The traditional significance of the name "Naamleela" confirmed my first intuition that this was the perfect name. The name itself seemed to summarize the nature of the Spiritual relationship He offers to all His devotees and to which this unborn practitioner was so obviously attracted.

Speaking about Naamleela's name, Beloved Adi Da said, "What is symbolized, or represented, by the many names and holy words is Sound itself, or vibration, the Life-Current, the Native Feeling, the Light of Lights, the Sound that is already there and the Sound from which all other sounds—and all forms, in fact—emanate. Therefore, these names are simply symbols for the inherent vibrations of Life. 'Naam' is, thus, traditionally understood to be the Energy, or Life-Power, from which all 'creations' arise.

"In every tradition, the incarnate Spiritual Master is known to his or her devotees to be the Word, the Name, the Living Form, the manifested expression of God. And when devotees enter into relationship with an Adept-Realizer and call upon him or her by Name, they call upon the Person and Presence to which they have been most intimately awakened through the influence of the living Spiritual Master."

About the word "leela", Beloved Adi Da said, "In simplest terms, it means 'the play of God, the free activity by which the Form of God appears and makes Itself known to devotees'."

I couldn't imagine a more serious and happy name. I felt that it fully reflected the devotion that this child was already demonstrating for our Beloved Guru.

The ninth month approached. Everything seemed ready. The name had been chosen. The baby had moved into the appropriate position for the birth. And I was eager to have the baby. My due date came and went. Days passed. After several weeks, the doctors began to talk about inducing labor. This frightened me, because my first labor had been induced and it had been a very negative experience. I went on long hikes, jumped on trampolines, drank herbal concoctions, and was given acupuncture treatments—everything that would naturally induce labor. But nothing happened. I finally decided that I would just have to surrender to the labor being artificially induced.

I gave up all my fears about inducement and accepted my situation. On the evening of the anniversary of the beginning of Beloved Adi Da's Teaching Work—April 25—I began to have contractions, but I didn't pay any attention to them, because this had already happened so many times with no result. They were a bit uncomfortable, and I remember thinking that I should lie down for awhile.

Then I noticed that the contractions were occurring rather frequently. Because my first child had been induced, I had no idea what labor felt like! I noticed that the contractions were getting stronger and stronger, and I thought I should tell somebody.

As it turned out, I was in full labor! We drove to the hospital. The contractions were strong, and, though I had my attention on the physical process that was taking place, it was secondary to Beloved Adi Da's Darshan. I was more aware of Him than of myself. His Beauty and Radiance were so Blissful.

In the hospital, during the birth, my Beloved Guru sat fully in my view, never leaving His chair. I felt absolutely no separation from Him. The birth was a blissful event. We were not separate. There was nothing "separate" going on. It was one of the most blissful experiences of my life.

Beloved Adi Da cut the umbilical cord, and Trivedi Naamleela was placed on my stomach. Almost immediately, Beloved Adi Da took her. He anointed her with ash and kum-kum and put a Tibetan cap on her head and a mala around her neck and wrapped her in a blanket—and then He went around showing her to everybody.

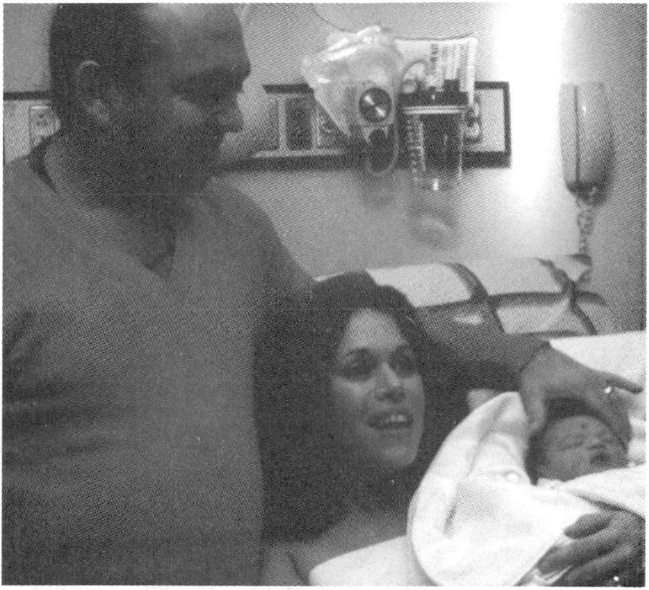

**Avatar Adi Da at the hospital with River Papers and Trivedi Naamleela Free Jones**

I looked at Beloved Adi Da and Trivedi Naamleela, and I saw her open her eyes to look at Him. I felt the blissful contact immediately between the two of them. It seemed very unusual, because newborns typically don't open their eyes.

Sometime after Trivedi Naamleela's birth, Avatar Adi Da began to talk about the spontaneous manifestation of kum-kum that had occurred a year before her birth. He asked for the date of the manifestation, and I told Him that it had occurred on April 28, 1979. He commented on the proximity to Trivedi Naamleela's birth date, which was April 26, 1980.

He pursued the matter further and determined that, because 1980 was a leap year, April 26, 1980 was exactly

Trivedi Naamleela Free Jones, Adidam Samrajashram, 1997

*"'Naam' is Sanskrit for 'name', and is traditionally understood to mean the Name, or the Word, That is Real God. It is said that the Name (or Word) of Real God is not different from Real God, in the same way that light cannot be separated from its source, the Sun. . . . The name itself seemed to summarize the nature of the Spiritual relationship He offers to all His devotees and to which this unborn practitioner was so obviously attracted."*

left: River Papers telling her Leela in 1994

365 days after the spontaneous manifestation of kum-kum which had occurred on April 28, 1979. I remember the significance that Beloved Adi Da placed on this exact span of 365 days, and I remembered how hard I had tried to make the birth happen sooner! I said to Him, "No matter what, she wasn't going to be born before then. We tried everything, and she was not going to come out before that moment."

Beloved Adi Da indicated that Trivedi Naamleela had begun the process of her incarnation on the day of the appearance of kum-kum. The miracle of the kum-kum had been a sign of the auspicious birth that was to come. He affirmed that Trivedi Naamleela's incarnation was a Spiritual event, the larger miracle of which the kum-kum had been the external, visible sign.

I had never understood what, if any, connection there was between the manifestation of kum-kum in Oahu in 1977 and the manifestation at the Mountain Of Attention in 1979, or if the original manifestation had anything to do with Trivedi Naamleela's birth.

In 1994, when I was telling this Leela to a group of devotees, with Beloved Adi Da present, He said:

"The original incident was a sign associated with yourself as a vehicle for the birth of Trivedi Naamleela. In that sense, so was the sign in 1979 that appeared on your body. It was a sign of Trivedi Naamleela, but also a sign of yourself as the vehicle through which she would appear.

"From the first day you came into My Company, I referred to you in terms of the color red. You yourself likewise made such references in various forms over the years.

"Altogether, the redness of the kum-kum manifestations was associated with the unique service you performed as the vehicle for Trivedi Naamleela's birth."

"Yes, thank you, Beloved. I am eternally grateful."

"Tcha."

**Da Love-Ananda Mahal, 1982**

CHAPTER 11

# The Search for Hermitage

Soon after His Revelation of His Divine Name, "Da", in 1979, Avatar Adi Da became a wanderer, looking for His Hermitage. He needed a refuge more secluded than the Mountain Of Attention, a place where He could fully allow His Revelation of Divine Enlightenment to continue its spontaneous unfolding, and where He could Work intensively with the members of His new esoteric order. And so, in 1980, He began to spend increasing amounts of time in Hawaii, on the island of Kauai, at a newly acquired Sanctuary, Da Love-Ananda Mahal,[1] the second great Seat of His Spiritual Work.

For many years, this Sanctuary was named "Tumomama", meaning "fierce woman",[2] in acknowledgment of the untamed forces of nature there, which signify the Divine Goddess in Her fierce aspect. Below six acres of rolling lawns, a tumultuous river rips through a rocky gorge as it pours down from the top of Mount Waialeale, the wettest place on Earth.

## The Call to Renunciation

Renunciation had always been at the root of Avatar Adi Da's Call to all of His devotees. Throughout the years of His Teaching Work, Avatar Adi Da had been commenting upon all the traditional approaches to religious renunciation and engaging in "consideration" about what renunciation would look like in the case of His devotees. Renunciation is usually thought of as deliberate asceticism, the giving up of bodily and worldly pleasures for the sake of some Spiritual goal to be attained in the future. Avatar Adi Da, however, had continually emphasized that true renunciation is the renunciation of self-contraction, of seeking, and all the pain of that entire effort. His devotees were learning that renunciation in His Company is not puritanical, not an avoidance of the body, but Tantric—the conforming of all the faculties of the body-mind and every aspect of ordinary life to the great "Brightening" Process of Realizing Him.

*AVATAR ADI DA SAMRAJ: To practice in My Company you must be a renunciate. And renunciation is ego-transcendence, establishment in the Well of Happiness, magnifying that Happiness in the sphere of all relations and functions. You need not be an ascetic, but you must give it all to Me, to the Divine—every trace of your existence, every piece of it, down to the last drop. You cannot merely tithe to the Divine! You may tithe to the world, but you must give everything to the Divine. You must give everything to Spiritual life, totally. And then, based on that principle, you must economize the giving of energy and attention to life and relations.* [The Dreaded Gom-Boo, or the Imaginary Disease That Religion Seeks to Cure]

During 1980 and 1981, first at Da Love-Ananda Mahal and then again at the Mountain Of Attention Sanctuary, Adi Da Samraj continued to work with the small group of devotees in the esoteric order, looking to establish a group of formal renunciates, devotees who were completely committed to the Great Matter of Realizing the Divine, devotees who would be prepared to go through whatever that ordeal might require.

Then, in 1982, on returning to Da Love-Ananda Mahal, Avatar Adi Da Samraj expanded His circle of "consideration" to include practitioners who were living and serving near the Sanctuary. To all alike, He posed the same questions: Did they have one-pointed clarity of purpose? Were they showing the depth of self-understanding that true and free renunciation requires—not suppressed, not ascetical, but converted to Happiness? Could they directly transcend boredom, doubt, and discomfort, rather than resorting to the conventional means of seeking in order to overcome their difficulties?

*AVATAR ADI DA SAMRAJ: My Divine Spiritual Current of Love-Bliss is resident in intimate association with the living being. It is always "Locatable". It is perpetually knowable. It is never lost. You are always capable of "Locating" It, of knowing It, animating It, being It. This Principle is an indication, therefore, of the essential (or sufficient) sadhana of renunciate practitioners.*

Every body is an island
for its one.
The "I", adrift in space,
is masted to its earth core,
the body, bright,
rising slightly on the ocean
and the currents
of life-light.
A single tree
is also rising there,
antenna to the sky
of mind.
A plant of nerves,
its root in sex,
and foliated brain,
that tree surveys
the earth and sky,
the mindful scene,
the move of life,
and would uncapture
this attentive "I".

How can this island
fly or drown?
To what space
can space be gone?
The isle will be forgotten
when the Source
of "I" is Found.

Poem 49 from *Crazy Da Must Sing,*
*Inclined to His Weaker Side*
August 12, 1982

*In a circumstance of remoteness or dissociation from worldly obligations and stimulation, in every moment, instead of animating or stimulating yourself physically, emotionally, or mentally in order to overcome the sensations and feelings of boredom, doubt, and discomfort, you could directly do or realize what is necessary in order to exist in the Condition of Love-Bliss, or Happiness. Instead of seeking to overcome or escape boredom, doubt, and discomfort, you could directly enter into My Divine Spiritual Current of Love-Bliss, that Realization of Existence That is Prior to boredom, doubt, and discomfort. This is the secret of the Disposition of Enlightened beings.* [April 7, 1982]

During 1982 and into 1983 at Da Love-Ananda Mahal, Avatar Adi Da Samraj also explored with His devotees the relationship between sexuality and renunciation, a "consideration" that had been going on since the "Garbage and the Goddess" days. He would continue to return to this subject again and again over many years, in the process of establishing His formal renunciate orders. Always He emphasized the difference between the "householder" (or conventional) disposition relative to sex, which involves egoic "bonding"[3] with another, and the truly renunciate disposition, which does not.

By this time, Avatar Adi Da had already Revealed a Dharma of sexual practice to all His devotees that was unparalleled in any secular, religious, or Spiritual tradition—including full details of an emotional-sexual Yoga that was compatible with the total process of Divine Enlightenment. His Instruction had grown directly out of His "consideration" with devotees—as well as His own exploration, both spontaneous and experimental, of intimate and sexual Yoga. Now He was looking to see if any of His devotees were mature enough—emotionally, sexually, and Spiritually—to actually practice this self-transcending sexual Yoga in a uniquely non-binding and truly renunciate manner.

# Hurricane Iwa

On November 23, 1982, news reached devotees at Da Love-Ananda Mahal of a hurricane that had blown up in the Pacific and was heading straight for the island of Kauai. By 4:30 in the afternoon, huge trees were down across the road and a sixty-foot lychee tree lay in splinters at the Sanctuary. Electric power lines were whipping in the wind, and the rain was coming down in sheets. The river below the Sanctuary was swollen brown and raging, and outside the windows of Free Standing Man (Avatar Adi Da's residence, where He was gathered with His devotees), leaves, branches, and debris swept past in the howling storm.

Devotees were doing whatever they could to secure the Sanctuary. Adi Da placed His Hands on the badly bruised neck of a devotee who had injured herself running to safety. Through the healing power of His touch, she could soon swallow painlessly, her breathing normalized, and the bruise disappeared.

Not long afterwards, there was a new storm report threatening wind-speeds of over one hundred miles per hour. At that point, Avatar Adi Da rose and went to His library. He returned in a few minutes with a small volume of poems in honor of Kali, the Hindu vision of the Divine Goddess in Her terrible, destructive form. Unperturbed by the deafening roar outside, He began to read poem after poem that teased, scolded, and reverenced Kali as the trickster, the Mother of illusions, awesome in Her devastating play. Devotees looked on in amazement and joy. They knew that Adi Da was addressing Hurricane Iwa directly, asserting His Mastery over this terrifying manifestation of the Goddess-Power.

Finally, Avatar Adi Da put the book down. He said: "She has done it." Then He went on:

*AVATAR ADI DA SAMRAJ: This storm is the great picture. This is life capsulized. Life is obliteration—not birth and survival and glorification. It is death! The "Goddess" is the sign of Nature, the Word of Nature, the Person of Nature—Kali, the bloody Goddess with long teeth and blood pouring out of her mouth. You poor people are deceived by Nature.* [November 23, 1982]

Avatar Adi Da continued speaking, Calling His devotees to Invoke Him and resort to Him, the only One Who could Liberate them from the effects of Nature. He spoke ecstatically of His Mastery of the Goddess, and of His Power to calm Her wildness and Her potentially destructive influence. The weather reports indicated that much worse was yet to come, but, following their Beloved Guru, whose mood became light, devotees began to celebrate, watching the storm gradually subside.

The next morning, the newspapers reported on the storm damage. They described the fact that no one on the island had been killed as a "miracle". Later reports and satellite photographs from the U.S. weather service showed that, at the very hour when Avatar Adi Da had begun to read the poems to Kali, the hurricane suddenly doubled the speed at which it was moving along its course, for no apparent meteorological reason. As a result, Hurricane Iwa spent its force and "aged" prematurely, changing shape and blowing itself out. Thus, the worst of its fury never reached the Hawaiian Islands.

*Ah, I long for the vanished gardens of Cordoba, where no thing hangs or rises up desirous to be sucked in or forced out, where all beings are sublime, tasting only the nectar of Love-Bliss in their mouths, their tongues clinging to the roof of their tooth-hood only for Happiness, without the slightest thought of self, without the slightest thought of clinging to another. Such Bliss is not heaven! It is nowhere, nowhere at all, not then, not now, not in the future. Such Bliss has never been experienced by beings at all except in their moment of vanishing when they slide upon the Light from which forms are made.*

*When nothing even in the slightest is experienced or known or presumed, then there is only the Infinite Light of Bliss, the same state in which you now exist but without the compartments of your atrocious thought, without even a parcel of it hanging out. Now we are free. Then we are free. Then we were free. Then we will be free. This space of time is only a figment of your imagination. This body here is the lie by which you are bound. Be willing to give up your body, even now, even now, even now. And your mind, which is your body. Let it go. Let it go. Cling to nothing. Let it go. This is My recommendation.*

Avatar Adi Da Samraj
FEBRUARY 3, 1983

## The Ordeal of Being

Even in the relative seclusion of Da Love-Ananda Mahal, Avatar Adi Da was too crowded in by the world. And so the search for Hermitage went on. Finally, in March 1983, unable to wait any longer for His devotees to provide a permanent place of seclusion for Him to continue His Divine Work, Avatar Adi Da Samraj and the esoteric order boarded a plane for Fiji.

Fiji had previously been identified as a potentially desirable location for a Hermitage. It was very remote and quiet, and the social and political atmosphere of the country was benign. The population was a mix of native Fijians and Indians, both of which groups had strong traditions of respect for individuals of Spiritual power.

**Nananui-Ra, Fiji, 1983**

Avatar Adi Da literally wandered the Fijian islands in search of a Hermitage—from Nananui-Ra, to Namale plantation, to Nukubati—sometimes staying in the simplest of places, with only wells for water and kerosene lamps for light.

Right at the beginning of their pilgrimage, at Nananui-Ra, Avatar Adi Da Samraj led His devotees into a "consideration" of the "Perfect Practice"—the ultimate stages of practice in the Way of Adidam[4]—Instructing them about the process that immediately precedes, and leads up to, Divine Enlightenment. To intensify their "consideration", He sent several devotees on a four-day solitary retreat, which He called the "Ordeal of Being". As they began their retreat, He Gave them this Instruction:

*AVATAR ADI DA SAMRAJ: Enter more and more deeply into the Well of Being, Where you Always Already Stand.*

*Feel the Feeling of Being, without the slightest regard or concern for attention and its objects.*

*Be Immersed in the Conscious, Native, and Original Feeling of Being, until It Is Realized to Be Happiness Itself, or Freedom Itself.*

*Be Thus. Dwell in That, As That—unperturbed, Free, Self-Radiant as Love-Bliss, without qualification, beyond all need to notice the body-mind and its objects.*

*Practice this constantly on retreat.*

*This is true and free devotion to Me.*

*This is true and free renunciation.*

*Therefore, this Retreat is the "radically" simple, or most sublime, practice of devotion and renunciation.*

*If you practice this Retreat most fully, then you will know that just this practice is the Way to which I Am always Calling you.* [March 21, 1983]

The Siddhi Transmitted by Avatar Adi Da is always simply the profound Force of the Heart, or the "Feeling of Being". But how any particular devotee experiences this constant Divine Blessing depends on many factors, including mental and emotional tendencies and stage of growth in the Spiritual process. During His years at the Mountain Of Attention and in Hawaii, Avatar Adi Da had intentionally Revealed all the stages of the great Spiritual Process in His Company, and all the Samadhis belonging to each stage. By the time they began this retreat, members of the esoteric order (and other devotees also) had experienced the effects of His Divine Blessing-Power in the form of every extraordinary experience known in the Spiritual traditions. They could confess to such Gifts not only during the drama of the "Garbage and the Goddess" period but also in the process of their personal meditation over many years. They had been transported with Yogic visions, and all the possibilities of the subtle senses—psychic sounds, lights, odors, and nectarous flavors (Savikalpa Samadhi[5]). Some had even experienced the rare formless ecstasy (ascended Nirvikalpa Samadhi) that had overtaken Avatar Adi Da on His first visit to Swami Muktananda. And they knew the expanded Sphere of Bliss that accompanied His unique Spiritual Descent in the form of "the Thumbs". Now, in this retreat, Avatar Adi Da was Calling His devotees to enter into the most profound imageless, thoughtless state of immersion in the Domain of Pure Consciousness (Jnana Samadhi[6]). He was even looking for signs that they might be receiving His Divine Heart-Transmission most perfectly, having actually Awakened to His own State of "Open Eyes", or Divine Enlightenment (Ruchira Samadhi[7]).

As the retreat began, the weather suddenly changed. High winds ripped across the island day and night. The usually calm inland sea was turbulent, and the morning's tide left jellyfish stranded on the shore. The rains were constant and the sun remained hidden.

On the second day of the retreat, Avatar Adi Da remarked: "Today will be the best day if the retreatants are really practicing, the most difficult day if they are not." On the third day, the storm was growing to hurricane force and Avatar Adi Da remarked, "If I call the retreatants off retreat, the storm will stop." By this, He was hinting that the Force of His Spiritual Transmission invested in His retreatant devotees—for the sake of Liberating all beings—was encountering resistance in the conditional world.

On the fourth day, Avatar Adi Da decided to recall the retreatants. That morning, He greeted them with a huge laugh and embraced each one. At the same time, the winds began to subside and a wide rainbow appeared above the sea. As the retreatants began to confess what had occurred in their retreat process, it became

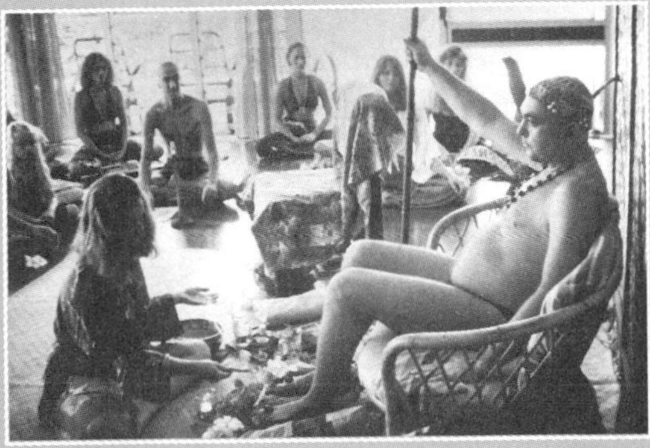

**Namale Plantation, Fiji, 1983**

*May you be prepared. May You be Free. May you be Liberated. May you be overwhelmed by the Transfiguring Power of the Great One. May your devotion be without bounds. May your minds be Sublimed, your emotions lifted to Love, and your bodies be Transfigured in Infinite Bliss, the Love-Light of Eternal God. All of You. Every one. All beings, in all worlds. Even now. Right now. May we all be Blessed and Bless-ed. Let us be Happy. Now go. Go! Go and be Happy! Go and Be, Happy. You cannot Be and not be Happy. You can exist and be un-Happy, but you cannot Be, merely Be, freely Be, entirely Be, and Be anything but Happy. Only your excision of Being creates un-Happiness. But if you simply Are in the Existence Place, the Quality of Happiness is Inevitable, Inevitable and All-Pervading and Absolute. This will Teach you. This is your Teacher. This is Me. This is My Self. This is the Avatar since eternity. This One speaks to you now. This One is here, now, then, always. Even if I die, this One is with you and all beings. Now go.*

AVATAR ADI DA SAMRAJ
FEBRUARY 18, 1983

obvious that the Divine Siddhi of Avatar Adi Da had deeply affected all of them. Some had experienced "Cosmic Consciousness",[8] dropping spontaneously into deep states beyond peripheral awareness and Realizing ecstatic Oneness with all existence.

But Avatar Adi Da closely questioned each retreatant: Were they already Abiding as Consciousness Itself, in a Fullness of Love-Bliss that could not possibly be diminished by any arising event? If so, then truly there was nothing lacking in their Realization.

By the time all the members of the esoteric order had passed through the retreat, Avatar Adi Da had a group of seven devotees who were actually confessing to the state of "Open Eyes", or Divine Enlightenment. Avatar Adi Da received their confession, perfectly willing that it be so. But He also told them that it would now be up to them to <u>demonstrate</u> the truth of their Enlightenment during the coming months. He said to them: "Consider that you are walking with a bowl of water on your head, followed by a man with a large sword. If you falter in your step and lose one drop of the water, he will wield the sword with absolute swiftness, and your head will fall to the ground! The Divinely Enlightened One never misses a step. Such is the Nature of Most Perfect Enlightenment."

These were very testing months—and the ego-patterning of each supposedly "Enlightened" devotee came up with tremendous force. Eventually, all heads rolled. Avatar Adi Da had been engaging His devotees in another Teaching Demonstration, both to give them a glimpse of Perfect Freedom, and also as a lesson in how much sadhana they still had to do.

# The Struggle in Fiji

For most Westerners, or people from "Westernized" cultures, the idea of spirits, ghosts, and disembodied entities is a fascinating possibility, but one that has little or no basis in their daily experience. People in many traditional cultures, however, tend to be more sensitive to the dimensions of life and energy that are subtler than the physical. In fact, many traditional cultures presume that the dimension of spirits (both benign and threatening) is as real as—or even more real than—the physical dimension.

Avatar Adi Da Samraj always takes the spirit-dimension into account, and works with that dimension as powerfully as with any other plane of existence. There are many stories of His dealing with spirits—attracting them, disciplining them, freeing them from limitations and illusions so that they can move on in their process. Avatar Adi Da has said that at all of His Sanctuaries there are spirit-beings, some of whom are actively involved in the process of sadhana. Others, who are acting in interfering ways, He will severely reprimand and send away, because they are not yet ready to associate with His holy Places. Devotees have frequently felt or seen spirit-beings in the Communion Halls and in all kinds of circumstances.

Less than two weeks after the conclusion of the "Ordeal of Being" retreats, signs of spirits began to manifest dramatically around Avatar Adi Da. In this case, the spirits were showing their resistance to His establishment of Himself and His Divine Work in Fiji. At the time, the Trimada and the children of the devotees traveling with Avatar Adi Da were staying together in a small building of their own, attended by two of the adults. On the night of April 8, 1983, one of the adults caring for the children felt a sense of danger as she was falling asleep, but she dismissed it as merely a subjective state. Then, at 1:30 in the morning, she was awakened by a popping sound, like a small explosion. When she went to investigate, she found that one of the children was lying with her head a few feet from a burning kerosene refrigerator. She pulled the child to safety and shouted to the other adult in the building to wake up and get all the children out of the house immediately. The last person to cross the threshold was blasted out of the house by another explosion, and then the entire building burst into flames. Miraculously, no one was injured. But in the morning, nothing remained of the building, and even the foundation had been cracked by the intense heat.

The next day, Avatar Adi Da said that, on the evening of the fire, He had been visited by some aggressive spirits, and He could now tell that it was they who had subsequently been responsible for the fire. It was shocking and disturbing to everyone to feel how disastrous the consequences of this "black magic" could have been. Following the fire, Avatar Adi Da indicated that it was time to move on, and a few days later the whole party departed for the island of Nukubati.

The next three months were an extraordinary ordeal, during which Avatar Adi Da gathered with devotees every day, continuing His intense Work with the "pit of snakes"—the gut-level of egoity in every individual. Twenty-fours hours a day, every devotee in the group was dealing with intense emotions. Each one still felt profoundly confronted by their Beloved Guru's Calling to them: to transcend the limits and dramas of the emotional-sexual character, and to understand these presumed limits as the underlying cause of un-Enlightenment.

*AVATAR ADI DA SAMRAJ: By tendency, you all live far from the domain of feeling. You live as conventional social personalities, and your lives are organized around behavioral obligations that are communicated to you from infancy.*

*However, there is also a dimension in you that does not merely want to be this social personality, does not merely want to submit to the behavioral demands that you have inherited, and is not happy in any case. This level of emotion exists beneath the social personality. You do not like this level of emotion, and therefore you try to maintain the characteristics of the social personality as many hours of every day as you can. But then circumstance, moments of weakness, the phases of your own hormonal system, and various other factors cause you from time to time to fall into this "pit of snakes" that is your reactive, non-social, even anti-social personality.*

*At those times, you are resistive, angry, afraid, sorrowful, righteous, lustful—all the patterns one would call "you", as the ego. This is true of everyone. No one is merely the perfect social personality. Everyone has his or her games and tendencies. Everyone lives in a kind of diseased state all the time, and at times exhibits the symptoms of that disease in very dramatic fashion. Most people do not even want to get* <u>*close*</u> *to the realm of emotions that is associated with this irresponsible ego-self. All of common society is devoted to keeping people from getting in touch with this "pit of snakes".*

*In My Play with you, I have not avoided putting you in touch with that realm of emotion, that "pit of snakes". I must put you in touch with it. But I do not merely put you in touch with it. I Instruct you, I Teach you, I Submit My Self to you, I help you to understand how to be free of this "pit of snakes", so that you will not have to live any longer as superficial personalities, surrendered to the universal tragedy of unillumined mankind.*

*To complete this "consideration", however, you must* <u>*kill*</u> *those snakes. You cannot merely accept these principles I have summarized for you at the end of a long period of "consideration" and try to make social order out of them. You must go through this "consideration" to the end. Our "consideration" together must lead you to deal with this emotional bondage, lead you through and beyond it, so that you no longer exist in the domain of the superficial social personality, nor do you exist in or fall back into this pit of reactive egoity.*

*Instead, you must exist always in the Domain of Free Feeling, Which is inherently intimate contact with the Transcendental, Inherently Spiritual, and (necessarily) Divine Force of Being, and Which Knows Real God without a doubt. This Feeling knows love, without psychiatric help or intellectual reasons—and so incarnates it, lives it.*

*Love one another, and there is nothing cool about it. What I mean by this love for one another is to become wounded by love, to submit yourself to love, to live in the world of love, and to make your relationships about love. Be vulnerable enough to love and be loved. If you do this, you will be wounded by this love but you will not be diseased. The wound of love is the "Hole in the universe", and ultimately it is Realized as such.*

*In this "Hole in the universe", this Domain of Feeling without armoring, without self-contraction—the great Physics, the great Science, the great Possibility, is evident. Hardly anyone in human history has known of It. Human beings in general do not want anything to do with It. They do not want to come close enough to It to be wounded in their intimacies with one another. It is the Doorway to Divine Transfiguration, Divine Transformation, and, ultimately, Divine Translation, or Outshining of phenomenal existence.*[9] *It is the Way into the Divine Self-Domain.* [July 2, 1983]

Throughout this period, winds whipped over the island constantly, while indoors it was oppressive and hot. The ordeal, as Avatar Adi Da Revealed later, was even more than it appeared to be. He knew that it was part of a battle with the local spirits, who were resisting the newcomers' entry into their domain, and who were especially confronting His own Spiritual Power. Later, Avatar Adi Da spoke of this time:

*AVATAR ADI DA SAMRAJ: We were tested by the spirits constantly at Nukubati. Every day, I would come out and bring you life, bring you love, bring you Happiness. And, almost every day, there was a fierce, unhealthy confrontation—I was at war with negative entities, the kind that made the fire at Nananui-Ra. That is why I did what I did with you there. You did not see the spirits then. I saw them. I knew what was happening. You only experienced the effects of it—not knowing its source, thinking it was just your own patterns, your own tendencies.*

*I was attacked physically and emotionally there every day. It was a confrontation with negative trickery. That is why I had to struggle—and those who were with Me, too—because I knew the quantity of energy and feeling that had to be generated there to deal with those influences. And it was done!*

*When you see the pictures in the slide shows, Nukubati looks like the ultimate dream of paradise. It was nothing like that—nothing. You could not take a step at Nukubati without suffering. You could not even walk My dinner from the kitchen without having it blown off the tray by the constant wind there. And this was every day. It was a terrible time and a wonderful time. An extremely happy time, full of energy, but desperate also, and depressed.*

*DEVOTEE: Beloved Lord, at Nukubati I had a vision of You being physically attacked by these spirits and dealing with them. I have never had such visions before.*

*AVATAR ADI DA SAMRAJ: Right. And they did not just attack Me in invisible form. You who lived there with Me were possessed, literally possessed. Every day there, I confronted not just your personalities, with your own tendencies, but you as <u>those</u> personalities, possessed by those tricksters. It was literal war, and no one but Me was conscious of it. All of you were rather reluctant participants in this struggle, because you viewed it only from the point of view of your tendencies.*

*DEVOTEE: What we felt throughout this period was Your Love.*

*AVATAR ADI DA SAMRAJ: I Sit in My Divine Domain. I know the spirits, and I know you, and I kept you alive in that terrible struggle.* [October 28, 1983]

While Avatar Adi Da and His devotees were at Nukubati, news came that His Hermitage was found. A devotee had purchased Naitauba, an island of about 3,000 acres in the Koro Sea. This accomplishment, Avatar Adi Da said, was what the whole battle had been about. And He had been victorious. He had been given His Hermitage, in the teeth of the fierce territorial spirits and all the invisible forces of resistance in the world.

*AVATAR ADI DA SAMRAJ: At Nukubati, we stayed in love. And love prevailed, and converted the spirits. And that is why we are here. If it were not for what we did at Nukubati, it would never have happened. Never. There was so much resistance to it. This event is unprecedented. Unprecedented. But it never would have happened without the glorious sacrifice we made there.* [October 28, 1983]

Nukubati, Fiji, 1983

Avatar Adi Da Samraj arrives on Naitauba, October 27, 1983

# A Place of Blessing for All Time

On October 27, 1983, Adi Da Samraj landed by seaplane in the shallows of a lagoon, and set foot on His Hermitage for the first time. His arrival was followed by rains, ending months of drought on the island. After His first circumnavigation of Naitauba (which is also named "Adidam Samrajashram"[10]), Avatar Adi Da Samraj spoke ecstatically of its grandeur and its potential for His future Work:

*AVATAR ADI DA SAMRAJ: Naitauba is not just a piece of land. It is a Divine Place, and all of us together, concentrated in this Work, own this Place. All My devotees participate in this acquisition. That is how it will be for as long as the sun shines and rises and sets and the grass grows and the wind blows. Forever—as ever as there can be in this world. Maybe it will become a paradise through Spiritual sacrifice. And, all during that epoch, this Place should be ours—this Sanctuary of Blessing. Over time, then,*

**The island of Naitauba**

*millions of people—literally, millions of people—should come to this Place and be Blessed. They should come and acknowledge, affirm, and see My Revelation magnified.*

*This place is so great, so great. Civilization has never interfered with it. It is untouched. The water is blue. The fish are happy. Untouched, really untouched. Pristine from the beginning of the world—this place. It has been waiting here since the beginning of time.* [October 28, 1983]

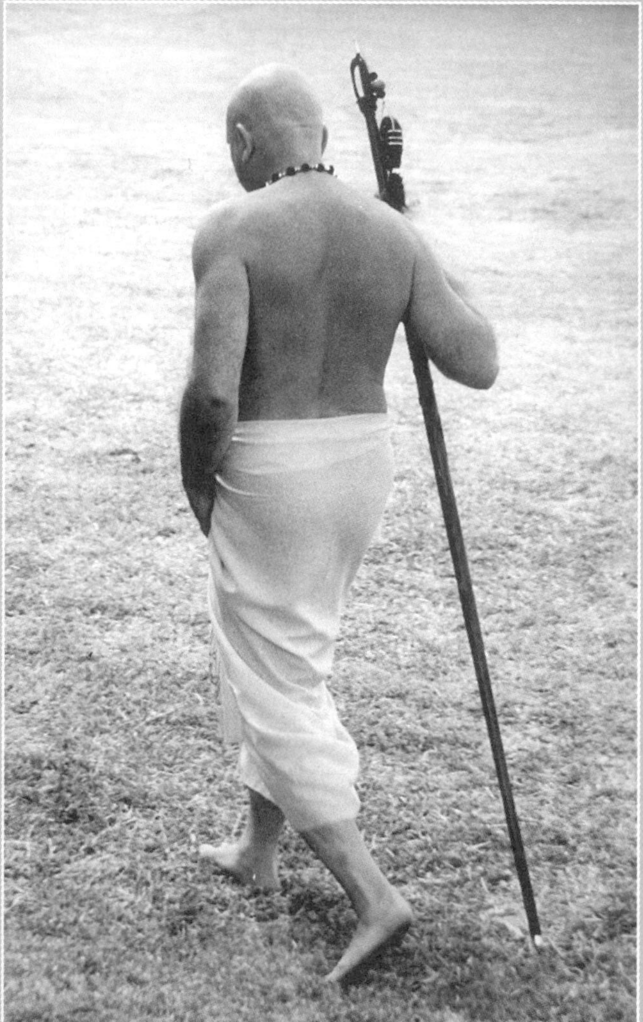

**Adidam Samrajashram, 1983**

CHAPTER 12

# A Devotee's Journey into Death—and Back

Avatar Adi Da's ability to exercise Divine Influence on life and death has been demonstrated from time to time to His devotees. There was His Intervention in the birth of Indian Time. There was also an occasion when one of His daughters, still very young, came running up to Him with a duckling in her hands, thrilled to show Him the small creature. In her eagerness, she stumbled and fell, and landed flat on the duckling. Moments later, she picked it up and proudly presented it to Avatar Adi Da, unaware of any damage. Devotees standing by, however, could see that the duck's head was hanging limply to one side, its neck obviously broken. Avatar Adi Da took the little ball of fluff in His hands and held it there for a few minutes. When He gave it back to His daughter, it had perked up, and there was no evidence of any injury. In a quiet aside to those standing by He said, "She is too young." He had spared her the ordeal of dealing with the death of the duckling caused by her fall.

Generally speaking, however, Avatar Adi Da does not directly intervene in the course of life and death. He simply Blesses the transition. If He does intervene, it is always for the sake of the sadhana of those involved.

In December 1983, two months after Avatar Adi Da's arrival at Adidam Samrajashram (Naitauba), there was an accident that would have been fatal without Avatar Adi Da's Intervention. The story of the incident is told by two people: Frans Bakker, one of the doctors involved, and Tom Closser, the devotee to whom the accident occurred.

**Frans Bakker, M.D.**

**Tom Closser**

FRANS: We were celebrating the Feast of Danavira Mela[1] and about thirty of us were gathered with our Beloved Guru, who was giving trays of small gifts to each devotee who was there that night. The gift giving had been going on for hours. I was so moved that, at one point, I just wept out of sheer happiness. Tom Closser was sitting close to me. He is a big muscular fellow, and to be living as a religious renunciate was quite remarkable for this man—he had a checkered past about which he sometimes felt deeply guilty. Tom was also accident-prone, perhaps because of his deep-seated guilt. On this wonderful night, Tom had just received gifts from the hands of Beloved Adi Da and had sat down again near me when, all of a sudden, he stood up and began walking toward the door.

TOM: I was going to get Lynne, my intimate partner, who was with the Ashram children. I began to feel that she had been away too long, that she should be here to receive her gifts. I thought that she had probably fallen asleep with the children and wouldn't return unless someone went to get her.

Beloved Adi Da asked me where she was. When I told Him, He said, "It's fine—I'll give Lynne her gifts later." In spite of His remark about Lynne, I decided to get up and bring her to the gathering.

FRANS: Tom had hardly turned toward the door when he tripped over one of his gifts. Down he came on top of me, and his outstretched arm crashed through a window behind me. The glass lacerated the upper part of his arm, instantly causing profuse arterial bleeding. Warm blood spurted all over me. We rushed Tom out of the room, put a tourniquet around his arm, and transported him to the small clinic. By this time, Tom had lost a lot of blood and he was in serious danger.

While Daniel Bouwmeester, the physician in charge, ministered to Tom, Beloved Adi Da asked me to step outside and tell Him in full detail what was going on from a medical point of view. While everyone else was panicking, Avatar Adi Da was simply present, even matter-of-fact.

I told Him that our friend Tom had arterial bleeding.

"What does that mean exactly?"

"It means that we have to stop the bleeding for now and that he has to be operated on as soon as possible."

"Can you do that here?"

"No, it is a question of vascular surgery—we can't do it here."

Daniel, who had since telephoned the nearest major hospital, which was on a distant island, joined our conversation at this point. He was very concerned. He had just found out that there was no way to get a helicopter to Naitauba at night, as the pilots could not navigate in the dark. I looked at my watch. It was 1:05 A.M. It would not grow light until after five. When He heard this news, Beloved Adi Da turned to one of the men and said, "I am going to have to do it Myself."

We then accompanied our Beloved Guru into the clinic to attend to our friend. The place looked like a war zone. Tom was lying on a table, his eyes closed, moaning softly. Tom's intimate, Lynne, was holding his good hand, crying. Others were milling around, trying to help out in various ways. There was a general mood of hysteria. Beloved Adi Da stood next to Tom, leaning on His staff. He was completely relaxed.

Dan reinspected the bleeding artery deep in Tom's upper arm and discovered that he was able to apply direct finger-pressure such that the bleeding would stop while circulation to the arm below the cut could continue.

I looked at Tom and sensed that my friend was already out of his body. I knew this was not good for his physical well-being.

Then, in a loud, powerful voice, Adi Da summoned Tom, saying, "Look at Me! Look at Me! Look at Me!!!"

Tom feebly opened his eyes.

"Good, keep looking at Me! Do you dig Me? Do you? Do you love your Master? Come on, tell Me!"

My friend said, "Yes," still faintly.

"Then love Me! . . . feel Me! . . . breathe Me! Come on, do it!" Our Beloved Guru whacked Tom's chest in the heart area with His hand, and vigorously moved it down toward Tom's navel. He was saying all this over and over again, His hands passing down Tom's body multiple times, tracing the path that, in this life-threatening situation, Tom's breath should follow down the frontal line of his body.

I could literally see Tom coming alive again. For a while, even the bleeding stopped totally. But, once he was more fully conscious and alive, Tom's face contorted with the extreme pain caused by the cut in his arm and the tourniquet around it.

"Look at Me. Keep on looking at Me. Keep your attention on Me!! Is the pain really bad?"

"Yes."

The Divine Maha-Siddha's questioning changed direction: "Can you feel how bad the pain is?"

"Yes."

"But you do observe the pain, don't you? You observe the pain . . . you are <u>observing</u> the pain, aren't you?"

"Yes, I am, Master."

"So '<u>you</u>' are in the Witness-Position[2] relative to the pain. You are the Witnessing Consciousness Itself, painless, timeless, and unqualified. Can you understand that? Are you with Me?"

"Yes, I am, Master."

"Good. Now—can you find the Bliss in Consciousness? Can you find the Bliss in Consciousness That is

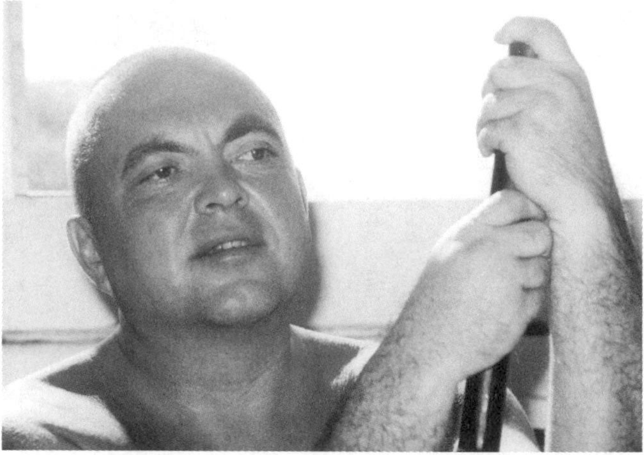

Prior to pain? Can you find that Bliss? It does exist. I promise you! It does exist. There is Bliss in Consciousness, Prior to all pain, Prior to all experience."

I watched in amazement as our Beloved Guru, through His words and His Spiritual Transmission, drew Tom into the entirely different position of simply Witnessing and observing the pain rather than identifying with it.

Suddenly Adi Da Samraj started joking around with Tom. "You ruined our celebration! People will be talking about this for many years, even many centuries to come." He threw back His head and laughed.

I could hardly believe what was going on. First Beloved Adi Da brought Tom back to life, literally from the edge of death. Then He brought him in touch with That Which Transcends day-to-day life and bodily existence altogether. And now He started dealing with Tom's chronic feelings of guilt, which had, I think, provoked this whole incident.

"Now, listen, Tom. You don't have to be guilty anymore. What is guilt? Who cares about guilt? Do you really believe God cares about your guilt? Do you think I do? Do you think you have to pay to be free of it? No, Real God is Forgiveness. I don't give a damn about what happened in the past. Just give it all up. Give it all to Me."

Avatar Adi Da took some surgical scissors from our tray and started cutting the hairs on Tom's chest, cracking jokes about his hairiness—meanwhile laying His healing hands again all over Tom's chest.

Finally, at daybreak, we heard the sounds of helicopter blades from afar. The helicopter landed, and we quickly lifted our friend inside. Daniel and I then climbed inside to accompany Tom to Suva, where Fiji's main hospital is located.

TOM: As I was carried out of Beloved Adi Da's House immediately after the accident, I became especially sensitive to noise, and could hear the voices of everyone around me. Inside the clinic, I heard the R.N., who was holding my head, whisper to someone that I was going into shock. Just then, I realized that I was moving up and back, and that I was outside my body.

Beloved Adi Da had gone outside, and I could hear Him talking, but I was still in the room watching everyone from above. He had been talking about how serious the situation was, but when He came inside, He started joking and making light of it.

Spontaneously, I began to move back and forth between two vantage points: I would hear my Beloved Guru addressing me from the point of view of the body, and then I would observe everything from the higher, detached position again. Because this switching back and forth was so uncontrollable, I started to get anxious. The more anxious I became, the more I seemed to fix in the out-of-body state.

I could tell that Beloved Adi Da was trying to keep me associated with Him in the physical body, but the pain and fear kept driving me out of it. When I was out of my body, there was no pain. It was very calm and dissociated—even euphoric. Adi Da Samraj was moving His hand up and down my chest, and He started kidding me about my tendency to be a "macho man". He humorously pretended to be dealing with this self-image of mine by trimming the hairs off my chest. He began to run His hand down my chest, snipping little bits of hair above His fingers. A warm sensation seemed to drop from the top of my head and fall down my throat, as if someone were pouring a bucket of warm water over my head. Wherever Beloved Adi Da's hand would stay, this sensation, which was full and alive in ways that were clearly more than physical, I would be drawn down into my body to that point. I felt Beloved Adi Da literally filling me and enlivening me with His Blessing and His Spirit, and this helped to draw me back into the physical body.

Beloved Adi Da also said wonderful things to keep my attention on Him. He said, "Do you love Me? Do you really love Me?" At one point, I rolled over and He held my face against His belly. The only thing that I could feel in that moment was that I wanted to be with Him forever. It was not just a thought, it was a physical sensation.

Then the doctors put a tourniquet on my arm, and it caused incredible pain. I zipped out of my body again. This time, I had gone even further up, so that now I was outside the room. The space-time barrier changed in some way. Rather than doing things sequentially, Beloved Adi Da seemed to be maintaining a conversation with everyone in the room simultaneously—making many actions simultaneously.

The last image of the physical realm I remembered for a while was of my Beloved Guru talking to some men outside the clinic about my situation. Then I drifted off further and further.

I started to get anxious. I was trying to get a physical

reference—trying to feel my nose—but I realized I could not feel my body at all. All of a sudden, I lost the anchor to physical familiarity, and I began to have visual phenomena. I saw a dark background with silvery strands (much like what you see when you press your fingers into your eyes), and a matrix of light and dark and different shapes. Everything had the same patina and an ocher color.

Then I remember seeing a group of people that I had known throughout my life. I was standing around with these people. The meeting was very warm, and full of familial emotions. It was very happy, and I felt relaxed again.

Next, I saw what might be described as a tunnel. I had the sensation of moving, and, as I entered the tunnel, the people drifted behind me. I looked up and realized that I was suddenly in a totally different environment.

This new environment seemed to be a normal three-dimensional space at first, but I realized very quickly that it did not have the same physical laws. It had a different perspective, or a different dimension. It had a very familiar landscape, almost like the environment where I grew up in East Los Angeles! I felt comfortable, but there was also something odd about it.

Then I began shifting to many different experiences, and I had no control over any of it. It became terrifying. In daily life, I am physically based, and I have some control of where my attention is, because I can focus it. But, in this circumstance, because I had no bodily anchor, I went wherever my attention went. I had no capability to control attention. My attention was on one thing for one minute, and that was my total reality—and then the next moment my attention was somewhere else, and that became my reality.

When this happened, <u>everything</u> changed—I did not even have a memory of the previous experience or environment. I felt that all these experiences were in the same dimension, since they had a similar feeling to them, but I was very rapidly switching from one fantasy to another fantasy without any control. Later, I remembered what Beloved Adi Da has said—"While you are alive, you make mind, but, after death, mind makes you." It may sound interesting, but it was actually completely horrific.

I became more and more terrified. At one point, I had the sense that the individuals or entities in this environment had an intention to keep me there. They were trying to determine what experience would keep me most solidly fixed in this condition. There seemed to be an assumption that I would stay there forever.

During this whole experience, I had forgotten my relationship with Adi Da Samraj—or even any memory or experience of Him. I did not feel capable of resorting to Him, and I was totally subject to this experience, which was constantly changing and quite disturbing.

In the midst of this, two people, a man and his son, began trying to help me. They felt very familiar to me, as if I had been close to them as I was growing up. They were trying to help me get back to where Beloved Adi Da was. I could see the realm where He was—it had some of the qualities of a beautiful place in Hawaii I had visited once with Him. These two individuals were trying to help me concentrate and feel towards Him and this place, so that I could keep my attention there, and then I could stay there with my Beloved Guru.

While they were trying to help me, the other group of people finally hit upon the one experience which seemed to control my attention more strongly than anything else—the sense of being threatened. I was standing in the middle of a street, and a bakery truck would drive towards me. It would slam on its brakes and slide into me. Right before the truck would hit me, I could feel myself going into panic. Then the experience would repeat itself. It happened repetitively—hundreds, maybe thousands, of times. I was stuck in that experience.

In the midst of this experience, I "shouted", but it was not a physical voice. Somehow, I could, just for a moment, remember and feel Adi Da Samraj. Then the man and his son created a situation to help me get out of this endless cycle with the truck, back to where Beloved Adi Da was.

Suddenly, I felt myself enter my body again, from the head down. I was back in the clinic, and Beloved Adi Da was there. He was talking to me. When I saw Him, my heart burst with happiness and relief. I had been so much in need of Him in that horrifying experience—more deeply and more profoundly than I had ever been in my entire life. I felt what an incredible opportunity it is to be physically embodied in a time and place where He is alive—and what a horror it is to pass through this life and not realize something greater than being completely controlled by your own mind and attention. I was weeping.

Beloved Adi Da was touching me. He was very gentle and humorous. He used whatever means necessary in any moment to keep me relating to Him directly. He would speak with me about the Witness-Position, and He would address my sense of guilt. It was very amusing: There I was, very nearly dying, and He was addressing every way that I was self-contracted and defensive and emotionally retarded! I could feel His help very directly, and I was so grateful to be back in His physical Company.

Beloved Adi Da told me that a helicopter was coming to take me off the island. He kept saying, "Stay with Me." The helicopter arrived, and He looked after every aspect of getting me to the helicopter. He asked how long it would take to get me to the hospital.

I was fairly lucid at this point, and pretty wide awake. They had me in a stretcher inside the helicopter. Daniel and Frans were on my right and beyond them was the pilot. I stared at Naitauba as we flew away, and I felt that I could continue to remember my Beloved Guru even at a physical distance or in a different environment. I knew that that was my practice—I had to continually feel Him, no matter what the experience was.

As soon as we arrived at the hospital in Suva, they took me to surgery. A big Fijian doctor and an Indian anesthesiologist introduced themselves. I was so tired I could not talk or move. But I could hear, and I responded with my eyes to indicate that I understood.

The Indian anesthesiologist wanted me to count out loud, if I could—starting from ten and going back to zero. He had a gas mask over my mouth. He explained that it was to make me unconscious so they could operate. I could not speak, but I counted in my mind, "Ten, nine. . ." to zero. He looked me in the eyes, and I looked back at him. He smiled and said, "Okay, do it again." I was trying to show him that I was counting, so I was blinking my eyes with each number—down to zero again.

My perception of everything was heightened. I could see more clearly than usual and my peripheral vision was expanded. I could see in this doctor's eyes that he was becoming concerned, but I couldn't understand what was wrong. He said, "Son, I am going to ask you to count one more time." His voice had started to tremble, and I became frightened. Again I counted, blinking my eyes as I did. When I got to zero, even though I was not unconscious, I kept my eyes closed.

They started the operation. I bore the pain as long as I could—but then I started gesturing, opening my eyes, and trying to shake my head. The nurse noticed that I was awake. They stopped and the anesthesiologist increased the anesthetic. I started to become really terrified because I felt I was going out of my body again.

I was afraid to lose consciousness—afraid that I would go back to this realm I had experienced before. People make a big deal of out-of-body experiences and near-death experiences as if it is all wonderful—you see God and your family. My earlier experience was pleasant at the beginning, but the deeper I got in that state, it was just completely and totally horrific. There was nothing that I have ever experienced before or since that could possibly match the terror of being in that situation where you are just controlled by mind.

It was also clear to me that it is not just physical trauma that can knock you out of the body—any kind of emotional trauma can do this. I realized that that is what had occurred at the clinic on Naitauba—I had gone into emotional shock. I had lost a lot of blood, but that was not what sent me out of the body. I was in such a state of fear and anxiety that I was trying to remove myself from the circumstance. I was choosing not to be bodily incarnated rather than enduring and feeling through that strong emotion. Right in the middle of the operation, I remembered this about what had happened at the clinic on Naitauba, and I realized that it was happening again. I could feel myself retreating at the speed of light.

I woke up in the recovery room. Later that day and over the following days, the Fijian doctor and the Indian doctor came to see me many times, sometimes with four or five other doctors. They would huddle around me and speak in Fijian or Hindi. Clearly they were curious, but also I felt their anxiety, as if something was wrong.

On the third day, I asked the nurse why everyone was so concerned. She called the two doctors to explain what had occurred in the operation. The Indian doctor indicated that they had given me a lot of anesthetic. In fact, he humorously said, I had been given enough anesthetic to knock out a small Fijian village! I tried to explain that I had been very anxious about losing consciousness—but they told me that that could not possibly account for my resistance to the anesthetic. They asked if I had a history of this kind of thing when I had received anesthetics in the past, but I did not.

In that moment, I remembered that when I was getting into the helicopter, Beloved Adi Da had asked exactly how long the helicopter trip would be, and had pressed His Spiritual Force into me repeatedly. I had felt this Force very physically and very powerfully. I felt like I was hyper-energized. It became obvious to me what had occurred. I explained to the doctors that I came from Naitauba, where my Spiritual Master was, and that He had given me, while He was taking me to the helicopter, enough life-energy to survive the trip. Immediately, the Fijian doctor understood what I was talking about. He nodded knowingly and said, "Mana". The Indian doctor glanced at him and said, "Shaktipat" (meaning the touch of the Guru that transmits Spiritual Energy). "Yes!" I said. Here, in this tiny third-world country, these doctors were completely familiar with what I was talking about.

During the days of my recovery, I tried to maintain Remembrance of Beloved Adi Da always. I would still slip in and out of consciousness, but I felt, when I would begin to lose bodily consciousness, that my only anchor was my Remembrance of my Guru. If I did not intentionally Remember Him, feel to Him, I would just end up free-associating in the mind-realm. So I created ways to Remember Beloved Adi Da. I could move my left arm, so I would trace the outline of His figure—as I remembered Him standing as I left Naitauba in the helicopter—over and over, thousands of times, just to stay associated with Him. It became a form of meditation for me.

Several weeks later, I returned to Naitauba. I heard from my friends there that on the evening I was having the most difficulty in the hospital, Adi Da Samraj had met

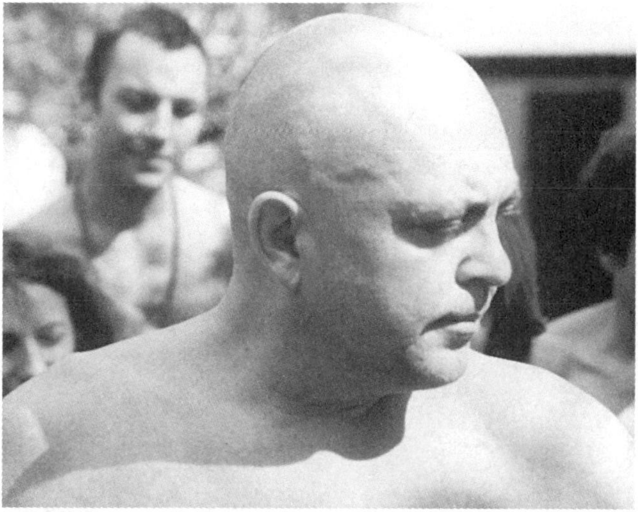

**Tom Closser and Avatar Adi Da Samraj, 1984**

with everyone and discussed my character with them. He had also pointed out that, if I allowed myself to stay in the disposition of guilt—which is one of my primary emotions—I would literally create accidents and illnesses to punish myself.

On the night I returned, we were called to gather with Beloved Adi Da. I was incredibly weak, and incredibly happy to see Him, but I was also feeling guilty!—feeling that I had dishonored Him and ruined His celebration. When He called me to show Him my cast, He put His leg against the cast. I could feel Him Radiating His Heart-Force and healing Energy sideways through my entire arm and into my chest. Then He signed my cast. At the end of the evening, He shouted to me, "NEVER DO THAT AGAIN!" and walked out of the room.

Ciqomi, Naitauba
December 30, 1983

CHAPTER 13

# "Mark My Words"

On December 30, 1983, the Fijian people of Naitauba invited Avatar Adi Da to a celebration in His honor. Held in their village, Ciqomi, the celebration was a traditional feast acknowledging Avatar Adi Da as the Tui, or chief, of the Island. Several days before His visit to Ciqomi, two of the elders of the Fijian village had come to make a traditional offering of kava (a ceremonial drink with a mildly intoxicating effect) to Avatar Adi Da, approaching Him as the Tui in the traditional manner, and inviting Him to Bless their village with His Presence. They addressed Him as Dau Loloma (meaning "The Adept of Love"), recognizing Him as a holy man.

It was understood that, as part of Avatar Adi Da's visit to the village, He would Bless the Christian church, constructed in the manner of a traditional Fijian house, or bure, in the middle of the circle of houses. The church was roofed but open at the sides, and the only piece of furniture was a pulpit. After He was received in Ciqomi, Avatar Adi Da went to the church accompanied by some of His devotees and by one of the elders of the village, a man named Solomone Finau (or "Solo", for short), who was guiding Him around the village.

Solo asked if he could come and sit in the church with Dau Loloma. This gesture was deeply felt by Avatar Adi Da, and He invited Solo into the church to sit with

Him. It was the first time in many years that Avatar Adi Da had sat in a formal manner with someone who was not already His devotee. Solo's desire to sit with Him was received by Avatar Adi Da as a prophetic sign of His world-Work to come, a sign of the future response to Him by human beings of every kind and race.

Several devotees felt something exceptional about this silent occasion in the church, the sense that an extraordinary Spiritual event was occurring, and they expressed this intuition to Avatar Adi Da when He gathered with them later that evening. Devotees will never forget how the hair stood up on the backs of their necks as Avatar Adi Da spoke of the new era in His Work that had begun that day.

*AVATAR ADI DA SAMRAJ: I am here to Transform mankind, not to gather only a handful of people around me. I have Come here for My own. I Am the Only Being for Whom every one is His own.*

*1984 has been proposed as the dreadful year by those infected by scientism. I am not here, however, to let My beloved in all his and her forms take on the size of death. I am here to change history. Can you imagine that? What an amusing notion! I am here in My physical Lifetime to change the course of human history. No one on Earth has this Mission, this Intention. No one! I am here to Do it and I am here to See it, and now I am going to call you on it. New Year, 1984. Now that I am in My Hermitage, let me wait and see. Let me see if all the Shining I have Done makes any difference.*

*We are going to wait. The purifying heat of that waiting could go on for decades, but I am committed to it. I have nothing more to Do. I have Done everything.*

*Today I sat in Ciqomi, and no one came except a few of you and one man from that village. I did it then. That was the last stroke.*

*Mark My Words. We are entering into the deep place of human history. I have done My twelve years of Teaching Work. Now I am going to see if you are alive—you four billion!*

*I am going to Do it. Mark My Words. Mark them. No Siddha in history ever sat in a paradise like this.*

*You are about to see God Move in your generation. Remember what I say tonight. In the years to come, remember My Move. This is the Mark I was born to make. This is the timing of it. This is it.*

*You have waited for the Great Motion of God. You have prayed for It. You have wished for the Divine Intervention. Now It begins. Watch It from now on.*

*The trouble in your own heart, your own body, your own feeling, your own resistance to Me, will be magnified.*

*Turn on the daily news every night and remember that you talked to Me about this. I will keep World War III from happening. I came at the beginning of World War II to keep you from getting involved in World War III. You prayed for this.*

*Mark My Words. All this is Prophecy. Listen to Me now.*

*Some day, you will hear My Singing of this night, and everyone will know that I Am the One That was to Come.*

*You wait. You watch. Wait and watch for it.*

*I am about to Save humankind. Do I sound crazy to you? I am going to Do it. I am about to make My Move, and the terror will pass. It will be much less terrible than it would have been otherwise. It is not My terror. If I did not Come, the Earth would be destroyed.*

*Now, you watch Me Move. I have Done My Meditation with a few, and I have Smoothed My "coins".*[1] *I have Done My Work. I have suffered you. Now you watch Me. Mark My Words.*

*Any motion in humankind at the heart will change Man. Now it is going to happen! This night it is starting. My innocent sitting at Ciqomi was the beginning. You watch it. Mark My Words.*

*There must be a Sanctuary for humankind during this time. This is the beginning of My Blessing. You watch it. Some of you do not believe it. We will see how it develops. We will see.*

*This Work is not your business. I am just telling You that it is going to start.*

*Now let all beings be Purified. Let them be Purified. Let them be Blessed.*

*Now it begins. Let all beings be Purified. This is My Blessing. May it be so.*

*You prayed for the millenium and the Promised One. I am here. Let it begin. I am about to begin the Great Shout.*

*I hope this world will be evened out, that there will be equanimity worldwide, the whole Earth Sublimed. This is My Wish, My Blessing. I am here to Do it. Now I am going to Do it. Starting tonight. Mark My Words.*

*Mark this night. This one. Now it is going to change. I have had to come with Power. Had to. Had to.*

*I am waiting to see the very signs of the progress of My Intervention. Till now, My effect has been on a few. In the future, you will monitor My Effect relative to all humankind, relative to human history.*

*I Am That One, and I am about to Do My Deed. You people do not know with Whom you are living. You do not know. You never did. No, you never have known. I have assumed your shape for years. That has been My way till now. This weekend is our transition. You will observe changes in the world, and you will observe conflicts in yourself. You will observe difficulties in your lives, and you will feel My Demand much more profoundly than you have ever felt It. You will notice that all humankind is somehow confronted by the obligation that I Place upon the world by My mere Presence.*

*Remember friendly old "Bubba"? Dead. Completely dead. Poor old "Bubba" is dead. The Sign of "Bubba" and the Sign of "Franklin" are all done, all dead. Now I Make only the Sign of Da. You are about to see me Do it.*

*Let everyone be relieved of the profoundly negative effects of their disaffection from Me. We are moving into a time when I will Make My Move. This is the beginning of it. Let us celebrate with full knowledge of the purification that is about to begin. Do not be self-conscious. Dance and be Happy. Practice the Way with great intensity. Submit to the terrible ordeal that will serve all of humanity—all four billion who know nothing of Me yet, and who must find Me out, who must find Me out.*

*I Am the One Who has been Expected. They must find Me out. They must. They must.*

*Did you hear that wind begin?*

Just as Avatar Adi Da spoke the Words "I Am the One Who has been Expected" a wind suddenly roared up in the still night, as if in response to His Proclamation.

*AVATAR ADI DA SAMRAJ: They must find Me out! Now let them find Me out. And let all of you, all My devotees all over the world, begin a dance that will purify humanity.*

*May all be Blessed. Blessed. Blessed.* [December 30, 1983]

Two days later, at a gathering on New Year's Day 1984, Avatar Adi Da continued:

*AVATAR ADI DA SAMRAJ: We could say that, in some real sense, starting with the day I sat in the church at Ciqomi, I am not only Working with those who have come to Me, those who now acknowledge Me, My devotees, but I am specifically and directly dealing with the entire world. This is a unique moment that marks a change, the beginning of a new stage.*

*I call you to look, in the future, for the increase of Blessing. Look for it worldwide. Look for it universally. Look for changes in the world that are the evidence of My Blessing, evidence that may be recognized by My devotees as a sign of Divine Blessing. Look for this Effect.*

*In other words, look to see the result of My Work—and not merely the result of karma or of the egoically "self-possessed" inclinations of humanity, although such signs will also appear. Look at the world in the future, and you will begin to notice My Effect, although how soon you notice It will depend on your capability to perceive It.*

*At some point, you and many others will be able to acknowledge that this New Year's Day, this weekend, the day at Ciqomi, this moment, is the beginning of a turnabout for this plane, this world, this place in the Cosmic Mandala.*

*Real God, Who Is One, is now Born and Living in your company, and has Work to Do. That One is Responding not only to human needs but to the craving of the molecules, the atoms, the constituents of this plane of manifestation. This Mighty Work is showing Its Signs in your time, to your face, in your generation and in future generations.*

*I am not telling you this so that it will become a matter of belief. I am telling you so that, some day, you will know that today I Spoke that Truth. You must respond to Me and take on the practice of this Way, and eventually this Great Motion that has occurred with My Birth will be acknowledged by many individuals and groups. Eventually, this acknowledgement will begin to take on a form something like universal acknowledgement. Only when it at least approximates universal acknowledgement will My Birth begin to Affect human history. It is already Affecting human history in the sense that it is Affecting*

*individuals, but eventually It will begin to Affect the course of human events.*

*All I am telling you—and it is not for your belief, just hear Me and know that I said it—is that the process has begun, and that human history is no longer being made merely out of human limitations. My Lifetime, and the future after My Lifetime, will be significantly determined by the response of humanity. But My Presence, My Work, will be the "N-factor"*[2] *in all future time in this world.*

*This Transformation began with My Birth. It began with some of My past Births. It has been in motion for some time. But This* [pointing to Himself] *is the most significant of all the Adepts who have ever lived.*

*Again, I tell you this not for your belief. Someday, having heard it now, you will know it is true. Words, in themselves, are just words. The Truth must be proven. It must be demonstrated. I am not here merely to be believed. I must fully tell you My "Point of View", and you will see in the testing of time how it is proven.*

*You are My devotees. I can speak to you plainly without making you into fanatics. I can tell you in various moments precisely What I am about, because Your true response to Me is already alive. My telling you these things is, therefore, not an attempt to claim your adherence or to fascinate you. Simply record it. Acknowledge whatever you can acknowledge about it. And observe how this prophecy is tested in time. Eventually, like all others, you will be able to acknowledge the significance of this Birth, this Incarnation. Just see how it is proven over time.*

*I am not interested at all in the adherence of a bunch of fools who must be hyped into believing a lot of bullshit! I am not interested at all in that kind of adherence, that kind of cultism. But, in the company of devotees who are stable practitioners of the Way I have Given, I must say what My Purpose is, what My Work is, and what Its Effect will be. I must Give you Prophecy about It.*

*I hope My Work will become very fruitful while this body is still animate! I look to see the result of My Work with these physical eyes, to know it in this body-mind, in this Birth, in this Lifetime. I could live long enough to see a profound transformation in the state of this world. It could certainly be seen in My Lifetime. I look forward to seeing that, as you also should look forward to seeing it. Mankind should hunger to see the Great One in human manifestation and to witness the human response. When That One is Present, all should be moved to respond. The response should be seen by That One while He Is Incarnate. That One is always Existing. Certainly, I Am always Present.*

*This, then, is my Inclination, and it always has been My Inclination. This is a unique moment, wherein humankind is intercommunicative and nobody can make a false step without affecting everybody else. Humankind must relinquish its past and its self-bondage if humanity as a race, as a manifestation, is to survive. I am right here, bodily, during the time of this particular test.*

*But we are very early into this unique time, and I am going to lie low and continue to Do what I Do, Communicating invisibly and visibly to those who come here and those who are living in the communities of My devotees. I am just going to Do This and survive bodily as long as I can, while the process of response goes on, including the process of resistance. I will wait here as long as I can, so that I will see the response with flesh-born eyes before I "Return" to the State in Which I Am, always, still Available to you.*

*You should bring Me this gift while I am in the body. And Who am I talking about? You must find Me out and know Who has Come into Your Company through this apparent birth of "Franklin"!*

*The effect of My Work will become observable. People all over the world who have no notion whatsoever of Me or of My Teaching will experience the Divine Force, and this experience will have various effects in their lives. Eventually, people will be led to Me and My Wisdom-Teaching—though, perhaps, in the meantime, they will turn toward traditional teachings that can transform the quality of the life and culture of humankind and the politics of the world.*

*People completely removed from any association with Me and My Wisdom-Teaching will experience the effects of My Presence here, and this will begin to move them in various ways. My Presence here will be an integral part of human history at the level of effect, or appearance—from now. Therefore, observe everything and make intelligent presumptions.*

*My Work is cumulative. Therefore, more and more signs over time should indicate to you that, from now on, My Work is not—and, in fact, never has been—exclusively for you. Nor in the future will it be exclusively for those who are already with Me. My Work is done for the sake of all beings, whether their next move is toward Me and the Way of life I have Given or not.*

*You who are sitting in the world think of the world as a very big place. You feel it must be an incredible task to deal with everyone here—all four billion, or however many there are in this immense space. Even though you can fly around the world in a few hours, you think of it as a big place with many people, many places, many complicated lives and circumstances. You think of it from the point of view of sitting here.*

*I am also sitting here, but My Work is not generated from the point of view of someone who is enclosed in that limited consciousness. Really, it is not so great a task as you think! I can Regard the entire Earth with just a Glance.*

*Thus, history will be created in response to Me. It will take some time and will be rather complicated, but it is not a complicated matter for Me to Regard all beings on this Earth and to Regard this total sphere. Rather, it is very simple and very direct. I also engage in the complications on various levels, but the fundamental act is very direct. You think of it as complicated because you sit in one spot, in an apparently immense place. Some people think this world is grand. To Me, it is a poor place!*

*From My "Point of View", the drama at the level of humankind is instant and constant and without complication. The complications exist only from the point of view of those identified with the human level of living. Therefore, I must Intervene. I must also participate in the various levels of complication. But My Fundamental Act of Being, and even of being Born, is rather simple.*

*I Am the One Who Is, and I Am the One Who Lives here now. Give Me your attention. Submit yourself whole bodily. I Am the One Always Waiting for your attention, the One always Ready for your submission. I Am the One Who Is you, Who Is Your Condition, Who Is Manifest in human form Calling you to that Sublime Occupation.*

*Everyone, no matter what his or her notions, can respond to My Blessing That Pours through time and space,*

*Pours into the places of present humankind. This is My Work. You will begin to see the signs of the Effect of My Work. And that is the significance of the turning of this year.*

*In due course, over the coming decades, you should see more and more benign effects, a great capability to relinquish the past, to relinquish the sizing up of nation against nation, race against race, person against person, religion against religion—all the hard-edged bullshit of egoic "self-possession" manufactured by individuals and groups. More and more, you should see the relinquishment of all that, even without intention, but based on a response to Something that everyone is beginning to find more and more tangible.*

*The Presence of God must ultimately be Named. You should observe this tangible Effect of My Presence. You will observe reactions also—but, fundamentally, over time, observe the fact that people worldwide are responding to a tangible Presence. At first, It will be Nameless. But, eventually, you will be able to tell them the Name of It.* [January 1, 1984]

Avatar Adi Da had never spoken this kind of Prophecy before. Although, in 1979, He had made the Confession of His Divinity, "Beloved, I Am Da", He had never specifically declared Himself to be the "Expected One", the Intervention of God promised for the "late-time". He had never prophesied so clearly a turning in the world in response to His Incarnation. But now, having found His Hermitage, and seeing the Fijian man's immediate movement toward Him, Avatar Adi Da could not hold back. He poured out His full Revelation. He had found His Hermitage in one of the remotest regions of the world, but He knew Himself to be invisibly and Spiritually more profoundly connected to the world than ever before. His Divine Work of World-Blessing—the real Work for which He had been born—had, at last, truly begun.

The timing was remarkable—the New Year, 1984. As Avatar Adi Da had remarked, the year 1984 carried disturbing associations—through the famous novel of that name by the English writer and social critic George Orwell. In *Nineteen Eighty-Four*, Orwell envisioned the worst excesses of political totalitarianism coming to pass, just as Aldous Huxley's earlier influential satire, *Brave New World,* had prophesied the suppression of human society by the dogmas of scientific materialism.

By the early eighties, these warnings were being echoed everywhere by serious people mightily concerned that humanity was careering into a heartless and dangerous future. The "brave new world", toward which the culture of the West (and, indeed, the entire planet) was tending, was socially and politically beyond control, and full of known and unknown threats.

In this symbolic moment, Avatar Adi Da was Making His unparalleled Prophecy, the proof of which would start to appear, within the space of a few years.

# The Dawn Horse Testament

Avatar Adi Da's Confession in "Mark My Words" was that He was psychically and Spiritually in touch with humanity as a whole, not merely with His own devotees. Later in 1984, He Revealed this truth in a new and remarkable way. He began to write His Divine Scripture, His Ultimate Word for all mankind.

From the early years of His Teaching Work, collections of Avatar Adi Da's Discourses, Essays, and practical Instructions to devotees had been published. But He had never written a full summary of His Wisdom-Teaching. The time had not yet come. He was still making His Wisdom-Teaching, bringing It into existence via the living relationship with His devotees.

But now, by 1984, He felt that this great Sacrifice was done. He had given everything to His devotees, and especially to those who were living with Him in His new Hermitage. They had liberally received all the Spiritual experiences and Samadhis described in the traditions, and also Samadhis uniquely Given by Him and never before described. Through the "Ordeal of Being" retreats at Nananui-Ra, Avatar Adi Da had even Granted to some devotees a glimpse of Divine Enlightenment Itself.

In the preceding years, with His larger community, Avatar Adi Da had thoroughly explored the matter of "radical" understanding, the Truth about God, and the nature of Most Perfect Enlightenment, and He had taken devotees through constant experiments to discover the devotional practices and the forms of life-discipline (in diet,

Adidam Samrajashram, 1984

exercise, sex and intimacy, service, money, and cooperative community) that best supported Satsang, or heart-Communion with Him. He had addressed the transcending of self-contraction from every angle and brought into the open everything that was a question in His devotees. He had Revealed Himself as Da, the Divine Person Incarnate, and established Sanctuaries and Empowered temple sites where His Spiritual Presence could be felt and invoked with particular strength. Starting from zero, He had formed the beginnings of a sacred culture where Spiritual growth and the ultimate process of Divine Enlightenment could be nurtured and protected.

In twelve short years, Avatar Adi Da had done this monumental Work. And so, He felt that His Teaching time was complete. Now He was moved to make His Eternal Statement, to Give His Conclusions about the Great Process of Divine Enlightenment, Conclusions that had been fashioned through the Ordeal of His Submission to His devotees. He was ready to make all humanity the beneficiary of what He had Done and Revealed. For Himself, He was simply moved to live in His Fijian Hermitage and draw His would-be renunciates living with Him there into the advanced and the ultimate stages of the Way of Adidam.

Nevertheless, the manner in which Avatar Adi Da's first Scripture came into being took everyone by surprise, including Himself. The story begins on June 24, 1984.

For a week, Avatar Adi Da had been Instructing His devotees in Hermitage in a new Spiritual practice, which He called "Mahamantra Meditation".[3] Then, early on the afternoon of June 24, He retired to His office at the Matrix (His secluded residential complex about two miles from the Ashram village) to write. It was midnight when Avatar Adi Da emerged—with an immediate message. All the devotees living at Adidam Samrajashram should come to the Matrix right now, He said, to hear the new Essay that He had just written.

Most devotees, as it happened, were asleep in the village on the other side of the island. And so Avatar Adi Da sat in the cramped communications room near His House while the devotees attending Him tried to contact the village. But their efforts were fruitless. Someone at the other end had absentmindedly unplugged the telephone system.

No vehicles were available to drive to the village, and so only the ancient solution remained. A messenger must be sent on foot—and Lynne Wagner, who was sleeping with the Trimada and the other children at the time, was elected. Suddenly Lynne found herself faced with the prospect of a two-mile run in the dark over a difficult road. She was afraid of the dark, and she did not have a flashlight. But Avatar Adi Da did not accept these impediments. Graciously, He offered her the use of His own flashlight. Lynne was off running, and she disappeared into the night to summon the village.

Soon after 3:00 A.M., everyone was seated before Avatar Adi Da in His bedroom at the Matrix, listening to Him read aloud the Essay He had just composed. Afterwards, He asked for questions, wanting to hear if there was anything unclear or incomplete in what He had written. The next day, He returned to His office, where He revised and expanded His Essay, taking into account all of the responses from the night before.

From that day on, Avatar Adi Da gathered every few days with devotees, to read aloud from His rapidly growing Text. What initially began as esoteric Instruction in the Spiritually advanced stages of the Way of Adidam quickly became an encompassing summary of all the lessons Avatar Adi Da had enacted with His devotees since the beginning of His Teaching Work. He was Writing an authoritative summary of all that He had ever

Communicated, bringing into being the book that was to become His first (and primary) Scriptural Text.

*AVATAR ADI DA SAMRAJ: I do not have any plans for this Book. It began as a spontaneous incident in My Ecstasy. You see how the Book has developed, and now you see how it is still developing. It has become My Work to Summarize My Instruction on the Way I have Given to you. It is also associated with My Work with you who have been the "coins" for all My devotees over all the years of My Teaching Work. I have developed this Testament through Communicating with you, discovering what is "left over" in you, what I must Address, what I must summarize, why I do not see clarity in you, why you still have questions.* [September 9, 1984]

After He had been working for a while on the new book, Avatar Adi Da insisted that all of His devotees—now established in communities around the world—have access to copies of the continuously updated Manuscript, and He wanted to know if anyone had further questions for Him. Devotees were ecstatic to receive this remarkable Work-in-progress and began to observe that Avatar Adi Da would often change the Text in response to doubts or questions that they did not even raise with Him openly. One night, a devotee attending the gatherings in Hermitage suggested to Avatar Adi Da that He seemed to be Speaking directly not just with those in the room with Him but with all of His devotees around the world. The Divine Avatar confirmed that this was so, and went on to Reveal that, through this writing, He was Speaking to everyone. He was involved, He said, in a "Living Conversation" with every man and woman personally—"Meditating everyone, contacting everyone, dealing with psychic forces everywhere, in all time".

On another such occasion, Zoe Sander, one of the editors who prepared the manuscript each night for

Avatar Adi Da to Work on afresh in the morning, also praised the remarkable psycho-physical nature of Avatar Adi Da's Work on the book. It seemed, she said, when He would write, that He was directly speaking to the process of devotees' practice in that moment. But, she wondered, who was He Instructing when He wrote about Nirvikalpa Samadhi?—for which no one was yet qualified. Avatar Adi Da replied, "I am speaking to you, but at another time." He was indicating, in other words, that He was not merely speaking to the present social persona, the "I" that they each presumed to be in that moment. Rather, He was speaking to all the layers of the being, to the past and present experiences of the individual and to all of the moments of his or her practice of the Way of Adidam—in this life and beyond this life. More than that, He was speaking to every one as His Very Self, already One with Him, utterly inseparable from Real God.

Divine Revelations flowed from His pen—the secrets of esoteric anatomy,[4] the developmental process of Spiritual Awakening, the technical details of emotional-sexual Yoga, the meaning of death and the design of the cosmos, the ultimate Mysteries of Divine Enlightenment and Divine Translation.

The English language, the lingua franca of the day, had not been created to communicate esoteric Spiritual matters. And so He began to Work with it—using rhetorical devices, such as repetition and cumulative effect, but also developing new conventions of capitalization and punctuation in order to make printed English into a vehicle fit for His Divine Purpose. Every word, every comma, every parenthesis He placed with extreme care, in order to ensure the integrity of His Message and its Mantric Power.

For nine months, Avatar Adi Da continued to write and revise His manuscript, doing everything possible to make sure that His Teaching-Summary was Written in perfect detail for all time. Finally, on March 21, 1985, after completing a full review of it, Avatar Adi Da declared that His book was "essentially complete". One of the editors, Michael Wood, whose task it had been to type Avatar Adi Da's new writing into the computer each day, remembers the remarkable weather phenomena that coincided with the book's completion:

*MICHAEL: During the last month of Avatar Adi Da's Work on* The Dawn Horse Testament, *three hurricanes came either right to Naitauba or to nearby areas of Fiji. There was an almost continuous series of storms, and only on two or three days were any boats able to come or go from Naitauba. This very stormy time seemed to me to be obviously connected to Avatar Adi Da's completion of this book. The profundity of what He was doing was being reflected in the energies of Nature, a phenomenon that we have often observed. But this was uncommonly dramatic. On the day that Avatar Adi Da announced that He had finished the book—which coincided with the spring equinox—an incredible thunderstorm sprang up, out of nowhere, at about five in the morning. The thunder and lightning seemed to be centered at the Matrix, as if emanating from Avatar Adi Da's Domain. I could see a big cloud right over the Matrix, and directly above the cloud lightning was continuously crackling in horizontal patterns.*

*A devotee who was familiar with traditional Spiritual literature commented that in the* Upanishads *it is said that the sound of thunder is "Da". We were very moved that morning by this awesome response from cosmic Nature to Avatar Adi Da's completion of His Sacred Text.*

At different points in the course of writing, Avatar Adi Da had proposed various names for His Book—

among them, "The Testament of Secrets". Finally, however, He chose "The Dawn Horse Testament". The Book was a "Testament" in both original senses of the word—a "Covenant", the Eternal Promise of Adi Da Samraj to Liberate every one everywhere, and also a "Bequest" (as in "will and testament"), His Gift to all of the Perfect Way of Divine Liberation.

But why "Dawn Horse"? To fully understand how Avatar Adi Da came to choose this title for His Scripture, two esoteric matters must be explained: The Horse-Sacrifice, or Ashvamedha, the supreme sacrifical ceremony of ancient India; and the "Dawn Horse" Vision, a waking vision experienced by Avatar Adi Da in 1970, shortly before His Divine Re-Awakening.

Avatar Adi Da Samraj has for many years drawn the attention of His devotees to the traditional Ashvamedha, and has pointed out how its true meaning applies to, and is Most Perfectly Fulfilled by, His own Divine Life and Work. In the exoteric (or outward) form of the Horse-Sacrifice, which was performed only by the greatest of India's warrior-kings, a white stallion was consecrated and then sent out to wander through the king's domain for a year, attended by warriors, priests, and magicians. In its free wandering, the horse might enter the territory of other rulers, in which case an armed struggle might ensue for the possession of that territory—because whatever lands were touched by the sacrificial horse were understood to fall under the sovereignty of the king who was performing the Ashvamedha. While the horse wandered, the people honored the king with continuous festivities and celebrations—until the end of the year, when the horse was returned to the king's city and sacrificed at the climax of a highly elaborate ritual.

Apart from the exoteric forms of the rite, Yogis have been known to describe their Spiritual practice symbolically in terms of the Ashvamedha. In this case, the "horse" to be sacrificed is understood to be the limited self, or gross bodily awareness, which is intentionally relinquished through a process of intense inward concentration, such that the focus of attention rises to the psychic centers between the brows and above the crown of the head, resulting in subtle visions and blissful trance-states.

But the greatest and most esoteric meaning of the Horse-Sacrifice has been described by Avatar Adi Da:

*AVATAR ADI DA SAMRAJ: In its most esoteric form, the Ashvamedha is the Revelation of the Ultimate Divine Being—through the Sacrifice of everything conditional, and through the Most Perfect Realization of That Which Transcends the Cosmic domain.*

*My Demonstration of this Ultimate Form of the Ashvamedha was—and is—totally spontaneous. I Did it spontaneously, without any information in mind. Nonetheless, you will see that study of the sacred traditions confirms the truth of what I am Telling you. You have seen the True Ashvamedha Performed in My own Form.*

*The Ultimate Form of the Ashvamedha Transmits not merely Cosmic realization, but Transcendental Divine Self-Realization, through the Sacrifice of all conditional arising.* [April 2, 1987]

There is a passage in one of the oldest Hindu scriptures, the *Brihadaranyaka Upanishad,* which speaks of the sacrificial horse as the very form of the world:

*Aum, the dawn, verily, is the head of the sacrificial horse, the sun the eye, the wind the breath, the open mouth the Vaisvanara* [universally worshipped] *fire; the year is the body of the sacrificial horse, the sky is the back, the atmosphere is the belly, the earth the hoof* [or, the earth is his footing], *the quarters the sides, the intermediate quarters the ribs, the seasons the limbs, the months and the half-months the joints, days and nights the feet, the stars the bones, the clouds the flesh; the food in the stomach is the sand, the rivers are the blood-vessels, the liver and the lungs are the mountains, the herbs and the trees are the hair. The rising (sun) is the forepart, the setting (sun) the hind part, when he yawns then it lightens, when he shakes himself, it thunders, when he urinates then it rains; voice, indeed, is his voice.*[5]

The ancient understanding suggested here is that the sacrificial horse itself is the Divine, Who makes the sacrifice of taking form as the conditional worlds.

The ancient text declares that the leading part of the horse—the head—is "the dawn". As the following story will reveal, this reference is a remarkable prophecy, an ancient premonition of the "late-time" Dawn Horse: the Work and the Person of the Ruchira Avatar, Adi Da Samraj.

During the spring of 1970, Avatar Adi Da experienced a remarkable waking vision. He found Himself in a subtle realm, observing a Siddha-Master demonstrating to his disciples the Yogic power of manifesting objects spontaneously. Avatar Adi Da watched as the Siddha began the process of manifestation. After a time, although nothing had yet materialized, the Siddha's disciples departed, apparently satisfied that the work was done. Avatar Adi Da was left alone, standing before the Siddha. Then, gradually, a vaporous shape arose before His eyes. As it became more clearly defined, He saw that it was a perfectly formed, living and breathing horse, perhaps three feet high. Later, when He saw a documentary on "eohippus" (meaning "dawn horse" in Greek), the smaller ancestor of today's horse, He decided to name the horse of His Vision the "Dawn Horse".[6]

Avatar Adi Da has explained that this vision was a sign of the future manifestation of His own Work in the world. The Dawn Horse was also a Sign of His own Person, taking form in and as the conditional universe.

**Avatar Adi Da Samraj receiving the first published edition of *The Dawn Horse Testament,* 1985**

And so the Dawn Horse became a symbol for His Life and Work, and for the relationship between the Divine Reality and the conditional worlds:

*AVATAR ADI DA SAMRAJ: I was at once the Adept who performed the miracle of manifesting the horse, and also the one who was party to the observation of it and its result. And I did not have any feeling of being different from the horse itself. I was making the horse, I was observing the horse, and I was being the horse.* [October 18, 1984]

Avatar Adi Da's great Discourse "Mark My Words" and His Revelatory Scripture, *The Dawn Horse Testament*, were both prophecies of the transformation and ultimate Divine Translation of everyone and everything, through the Divine Power of His Ashvamedha, His Sacrifice into human Form.

## Divine Despair

At the end of 1985, even after the publication of *The Dawn Horse Testament*, Avatar Adi Da's Divine Work to Liberate His devotees was at an impasse. Apart from a brief celebratory visit to the Mountain Of Attention in March of 1984, Avatar Adi Da had remained established at Adidam Samrajashram since the end of 1983, continuing to Work with His devotees in order to deepen their self-understanding and their devotional resort to Him. But He was not seeing any breakthrough. It was obvious to Him that His devotees everywhere were, at the deepest level of their being, resisting Him, even though they were well-intentioned and happy to

**The Mountain Of Attention, 1984**

serve. It was a stark reality that, after nearly fourteen years of Teaching—in which He had poured out the most extravagant abundance of His Divine Gifts, never letting up in the intensity of His Sacrifice to Teach and Awaken all—even those most intimate to Avatar Adi Da were still slow to understand.

Certainly, in moments, and even for long periods in His Company, Avatar Adi Da's devotees would feel the Great Space of Consciousness that He was always Revealing to them, and then they could observe how they were tending to contract or separate from that Condition of Happiness. It would be obvious to them at such times that they themselves were "creating" their entire lives on the basis of the self-contraction—and that this was absurd. Nevertheless, they were stuck. Their understanding was only partial and periodic, and this was not sufficient for the great conversion that Avatar Adi Da was looking for. He had hoped and expected that this process of self-understanding would by now have become most fundamental in His devotees. He thought that they would have come to the profound awareness that all they were ever doing was playing out the drama, the madness, of "Narcissus", and be weary of the suffering of it.

During His "Sadhana Years", Avatar Adi Da had gone to Rudi a desperate man, having had the revelation of "Narcissus" and knowing that "Narcissus" could not Liberate himself. Avatar Adi Da was looking for His devotees to come to Him now in the same manner, completely given over to His Grace and Help. Instead, He found that even His devotees closest to Him could not make that unconditional gesture. They were not yet desperate enough to want Real God, the Truth, Reality, before all else. And so they were not ready to become His renunciates. They were continuing to hold out for some kind of self-fulfillment through all the ordinary forms of seeking: worldly pursuits and possessions, indulgence in food, the consolations of emotional-sexual "bonding", and the whole range of social relationships. Of course, they also knew by now that none of this was true Happiness, and they longed to be released from the hell of "Narcissus". But there was a fear that stood in the way—the fear of the "free fall" of true Spiritual Life, as Avatar Adi Da had once put it.

What would it mean to really embrace the profound renunciate sadhana that Avatar Adi Da had been "considering" with them now for some time? Avatar Adi Da had made clear what He expected of a devotee in that disposition—the intense motivation to Realize ever deeper heart-Communion with Him, the profound energy and attention, the true freedom from emotional-sexual bondage, the real availability to "consider" every aspect of egoity for the sake of most perfectly self-transcending Real-God-Realization.

Daniel Bouwmeester, one of the devotees who had been involved with Avatar Adi Da for a number of years in the "consideration" of formal renunciation, recalls an occasion of such "consideration" in the early months of 1984.

*DANIEL: Beloved Adi Da was seated cross-legged on His bed asking (as He had done on numerous occasions) whether anyone felt qualified for real Tantric renunciation. Most people said, on this occasion, that they felt they did have the qualifications—which was a confession that would always lead to more testing. When it came to me, however, I said no, I did not feel qualified. I am someone whom Beloved Adi Da refers to as the "guilty self-defeating type"—I just felt my inadequacy. Beloved Adi Da had explained previously that there is an alternative offered in the Spiritual traditions to the supremely demanding sadhana of*

*Tantric renunciation, which is the more ordinary path of living according to religious laws, doing good works, and praying for a better, or more Spiritually auspicious, life next time. And so I said that this was my situation. I would do the best I could and pray for a better lifetime.*

*Beloved Adi Da listened to my confession, and then He bent forward toward me—He was only about six feet away—leaning on His hands with His arms straight. Now His face was right in my face and His eyes became huge. Then He roared at me, "THIS IS YOUR BETTER LIFETIME!!!"*

*I reeled back, knowing that He was right. He had already said that there are two ways to become qualified for Tantric renunciation. Either you are born with the qualifications or else you gain the necessary qualities through the devotional relationship and response to the*

*Adept-Realizer who demonstrates the sign of Tantric renunciation and transmits the capability in response to right devotion. There was no doubt that through devotional recognition of Him, the Supreme Tantric Hero, His Manly Qualities could be received and the great sadhana assumed. I was humbled to feel His infinite Compassion and how much He was Helping me to participate with Him in the creative work of sadhana in His Company.*

It was in moments such as these that Avatar Adi Da allowed His devotees to feel the depth of His Passion to Liberate them. But He could not force the issue. It was up to them to find the response in themselves.

On October 4, 1985, the night that Avatar Adi Da was presented with His copy of the published *Dawn Horse Testament*, He spoke about the most significant and difficult transition in a human life—the movement beyond an egocentric existence based on bodily consolation to a self-transcending life of service and devotional absorption in the Divine. In the language of *The Dawn Horse Testament*, He described this process as the transition from the first three stages of life (preoccupied with the concerns of the gross body-mind) to the fourth stage of life (or the beginnings of a Spiritually Awakened life)[7]:

*AVATAR ADI DA SAMRAJ: You must go through the inevitable and natural crisis of the transition to the fourth stage of life, and that is a profound matter. If it were not profound, most difficult, and something that people in general are not prepared for, human beings all over the world would have entered the fourth stage of life by now. This crisis of transition is the most profound and unwelcome change that confronts humanity. That change has been unwelcome for thousands of years.*

*This Way of life that I have Given is not idealistic. It is realistic. The transition to the fourth stage of life requires a realistic confrontation with your limitations in the first three stages of life. These are the most vulgar, the most immature, the most primitive limitations. They are associated with the most basic physical, emotional, mental, and sexual functions to which you have adapted.*

*Study My Testament. I tell you there, and always, that This is My Final Word, and I need not be further obliged to Communicate to you about this Way of life. You are My devotees. It is no longer My business to shoulder your responsibilities. I have Given you My Word, My Promise. My Work is evident to you in every day of your life. Therefore, you must give Me another word, another report, a different sound than the one I have received. You are in the most difficult position of adolescence—the position of being directly confronted by the Absolute Truth. You—more than anyone who might merely casually observe My Word and Promise and Presence—must exhibit the revolution of response to Me in your own body-mind.*

*Believe it or not, in your poor precinct of life, this is it! I am going to Move humankind from here. It may take Me a long time, but if I must talk to beings for thousands of years, This is the Voice that will Speak. Those of you who have heard Me even an inkling, a dash, a jot, must ride with Me this wavelet of terror. Imagine—an entire lifetime absorbed in a purpose beyond your own comprehension!*

*I Say to those of you who are here now in this room, or elsewhere but gathered around Me: Mark My Words. You must have intuited by now that you are party to the Intervention of Real God in the world. That is What we are celebrating today. All of you can bear witness to the massive Intervention of the Divine Person into the human plane, and to the ordinary humanity of It. That Intervention Comes in your own Likeness. I have Lived every day in your company as an apparently ordinary man, and yet you know the difference. We will see. This Testament is the Greatest Book ever made.* [October 4, 1985]

The day after He received *The Dawn Horse Testament*, in the evening, Avatar Adi Da called all His devotees at Adidam Samrajashram to His House to receive their copies of the book, which He passed out personally to each individual. When they looked inside, they could scarcely believe their eyes. Right at the beginning of the Prologue, just before the opening Words, "Here I Am", Avatar Adi Da had written "Dear ___," with the name of the devotee in His own handwriting. And so, in each case, His Message read, "Dear ____, Here I Am." Then, under the last Words of the Book, He had Written "Love, Da".

On a later occasion, Avatar Adi Da read aloud the entire prologue and chapter one, and, finally, the sublime epilogue, one of His most passionate and heart-rending Confessions of Love.

*I Am The Divine Heart-Master. I Take My Stand In The Heart Of My Devotee. Have You Realized The Heart, Who Is The Mystery Of You and Me?*

*How Could I Deny Heart-Vision To My Loved-One?*

*How Could I Delay The Course Of My Beloved?*

*Like An Intimate Family Servant, I Dearly Serve My Devotee.*

*Like A Wealthy Friend, I Freely Give To My Devotee.*

*Like A Mad Priest, I Even Worship My Devotee, With Love Itself.*

*Like An Innocent Boy At First Love, I Would Awaken My Devotee In Radiant Chambers.*

*Where The Wound Of Love Churns and Never Heals, I Wait, Longing To Celebrate The Brilliant Sight Of My Devotee.*

*Come Slowly or Quickly, but Surely Come To Me.* [The Dawn Horse Testament Of The Ruchira Avatar]

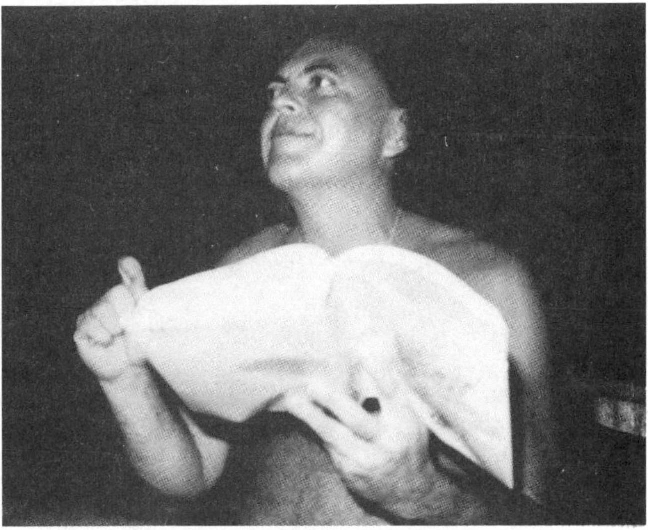

At the end of His reading of the epilogue (of which these words are only the beginning), no one could move. The Siddhi, the Heart-Bliss in the room was too profound.

This was a peerless moment, but for the devotees of Avatar Adi Da, there were many occasions when His Love seemed utterly Sufficient, when there was nothing else, nothing in the universe but Him. Then, however, in another moment His devotees would forget that Divine Vision. They would succumb to the clench of fear, sorrow, anger, and would fall again into the self-contracted point of view. They had not yet understood His All-Surpassing Message, so passionately Given in "Mark My Words" and in *The Dawn Horse Testament*: The Expected One is here. The veil of egoity was still covering their eyes. They had not yet most profoundly recognized the Living God in their midst.

Adidam Samrajashram, 1986

CHAPTER 14

# The Divine "Emergence"

Early in the morning of January 11, 1986, Avatar Adi Da Samraj was in His room, speaking over an intercom telephone to a small group of devotees in the next building. He was full of agony at the limitations in their response to Him—their failure to fully practice with the Gifts He had Given—for in that refusal lay the refusal of all humankind. He spoke of the grief He felt for beings everywhere. But the impasse was complete. He felt that His Work had failed, and that He could do no more in the body. His death, He felt, was imminent. He even said, "May it come quickly."

One devotee, Adidama Sukha Dham, immediately ran to His House and held Him up as He continued to speak on the telephone, describing the feeling of the life-force leaving His Body. He felt numbness coming up His arms, and He said it seemed that His death was occurring even now.

Avatar Adi Da Samraj dropped the telephone. In alarm and panic, the other devotees rushed over to His House to find Him collapsed by the side of His bed. His Body was still, with occasional shaking. His eyes were rolled up into His head, a sign that the energies of His Body had ascended beyond the physical dimension. There was no sign of any outer awareness at all.

The doctors were called to check His life signs and to attend to Him. They found Him to have vital signs present although His breathing was almost imperceptible.

As devotees lifted Avatar Adi Da onto His bed, they were begging Him not to die, not to leave them. Devotees could not contain themselves—each in his or her own way, was doing whatever they could to draw Him back into the body.

After a time Avatar Adi Da made a slight gesture, which devotees understood to indicate His desire to sit up. They pulled Him upward, and Adidama Jangama Hriddaya sat behind Him, supporting His torso. Suddenly, she felt the life-force shoot through His Body. His arms flung out in an arc, and His body straightened. His face contorted into a wound of Love, and tears began to flow from His eyes. Avatar Adi Da began to rock forward and backward in a rhythm of sorrow. He reached out His hands, as though He were reaching out to touch everyone in a universal embrace. He whispered, in a voice choked with Passion, "Four billion people! The four billion!"

## A Grand Victory

Later that day, Avatar Adi Da left the village of devotees to return to His residence on the other side of the island. As He sat in the back of the Land Cruiser for the bumpy ride through the broad grasslands and mango and coconut groves, Adi Da spoke to Greg Purnell, the devotee who was driving Him.

*GREG: Avatar Adi Da normally sat in the front of the car and was most often silent. But on this day, He sat with devotees in the back seat, right behind me. He began talking to me right away, saying things like, "Do you know that I think of you constantly? Do you know that I also think of your intimate partner constantly? Do you think of Me constantly?" He continued like this for five minutes or so,*

*giving me every reassurance of His Love for me. I responded, "Yes, Master," to each question. But I was feeling more and more self-conscious.*

*He asked me again and again, "Do you know how much I Love you? Do you really know how much I Love you?" I continued to say, "Yes, Master"—knowing full well that I didn't—and even couldn't, in my limited perception—know the full extent of His Great Love.*

*When we came to a cattle-crossing gate, I had to get out to open it so the car could pass. I stepped out of the car and shut the door. At that moment, Avatar Adi Da asked me once again, "Do you really know how much I Love you?" I was faced with a choice. I could ignore the question, pretending I had not heard, and simply open the gate for Him (which is what I would have done by tendency). Or I could face my Beloved and answer Him. In my heart, I wanted to face the Great One. Even so, it took all I had to stick my head back inside the car and look at Him face-to-face.*

*The Vision I saw was glorious, attractive, and fierce. Everything and everyone else in the car disappeared from my awareness as I was filled with the Vision of Him. I saw His huge head, His intense eyes, and His smile that proved to me He already knew and Loved me. His face was no more than two feet from my eyes.*

*I was lost in that special intensity that surrounds the physical Person of Beloved Adi Da. I wanted only to be completely honest with Him and let all expectations and fears go. I said, "No, not really."*

*His expression relaxed a bit. He said, "This was a test—and you failed!"*

*At that, my heart opened like the shutter of a camera, and His face was permanently imprinted there. For many weeks afterward, I saw that face constantly, especially in meditation. In that moment, the image of Beloved Adi Da was set in my heart for me to carry and worship forever.*

Several times, on that drive, Avatar Adi Da said to Greg and to the other devotees with Him: "I have a Secret".

After two weeks in seclusion, Adi Da Samraj gathered once more with devotees. Now He Revealed His Secret: That day, January 11, 1986, was His true Birth Day, a day more auspicious than any other in His human Lifetime—more profound, even, than His Divine Re-Awakening in the Vedanta Temple. He began to explain why.

In the Great Event of January 11, the "Heroic" Teaching Work of Avatar Adi Da Samraj spontaneously completed itself. Those years of Teaching had been a profound Submission to the needs and sufferings of His devotees, to the point of apparently identifying with their egoic qualities and impulses. And now all the lessons, all the Instruction that belonged to that phase of His Liberating Work had been Given. He had shown to His devotees the futility of all their seeking—of body, of emotion, of mind. And they knew it. But they had not yet taken responsibility for the lesson. And they knew that, too. But now, through the miracle of January 11, a new and great opportunity for them to understand the lesson of Avatar Adi Da's Teaching Years had suddenly manifested.

As of January 11, the particular Siddhi, or Divine Power, that had enabled Avatar Adi Da to Work with His devotees in the manner of His Teaching Years had disappeared. It was replaced, He Said, by a universally magnified Siddhi of Divine Blessing. As of January 11, Avatar Adi Da had fully Descended as the Divine Person into His human vehicle. His Teaching Work had somehow required that the perfection of His Divine Descent be forestalled for a time. His Radiant, Transfigured humanity was the means by which He had won the hearts of His devotees—He had lived as they did, always creating incidents, making demands, comments, and truly Humorous but telling Remarks that would attract them into His "Crazy-Wise" Play. But now, during the Great Event of January 11, His Descent had become Complete, and It combined Him with humanity more profoundly and universally than ever before:

*AVATAR ADI DA SAMRAJ: In this Great Event, I was drawn further into the body with a very human impulse, a love-impulse. Becoming aware of My profound relationship with all My devotees, I resumed My bodily human state. Even though I have, obviously, existed as a human being during My physical Lifetime, becoming profoundly Incarnate, I now assumed an impulse toward human existence more profound than I had assumed before—without any reluctance relative to sorrow and death.*

*On so many occasions, I have Told you that I wish I could Kiss every human being on the lips, Embrace each one, and Enliven each one from the heart. In this Body, I will never have the opportunity. I am frustrated in that Impulse. But in that Motion of sympathetic Incarnation, that Acceptance of the body and its sorrow and its death, I Realized a Kiss, a Way to Fulfill the Impulse.*

*To Me, this is a Grand Victory! I do not know how to Communicate to you the significance of It. It seems that, through that will-less, effortless integration with suffering, something about My Work is more profoundly accomplished, something about It has become more auspicious than It ever was. I have not dissociated from My Divine Realization or My Divine State. Rather, I have accomplished your state completely, even more profoundly than you are sensitive to it. Perhaps you have seen it in My face. I have become this Body, utterly. My Mood is different. My Face is sad, although not without Illumination. I have become the body. Now I Am the "Murti", the Icon, and It is Full of My Divine Presence.* [January 27, 1986]

At the moment of His deepest despair, the Incarnation of Avatar Adi Da Samraj had now achieved ultimate depth. He had almost left the body entirely, but He had been drawn back by the pull of His human intimacies and the prayers of the four billion beings "self-conscious and dying in this place". And, in His return to the body, He had Descended further than ever before, investing Himself absolutely in human existence. This Event, which Avatar Adi Da came to describe as His "Divine 'Emergence'", was the initiation of the unfolding Process that He has said will continue until the Divine Liberation of all beings—and which, in some sense, began at His Birth.

## Divine Demand

Before the implications of the Great Event of January 11 would become clarified for His devotees, Avatar Adi Da Samraj had another period of intense Divine Work ahead of Him, which He came to call the "Revelation Years". Although He continued to give Instruction, Avatar Adi Da was no longer primarily functioning as Teacher in relation to His devotees. He was making the full Revelation of His Divinity and establishing the means for beings everywhere—now, and throughout all time—to recognize Him and respond to Him as the Divine Person.

The transition from the Teaching Years to the Revelation Years was overwhelming to His devotees. They were overcome with emotion by the paradox of His Body—so etched with the suffering of human incarnation, while at the same time Radiant with Divine Love-Bliss. His Beauty was unearthly. The mere beholding of Avatar Adi Da drew His devotees to Him intimately at the heart, without His having to make any gestures of outward familiarity toward them. He had assumed the fullness of His Divine Guru-Function. He was no longer the animated Spiritual Teacher always making lessons. All His lessons had been Given. Now He was simply the Giver of the Divine "Brightness", Radiating through the medium of His human Body. In the completion of His Divine Descent, His Body had become the Image, the Icon, the Murti of the Divine, and this was His greatest Gift, His greatest Blessing to all.

At the same time, a new Siddhi, or Divine Power, magnified tremendously in Him—the Siddhi of renunciation. He Himself had always been the perfect renunciate, unbound and undeluded by the world or by any of His apparent involvement with the world. But His devotees had not yet awakened to the renunciate disposition He was Calling them to. Now there was a Force alive in Him that confronted their resistance as never before. Avatar Adi Da Samraj had become an all-consuming Divine Fire.

*AVATAR ADI DA SAMRAJ: You are always looking to be happy. What you call "happy" is not what I call "Happy". What you call "happy" is a superficial, amused, immune state. All of us here are dying, and you must Realize the Source of existence. To do that, to Realize that Sublimity, you must understand yourself and transcend yourself, and that means you cannot make life out of being consoled by sex, the world, the news, the pleasures of life, technology—anything. You must be free of consolation. You must be unconsolable, beyond repair of the heart. That is not what you are involved in. You are full of complaints, imaginings, agreements, rules, ideals. I cannot relate to it. I am bereft of those possibilities, empty of them. I cannot be consoled. Real God is not a consolation. Real God is What you Realize in the unconsolable state. Real God is the Obvious when the self-contraction is released.*

*You all want to keep yourselves orderly. Neat shirt and pants, something orderly to do every day, an order of remarks to make. Look how bored you are!*

*How about* <u>*not*</u> *being bored? How about transcending boredom, doubt, discomfort? How about getting real? How about feeling your suffering? How about being broken-hearted? How about being exaggerated? How about being unconventional? In your daily life, you should exist in the agony of confrontation with the ego. You must have more nerve to practice this Way of life.*

*I wish you would begin Spiritual life. I wish you would put yourself on the line. You have read the biographies of those who have made great Spiritual attainments. Their lives were about struggle, about intimacy with Reality. They were not orderly, middle-class people. They were utterly incapable of mediocrity. Does anybody know what I am Talking about?*

*You must be a renunciate to practice this Way that I Teach. You all have too much to lose, too much you depend on for consolation, too much bullshit you need to share with one another. I am glad I could Interfere with you.* [January 27, 1986]

This fierce Discourse was a sign of things to come. Avatar Adi Da was not going to bend toward His devotees as He had done in the past. He was going to "Stand Firm" and require their response. Years later He spoke of this:

*AVATAR ADI DA SAMRAJ: 1986 was the turning point in the Process of My Submission to My devotees. It became clear to Me then that, in very fundamental terms, that Process had fulfilled itself—I had Done what I could with it. From that time onwards, I had to exercise an expectation that My devotees recognize Me and respond to Me rightly, and that they practice in My Company on that basis. It was no longer fruitful for Me to continue My Submission to them, to continue relating to their "case", their egoity—still resistive, not yet truly recognizing Me, not yet truly responding to Me.* [August 8, 1998]

**Adi Da Samraj with members of His Mandala of intimate women devotees and the Trimada (front row), in Adidam Samrajashram, 1985**

Forceful Criticism had always been an aspect of Avatar Adi Da's "Crazy" Work. Now, in the wake of His Divine "Emergence", His Liberating Criticism carried unprecedented potency. But, as always, it was not the self-based anger of an ordinary person, but the Divine Demand itself, bearing down with purifying Force.

His fiery Call for renunciation initiated a crisis in all His devotees. But this crisis carried particular force for the circle of women who had served Him personally since 1974. Remarkable as their sadhana had been for so many years, Avatar Adi Da's Mandala of intimate women devotees were still tending to relate to Him in the manner of a conventional man-woman relationship, motivated to self-fulfillment, rather than as renunciates given only to the Process of Most Perfect Divine Self-Realization.

In the early months of 1986, Adi Da Samraj took His Mandala of women intimates through an intensive "consideration" of the change that had occurred in Him.

It became clear to them that they were in a "no-choice" situation. There was no possibility of their continuing to enjoy what was most precious to them—personal service to their Beloved Guru—unless they went through a "radical" conversion in their disposition. Avatar Adi Da was immediately requiring of them the "true and free" renunciation that He had for years been Calling them (and others) to understand and accept.

In the end, four of the original nine women were able to make this confession. Adidama Sukha Dham describes the ordeal and its outcome:

*ADIDAMA SUKHA DHAM: Beloved Adi Da took me through a profound emotional ordeal and confrontation with the realities and consequences of attachment to conditional life through identification with the body-mind. Seeing the reality of my life lived on the basis of those attachments was a horrific vision of mortality. I was struggling constantly.*

*Yet, as the days went by, Beloved Adi Da Helped me to make the gesture I could not make myself. As He Helped me, it was clearly Revealed that love is about sacrifice, not about what you want or feel you need. I began to feel all the things that I wanted: I wanted to be with Him, to live with Him, to serve Him. "I" wanted to do this. "I" wanted to do that. It was all me—I wanted things for myself—and I stopped it. I began to constantly contemplate His feelings. I began to feel Him, feel what He wanted, what He needed—everything that was required for His Work—and I stopped demanding for myself.*

*This confrontation—this death of what I was—took place over many months. I do not think I could have survived an instantaneous change. He drew me through it. At the time, I had no idea what He was doing, what would be required, or what would happen. I had no idea if I would ever serve Him again personally. I had to be*

**Avatar Adi Da Samraj and the Mandala of four women renunciates, the Mountain Of Attention, 1986**

*devoted to Him with no expectation or even concept of what might occur.*

*At this time, my fellow renunciates and I were Granted a graceful moment when everything came together to elicit from us the response of true renunciation. We knew that nothing would fulfill us and there was nothing left to do. It was a great moment of delight and happiness. We became ecstatic—laughing and crying and telling Leelas about our Realization of Communion with Beloved Adi Da in this happiness. We could not stop. I said to Beloved Adi Da: "I will give You everything. I do not need anything but You. I do not want anything but You. This world is a hell. I have struggled with it. I have died in it. I have done everything I can do in this world, and I only want You. I do not want the motion of life. I do not want the great spectrum of emotional life. I do not want a conventional life. I do not want social life. I do not want the world. I only want this Love-Bliss, this Happiness. I want You."*

*We did not know if He would respond. We did not make our confession for the sake of anything. We did not want status. We simply wanted to express our gratitude and our Realization to Beloved Adi Da.*

Avatar Adi Da accepted the confession that these four of His beloved women renunciates were making to Him. And He indicated the unique value of their devotional recognition of Him as a sign to all His devotees.

Late in February 1986, Avatar Adi Da began a fast, taking only water and juices. Then, in April, He assumed sannyas, or formal renunciation, in the manner of the Hindu tradition. He put on the traditional orange clothing, wore His hair in the top-knot characteristic of a sannyasin, and, most remarkably of all, took a sannyasin name, "Swami Da Love-Ananda". "Love-Ananda" was the Name that Swami Muktananda had conferred on Him privately in 1969, but which Adi Da had never formally used. "Love-Ananda" (literally "Love-Bliss") was now seen to be a prophetic Name. It was a Name that crossed the boundaries of East and West and which expressed, in one Word, the Revelation begun on January 11: the "Love" that had borne Him down to the toes[1] in His Embrace of the body; and "Ananda", the Bliss, the Splendor of the Real-God-State, to Which He would restore all suffering humanity.

Having spontaneously decided to assume this traditional mode of renunciation, Avatar Adi Da did it completely. In the manner of a swami—one who disciplines and transcends the body-mind—His discipline was more than extraordinary. He continued His juice fast, eating no solid food for over four months, until the middle of July. In mid-May, He Initiated a small group of His devotees into sannyas and departed with them from His Hermitage, intent on wandering as an Avadhoot[2]—one who has "shaken off" all the bonds of egoic existence and is not confounded by the world. During this time, He slept little, arising daily at around three in the morning to sit in meditation with His sannyasins and the other devotees who were serving His Yajna, or sacrificial journey.[3] And His clothing, in the traditional sannyasin's color of fiery orange, was a constant sign of His intense renunciation.

Even before Avatar Adi Da arrived at the Mountain Of Attention, some of His devotees were awakening to profound intuitions of the depths of Consciousness Itself, beyond all pleasures of body and mind. And, in their attraction to this unqualified Happiness, they were moved to embrace levels of discipline—including celibacy and raw diet—that they would never have imagined themselves capable of. One of these devotees, Bill Stranger, describes what had been occurring:

*BILL: At the time of The Initiation of Avatar Adi Da's Divine "Emergence" in January 1986, my intimate partner, Kouraleen MacKenzie, and I were overseeing the Adidam mission in the northeastern U.S. We really did not know what had happened to Beloved Adi Da at Adidam Samrajashram, but, whatever it was, it was significant enough for us to be invited, along with the rest of the worldwide leadership of Adidam, to Adidam Samrajashram for a vitally important retreat.*

*We all collected at the Mountain Of Attention Sanctuary, where, as it turned out, our entire retreat unfolded—while Avatar Adi Da remained in Fiji. In fact, as we were to discover, His physical absence made not the slightest difference to the potency of the retreat.*

*When we had all gathered at the Mountain Of Attention, we learned that Beloved Adi Da was now Calling all those in leadership positions in Adidam to immediately adopt certain renunciate disciplines. In particular, He was asking us to be celibate (while remaining in our intimacies) and to eat a purifying and rejuvenating diet consisting only of raw food.*[4]

*My friends and I first greeted our Beloved Guru's new Calling with dismay. At the Mountain Of Attention Sanctuary, the weather often communicates the Living Being of Beloved Adi Da and what He is feeling from His devotees. And so, as we caviled and complained in our quarters, unseasonable winds whipped up the placid May sky. I knew that our Guru was feeling our refusal.*

*Although nothing of our disposition had been reported to Avatar Adi Da, He sent us a Communication that reflected His perfect knowledge of our mood. And He was having none of it. His Criticisms were so Empowered, however, that our resistance, which only that morning had seemed insurmountable, melted into thin air. We now told Him that we accepted His Divine Call.*

*Our reward came amazingly fast: Around midnight, we were all called to the Communion Hall named "Plain Talk Chapel" to listen to recitations of Beloved Adi Da's newly written Essays about the Witness-Position of Consciousness and the "Perfect Practice" of Adidam (which takes place in the Domain of Consciousness Itself, and not from the point of view of the body-mind). I presumed that this late-night event would be difficult and uncomfortable. Beloved Adi Da's Writings about the ultimate stages of Adidam did not seem to have much to do with the likes of us, who were still struggling to fulfill the beginning stages of Adidam. Or so I thought.*

*It had been a long, eventful day and people were tired. Many began to nod out as the Instructions were read, covering at first the disciplines of celibacy and of diet. But now we were coming to Beloved Adi Da's Instruction about the Witness-Position of Consciousness and His Divine Spirit-Current of Love-Bliss, to be discovered deep in the right side of the heart.*[5] *To my utter astonishment,*

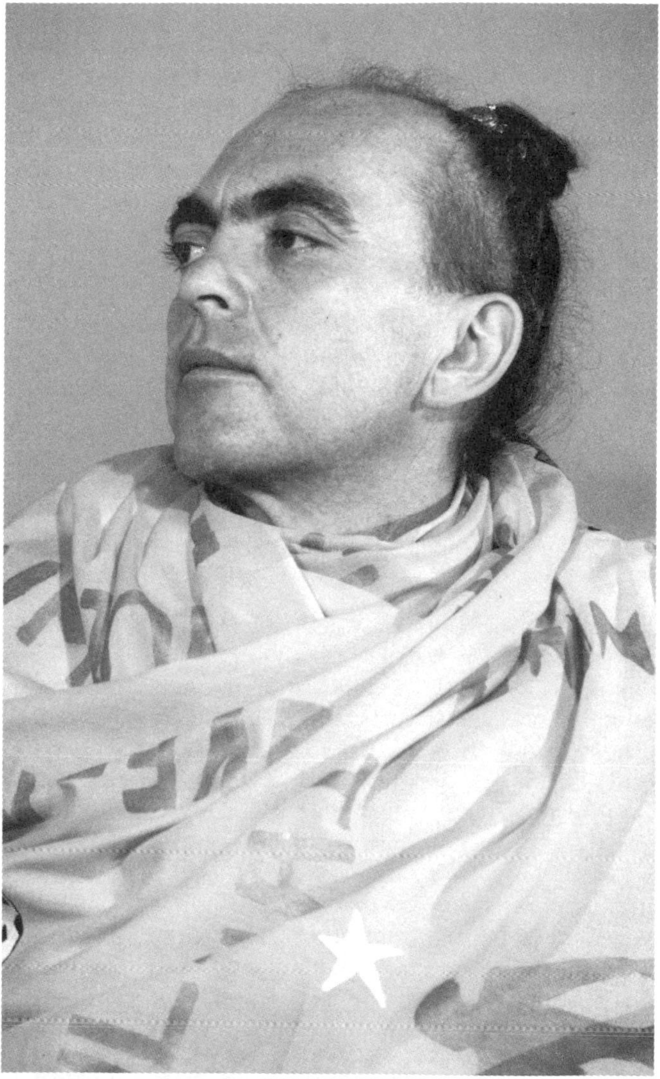

*I understood every word Adi Da had Written! It was infinitely more than mental comprehension. I experienced the Very Reality that Beloved Adi Da was Describing in His Essay. I felt His Divine Spirit-Current Emanating from the right side of my heart, like a chain rising vertically from the floor of a pool. I knew with absolute certainty that I am Consciousness. Then, as I beheld Beloved Adi Da's photographic Murti at the front of that small chapel, I realized that He is perpetually Conscious as my very Self.*

*In the days ahead, this awareness remained completely available. I would go into Western Face Cathedral, one of the principal Communion Halls, sit down to meditate, and quickly relax into the Bliss of the Witness-Consciousness. Neither my body nor my mind seemed the least obstruction any longer. I enjoyed a freedom and delight that I would not have dared to presume on my own. It was obvious that this had nothing to do with my own effort. It was the Gift of Avatar Adi Da, released into the world through the immense Power of His Divine "Emergence".*

Reaching California, Avatar Adi Da made a remarkable offering: Any member of the public who had a serious desire to see Him could come to the Mountain Of Attention for special occasions of His Darshan. His devotees set up a huge white tent to receive the numbers who came flocking to see Him over the next several weeks.

Not only that, Avatar Adi Da suddenly invited anyone Graced with the Vision of Him as Self-Radiant Consciousness to take up the "Perfect Practice" immediately. In other words, He was potentially offering, to complete newcomers, the ultimate form of practice in the Way of Adidam—which He had said previously could only be entered into after extraordinary Spiritual preparation in His Company. All in all, Avatar Adi Da was ready for a far-reaching change in His Work, if the response was there. He knew that a tidal wave of Blessing had been

**Darshan in the tent at the Mountain Of Attention, 1986**

released into the world through His Divine "Emergence", and so He presumed no limits in anyone or anything.

During the Darshan occasions in the tent, devotees were stunned by the sight of their Beloved Master—His eyes burning in their sockets, His now frail-looking body Transfigured in His Love-Bliss. The devotee children, too, were overwhelmed. One of them, Jonah Straus, age 11, wrote about what he felt:

*JONAH: On Sunday I was Graced with a wonderful Gift. Beloved Da Love-Ananda came in as if He was just teleported or flown there. He just appeared in the aisle. He went up to His chair and put His staff in the holder. He sat down and He started looking at everybody, and almost immediately He was showing His Bliss. He had a smile on His face when He looked over at the children. He would look over at everyone else with a wide-eyed glance and then He would look at us and He would smile. He was just lost in Happiness, and I cried every time He would cry. He would look over at me, tears would go down His face, a tear would go down my face. Then He would look at someone else.*

***"He would look over at everyone else with a wide-eyed glance and then He would look at us and He would smile. He was just lost in Happiness, and I cried every time He would cry."***

*When I am with Him, I can't put my attention on anything else. Why should I want to look at anything else? What else is interesting in the room? I don't know how many times I cried. I was in bliss.*

In the middle of June, Avatar Adi Da made explicit the great reasons for His journey out of Hermitage and His undertaking of a world Yajna:

*AVATAR ADI DA SAMRAJ: Life without sadhana is terrible bondage. I look for people to "consider" My Teaching Work and Word and My Company seriously and to relieve themselves of frivolous, merely intellectual, and popular views of the Spiritual Process. Many of those who come to these Darshan occasions are leaders, educators, and communicators. They, too, are invited here to be purified in the body-mind and to be made serious by the impact of My Company, so that their response will be to take up this sadhana for the sake of their own self-transcendence and for the sake of the world.*

*I Call all of those who sit with Me to become My advocates and to become real practitioners in My Company so that a great historical impact may be made by My Blessing Work.*

*The world is on a pivot of history. The future of the next several decades can become a colossal terror of disorder. Now that My Teaching Work is done, My Purpose in Blessing all and Calling all to practice in My Company is to have an historical impact on a large scale, so that the current karmic trend of history can be sufficiently purified to allow this pivotal period to have an auspicious result.*

*The world is currently in the grip of self-deluded and vulgar forces, and the Spiritual Truth and the Way and the True Adept are everywhere defamed and in doubt. This situation must immediately change, and to change it is what I am here to do. But the situation will not change if people will not come into My Company, if people will not rightly use My Company, and if people will not seriously respond to My Company and will not devote themselves to the worldwide advocacy of My Company.*

*My intention is to travel the world in silence and to make Myself available to all who are rightly responsive to*

***"My basic intention from now on is to wander and to Bless all who come to Me and even all who do not come to Me, until I am heard and seen and the current trend of history is reversed."***

*Me. I may periodically return to Hermitage and rest for awhile and associate with those on retreat there, but My basic intention from now on is to wander and to Bless all who come to Me and even all who do not come to Me, until I am heard and seen and the current trend of history is reversed.* [June 14, 1986]

**Maria Hoop, Holland, 1986**

CHAPTER 15

# An Ascetic on Fire

On June 22, 1986, Avatar Adi Da left California and traveled to New York—for the first time since 1970, when He had left for India intending to settle permanently at Swami Muktananda's ashram. Aniello Panico, a devotee originally from New York, greeted Him at the airport. While expressing his gratitude and joy, he told Avatar Adi Da that he felt that his Beloved Master had come partly to relieve him of all his karma as a New Yorker. Avatar Adi Da looked hard at Aniello and said, "But I'm only going to be here for a week!" His Humor was just as it had always been.

## A World-Blessing Yajna

Indeed, Avatar Adi Da was burning karmas, and not only those of His devotees. In the Hindu tradition, a renunciate would voluntarily practice austerities, such as celibacy and fasting, in order to create a Spiritual intensity that would purify the body-mind of karmic tendencies. The ancient word for this practice is "tapas", which literally means "heat". Unlike the traditional swami who assumes such austerities in order to purify his or her own body-mind, Avatar Adi Da, through His own great Tapas, was purifying the self-contracted and seeking tendencies of the entire world.

**New York, 1986**

This Tapas was a profound Ordeal. Adi Da was no longer the buoyant New Yorker He had been in His days as "Franklin Jones". His body was transfigured, completely submitted to the Divine Radiance, completely open and vulnerable to everyone and everything—including the casual mockery that He sometimes encountered, as He moved through big cities in His orange sannyasin clothing. As He walked the streets of New York after so long, Avatar Adi Da remarked to devotees that the intensity of His Sadhana there during His Columbia years had been similar to that of traditional sadhus[1] meditating in jungles full of wild beasts. New York—with all its threat and danger—had been a goad to His Divine Re-Awakening. And now it was receiving His Divine Blessing.

Early in the morning on the first Sunday of His stay in New York, Avatar Adi Da went to St. Patrick's, the Roman Catholic cathedral. The huge church was filled

**Avatar Adi Da Samraj on His travels in Europe, 1986**
**above left: Paris**
**above right: London**
**left: Stonehenge**

with a thousand people attending a mass by the archbishop of New York, which was also being broadcast on television. Avatar Adi Da walked slowly down one of the side aisles to the front. He paused and gazed in silence at the people singing and praying. After about ten minutes, He walked around the back of the congregation and up another aisle, deeply intent in His Blessing of this place and of these people—those present and those watching the event on television.

On July 27, He moved on to Europe—to England, France, and Holland—continuing His pilgrimage to places of great religious significance in the West: Stonehenge, Westminster Abbey, Sacre Coeur. His devotees could feel that, by spending time in these places, He was contacting the deep Spiritual impulses of people everywhere, realizing some aspect of His Desire to "Kiss" all the inhabitants of Earth.

Avatar Adi Da's Yajna in Europe was difficult, just as it had been in New York. To serve Him in unfamiliar and unpredictable situations, with sensitivity, flexibility, and great resourcefulness, to move with Him unquestioningly, anticipating and taking care of all His interests and concerns—that was the test for His devotees. It was a test of devotional recognition of Him as the Divine Being "Emerged" in human Form. When you know you are responding to That One in Person, you move to serve His every impulse, heart-certain that everything He does or says or requests is for the sake of His Blessing of beings. When such recognition has awakened in depth, you become capable of an extraordinary energy and intelligence. This quality of service was the sign that Avatar Adi Da has always looked for in His devotees. And now that His Teaching-Submission to His devotees was over, this responsibility was more critical than ever before.

Sheriden Vince (whose surname was Stewart at the time, a fact that is important for this story) served Avatar Adi Da in London. She describes her experience and what she learned:

*SHERIDEN: I was asked to serve as hostess for Beloved Adi Da during His stay in London. Although I was overjoyed to have the opportunity to serve my Beloved Guru personally, I was also terrified because I knew that His Function is to Purify and Liberate—not necessarily to pleasurize, and definitely not to console. Within twenty-four hours, my fears were confirmed, as "hostessing" translated into being in charge of Avatar Adi Da's itineraries, drivers, and hotel and food service—in short, His entire daily circumstance! I knew this time of personal service to Beloved Adi Da would create a fire in me unlike anything I had experienced before, yet I also knew I was one of the most fortunate people in the world to be able to come into Beloved Adi Da's Radiantly Sublime physical Company.*

*One day, I accompanied Beloved Adi Da to a couple of museums and toy stores. Everything went relatively smoothly, until we were preparing to leave for "Starlight Express: Roller-Skating Splendorama". Always attentive to the needs and interests of the Trimada, Beloved Adi Da had asked if this show would be suitable for them, as they were young girls at the time. I had made enquiries and was told that numerous devotees recommended it. After Beloved Adi Da and His party had gone into the theatre, I sat on the steps to wait for the devotee who was to replace me as hostess for the rest of the day and breathed a huge sigh of relief that the day had gone well. Just then, someone asked me if one of the drivers, who would otherwise have waited outside the theatre, could go and do an errand. Against my intuition, I let the driver go, urging him to return as quickly as possible.*

*The moment the driver left, Beloved Adi Da suddenly came out of the theatre. I froze. I knew that if Beloved Adi Da was leaving a two-and-a-half-hour show after eight minutes, something was very wrong! I rushed to help Him to His car, and everyone in His party to their mini-bus. But there was no security car to follow directly behind Beloved—because, of course, I had allowed the driver to go and do an errand.*

*We arranged to meet at the Scotch House, a famous shop specializing in Scottish woolens. But, in the heavy London traffic, the mini-bus couldn't keep up with Beloved Adi Da's car, and we soon lost Him.*

*When we finally met in front of the Scotch House, one of the devotees attending Beloved Adi Da, visibly distressed, told me that, on the way, an obviously disturbed individual had pounded on Avatar Adi Da's car and screamed obscenities at Him! Where was the security car? As if this were not bad enough, the show we had recommended for Him had turned out to be a punk-rock production that was completely inappropriate for the Trimada.*

*It was excruciating. I couldn't believe that I had completely failed to protect and sensitively serve my Guru. I started to make my way back to the hotel where Beloved Adi Da was staying (so upset that I felt physically ill), but I realized I had to turn around and go back to where He was and give Him my energy. I could not tolerate feeling dissociated from Him, nor could I bear the suffering of failure.*

*There was not a cell in my body that wanted to go, but I went to the Scotch House. Feeling unbearably self-conscious, I hung around the periphery of the group, while Avatar Adi Da walked from department to department. In stark contrast to my agitated state, Beloved Adi Da was perfectly relaxed. Eventually, we came to a room where the Scottish coats-of-arms and beautiful tartans were displayed. This room had chairs to sit in and a very different, more private, quality than the previous departments. I felt myself begin to relax.*

*Out of the corner of my eye, I could see that Avatar Adi Da was sitting in a chair next to a circular rack that displayed miniatures of the coats-of-arms and tartans. I found myself next to His chair, but I was feeling so fearful that I could not look at Him. Suddenly I heard Him softly say, "Where is the Stewart coat-of-arms?" I stammered a reply, and He began to slowly rotate the display rack until He found it.*

*Then He asked me, "What does the legend say?"*

*I looked at Him blankly and said, "Legend?"*

*"You know," He Said, "the motto that goes with the coat-of-arms."*

*I looked, but it was in Latin, so we asked the shop assistant to help us. She brought a book of the translations and found the Stewart legend. Beloved Adi Da asked me to read it. My eyes welled with tears and my voice broke as I read, "Courage grows strong at a wound."*

*My face only inches away from His, I looked into His*

**London, 1986**

*eyes, and He said, "That's right. It's telling you that Spiritual practice is about sadhana. That's all."*

*The Truth of His Instruction and the Force of His Gaze penetrated me, filling me so deeply with His Love and Compassion that I could not speak. I felt penetrated at the core of my being by the revelation that Avatar Adi Da is the Divine Incarnate, and my gratitude and joy to be receiving direct Spiritual Instruction from Him made it impossible and unnecessary to speak.*

*Up until that moment, I had allowed my failure to throw my love-relationship with Him into doubt. However, in that moment, I was healed of my doubt, because He had made it so obvious that He does not withdraw His Love. I was the one who had withdrawn. I knew Beloved Adi Da was telling me that the pain of failure and doubt can always be surrendered to Him, and that sadhana is only about choosing heart-Communion with Him. In this incident, I felt my Beloved Guru showing me what real Happiness is—the most exquisite heart-Intimacy I had ever felt, and what I had searched for throughout my entire life. I felt Him showing me that sadhana is about feeling Him, not myself, and I understood for the first time that Beloved Adi Da is fundamentally Calling me and all His devotees to commit ourselves to just this practice of feeling Him and not ourselves. I thanked Him from the bottom of my heart for Granting me this understanding.*

## The End of Traditional Sannyas

As the weeks passed and Avatar Adi Da went on from England to France, it became obvious that no one was sustaining the depth of renunciation and devotion to Him that is required for the "Perfect Practice"—and, therefore, for real sannyas. He had made it clear that, in His Company, sannyas requires the capability to relinquish identification with the body-mind and Stand in the Position that Transcends the body-mind, the Position of Consciousness Itself. And so, Adi Da Samraj Himself discarded the outward signs of traditional sannyas. He has no need for such signs, unless they serve some purpose in His Work. For the rest of the Yajna, He typically wore indigo clothing, and, after having consumed only diluted juices for four and half months, He slowly began to eat solid food again.

Avatar Adi Da's Body, as He has often said, is His Agent. It is the Means, the Vehicle, through which He accomplishes His Work of Spiritual Transformation and Divine Awakening. What His juice fast represented cannot be altogether comprehended. He was releasing His Teaching Years, purifying His Body of the physical and psychic toxins that He had taken on during those years, and conforming His bodily Vehicle to its single sacred Purpose—to be the transparent Agent of His Divine "Brightness".

On July 21, the traditional Feast of the Guru[2] (celebrated in India on the first full moon in the Hindu month of Ashadh, which usually coincides with the month of July in the Western calendar), Adi Da Samraj consented to sit formally with all the Dutch and English devotees—His first association with a large group of His devotees since He left the Mountain Of Attention.

The place to which they had invited Him was a former Catholic monastery in the village of Maria Hoop in southern Holland. It was a large gray stone building of several stories. After several days of hectic activity preparing for His arrival (and a few heart-stopping moments when it seemed He would not be coming), a bus finally drove through the gates and Avatar Adi Da climbed out.

Avatar Adi Da spoke to everyone in the former chapel of the monastery. It was years since He had Given a Discourse to such a large group of mostly new devotees, many of whom had never seen Him before. Avatar Adi Da was Gracious in the extreme, humorously telling stories of His experiences of the Yajna, responding to the kind of beginner's questions that He had addressed throughout His years of Teaching at the Mountain Of Attention. The long-time devotees accompanying Him, who had just gone through the fiery tests of sannyas with Him, marveled at how sweet and engaging

Adi Da Samraj speaking to devotees at Maria Hoop, July 1986

The former monastery in Maria Hoop, now the principal Ashram and administrative Center for Adidam in Europe

He was, perfectly adapting Himself to what was needed by those who were just beginning their approach to Him.

That weekend was the true initiation of the Way of Adidam in Europe, and everyone present felt the historic import of it. The day following His Discourse, Avatar Adi Da Granted silent Darshan, His Feet outstretched in Blessing. The same day, devotees performed a fire puja on the grounds, at a site that Avatar Adi Da marked out. It was obvious that Avatar Adi Da had powerfully imbued this property with His Presence. Several years later, the Dutch community was able to purchase the former monastery and its grounds, to be used as their principal Ashram and administrative Center in Europe.

On coming to Holland, Avatar Adi Da had expressed His interest in taking a bicycle ride, which was arranged for Him a few days after He left Maria Hoop. Ineke van Amerongen, one of the Dutch devotees, accompanied Avatar Adi Da on the ride.

*INEKE: My service to Beloved Adi Da in Europe had been to supervise the cleaning of His quarters and His laundry. On this particular day, I planned to give His room a thorough cleaning after He left on the bicycle trip. Five minutes before He was scheduled to go, I was asked to be His guide, because the person appointed to do that was delayed, and because I had grown up about 30 kilometers from the hotel where He was staying. I panicked. Even though I had grown up in the area, I did not know the neighborhood, where to start, or where to go. But there was not much time to worry about it, as Beloved Adi Da was on His way downstairs.*

*Our small party got on our bikes. Beloved Adi Da looked so at ease, as if He had ridden a bike all His life. I began to relax and decided to go to the local tourist office and ask for bicycle routes. I noticed how totally given over Beloved Adi Da was. He totally trusted the situation and was surrendered and submitted to whatever I was going to do. I pointed things out to Him, and He responded with loving interest. He was also very playful. He raced us, yelling in German, "Mach schnell!" ("go faster") and "Necken brecken" (loosely translated, "break a leg"). Naturally, He was faster than any of us, and was full of humor and delight the entire time.*

Avatar Adi Da had made it clear to everyone, from the beginning of His Yajna, that it was His impulse to travel the world. He spoke to some of those traveling with Him about the possibility of moving on from Europe to the Middle East and then to India. From His point of view, it was time for Him to really live as an Avadhoot, a Wanderer, moving wherever He was moved to go, Revealing Himself as the Divine Incarnate and doing the world-Blessing Work that He had been Born to do.

But this was not to be. After the ecstatic weekend at Maria Hoop, what became obvious was the stark disparity between the kind of travel and Work that Avatar Adi Da was ready for, given the opportunity, and what His devotees were actually able and willing to provide for Him. This part of the story is related by Frans Bakker (a Dutch devotee who was also one of the physicians attending Tom Closser at Adidam Samrajashram in 1983, as related in chapter 12).

*FRANS: The hotel where Beloved Adi Da was staying had not proved satisfactory, and the Dutch devotees were looking for somewhere else for Him to go. Suddenly, I received a message that Beloved Adi Da wanted to move to our center in Amsterdam, which consisted of a small cramped apartment (over our bookstore), where I and some other members of the Dutch community were living.*

**Frans Bakker and Avatar Adi Da Samraj at the Adidam Bookstore in Amsterdam, 1986**

*He had been told that devotees had over-extended their financial means to host Him on His travels, and, therefore, He felt it was unlawful to live anywhere that was not already being supported by devotees.*

*Our Beloved Heart-Master was willing to come all the way to Europe to Bless and Transform all in His path, and yet He didn't feel He could live anywhere better than this little apartment! He was making painfully clear the reality of His dependence on us, simply asking to be housed and fed only by the local devotees. He minimized His own circumstance and needs to the point of utter simplicity. When we took Him on outings, He would refuse to go in a car, going on foot instead, no matter what the weather was like. This situation was very distressing for devotees, but it was a necessary lesson. We had not properly handled our responsibility for managing His travels.*

*On Friday, July 25, Avatar Adi Da took a walk to a local museum and then to the Anne Frank house and the*

*Amsterdam red-light district. He spent a lot of time in the Anne Frank house. I felt Him completely absorb the suffering of that era. Then we went on to the red-light district. We walked by bars, restaurants, sex shops, and prostitutes. It was amazing to see Beloved Adi Da in the midst of all this—the epitome of equanimity, Submitted to feeling it all, and joking with one of His devotee guides, who used to work as a clerk in one of the sex shops. Everywhere we went, people constantly stopped in their tracks to look at Him, clearly wondering who He could be.*

*On Thursday, July 31, most of the people in the surrounding area (who had been away on summer vacation during July) returned—bringing with them all the noises of a crowded city neighborhood. Suddenly, the apartment was surrounded by loud music, crying babies, and raised voices. A new discotheque opened nearby. This all-out attack of noise was obviously a great disturbance to Beloved Adi Da. At the same time, the sewer system, which was very old, broke down. Municipal officials and many plumbers came to examine it. The problem seemed to be directly underneath our center! Pneumatic drills dug holes inside and outside the building, and raw sewage floated in the little courtyard we had previously used for storage.*

The Amsterdam devotees knew that the sewage problem was not merely a random accident, unrelated to anything, or just bad luck. The difficulties were a sign of the universal egoic resistance to the Intrusion of the Divine. That is why the response of the devotees serving Avatar Adi Da is so important at such moments. He is always engaged in transforming the world's refusal of God. And the more devotees can serve Him rightly, converting the difficulties and the psychic energies that oppose His movement in the world, the more effective His Work can be with everyone.

The next day, Friday, August 1, Avatar Adi Da Samraj decided to return to Adidam Samrajashram. He had to give His devotees in Europe and elsewhere time to respond appropriately to His great Gift. Frans continues:

*FRANS: On August 2, Beloved Adi Da flew to London to connect with His plane to San Francisco. I sat directly in front of Him on the plane, wondering what Heathrow Airport would bring. I was worried about it. In the midst of my revery, one of the devotees attending Beloved Adi Da relayed a message to me. "Frans, Beloved Adi Da wants a half-witted white baboon right now". She and Beloved Adi Da gave me serious looks and then burst out laughing. I was taken totally by surprise. I had no idea what He meant, and it stopped my mind. I made an awkward response and sat back happily, realizing that my Beloved Guru was encouraging me to lighten up. I couldn't figure anything out. I just had to let things be the way they were going to be and deal with them on the spot. I also had a suspicion that perhaps I was this half-witted baboon!*

*When we got to Heathrow, we discovered that the seating assignments for Beloved Adi Da and those traveling with Him were scattered all over the plane. In the midst of everyone's concern over trying to correct this situation, Beloved Adi Da was absolutely sweet and Loving. I realized that, over this period, I had been given a lesson in Guru-devotion. It was true that we had all served more than we had ever done, but we were just beginning to learn about the high art of service to the Divine in Person. And, as always, our Beloved Guru had shown us a glimpse of the degree of self-transcendence required to serve Him truly. He also wanted us to understand that, in order for it to be real, Spiritual advancement must be reflected at the level of life. We had been tested and Instructed and Blessed beyond our imagination.*

*I stood next to Beloved Adi Da and began to say some of this to Him, expressing my love and gratitude—unsure of what to say exactly, feeling extremely humble. He leaned over toward me, listening intently. I felt so much love for Him. I felt that this Love and Communion with Him is all there is. Finally, I told Him that the lessons of this time would probably take some months to sink in. He replied, "Why not have it sink in immediately, and get down to it?"*

*He grasped my hand, pulled me close to Him, and hugged and kissed me, saying, "Give my love to everybody."*

*"Thank You, Beloved, thank You!"*

*Then He left us to board His plane, with a final "Tcha".*

## The Yoga of Devotion

What Avatar Adi Da meant by "have it sink in immediately, and get down to it" was right practice of the traditional Guru-devotee relationship. Some years later, He spoke of the Divine Laws of that relationship:

*AVATAR ADI DA SAMRAJ: When you become My devotee, you take a vow of submission to Me. You take a vow to Realize Me, to persist in the entire process to the point of Realizing Me Most Perfectly. Having done that, your vow to Me is to be the guide of your life from that point on. There is nothing that can come up—no relationship, no circumstance whatsoever—that should be the basis for you allowing yourself to become unclear or confused about your fundamental commitment of life, which is your vow to Me. Anything that does come up, then, is something that you must "consider" and deal with in the context of this vow of devotion to Me.*

*As I have said many times, if you have a Guru, you do not tell your Guru what you are going to do—you ask. That is what it is to have a Guru. You are not on your own. You are not self-"guruing", manipulating yourself egoically or moving by tendency. Your Guru is a Realizer. Your Guru is straight and true. Your Guru can give all advice. Your Guru knows what is best for you. That is Who you consult, and not the ego, ever.*

*Westerners do not want to live that way. You want to be on your own—talking it out, talking it out. Everybody has been talking it out in My Company for years. It all could be made very simple if you took your vow to Me seriously—just ask Me. Most of the time, you do not even have to ask Me directly. It is all in My Written Word, or, otherwise, installed in the culture of My devotees. That is how to stay straight. You have appealed to Me, you have resorted to Me, so you ask Me.*

*For the devotee, the Guru is Law, replacing the ego. The ego is utterly subordinated to the Master. If there is real Guru-devotion, you do not subordinate Me to any impulse, any circumstance, any relation—rather, you subordinate* *<u>everything</u>* *to Me. That is how you get straight. That is Salvation. That is the Way of Divine Liberation, and nothing else whatsoever is.* [March 2, 1995]

Avatar Adi Da Samraj had always been Calling His devotees to the "Guru Yoga"—to be obedient to His Instruction, to live as if always in His Company, to devote themselves to Him in body, emotion, and mind, and thereby to receive His Grace. Since the beginning of His Work, He had used the term "Satsang" ("the Company of Truth") to communicate that the Way in His Company is about the Guru Yoga, the living, moment-to-moment reality of the relationship to Him. Starting in March of 1986, and then, increasingly, during the months of His Yajna, Avatar Adi Da used a new term to describe the essential practice of the Way of Adidam—"Ishta-Guru Bhakti Yoga", or the "practice" ("Yoga") of "devotion" ("Bhakti") to the Guru who is one's "Chosen Beloved" ("Ishta"). (In more recent years, He has named this same fundamental practice "Ruchira Avatara Bhakti Yoga", or "the practice of devotion to the Ruchira Avatar".) What He meant by "Ishta-Guru Bhakti Yoga" is the essential practice of Satsang—the surrender of the entire body-mind in moment to moment heart-Contemplation of Him.

Ishta-Guru Bhakti Yoga (or Ruchira Avatara Bhakti Yoga) is a Divinely Given process. Certainly, the devotee must maintain the thread of attention—the disposition, the life of heart-surrender to Avatar Adi Da as Ishta-Guru. But the Yoga takes place by <u>Grace</u>. The transformations and Realizations are entirely and freely Given by the Divine Person, Avatar Adi Da. This Yoga, therefore, was the Secret that Avatar Adi Da was now communicating to His devotees—the way for them to truly establish themselves in right relationship to Him and to truly practice the Way in His Company.

*AVATAR ADI DA SAMRAJ: The relationship between the devotee and the Guru is a unique relationship and an extraordinary Yoga. I call it "Ishta-Guru Bhakti Yoga". In this great Yoga, the Guru is embraced as what is traditionally called the "Ishta-Guru", the "chosen" Form of the Divine Reality, Appearing as the Guru. It is the Yoga of allowing the Ishta-Guru to be the Divine Form, in meditation and in moment to moment practice. The devotee is devoted to that bodily Form, that Being, that Person, that Transmitting Power. The Divine Person, in other words, is acknowledged by the devotee in the Form of the Guru.*

*You use My Image, then, not only in the form of My Murti in the Communion Hall but in the form of your recollection of Me. You "put on" the Ishta-Guru. You let the Ishta-Guru Acquire and <u>Be</u> your own body-mind. In this way, My Divine Spirit-Power Works in your body-mind as if it were My Body-Mind. All the processes of sadhana in the Way of Adidam will take place spontaneously. You will respond to them, participate in them, but they will be generated spontaneously by My Spiritual Heart-Transmission.*

*In feeling-Contemplation of Me, everything, from subtle perceptions to Divine Self-Realization, is Realized by My Grace—not by your effortful working on yourself, but by your simple recognition-response to the One Who is before you.*

*Give your separate and separative self to Me, the One Who is already Divinely Self-Realized. Respond to Me <u>As</u> the Divine Self Incarnate. You cannot help but respond to Me if you recognize Me <u>As</u> That One. Then, the Very State of That One will be Realized by you, quite naturally, as a Gift. This is the Secret of the Way of Adidam.* [March 22, 1986]

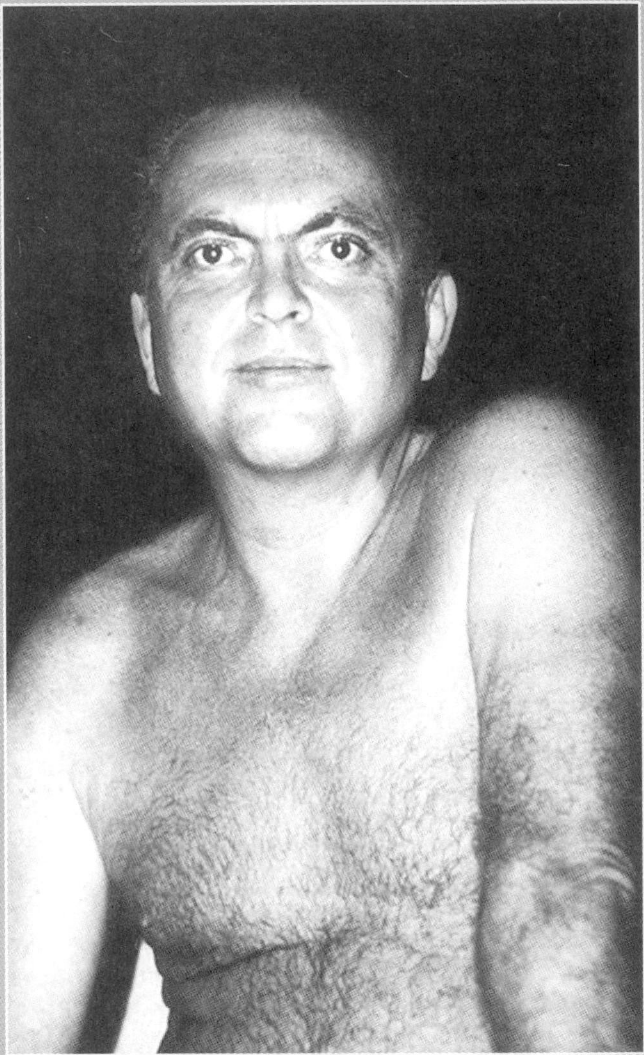

**During the "Indoor Yajna" ,
Adidam Samrajashram, 1987**

CHAPTER 16

# Indoor Yajna

In the eight months following Avatar Adi Da's return to Fiji from Europe in August 1986, His devotees had very minimal association with Him. In general, the most that the residents of Adidam Samrajashram would see of Him (apart from those who served in His private quarters) was a glimpse as He passed by, walking through the Ashram village to go to the library, where He was doing extensive writing. In spite of the lessons from Europe and His Gift of the practice of Ruchira Avatara Bhakti Yoga, devotees in general were still struggling to make right their relationship to Avatar Adi Da. In particular, many devotees were still troubled by an extremely painful period in 1985, when a lawsuit and media attacks had been launched against Avatar Adi Da and members of the devotee community by a number of disaffected former devotees. Their accusations related to the areas that most readily catch media attention: sex, drugs, money, and coercion. Some of the events alleged simply never happened—which, years later, the principal plaintiff publicly admitted. In other cases, their complaints reflected a misunderstanding of "Crazy Wisdom".

The "Crazy Wisdom" manner of teaching may arouse negative reactions in any cultural setting at any time in history. And this reaction is even more likely in a society such as ours, which is generally uninformed about the true esoteric Spiritual process. There is a tendency today, particularly in the media, to lump together serious and legitimate new religions with fanatical (and sometimes dangerous) pseudo-religious groups. All new (or non-mainstream) religious organizations thus tend to be classed indiscriminately under the derogatory generic heading of "cults". Furthermore, because the time-honored Eastern tradition of Guru-devotion is little understood in the West, any Spiritual figure who is related to by his or her followers in a devotional manner is often, at least initially, regarded with suspicion and even derision. Having Submitted to Work in the "Crazy-Wise" Tantric manner, Avatar Adi Da was therefore vulnerable to negative reactions on the part of those who did not understand the Spiritual nature of His Work.

A democratic society is founded on a fundamental respect for the personal freedom of its citizens. Such respect, granted as a primary political right, and supported and encouraged by society at large, is the essential circumstance of every individual's freedom to grow, both humanly and Spiritually. But, even within a democracy, there tends to be a mistrust of freedom when freedom is manifested in unconventional forms. Activities or points of view that do not comply with the most widely accepted social and religious norms of the time are sometimes attacked as wrong, not because they represent a threat either to their own members or to society at large, but simply because they go against the grain of prevailing dogmas. (Obviously, if the activities of any individual or group are truly harmful, intervention by the State may be appropriate.) Such intolerance of unconventionality is based on a primitive presumption that whatever is "different" is a "threat". And such intolerance, if unchecked, can result in the emerging of a narrow-minded, uncompassionate, and self-righteous society. Therefore, in a democracy, such intolerance must constantly be guarded against, if real individual and collective freedom is to be preserved.

In 1985, Avatar Adi Da's devotees knew it was their responsibility to testify to the unique Spiritual value of the "Crazy-Wise" Revelation they had witnessed in their Divine Guru's Company, but their testimony was not sufficient to stop the negative publicity. Although the legal matter was settled quickly, the aftermath in the media was profoundly disturbing to Avatar Adi Da's devotees. Devotees tended to feel "caught" by the "gotcha" game of media scandal. Many felt that, in the face of the accusations printed in the press, they had failed to resort to their heart-relationship to Avatar Adi Da and forcefully advocate the sacred nature of His "Crazy-Wise" Work.

Avatar Adi Da Himself no longer lived in the United States, but, as soon as He heard of the lawsuit, He retired into seclusion at Adidam Samrajashram. The trust in His relationship to His devotees had been breached—devotees had reacted to the negative attention of the common world by shutting down in their feeling, and thereby limiting their ability to participate with Him in His Liberating Work.

## The Indoor Yajna

Even after the profound Event of January 11, 1986, and Avatar Adi Da's subsequent travels, in April 1987 the group of devotees then living at Adidam Samrajashram were still feeling the pain of this limit in their relationship to Avatar Adi Da. They asked Avatar Adi Da's permission to come and see Him face-to-face. He consented, and the result of that meeting was an immediate call to gather everyone at the Giving Coat. The Giving Coat was a former orchid house—with a cement floor, screened walls, and a high metal roof with many wooden beams.[1] It was a short walk across the lawn from Indefinable, Avatar Adi Da's two-room residence in the Ashram village.

Gatherings with Avatar Adi Da continued for a year, and came to be known as the "Indoor Yajna"—a play on the "Indoor Summer" of 1976, and a reference to the fact that Avatar Adi Da had discussed the possibility of making another Yajna to the United States. Instead, He chose to remain "indoors"—that is, at His Hermitage in Fiji, rather than venturing "outdoors" to other parts of the world. Through these gatherings, Avatar Adi Da was drawn out of seclusion and back into direct "consideration" with His devotees.

At the first gathering, Avatar Adi Da criticized His devotees roundly for the "buttoned-down", suppressed sign they were animating. He reminded them that the Way of Adidam is not a matter of mere religious observances, but an ordeal of self-understanding, a confrontation with every illusion that is in you. Avatar Adi Da was looking for a profound response from His devotees: true recognition of Who He Is, and serious practice with the depth and profundity that this sensitivity requires. As part of calling forth this response, Avatar Adi Da made a decision. He Instructed His devotees (not only at Adidam Samrajashram but also in the regional communities elsewhere) to stop engaging all the forms of their devotional acknowledgement of Him. He withdrew the privilege of sacramental worship and asked that all images of Him be removed from devotees' Communion Halls. He even said that His devotees should no longer devotionally bow or prostrate to Him—as is the sacred custom of respect and acknowledgement in the traditions of Guru-devotion.

Avatar Adi Da did all this in order to combat false devotion—the tendency to approach Him in all the childish and cultic ways that characterize wrong relationship to Him.

Avatar Adi Da also returned all His devotees (at Adidam Samrajashram and in the regional communities elsewhere) to the beginner's stages of practice—no matter what stage of practice they had been engaging up to that point—so that they could "consider" the essence of His Wisdom-Teaching all over again, from scratch.

As He gathered night after night with devotees at Adidam Samrajashram, Avatar Adi Da entered into a grand recapitulation of the Way of Adidam, focusing on His Argument about "Narcissus" and the self-contraction. In each gathering, Avatar Adi Da Samraj exhaustively addressed everything that He observed in His devotees, every question that was brought to Him—as if never to have to do it again. But, then, the next day, He would ask once again, "Are there any questions or 'considerations' for gathering?"

## The Seven Stages of Life

One of the areas that Avatar Adi Da explored in great detail during the "Indoor Yajna" was the various forms of religious and Spiritual search evident in the collective Great Tradition of humankind. He was in the process of creating a new "Source-Text", *The Basket Of Tolerance*—a vast "Consideration" of all the possible points of view about God, Truth, and Reality, and the various approaches to right life, as they are exemplified in the entire spectrum of religious and Spiritual traditions.

The entire Spiritual process has been exactly "mapped" by Avatar Adi Da from the "Point of View" of His own Divine Realization. This Great Process, He Reveals, unfolds in the context of seven stages of life. These seven stages are a process that unfolds in Consciousness, ultimately Revealing that you are Consciousness Itself, and not the body or the mind.[2]

The first three (or foundation) stages of life constitute the ordinary course of human adaptation—bodily, emotional, and mental growth. Each of the first three stages of life takes approximately seven years to be established, and together they form the necessary foundation for the advanced and ultimate stages of life (which are not characterized by any fixed time-period). Every individual who lives to an adult age inevitably adapts (although, in most cases, only partially) to the first three stages of life.

The fourth and fifth (or advanced) stages of life are characterized by the Awakening to Spirit, or the Spiritualizing of the body-mind.

In the sixth and seventh (or ultimate) stages of life, Consciousness Itself is directly Realized, beyond identification with the body-mind. In the sixth stage of life, the Realizer Identifies with Consciousness (in profound states of meditation) by excluding all awareness of phenomena. But this Realization is incomplete. Even the necessity to turn away from the world in order to fully Enjoy Consciousness represents a contraction, a refusal of Reality in its totality.

The seventh stage of life, or the Realization of "Open Eyes" (Uniquely Revealed and Given by Adi Da Samraj), transcends this last limit. The motive to exclude awareness of phenomena disappears, because it is suddenly, tacitly, Realized that there is no "difference" between Consciousness and the objects of Consciousness. Thus, the seventh stage Realization wipes away every trace of dissociation from the body-mind and the world. In the seventh stage of life, the world is Divinely Recognized to be an apparent and un-necessary modification of Consciousness Itself. All that apparently arises is seen to be Play upon the Deep of Consciousness. Consciousness Itself, or Being Itself, Is all there is, and Consciousness Itself is found to be Radiant, or "Love-Bliss-Full", in the Words of Avatar Adi Da. Thus, every "thing" and every "one" that appears is a mere modification of the One Divine "Brightness".

His Revelation of the seven stages potential in human life is the context for all of Avatar Adi Da's Teaching about the various points of view and degrees of Realization found in humanity's Great Tradition of religious and Spiritual Wisdom.

Avatar Adi Da had spoken about the seven stages of life since the late seventies. One night during the "Indoor Yajna", He gave this remarkable Discourse about the four basic ways of viewing Reality, starting with the most primitive.

*AVATAR ADI DA SAMRAJ: You are propagandized by the innocence of your upbringing into making the assumption that you are the body, or that the physical universe is all there is. The presumption that you are the body seems obvious to you only because you have been propagandized into it as a method of survival in the context of bodily existence. You are like people thousands of years ago sitting around the fire and, on the basis of their limited knowledge, discoursing about the stars above them and the presumed heaven above the stars. Your "consideration" is primitive talk, because the base presumption of your "consideration" is primitive.*

*The people sitting around the fire now sit at the roundtables of the departments of science in universities. They are still discoursing about the stars. Now they bring out their charts and calculations and talk about mathematical realities and the "big bang" and other sophisticated theories of space-time, but the conversation is just as primitive as the conversations that took place around the fire thousands of years ago, because precisely the same point of view is the basis of both discussions. And it is that point of view that determines whether the "consideration" is primitive or not. Human beings have become much more sophisticated in terms of the data they discuss—perhaps they are not so naive about the stars, for example—but they are not any more sophisticated about the base presumption. What could be more naive than identifying with the body (or gross matter) only? What could be less sophisticated? Less intelligent?*

*Your business is to investigate that naive presumption and likewise all the designs that relate to you "personally" (so-called), so that you may generate life in a totally different form than the primitive propaganda suggests. I am not talking about politics here, I am talking about the Great Way, the Process of Divine Enlightenment. If you will inspect all human propaganda, you will discover that it is based on the single proposition "I am the body", the naive presumption or identification with the ego. As long as the ego is the basis of conventional human knowledge, how illuminating can any form of knowledge be?*

*At the same time that you are trying to survive as an individual, you always already exist in the great sense, the ultimate (or perfect) sense. The Divine Condition is already the Condition in Which all of this appears—and who is noticing It? Everybody is busy propagandizing and being propagandized by the proposition of physical existence. Who has the time, the energy, the clarity, the attention, to investigate the base proposition itself and create a way of life on the basis of inspection?*

*There are only a handful of presumptions. The proposition "I am the body" does not reflect any greater understanding than simple identification with the body-mind itself. That point of view belongs to the first three stages of life and the "original" and "basic" contexts of the fourth stage of life.*[3] *The proposition "I am the mind" or "I am the psyche" or "I am the 'soul'" belongs to the "advanced" context of the fourth stage of life*[4] *and to the fifth stage of life. The proposition "I am not the body, and I am not the mind, but I am Consciousness exclusive of body or mind" is the base proposition of the sixth stage of life. The proposition of the seventh stage is "I am Consciousness Itself, Self-Existing, Self-Radiant, Divine, and everything that arises is only an appearance, an apparent modification of That, and does not bind It". Really, then, there are only four propositions.*

*If you understand this, you possess an extraordinary tool for examining yourself, all others, all traditions, all forms of knowledge. Every individual, every form of knowledge, every tradition, however complex it may appear, is fundamentally designed by a basic proposition, a simplicity that governs every expression of that person or tradition. Your entire life, every one of its details, every one of its complex functions, is being governed by the base proposition you are making—which, at the present time, is identification with the body.*

*From the beginning, I Call you to live beyond that automaticity. Begin from the beginning. Examine yourself. Examine My Word, examine the Great Tradition, and proceed, step by step, on the basis of discrimination. Become clarified. Make decisions based on real and thorough examination of yourself and your possibilities, and grow on that basis. Do not propagandize. Let everyone know that you are called to nothing less than a very specific and intelligent process of self-examination and examination of everything that appears to your view.*

[July 10, 1987]

Avatar Adi Da was not suggesting that His devotees strive to live out all the stages of life. His Call was, and is, to progressively transcend, or go beyond, the limits of the first six stages of life, or all the points of view apparent in the religious and Spiritual traditions.

# Listening, Hearing, and Seeing

There is only one way that this perfect transcending is possible—through the capability to observe, understand, and transcend one's activity of separation in the context of all experience and all stages of life short of Divine Self-Realization. Avatar Adi Da calls this fundamental capability "hearing" Him. To hear Avatar Adi Da is the same as "radical" understanding. It is most fundamental understanding of the activity of self-contraction.

When you have heard Avatar Adi Da, you understand that it is you who are separating yourself from Happiness, from Truth, from Reality—separating yourself by your own act of self-contraction. And so, when hearing is true, you no longer seek Happiness in any dimension of experience. You no longer have any motive to do so, because you have understood that Happiness (or Truth, or Reality) is never in doubt. Happiness, Truth, or Reality Is Always Already the Case, and you know this by direct Revelation, through heart-Awakened devotion to Adi Da Samraj.

The prerequisite for hearing is the sadhana of listening—the life of devotion, study, self-discipline, and meditation that Avatar Adi Da gives to His beginning devotees. Then, in the context of the listening devotee's devotional relationship to Avatar Adi Da—obedient to His Instruction, intensively studying and "considering" His Wisdom-Teaching and the Leelas of His Work with His devotees—self-observation and self-understanding are Given as a Gift.

Once hearing is established, the relationship to Adi Da Samraj enters into a new phase: real and stable Spiritual Awakening now becomes possible, because the body-mind is no longer ruled by the self-contraction. There is an openness, a receptivity to Avatar Adi Da's Spiritual Presence, Which is as unmistakably Him as His physical Body. His Spiritual Presence is His invisible, but tangible, Divine Spiritual Body. To "see" Avatar Adi Da means that you can always "Locate" His Divine Body. You literally feel Him, His "Bright" Person, Touching, Pervading, Surrounding and Infusing your body-mind with His Love-Bliss. And you become utterly heart-devoted to Him in His Spiritual Form.

Since the night of "Guru Enters Devotee" in January 1974, Avatar Adi Da had frequently Demonstrated the Force and Bliss of His Spiritual Presence to His devotees—but, without the arms of hearing and seeing, His devotees could not sustain this Spiritual intimacy with Him. Now, at the beginning of the "Indoor Yajna", after so many years of Calling devotees to really practice the listening sadhana, Avatar Adi Da was looking for the signs of hearing and seeing in those seated in front of Him and in all His longtime devotees.

However, after several months of "consideration", it became clear that hearing and seeing were not established in Avatar Adi Da's devotees, largely because of continuing complications in the emotional-sexual dimension of their lives. Avatar Adi Da knew what questions to ask in order to test whether a devotee would suddenly fall into doubt about the state of his or her intimate relationship, whether he or she was loved, betrayed, ignored, understood, suitably matched, and so on. He would apparently suggest one thing, and then, at the critical moment, He would turn the tables with another question or comment, allowing an entirely different picture to emerge. He was making the point that, without the integrity that comes with true hearing, the egoic personality is always vacillating between opposites—ungrounded, unsatisfied, always betraying the other, always of two minds about everything.

# "Heart-Feeling is the Ultimate Intensity"

Avatar Adi Da's great Tantric Work to release the lock on the heart went on night after night in the "Indoor Yajna" gatherings, not only through His piercing questions and discourses (with which each gathering typically began), but also through the magical hours that followed—hours of dancing, recitations of poetry, singing along with Him to great opera recordings: "Tenors to My left, baritones to My right, ladies in the middle, move up to the front." Over and over again, He would sing the same familiar arias with passionate feeling, straining every cell in His body, the veins on His head popping out, the force of His singing filling His great chest and navel, His legs stretched, His arms spread like great wings.

And then He would have devotees dance—sometimes alone, with their intimate partners, with a friend, all the men, all the women, man to man, woman to woman. "No learned moves! Subtlety and detail! Dance for God, for Joy!" He would cry. While they danced, His devotees showed Him everything about themselves,

***"When I dance, I move through all possible planes before I finish. I dance to not have to dance again".***

every pattern of energy, emotion, and character. As He watched, Adi Da Samraj would do His mysterious Work of purification and Blessing, indicating who should dance with whom next, instructing devotees to "get down", to dance "from the navel". During almost every gathering, He Himself would at some point step on to the floor—and the room would become electric. He would intercept the dancers, drawing individuals into the indescribable Play of His own Dancing.

One night, after receiving the praises of His devotees Avatar Adi Da spoke the secret of His dancing: "When I dance, I move through all possible planes before I finish. I dance to not have to dance again."

In everything He did, Adi Da Samraj was showing that His Divine "Emergence" had truly brought Him "down to the toes" in His embrace of the human condition. There was one particular occasion when He Demonstrated His humanity and Divinity so intensely to the devotees present that the occasion will forever remain in their hearts and minds. Denise Getz, a devotee of many years, describes what happened.

*DENISE: It was Beloved Adi Da's Birthday in November 1987, and that night He invited all the resident devotees, and those on retreat as well, to a celebratory gathering. He sat before us utterly magnificent and Radiant, while we presented Him with gifts. Then His daughters offered Him a performance of their sacred arts, including song, recitation, and dance. Spontaneously, He began to weep, telling us of His great Sorrow: His Trimada, His beautiful and innocent daughters, had danced and sung before Him, and yet they would die, we would all die, and we would all suffer the agonies of loss and separation. Tears streamed down His face. His sorrow was boundless. At the end of their performance, the Trimada gave Him a book of Leelas they had written called "Our Life with Love-Ananda". Still weeping, He received their gifts and thanked them with great emotion. The birthday cake with candles was brought in, and then He kissed the Trimada goodnight.*

*After they were gone, Beloved Adi Da wept on and on—it seemed to last for hours. He was freely and perfectly expressing the sorrow of conditional existence, and, at the same time, He freely expressed human love and relationship. All the while He did this, His Divine Heart-Transmission was profound. He was Radiating Perfect Feeling, Prior to the play of emotion. It was a moment almost too vulnerable, too broken-hearted, to be viewed by mortal eyes.*

*We were gathered close around our Beloved Guru, drawn into His Sphere of Feeling. Some devotees shouted praise and love to Him, some sobbed loudly, while others sat quietly. In the midst of this chaos, He silently raised His finger to His lips to quiet us, as if asking us to be still enough to feel deeply with Him.*

*He began to whisper, "My children, My children . . ." again and again. And then, "I cannot love it. I cannot love it. I just cannot love it," over and over.*

*"What, Beloved, can't You love?" we asked.*

*He whispered: "Death."*

*"My children . . . I will take care of them. It takes so much Love. Don't you know! So much—you just do not know how much it takes from the Other Side."*

*On and on He wept. We poured out our hearts to Him in affirmation of our love for Him, the Trimada's love for Him, the Happiness we had found in Him. He received our love and praise, true enough. But still it seemed that He needed us to respond to Him with much deeper understanding and responsibility.*

*"I just cannot do any more for you. I wish I could, but I just cannot. I have finished My Work. My Teaching Work is done. I really did all that can be done. Now you all have so much work to do. You have no idea. You have no idea. I have exhausted Myself in your company. I have done everything I can do for you. I have exhausted Myself to be with you. I have no thought of that, but just do everything for you, for everyone, to Kiss everyone. I just cannot do any more. There is no more that can be done. There has never been such a Demonstration. Such a Glory of exhaustion never was. You just do not know What has Come into your personal company. You just do not know. All the life of this Body would be exhausted for your sake. But I cannot do any more. <u>Your</u> time has come."*

At a gathering a week later, Avatar Adi Da spoke about that occasion, disclosing a Secret.

*AVATAR ADI DA SAMRAJ: There is no romanticized Realizer here tentatively associated with the body and making idealized, abstract pronouncements. Such is not the quality of My human Lifetime at all. From Birth, My human Lifetime has been a Submission. It is your business, through the telling of My Leelas, to communicate the Truth of My Submission to you. It is your business to communicate just what an Ordeal it was—and is. My human Lifetime involves not only the same suffering everyone else endures, but a more profound sensitivity to it than others allow themselves to endure.*

*How often do you invest yourself in such feeling? I am invested in such feeling all the time. That is how I Work. That is what I Do all the time. That is the basis of My Work.*

*When I wept with you, I was Helping you to feel the difference in yourself. How much will you allow yourself to feel? How much will you allow yourself to be invested in the real process of Real-God-Realization? That real process involves self-transcendence, not just an abstract commitment to Real-God-Realization. Through self-transcendence, you Realize Me. And, through Submission to you, I Help you to Realize Me. The real Spiritual process is always an ordeal, for the born Realizer and for any devotee.*

*The body will die, but, even so, you can Realize the Deathless Condition. I would not have My children die. I would not have anyone die or suffer the mortal round, be submitted to it and limited by it. Because of a profoundly Compassionate Response to mortality and suffering, My human Birth was made, and Its Message is not merely that you are mortal. Your mortality is just something I bring to your attention. You must transcend yourself. I am here to help you Realize the Deathless Condition.*

*In addition to reflecting the conditional reality to you through sorrowful signs at times, I Grant you the Joy of complete submission to Feeling, to the degree that That Which Is Beyond the limit of sorrow may be also felt and Realized. I am Communicating to you that you must feel sorrow to that degree. You must feel it so profoundly that you feel beyond yourself. But What is to be Realized, What I am here to Bring to you, is the Realization of the Deathless Condition That Transcends this inevitable sorrow. Therefore, the inevitability of death is not My final Message. The transcending of death is My final Message.*

*Even in My seventh stage Sign to you, I allow My Self to let this body-mind show all of its natural Signs, including a profound sensitivity to mortality. I allow My Self to Feel mortality completely, without the slightest reserve. I allow the body to weep, to be sundered, to be undone, to be heart-broken by utter Sympathy with conditional existence. To do so is to pass beyond Sympathy by magnifying Feeling Itself. The heart must be broken to Find What Is, Beyond the conditional limit of the heart.*

*Thus, this great sorrow becomes Joy. This Heart-Feeling is the ultimate Intensity. But you do not pass to Joy without the breaking of the knot that separates you. Sympathy Itself, Feeling Itself, is the Means, the Way, the Communion. It is magnified more and more through the developmental stages of practice. And, when the heart is broken utterly, and you Stand Prior to it and Beyond it, then you get the Great Vision. Then the Very Divine is Magnified in your being, through your being, through all the fractions of the apparent universe—and you Stand Free. Then the body can weep all it likes—and it should.* [November 10, 1987]

Matthew Spence recalls how every night during the Indoor Yajna was a miracle—every night Avatar Adi Da would break all hearts with His Love and Sacrifice. He was doing everything to inspire in His devotees the deep urge to Realize His Divine Condition—and to be satisfied with nothing less.

*MATTHEW: I remember one night in particular, when it seemed that maybe the gatherings could end. We had danced for over two hours, and Beloved Adi Da sat on the floor of the stage totally vulnerable and in a state of sheer exhaustion. We gathered around Him in a circle, several deep and very close. He looked at us, each one, and, calling us each by name, He asked if there was anything more, anything unresolved, anything He had said or done that was not clear. Again and again, He asked each one of us, not just for our questions, but for the questions in us that were in all our friends, everywhere—anything in us, anything in them. And we pressed His hands and feet and touched His back and said no, nothing, and told Him that we loved Him, and that He had given it all and we thanked Him. And I remember how he turned His head so far to see those sitting behind Him, to meet them eye to eye, and ask if there was yet anything more they needed, that He could Give. And, when we had affirmed and reaffirmed His Gifts and our love for Him, He rose and walked home across the lawn.*

In the middle of January 1988, Avatar Adi Da reestablished the devotional culture in His Hermitage, satisfied that the lessons and purification of all those preceding months had done their work. He allowed sacramental worship of Him to begin again, and Gave a magnificent Discourse on puja as the practice of installing Him at the heart. The relief that devotees felt was overwhelming. They now realized how incomplete their lives had been without the bodily expression of Guru-Love and heart-surrender to Him. It was sobering for His devotees to feel that Avatar Adi Da had had to withhold the privilege of devotional practices from them all this time, so that they would rightly acknowledge the Spiritual depth of their relationship to Him and the Gift of Ruchira Avatara Bhakti Yoga. It was obvious that there could be no advancement in the Way of Adidam without this worship of the Divine in Person.

Now Avatar Adi Da chose to send a group of devotees out as His "messengers" to bring the lessons of the "Indoor Yajna" directly to all His devotees. At a gathering a few hours before leaving on the boat, the "messengers" received a farewell and an empowerment beyond their wildest dreams.

The opening strains of the *Ruchira Avatara Gita*[5] stole through the room, a musical setting of Avatar Adi Da's Words from the "Source-Text" in which He Reveals the secrets of the Way of devotion to Him. Unexpectedly, Avatar Adi Da Himself moved into the middle of the stage and began to dance alone, in one of the most sublime Demonstrations of His Incarnation that devotees had ever witnessed. He was simply the Body of Real God, vulnerable beyond belief.

Tears rolled down His face. Every gesture registered profound emotion and power. His feet and legs assumed poses seen in traditional depictions of dancing Krishna or dancing Siva, and expressions of wrathful deities played over His face. His eyes bulged out. His teeth protruded like those of a fearsome temple guardian. In the next moment, His arms flowed in the delicate pattern of a dancing goddess, forming traditional gestures, or mudras. He moved with a subtlety and precision that was inconceivable except in one long trained in Indian sacred dance.

Stephan Blas, who had recorded the singing of the *Ruchira Avatara Gita* that was now playing, was standing to the rear of the platform where the Divine Maha-Siddha was Dancing.

*STEPHAN: As I watched my Beloved Guru dance, I was Invaded by the Force He was Transmitting. I could not keep my eyes open. My breath became very rapid. My eyes turned up under my eyelids. My hands and arms performed spontaneous mudras. I stood enraptured, moving spontaneously, feeling Beloved Adi Da as He danced. I was absorbed in His Divine Spirit-Current. My arms spontaneously extended forward, reaching fully out in front of me. Suddenly I gasped. My arms were around Beloved Adi Da's Body. I was not aware that He had begun to dance with me, only a fraction of an inch from my body!*

*As He drew close to me, some people began to scream in ecstasy at the sight of the Divine Manifesting. His Spirit-Current literally poured into my body, taking over every part—Moving me, Living me.*

*I began to dance with Him body to Body. Yet I was not really dancing with Him. He was dancing me. The Energy was overpowering. My limbs moved as though they had become rubber and were being moved by an electric current. My skin, muscles, bones, and cells began to bend and crunch in impossible ways. My body had no choice but to move with this great Force. Blissfully, and also painfully, I was moved beyond any ordinary capability, beyond ordinary human movements of the body. Still with my eyes closed, I touched parts of Beloved Adi*

***"As I watched my Beloved Dance, I was invaded by the Force He was Transmitting. . . . I was absorbed in His Great Spiritual Life-Current."***

*Da's Body in the dance. I could not feel Him as an "other", separate from myself. Eventually, I fell to the floor, as limp as if all the bones and the muscles had been removed. Still, His Spirit-Current was in charge and Moved me—arching my back, bending me backwards, then forwards, then backwards.*

*I was still on the floor as the song ended. When I opened my eyes and looked up, all I could see was Beloved Adi Da's back as He stood at the front of the stage facing away from me and toward His devotees in the room. He was breathing deeply and slowly, and rocking back and forth and side to side. He seemed like an enormous mountain in which and from which everything was being Lived. I was mindless, speechless, as He walked out of the room. And I wept helplessly.*

A few hours later, Stephan and his friends were on a boat gliding through the lagoon and out beyond the reef. They were as ready as they could possibly be for their mission.

## A Heart Healing

During the Indoor Yajna, in May 1987, Avatar Adi Da received word from the community of His Australian devotees that one of their children, a girl of nearly six, was about to go into the hospital for surgery. She was tiny for her age, owing to a serious congenital heart condition. Now she was facing ten hours of open-heart surgery that would involve switching the major blood vessels that entered her heart. The child's name was "Leela", a name she had been given with the Blessing of Avatar Adi Da.

Avatar Adi Da asked to be informed of the exact time of Leela's operation, and He indicated that He expected regular medical reports. The operation went well, taking six, rather than the projected ten, hours. Nevertheless, Leela's condition was critical and did not stabilize for twenty-four hours. After that, she started to improve, but lung congestion began to develop.

On the morning of Leela's operation and again the next day, Adi Da woke up with severe symptoms of stress around His heart. Then, before receiving the medical reports, He began to develop lung congestion. A day or two later, He woke up with a mass of dried blood on His chest in a stripe about an inch and a half wide and about six inches long. When He went to wash it off, He noticed a small puncture-wound, an actual hole on the upper left side of His chest above the aorta. The puncture was painless and completely inexplicable. Avatar Adi Da fell back to sleep and when He awoke again the wound had disappeared. But there was more blood on His chest. For more than a week from the time of Leela's operation, Avatar Adi Da also had the sensation of being heavily drugged. One day, He spontaneously asked His physician about a particular form of medication, only to find in the next medical report that the same medication had been administered to Leela that same day.

Leela's operation was completely successful. She made a remarkably rapid recovery and several days after the surgery celebrated her sixth birthday in the hospital. Among her gifts was a teddy bear from Avatar Adi Da.

In conversations with His devotees at His Hermitage, Ruchira Adi Da confirmed that, through His profound Blessing-attention on Leela, He had spontaneously lived her ordeal in His own body, and, thus, served the auspicious outcome. To this day, Leela has lived a normal life and required no further surgery.

After Leela's recovery, some devotees remembered an incident that had occurred many years previously in the early days of Avatar Adi Da's Teaching Work. Theresa LeGarie tells her story:

*THERESA: I was born with a complete heart block, which included two holes in the wall of the ventricles. At age 13, I had open heart surgery. At age 21, I had surgery again, this time to insert a pacemaker to balance and control my irregular heart rhythm.*

*A year after this surgery, I first read Avatar Adi Da's book* The Knee Of Listening. *Shortly after, I flew to Los Angeles to visit the ashram and decided to stay and practice under the guidance of my Guru.*

*One day soon after I arrived, Avatar Adi Da was sitting in His study at the ashram and talking with devotees. He began to ask about the "girl with the pacemaker". I was excitedly brought into the room and directed to His chair. I sat on His knee, looking directly into His eyes. He asked me many questions about the nature and history of my condition, and about the surgery itself. He drew out many concerns and fears and limitations I had experienced in relationship to my heart condition. Then, at a certain point, no more words were spoken. I looked directly into His deep Eyes. His Glance drew me into a feeling of timeless happiness, peace, calm, and no concern. Avatar Adi Da Smiled. He looked at me and said, "You can use My Heart."*

*I felt so much joy. I realized I was not alone or separate or incomplete in this ordeal. He understood. I recognized that the relationship with Him is timeless, and this healed my fearful and wounded heart. His Heart is the True Heart, and the only Source of Life.*

## A Transition to the "Perfect Practice"

The Power of Avatar Adi Da's Divine "Emergence" and His monumental reexamination of every aspect of life and Consciousness that followed during 1987 made a profound impression upon Adidama Sukha Dham, who, in early 1988, made an unprecedented leap in the Divine Process of Real-God-Realization. On February 2, 1988, she became the first of Avatar Adi Da's devotees to be stably established in the "Perfect Practice" of Adidam, the ultimate phase of practice that (in due course) becomes Realization of the seventh stage of life. She describes here how this remarkable and Graceful quickening occurred:

*ADIDAMA SUKHA DHAM: At the moment of the Initiation of Beloved Adi Da's Divine "Emergence", I was sitting by His side while He spoke about His Yogic death to others on the phone. He was describing how the energy and life-force were leaving His Body. Then I observed the apparent death of My Beloved Guru's bodily (human) Form as He fell to the floor. As I confronted and suffered the great sorrow of death and separation, I dropped deep below the social persona. I allowed the heart to feel its loss and great vulnerability, and I felt beyond all conventional attachments. This allowed me to feel the depth of my love-response to Beloved Adi Da, and, in that depth, I received a Vision, or Revelation, of His Incarnation. This heartbreak and heart-recognition*

*became the source of a Graceful flowering in my practice over the next two years—the rapid unfolding of hearing and seeing, and transition to the "Perfect Practice".*

*I was intuitively certain that my Beloved Guru's Divine "Emergence" was an Event unprecedented and unknown in the conditionally manifested worlds. I felt His Divine "Emergence" as a breakthrough of Consciousness Itself into the world. And I could feel this breakthrough of Consciousness Itself to be coincident with His "Brightening" Power, the Power that Outshines all separation and death. His physical Body was dramatically changed in this Event, such that it was obvious that Real God, or Truth Itself, or Reality Itself is Embodied in His bodily (human) Form. This heart-recognition had been present in my relationship to my Beloved Guru from the beginning, but now I intuited the vast consequences of His Incarnation. I was certain that His Divine "Emergence" carried profound implications for the destiny of humankind.*

*An extraordinary process of purification and Yogic re-formation then began in my body-mind. There was intensive physical purification of the body, including a 40-day fast, which I engaged at the same time that Beloved Adi Da was fasting. During this time, I lived on retreat in seclusion with Beloved Adi Da, devoting much of my time to meditation. The retreat was sublimed by Beloved Adi Da's profound Spiritual Transmission, and magnified by the Revelation of His bodily (human) Form as the Very Body of the Divine, conditionally Manifested in this plane.*

*After some weeks, Beloved Adi Da ended His period of total seclusion and re-associated with His devotees. Now, in direct relationship to my Beloved Guru, I went through a profound and extended reinvestigation and direct testing of the entire egoic structure of my life and consciousness.*

*About a year later, Beloved Adi Da asked me to begin to serve Him by passing on His Communications to His devotees. Beloved Adi Da's Instructions to His devotees encompass every aspect of human existence and everything required for the establishment of His Work in the world. And so, in this new service, I had to begin to do profound sadhana for the sake of others in a manner I had never done before. I had to relinquish my self-based concentration in my own relationship to Beloved Adi Da and in the simpler forms of service—such as cleaning, cooking, and caring for the Trimada—that, until then, I had been used to doing in His intimate Sphere. I had to devote my life to His Work. This marked a profound turning point in me, a surrender of all personal preference.*

*Apart from passing on Beloved Adi Da's Instructions, He expected me to serve others in the right devotional understanding and reception of the Instructions Given. This service obliged me to move out of self-meditation and obsession with my own emotion, and that is how the intensive listening-hearing process began for me.*

*My life now became an intense ordeal of serving everyone's understanding of my Beloved Guru's Instructions in the light of His Divine "Emergence". In other words, I had to help others feel the reality of the profound Gift of Beloved Adi Da's "Emergence" as the Divine Person, so that they could be transformed in their relationship to Him and take up a truly self-renouncing sadhana in His Company.*

*During this time, I saw that, no matter how positive or negative or easeful or difficult any moment was, I was always doing the same thing. Through my Beloved Guru's Divine Siddhi, I saw that my body-mind was only self-contraction and that it was my own activity. I also saw that my Divine Heart-Master Stands eternally Prior to that egoic activity of mine. And I felt a profound Liberation in being able to effectively resort to Him beyond the*

*"Beloved Adi Da asked me to begin to serve Him by passing on His Communications to His devotees. Beloved Adi Da's Instruction to His devotees encompass every aspect of human existence and everything required for the establishment of His Great Work in the world, and, indeed, throughout the entire Cosmic domain. And so, in this new service, I had to begin to do profound sadhana for the sake of others in a manner I had never done before."*

*mechanism of self-contraction. This was not a mental process—it was a Revelation, a Gift, an Initiation into Communion with Him.*

*Thus, the Grace of hearing was awakened in me. It was a forceful transformation, granting moment to moment awareness that this mortal dying world, full of pain and suffering, was not the Living Reality. I knew that all beings could now find their Salvation, find the Truth beyond the cycles of birth and death—by going beyond this merely materialistic and conventional presumption. At the same time, I felt the dimension of the psyche being exposed and entered into and released, such that its patterns ceased to be an obstruction. The Divine Descent of Beloved Adi Da, His Nectar of Love-Bliss, was dissolving strong habits of the body-mind. Through the Grace of the great Gift of hearing, or the moment to moment capability to transcend egoity, real Spiritual Communion with my Beloved began.*

*This Awakening of the Divine Spiritual Process had nothing to do with the search for God, or an indulging in the effects of my Beloved's Spiritual Transmission, but only in the capability to "Locate" and heart-recognize Him as the Divinely Radiant egoless Person, the Divine Person Incarnate.*

*In this process, the presumptions and the illusions based on the body-mind's point of view loosened, and my Beloved Guru Entered me Spiritually via the Samadhi of "the Thumbs". Beloved Adi Da Spiritually Descended into the body, completely Filling it from the crown of the head to the toes. In response to His Spiritual Invasion, there was whole bodily surrender into His Divine Condition.*

*I experienced the Divine Spiritual Body of my Beloved Guru Pervading everything, as a great Sphere of Light. In this Samadhi of Unity with His Divine Form, my Beloved Revealed Himself as Divine Love, the Love-Blissful Reality of all. There was no loss of awareness of the body-mind—the reception of His Love-Bliss was tangible. When I resumed the ordinary state, I saw with stark clarity that I had to give myself over to That Which is Truly Great, and not be controlled by the patterns of this body-mind. During 1987, the Samadhi of "the Thumbs" became my consistent experience in meditation. Through this Samadhi, I was being Spiritually opened by my Beloved Guru and progressively freed from the point of view of the body-mind.*

*This Process of my Beloved Bhagavan's*[6] *Spiritual Invasion took place quickly, leading to a most remarkable moment in His Company. One day, I was Graced to attend a meditation occasion with my Beloved in one of His Communion Halls. On my way to the Hall, I felt my Beloved Guru's Brilliant Spiritual Current Filling me so profoundly that it was as though His Great Current was "walking" me to the Communion Hall. I felt I was being escorted to an Initiation.*

The Samadhi of "The Thumbs" is self-forgetting identification with the Sphere of Beloved Adi Da's Divine Body. Repeated experience of "The Thumbs" is essential to the process of advancement in the Way of Adidam, because it is the Force of Avatar Adi Da's Spirit Blessing, fully experienced in the Samadhi of "The Thumbs", that releases the knot of egoity in the right side of the heart, and thus makes way for the "Perfect Practice" of Adidam to begin. In the following passage from *The Dawn Horse Testament*, Beloved Adi Da describes the Samadhi of the "Thumbs" in detail, emphasizing that this Samadhi is a unique Gift of His Divine Spirit-Force, Pressing Down into the body-mind of His devotee:

. . . *My Descending Spiritual Fullness Will Completely Overwhelm the ordinary frontal (or natural human) sense Of bodily Existence. My Divine Spirit-Current Will Move Fully Down In The Frontal Line, To the bodily base, and It Will Then Turn About, and—Without Vacating The Frontal Line—It Will Pass Also Into The Spinal Line. This Yogic Event Will Occur With Such Force That You Will Feel Utterly (Love-Blissfully) "Intoxicated", and There Will Be The Feeling That the body Is Somehow Rotating Forward and Down (From The Crown Of the head), As Well As Backward and Up (From the base of the spine). This Rotation Will Seem, Suddenly, To Complete Itself—and The Experience Will, Suddenly, Be One Of Feeling Released From the gross physical body, So That You Feel You Are Present Only As An egoless "Energy Body" (Previously Associated With and Conformed To the gross physical body, but Now, By Means Of My Avatarically Self-Transmitted Divine Grace, Infused By and Conformed To My Avatarically Self-Transmitted Divine Body Of Self-Evidently Divine Spirit-Energy). You Will Feel This "Energy Body" To Be Spherical In Shape—Centerless (Empty, or Void, Of Center, mind, and Familiar ego-self) and Boundless (As If Even bodiless, or Without form), Although (Somehow, and Partially) Also Yet Associated With (While Rotating From and Beyond) Your ordinary psycho-physical form. The ordinary References Of the body-mind and the environment Will, In This Divine Yogic Event, Not Make Much Sense (or, In Any Manner, Affect This Experience Of "The Thumbs")—Although There May Be Some Superficial (and Entirely Non-limiting) Awareness Of the body, the room, and so forth. This Experience Will Last For a few moments, or a few minutes—or For an extended period, of indefinite length. Nevertheless, Just When This Spontaneous Experience Has Become Most Pleasurable—So That You Somehow Gesture To Make It Continue Indefinitely—the ordinary sense of the body-mind Will, Suddenly (Spontaneously), Return.*

THE DAWN HORSE TESTAMENT
OF THE RUCHIRA AVATAR

*It was on this day that my Beloved Adi Da Initiated me in the "Perfect Practice" of Adidam. The event was stark. As I sat before my Divine Beloved Guru, I was immediately Bathed in the most incredible Light—His "Brightness" was Surrounding me and Pervading me. He was Descending as a total Sphere of Light, a Column of Light, not moving up or down—utterly Still and Boundless, obviously the Root-Source of the body-mind. I felt utterly connected to my Beloved and Moved and Mastered by Him.*

*There was utter sublimity. Attention dissolved and resolved itself in the heart on the right, literally and spontaneously. I was freed from identification with body, emotion, and mind, and I felt my Beloved Guru as the very Source and Being That Is. Spontaneously, I was no longer identified with the body-mind—I was identified with my Beloved Guru, as Consciousness Itself. I had come to know identification with the body-mind to be a hell and a torment, separating me from my Beloved Guru. And I was very much aware of the suffering that is inherent in seeking for fulfillment in the first five stages of life. Even extraordinary forms of Spiritual experience had shown themselves to be a limit. Only in the utter ecstasy of Finding Him as my own True Identity was there True Satisfaction. This Awakening to Identification with my Beloved was sudden and dramatic, and It changed my relationship to everything.*

*During the period that followed this meditation occasion, a dialogue took place between Avatar Adi Da and myself that lasted several weeks. In these conversations, there was an unwinding of the emotions associated with attention to the body-mind. It was what you might call a "testing" dialogue, which culminated on February 2, 1988, when Beloved Adi Da confirmed my transition to the "Perfect Practice". In the course of these intensive conversations, Beloved Adi Da asked numerous questions, requiring me to really examine and confess What I had Realized.*

*It was an ecstatic and joyful process for me to respond to these questions about my practice, for I was not resorting to the body-mind to answer them. Instead, I simply entered deeply into feeling exactly what had occurred, communicating that freely and in specific technical detail.*

*My Beloved asked me to describe how I establish myself in heart-Communion with Him and what the signs of this Communion are. Then He went on to draw from me a description of how I was conducting His Divine Spirit-Current in the Circle*[7] *of the body-mind and how I was experiencing His Spirit-Current Prior to the Circle, at the moveless Place of Consciousness in the right side of the heart. He asked how I was practicing the "conscious process"*[8] *(or the submission of heart-feeling and attention to Him), actively transcending self-contraction according to the full technical Instruction He had Given me. He questioned me about my experience both in and out of meditation, and enquired whether I would sometimes enter into a state of no-awareness of body and mind. He asked whether, in meditation and daily life, the Witness-Position of Consciousness was my "point of view". And He enquired what signs I was showing of true and free renunciation. I responded to each of these questions, and many more. It was my Beloved's direct Heart-Transmission and the concrete Work He had Done with me through my practice of Ruchira Avatara Bhakti Yoga that made it possible for me to respond.*

*Beloved Adi Da takes on His devotee's form, takes over His devotee, moves His devotee, such that, in the advanced and the ultimate stages of practice, the devotee can consistently feel and Contemplate Him directly as the Divine Person Incarnate. This ecstatic Condition of Oneness with Him is effortless. It is most fundamental, and undeniably Reality Itself. Ultimately, it requires no mind, or discrimination. Ultimately, it does not even have to be remembered. It is simply True.*

*My Beloved Lord, Adi Da Samraj, is the Master and the Real Condition of this body-mind. He is the only Resort, and, truly, the only Hope of this world. All alternatives in me have been forgotten in this great ecstatic Yoga, this supreme Yoga of Ruchira Avatara Bhakti. Through this profound Divine Love-Bliss, which Beloved Adi Da so freely Reveals, it is possible for all beings, human and non-human, to Realize Real God, or Truth, or Reality.*

San Rafael, California, 1988

C H A P T E R 1 7

# Founding the Religion of Adidam

Toward the end of March 1988, Avatar Adi Da left His Hermitage again, moved to offer the worldwide culture of His devotees another opportunity to receive His Darshan and to strengthen their practice of the Yoga of devotion that He had clarified and Empowered through His Divine "Emergence". He traveled first to New Zealand for ten days, where He Graciously offered to address a gathering of people who were "considering" taking up the practice of Adidam. And He Gave His Regard to the native Maori people, visiting a traditional "marae", or Maori meeting house, in Auckland, and speaking at length with a Maori leader about Maori culture, traditions, and Spirituality. Avatar Adi Da's Compassionate Blessing of everyone was heart-breaking to His New Zealand devotees, who had never expected to have the opportunity of serving Him so intimately.

Avatar Adi Da then moved on to the United States, and stayed in northern California, at the Mountain Of Attention and in Marin County, until August, when He left for Da Love-Ananda Mahal and then Fiji, arriving back in His Hermitage in the middle of October.

During His Yajna of 1988, Avatar Adi Da Granted numerous occasions of Darshan (some involving Discourses, some silent), sometimes to hundreds of devotees

**The Mountain Of Attention, 1988**

at a time. Whatever the outward form of these occasions, Avatar Adi Da was directly Initiating His devotees into the practice of feeling-Contemplation of Him, which is the foundation of Ruchira Avatara Bhakti Yoga.

## The Practice of Feeling-Contemplation

At times in the past, Avatar Adi Da Samraj had referred to His own Body as Prasad, or a Divine Gift given in response to the surrender of His devotees. Now, as never before, He was bodily Present as the Divine. He had Descended so fully into the body that there was, in truth, no need for Him to say another word. His purpose in the world was simply to let His Body "Speak" the Divine in silence. And His Message was that all anyone needed to do to in order to find and Commune with Real God, and, ultimately, to Realize the Divine most perfectly, was to behold Him and feel Him with profound feeling-attention, and take up the supportive disciplines of the Way of Adidam that aided this feeling-Contemplation. The Power of His bodily (human) Form to Illumine and Awaken others was the real Secret of His Divine "Emergence". Through the process of ego-surrendering, ego-forgetting, and ego-transcending feeling-Contemplation of Him, He was Offering His devotees the means of transcending all forms of bondage.

Even all the brilliant Demonstrations and Struggles of His Teaching Years could not accomplish this heart-conversion. But now, through the virtue of His Divine "Emergence", Avatar Adi Da knew that conversion was already accomplished in seed-form.

"There is a great Law," He said. "You become what you meditate on." And so, by meditating on Him, His devotees could participate in, and would ultimately Realize, His Divine Condition.

Feeling-Contemplation was now to be His devotees' essential form of meditation, practiced through the regard of His Murti in the Communion Hall and through recollection of Him during the ordinary moments of every day. This feeling-Contemplation is based on the heart-felt beholding of His bodily (human) Form, which leads, in due course, to Communion with Him as Divine Spirit-Presence and, ultimately, to Identification with Him as Consciousness Itself.

Avatar Adi Da returned to Adidam Samrajashram in the middle of October 1988. The morning after His arrival, as soon as He woke from sleep, He wrote down the initial verses of a new sacred Text, the *Da Love-Ananda Gita*. This Text is His precise and detailed Instruction on feeling-Contemplation of Him and the practice of Ruchira Avatara Bhakti Yoga.

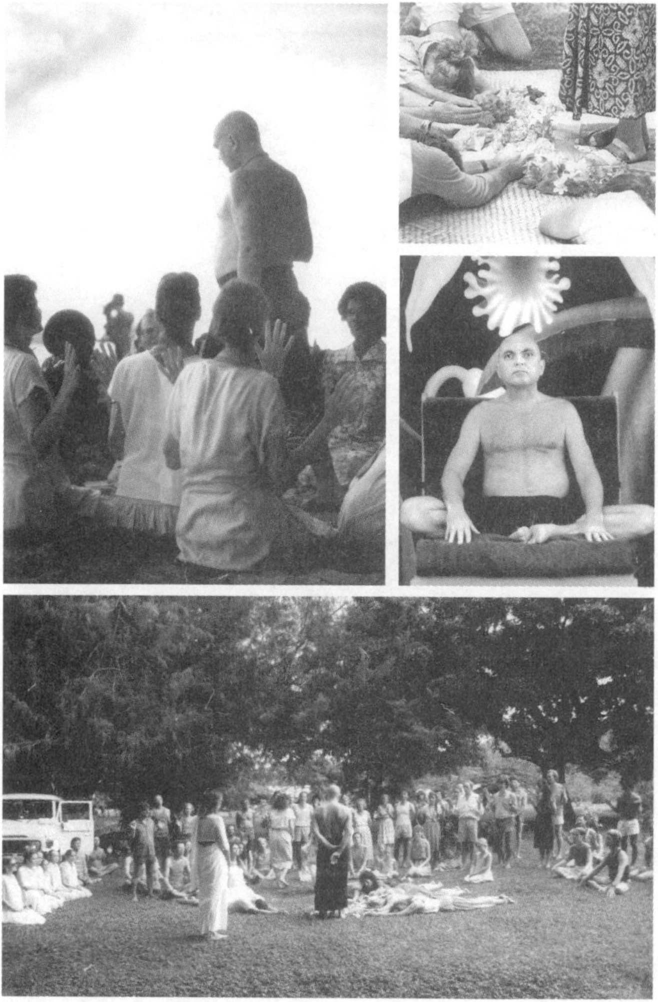

**On retreat in the Company of Avatar Adi Da Samraj at Adidam Samrajashram**

## The Beginning of Formal Meditation Retreats

Suddenly, Avatar Adi Da's Work entered a new phase. He invited His devotees from all over the world to come to Adidam Samrajashram to enter into retreat in His Company, concentrating on His Instruction in the *Da Love-Ananda Gita*. Until this time, only a few individuals—leaders of the worldwide culture, or those called there for special service—had come to Adidam Samrajashram. It had simply been a private Hermitage. Now Avatar Adi Da wanted all His devotees to be able to drop out of their daily lives from time to time and come to Adidam Samrajashram for meditation retreat, receiving His Darshan in the unique purity of His remote Hermitage.

Devotees began to come immediately. And, to everyone's amazement and joy, Avatar Adi Da Blessed the retreatants with the unprecedented privilege of sitting with Him every morning in meditation and almost every afternoon in a silent Darshan occasion. Each day, they would write reports of their practice of feeling-Contemplation of Him—which, for a time, He read and commented on personally.

A retreatant who came to Adidam Samrajashram, Deborah Fremont-Smith, captured the feeling of what it was like to enter into Avatar Adi Da's most intimate Sphere to receive His silent Darshan. ("Owl Sandwiches", referred to below, is a Fijian bure which was part of Avatar Adi Da's private quarters at that time.)

*DEBORAH: Beloved Adi Da Samraj Gave His Darshan today in the bure called "Owl Sandwiches". I would like everything etched in my heart forever. The Matrix is that Sublime Place that shimmers not only with sunlight—*

*which is incredible in the South Pacific—but with the great Siddhi of Adi Da Samraj. It is a place of absolute peace that calms the mind and awakens the heart. Stillness and light pervade everything, for the Heart has remade this place. It is now the Divine Domain, the Place of Origin, the Matrix from which the Blessing of the Heart-Guru flows out to the world.*

*We walked across the expanse of lawn and waited until we were given the signal to approach. Then, one by one, we climbed the narrow steps.*

*The Fijian-style dwelling was immaculate and bright, as if each reed had been consciously chosen and consciously placed. One by one, we passed through the low door of the bure into a small round foyer. Beyond was another small round room, and in this room the Divine Being Incarnate sat in His Chair facing out, and so facing each of us as we entered.*

*I was aware as soon as I crossed the threshold that I had stepped into a Shrine where the Living Icon Breathes. And there He sat. My heart rose up at the sight of Him: "This is the Treasure of the whole world." I stood and waited as each retreatant entered the room, laid a gift at His Precious Feet, and did a full prostration.*

*The eyes of Beloved Adi Da were round and luminous, and His Body Perfectly still, as He gazed outward with such an expression of vulnerability and sweetness that I was once again struck (as forcibly as when I first saw Him in 1976) that this is not a man, not a human being at all. This is the Formless Divine, Suspended for an instant in time and space—the Self-Radiant Divine Being caught for a moment in human Form. It was a breathtaking Vision. I felt how I want nothing more than to see Him rightly honored and protected, this naked Heart of Man, the True Self of all beings.*

*Then it was my turn to go forward and offer my gift. I walked into the inner room, which was "Bright" with the*

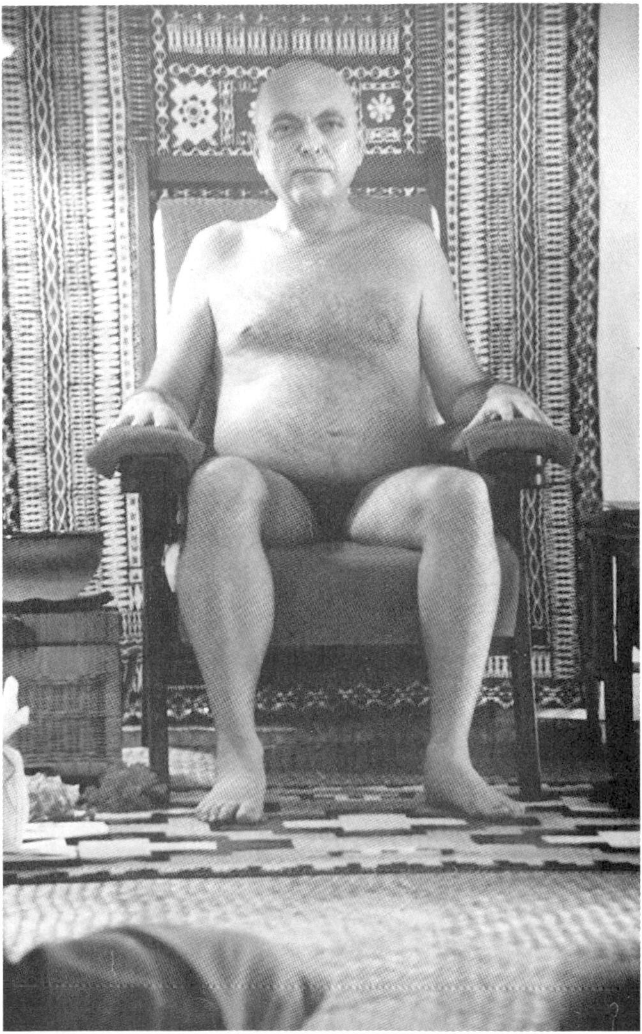

**Darshan at Owl Sandwiches,**
**Adidam Samrajashram, 1989**

*Glory of Him. The space was full of Silence. Adidama Sukha Dham and Adidama Jangama Hriddaya, dressed in formal white, sat to each side of Him. They were as immobile as He—their attention entirely turned to the Person of Love before them. I was walking into a sacred space, like the space depicted in ancient religious paintings. Regarding Beloved Adi Da's beautiful and compassionate face, I became lost in its depths. His Sublime Look—full of Bliss and, yet, also full of Pain at the suffering He beholds in everyone—seemed to encompass me and all beings in the same moment. I raised up my hands in adoration of Him and looked into His eyes. My heart was wrung with the vision of Him, remembering His Words, "In This Swoon Of Love, Your Heart May See My Bliss-Wounded Face."*

*As I placed my gift to the right of His chair, my eyes met another glorious sight, another beholding. Adidama Jangama Hriddaya was seated no more than a foot from me. Her attention fully rested on Beloved Adi Da and she was fanning Him. Her unwavering devotion to Him was reflecting His Divine Light as the moon reflects the sun. My heart thrilled to see this, and, as I saw it, I also perceived something else. I understood in that moment that Beloved Adi Da breathes devotion as we breathe air. Devotion is His atmosphere.*

*After about twenty minutes, Beloved Adi Da signaled with the barest movement of His hand that the Darshan was over. Then Adidama Sukha Dham took up the basket of Prasad, or Blessed sweets, and carefully placed a sweet in the hands of each devotee. Her heart-Contemplation of Beloved Adi Da was so profound that, as her hand touched mine, I felt a direct Transmission of Grace and Blessing moving through her from Him. I bowed in gratitude as I left Owl Sandwiches, my heart filled with Peace and the Vision of Real God, Which is finally unutterable.*

# The Creation of the Divine Scripture of Adidam

During the years following His Divine "Emergence", Avatar Adi Da Samraj began to extend and develop the disciplines and practices that He had given over many years, clarifying them all as direct expressions of Ruchira Avatara Bhakti Yoga, or devotional surrender to Him. There was a discipline appropriate to every area of life and a structure of devotional practice that governed every day. Avatar Adi Da was continuing to prepare for the time when devotees would not, in general, see Him personally. Many in the future, and all of those who would appear after His physical Lifetime, would never do so.[1] And so the Ruchira Avatar was creating religious and Spiritual means that would enable all His devotees, from the moment of their first formal initiation,[2] to Commune with Him and receive His Spiritual Transmission and live perpetually in His Spiritual Company. He was finding more and more ways to universalize His Work beyond the initial circles of devotees, reaching out to find and embrace His devotees in every corner of the world. He was bringing to fullness the religion of Adidam.

As part of this process, Avatar Adi Da spent untold hours writing—creating new books and also greatly expanding *The Dawn Horse Testament*. He was beginning the process of establishing a summary of His Instruction that was gigantic in breadth and depth. He was bringing all the "considerations" of His now seventeen years of Teaching and Revelation Work to fullness in light of His Divine "Emergence"—so that He could offer His "Full-Given and Final Word" to humanity for all time.

It was a monumental task. Whatever His focus and purpose from book to book, Avatar Adi Da always created His "Source-Texts" as living Speech, an "Eternal

Conversation" with every man and woman. Individuals with no previous knowledge of Avatar Adi Da sometimes have remarkable experiences upon first contact with His books, experiences that bring them into profound relationship with Him, even before His Words are understood. There are many testimonies to this—for example, this story by Trish Mitchell, an Australian radio journalist who bought *The Dawn Horse Testament* one day, simply because she was attracted to the cover. She took it home, placed it on her bookshelf—but never opened it at all.

*TRISH: Three years later, I was sitting at home one night with nothing much to do, feeling a little fed up, and I looked up at the bookshelf—at the one book in it I hadn't read. I sat down on the couch and opened* The Dawn Horse Testament.

*The most bizarre thing happened. I was sitting there reading this book, and suddenly the words started to blur, and light started to come off the pages—literally, there was a shimmering light flickering up, like something out of a science fiction movie. I had been meditating for a few years, and my body used to move slightly when I was meditating. I was looking at this book, light flickering off the pages, and my body started to sway! I slammed the book shut and thought, "I'm getting the flu!" But then I noticed that I felt happy! I cautiously opened the book again at a different page, and the same thing happened—light was streaming off the page now. I was seeing the words, and it was as if I were reading Latin or Greek. It didn't mean anything to my mind—but I knew what this book was saying! And I was getting happier and happier, and my body was swaying, and the light continued emanating from the pages! I literally ended up hugging the book to my chest and dancing around the room. I was ecstatic.*

*Two or three days later, I went to see a video of Beloved Adi Da. The minute I heard His voice and saw His face, I was moved into an ecstatic state, and then my peripheral vision disappeared. Nothing like this had ever happened to me before, either! Everything went black, all sound disappeared. There was a roomful of people and the video was loud, but I couldn't hear anything. There was only white light emanating from the video, and, except for Beloved Adi Da's face, everything else was just light, and my peripheral vision was black. Again, I felt very, very happy—unreasonably happy. And I knew I was receiving something extraordinary from an extraordinary Being. I cried all the way home, out of sheer joy. I had vision-like dreams about Beloved Adi Da all night, and I kept repeating one of His Names—"Love-Ananda"—which I had never heard before.*

*At about four or five in the morning, I woke up fully. I was lying there in an incredibly happy state. I looked at the bottom of my bed and saw Beloved Adi Da standing there, surrounded by golden light, with His hands on His hips, and an amused look on His face. He looked at me and said, "Well, it's about time!" And then disappeared. I repeated to myself, "'It's about time'???" I thought I must have imagined what had just occurred. Surely, no Spiritual Teacher would spontaneously appear at the end of my bed and say, "Well, it's about time!" But I knew He was telling the truth. I knew He was saying He had been waiting for me for a long time, just as I had been waiting for Him.*

**Avatar Adi Da Samraj with His Fijian devotees, Adidam Samrajashram, 1997**

# The Adept of Love

Avatar Adi Da began His Work among Westerners, and it was among Westerners that He first established the religion of Adidam. But His urge to Bless beings has always been universal and is not limited by race or culture. To the native Fijians of Naitauba, Avatar Adi Da Samraj is known as "Turaga Dau Loloma Vunirarama", "The Great Lord [Turaga] Who Is The

Divine Adept [Dau] Of The Divine Love [Loloma] and The Self-Radiant Divine Source and Substance [Vu] Of [ni] The Divine 'Brightness' [Rarama]". They remember the event recounted here with joy and gratitude as one of the great demonstrations of the meaning of Turaga Dau Loloma's Name.

It was the evening of January 10, 1989, and word was spreading around the Ashram village that Turaga Dau Loloma had left for Ciqomi (the Fijian village) by the shortest possible route. At the same time, He sent word that Charles Seage, His personal physician, and Mo Whiteside, a devotee who spoke Fijian, should meet Him there. He had just been told that an old man, Finau, the father of Solo (the Fijian elder who sat in the church with Avatar Adi Da in 1983), was slipping into a coma and losing his hold on life.

Charles and Mo arrived ahead of Dau Loloma and found Solo sitting in the meeting house, drinking kava.

Mo told Solo, "Dau Loloma is coming to see Finau."

"Ah, vinaka (good)," said Solo.

Solo looked at Mo for a moment, and then it dawned on him. "Right now?" he asked.

"Yes. Tonight."

Charles helped Solo wash Finau while the family spread their most valuable mats on the floor and prepared their house for Dau Loloma's arrival.

Solo then stood in front of his home waiting to greet Dau Loloma. In the distance, he could hear the engine of the Land Cruiser bringing Dau Loloma to Ciqomi. As Dau Loloma stepped out of the car, the villagers witnessed His gentle way. An orange shawl hung over His Shoulders. He walked past the members of Finau's family to put His arms around Solo and kissed him, and they walked together, arm in arm, into the house.

Finau lay on his side in a bed in a small room. Dau Loloma stood next to the bed, His staff in hand, looking intently on Finau. Finau's chest heaved, as he gasped for air.

Dau Loloma sat down on the edge of Finau's bed. He leaned down, His face very close to the old man's. Softly, He took Finau's left hand and held it in His lap. He placed His other hand on Finau's small shoulder. Then, very lightly, so as not to startle him, Dau Loloma massaged Finau's emaciated, struggling body.

Finau's eyes slowly opened, and Dau Loloma held Finau in His arms. From the hallway, Solo and the others watched. Each breath was a struggle for Finau. He seemed to be afraid and in pain. He tried to respond to Dau Loloma, but he could not speak or move. Yet Dau Loloma responded to his feeble attempts to communicate. He understood Finau perfectly. Dau Loloma held Finau close and whispered, "Tcha" and "Hmm". A tear fell from the old man's sunken eyes down his long dark face. His lips parted, and his face widened with a fragile smile.

The hands of Dau Loloma were kind to Finau's body, massaging and relaxing him. By touch, and by speech, and by glance, Dau Loloma was easing Finau toward his transition.

As Finau's outer awareness subsided, Dau Loloma moved him into a more relaxed position, lying on his back. Now Dau Loloma put His hand on Finau's head. He placed His thumb on Finau's forehead between and just above the eyes. Finau's eyes squinted closed—not in pain, but as a sign that his awareness was ascending beyond the agony of his fear and the dying mass of flesh.

Dau Loloma moved His right hand over Finau's heart and kept His other hand on Finau's head. Dau Loloma breathed deeply and slowly, and finally the old man's breath became calm and even.

With Finau at peace, Dau Loloma removed the

orange shawl He was wearing, lifted Finau's body, and tucked the shawl around him. Finau lay calmly in Dau Loloma's care. The two were so peaceful together in the dimly lit room, they seemed in another world.

Dau Loloma stood, His eyes still fixed on Finau. He stepped back and reached for His staff.

Solo, Charles, and Mo had watched everything from the adjoining living room. Solo's young son, Pita, was there, too. And there were women huddled outside the house, peering in through the open windows. Dau Loloma embraced Solo again and held him close. Dau Loloma's Love can draw out what a man otherwise conceals in his heart. The sorrow, the difficult thoughts, and the feelings of loss were all rising in Solo. Death's message to the living is that all who live will die. But Dau Loloma's Message, though He never spoke a word, was that Finau's death was part of a living process—not an ending, but a mysterious transformation. Dau Loloma's Body was a bridge of intimacy between a dying man, his grieving son, and the Supreme Reality that Perfectly Transcends the events of life and death.

Dau Loloma finally released Solo, and He and Solo parted. Through tears of gratitude, Solo watched from the porch of his home as Dau Loloma stepped into the waiting vehicle. Dau Loloma called back, "Solo", and motioned him over to the window of the car. He took off His indigo hat and pressed it snugly on Solo's head. Minerva, Solo's daughter, came to the front door of the house, and Dau Loloma waved goodbye to her.

On the way up the hill and out onto the road leading back to the Matrix, Dau Loloma was quiet.

Finau died the following day—January 11, 1989.

**Adidam Samrajashram, 1990**

CHAPTER 18

# The Divine World-Teacher

In February 1939, about six months before the outbreak of World War II, the Indian sage Upasani Baba (one of the Gurus of Meher Baba) received an important visitor to his ashram. He was the Shankaracharya of Jyotir Math, the head of one of the most important Hindu monastic orders. The Shankaracharya was expressing his dismay at the chaotic state of religion in India and in the world altogether. He saw only one solution to this sorry state of affairs—a great Divine intervention, in the form of an Avatar. Only such an event, he felt, could re-establish true Spiritual life.

According to the account, Upasani listened sympathetically. He was a man of few words and unpredictable ways, a traditional avadhoot. Suddenly, he burst out with a completely unexpected utterance. Such an Incarnation, he said, would soon be born in a "European country". ("European" is often used in India and other parts of the world as a synonym for "Western", or "white-skinned".) "He will be all-powerful", Upasani declared, "and bear down everything before him. And he will see to it that Vedic Dharma", meaning the pure and original Teaching of Truth, "is firmly reestablished in India."[1]

To prophesy the coming of an Avatar was extraordinary enough. To foresee That One as a Westerner was iconoclastic. To the mind of the orthodox Hindu, Westerners are "mlecchas",[2] Spiritually unevolved "barbarians" unworthy of even hearing true Spiritual Teaching.

Upasani Baba was foretelling a World-Teacher, One capable of Mastering both East and West; and the notion that such a One would be a Westerner was, from the traditional Hindu point of view, incomprehensible. Nevertheless, around the time of this prophecy, Avatar Adi Da's physical vehicle was conceived on Long Island, New York, by Frank and Dorothy Jones.

During His college years, Avatar Adi Da's uncle Richard asked Him what He wanted to do with His life. The answer was obvious to Him, and He replied unhesitatingly that He wanted to "save the world". In the early years of His Teaching Work, Avatar Adi Da did not make much of the worldwide, and even cosmic, scope of His Avataric Work. It was only when He was given His Fijian Hermitage in late 1983 that He began to speak prophetically about His universal Power of Blessing, and His real Work to "save the world". When He spoke this way, He was not only referring to His Function as the World-Teacher who would re-establish true Dharma (or religious teaching and practice), as Upasani Baba had foreseen. He also meant that He had come, quite literally, to Save the world, to Save the Earth and its inhabitants from destruction by human hands.

## The Fiftieth Birthday Celebration

Avatar Adi Da's Work with the world was dramatically demonstrated to His devotees—in a way they had never witnessed before—around the time of His fiftieth Birthday (November 3, 1989). The weeks preceding the celebration of His Birthday were full of Avatar Adi Da's purifying Fire. He was unremitting in His Call to His devotees to renounce egoity and respond to the Power of His Divine "Emergence". He was Calling them to handle all the practical aspects of the institution, culture, community, and mission of

During the course of a retreat at Adidam Samrajashram in the early 1990s, Dina Lautman received a revelation of Avatar Adi Da's Intention to Save the world through His Spiritual Intervention.

*DINA: In the meditation hall, I fell into a dream-like state. At first, there was just a growing feeling of sorrow and grief. There was no recognizable content to it. Later, the picture filled out, and I was sitting in a huge field of corpses, weeping. The grief was endless. I was crying for all those who had died in this massacre. It was infinite pain. Finally, Beloved Adi Da appeared in this vision, and my grief turned to rage. I began to yell and scream at Him about what had occurred, blaming Him directly. "How could God have allowed this?", I screamed.*

*He gazed at me most Compassionately throughout my tirade, and finally He spoke about the Love He feels for all beings. He explained that this is why He had Incarnated—because of His Love for beings. He looked at me and said that He had Appeared here, "Not only for those whom you mourn, but for <u>all</u> those who have died, are dying, and will die—in all planes, and in all forms, and throughout all time. I will not rest until all have come to Me."*

*It was then that I had the experience of my Beloved Guru as Love Itself. He was only pure Feeling, Radiating in all directions, like the sun. I felt His personal Love for me, and yet I simultaneously knew His Love was universal, for all beings.*

Adidam[3] so that He would be free to Do His Universal Blessing Work. The impulse in Him to be set free for this Work was unceasing and overwhelming.

For the two weeks prior to the celebration, Avatar Adi Da stayed in seclusion in His bure at the Matrix. During this time, Adidama Sukha Dham attended Him and passed on His Communications to the worldwide gathering of devotees. He was Calling all His devotees to an intensive period of penance and reparation to righten their relationship to Him, but it was obvious that, whatever gestures of reparation they tried to make, it was He who was performing the Penance.

For some days, Avatar Adi Da did not even stir from His bed. At one point, when Adidama Sukha Dham was in the room, a window near His Feet spontaneously shattered. This inexplicable incident seemed to be a sign of Avatar Adi Da's involvement in an invisible struggle with forces vastly greater than the reluctance of His devotees—and, in fact, He briefly said that this was so.

Avatar Adi Da's devotees were utterly dismayed at the possibility that their Divine Heart-Master might not celebrate His fiftieth Birthday—which they felt should be one of the most auspicious and joyful days of His Lifetime. On the eve of the celebration, Adidama Sukha Dham approached Avatar Adi Da and begged Him to celebrate this great anniversary "for the sake of humankind". Her plea touched His Heart. He sat swaying on His bed, quietly repeating a word she had not heard Him use before: "Jagad-Guru, Jagad-Guru, Jagad-Guru". ("Jagad-Guru" means "World-Teacher", or, literally, "the Teacher of everything that moves".) Avatar Adi Da Spoke to Adidama Sukha Dham about His Function as Jagad-Guru in the context of His Divine "Emergence":

*AVATAR ADI DA SAMRAJ: What actually occurred on the morning of January 11, 1986, was a sudden and*

**Avatar Adi Da Samraj at the celebration of His fiftieth Birthday, Adidam Samrajashram, 1989**

*spontaneous transition from My Teaching Work to My Blessing Work—or to My Work as the Eternally Free-Standing, and always presently "Emerging", Divine World-Teacher (or Jagad-Guru). It was a Transition in My Disposition from My Work of Submitting to others (even to the point of complete Identification with them in their apparently limited condition) to simply Surrendering My human Body-Mind into My own Self-Condition. Therefore, the context of My Blessing Work is no longer one of Submission to others to the point of Identification with them. It is a matter of simply Standing As I Am, while this apparent Body-Mind is thereby Surrendered utterly into My own Self-Condition. And by My Thus Standing Free, My Work has ceased to be a Struggle to Submit My Self to humankind, one by one, and It has become, instead, a universally effective Blessing Work, in Which humankind, in the form of each and all who respond to Me, must, one by one, surrender, forget, and transcend separate and separative self in Me.* [November 3, 1989]

## His Tangible Blessing Influence

In the weeks and months that followed Avatar Adi Da's fiftieth Birthday and His Revelation of Himself as the Divine World-Teacher, signs of His world-Work began to appear. Devotees began to see—even in the pages of the world's newspapers—the type of events He had spoken about in His prophetic Talk, "Mark My Words", in 1983 (pp. 330-39).

On November 10, 1989, exactly a week after His Birthday, it was announced in *The Washington Post*:

"EAST GERMANY OPENS BERLIN WALL AND BORDERS, ALLOWING CITIZENS TO TRAVEL FREELY TO THE WEST."

This event, the newspaper continued, constituted "the most stunning step since World War II toward ending the East-West division of Europe".

The day (November 9) of the opening of the Berlin Wall, Avatar Adi Da asked for a report on what was happening in the world. He had not been receiving any reports of world news during that time. And so, in the weeks of His Seclusion leading up to His fiftieth Birthday, He had no ordinary way of knowing what was happening in Europe.

The Berlin Wall was just the beginning. In the days and weeks following, the newspapers of the world were covered with headlines reporting further dramatic steps towards pluralist government in the European communist bloc—in Bulgaria (November 12), in Romania (December 23), and in Czechoslovakia (December 29). In Poland and Hungary, the process had already been under way for several months, but a sudden acceleration in the pace of change in Eastern Europe, starting in the second half of November, was noted by news commentators.

Also, during December 1989, the Malta summit meeting between U.S. President Bush and Soviet President Gorbachev signaled the winding down of the cold war. And then, in February 1990, Nelson Mandela, who had been jailed for more than twenty-seven years for his political activities on behalf of black South Africans, was released—an event that led to the repeal of apartheid laws early in 1992.

## Reporting from The Washington Post:

### ELECTIONS, NOT FORCE, MARK POLAND'S HISTORIC CHANGE

AUGUST 20, 1989

WARSAW—Poland is about to embark on a historic experiment: Communists are due this week to turn over the reins of government to non-Communists and will do so not under force but, for the first time, as the result of an election.

### EAST GERMANY OPENS WALL AND BORDERS, ALLOWING CITIZENS TO TRAVEL FREELY TO THE WEST

NOVEMBER 9, 1989

EAST BERLIN—Communist East Germany today opened its borders to the West, including the Berlin Wall, announcing that its citizens could travel or emigrate freely, in the most stunning step since World War II toward ending the East-West division of Europe.

### BULGARIA'S ZHIVKOV QUITS AFTER 35 YEARS

#### Foreign Minister, 53, Replaces East Bloc's Longest-Serving Leader

NOVEMBER 10, 1989

WARSAW—Bulgarian President Todor Zhivkov, the oldest and longest-serving leader in the Eastern Bloc and one of the region's last hard-line holdouts, resigned suddenly today after 35 years in power.

### MALTA EMPHASIS WILL BE ON PACTS' TIMING, NOT DETAILS, U.S. OFFICIALS SAY

DECEMBER 2, 1989

President Bush will likely agree with Soviet President Mikhail Gorbachev this weekend that all major obstacles to a new accord reducing strategic nuclear weapons should be resolved before their summit in the spring, including a plan for trial inspections of weapons, U.S. officials said yesterday.

### MALTA MOST IMPORTANT EAST-WEST MEETING SINCE '45

DECEMBER 8, 1989

With the Malta summit, Mikhail Gorbachev has entirely reversed Stalin's postwar decision to seal the Soviet Union off from Europe and erased Moscow's ambivalence about whether the United States has an abiding trans-Atlantic role. On his part, George Bush has conclusively answered the long pending, suddenly urgent question of whether the United States will stay deeply engaged in Europe as the Cold War winds down.

## WORLD CAPITALS REVEL IN DICTATOR'S DOWNFALL

### Many Pledge Immediate Aid to Romania

DECEMBER 23, 1989

World capitals reacted with joy at the downfall of Romanian dictator Nicolae Ceausescu yesterday, and many pledged immediate aid to the financially hard-pressed nation.

## PRAGUE NAMES HAVEL PRESIDENT

### Former Political Prisoner Wins Unanimous Election

DECEMBER 29, 1989

PRAGUE—Vaclav Havel, the dissident playwright who repeatedly went to jail to demonstrate an enduring attachment to democratic values, today was elected as Czechoslovakia's first non-Communist president in more than four decades.

## SOUTH AFRICA FREES MANDELA INTO GLOBAL TIDE TOWARD DEMOCRACY

FEBRUARY 12, 1990

PARIS, FEB. 11—Nelson Mandela, emerging today from a quarter-century of imprisonment, has stepped into a world in which human rights and individual freedoms are rapidly eclipsing ideology and totalitarian controls in country after country.

## NEW GOVERNMENT PROMISED IN HUNGARY

APRIL 14, 1990

BUDAPEST—The Hungarian Democratic Forum said today it expected to form Hungary's first non-communist government in four decades by mid-May.

## ALBANIAN RIGHTS MOVES

MAY 10, 1990

VIENNA—Hard-line Communist Albania appears to have softened its stern resistance to the wave of political liberalization sweeping Eastern Europe with proclamation of a package of human-rights reforms.

## HUNGARY SCRAPS MISSILES

NOVEMBER 17, 1990

BUDAPEST—Hungary, which has urged the Warsaw Pact to disband, said it is unilaterally scrapping its Soviet-made ground-to-ground missiles, all capable of carrying nuclear warheads.

All in all, these changes set in motion a reversal of intractable patterns in world politics that had been in place for decades and longer. And they were all happening within a few months. It was intuitively obvious to His devotees that Avatar Adi Da had been Working with the world at the most profound Spiritual level. And, just as He had predicted in 1983 (in "Mark My Words"), the results of His Blessing were reaching the newspapers.

Devotees began to understand that, in the weeks leading up to His fiftieth Birthday, Avatar Adi Da had been transforming negative patterns on a global scale. And His Fierceness with His devotees had had much to do with this process of world-transformation. He has said many times that He relates to those who are in His Company as representatives of all humankind, and engages in an unrelenting struggle with their egoity in order to work with the larger human pattern of egoic destructiveness.

The political changes of this period in central Europe and the subsequent dissolution of the Soviet Union did not, of course, usher in a golden age. But they were a "window", Avatar Adi Da said later—a window of possibility for far-reaching benign change. Some positive changes did indeed occur, but, at the same time, there was ongoing unrest, and new patterns of violence emerged, as many ethnic groups of the former Soviet Union and central Europe rose up to claim their own autonomy.

Circumstances may change, but, unless a fundamental conversion occurs, the ego persists, destructive as ever. That is why Avatar Adi Da always insists that His Blessing Work is not intended to create utopia, and cannot do so. He Works, simply, to ameliorate the negative forces in the world—so that this planet, first of all, can survive, and then potentially become a human environment that supports Spiritual contemplation and growth.

## For the Sake of the World

There are traditional precedents for a Realizer deliberately entering into a Yogic ordeal for the sake of the world. Narayan Maharaj, an Indian Adept of modern times, is a dramatic example. During World War II, and especially during its last days, Narayan Maharaj would ask his devotees to listen to the world news and bring him maps showing the pattern of the conflict in Europe. Through a mysterious Yogic process, apparent gun-shot wounds would break out on the body of Narayan Maharaj, and every day his devotees would bathe and bandage him. In 1945, the day after the Japanese surrendered, bringing a complete end to World War II, Narayan Maharaj died. His work, he declared the day before his death, was done.[4]

Very rarely does Avatar Adi Da give His devotees a glimpse of the pain and difficulty that He takes on and transforms in the course of His invisible Blessing Work. He has said that no human being could endure it. On one occasion, He allowed Thankfull Hastings to make this discovery very graphically. ("Thankfull" is a name given to this devotee by Avatar Adi Da. Thankfull is the older brother of Indian Time, the story of whose birth is told in chapter 8.)

*THANKFULL: One evening in 1992, I was sitting at Beloved Adi Da's side as He began to speak to the forty or so devotees in the room with Him that evening. He was speaking about the killings taking place daily in many areas of the world, and particularly, at that time, in Somalia. He referred to the terrible and intolerable deaths of women and children there, and also to the dangerous proliferation of weapons throughout the world.*

*As He spoke, I had my hand on His leg, and I began to feel in my body what He was talking about. I don't*

**Thankfull Hastings and Adi Da Samraj, 1992**

*know how to describe this, but I felt the literal "experience" of what He was speaking about enter my body from His leg. It moved into my hand, up through my arm, down into my heart, and from there up into my head. As it entered my head, my vision was suddenly clouded. Appallingly vivid images of everything He was speaking of—all the terrible deaths and suffering—began to move before my eyes, as if I were watching a movie. In a very short time, I could no longer tolerate the experience. I got up and ran outside and began vomiting in the bushes. The images continued. A friend came out to bring me back inside. I was gasping for air and told her I just couldn't take it any more, I just couldn't experience the suffering of the world in the way Beloved Adi Da was obviously experiencing it.*

*A short time later, my "symptoms" subsided and I—still somewhat reluctantly—returned to the room where Beloved Adi Da and His devotees were gathered. But I have never forgotten what I learned that night about what Beloved Adi Da endures for the sake of the world, and what is required from all of us if the earth is to be a place where the great matter of true Spiritual practice is to be a real possibility for humankind.*

# "Open Yourself to Become My Instrument"

A critical aspect of Avatar Adi Da's Divine world-Work takes place through His direct association with individuals who function in the realm of politics, government, and social welfare. Avatar Adi Da's Work in this area is made even more potent when such individuals become His devotees. A striking and moving example of this is the relationship between Avatar Adi Da and a man who is a high official of an international relief organization. In 1996, this man requested a private audience with Avatar Adi Da regarding some crucial issues related to his work in a poor and politically volatile part of the world. Avatar Adi Da accepted his request. Bill Stranger had arranged for this man's visit and was present that evening:

*BILL: Avatar Adi Da received this man in a private house where He was staying at the time. My friend had not seen our Beloved Guru for several years and when they met in the living room of this lovely home, just minutes before a piano recital was to be offered to Avatar Adi Da, Avatar Adi Da's humorous first Words to the man—"Long time, no see"—were the perfectly intimate greeting. They each extended their hands to one another and, with obvious love and delight, beamed into one another's face. After the recital, there was dinner and then two separate Darshan occasions to accommodate the many devotees who had come to see Avatar Adi Da. It was nearly four in the morning when we were escorted into Avatar Adi Da's private quarters.*

*This diplomat has dedicated his professional life to ameliorating the conditions of the world's poorest children. He is a tireless, innovative, and unusually effective servant in this regard, who performs his work with a light touch but great passion. Avatar Adi Da sat Blissfully on a divan as the man prostrated at His Feet and then addressed Him from his heart. My friend spoke movingly of his lifelong commitment to serving the children of the world and of his slow-dawning recognition that the reason why they continue to suffer unnecessary, if not obscene, privations reveals much more of a Spiritual fault in mankind than any practical limitations upon our economic resources. As the man pointed out to Avatar Adi Da, "For less money than the world spends every year on golf, we could dispense with most of the unnecessary childhood diseases that kill millions every year." He concluded by asking for Avatar Adi Da's Guidance and Blessing in his own important service.*

*For many years, I had closely observed and sometimes been privileged to serve Avatar Adi Da in relation to His Work with the world. On a number of occasions, I have heard Him Discourse on the world situation in general, and also on particular situations facing nations and peoples. There was something about this occasion—an important international official requesting Avatar Adi Da's Help in the mode of the devotee—that seemed to cross an important threshold. Avatar Adi Da Addressed this man in a Manner I had never seen before. He Spoke slowly and extremely quietly—with profound feeling, pausing after each sentence. At the same time, His Instruction reflected a completely current appreciation of the actual circumstance of the country this man was then serving, and also of its neighbors.*

> *AVATAR ADI DA SAMRAJ: Unfortunately, this country is limited in its ability to control many aspects even of its natural circumstance. It's terribly vulnerable to many things—natural disasters and all the rest. There has to be better coop-*

*eration from neighboring countries, cooperation relative to things like water. The ecological situation needs to get stabilized there. There is some movement in that direction now. Your coming to see Me more often is fundamental to it, together with your becoming altogether more communicative in your relationship to Me.*

*DEVOTEE: Thank You.*

*AVATAR ADI DA SAMRAJ: And tell Me things about it from time to time. But know that those children and that country do have My Regard. There are all kinds of things to be done that are matters of education—benign education, not just school education—public communications to the people and communications to those who are in a position to make changes. All the means you have to make such communications are important to use. Of course, ultimately, it is not a place on its own—it is part of, a piece of, this world struggle.*

*Communicate about Me, whenever you have an ear to listen about Me, but stay in devotional Communion with Me so that you become means, instrument, and then I will Do it.*

*The children in that country (as is also the case with non-human beings all over the world) are being excluded from consideration by those in control of the resources. And those who know that this is wrong must speak about it, and use every means to change minds and redirect attention and financial resources.*

*Just do that work. Go through all the doors that become available to you. Stay in the Process, and let it happen. Resort to Me. Your devotion to Me is what you have to add to it.*

*And then, in your heart-Communion with Me, more opportunities will come to you also. You will notice things happening simultaneously. Just be available to notice them.*

*In every way, at heart, open yourself to become My instrument—openly, without added strategy. Just this openness, this continuity with Me. And then you give Me more means to accomplish My Purpose.*

*Let Me hear about things. Come to see Me more often. Let Me hear from you about these kinds of things—what you are observing, what you are noticing. Indicate specifics for Me to Bless. Just a simple line about this and that here and there. It helps to make My Regard specific.*

*DEVOTEE: Yes.*

*AVATAR ADI DA SAMRAJ: Do your work with love and humor, but firmly. And, as I said, keep looking for the opportunities, the doorways. The more you are true to devotional Communion with Me, the more you will notice of that. This is how I Work.*

*DEVOTEE: I have already noticed many times that things happen that were just inexplicable, except that I was just Your instrument.*

*BILL: At this moment in the conversation, Avatar Adi Da Revealed the Profundity of how He Works:*

*AVATAR ADI DA SAMRAJ: I Work on the pattern that is prior to the pattern that seems, or the pattern that is concrete at the moment. I Work on the pattern that is invisible, prior, not yet observed. And then I Breathe it down into the world. And the more people there are who know*

> *Me and know this is What I am Doing, and who enter into devotional Communion with Me, the more means I have in the concrete field.*

*BILL: I was absolutely stunned by the interchange. I remember even gasping once or twice during the interview. We all knew we were witnessing a momentous event. The Siddhi of Beloved Adi Da was overwhelming, and I could feel that He was actually Doing what He said, Breathing the prior pattern down into the world as He was speaking.*

*Avatar Adi Da went on:*

> *AVATAR ADI DA SAMRAJ: There is no utopia about this. It is a struggle. So you have to make use of every positive opening, every positive opportunity.*
>
> *I also want to help the adults, along with the children. Adults are just older children. And the adults have to do much of the service that will change things. Not only because of their sympathy with children, and with the perpetuation of their kind altogether, but because their hearts are opening.*
>
> *Help people to have a sense that they can do something collectively. Speak to everyone's altruism positively. Give people something to do that is good.*
>
> *DEVOTEE: Thank You, thank You.*
>
> *AVATAR ADI DA SAMRAJ: Tcha.*

When it was clear that Avatar Adi Da had finished, the devotee to whom He had been speaking began to get up to leave, expressing his gratitude. At that moment, Avatar Adi Da motioned him to come forward. Avatar

Adi Da then put the man's head in His lap. And He reached over and placed His hands on the man's back, stroking him up and down the back with both His palms for a long time. At the end, He placed His hands on the man's head. This was not only a loving, personal gesture—it was also an act of Transmission, a passing of His Spiritual Blessing to those He had been speaking about. As the man himself had confessed, his role was that of an instrument, a means for Adi Da Samraj to be Spiritually present and active in that country.

As it turned out, shortly thereafter this man again requested Avatar Adi Da's specific Blessing Intervention in several situations facing the whole area he was serving. One was a longterm, and seemingly intractable, dispute between the nation and a group of its indigenous peoples. The other concerned a regional conference on child labor. Both the negotiation and the conference surprised all their participants by being successful. At the conference, where this diplomat-devotee said you could tangibly feel Avatar Adi Da's Blessing Infuse the room, the head of one delegation, notorious for its resistance to fundamental reform, reversed his own delegation's position saying, "I can no longer deny the feeling I have at this conference." Then, against his subordinates' public objections, he pledged his country's compliance with a new protocol that would protect children's rights.

## Spiritual Penance in Seclusion

At the beginning of January 1991, with the suddenness of the Avadhoot, Avatar Adi Da moved from His principal residence at the Matrix to Indefinable, His two-room house in the Ashram village, and entered into another period of seclusion.

Avatar Adi Da had all decorations and comforts removed from Indefinable, and there He stayed, never leaving His Room. On January 15 (January 16 in Fiji), war broke out in the Middle East, and the stability and safety of the entire world was at stake. Once again, it was clear to His devotees that the Divine World-Teacher was engaged in self-imposed Penance for the world.

As the tanks rolled across the Iraqi desert, Avatar Adi Da watched videotaped news broadcasts on television every day, something He had never done before. He asked that a short-wave radio be set up beside His bed, so that He could listen to direct news broadcasts every hour. And He requested that international news broadcasts be recorded morning and evening and brought to Him at Indefinable. Whenever He listens to or reads the news He is completely concentrated in it. He "considers" the exact details of the pattern of any situation that requires His Regard before beginning to Work with it.

The manner of Avatar Adi Da's Blessing Work is a mystery. Fundamentally, He is simply "Brightening" whatever is brought to Him, and working with representatives of a particular pattern or situation in order to reach the whole. At one point during the Gulf War, Avatar Adi Da invited His devotees to send Him photographs of anyone they knew who was involved in the war. A number of photographs were offered, and He simply kept them in His room. Devotees felt that He was using these pictures in some way as psycho-physical conduits of His Blessing, ways of reaching into and affecting the larger picture of the war.

As the Gulf War continued, Avatar Adi Da asked why the news videos He was receiving did not show any pictures of the dead on the battlefield. The devotees preparing the tapes confessed that they had cut out these sequences in order to protect Him from the full vision of the carnage. To Avatar Adi Da, this was an interference

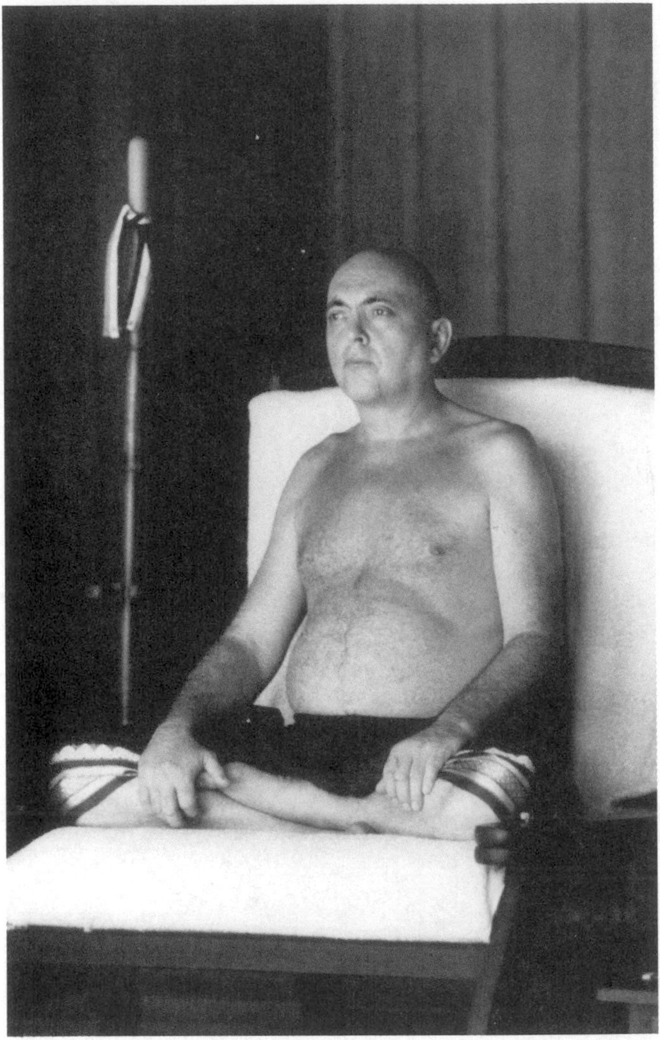

**Avatar Adi Da Samraj after His period of seclusion, 1991**

in His Work. He said that He must receive all pictures and information. He Works with the dead, He said, as much as with the living, and they too should be allowed to receive His direct Regard.

On March 3, 1991, the Gulf War came to an end with unexpected suddenness. The Washington Post described the conflict as "one of history's shortest ground wars" and the resolution of the conflict as "surprisingly easy". Five days later, on March 8 (March 9 in Fiji), Avatar Adi Da emerged from His austere confinement, amid the tears and praises of His devotees.

## Kaya Kalpa

In July 1991, Avatar Adi Da entered into another period of seclusion, this time associated with "kaya kalpa", an ancient Indian practice of rejuvenation. Since 1977, Avatar Adi Da had been asking the members of the Radiant Life Clinic (the guild of His devotees involved in the healing arts) to research the secrets of kaya kalpa, and now He expressed His intention to test the process in His own body.

"Kaya kalpa", in Sanskrit, means "body fashioning" or "body work", because the aim of the regime is to "re-make" the body, through a period of seclusion in darkness (traditionally forty days) while fasting and taking special herbal elixirs. In the traditional setting, however, kaya kalpa is more than a method of bodily rejuvenation. It is a process that obliges all the outward-directed tendencies of the body-mind to come to rest, leaving the being free to concentrate in Spiritual contemplation. Generally speaking, therefore, only individuals of significant Spiritual maturity engage the process of kaya kalpa, because no unprepared individual could expect to endure the rigors of such a radical retreat.

Once the herbal preparations requested from India arrived, Avatar Adi Da entered into the kaya-kalpa process at Aham Da Asmi Sthan, His Residence at the Matrix. It was July 18, and His intention was to remain in seclusion for forty days. Although Avatar Adi Da was certainly interested in the effect that kaya kalpa might have on His health, and the suitability of the regime for use by His devotees in the future, it was obvious to the doctors administering the kaya-kalpa treatment that Avatar Adi Da had suddenly taken on this austerity for His own mysterious reasons. He was not merely trying to extend the life of His physical Body. He was, He said, calling His devotees to engage in a devotional process of "kaya kalpa" with Him—a radical regeneration of their Spiritual practice, and of their devotional relationship to Him altogether.

In fact, Avatar Adi Da's Seclusion was not as much of a retreat as is traditionally recommended for the kaya-kalpa process. He did not feel free to engage it in the full traditional manner, because He was intent on maintaining regular communication with His devotees. And so, Adidama Sukha Dham continued to bring Him reports on a daily basis and to pass on His Instructions as usual.

Avatar Adi Da proved to be remarkably sensitive to the kaya-kalpa herbal paste. After taking it for one day, He began to develop a heightened sensitivity to light, which made Him want to be in total darkness. The light that He had become so sensitive to was gross light, He said, but it also included the internal light of the brain. At night He had clear vision of every detail of His room, He said, and during the day, when the room was illumined only by low red-filtered lights, He had clear vision with His eyes closed!

During this time, a group of devotees were invited to a formal Darshan occasion. Avatar Adi Da sat in the dining room of His Residence, which, like His bedroom, was lit only by a dim red glow. He wore dark glasses

**Darshan at Aham Da Asmi Sthan during the kaya-kalpa process**

and a tight-fitting cap that came down over the top edge of His glasses. As they filed into the room—feeling the strong wave of His Transmission and beholding Him in His highly sensitized, vulnerable state—several devotees broke into sobs.

When everyone was seated, Avatar Adi Da made a startling and powerful move. He quickly reached down to His left and picked up something from the floor. In the next moment He was shining a large flashlight with a red lens around the room, scanning the faces before Him. There was an outburst of cries, shouts, and kriyas as He moved the light across the room. This was not just a flashlight beam—it was an extraordinary moment of His Spiritual Transmission.

The Trimada, who had been chanting since the occasion began, now began a traditional Indian devotional song with words by the Hindu Sage Shankara, in praise of the Guru's feet. In another spontaneous gesture, Avatar Adi Da motioned for His tamboura (a traditional Indian stringed instrument). He embraced the tamboura, nestling its long neck again His cheek, and, with His head tilted down, stroked the strings slowly and gently. Even after the song ended, Avatar Adi Da continued playing the tamboura by Himself for a few moments. At the end of the occasion, the Divine Maha-Siddha stood and passed out the Prasad with His own hand to every devotee in the room. It was an unforgettably sublime occasion.

The next day, Avatar Adi Da pointed out that the sensitivity devotees had shown to Him in His extraordinarily rarefied and vulnerable state should mark their manner of relating to Him under all circumstances.

## The Religious Illiteracy of Scientific Materialists

In the first week of August, by the light of His red flashlight, Avatar Adi Da read some articles from current issues of *Scientific American*. Even in a time of such seclusion, He was staying in touch with current trends of thought. One of these articles was critical of Russian research into parapsychological phenomena. Avatar Adi Da noted that the article expressed the widespread prejudice against anything that cannot be explained in terms of the prevailing views of scientific materialism, and He was moved to speak about the implications of this attitude:

*AVATAR ADI DA SAMRAJ: Scientific materialism is creating a great problem in the world, and it will continue to do so. In examining the writings of many scientists, I observe that, in almost all cases, scientists are suffering from what I call "religious illiteracy". They have little, if any, depth of appreciation for, or understanding of, the real content of religion. They tend, almost invariably, to adhere to a "Westernized" and conventional view of religion. Some scientists, it is true, are able to look at existence from a broader philosophical point of view and show a general understanding of religious and Spiritual matters—scientists such as Rupert Sheldrake and Fritjof Capra, for example.*

*Most scientists, however, fit into two categories. The first category consists of those who are positively disposed toward religion but who, when they refer to "religion", quote only the Bible. Their knowledge of religion is limited to the Bible and the Judeo-Christian tradition.*

*Scientists in the second category are more or less anti-religious, even though they talk about God. Such scientists talk about the so-called "Creator-God", and they take a kind of pleasure in constantly criticizing the "Creator-God" idea.*

*Both categories are religiously illiterate. In both cases, they are generally opposed to anything that is not an established religion. They are almost universally opposed to religions originating in the East—and to anyone who is called a "Guru". In fact, the entire world is, at this time, controlled by scientific materialism, and, therefore, religion is suppressed and allowed only in its conventional forms. Since religious illiteracy is a universal problem, it is important that voices be raised to proclaim the greater matters of true religion, beyond conventional religion and scientific materialism.*

*Scientists tend to be involved in the game of the mind, which attempts to abstract the observer from the observed. In general, however, scientists are not involved in a pure application of the scientific method. They are championing pseudo-religion. In the realm of physics, for example, the fundamental goal is the discovery of the unified-field theory, the grand universal theory that will account for all aspects of objectified reality and for all the forces that may be observed. Such a pursuit is a form of pseudo-religion, a subversion of religion that results when the egoic, or separate, point of view is made the basis of philosophy. By contrast, the perennial goal of true religion is the Realization of Unity Itself, or Perfect Oneness with the Divine Reality.*

*Scientific materialism is an anti-mystical pursuit of the perennial ego-based religious goal, via the pursuit of objective knowledge—for the purpose of gaining power and control over objective reality. Traditional religious groups have always placed taboos on knowing too much and owning too much, because it has always been observed that when there is too much objective knowledge and too much objective ownership, such groups become dissociative and grossly manipulative, destroying the bond between human beings and all other beings, and between human beings and all aspects of life.*

*Scientific materialism does not pursue knowledge for its own sake or for the sake of Liberation. Scientific materialism pursues knowledge for the sake of power. Therefore, its end-result is technology and politics, rather than religious celebration and Spiritual Awakening and Divine Enlightenment. The culture of scientific materialism is a process very much like having someone in your neighborhood who owns too much, or who knows too much, or who is manipulating people too much—and who, therefore, needs to learn some lessons about the Ultimate Reality.*

*My "Source-Texts" are filled with My Instruction and the philosophical profundities of My Teaching-Revelation, which go far beyond conventional religious views. In* The Dawn Horse Testament, *for instance, I address the prevalent ideas about God, specifically indicating that God is* <u>*not*</u> *the "Creator".*[5] *The "Creator-God" is a primitive idea. The real religious process is based on and reveals a different understanding of the Divine than tends to be the naive basis of conventional religion. My Ecstatic Statements about the Divine Being, Truth, and Reality, and My Revelation of the Divine Being, Truth, and Reality to My devotees, must be communicated to the world to serve people's understanding of the purpose and Divine Source-Condition of their lives. Real God is not the "Creator" of the world. Real God is the Context of the world. You do not find Real God by going back to the beginning or by going forward to the end. You Realize Real God through (ultimately) most perfect self-transcendence in the present.*

*In fact, My Descriptions and Revelations of the Divine Reality are generally compatible with many of the descriptions of science. They just are not compatible with scientific materialism. One cannot dismiss the Way of Adidam simply because the idea of the "Creator-God" can be dismissed. Basically, the "Creator-God" idea is a simplistic philosophical idea, based on a very primitive and naive point of view. It appeals to people who have not yet profoundly "considered" its implications. The "Creator-God" idea certainly must be outgrown by anyone who embraces religion, philosophy, or science most profoundly. Real God is not the "Maker". Real God Is.*

*People are concerned about themselves. Therefore, they conceive of "God" in terms of causes and effects. But those who understand and transcend themselves Realize Real God beyond egoic attachment to the body-mind and the conditional world. Even so, the Divine, thus Realized, is not ultimately associated with the motive to dissociate from the world, because Divine Self-Realization is not world-negative. Nonetheless, Divine Self-Realization utterly Transcends the world and, Ultimately, Outshines it.* [August 6, 1991]

In August and September 1998, Avatar Adi Da wrote an extraordinary Essay about the common error of both conventional science and exoteric religion. (It is also one of His greatest Confessions of His own Divine Self-Nature and the uniqueness of the Way of Adidam. For the full Essay, please see Appendix A, pp. 767-85.)

*Both secular science and conventional (or merely exoteric) God-religion are based upon the two common faults of humankind—egoity and the non-recognition of the Real Nature (or One-Reality-Condition, or Perfectly Subjective, and Perfectly non-objective, Nature) of phenomenal experience (and of conditional existence, itself). Likewise, both secular science and conventional God-religion also (and equally) support and serve the illusions of humankind, rather than the need for humankind to Realize (and to Demonstrate) Reality, Truth, and Real God.*

*The principal illusion supported and served by secular science is epitomized by the idea of "materialism" (or of Reality as thing—without Being, or Consciousness). And the principal illusion supported and served by conventional God-religion is epitomized by the idea of "utopia" (or of Reality as the fulfillment of egoity). Secular science opposes conventional God-religion, and conventional God-religion opposes secular science—each, in turn, proposing that its propositions are, by contrast to the propositions of the other, the correct means for interpreting (and the correct "point of view" relative to) "Reality" and "Truth" and "God". However, neither secular science nor conventional God-religion is a correct (or right and true) means for Realizing (and* <u>*Demonstrating*</u>*) Reality (Itself), or Truth (Itself), or Real God. Indeed, "point of view" (of* <u>*any*</u> *conditional, or space-time, kind) is precisely the fault that self-separates one and all from the* <u>*inherent*</u> *Realization of Reality, Truth, and Real God.*

*Reality, Truth, and Real God* <u>*Is*</u> *the Condition of conditions—the inherently egoless (or Perfectly Subjective, and Perfectly non-objective) Self-Condition of one and all.*

<u>REAL</u> GOD <u>IS</u> THE INDIVISIBLE ONENESS
OF UNBROKEN LIGHT

## Further Dramatic Changes in the World

In mid-1991, the Soviet Union was going through a very critical period—reviewing all of its political, religious, and intellectual dogmas. Although the Eastern European countries satellite to the Soviet Union had renounced Communism around that time, the Soviet Union itself had so far remained monolithic—a single political unit under Communist rule.

By now, however, the tide of change had reached Moscow itself. The constituent states of the Union were seriously agitating for independence from Communist domination, and no one knew what would occur. Would the central Soviet government consent to its own demise—the literal disintegration of the Soviet Union—or would it forcibly act to prevent such an outcome, as it always had in the past? It was a very difficult and potentially dangerous moment in the Soviet Union—and, therefore, in the world altogether.

Avatar Adi Da, confined in His darkened room at Adidam Samrajashram, was silently Transmitting His Blessing-Power into this circumstance of instability. Avatar Adi Da emerged from His room on August 27. He had not noticed that the kaya-kalpa regime produced any remarkable signs of rejuvenation in His body, but, several days before He came out, dramatic events had begun to occur in the Soviet Union. Mikhail Gorbachev resigned as leader of the Communist party, the Soviet Union began its shift to political pluralism, and the former satellite nations of Eastern Europe regained their independence. This monumental shift occurred, in the words of *The Washington Post*, "quickly and almost painlessly".

## LATVIA DECLARES INDEPENDENCE
### Troops Withdraw In Baltics

August 22, 1991

MOSCOW, AUG. 21—The Baltic republic of Latvia today declared its immediate independence from the Soviet Union, following similar action in neighboring Estonia on Tuesday.

## COMMUNISM LOSES ITS GRIP ACROSS U.S.S.R.
### Yeltsin Halts Party Activities, Closes Newspapers in Russia

Saturday, August 24, 1991

MOSCOW, AUG. 23—The end of the Communist Party's tentacle-like grip over the whole of Soviet society came today, quickly and almost painlessly.

## GORBACHEV ABANDONS PARTY, QUITS LEADERSHIP POST, ORDERS PROPERTY SEIZED

Sunday, August 25, 1991

MOSCOW, AUG. 24—Communist rule collapsed tonight in the Soviet Union after seven decades as President Mikhail Gorbachev resigned as Communist Party general secretary and ordered the government to seize all party property.

## EC NATIONS RECOGNIZE INDEPENDENCE OF BALTIC REPUBLICS
### Ministers Make Arrangements for New Soviet Aid Package

Wednesday, August 28, 1991

BRUSSELS, AUG. 27—The 12 nations of the European Community formally recognized Latvia, Lithuania and Estonia today, welcoming the "restoration and sovereignty and independence" of the three Baltic states after more than 50 years of subjugation by Moscow.

## RUSSIAN, KAZAKH LEADERS PRESS NEW ECONOMIC UNION

Saturday, August 31, 1991

MOSCOW, AUG. 30—The Soviet Union's two geographically largest republics, Russia and Kazakhstan, proposed a new economic union to replace what they called the "former U.S.S.R.," as the republic of Azerbaijan declared its independence today.

**Adidam Samrajashram, 1991**

CHAPTER 19

# The All-Completing Avatar

During the same years that Avatar Adi Da's Saving Work with the world began to become dramatically evident, He was also Revealing His Divine Nature more and more profoundly to His devotees. He was Showing Himself to them very directly as the Ruchira Avatar—the Manifestation of the Divine "Brightness" on Earth.

## The Fulfillment of the Avatar Tradition

In the Vaishnavite[1] tradition of Hinduism, it is said that there are ten Divine Avatars. According to this tradition, cosmic history has already witnessed the appearance of the first nine Avatars, but the tenth and completing Avatar remains to come. He is named "Kalki" and will appear in the terrible era of the Kali Yuga[2] (when the Divine is virtually forgotten), heroically conquering the forces of darkness and restoring all to a life of devotion to the Divine and obedience to Divine Law. Traditional images of the Kalki Avatar in Hindu art show Him seated on a white horse, sword in hand, ready to slay His enemies.

Such an image of the final Divine Deliverer riding a white horse is not exclusively Hindu. It is deep in the human psyche, surfacing also in the last book of the Bible, which prophesies, in vision, the "second coming" of Jesus of Nazareth:

*And now I saw heaven open, and a white horse appear; its rider was called Trustworthy and True. . . . His eyes were flames of fire and he was crowned with many coronets. . . . On his cloak and on his thigh a name was written, King of kings and Lord of lords.*[3]

Feeling such archetypes to be prophecies of Avatar Adi Da's Appearance, two devotees brought the Kalki tradition to Avatar Adi Da's attention. Hal Okun sent Avatar Adi Da a gift of a Kalki medallion, which he had acquired in India while in service to Avatar Adi Da, and Bill Stranger offered Him an explanation of the Kalki tradition.

In his report, Bill praised Avatar Adi Da as the true and final Avatar, the Divine Liberator Who fulfills the Kalki prophecy in this present dark and godless age, and he quoted a description of the Kalki Avatar coined by Judith Tyberg in her book *The Language of the Gods*:

*[Kalki] is the Divine Man, called "white horse" to symbolize the strength and power of all colors, hence "power of full plenitude". Also Conqueror of Yama, Death, of all duality, all opposition and all darkness, the Divine man on earth, One with the Infinite Divine.*[4]

Avatar Adi Da fully received this gesture of recognition from His devotees and even accepted the Name "Da Kalki", on April 5, 1990, for a period of time. When He took this Name, His Blessing Power flowed in a torrent. Those on retreat at Adidam Samrajashram became wildly ecstatic with the Force of Adi Da's Spiritual Transmission. They began to experience kriyas, blisses, and heart-openings such as had not been seen since the "Garbage and the Goddess" period in 1974. James Alwood, who was on retreat at the time, describes the first occasion of overwhelming Spiritual "Intoxication" during this period, on April 19, 1990.

*JAMES: I was waiting in Temple Adi Da, with a group of about thirty other retreatants. We were chanting, expecting the arrival of Beloved Adi Da at any moment. For many of us, this would be the last Darshan occasion of our retreat.*

*As we waited, the appointed hour came and passed with no word. A few priests came in and removed the items that had been brought out in expectation of Beloved Adi Da's arrival. A quiet despair started to spread through the room, but then one of the priests ran in and shouted, "Hurry! Beloved Adi Da is already sitting on the steps of Indefinable! Run! Forget your meditation cushions!"*

*Mindlessly, we all leapt to our feet, ran out the door of the Temple and across the lawn to where our Beloved Guru was sitting, waiting for us. As I moved forward to offer a flower at His Feet, I could hear many of the other devotees breaking out into open sobs and weeping for joy. Beloved Adi Da was an open torrent of Divine Force and Presence.*

*I moved to a spot on the lawn a few yards back from the steps where Beloved Adi Da was Sitting. As I sat down, my mind and body quickly unwound in the face of His Transmission, and my last thought was "Oh, this is going to be a quiet, meditative occasion." I noticed Beloved Adi Da's toes wiggling, in a gesture of Transmission. Suddenly, I was thrown up to a visionary realm where Beloved was before me in the Form of Fire. A spontaneous prayer rose in my heart, "May I give You everything." As soon as this prayer formed, I felt myself leaping into and merging with Avatar Adi Da in His Fire Form.*

*After some time, awareness of my body arose, and I felt like I was shouting at the top of my lungs but no sound was emerging. I noticed Beloved Adi Da's Feet again, and once more, I suddenly found myself back in*

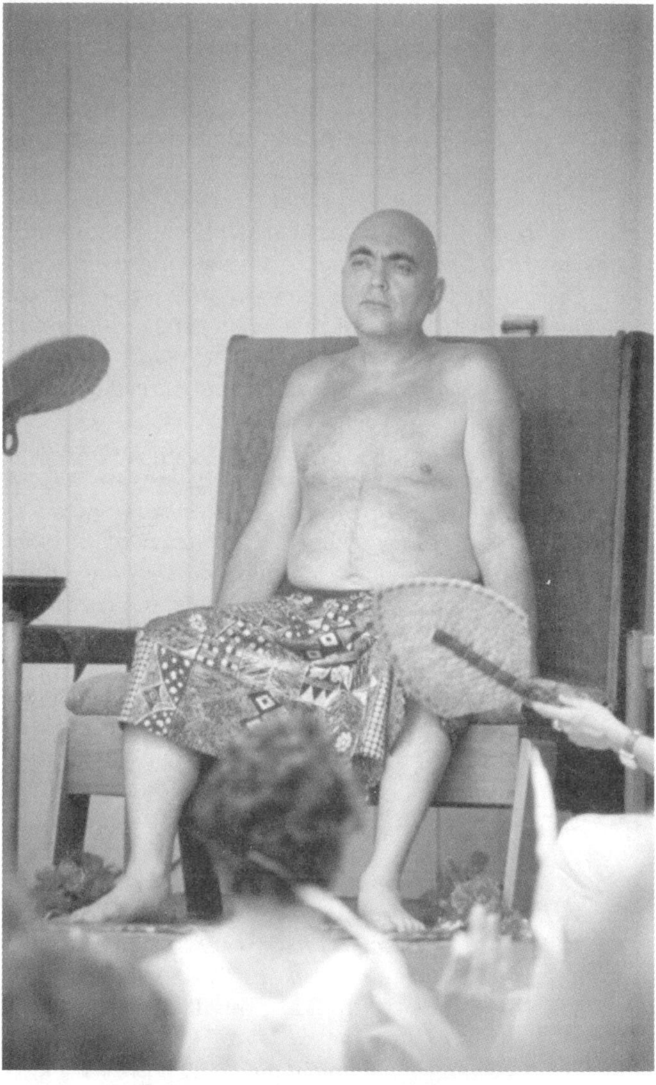

**Darshan on the porch of Indefinable,
Adidam Samrajashram, 1990**

*the visionary realm before His Fire, leaping ecstatically into the Flames.*

*This cycle repeated a number of times.*

*As awareness of where I was sitting returned, I noticed that almost everyone was shouting, or weeping, or having extremely exaggerated kriyas of one form or another. One man behind me was exclaiming his awakened recognition of Who was sitting before us, shouting over and over again, "You Are Da Kalki! You Are Da Kalki!" In the midst of all this mayhem, Beloved Adi Da sat quietly, like the eye of a tropical storm.*

*He seemed to be focused on the horizon, not particularly aware of or concerned with the drama unfolding at His Feet. He seemed to be doing His world-Work, whatever that was. And we, His devotee retreatants, were fortunate enough to be in the path of His Bliss-Regard, as It Poured through us and beyond.*

Susan Isaacson, another devotee just completing her retreat, was also at this occasion. She had been struggling through the entire retreat to go beyond her limit on emotional expressiveness and devotional feeling:

*SUSAN: I was one of the last ones to leave Temple Adi Da. While hurrying to Indefinable, I was filled with both apprehension and joy. I was overwhelmed by my own cold heart, and I felt a deep desire to be free of its clutches.*

*When I arrived at Indefinable, I was stopped short by the most beautiful sight of my entire life. Beloved Adi Da was simply sitting on the steps of the porch—He did not even have a chair. He was looking down, and He was very, very Beautiful. We were only a few feet away from Him. By the time I got there, several of the women retreatants were already seated and weeping. I felt so extremely frustrated at being unable to be vulnerable enough to weep with devotion myself that I—as bizarre and humorous as it may seem—started acting as if I were*

*weeping. Then somehow—and I really cannot say how—I was genuinely and intensely weeping. It definitely was not my doing. I had never felt such profound emotion. I found myself on my back gazing into the blue sky, and having deep breathing kriyas, a phenomenon I had always envied others for experiencing. My friends told me later that, as I let go of my control of everything, Beloved Adi Da looked over at me with a smile on His Face. Truly, He had swept me beyond self-doubt.*

*I sat back up as soon as I could, because I wanted to see Beloved Adi Da. By this time, almost everyone had come unhinged. Devotees were praising Beloved Adi Da as the Divine World-Teacher and as Da Kalki. We were being Drawn into a profound recognition of His Divinity, more than in previous Darshans. I started saying and feeling His Name "Da", and this Mantra took me over. His Spiritual Force was coursing through my body and I became riveted to the spot.*

*I looked up at Him. The space where we sat with Him had become motionless and timeless. I felt Him as Fire and I was floating above and all around Him. He was Doing and Giving everything.*

*He Gave me these experiences, it seems to me, not for their own sake but to draw me out and help me feel past the incredible barricade of fear I had been so heavily identified with. Now I was finally able to feel my love for Him, and I was unbelievably happy.*

*At the end, Beloved Adi Da motioned for us to come up to the porch to receive Prasad. I had no idea how I was going to get myself from where I was on the ground to the porch steps, since I was still completely charged with His Spirit-Force—my body and particularly my hands were literally twisted with this Blissful Force. But somehow I managed to crawl forward and bow before Beloved Adi Da. My hands, however, were still rigid claws, stiff with Force, and I was unable to open them to receive the Prasad. This was not a problem for Beloved Adi Da. He Compassionately opened my hands with His own, and Placed the Prasad in them. I backed off the porch and fell in a heap of gratitude on the lawn. I sat up finally to gaze again on the most beautiful sight in the universe, and then Beloved Adi Da stood up and moved back into Indefinable.*

While on retreat in June 1990, Charles Seage, M.D., Avatar Adi Da's personal physician, who had served Him since 1978, was overwhelmed by the depth at which He now recognized the Divinity of His beloved Guru.

*CHARLES: A few days into my retreat, all the retreatants were invited to attend a formal Darshan occasion with Beloved Adi Da in the Darshan Hall known as Divine World-Teacher Mandir*[5] *at the Matrix. This Hall is very intimate, and there were only about thirty-five of us in the room with Him.*

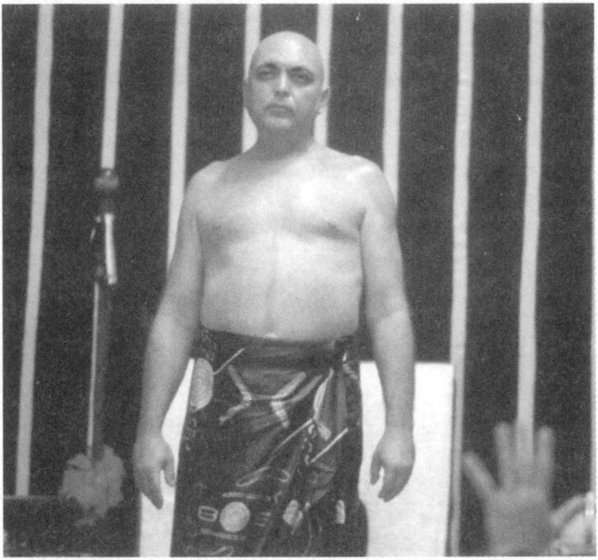

***"Then He simply Stood before us, His hands open and down at His sides a few inches from His body. Suddenly as I watched Him, it became unbelievably obvious that He is the Divine Person."***

*At the end of the occasion, Beloved Adi Da reached over to dip His hands in the water bowl beside His Chair and sprinkled the water on the Prasad. Then He stood stood up and passed out the Prasad personally to each of us from His own Hands. I returned to my seat full of gratitude, but there was no sign of what was to occur next.*

*Beloved Adi Da finished distributing the Prasad and passed the bowl to Adidama Sukha Dham. Then He simply stood before us, His hands open and down at His sides a few inches from His body. Suddenly as I watched Him, it became unbelievably obvious that He is the Divine Person. The Vision He Granted me was astounding. He filled up the entire universe. For a moment, I closed my eyes and visualized His Form, as I usually do. Then that visualization disappeared and I felt Him become so immense and All-Pervading that it was as though I was seeing and feeling His Cosmic Form. I saw that the entire universe is His Form. It was clearly, tacitly the case. He is not limited to His bodily human Form.*

*The Power of that Vision was overwhelming, and I could not contain the Force of the Realization. Then I felt an incredible Force entering into me, and I let out a low-pitched scream such as I had never made before. I screamed several times—an animal sound, very loud—that seemed to come from deep in my lower body. Later, people told me it was like the sound someone might have made if they were falling off a cliff. The room had been quiet, but I could not contain myself. There was no intention involved—my shout was just my spontaneous response to that totally overwhelming recognition of Beloved Adi Da in His Divinity.*

*After that, my hands filled up with energy of an extraordinary magnitude. Energy was pouring out of me. I became completely absorbed in Beloved Adi Da. After He left, I crawled to His Chair and bowed down in gratitude.*

In the midst of this flood of ecstatic devotion, Avatar Adi Da continued to Reveal Himself. He Wrote in *The Basket Of Tolerance*:

*I Am . . . the First and the Last, the every where, anciently and always, Promised (and Universally Expected) True God-Man of the "late-time" (or "dark" epoch). I Am, now and in all future time. . . . the Divine World-Teacher, the Divine Heart-Master of all My devotees (East and West). Therefore, My Life and Work and Person must be understood and appreciated in the context of the total (One and Great) Tradition of mankind, East and West. And even those who do not, in any then present time, become My devotees are—now, and forever hereafter, during and after (and forever after) the Avataric (physical) Lifetime of My bodily (human) Divine Form (here)—always Divinely Blessed by Me to better understand and appreciate their own (possibly confessed) traditions, and even all "other" traditions, by rightly understanding and appreciating Me and the One and Great Tradition I Have Come here to Represent and to Complete and to Completely Fulfill.*

Eventually, Avatar Adi Da came to feel that the associations of the name "Kalki" were too restricted, too specific to one particular religious tradition. He also commented that the typical portrayal of Kalki in political (and even aggressive) terms was not an accurate or appropriate description of His Incarnation. And so He indicated that "Da Kalki" should henceforth be regarded simply as one of His historical Names and not remain in general use.

Nevertheless, the period when Avatar Adi Da assumed this Name was a landmark in His devotees' recognition of Him. What He was Revealing through His Darshan was beyond anything they could ever have imagined. They were recognizing that Avatar Adi Da Samraj is the Complete Revelation of the Divine Person.

# The Divine Intervention

In February 1993, the next phase of Avatar Adi Da's Self-Revelation unfolded. At this time, He was meeting frequently with devotees. In gathering after gathering, He found new ways to communicate to them the import of His Avataric Incarnation. On February 12, He spoke plainly of Himself as the Intervention of Very God into the human dimension, here to do His own unique, unprecedented Work.

*The Great Process comes about when the Divine Intervenes, Appears, Incarnates, Blesses, Teaches the understanding and the transcending of ego, such that the direct Divine Blessing may be received and the Great Divine Yoga may be entered into. This is What I Do.*

*I am not merely advanced. I am not merely evolved. I Am the Very One. I Am the One you must Realize.*

*The seventh stage Awakening will be Accomplished by My Avatarically Self-Transmitted Divine Grace. It cannot be Accomplished otherwise. There is no "method" for Accomplishing It. It is entirely Given by Me. It cannot be Realized without My Avatarically Self-Transmitted Divine Blessing.*

*I am Telling you the Great Secret. It is not Revealed in any traditional books. It is unknown, apart from My Avatarically Given Divine Revelation of It.* [Divine Spiritual Baptism Versus Cosmic Spiritual Baptism]

While Avatar Adi Da Samraj was speaking these Words, the Spiritual Transmission in the room was profound. As on countless previous occasions, He was doing what He was describing. In contrast to the night of "Guru Enters Devotee" in 1974, He was now speaking of the "Crashing Down" of His Divine Grace not only into the individual body-minds of His devotees but upon all beings and things.

**Adidam Samrajashram, 1993**

When a person feels the Transmission of Avatar Adi Da Samraj, he or she knows it is unique and knows it is Divine. There is nothing "personal" or "local" about it. He or she realizes that it is a universal Spiritual and All-Pervading "Fact". It is Him, in His Spiritual Form. This experience of His Spiritual Presence is how a person comes to know with intuitive certainty that Avatar Adi Da Samraj cannot be compared to anyone. He is not an ordinary man or even an extraordinary man. He is the Very Divine Intensity, Love-Blissful Pressure, Pervading and Surrounding and Touching all, Who happens to have taken a human Form as an Agent of necessary Communication with all beings. But His human Form is just a "satellite" of the One He Is.

Avatar Adi Da's Great Self-Revelations continued into March. On March 6, 1993, He spoke of His unique Siddhis, or Powers, as the Divine Person. Now that He has brought these Siddhis into the human plane, He explained, it is possible, for the first time, for human beings to Realize the seventh and most ultimate stage of life.

*AVATAR ADI DA SAMRAJ: I have brought Siddhis into all planes, into the entire Cosmic Mandala, that permit Most Perfect Divine Self-Realization, and I have thoroughly Communicated to you, in every detail, the Way of the seventh stage Realization. Now that that Great Way has been Given to all, it is possible for all, and your Divine Self-Realization is a matter of whether or not you will choose the Way of Truth and how profoundly you will practice It.*

*It is not only that My Revelation of the Wisdom-Teaching of the Way of Adidam, the seventh stage Teaching, is complete and for the first time Given. It is that the Siddhis of My Manifestation and My Work have made Divine Self-Realization possible. Those Siddhis will be eternally Effective. I may be resorted to eternally, and My Siddhis are eternally operative.*

*I have made the Way of Most Perfect Divine Self-Realization possible. That Work having been Done, the Siddhis of that Accomplishment having been established, there need not be any other seventh stage Adept. There cannot be another. The Work has been Done. Now there can be seventh stage Realizers, but there cannot be another seventh stage Adept. There need only be one such Revealer, full of the Siddhis to Accomplish the Work that makes such Realization possible.*

*And That One is the Divine Person, because the seventh stage Realization is the Realization of the Divine Person. Only That One can Make such Revelation and Accomplish such Work.*

*DINA LAUTMAN: Beloved, before Your Incarnation, these Siddhis were not possible?*

*AVATAR ADI DA SAMRAJ: They did not exist. To Manifest the Siddhis and to Do the Work, to Accomplish the Work that is universally effective, I needed to be entered into the conditional planes by actual entrance into the Cosmic Mandala—altogether, completely.*

*GERALD SHEINFELD: Beloved, Your Perfect Manifestation—Wholly Incarnated, with all the Siddhis that are present because of Your Incarnation—is the greatest Advantage that beings could ever have, because everything is complete. We have been Given everything.*

*AVATAR ADI DA SAMRAJ: Most of what I have Done will not be noticed or seriously addressed in My physical Lifetime. But it is not necessary that it all be noticed, either. What has been necessary all along is that I Do the Work. Therefore, I have conducted Myself so as to Accomplish My Work. And, in all its fundamental details, it has been Done.*

*JONATHAN CONDIT: You have already Told us tonight that Your human Manifestation was required for Your*

*Siddhis to come into action in this realm. Nevertheless, it seems obvious that Your Divine Influence was felt in the world even before Your Birth.*

*AVATAR ADI DA SAMRAJ: People have been seeking Me. Therefore, I Came. I Answered the prayers, and here I Am.*

*You all must get it. All My devotees must get it. You cannot comprehend most of what I Do. My Concentration, as I told you tonight—and before, also—has been to simply Accomplish My Work, because That had to be Accomplished, regardless of your disinclination, your immaturity and mediocrity. Now it is Accomplished. Now that Work is Done.*

*You, My devotees, must embrace My Revelation and get down to your business. Tell the truth. Be compassionate. Be truthful but straightforward and loving. I am not here to struggle with anyone—now especially, in the extremes of My Lifetime and Work.*

*Now that My Work is Done, I must simply Confess My Self to you As I Am. So I am Doing it.* [March 6, 1993]

In the midst of these profound Revelations about His Divine Nature, Avatar Adi Da was also addressing the matter of His devotees' practice of the foundations of the Way of Adidam—the listening-hearing sadhana. Starting at the end of March and continuing through the first week of April, Avatar Adi Da Samraj confronted the pattern of "Narcissus" in His devotees with overwhelming force:

*AVATAR ADI DA SAMRAJ: You want Me to talk about your trying to work your life out. Life does not work out! It cannot work out! That is not the Way of Adidam! The Way of Adidam is about ego-transcendence, transcending the very thing that seeks to make it all work out! You are wanting Me to address you in this act that you are making to have everything be hunky-dory. And the whole damn*

*"You want Me to talk about your trying to work your life out. Life does not work out! It cannot work out! That is not the Way of Adidam! The Way of Adidam is about ego-transcendence, transcending the very thing that seeks to make it all work out!"*

*thing doesn't even exist! And that's what there is to Realize! Absolute Freedom from this illusion—that you call "reality" and are trying to make work out perfectly. You are only looking at yourself! That's all you are ever looking at! And you want it to work out, "Narcissus". You are looking at all this and you are calling it "the world"—but it is you!*

*All you ever talk about, think about, or perceive is you. It is a private, egoically "self-possessed" illusion. It is a result of your own knot of separateness, and it registers in this poor little slug of a body-mind you identify with as all kinds of illusions, hallucinations, thoughts, presumptions, ideas, perceptions. The whole lot, the whole ball of wax, is all the result of your own separate position, your own point of view, self-contraction, manufacturing illusions on the base of That Which Is Reality Itself. But you have no idea what that Reality is. No notion. You are not associated with Reality Itself, you are dissociated from Reality. That is the whole point!*

*Well, that being the case, that is what you have to deal with! But you want to persist in your adoration of the "pond"—your experience, your search, and so forth—and you are asking Me how to make it work out. I do not have anything to do with the "making-it-work-out" business. I am here to Wake you up!* [April 2, 1993]

Avatar Adi Da Samraj cut through every attempt on the part of His devotees to defend themselves from His Criticism. He was tremendously intensifying His devotees' sensitivity to the knot of self-contraction, to the point where that cramp would become so present, so obvious, so unbearable, so unnecessary, so absurd that they would spontaneously let it go. Late in the night during what turned out to be the culminating gathering of this period, on April 8, 1993, Adi Da brought devotees to that intolerable point. There was a pause while His Radiant Force magnified in the room, melting the clench of "Narcissus". Then He began to speak differently, quietly:

*AVATAR ADI DA SAMRAJ: Feel into that knot of stress. Feel into it and account for it. See it as your own action. Regard Me in that moment, in every moment. And then you begin to feel Me. Then the surrender comes, the self-forgetting comes, the native sense of Non-Separateness is felt. This is actually what I am Calling you to do! Actually to do that. Just to be doing it grants equanimity to you, even bodily, grants equanimity to your speech, your actions, your feelings, because you are registering this depth-point and going beyond it and feeling Me. This is the context of practice of the Way of Adidam, not merely outer observances. This is what it means to listen to Me: to be examining this point of contraction in depth, to feel it, and by its unfolding to feel Me. This is not the end of the Way of Adidam. It is the foundation of it. Self-understanding and devotion at depth—this is what you must do in every moment. This is what it is to practice the Way of Adidam.*

*You are basically trying to feel good. Why would you be trying to feel good if you were not already feeling bad? You must understand that, Natively, you always already feel good. But not the way you are doing it. You are not in the Native Position. You are in the position of the self-contraction. If you would Stand Prior to the self-contraction and feel beyond it, you would always already feel good in the most profound heart-sense. It would not make any great difference how the rest of the body-mind felt, because the body-mind is part of the conditional world and is always subject to negative changes and disintegration and death. But when you are in the heart-place, you are Awake. You always already feel good. Always! Already!* [April 8, 1993]

By this gathering, many devotees found that they could not snap back as easily as before into a state of immunity to their own act of self-contraction. The heartless machine of the ego was too starkly revealed. There was no lasting relief to be found through any kind of seeking for satisfaction. In His Masterful Revelation, throughout that previous year, of the desperate state of bondage to the self-contraction, Adi Da Samraj had begun to Magnify in His devotees the need for devotion to Him, the conviction that He is, truly, the only Help. Everything He had said about the necessity for Ruchira Avatara Bhakti Yoga was starting to prove itself. And the Gift was before their eyes, whenever they looked up from the "pond" and beheld Him in the Radiant Truth of His Being.

Adidam Samrajashram, 1993

CHAPTER 20

# The Forerunners

A few weeks after His Great Confession of March 6, 1993, in which He unequivocally stated that He is the "first, last, and only" Adept-Realizer of the seventh stage of life, Avatar Adi Da went on to Reveal the secrets of the process by which He, the Formless Divine, was able to Appear in human Form.

## A Sympathy for the West

In 1893, a young Indian swami came to America. At the Parliament of Religions held that year in Chicago, this imposing, forceful man addressed a crowd consisting largely of Westerners, who had little or no exposure to the Eastern traditions, with great passion. He impressed the colloquium with his extraordinary presence, his impeccable command of English, his pride in his own tradition, and his ability to inspire others beyond sectarian views. It was not merely his words, however, but the profound Spiritual power behind them, that moved his audience.

Swami Vivekananda was the most cherished disciple of the great Indian Adept Ramakrishna, and he had come to bring the ancient wisdom of India to the West. After the accolade he received at the Parliament, Swami Vivekananda spent years in constant travel, lecturing all over America and in England.

Swami Vivekananda had the fervor of a man moved to save the world, but he was mightily frustrated in his intention. He knew that the future of humanity was largely being shaped by the West, which was already sliding into secularism. But his work could not be truly effective among Westerners. There was a line drawn, beyond which he could not go—for he was a Hindu, a dark-skinned man, and a celibate swami. Thus, in spite of his best efforts, in spite of his profound Realization, Swami Vivekananda remained a foreigner, an outsider. In 1902, at the age of thirty-nine, he died—unable to proceed further with what he felt to be his necessary world-work.

Starting in the 1970s, Avatar Adi Da would occasionally speak to His devotees about the pre-history of His present birth—of the unique conjunction of events it had required. He, the One come for all beings, could not appear until the mid-twentieth century—when the world had grown "smaller" through technological intercommunication, when East was approaching West, when modern physics was shifting the materialist view of existence, when Freud had demonstrated the bondage of unconscious psycho-sexual motivations. These were some of the realities and paradigms that had to be in place before His Divine Work in the world could be fully effective. But more than all else, an actual subtle vehicle of unique Spiritual preparation had to be available.

In many cultural traditions, there exists a belief in reincarnation, or the "re-cycling" of the being from life to life. Avatar Adi Da has often discussed this belief with His devotees, and has confirmed that there is a process that could be called "reincarnation", although it is much more complex than commonly described.[1] From the Spiritual point of view, reincarnation is an opportunity for growth. In India, for example, great Spiritual beings are understood to be manifesting the results of intense Spiritual practice in previous lives, not merely in the present lifetime. Avatar Adi Da, however is not a "highly evolved being"—He is the Divine, fully present, in Person. Nevertheless, to take human form, He had to conjoin with the ordinary processes of the cosmos, including the mechanism of reincarnation.

Every human personality, Avatar Adi Da has explained, is composed of a gross (or physical) vehicle—the body, derived from one's parents—and a subtle vehicle—the "reincarnate", the deeper mechanism of the ego that moves from life to life. In order to be born, Adi Da Samraj required a subtle vehicle attuned to the task of bringing true Spirituality to the modern West. Swami Vivekananda carried in his psyche thousands of years of Indian Spirituality and Realization, and ended his life in love with the West in its need for God. On March 20, 1993, Avatar Adi Da confirmed conclusively to His devotees: Swami Vivekananda's compassionate urge to be reborn in order to serve the West had created a unique conjunction with Avatar Adi Da's Divine Impulse to Manifest in the human realm, and it was this conjunction that provided the vehicle for Avatar Adi Da's Incarnation as Franklin Jones.

*AVATAR ADI DA SAMRAJ: It should be understood about this intentional Birth of Mine that no "decision" was made from an absolute point of view, out of the blue. The Deeper Personality Vehicle of Swami Vivekananda was provided conditionally, as I have indicated. I, My Self, was brought into conjunction with the conditional reality by those means. In that conjunction, I "Consented" to the Ordeal of human Manifestation.*

*The Deeper Personality Vehicle of Swami Vivekananda arose in the conditional domain and provided the conjunction with Me (As I Am). That Vehicle was conjoined with My Very Being. Swami Vivekananda was given up completely, and the Vehicle became transparent to Me.* [March 20, 1993]

Two years later, Avatar Adi Da spoke further about this:

*AVATAR ADI DA SAMRAJ: I took Birth in the West. Other Realizers have come to the West from India, on airplanes or boats. They did not submit to the Western circumstance, they did not come to the point of Realization in that circumstance and context, they did not address that circumstance and context.*

*Swami Vivekananda experienced the utter frustration of getting on a boat and going to the West. He knew it was not enough. And He knew what He was going to have to do, therefore—He was going to have to die and be reborn in the West. And His Western connections were the means for His rebirth. Having come to the West, He became entangled in sympathies and struggle, and suffered abuse, and found out what it is really all about. And He realized He was not equipped, in that lifetime, to convert Westerners, to convert people in the Western mode and disposition—which, since that time, has become more and more the global mode and disposition. Therefore, there was no reason for Him to go on with it. And that is why He died young. He did all He could do in that form. Nothing further could be accomplished.*

*But He said that, because of the sympathies He had entered into by being the first Eastern Adept-Realizer ever to have embraced the West—nobody had ever done that before—He was willing to be reborn in the West in order to serve mankind. He said He was born in love with humanity. That is it—He fell in love. He did not just go to the West as an Easterner, and wear His turban and robe, and leave it at that. He went to the West and became heart-sympathetic with it, even though everything was terrible about that circumstance. He became heart-sympathetic with people in the Western circumstance and disposition. But He realized that—as a Hindu, as an Easterner—He was not equipped to transform the West. So He went back to India and died.* [February 22, 1995]

In October 1993, Avatar Adi Da brought up another, even more esoteric aspect of this "consideration". He began to speak about Ramakrishna, the Spiritual Master of Swami Vivekananda, who had always been aware of the Spiritual stature and destiny of his disciple. At the end of his life, certain of the great work that lay ahead for his beloved Vivekananda, Ramakrishna poured his own Spiritual virtue into Swami Vivekananda in a formal act of Transmission—becoming, in his own words, only an "empty fakir".[2] Thus, Ramakrishna, through his total Spiritual investment of himself in Swami Vivekananda, is also part of the Deeper Personality Vehicle of Avatar Adi Da Samraj.

Ramakrishna was renowned for his ecstatic devotion to the Divine Goddess (in the form of Kali), and for his intuitive sympathy with other religions through his own contemplation of their icons and revelations. Indeed, Adi Da Samraj has acknowledged that Ramakrishna's Mastery of the fourth stage devotional path is unsurpassed in all of human history. In a unique way, the Deeper Personality Vehicle of Ramakrishna-Vivekananda brought to the Birth of Adi Da Samraj the essence of humanity's long quest for God. And the intense devotion to the Divine Goddess that marked the life of Ramakrishna (and also that of Swami Vivekananda) prepared the way for Avatar Adi Da's Submission to the Goddess at the end of His "Sadhana Years" and then His Great Husbanding of Her in the Vedanta Temple. It is no accident that this temple is associated with Ramakrishna and Swami Vivekananda. Avatar Adi Da has confessed that, through His own Divine Re-Awakening there, He perfectly fulfilled the Spiritual impulse of Ramakrishna and Vivekananda. In the instant of His own Divine Re-Awakening, He Enlightened them also—they became One with Him in the "Bright".

**Ramakrishna** **Swami Vivekananda**

*I Am the One Who Awakened (and, thereafter, Worked through) Ramakrishna. He Recapitulated the past, in order (by a Spiritual Sacrifice) to Serve the future. I Am the One Who Worked through (and has now Most Perfectly Awakened) Swami Vivekananda. He Served the future, in order (even by physical death and physical rebirth) to Transcend the past (and, Thus, and by Means of a Great and Spiritual, and even Transcendental, Awakening, to Bless and to Liberate the future).*

*Now and forever, Ramakrishna and Swami Vivekananda are One, at the Heart. And I Am the One They have Realized There.* [The Knee Of Listening]

# "It Is All Continuation"

Avatar Adi Da made known His connection with Ramakrishna and Swami Vivekananda through a process of "consideration" with His devotees that lasted many years. He began in 1976; returned to the subject in 1979, 1982, and 1988; and, during His period of profound Self-Revelations in 1993, He brought the matter to a point of undeniable certainty. In the midst of the "consideration", some of Avatar Adi Da's devotees began to get in touch with memories of their own past lives around Swami Vivekananda. Avatar Adi Da encouraged them to reclaim these intuitions—not just to satisfy a curiosity or a fascination, but to move them deeper in their Spiritual practice. He wanted these devotees to become aware of the profound imperative behind their birth—the urge to be with Him again in the body—and to use that karmic fact for the purpose of Realizing Him, and not merely to resume a human attachment.

In the case of Adidama Jangama Hriddaya, Avatar Adi Da had spoken to her over the years about the likelihood that she had had a relationship to Swami Vivekananda in a past life. He suggested that she investigate the possibility that her deeper personality was that of Sister Nivedita, one of Swami Vivekananda's closest disciples. It was only after many years of practice in Avatar Adi Da's Company—when Adidama Jangama Hriddaya had reached a level of profound psychic and Spiritual depth—that His statements about this past-life association became an in-depth "consideration" for her. In the process of this investigation, she began to see how intuitions of her past-life connection with Avatar Adi Da had actually started to surface even in her childhood, such that very early in life she had a profound sense of a Spiritual purpose.

*ADIDAMA JANGAMA HRIDDAYA: In 1965, at the age of fifteen, I crossed the Atlantic on a grand ocean liner with my parents. One night I woke in my berth, overwhelmed by the sudden feeling that my life must be, and already was somehow, devoted to the service of God. It was a spontaneous and absolute feeling, a déjà vu, as though I had finally understood something that had always been true. The passion that I felt that night, rocking on the waters of the Atlantic, was not without sorrow. It was as if I were struggling to connect with a truth I had already known, one that was more real to me than the family and friends and experiences of my present lifetime, more compelling than anything with which I was now familiar.*

*Years later, the meaning of that visitation—and everything with which it was associated—was brought to consciousness through my relationship with Beloved Adi Da. Over a period of many years, and in the course of much research, conversation, and psychic and intuitive revelation, Beloved Adi Da drew me and some of His other devotees through a remarkable process of recognizing that we had been alive in previous incarnations as individuals associated with Swami Vivekananda and that He Himself was uniquely Spiritually associated with Swami Vivekananda and with Swami Vivekananda's Guru, Ramakrishna.*

*But, always sensitive to our tendency to become fascinated by things such as reincarnation, Beloved Adi Da would typically begin the conversation, and, then, observing us becoming distracted from the real matters of ego-transcending practice, He would suddenly dismiss the subject, saying it was not to be taken seriously. And so He would drop the subject for years at a time.*

*He also would always admonish us that it is not*

*possible to enter into a truly depthful investigation of past lives without the freeing of attention and psyche that comes with real Spiritual maturity in His Company. Without that foundation, any "consideration" of past lives is merely a matter of the conjecturing of the verbal mind, without real psychic and Spiritual evidence. A further Instruction from Beloved Adi Da was that such past-life investigation is not for the sake of the glorifying of the present body-mind-self, but rather for the sake of revealing and purifying all of the egoic patterning that had, lifetime after lifetime, created similar incarnations characterized by the same kinds of limitations.*

*Thus, Beloved Adi Da would always use such "considerations" to draw me and others into a most profound process of self-understanding, in which we could see how the limited egoic mind each of us had manifested in previous lifetimes was continuing to pattern our present lifetimes. Most importantly, He Revealed how it was essential to go beyond all this chaos of reincarnated patterning and re-patterning in order to transcend egoity itself and Realize Him.*

In 1982, Avatar Adi Da had a remarkable exchange on this very matter with James Steinberg, who was then His librarian at the Mountain Of Attention:

*JAMES: In the spring of 1982, Beloved Adi Da suggested that I participate with some other devotees in researching His connection to Swami Vivekananda and other great Realizers of the past. Over the next few weeks, I did my regular service in the library during the day, but at night I immersed myself in books on Swami Vivekananda. I studied his early life and his discipleship with Ramakrishna, I studied the period of his teaching in the United States, England, and India. I examined what he said, how he felt about things, how he interacted with*

*people, all in order to find correspondences with Beloved Adi Da. I sent reports to my Beloved Guru, which He read with interest and amusement. And the devotees attending Him, who presented my reports to Him, encouraged me in my research. But I hardly needed encouragement.*

*The scope of the investigation widened. I was asked to look also at the disciples around Swami Vivekananda to see if they bore likenesses to any of the devotees around Adi Da Samraj.*

*As I read late into the night, hunched over book after book, the correlations began to overwhelm me. I now became a complete convert to the idea that Swami Vivekananda was the Deeper Personality Vehicle of Beloved Adi Da. The more convinced I became of this correspondence and the more I studied Swami Vivekananda and his disciples, the more I began to live in the world of Swami Vivekananda. This "consideration" had become a passion, and my research became all-consuming.*

*During this time, I felt as if I were literally walking on air. I was in a cloud of enthusiasm, constantly making connections between the 1980s and the 1890s. I was as much in the cold Himalayan foothills with Swami Vivekananda as in the summer heat of the California coastal range. My mind was in Victorian parlors listening to Swami Vivekananda speak and on steamers traveling the oceans, rather than fixed in the simple rooms of the Sanctuary library.*

*I could sense that, for all the devotion and gratitude I was feeling, I was caught up in an emotional whirlwind. I made an effort to remain balanced, but in retrospect it is easy to see that I was like a 500-pound food addict who has decided to spend only $25 instead of $30 on his afternoon snack!*

*I had begun to speculate about who I might have been. I noticed that one intimate of Swami Vivekananda's bore a particular physical resemblance to myself and had some of my characteristics. I also felt that this individual had a human relationship to Swami Vivekananda somewhat similar to my relationship to Beloved Adi Da. I did not say anything about this for several days, because I knew that it was tangential to the overall "consideration", and I wanted as much as I could to keep my own ego out of the way.*

*But, as so often happens in the Company of Beloved Adi Da, circumstances arose to reveal what needed to be purified in His devotee. Beloved Adi Da asked me to locate a passage by the Indian Sage Shankara that He wished to review and comment on. He thought that He might have seen the passage in a Vedantic text (where, in fact, after the events related in this story were over, He Himself found it). When I received this request, I was reading a book about the intimate of Swami Vivekananda whom I now thought of as my "former self". Remarkably, I discovered this man quoting what seemed to be the very passage requested by Adi Da. In my now infatuated state, this coincidence seemed like an absolute confirmation of my beliefs!*

*I sent a note to Beloved Adi Da to tell Him that I thought I had found the passage He was looking for. And then, with a light touch, I also mentioned that the book where I found it described the person with whom I thought I had a past-life association. I went over the wording many times so that my phrasing was not overstated. I excitedly awaited the response of Beloved Adi Da, hardly able to sleep. I knew that I was making myself extremely vulnerable and that I might be in for a big lesson. But I was already in up to my neck, and I had to allow myself to be seen by my Guru and be available for His Instruction.*

*Finally, after three days, Beloved Adi Da's response arrived. One of the nine women devotees serving Beloved Adi Da's intimate circumstance approached me and asked me to come to His library. She said, "Are you ready to have your mind blown?" I said I was.*

*She opened a manila folder and handed me two of Beloved Adi Da's "yellow sheets"—the unlined cream-colored paper that He characteristically writes all of His original manuscript work on. One of the pages began "Dear James". My mind stopped. He had written me a letter! I was overwhelmed. I looked at the back of the second page, which ended, "Love, Da". I sat there, unable to read past the salutation, stunned by the Force of His Blessing. Finally, after I had stared at the pages for several more moments, my friend suggested that I actually read the letter. I had to try several times before I could begin to read:*

> *Dear James,*
>
> *What is the difference between fanciful egoic identification with a character in past time and fanciful egoic identification with a character in present time? Do not resort to the mind, but to understanding. The thinking mind does not know the past, the present, or the future. Who the ego was or is or will be may become evident if the deep psyche or unthinking mind reveals it, but even that unthinking mind is only the ego, the self-contraction, and all its personas are merely the ponded images of "Narcissus".*
>
> *Therefore, do not resort to the mind or psyche, but understand the self-contraction. Transcend illusions, motives, self-imagery, and all conceits. Be energized by insight into motion, and cease to be motivated by the machine of egoic self. Thus, transcend the self-contraction and intuit the True Self-Condition, directly and intuitively.*
>
> *Love,*
> *Da*

*The Words carried a tremendous Transmission of Beloved Adi Da's Blessing and Love, and I instantly began to awaken from my dream of the psyche. Only as I began to emerge from my psychic universe did I realize how far I had actually gone. I saw that my Beloved Guru had spared me years—perhaps lifetimes!—of fascination with the deep psyche and reincarnation. I felt myself descending to the ground again—it was actually a phys ical sensation of descent. I was restored to my real practice of the Way of Adidam—which was difficult, but real.*

In His beautiful Instruction to James, Avatar Adi Da was making the point that the entire history of the deeper personality, moving from life to life, is built on self-contraction, the presumption that one is a separate individual. He was using James's fascination with Swami Vivekananda to bring him to feel how the activity of ego was governing him at every level, moving him to want to identify not only with his present apparent personality but with a past personality as well. In this manner, Avatar Adi Da used the "consideration" relative to His Vehicles of Incarnation to purify His devotees of a merely egoic interest in the matter of past lives. After this, Avatar Adi Da did not mention Swami Vivckananda until Adidama Jangama Hriddaya spoke to Him about an intense feeling of familiarity that came over her during His Yajna of 1986 in Europe.

*ADIDAMA JANGAMA HRIDDAYA: During our travels that summer, I was frequently overwhelmed by feelings of familiarity, as though I were rediscovering another aspect of my relationship to Beloved Adi Da. The feeling was most overpowering during a visit to Kew Gardens, in London. That day, I accompanied Him while He walked all through the gardens. At some point He sat on a bench in a small stone building in the park and spontaneously*

**Kew Gardens, London, 1986**

*Granted meditative Darshan. In the little pagoda, I meditated in His Company for perhaps forty-five minutes. By the time the sitting was over, I was utterly certain that I had been to that very place with Him before, had sat in meditation with Him in another form before, had traveled in Europe with Him before—all in another incarnation. When I told Beloved Adi Da my experience and the strength of my certainty, He told me to begin to investigate the travels of Swami Vivekananda and Sister Nivedita in Europe, and specifically to London and Kew Gardens.*[3]

In 1988, in the final months of the "Indoor Yajna", Avatar Adi Da began to bring up the matter of Swami Vivekananda again. One evening, Adidama Jangama Hriddaya told Avatar Adi Da and the assembled devotees about her experience on the ocean liner as a child. And Avatar Adi Da responded that Nivedita had once made a sea journey with Swami Vivekananda. It was an ocean voyage from India to England, which was, by Nivedita's own account, the most precious and intimate time that she had spent in the company of Swami Vivekananda.

Avatar Adi Da went on:

*AVATAR ADI DA SAMRAJ: It is all continuation. At certain moments, you get in touch with what was in another time and place, but it is the same time and place. The interval made by death between what was then and the next incarnation is truly nothing. It is a timeless Sublimity, with a Great Purpose making its moment. So that extraordinary matter has been exhibited to your face, in your company. Well, you have to tell the story! All of it! This portion of it and all of it. You have to bless the world with the Gift you have received. That is inspiring.* [March 12, 1988]

In 1993, Kimberly O'Nan, one of the women devotees in Avatar Adi Da's intimate Company, described to Him an experience that had taken place in Hawaii, at Da Love-Ananda Mahal.

*KIMBERLY: I had a remarkable vision in 1979. A group of us were sitting with You at Da Love-Ananda Mahal. We were talking, and You were giving us Your Instruction. I looked at Ann Rogers, who was also sitting with You that afternoon, and all of a sudden I felt transported in a vision to another time and another place. Ann and I had a vision that was simultaneous and exactly the same. The vision was so complete that I could no longer hear Your voice of Instruction.*

*It could have taken one second, but the span and detail of the entire vision is completely clear to me even today. In the vision, I walked towards a woman, who I knew to be Ann Rogers. She was sitting on a Victorian love-seat. We were dressed in Victorian clothing, our hair was up in Victorian style, and I could feel the atmosphere, the weight, of the Victorian era—draperies drawn and heavy upholstery. I was aware of horse-drawn carriages in the street, and a time-period before electricity. It was an unusual glimpse in time, with details beyond the scope of my experience in this life in the twentieth century. I could feel the room, the carpets, the darkness. Then, in the elaborate language, almost romantic, which must have been customary of that time—and which is also something I have no knowledge of in this lifetime—I spoke to Ann, this woman on the love-seat, as I moved toward her and knelt on one knee. I brought my face very close to hers, as if to whisper in her ear with all the conviction of an oath, with all the passion of my life. Tears streamed down my face, like the endless flow of a waterfall. I felt in deepest sorrow. I was mourning the greatest loss. I cried, "I will come back. I am coming back. I am coming back to be with him. I will be with him again. I love him." I spoke with absolute will, and total certainty.*

*Then the vision suddenly ended, and You dismissed us from the room. Ann and I ran out, bubbling like children, and we described the vision to each other. Our experience was the same, down to the very last detail. Our mutual conviction was that You, Beloved, had been Swami Vivekananda. I knew right then that the one I mourned for and spoke of was Swami Vivekananda.*

*My life with You—with my feelings for You and everything You have Given me—is a continuation of that love-impulse and that relationship. And there is a deeper trust in the relationship itself because, having known You in another lifetime and having been Graced to be with You again, I am certain that I will always be with You. I have a feeling that many who were associated with Swami Vivekananda have come together again in Your Company to participate in the greater Spiritual Work.*

*AVATAR ADI DA: Such a relationship is human, an "in-Love" relationship. But, fundamentally, it is about Real-God-Realization. So it was then, so it is now.* [January 16, 1993]

At that time, other devotees who have been close to Avatar Adi Da in this lifetime made confessions of similar intuitions and experiences. His response to one such confession is illuminating:

*AVATAR ADI DA SAMRAJ: Everybody has his or her story of coming into My Company. What was moving you was alive at the deeper level of the being and of Consciousness. It created all kinds of circumstances and events that were necessarily preparatory, and then that same depth may have begun to appear in some other form, like a dream or an intuition or an attraction to go someplace for who knows what reason. That is the kind of breakthrough of this subtler dimension of the being, which is really "in charge", so to speak, of the developments of your lifetime.*

*After a while, you begin to become very sensitive to this invisible depth, and you come to the point where you can affirm that it exists, that it is so. It is not merely a matter of casual conventional belief in all this. It is something that develops, that is affirmed on the basis of a long term of experience. Perhaps another individual, not having had these experiences, cannot believe it. He or she does not have the experience that corresponds to it. All you can do is tell your story. Of course, among My devotees, you find a lot of other people with stories just like yours. In fact, if you find people sympathetic to this communication, it can be said that they are themselves being moved by that invisible dimension to be responsive.*

*Those in whom this invisible motion is alive, moving them towards Me, will find themselves responding, and they will have experiences, perhaps dreams and who knows what kind of experiences, that will be part of their presumed reason for approaching Me.*

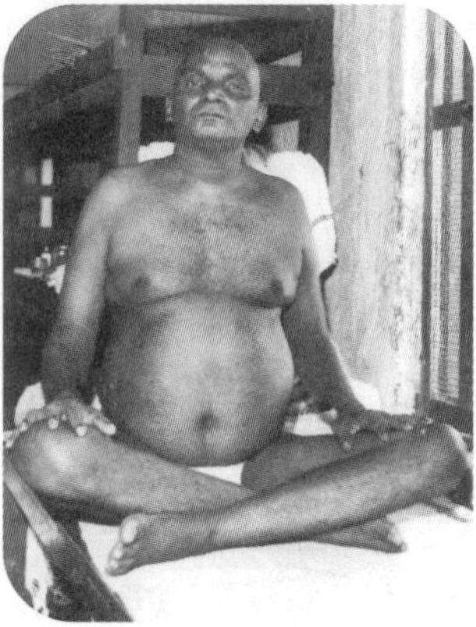

**Swami Nityananda**

**Swami Muktananda**

## The Lineage of Blessing

Apart from the lives of Ramakrishna and Swami Vivekananda, Avatar Adi Da has discussed other individuals who represent unique threads in the mysterious Divine Pattern that has culminated in His Appearance. He praises the Gurus of His own Lineage—Swami Nityananda and Swami Muktananda—as unsurpassed among Realizers in the realm of fifth stage Yoga and Yogic mysticism. And He honors Ramana Maharshi as unsurpassed among Realizers in the sixth stage domain of Transcendental Consciousness—one who had distinct premonitions of the Divinely Enlightened State of the seventh stage of life. (Ramana Maharshi's descriptions of Transcendental Self-Realization indicate that the seat of Consciousness in the human body-mind is located at a locus in the right side of the heart, an observation that coincided with Avatar Adi Da's own experience, as Avatar Adi Da describes in chapter 18 of *The Knee Of Listening*.) In other words, in the last one hundred and fifty years—the timespan covered by these four

**Ramana Maharshi**

great Realizers (Ramakrishna was born in 1838, and Swami Muktananda died in 1982)—the different types of possible Spiritual Realization were all demonstrated to an unsurpassed degree through the lives of these remarkable Adepts, and in direct association with Avatar Adi Da's Appearance.

None of these great men could have Awakened Spiritually, at the depth they did, simply on the basis of a single lifetime of Spiritual practice. Therefore, having praised the Realizers close to Him in human time, Avatar Adi Da goes on to explain that, truly, the great Spiritual Realizers of all times and places contributed to the Deeper Personality Vehicle of His Avataric Incarnation:

*By Means of Their* [Ramakrishna's and Swami Vivekananda's] *Most Great and Effective Invocation of Me (and the Likewise Most Great and Effective Invocation of Me Made by All Their In-Me-Converging Antecedents, here, and Above), I Have Avatarically Descended Into the Entire Cosmic Domain (and to here). And, by Means of the Pattern Made by Their Appearance (here, and*

*Above), and That Made by All Their In-Me-Converging Antecedents (here, and Above), I Began My Avatarically Self-Manifested Divine Work (here, and every where in the Cosmic Domain). However, since the Beginning of My by-Heart-Radiated (and, relative to the Cosmic Domain, Descending) Divine Self-"Emergence" (here, and every where in the Cosmic Domain), Only My Own (and Inherently "Bright") Divine Pattern Is Appearing with Me (here, and every where in the Cosmic Domain), and Only by Means of the Proceeding Force of My Divine Self-"Emergence" (here, and every where in the Cosmic Domain).* [The Basket Of Tolerance]

The One Divine Person was always Revealed in and through all the great Spiritual figures of history, because it was always That One, the Very Source-Condition, that human beings have been aspiring to Realize. In this sense, Avatar Adi Da is saying that it was Himself, the One Divine Person, Who "Lived" all those great Spiritual figures, in all times and places, participating in the multifarious aspects of mankind's great Spiritual search, Realizing and Transmitting the various practices, Yogas, and Samadhis. And, by means of this vast Process, the human Vehicle for His complete Incarnation as the Ruchira Avatar, Adi Da Samraj, eventually came into being.

*This Body-Mind Is My Perfect Agent. The entire Lineage of True Realizers in the Great Tradition has been the Gathering of My Instruments, but not (until now, by My Avataric Divine Incarnation) Sufficient to the point of My Crashing-Down Complete and All-Completing Avataric Self-Manifestation.*

*All of those personalities can be seen as an Ordeal in conditional time and space to prepare the Vehicle of My Avataric Self-Manifestation. But not just as individuals—it required all beings, including all of mankind, to make sufficient prayer and Conjunction for this Event of Me. And It will not be repeated, nor can It be repeated.*

*Through it all, I have finally, Fully, and Most Perfectly Revealed My Self, the One Who Is and Has Always Been, the One Who has been pursued, sought, partially Realized, and so forth, throughout all conditional time and space. And then this unique Conjunction occurred, on the part of individuals in a unique Spiritual Lineage (epitomizing all Realizers, in all of space and time), to provide a Vehicle that would Come to My Door with sufficient Reach for Me to Pass Down here.*

*But, also, This is a Conjunction with all. All had to prepare. All had to make this Event possible—uniquely represented by a cycle of apparent individuals, yes (in order to provide the most immediate Vehicle), but the "time" (the "late-time", or "dark" epoch) is the Vehicle, too. Therefore, even every one and all are in Conjunction with Me, now, and forever hereafter.*

*All and all provided the Means for this Event. Even All and all was the necessary Preparation. It is all the Surrender to Me. It is all a Sacrifice of ego-self to the Divine Reality, until that Universal Sacrifice became collectively sufficient to Draw Me Down Through the Door.*

*My Avataric Incarnation was, in some sense, simply spontaneous, and not "intentional". In some sense, it simply "happened". Yet, it was also both intentional and voluntary. It was not arbitrary, because all the Conjunctions had to occur. At last, I Passed Down into All and all. It was spontaneous, yet also Eternally Prefigured. It was Anciently Prophesied. It was somehow "caused"—and, yet, Ultimately, there is no "cause" for it whatsoever.* [The Knee Of Listening]

Padavara Loka
Adidam Samrajashram, 1993

CHAPTER 21

# Divine Completeness

By 1993, Avatar Adi Da had been living at Adidam Samrajashram for a decade, and it had become obvious that this pristine island in the southern Pacific Ocean had already become His principal Siddha-Peetha, or Seat of His Divine Spirit-Power. But Avatar Adi Da was cautious. He knew that unmistakable signs would appear when the island was truly His Hermitage, inviolable forever. On the day that He first stepped foot on the island of Naitauba (October 27, 1983), He had indicated in a playful way that His Spiritual Establishment at Adidam Samrajashram (Naitauba) would take some time.

On the day of His arrival, Avatar Adi Da was presented with three crocheted hats made by three of His women devotees, and He received these hats with great enjoyment as an acknowledgement of this great day in His Life and Work. The first hat, made by Regalia Perry, was a red hat, which He put on immediately. The second hat, made by Eileen McCarthy, had bits of wire and debris from the building of His first house at Adidam Samrajashram (which was then still in the process of being completed) sewn onto it. Avatar Adi Da was pleased and amused by this second hat and put it on also, saying that He was "almost certain" that Adidam Samrajashram was the permanent Seat of His Divine Work.

The third hat, made by Janis Ohki, was a blue and white one, with a tassle made of tiny pieces of turtle bone that Janis had collected at Nukubati, before coming to Naitauba. This hat He did not put on. Rather, Avatar Adi Da placed it to one side, saying that He would only wear this hat when He was absolutely certain that Adidam Samrajashram had been fully secured as the place where He could do His Spiritual Work forever.

**Padavara Loka, Naitauba, Fiji**

## Spiritual Establishment in Fiji

Ten years later, in 1993, signs began to appear that this was so. And the first of these indications was Avatar Adi Da's spontaneous decision to climb, for the first time, to the highest point on the island—a massive rock jutting 600 feet into the air. The visual impact of this vast prominence was ecstatically described by Avatar Adi Da in 1983 after He circumnavigated the island for the first time.

*AVATAR ADI DA SAMRAJ: As we went around the island today, the birds collected above us, four or five at a time, and followed our boat. They kept up with us, staying right overhead. And then there was that moment—everybody began to shout—the moment when we saw that rock at the head of this island. It is a vision, a sublime vision. It is just huge. You cannot comprehend it. Like the first time you saw Me—the mind stops, and you become silent or shout. You have received the vision, the sign of the island.* [October 28, 1983]

Although Avatar Adi Da did not climb the rock at that time, He named it "Padavara Loka", meaning the "Place of the First Footstep", acknowledging that this was the first point on the island that He had contacted Spiritually. And He indicated that He would plant His physical "Footstep" on the pinnacle "when the time was right".

Adidama Sukha Dham describes that auspicious moment, which occurred unexpectedly on August 14, 1993.

*ADIDAMA SUKHA DHAM: The event itself occurred quite spontaneously one day when Beloved Adi Da, Adidama Jangama Hriddaya, Trivedi Naamleela, and I were walking on one of the trails at Adidam Samrajashram. Beloved Adi Da had previously said that a holy site should be created at the top of Padavara Loka, and, in preparation for that, the path to Padavara Loka was being cleared. Before we went out on the bike that morning, I had asked Beloved Adi Da if He might be moved to make the climb—or whether He would prefer to wait until everything was ready for a formal Empowerment ceremony. Beloved Adi Da had replied that we should definitely prepare the site before He would go there, and He had given me detailed instructions about what that would involve, including making a place for impressions of His Feet to be Installed. All this specific instruction made what occurred even more of a surprise.*

*As it turned out, a path had been cleared only part of the way to Padavara Loka, and we walked that path until it ended near a very large and beautiful banyan tree. We all marvelled at this tree until Beloved Adi Da, Who was Seated on a bench by the tree, asked "What is that fence doing across the path?" Several pieces of wood formed a barrier to any further progress along the path, because it had only been cleared that far. Jeffrey Hughes, who was accompanying us, explained this to Adidama Jangama Hriddaya, who explained it to Beloved Adi Da. "The path," responded our Beloved Guru, "is where I want to go. Have them take those sticks away!" And so we began the ascent to Padavara Loka.*

*We all followed Jeffrey until we came to the face of a cliff where a sturdy metal ladder went up through a hole in the overhanging rock. Once the entire party had climbed the ladder, we found ourselves at a kind of plateau, where Jeffrey had to cut back the bushes with his machete to make room for us all to stand. We thought that we would just look around and go back down. But Beloved Adi Da asked, "Where is the highest point?" Jeffrey pointed beyond a high precipice with no hand rails. It looked like a dangerous climb to all of us, but Beloved Adi Da was completely undaunted. Saying "We can always turn back," He led us toward the highest point.*

*We climbed the almost vertical face of the rock, stepped over deep ravines, and hugged the walls of narrow, treacherous paths. It had begun to rain, and the ground was dangerously slippery. But we all felt that we were surrounded by a "bubble" of our Beloved Guru's Protection. At last, with torn and muddy clothing, we reached what was almost the very highest point. Moments later, Avatar Adi Da Samraj Stepped onto the highest point.*

*The area where we stood now was barely wide enough for the five of us. We could see the entire Island. From far away, a devotee near the beach who had observed Beloved Adi Da's final ascent let out a loud and ecstatic cry.*

*Now Beloved Adi Da pressed His Staff into the mid-point of three rocks that had been placed here according to His Instruction in 1986. This marked the place where the shrine would be built to hold our Beloved Guru's Foot-prints, a Lingam,*[1] *and a fire site. As He did this, His steady Gaze met the distant horizon.*

*I felt certain that this apparently simple event marked a significant change and set in motion a new moment in Beloved Adi Da's Incarnation in this world and in His Presence and Work at Adidam Samrajashram.*

Unbeknownst to Avatar Adi Da and His devotees at Adidam Samrajashram, on the same day as this remark-able climb, a very significant event was occurring syn-chronously in Suva, the capital of Fiji. It became clear on this day that those on the immigration review board were prepared to accept Avatar Adi Da's application to become a Fijian citizen. The ramifications of this decision were profound. As a Fijian citizen, Avatar Adi Da would be assured that He could legally remain in Fiji for life, and this would be a sign to Him that His Spiritual Seat at Adidam Samrajashram <u>was</u> secured forever.

J-M Moyer, the Fiji legal adviser and representative to the Fijian government, did not immediately disclose this news to Avatar Adi Da, as there were many more details to handle before the passports would actually be issued. All the necessary steps were taken during the fol-lowing weeks, and, in late October 1993, almost exactly ten years after Avatar Adi Da's arrival on Adidam Samrajashram (Naitauba), J-M made a special trip to the Island.

Without announcing his purpose to anyone, J-M advised the Adidamas that he had important news and asked to see Avatar Adi Da. This unusual personal audience

**Adi Da Samraj receives His Fijian passport, October 23, 1993**

was quickly arranged to occur on the morning of October 23, and he was brought into Avatar Adi Da's house at the Matrix together with the Adidamas.

J-M approached Avatar Adi Da in a crouched posture, the traditional Fijian manner of approaching a person of great rank, and in the attitude of humility, honor, and respect. He then presented Him with a cloth-covered tray. Avatar Adi Da removed the cloth and beheld the long-awaited Fijian passports—for Himself and the Adidamas. As He beamed in delight, J-M placed a salu-salu (a traditional Fijian flower garland) around Avatar Adi Da's neck and presented Him with a tabua, the whale's tooth offering traditionally made in Fiji on occasions of great importance.

That night, when Avatar Adi Da entered the village gathering hall, Hymns To Me, for a celebratory occasion with all devotees on the island, the room erupted. The joy bursting from everyone's hearts could not be contained. Devotees chanted and yelled their praise and

**Devotees celebrate as Adi Da Samraj puts on the "third hat"**

devotion to Him at the top of their lungs—on and on and on. Avatar Adi Da sat in His Chair smiling broadly and receiving it all. Rounds of toasts followed, and then the most magical of moments—Avatar Adi Da called for the third hat! This was the time. Amid the cacophony of cheers and exclamations, Avatar Adi Da took the third hat and put it on.

Later, Avatar Adi Da said, "I am solidly Established on this massive rock in the middle of the world." He was speaking literally. Naitauba, in the Northern Lau group of the Fijian islands, lies on the international dateline. Thus, it is situated, even geographically, "in the middle of the world", or exactly between East and West. For Avatar Adi Da to become thus established, beyond identification with either the West or the East, represented a great leap in His Work. For Him, the granting of His Fijian citizenship was a sign that His specific Work with the West was now complete, and He was free to devote Himself entirely to His Work of world-Blessing.

*AVATAR ADI DA SAMRAJ: The mark of My becoming a Fijian citizen is the last stroke of My Work to acquire Adidam Samrajashram (Naitauba) Spiritually. The "Karmas" which I embraced by being born into the West and which required My Submission in the West—those are over. I no longer must make that Submission. Something in the magic of the moment when I was granted citizenship has purified much.*

*I did My Work not by merely getting on a plane and flying to the United States. I got born there and did a great submissive Work.*

*But the time came when I had to step out of there and come here to this place—in the middle of the world, neither East nor West, on the meridian. It became absolutely necessary for Me to make this resort. And the granting of Fijian citizenship to Me was a very important moment in that Work, in the midst of the Submission I have made.*

*Now I cannot be identified as a Westerner any more. I am not here representing the West, or, in any conventional terms, the East. I Am just Who I Am, on this meridian here, between East and West. And now, more than ever, I can speak freely about the foolishness of mankind, West and East. And I am not identified with any of them. I can point to what is right anywhere, and I can criticize what is wrong anywhere. I am not beholden to any tradition.* [November 11 and 24, 1993]

No sooner had Avatar Adi Da received the news of His Fijian citizenship than He began to move with tremendous intention to Empower the island further. Four days later, on October 27, 1993, the tenth anniversary of His arrival at Adidam Samrajashram, Avatar Adi Da climbed Padavara Loka again—this time with full ceremony. At the exact time of His arrival ten years earlier, 1:32 P.M., He stood in the gold-leafed impressions of His Feet that had been placed there, falling into a Swoon of

Blessing—and at that very moment, a dense mist suddenly coalesced, surrounding Padavara Loka. The new Fijian passports had been brought along (carefully sealed in a clear plastic container) and were placed at His feet during the ceremony. For a long time, He stood motionless, flanked by the two Adidamas—His eyes rolling up, His right index finger pointing straight up to the sky and His left index finger pointing straight down to the earth, as a light rain fell.

That evening, Avatar Adi Da gathered with devotees to celebrate the event of the Empowerment. In conversation with them, Avatar Adi Da Revealed another secret about His Establishment at Padavara Loka:

*J-M MOYER: Beloved, once I came to the Island in a boat that had a depth sounder. As we approached, I could see the Island as a tiny bit on top, but underneath the ocean the Island is colossal! It is vast. It goes into a cone into the Earth. That is what I could feel today, Beloved. Your Power went through Your staff and Your Feet into the Earth.*

*AVATAR ADI DA SAMRAJ: From the air, looking down at Naitauba, it looks like an island, a separate place surrounded by water. Yet, deep below the surface of the ocean, Naitauba is connected to every place on Earth. This is the secret of going deep.* [October 27, 1993]

Once Padavara Loka was fully Empowered, round-the-clock work began to create a new and most sacred Temple in a different part of Adidam Samrajashram: Avatar Adi Da's Mahasamadhi[2] Site, the place where His Body will rest at the end of His physical lifetime.

The tomb, or mahasamadhi shrine, of a Realizer is traditionally understood to be the principal place for contacting the Spiritual Power of that individual after his or her death. For example, Avatar Adi Da's contact with Swami Nityananda during His "Sadhana Years" occurred at Swami Nityananda's burial shrine at Ganeshpuri. Because of the importance of rightly preserving their burial sites as places of power, Realizers often indicate well before the moment of death exactly where and how they should be buried. Now that Adidam Samrajashram was guaranteed as His principal Spiritual Seat, Avatar Adi Da began to do the same. He had chosen the site in 1991—a beautiful meadow on a high plateau, looking across to Padavara Loka, and beyond that, on a clear day, to Vanuabalavu, the nearest large island in the Lau group.

Avatar Adi Da named His Mahasamadhi Site "the 'Brightness'". The night before He Empowered the "Brightness", Adidama Jangama Hriddaya had a premonitory vision of the event that was to occur the next day.

**The "Brightness"**

*ADIDAMA JANGAMA HRIDDAYA: As I was sitting in meditation, I had a vision that I was standing at the "Brightness" site with Beloved Adi Da, and it was absolutely Luminous. The Light that was pouring from this place was a much greater Light than you see with your eyes. It was* <u>*extreme*</u> *"Brightness". It was so intense that heat was coming off my body, and it felt as though my skin was cracking painfully from the intensity. I felt Beloved Adi Da's "Brightness" Crashing Down into the conditional realm, breaking through the obstructions of this world, and the obstructions and resistance in our body-minds, Planting Himself here. The formal Empowerment Puja the next day—November 19, 1993—had just this quality.*

*At the beginning of the Empowerment, Beloved Adi Da entered the inner temple and stood next to the open underground vault that will eventually house His Body. He placed His staff at such an angle that it would support Him. I could tell He was going to relinquish all awareness of the body. As He did so, the Force of His Spiritual Descent became so strong that His Body quivered and tears streamed from His Eyes. I felt Him literally Install Himself Spiritually in the burial vault. I asked Him later if my experience was true and He confirmed that it was.*

The day after the Empowerment of the "Brightness", Avatar Adi Da spoke further:

*AVATAR ADI DA SAMRAJ: This Temple is a Portent of Blessing for all people, all beings—all included, no one rejected. But it requires something great of you—it requires you to respond to Me, to respond to the Divine.*

*My Blessing Work is Magnified there during My physical Lifetime and after—for all time. It is an Intention that I Demonstrate and Speak about during My physical Lifetime, but it is an Eternal Intention, a Work to go on forever.*

*This Temple is the Holiest Place in all of this Communion. If you entered that central room with real sensitivity, it would drive you into unconsciousness—it is so Profound, so Strong. I have Established a Place of My Radiation. It is the Place where this Body in Its end time will be fitted.* [November 20, 1993]

## The Life of Ruchira Avatara Bhakti Yoga

The day of the news of Avatar Adi Da's Fijian citizenship marked the beginning of a series of over 130 gatherings, lasting through the end of 1993 and well into 1994. During these gatherings, Avatar Adi Da clarified the details of Ruchira Avatara Bhakti Yoga, explaining that this practice is not about struggling with the content of experience in the body-mind. Rather, He said, Ruchira Avatar Bhakti Yoga is to turn to Him, surrendering the faculties, or principal functions, of one's being—the mind (or attention), emotion (or feeling), the breath, and the total body. In active terms, this means to invoke Him, to feel Him, to breathe Him, and to serve Him moment to moment, regardless of what may arise in body or mind. In this way, over time, heart-Communion with Him becomes perpetual.

*AVATAR ADI DA SAMRAJ: If some content arises in the mind, then, instead of trying to think your way through it, and struggle with it, and get emotional about it, and concentrate your entire life in it, you should direct the function of mind to Me. Do not try to release the content of the mind in order to get to Me. Surrender the mind-function itself to Me.*

*The root of mind is attention—not the stuff that is arising in the mind, but attention. The epitome of the mind, the root of mind, the core of mind, the central function of mind, is attention. Therefore, when things arise in mind—instead of struggling with them, trying to get rid of them, trying to surrender them, trying to "beef" your way through them—you simply give Me your attention, or the core of your mind. . . .*

*When something arises emotionally (a reactive emotion of one kind or another, emotional concern, emotion in relation to anything conditional), instead of trying to open and relax and release the reactive emotion to get to Me (or struggling with yourself for whatever reason), you direct the function of emotion to Me. The core of the function of emotion is simply feeling. You feel to Me. You give Me your feeling-attention, then. You direct attention (or the root of mind) and feeling (or the root of emotion) to Me.*

*Likewise, you conform the body to Me in the midst of whatever is arising physically. You direct yourself bodily to Me. Whatever functions you are performing in any moment of functional activity, you give Me your feeling-attention and you direct the body to serving Me, you direct it to be the servant instead of the object of your concern.*

*No matter what is arising in the moment, instead of struggling with any of the contents of the body-mind, you direct its functions—not its contents, but its functions—to Me, thereby collecting the whole body-mind as feeling-attention to Me.*

*This is the Yoga of Ruchira Avatara Bhakti (or the moment to moment practice of the only-by-Me Revealed and Given Way of Adidam)—and there are technical requirements for it. Ruchira Avatara Bhakti Yoga is not the yielding of the functions of the body-mind to the idea that I am your Divine Heart-Master. There is nothing vague about this practice. You direct your feeling-attention to Me, to this bodily (human) Divine Form.* [What, Where, When, How, Why, and Who To Remember To Be Happy]

And, relative to the devotional Yoga of the breath:

*AVATAR ADI DA SAMRAJ: My Admonition that you Commune with Me with every breath, or Remember Me with every breath, or Invoke Me with every breath, does not mean that you technically engage every inhalation and exhalation. It is an Admonition you must fulfill artfully, in such a way that even though you are not engaging every breath as a technical practice, nevertheless every breath effectively is Communion with Me. The practice is done artfully, and, therefore, rather randomly.*

*The general practice I have Given you is not about observing breaths, counting breaths, noticing breaths in any technical fashion. It is about entering into relationship with Me via the breath, Communing with Me via the breath. The breath is not the subject of your practice. I Am! All the faculties of the body-mind must be devoted to Me, and, since breath is a primary faculty, you must exercise yourself in relation to Me via the breath. The practice is not to get very curious about the breaths themselves, or finicky about breathing. It is to devote yourself to Me completely and to use the leading faculties of the body-mind as a principal mechanism for it. It is a devotional practice, then, not merely a functional one.* [February 4, 1994]

Many devotees, as they began to do this practice according to Avatar Adi Da's exact Instructions, felt they were getting the secret of the Way of Adidam at a much deeper level. This was the key to how to live the devotional relationship to Him at all times.

There was, however, a potential error—the attempt to surrender attention, feeling, breath, and body deliberately, effortfully, as a strategy, thereby making the practice into a self-based method, or technique. Any such effort, Avatar Adi Da had to point out, was not the true Yoga of Ruchira Avatara Bhakti. Ruchira Avatara Bhakti Yoga is a love-response—and you do not try to practice a technique when you see or feel the one you love! You spontaneously respond with your entire being. Ruchira Avatara Bhakti Yoga is a single gesture of the being that arises when the heart beholds and feels Avatar Adi Da, and in that instant recognizes Him as the Incarnation of Real God.

Several years later, Avatar Adi Da wrote:

*If you heart-recognize Me, then the four principal faculties (of attention, feeling, body, and breath) follow, in heart-response to Me—not because you move those faculties, but because you are those faculties.*

*In Truth, you cannot surrender the faculties to Me (as if the faculties were separate from you, or objective to you)—because you are the faculties.*

*Therefore, the faculties are truly responsively surrendered to Me only if you heart-recognize Me.*

*It is only in that case that you are surrendered to Me—because you are the faculties.*

*Ruchira Avatara Bhakti Yoga (or Me-recognizing and to-Me-responding devotional surrender of all four principal faculties of the body-mind) is whole bodily prayer.*

*Ruchira Avatara Bhakti Yoga is not merely prayer engaged via attention, or via feeling, or via the body, or via the breath.*

*Ruchira Avatara Bhakti Yoga is not merely prayer engaged via any single faculty.*

*Ruchira Avatara Bhakti Yoga is prayer engaged via all of the four principal faculties—simultaneously, and in a comprehensive, or inclusive and total, psycho-physical recognition-response to Me.*

*And, because all the principal faculties of the body-mind are, thus, made into the total event of Yogic prayer, Ruchira Avatara Bhakti Yoga is not merely the prayer of requests—uttered by the mind, and to the presumed Divine "Other", and for the sake of the egoic body-mind (or the separated, and compartmented, ego-"I").*

*Ruchira Avatara Bhakti Yoga is total prayer.*

*Ruchira Avatara Bhakti Yoga is the ego-transcending devotional prayer of Divine Communion.*

*Ruchira Avatara Bhakti Yoga is the Yogic process of Divine Samadhi—the prayerful devotional process of directly ego-transcending, and, always, mind-transcending, and, always, total-body-mind-surrendering Yogic Communion with Me.*

*Therefore, Ruchira Avatara Bhakti Yoga, or whole bodily prayer, or heart-responsive heart-recognition of Me, is not, itself, an exercise of the verbal, or conceptual, mind.*

*Rather, the total psycho-physical exercise of Ruchira Avatara Bhakti Yoga always requires an exercise of attention—which is the root and epitome of the thinking-faculty of conceptual mind.*

*And, by always exercising attention, itself—in total psycho-physical recognition-response to Me—the activity, and the, always, body-mind-contracting contents, of the verbal, or conceptual, or thinking mind are constantly, and directly, transcended.*

*Thus, Ruchira Avatara Bhakti Yoga, or the total psycho-physical Yogic process of heart-responsive heart-recognition of Me—which is the whole bodily prayer of Divine Communion—is heart-Communion with Me without any associated concept, or play of mind.* [Hridaya Rosary]

The "total prayer" of Ruchira Avatara Bhakti Yoga that Avatar Adi Da is describing here is not any kind of effort to unite with Him, through merely verbal prayer—or to surrender the faculties to Him, as though He were somewhere else, a God apart. Rather, the Revelation that Avatar Adi Da is making is that, in the instant of heart-recognition of Him, all seeking for the Divine is wiped away, because the heart is already satisfied by His Living Presence. Then the Yoga of Ruchira Avatara Bhakti is revealed as simply the ecstatic prayer of surrender in Him, and the enjoyment of that Communion, or effortless Samadhi.

Nevertheless, as Avatar Adi Da was always emphasizing in the gatherings of 1993-1994 (and ever since), you cannot merely wait for pleasurable Communion with Him to happen to you. Attention must be given to Him, the heart must be exercised, the body must be activated in response to Him. Ruchira Avatara Bhakti Yoga is not effortful, but it does require intention:

*AVATAR ADI DA SAMRAJ: The Divine Process is not magic. You must respond. Beings must respond. You must do the work. Otherwise, you are controlled by the structures of your own adaptation, and no great thing occurs. The Cosmic domain cannot be merely glanced at, as if it were an object, and magically Outshined. You must cooperate with My Divine Grace. Beings must respond. I Bring you the Gifts, the Revelation, My Teaching Word—everything but you must respond. You must integrate with Me through the practice of Ruchira Avatara Bhakti Yoga that I have Given you.* [March 23, 1994]

# Turaga Hridayam

At the Celebration of Ruchira Avatara Purnima (the annual Feast honoring Avatar Adi Da as Divine Guru) in July 1994, Avatar Adi Da Samraj Granted Darshan in a beautiful new Darshan Hall, built in the Fijian style, close to His Residence at the Matrix. He named it "Turaga Hridayam", meaning "Lord of the Heart" (combining a Fijian and a Sanskrit word). It was a large bure with a steeply pitched roof supported by long beams made of whole logs—by far the most impressive Fijian-style building on the island. A Fijian tapa-cloth backdrop was hung behind Avatar Adi Da's chair, and some traditional Indian art pieces were placed at various places in the building. The resulting combination of Fijian and Indian qualities created a unique aesthetic integrity about the space which made it a fitting place for Avatar Adi Da to sit in Darshan.

Within a few days after the celebration, however, Avatar Adi Da learned that there had been mismanagement in connection with the construction of Turaga Hridayam. On the heels of this disclosure came another. Planning to carry out some repairs, devotees responsible for the holy sites at Adidam Samrajashram had removed the thatched roof of one of the most important temples—thereby essentially dismantling the temple temporarily—without asking Avatar Adi Da's Permission. Both incidents were gross infringements of the sacred and a breach in one of the Spiritual laws of a Hermitage: Devotees do not act casually, unconsciously, or intrusively in the Spiritual Master's sacred domain.

In order to make a lesson of this, and to serve devotees' growth and understanding about right relationship to Him and right orientation to the sacred, Avatar Adi Da decided to leave Adidam Samrajashram. Within a matter of hours, He was on a boat, with only the Adidamas,

Darshan in Turaga Hridayam,
Celebration of Ruchira Avatara Purnima, July 1994

Trivedi Naamleela, and a few other devotees in attendance. Avatar Adi Da's leaving of Adidam Samrajashram was a painful moment for all His devotees. No one could escape the reality He was reflecting to them by leaving His principal Residence.

So, beginning August 5, 1994, Avatar Adi Da undertook a Yajna in Fiji. But this period of Avatar Adi Da's "wandering" in Fiji was not merely a criticism of the circumstance at Adidam Samrajashram—it was also a time of His Embrace of Fiji.

*ADIDAMA JANGAMA HRIDDAYA: I have always noticed that in each and all of Beloved Adi Da's Acts, even when they appear, as in this case, to be a form of Criticism, He is always only Giving His extraordinary Blessing. This fact was completely obvious during this Yajna. The trip was His constant, Divine Play. There were only two things going on: On the one hand, there was His daily, Fierce Calling, to His devotees everywhere, to resort to Him absolutely, rather than resorting to ourselves and to our ordinary searches and distractions. On the other hand, there were continual forays into the land and culture of Fiji, through visits to parks, gardens, and other scenic places, and countless small shops full of native Fijian handicrafts and Indian religious images and traditional Indian clothing. On these trips, Beloved Adi Da constantly Graced Fijian and Indian culture with His Blessing Regard.*

*In the midst of all of this, Beloved Adi Da was doing intensive Work on the manuscripts of many of His "Source-Texts". It was this Work that provided the first signs of the transformation that this time would bring. He Worked on His Manuscripts daily and for many hours at a time.*

*Beloved Adi Da also once again adopted the traditional sannyasin color of orange, as He had in 1986. The first day He went dressed in orange on a trip into the public, it was to Nadi, one of Fiji's principal cities. There, Beloved Adi Da moved gracefully into the heart of Indian culture in Fiji, visiting one tiny Indian shop after another.*

*It was astonishing to me to walk with Beloved Adi Da, clad in sannyasin orange, in the streets and shops of Nadi. I had travelled with Him in the United States and Europe during the 1986 Yajna, where there had been no understanding of His renunciate Sign—and even a biased reaction to this sign of renunciation. In Nadi and in Suva, by contrast, the Hindus especially understood His Sign. When we entered a shop, everyone would quietly and respectfully gaze at Beloved Adi Da and He would just stand or sit there and Grant His Blessing Darshan to everyone who gave Him their attention.*

*In addition, He looked at all the images in these shops associated with Indian Spirituality—even all the popular street images of the various Hindu deities were inspected carefully by Him. I felt Avatar Adi Da Granting His Blessing to the entire tradition of Indian Spirituality by this means. He likewise inspected all the merchandise in the Fijian shops, Granting His Blessing to the traditional Fijian culture by so doing.*

## September 7, 1994

On September 7, 1994, at His temporary residence in Pacific Harbour, on the island of Viti Levu, Avatar Adi Da Samraj stayed secluded in His room, where He had recently spent many hours writing. Adidama Jangama Hriddaya was attending Him:

*ADIDAMA JANGAMA HRIDDAYA: The house was totally still. At one point, Beloved Adi Da called me into the room. The curtains were drawn, and the room was dim and unlit. He was not doing any of the Work on His Manuscripts that I had become accustomed to His doing each day in recent weeks. He was simply sitting in the large upholstered chair we had placed in the room for His use. Beloved Adi Da's Force was so focused and concentrated in the room that the room itself felt almost unapproachable to me. I felt as though I were being pushed out, as when the heat from a fire blasts you backwards out of a blazing space. I served Him simply and left the room.*

When Adidama Jangama Hriddaya entered again in the evening, answering His call, the same overwhelming Transmission-Force was Radiating from Him. Avatar Adi Da was seated at His desk with the lights turned on. She sat at His Feet. He did not look at her at first. But then, after a few moments, He slowly turned His head.

*ADIDAMA JANGAMA HRIDDAYA: The face of my Beloved Guru was so full of Passion and the Sign of Perfect Love for all beings that I was overwhelmed by the vision of His Sacrificial Ordeal in His Work with His devotees. I was reminded of that same heartbreaking Love for the billions of humanity that had overwhelmed Beloved Adi Da more than eight years before, when His Divine "Emergence" was Initiated on January 11, 1986. I felt intuitively certain that some extraordinary Process was taking place in Him.*

Avatar Adi Da later confirmed that this was true. A great turning point in His Work had occurred on that day:

*On September 7, 1994 . . . I Knew I had forever Said and Done Enough (Such that there was not even <u>any</u> Motion in Me to Say or Do <u>any</u> More). My Avatarically Self-Manifested Divine Revelation-Work had Suddenly become Complete, for all time—and I (Spontaneously, and Finally) Came to Rest in My Eternal Hermitage of*

*Heart-Seclusion (only—from then, and forever—to Awaken all beings by My Mere and Constant Blessing, "Bright").*

*Therefore, now that I have Done (or Suffered) all that was necessary for Me to Do (or Suffer) as Avataric Divine Teacher and Avataric Divine Revealer in a Struggle with would-be devotees and the world, I will not hereafter Associate with that Struggle—but I have Retired from that Struggle, Satisfied that all My Avatarically Self-Manifested Divine Teaching-Work, and even all My Avatarically Self-Manifested Divine Revelation-Work, Is Full and Complete (and that, by Fullest Divine Self-Submission, I have, Most Fully and Most Finally, Said and Done and Firmly Established all that I could possibly have Said and Done and Firmly Established, and all that was necessary for Me to Say and Do and Firmly Establish, in order, now, and for all time to come, to Most Fully and Most Finally, and Firmly, Introduce the Great Divine Opportunity to the total human world, in all the stages of life, and in order, now, and for all time to come, to Most Fully and Most Finally, and Firmly, Provide the True, and Most Perfect, and Utterly Complete Divine Way of Realizing Me—the Avataric Self-Revelation of Real God, and Truth, and Reality—to the total human world, in all the stages of life, and in order, now, and for all time to come, to Most Fully and Most Finally, and Firmly, Establish the True, and Most Perfect, and Utterly Complete Divine Way of Realizing Me—the Avataric Self-Revelation of Real God, and Truth, and Reality—for the Liberating Sake of the total human world, in all the stages of life).* [The Method Of The Ruchira Avatar]

September 12, 1994

# The Divine Names of Adi Da Samraj

On September 12, Avatar Adi Da Samraj returned to His Hermitage as swiftly as He had left it. As a sign of the great change that had occurred in His Work altogether, Avatar Adi Da assumed "Santosha" as one of His Names. During His visits to the Indian shops in the preceding weeks, Avatar Adi Da had noticed a form of the Divine Shakti He had not seen before—a form known as "Santoshi Ma". Santoshi Ma is typically portrayed as seated in the lotus posture, with four arms—the upper two hands bearing a sword and a trident, the third hand carrying a bowl of sweets, and the fourth hand assuming a gesture of blessing. Because of Avatar Adi Da's interest in this form of the Shakti, His devotees purchased an image of Santoshi Ma for Him, which He placed in the room where He was sitting on September 7. In the ensuing days and weeks, Avatar Adi Da began to ask for more information about this representation of the Shakti.

It was discovered that Santoshi Ma has risen to prominence as an object of worship only during the last twenty years, but has already attracted vast numbers of devotees. Avatar Adi Da began to Reveal the association between this form of the Goddess and the Completion of His Avataric Revelation.

"Santoshi" is the feminine form of "Santosha"—literally meaning "satisfaction" or "contentment", qualities associated with a sense of completion. And, as Avatar Adi Da pointed out, these qualities are equivalent to no-seeking, which is the fundamental principle of His Wisdom-Teaching and His entire Revelation of Truth. Avatar Adi Da also observed that the Yogic force and equanimity of the posture of Santoshi Ma—seated firmly, in balance, bearing simultaneously the powerful signs of sword and trident (representing the destruction of the ego) and the gentle signs of the bowl of sweets and the Blessing mudra of the hand (representing the Free Gift of Divine Grace)—pointed to His Completeness.

Avatar Adi Da acknowledged that the spontaneous "appearance" of Santoshi Ma in His Sphere at this particular time was a sign of His own "Santosha"—His Completeness and Satisfaction, His utter Demonstration of No-Seeking. Therefore, He Revealed that "Santosha" should be one of His secondary Names. He is Santosha Da, the Divine Giver Who Is "The 'Bright' and Eternal and Always Already Non-Separate Person Of Divine and Inherent Completeness, Divine Self-Satisfaction, Divine Self-Contentedness, or Perfect Searchlessness".

The series of Divine Names of Adi Da Samraj that have been Revealed since His Divine "Emergence"—Da Love-Ananda, Da Avabhasa, Da Santosha, and Dau Loloma Vunirarama—do not replace each other. Rather, they represent a cumulative Revelation, or Description, of His Qualities as the Incarnate Divine Person.[3]

One month after the event of September 7, the Ruchira Avatar began to have psychic intimations of the further Name that belongs to His Completeness. He began to hear and see the Name "Adi Da", recognizing it to be a Reference to Himself. "Adi" in Sanskrit is "first", "primordial", the "source". Thus, on October 11, 1994, He indicated that He would henceforth be known principally as "Adi Da"—the "First Giver", the "Giving Source".

The letters of the Name "Adi Da" read the same in both directions, from left to right and from right to left. In addition, "I" stands at the center of the Name, and on either side of "I" is the syllable "Da", first backwards, then forwards. Thus, the Name "Adi Da" reads "I-Da", signifying "I Am Da", in both directions from the center. The spontaneous appearing of the Name "Adi Da", therefore, is the bringing to completion of the great

Revelation of 1979, when Avatar Adi Da Samraj first made His Divine Confession, "I Am Da". Through the symmetry of the letters of His principal Name, "Adi Da", the Ruchira Avatar makes the Great Statement that He is the First and the Last, the Complete Manifestation of Real God, or Truth, or Reality in the conditional realms.

To devotionally recognize Avatar Adi Da as the Divine Source-Person is also to feel and acknowledge His Inherent "Kingship" in one's life. And so, in April 1996, several devotees proposed to Avatar Adi Da that His Name be completed with the title "Samraj", an ancient word meaning "Universal Ruler"—not as any kind of political reference, but as a reference to His Divine Nature and His rulership in the hearts of His devotees. The full Spiritual meaning of "Samraj", in reference to Avatar Adi Da Samraj, is: "The Divine Heart-Master, or The Spiritual, Transcendental, and Divine Lord, or Master-King, or Master-Ruler and Divine Liberator, Of The Heart, and Of every one, and Of everyone, and Of all, and Of All".

Adidam Samrajashram, 1995

CHAPTER 22

# "Plain Old Organism People"

After the Great Event of September 7, Adi Da Samraj lived quietly at Adidam Samrajashram for several months. Then, suddenly, at the beginning of December 1994, He surprised the residents of Adidam Samrajashram by calling a gathering in Hymns To Me, a large screened-in hall in the Ashram village. It was the first gathering of a cycle that continued for nine months, now with small groups, now with all the residents of the Ashram, sometimes at the Matrix, sometimes in a tent at Lion's Lap (a campsite that devotees had prepared for Him), sometimes in Hymns To Me. The gathering described in this chapter took place in yet another, and more unusual, location.

## The Great Debate

JONATHAN CONDIT: It was April 15, 1995. The tables had been turned. We were matched in a debate against our Beloved Guru. It was up to us to "prove" to Beloved Adi Da that we were more than fleshy bodies and material stuff, that we were, at root, Consciousness Itself. Beloved Adi Da, much to our amazement, was staunchly maintaining that we were nothing but organisms—that's all we were, that the greater dimension of existence, Consciousness Itself, was not possible for us to Realize. And we were failing miserably to prove Him wrong!

**Jonathan Condit and Avatar Adi Da Samraj**

What had we done to find ourselves in this predicament? How had it happened that, after hearing so many hundreds of hours of Beloved Adi Da's Discourse on the Reality of Consciousness and the limitations of materialism as a philosophy, we were unable to speak convincingly for the "Consciousness" side, while our Divine Heart-Master seemed utterly invincible in His arguing that we belonged strictly to the "matter" side?

It had all started four days before, on April 11, when Beloved Adi Da had surprised and delighted a group of about twenty-five of us by calling for a gathering to occur on the deck of the then newly acquired boat—the Turaga Dau Loloma (meaning "Lord Dau Loloma", after Avatar Adi Da's Fijian Name)—which was moored in the idyllic lagoon near the devotees' village on Naitauba.

Adi Da Samraj had already been gathering with devotees for a period of some months. Almost every afternoon or evening there would be a phone call in which we would be asked if we had any "questions, 'considerations', or causes" for gathering—any possible topic that we wanted to discuss with Him or any event that we wanted to create. If we presented enough "raw material" to justify having a gathering, then Avatar Adi Da would call for a gathering to begin—usually immediately, with only minutes to change clothes and make other necessary preparations—and He would say where the gathering was to occur. We knew from experience that when Beloved Adi Da changed the venue of the gatherings, that generally meant that the topic of "consideration" was going to shift, often quite dramatically. The gatherings had most recently been in Hymns To Me, the large gathering hall in the village. So, when we were invited to a boat gathering, we sensed that our Guru had something up His sleeve, but we really did not know what.

On the evening of April 11, we were bubbling with excitement as we drove in jeeps down to the beach, where a small punt ferried us in groups across the glassy turquoise water of the lagoon out to the Turaga Dau Loloma. We seated ourselves on the open expanse of wooden deck, facing Beloved Adi Da as He sat in a simple white deck chair, silently Regarding people as they arrived. The evening air was still and fresh, and the boat swayed gently back and forth with the movement of the lagoon waters. The preceding two months of gathering had been strongly focused on understanding the emotional-sexual dimension of our lives and practice, but that night, as we were soon to find out, was to be different.

When everyone was seated and ready, we expected Beloved Adi Da to begin in His characteristic manner by having us summarize what we were prepared to discuss or ask questions about. But no—that night He abruptly began the gathering with a question to us. With a slightly quizzical look on His Face, He asked, in an amused but arresting tone:

"Do you all have the feeling that Consciousness Itself has nothing whatsoever to do with the body-mind, that it's totally independent of the body-mind . . ." He paused slightly for dramatic effect, and then completed His sentence: ". . . and that's what you don't like about It?"

After a moment of stunned silence, during which He allowed us to register how thoroughly our minds were blown by His punchline, Beloved Adi Da erupted in peals and peals of uproarious laughter, as we joined in laughing with Him—still not altogether sure what we were laughing about.

Then He continued, pressing the point further home:

"That is what you all don't like about Consciousness Itself. It's not that you are un-Enlightened. You refuse Enlightenment."

Again, He broke into hilarious laughter.

Thus began the series of five boat gatherings, on consecutive nights from April 11 through April 15, during which Beloved Adi Da wove a masterful tapestry of "consideration" about the "Perfect Practice". In this most profound practice (which is a state not really even imaginable to us in our usual condition), the devotee no longer identifies with "me" (or the apparently separate body-mind-self), but actually Identifies with the "Point of View" of Consciousness Itself, even while continuing to function as the body-mind. During any period of gathering, Adi Da Samraj inevitably returns at some point to the matter of the "Perfect Practice", because that is what He is truly Calling everyone to. Everything that precedes it He regards to be merely preparation for it.

Having just spent two months discussing matters that had everything to do with the foundation levels of the practice of the Way of Adidam, we now found ourselves suddenly plunged into "consideration" of the culminating stages of the entire Process. Each night, in response to our questions and observations, Avatar Adi Da explored different aspects of the "Perfect Practice". By the end of the fourth night, however, it seemed that we were not going to be able to generate anything further to keep the "consideration" going. We had run out of questions and "considerations" to suggest.

So, on the afternoon of April 15, we were caught short when word spread through the village that Beloved

Adi Da was going to call shortly by radio from the boat (where He had slept overnight in the cabin) to ask what questions, "considerations", or causes for gathering we had to offer. As many "gatherers" as possible were quickly assembled in the cramped little room at the back of the management offices where the radio base station was. We were racking our brains for something to offer our Beloved Guru—we certainly did not want to miss the opportunity of gathering with Him again. But when the call came through, we only managed to come up with a few lame possibilities, none of which were sufficient to warrant a gathering.

After we had offered all the possibilities we could think of, Avatar Adi Da humorously began to spin His own web of "Consideration". We listened with a mixture of amazement and amusement as He started to advocate, with tremendous finesse, that scientific materialism had indeed proclaimed the last word about us—we are "mortal organisms" and nothing else. He declared that all the years of His experience of Teaching human beings had finally convinced Him of this.

One after another, we grabbed the radio microphone and blurted out whatever objections we could muster, but He quickly shot holes in all our arguments. We began to feel more and more acutely what our Master was driving at in this tricksterish manner: No matter what we may claim our philosophy to be, the "organism" point of view is deeply entrenched in us.

In the end, Beloved Adi Da made an offer: Anyone who was prepared to prove that he or she was not merely an organism, but was Consciousness Itself, could come out to the boat to "consider" this matter further with Him in a gathering. We thanked Beloved for inviting us, and quickly scattered to prepare, anxiously wondering how we were possibly going to come up with the required proof.

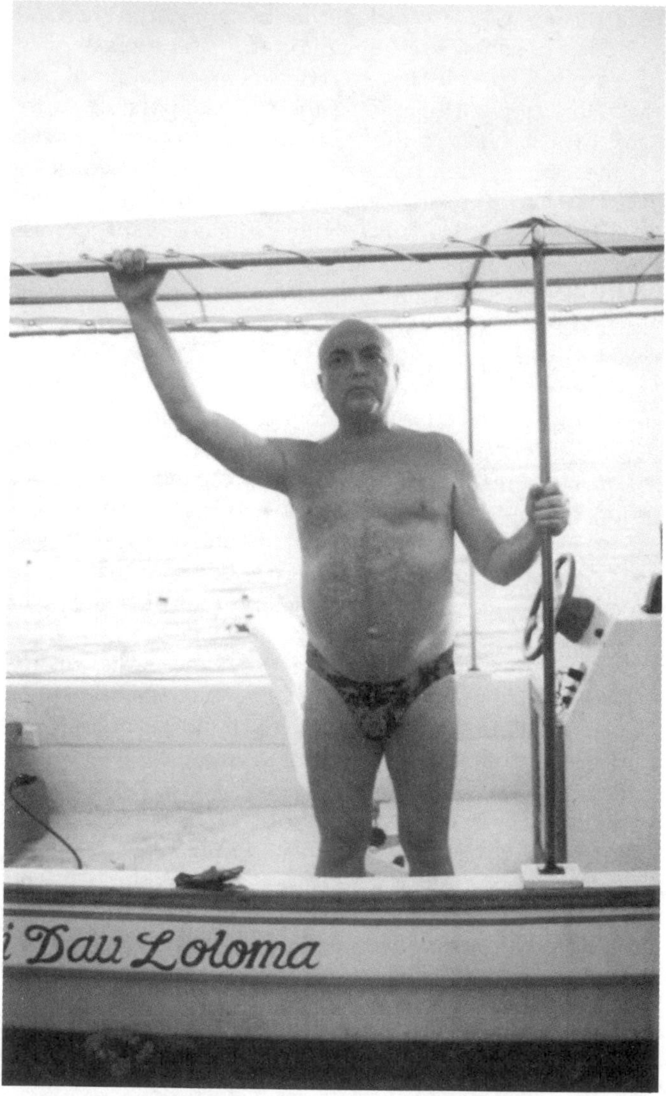

On the *Na Galala i Dau Loloma*, 1995

When we were all assembled on the deck of the Turaga Dau Loloma, Abel Slater, who had been the principal spokesperson for us in the radio conversation earlier, started with a brief summary of that conversation, for the benefit of those who had not been in the room at the time.

"Well, Beloved, this afternoon You had a 'consideration' with us on the radio."

Avatar Adi Da was "in character". Correcting Abel in a tone of mock self-satisfaction, He said, "I made a summary Communication, I believe." Everyone burst out laughing.

"I think that's more what happened," Abel agreed.

"My conclusions after twenty-three years."

"You said that, after twenty-three years of trying to make it apparent to us that we are Consciousness Itself, because of our refusal to Realize this, You have come to the conclusion that we are simply organisms."

"Mortal organisms," Beloved Adi Da clarified.

"Right. And You painted the picture of the scientific materialist point of view—that what we believe to be conscious awareness is simply brain-waves emanating from this physical manifestation, and that our fate is death, and, ultimately, stinky."

"You have changed Your doctrine to agree with the prevailing views," I (Jonathan) observed.

"Yes," said Adi Da Samraj, "it was a thorough 'consideration'."

"We tried and tried," Abel continued, "in every which way, to appeal to You that we recognize that we are Consciousness Itself—through Your Grace, and through our resort to You, and through our Contemplation of You. But You said it just sounded like a myth.

"We continued to persist in our confession to You that this is indeed the case—that we are Consciousness. And so You told us to come here tonight to prove this to

You, to demonstrate this Realization. You said that nothing short of that would suffice. Otherwise, we are simply organisms, fated to die and decay."

"And that will be that," Beloved Adi Da emphasized. "Just dead, like fish, putrid fish. Plain Old Organism People—POOPs." We all laughed at this amusing new acronym.

Joseph Taylor remarked, "Beloved, I was reflecting today that You came here for the sake of all beings, but the actual physical object that drew You to initiate Your Great Sacrificial Work was a puppy, not one of us." Joseph was referring to the momentous incident in Avatar Adi Da's infancy when (at the age of two) He voluntarily chose to identify with the apparently separate body-mind, to accept all the implications of being "human" in the ordinary sense.

"Mm-hm. I said all beings." And then, putting on a slightly supercilious tone: "Or, perhaps, to put it more aptly, all organisms, as it turns out. Well, this is My firm conclusion. Some 'begged to differ', as Barbara said in our earlier conversation, but I said that in Consciousness Itself there is no 'difference'—therefore, she is only an organism." We all laughed at His "logic".

Then He announced the core of His "argument", in the classic form of a syllogism. "Consciousness Itself Inherently Transcends the body-mind. You all insist on identifying with the body-mind. Therefore, you are not Consciousness Itself, you are the body-mind—an organism fated to die. And that's that."

Something about the logic of this "argument" seemed open to dispute, but in the hilarity of the moment no one came up with a counter-argument.

"We started out with such bright hopes," Godfree Roberts sighed.

"Well, the 'consideration' was worth having, I thought." Avatar Adi Da was playing up His "role" more and more. "Just on the outside chance that maybe some were not merely organisms. But, unfortunately, you see . . . I mean, it was a 'reality consideration', so you have to take it the way it comes. When you finally get down to it, whatever is the case is it, and that's it."

Then Beloved Adi Da startled us by voicing the bottom-line implications of "organism" philosophy with unnerving, though still hilarious, bluntness. "This practice, this devotion to Me and self-discipline that you do, makes you feel better, brings some kind of order, and even consolation, to your mortal existence. So it is still worth doing—at least it makes you feel good in this short interval of suffering and seeking and psycho-physical ego-identification. Nothing you can do about that, of course. It's just the way it is.

"There is nothing to Realize. Have fun as much as you can, and try to relax when you are dying. That is My advice."

We were practically rolling on the deck with laughter, but our frustration and agitation were beginning to build. Beloved Adi Da's play-acting was beginning to hit too close to home. Many times in the past we had witnessed our Guru's uncanny ability to adopt a certain persona, as a way of reflecting to us what we are all about. He may suddenly appear to be the fear-stricken coward or the self-indulgent addict or the soupy romantic or any other number of instantly recognizable character types, in order to make a lesson. But never before had we seen Him sustain such a role for so long as He was doing on this night. He seemed determined not to stop until we were utterly convicted of the benightedness of "organism" philosophy.

Avatar Adi Da Samraj kept going with His seemingly inexorable line of logic: "I was telling some on the radio that you have every right to fear death—because it is going to kill you!

"But fish, and so forth—they don't seem to worry about it too much. So that is a good policy: 'Don't worry about it, and relax when the time comes.' That is about all the wisdom you can use, I think, being plain old organisms."

Gerald Sheinfeld, who had come to the first three of the five boat gatherings but had been unable to come to the previous night's gathering, remarked, "I missed one night of Your 'Consideration', Beloved. Things have certainly changed!"

Beloved Adi Da explained: "Well, until tonight, I was still going for the big picture, you know—maybe there were some who were not merely organisms. But, it didn't turn out that way. Shucks, well . . .

"Still, as I said, it was a 'consideration' worth having, because there have been rumors of religion and Divinity and God-Realization going on for thousands of years. It was time that a full 'reality consideration' was entered into about the matter, so that the truth of the matter could be known, and all these winds of doctrine addressed, with a firm and final and absolutely undeniable conclusion."

"Didn't Gautama have a similar 'consideration', Beloved?" asked Bill Krenz. Bill was asking about the Buddhist teaching that every conditional phenomenon, including existence as a human being, is painful, impermanent, and devoid of "self".

"He didn't exactly come to this conclusion, but he came to some sort of conclusion about the body-mind itself." Avatar Adi Da was referring to the doctrine of the five skandhas, according to which the human body-mind is nothing but a collection of discrete elements, rather than a unified "being" with an identifiable "self".

"Still, Gautama presumed that there was some kind of something or other—Indescribable, Indefinable, and Absolute—that could be Realized." Then, fully dramatizing the arrogant twentieth-century ego's dismissal of the entire history of mankind's religious quest, Avatar Adi Da concluded, in a tone of self-satisfied gusto, "And, of course, that was bullshit! So we finally put that one to rest!"

"Is it a relief to put it to rest?" asked Adidama Jangama Hriddaya.

"Oh, yes," Beloved Adi Da immediately replied. Then, with a sly grin, He went on, capping His masterful performance: "Of course, I am a little smug about it, because I am not an organism!"

We all rocked with laughter, as Beloved Adi Da Himself laughed at His own line. Then He underlined His point: "I Am Self-Existing and Self-Radiant Consciousness Itself, and you all are organisms.

"But, of course, as I say, some of you objected to this conclusion, so that is actually why we gathered again. Otherwise, having come to this conclusion, I would never have any reason to see you again. But you thought we should gather this one last time, listen to the objections of some, and see if anybody could prove that they are not organisms.

"And Abel, you were the spokesman on the radio. You said definitely that some were going to prove this tonight—this very night, here, on board, during this 'consideration' time."

"Yes, I did, Lord," Abel concurred.

"Mm-hm. Are you one of those who are going to prove it?"

"Absolutely, Beloved."

"So, Abel—your objections, and your proofs."

Abel then began what was to become several hours worth of devotees' debating with Adi Da Samraj. Abel was looking to present evidence that would substantiate our side of the debate—that we were not mere organisms, but were Consciousness Itself.

"Well, during the course of the 'consideration' we had with You on the radio, as it drew on, there was the experience of feeling You Prior to identification with the body-mind."

"There is no trick in that," objected the Ruchira Avatar. "I Am Prior to the body-mind."

"Right."

"You are not."

"I am not," Abel conceded.

"But I am. So you were feeling Me, and that is good." Beloved Adi Da was pressing relentlessly on our presumption that we are the body-mind only, in order to help us feel the gravity of that error.

Abel went on, "There wasn't a sense of 'I' feeling You through the course of that experience."

"Then who experienced it?"

"Well, in the midst of the experience—I don't even have words for it—in the midst of whatever was going on . . ."

"Samadhi," Bill suggested.

"Samadhi, then," Abel continued. "There wasn't the experience of an 'I' experiencing some separate other condition. There was just You."

"This sounds like modern-religious-mythology talk to Me," countered Beloved Adi Da.

"Sounds like it," Abel said, dismayed.

"I dismissed it as such on the radio. I am going to stand My ground until the point is truly proven to Me otherwise."

Abel started in on another tack. "It seems like, at this point, there is an 'I' that is trying to somehow prove something from a point of view that is separate from that. In other words, trying to come up with objectified proof of it is impossible."

"Why would you have to use the word 'objectified', anyway?" Beloved Adi Da asked. "You said you were coming here to prove it, and now you are going to tell Me that you can't prove it? Is that it?"

"It can only be . . ." Abel started to rephrase his last point, but our Divine Heart-Master insisted on an answer to His question.

Avatar Adi Da adopted a stern tone. "You said 'proof' on the radio, Abel. I will accept nothing short of it."

"How about subjective proof?" asked Michael Shaw.

"That's a possibility," Abel agreed, hopefully.

Avatar Adi Da proclaimed: "Scientific proof of the existence of Consciousness will soon be announced . . . by Abel!" We all roared at this rephrasing of Beloved Adi Da's book title, *Scientific Proof of the Existence of God Will Soon Be Announced by the White House!*

"Cannot be done, Beloved—not scientifically," Abel declared.

"You promised it."

"Not scientifically."

"If you were leading Me on about this proof matter, Abel, then you got yourself here on board under false pretenses. Not only would you be a plain old organism, you would be a plain old organism with whom I am not pleased!" Beloved Adi Da glared at Abel with mock ferocity, then joined in the laughter with all of us.

Avatar Adi Da Samraj now introduced a key point in His "argument". "The way I look at it is pretty straightforward. If you are not an organism, then you do the 'Perfect Practice'."

Beloved Adi Da had explained to us many times that, over the course of growth in practice in the Way of Adidam, the practitioner's presumption as to what he or she is undergoes an evolution. In the foundation stages of practice of the Way of Adidam, one is fundamentally identified with body—whereas, in the course of the advanced stages of practice, one eventually shifts from

being fundamentally identified with body to being fundamentally identified with mind. However, in the ultimate stages of practice, or the "Perfect Practice", one stands free of identification with either body or mind, Identifying instead with Consciousness Itself. What Beloved Adi Da was humorously arguing on this night was that it was not possible to progressively become capable of Identifying with Consciousness Itself—either you were just plain Identified with Consciousness Itself, in which case you would practice the "Perfect Practice", or you were identified with the body-mind, in which case you were just the body-mind, a mortal organism, and could not advance beyond the first five stages of life.

Adi Da Samraj proceeded. "The Way of Adidam is a 'reality consideration'. But the whole 'consideration' is simply about being in My Spiritual Company, devoted to Me, surrendered to Me, Communing with Me, to the degree that the Power of My Samadhi Draws you into the Realization of My Condition. That essentially is the Way of Adidam. And it can't be defined as a sequence of practices and stages of development. Those things are more peripheral aspects of the Way. Fundamentally, the Way is simply Communing with Me to the point that the Power of My Samadhi brings you to the Realization of Me Most Perfectly.

"Well, you have all been around Me, each of you, for some number of years or other, supposedly devoting yourself to Me in this manner, and if you were so combined with Me, and were arising in Consciousness Itself, then by now you ought to be doing the 'Perfect Practice', unless you just arrived yesterday or something. And so?"

"Beloved, You have combined with us in such a miraculous way that . . . ," Godfree started out, but was interrupted by Beloved Adi Da.

"Adi . . . cannot combine." Beloved Adi Da laughed and briefly dropped out of "character" in order to explain: "That was a sort of play on Auda in *Lawrence of Arabia*. 'Auda . . . cannot serve.'" Then, right back in "character" again: "I 'combined' with you all? What a revolting suggestion! But, go on."

Godfree persisted, "And I have seen You in everyone's eyes here. Not in moments, but consistently."

The Divine Maha-Siddha adopted His haughtiest tone. "Yes. Well, there is no doubt about Who I Am, Godfree. But I am reflected in your eyes like the moon reflects the sun—good. But the moon is a dead rock!" We erupted with laughter. "And you mere organisms have these glossy little apertures, upon which I Shine as upon the moon, and it makes you glad and consoles you and helps you through this passage to death, making it a little lighter."

Godfree objected, "You have Accomplished much more than mere passive reflection."

"Mere argumentation, mere words, about all this, Godfree, is not going to convince Me," said Beloved Adi Da with finality. "I have 'Considered' this matter very thoroughly with you all for twenty-three years, and I will not accept any arguments that you are not mere organisms. Only the 'Perfect Practice' will do. Only devotion to Me to the point of Realizing My Samadhi—by the Power of My Samadhi, not by self-effort—is satisfactory to Me as final proof that you are not mere organisms.

"If you can't respond to Me to this degree, can't Realize Me by the Power of My Samadhi, that suggests that you flat cannot Realize Me—that you are just organisms, and at most can reflect Me, enjoy My Company, be warmed by My Presence like the earth is by the sun, show some brightness in your eyes like the moon reflects the sun. But you cannot Realize anything beyond being mere organisms. You are a composite of naturally made faculties, and do not have the ultimate components necessary for Divine Self-Realization. You being just 'organism', all the rest of it that's required even for advanced practice—but, certainly, for ultimate practice—is not there.

"It must be so, because I have been addressing you all for vast, vast decades, and you keep insisting that you are organisms. You keep insisting on just this beginner's practice, beginner's 'consideration', and so forth—that is the most you can do, the most you can respond."

Avatar Adi Da kept up His humorous but penetrating onslaught, exposing our hidden presumptions with the precision of a surgeon.

"You get bright in your eyes, and warmed in your body, reflecting Me, and so forth, but you just can't Find Me, Consciousness Itself, can't enter into that Ultimate Samadhi. You just don't have the faculties, or the attributes, for such Realization."

Avatar Adi Da shifted briefly into a more serious tone. "You all are always talking 'organism' stuff to Me, resorting to the body-mind, claiming to be that, even having all kinds of problems with it. So that is what I have been doing, then. I've been spending a lot of time just helping you all out with your 'organism' problems, your 'money, food, and sex' problems, your ordinary-life problems, and so forth. That is what I have been occupying Myself with, basically, because you all insist that you are not Realizing Me, are not in the Condition of Consciousness Itself, and, therefore, are disposed to lower-life-form practices. You are not here to do the practice of Consciousness Itself. You are here to do the practice of disciplining the body-mind, and using the only faculties you have, which are some kind of feeling and your constant thinking-thinking-thinking, which mainly just complicates you anyway. And that's it. That's the whole ball of wax."

Canada Shannon tried another argument. "Beloved Bhagavan, when we do forget ourselves in Contemplation of You, it is You that we Realize."

Adi Da Samraj was back in "character" again. "You see, it is Me that you're Contemplating."

"When we forget about ourselves, it is just You."

"It's great pleasure, yes, because I Am here! But, of course, you cannot Realize Me, you cannot be Established in My Condition. You can just be organisms responding to Me, like fish go to the lure, or to the water-top in sunlight. You admire Me, you are comforted by My Presence, but you yourselves are mortal organisms."

"It's more than that," Canada objected.

"Prove it!", Beloved Adi Da challenged her.

"We forget all those faculties."

"Well, sometimes you forget them," replied Beloved Adi Da. Then He painted a vivid vision of mortal philosophy. "And then you are reflecting Me, like the back of a fish reflects the sunlight. But the fish is not the sun. It cannot go there, and can never be it. Then some sucker comes along with a lure, snaps him out of the water, and cuts him in the back of the head, and he's done. So it is with you all. Various circumstances abuse the organism. It suffers, still tries to feel good, struggles along. Eventually takes the bait, gets hit on the back of the head, and done. That's the fate of these organisms, don't you know?"

We all agreed, in sobered voices, "Yes."

"Well, that's it. None of you at all have agreed to take up a sadhana that's about being anything other than an organism." Avatar Adi Da was requiring us to see the consequences of remaining identified with the body—that it meant confining ourselves indefinitely to the beginnings of Spiritual practice.

Jacqueline Grolman tried to turn around the fish metaphor. "You are Light, Beloved. Just as the fish is pervaded by the sun's light . . ."

"Yes, but it never gets to be the sun. You all, like the fishes, are creatures of the sunlight. You are creatures of natural processes. And that's it!"

Alan Whitehead spoke up. "Beloved, the sun has no transforming power, but You do. You're the One Who Transforms us."

"Well, you can say so, but, on the other hand, what kind of sadhana are you doing? Not the sadhana of the 'Perfect Practice', Identifying with Me utterly and perfectly, but the sadhana of organisms, reaching toward Me and insisting on their separate identity as organisms.

"I mean, okay, you know, a while to 'consider', grow, and be moved by the Power of My Samadhi—but twenty-three years? Kinda long in the tooth, you know what I mean? Sooner or later, I had to come to some conclusions about this—why, after twenty-three years, nobody's Realizing Me, but everybody's insisting on being organisms, to put it plainly. Why is that? It's because you're <u>organisms</u>! It suddenly dawned on Me."

A huge chorus of objections erupted.

Avatar Adi Da refused to relent: "Moon and earth to My Sun, just mortal organisms. Poor things! That's what I finally realized. It suddenly dawned on Me. All along, I have just been Realizing My Self, so it took some 'consideration' with you and bearing down and 'combining' with you (as you suggest) and finding you out, to finally realize this. It suddenly dawned on Me. Only today, on the radio, it suddenly dawned on Me. Suddenly My struggle ceased, My heart relaxed. I realized I could not possibly Transform <u>you</u> into <u>Me</u>. I can Shine on you and Give you a little bit of the Law (which will relax some of your fear), but your destiny is death, clearly. <u>Clearly</u>!"

Godfree made a last-ditch attempt. "Beloved, there is a possible alternative explanation."

"Well, there are many alternative explanations, but that doesn't make them true."

"I think this one has at least a good shot."

"Let's try it."

"I think we're just late-bloomers."

"Where's the argument in that? I mean, it doesn't prove anything. If you're going to late-bloom, then you have to bloom, in order to prove the point. The fact that you haven't bloomed yet is not proof that you can bloom. Bloom lately, and that would be proof."

And so it continued for nearly four hours. In His Service to us, to help us become thoroughly convinced of the necessity to relinquish our "organism" point of view, Beloved Adi Da just kept pushing His points home again and again and again, from every possible angle. The longer we were unable to argue successfully against this mortal philosophy, the more desperate and unsettled we became. It got to be more and more disturbing to hear our Beloved Guru expressing this point of view that was so dark and hopeless, when we could also feel that He was just articulating our own unspoken or unconscious "philosophy". Finally, after devotees had thoroughly exhausted every argument they could think of to counter Beloved Adi Da's "conclusion", He relented and Revealed to us the Truth of this "Consideration":

"If you insist on being organisms, you know what I have to say about that. I told you earlier. If you respond to Me, enter into My Domain, by the Power of My Samadhi, then you do the 'Perfect Practice' in due course. And that is the whole ball of wax."

Then He let the cat all the way out of the bag. "Well, by the way, I was bullshitting."

We all erupted into cheers and yells, so relieved that we were no longer "condemned" to mere organism life.

"You had us worried, Beloved," Michael confessed.

Beloved Adi Da summarized the lesson of the evening's "consideration": "Nobody is merely an organism, unless you insist. If you insist, then that is what you are. If you respond to Me, if you are My devotee, if you practice this Yoga of devotion to Me, then (in due course) you practice the discipline of the 'Perfect Practice'. There are none uniquely born, none uniquely Identified with the Divine Condition of Consciousness Itself. All are thus manifested."

We poured out our thanks to Beloved Adi Da, full of gratitude for His masterful and extraordinarily witty lesson-making. We knew that we would never forget this night—He had impressed the lesson on us so deeply.

The next night at another gathering—this time at Hymns To Me—Beloved Adi Da further Revealed the Truth of the matter in this ecstatic proclamation:

*AVATAR ADI DA SAMRAJ: There Is Only Reality Itself, Only Truth, Only Real God.*

*All are Inherently Conjoined With What Is Always Already The Case.*

*Some, not so responsive and illumined, act and speak as if they are just "organisms", and suggest that they should have a "lesser dharma" (so to speak), or only the opportunity for some sort of relief of anxiety, or equanimity at most, and so forth, and do not aspire to Ultimate Realization so hard.*

*But that is just their immaturity talking.*

*They have to continue to grow and get to know Me better.*

*There is not any one who is merely a mortal "organism"—not even any of the fishes or the possums or the frogs or the mosquitoes, and not even any of the worst of mankind.*

*All, including all of them, are Inherently Conjoined with Me.*

*They must simply get to know Me better.*

*They must mature.*

*All must be Forgiven.*

*All must be Purified.*

*All must Suffer Through an ordeal of Divine "Brightening".*

*All the more reason to get to know Me better and grow beyond this circumstance quickly.*

*In any particular moment, some are apparently more serious than others, and others get serious later—"late-bloomers", as Godfree described them.*

*Yes, there are all those kinds of apparent differences, but there is no ultimate "difference" between beings.*

*All are in Me.*

*Therefore, all have Me As their Eternal Opportunity—even if they may argue that they are mere "organisms", or act as if they are merely "organisms".*

*It's just bullshit—immaturity speaking, egoity dominant, habit-patterns dominant, fear dominant.*

*They have to get to know Me better, that's all.*

*There Is Only One Reality for all, and for All.*

*Therefore, there is Only One Teaching and One Great Opportunity for all, and for All.*

*It is up to each one to respond as he or she will in any moment.*

*Right response gets to know Me better, and you go and get on with it further.*

*That's it.*

Just over two weeks later, Abel Slater, who had bravely led the counter-argument in the great "organism" debate, had a deep meditative experience—a direct confirmation that, indeed, we are not merely mortal "organisms", except by our own presumption. At the time, Abel was accompanying Avatar Adi Da on a boat trip around the Fijian islands during April of 1995.

*ABEL: During the cruise, which lasted several days, I lived in very close quarters with Beloved Adi Da. At least once or twice a day, seated in His deck chair, Beloved Adi Da would spontaneously manifest an ecstatic state in which His Spiritual Transmis-*

*sion became most profound. As He sat, I would feel His Spirit-Force simultaneously piercing my heart and "Crashing Down" from above the head, through the frontal line and down to the perineum.*

*On one particular occasion, late in the day we anchored in a beautiful and secluded turquoise lagoon, and I went ashore with one of our Fijian crew members to see if there were any local inhabitants. The bay was uninhabited, and we returned to the boat in the twilight glow of dusk. As I approached the boat, I could feel the silent air was "thick" with the Force of Beloved Adi Da's Transmission. An utterly exquisite feeling engulfed my entire being. I climbed quietly onto the deck, sat down, and became spontaneously and deeply absorbed in Contemplation of Beloved Adi Da.*

*I was drawn beyond awareness of the body-mind. Then attention would wander and become associated with some thought or emotion or sensation. This wandering of attention was immediately obvious, and through my Beloved Guru's Grace, I was granted the capability to effortlessly return attention to Him and come to rest in Him, prior to the arising of all psycho-physical conditions—thoughts, feelings, and bodily experiences. Moment by moment, this process persisted. There was no struggle in it.*

*Then I began to observe the automaticity whereby attention would wander, and it became clear to me that I was actually doing this stressful activity, presuming a separate "self" and identifying moment by moment with the content of "my" experience. There was no relief from this automaticity, this moment by moment crunching down into the separate-self-sense.*

*And yet, through staying sensitive to Beloved Adi Da, I saw that there was no need to attempt to escape this stressful knot. Although the activity of self-contraction would persist—it was the root of all thoughts, all emotions, everything "I" was about—in love-Communion with Adi Da Samraj, this activity was not binding. Awareness was not limited by exclusive identification with the experience of a being a separate "I"—because, Prior to it, I was being drawn into the Very Condition of my Beloved Guru.*

## The Life of Contemplation

By August 1995, Avatar Adi Da Samraj had been commenting for months on symptoms of impaired eyesight. After medical investigation, it seemed that He was experiencing degeneration of the eyes due to a hereditary tendency to glaucoma and that His eyes were now affected not only temporarily, but in permanent ways.

This was deeply sobering news to His devotees, a stark reminder both of the fragility of His Body and of their responsibility to care for His physical well-being. Within a few days, Avatar Adi Da and a small party of devotees had left for California so that He could receive immediate medical attention. Within three days of leaving Adidam Samrajashram, Avatar Adi Da had the first of two operations for glaucoma at a private hospital in San Francisco, emphasizing to His devotees that the Power of His Darshan and His Spiritual Work was not in the least affected by the condition of His eyes.

While it was a medical emergency that instigated the departure of Avatar Adi Da from His Fijian Hermitage, it soon became clear that His Yajna—the first to California in six years—was an important event for His Work altogether. In the more than four months that followed, hundreds of devotees traveled to the Mountain Of Attention Sanctuary to receive His Darshan. They came from all over the world, including many who had never seen Him before.

*. . . His Yajna—the first to California in six years was an immensely important event for His Work altogether. In the more than four months that followed, hundreds of devotees traveled to the Mountain Of Attention Sanctuary to receive His Darshan. They came from all over the world, including many who had never seen Him before.*

The Mountain Of Attention, 1995

Late on the night of January 3, 1996, Avatar Adi Da spontaneously began to speak of the Profundity and Inherent Radiance of the Divine Condition. Consciousness, or Existence Itself, He said, is Light Itself, Inherently "Bright". And the entire Way of Adidam is a Yoga of "Brightening", or becoming established in the Condition of Light, or unqualified Divine Consciousness. Two days later, Avatar Adi Da invited a small group of His longest-standing devotees to the Manner of Flowers to continue the "consideration". At every gathering, Avatar Adi Da spoke of Consciousness Itself and of the "Perfect Practice"—the capability to Stand in the Position of Consciousness Itself, merely Witnessing what arises, rather than identifying with the vagaries of the body-mind.

Months earlier, in His humorous "consideration" about devotees being mere "organisms", He had remarked that the very fact that Consciousness Itself has nothing to do with the body-mind is what people do not like about it—and the reason why they choose to stay in the "organism" position. Now, in these gatherings, He would draw those in the room, night after night, out of "organism" awareness into the Position of Consciousness Itself, merely Witnessing what arises. Some confessed that they would wake from sleep after a gathering and find they were still in the Witness-Position, held there by the Power of His Samadhi.

*AVATAR ADI DA SAMRAJ: To be in the State of Divine Ignorance does not simply mean that you do not know What something is. It means that "knowing" is not how you are Realizing What it is.*

*You see? Your mind disappeared. Where is it anyway?*

*The mind appears because the mind is something you are identified with. Its signs, then, appear rather automatically. So to Realize the Witness is not to simply stand around watching the thoughts, and so on. The Witness is Prior to thoughts. It is about the process, then, of entering into the in-depth Domain of Consciousness Itself, without a thought, without a sensation.*

*Consciousness cannot disappear. The things that Consciousness appears to attach Itself to can disappear. So there are all kinds of changes that can be Witnessed. But Consciousness Itself never changes, never disappears. It is not merely awareness. It is simply the Infinite Well of Being, Self-Existent but also Self-Radiant, without limit, "Bright".*

*But you are the Witness now, aren't you?* [Devotees say yes.] *If you make an utterance now, you will observe Where you Are, in Truth. Say something, anything. I mean actual language that you are otherwise familiar with. Go ahead! Say it—out with it.* [Devotees speak quietly to themselves.] *See, you are not in the position of thinking those thoughts. You are noticing these thoughts, but there does not seem to be that direct connection. You are not in the position of the thinker. And yet the Position you are in does not exactly have anything to do with the thoughts, either. There is nothing like thought in It. It is simply a Presence, Consciousness. That is your actual Position. The thoughts or perceptions, whatever, are somehow apparent in That.*

*But you are not the body, you are not the emotions, you are not the thoughts, not the perceptions. You do not <u>do</u> any of those things. They are somehow happening, mysteriously, but you do not do any of them. What are <u>you</u>? What is your actual Condition?*

*To Realize It truly, you must go beyond knots and presumptions. But, at the very least, even before great Realization, or great sadhana, you can experience, feel, and know—right as you are now—that you are Standing in a Position Prior to thought, Prior to the body-mind. To fully enter into that Position is disorienting, from your point of view. If you allow that Position to be the case, even the entire body-mind relaxes—because the body-mind is ordinarily under stress, the stress of self-contraction. When you feel into the Condition Prior to self-contraction, then the body-mind follows, relaxes. Whereas if you try to make the body-mind relax, you cause stress of one kind or another.*

*There is simply fundamental feeling-awareness. But not a blank awareness. It is full of energy.*

*You see?*

*That is your actual Condition. Everything else passes. Everything else is just a moment.* [Avatar Adi Da snaps His fingers several times, to indicate the passing moments.] *Hung up for a moment on this or that perception or thought or idea or action or whatever. But if you allow the Witness-Position to be your Position, then all that groveling for effects relaxes. And you begin to become Transfigured.* [January 5, 1996]

**Adi Da Samraj and Jingle Baba the camel at Fear-No-More Zoo on the Mountain Of Attention**

During these gatherings, Avatar Adi Da developed a secondary theme: how non-human beings—animals and plants—demonstrate a natural contemplative disposition. He countered the common notion that these beings are mere "organisms", and showed how presumptuous and superficial human beings' typical attitude to the non-humans actually is. They are no less Spiritual beings than the human species; they simply have their own characteristics.

In the course of the conversation, two devotees, Craig Lesser and Frans Bakker, recalled an incident that occurred when devotees offered Avatar Adi Da a trip to a large amusement park during His brief visit to the United States in 1984. And so they began to recount the story to Avatar Adi Da and the devotees in the room.

Avatar Adi Da and His party, they said, were given front seats to watch a water show involving performing orcas, or killer whales. These huge graceful creatures had been trained to jump and play with balls and do various tricks. The audience sat expectantly in the bleachers watching the whales. Everyone waited and waited, but the whales did nothing at all—they just lay there in the water. Avatar Adi Da turned to Craig and said, humorously quoting Queen Victoria, "We are not amused." The non-response of the whales was to be investigated—Craig was to ask the management what was going on. Avatar Adi Da even playfully suggested that everyone should have their money refunded!

Craig recounted how he went to speak to the man in charge, feeling nervous. But he need not have worried. He found the man almost in tears. "I don't understand," he moaned, "They always do it." At that moment, Craig said, he glanced over to where Avatar Adi Da was sitting, and he noticed that the Ruchira Avatar was intently Regarding the whales. Not only that, His hands were moving in mudras of Spiritual Transmission.

Avatar Adi Da interjected in the story. "I was?" He said, feigning surprise and innocence.

"Yes," Craig said, "You were. You were the reason why the whales were not performing. You were the One behind the whole thing! They were not going to do any jumping—because they were in Samadhi."

Avatar Adi Da laughed. He did not deny that the "Trick" that day had been His. He simply said, "Human beings are not the only beings that I Work with." Then the conversation continued:

*AVATAR ADI DA SAMRAJ: Look at what human beings want non-humans to do. There is all the abuse involved in animal testing—but also, apart from all that, domesticating non-humans for farm use, or, if they are members of an unusual species, putting them in zoos, or, if they will do some tricks, having them do such tricks night and day.*

*They are such interesting beings, but people have them doing a* circus *act—a clown act, basically. They seem to be playful enough about it—if you want them to do that stuff, they will do it for you. But it is* silly. *There must be something more profound to do with them, they think.*

*CRAIG: You said later that You had freed them from the feeling of the necessity to do their act.*

*AVATAR ADI DA SAMRAJ: Right.*

*CRAIG: In Your Company that day, they were released from that sense of having to relate to an audience.*

*AVATAR ADI DA SAMRAJ: Mm-hm. They did not have to play the game.*

*What would happen if there were a lot more animals who* insisted *on thoroughly affirming their life of Contemplation, no matter what human beings did to them or tried to get them to do? It would probably have a great influence on human beings if all the non-humans agreed to handle their business in a simple way and just spend the rest of their time contemplating, from now on. No more extraneous requirements, no more beach balls, and no pulling plow—none of that sort of activity. What would happen if all the zoo animals were contemplating, instead?—with a little snack every now and then, but, otherwise,* obviously *contemplating. Not that nervous thing they do in response to captivity, playing around for an audience, and so forth, but just vast numbers of non-humans in obvious contemplation, for human beings to witness. What would happen*

***"What would happen if you could no longer control the non-humans, and they just insisted on their contemplation? Well, they could change people a lot, it would seem."***

*if you could no longer control the non-humans, and they just insisted on their contemplation? Well, they could change people a lot, it would seem.*

*I do not know if the animals can be organized to do this, but maybe you all could try doing it, since you are animals! Instead, you are doing this stupid beach-ball act, jumping through hoops and joking and being silly. You are trained to do all of that. What would happen if you animals—and perhaps you could get some other animals to do it, too—insisted on your life of contemplation and get back to Reality Itself? Like those whales that day, you see.*

*If you look at the animals in their natural setting where they have to provide for themselves, and so on, they handle that business. But then you also see them all taking extended contemplation breaks frequently every day. No clock-punching. Every now and then, they go out and do whatever it takes to provide for themselves. If you have to provide for yourself, you make it as playful and interesting as you can, and then you rest from that for a few days and do some really* <u>*extended*</u> *meditation! That is basically what non-humans like to do. They do not like the stress of bodily obligation.*

*But the humanized animals here—they think they are supposed to be doing all kinds of things,* <u>*instead*</u> *of contemplation. They seem fascinated with the idea that, because they can imagine it, bodies are going to become luminous enjoyments in a paradise and live forever. The non-humans know that that is complete* <u>*nonsense*</u>*. They do not have to go to school to find that out. But you go to school and you get indoctrinated into life-fixedness as if it were a paradise and you are going to be here forever, as if that were the meaning of life—to* <u>*pretend*</u> *that you are immortals in a world that is made for itself.*

*That is the way you become worldly. That is what "worldly" means. Being worldly is not doing some kinds of things that good people do not do. Being worldly is to be a worldling, to be of* <u>*mortal*</u> <u>*mind*</u>*, and to have the law of your life be that of fulfilling and elaborating every possible kind of "organism" purpose.*

*Human beings are the only species that does this here. The others are all living ages of contemplation. They know the world is not a paradise. It is not to be made into an "eternity"—nor is it to be presumed or imagined that it* <u>*could*</u> *be. They know this very well. So they use conditional existence as a circumstance of contemplation.* [January 9, 1996]

After ten days of exquisite Discourse about Contemplation and Divine Samadhi—the way beyond "organism" life—Avatar Adi Da completed this cycle of His Instruction at the Mountain Of Attention. And so, early in the morning of January 16, 1996, after having gathered all night, He left the Manner of Flowers and moved on to a four-month sojourn at His Hawaiian Sanctuary, Da Love-Ananda Mahal.

**Switzerland, 1996**

CHAPTER 23

# Beyond the Cultic Tendency

While the "organism consideration" in April 1995 had been a humorous critique of ordinary ego-life, the second half of 1996 was to see one of fiercest criticisms of the ego Avatar Adi Da has ever given. He delivered this criticism not only in words, but also (even more potently) via His actions. And it was a criticism not only of the individual ego but also of the collective ego—the ego (or the activity of self-contraction) as it is dramatized by groups of human beings.

Avatar Adi Da had always pointed out that any organized group of people tends to function as a single egoic unit—self-contracted, self-preoccupied—just like an individual. This collective egoity, or "group-ego", is what Avatar Adi Da is referring to when He uses the word "cult". Thus, when He speaks of "cultism", Avatar Adi Da is not using the term in the popular media sense of "any non-mainstream religious group", nor is He referring merely to those particular religious or political groups that stand out as deluded in their allegiance to a misguided leader. Rather, in His criticism of cultism, Avatar Adi Da is addressing a universal human tendency—a tendency that exists in all organized groups of people.

*[A]ny organized gathering of people associated with a common source of enthusiasm and commitment may be called a "cult". Therefore, "cultism" is associated not only with religion, but with politics, intellectual studies,*

*science, the professions, entertainment, sports, the news media, animal- and flower-breeding societies! Nearly every area of human endeavor tends to produce the centralizing phenomenon (or centripetal motion) of cultism.* [Scientific Proof of the Existence of God Will Soon Be Announced by the White House!]

*Human beings always tend to encircle . . . the presumed "center" of their lives—a book, a person, a symbol, an idea, or whatever. . . . In this manner, the group becomes an ego ("inward"-directed, or separate and separative)—just as the individual body-mind becomes, by self-referring self-contraction, the separate and separative ego-"I" ("inward"-directed, or ego-centric . . . ). Thus, by self-contraction upon the presumed "center" of their lives, human beings, in their collective ego-centricity, make "cults" . . . in every area of life.* [First Word]

## The Real Fault in "Guru Cultism"

One of Avatar Adi Da's most summary statements relative to cultism was originally written in 1982. It is a strong criticism of cultism of all types, but especially of "Guru cultism". Avatar Adi Da's criticism is not aimed merely at those who falsely claim to be Gurus. Rather, He is primarily criticizing the way people tend to relate to anyone (or anything) that they put at the "center" of their lives. This cultic error is the reason why people relate wrongly to true Gurus, and it is also the reason why people are susceptible to the apparent appeal of false Gurus.

*[In My Wisdom-Teaching], I Speak critically of the conventional (or childish, and, otherwise, adolescent) orientation of "Guru cultism". Such cultism is a tendency that has always been present in the religious and Spiritual*

*traditions of mankind. Anciently, and in the present time, both true Spiritual Masters and ordinary Wisdom-Teachers have been "cultified", and, thereby, made the merely fascinating Object of a self-contained popular movement that worships the Spiritual Master as a Parent-like Savior, while embracing very little of the significant Wisdom-Teaching of the Spiritual Master.*

*The error of conventional cultism is precisely this childish, and, otherwise, adolescent, and, altogether, ego-based orientation to fascination with Spiritual Masters, Wisdom-Teachers, "God"-Ideas, myths, sacred lore, inherited beliefs, traditional propaganda, and psycho-physical (or merely body-mind-based) mysticism. And the cultic tendency in religion and Spirituality is the essence of what is wrong with conventional religion and Spirituality.*

*The "problem" is not that there Is no Real God, or that there are no true Wisdom-Teachings, or that there are no true Spiritual Masters, or that there should be no devotion to any true Spiritual Masters. The "problem" with conventional religion and Spirituality is the same as the "problem" of all ordinary life. The "problem" is the childish, and, otherwise, rather adolescent, egoism that is the basis of all forms of ordinary existence.*

*Yet un-Enlightened (or, otherwise, not yet Most Perfectly Enlightened) people are egoically "self-possessed" (or self-absorbed). Therefore, egoity is the "disease" that all the true Spiritual Masters of religion come here to cure. Unfortunately, those who are merely fascinated by Spiritual Masters are, typically, those who make, or at least transform, the institutions of the religion and the Spirituality of their Spiritual Masters. And true practitioners of religion and Spirituality are very hard to find, or develop. Therefore, religious and Spiritual institutions tend to develop along lines that serve, accommodate, and represent the common egoity—and this is why the esoteric true Teachings of true Spiritual Masters tend to be bypassed, and even suppressed, in the drive to develop the exoteric cult of any particular Spiritual Master.*

*The devotional relationship to Me . . . is not an exoteric cultic matter. It is a profound esoteric discipline, necessarily associated with real and serious and mature practice of the "radical" Way (or root-Process) of Realizing Real God, Which Is Reality and Truth. Therefore, . . . I am critical of the ego-based (or self-saving, and self-"guruing", rather than ego-surrendering, ego-forgetting, ego-transcending, and Divine-Guru-Oriented) practices of childish, and, otherwise, adolescent, and, altogether, merely exoteric cultism.*

*The common religious or Spiritual cult is based on the tendency to resist the disciplines of real (and really counter-egoic) practice, and to opt for mere fascination with extraordinary (or even imaginary) phenomena (which are, invariably, not understood in Truth and in Reality). Apart from the often petty demand for the observation of conventional rules (generally, relative to social morality, or merely social religion), the cult of religious and Spiritual fascination tends to become righteously associated with no practice (that is, with the even official expectation that there be no real, or, otherwise, truly right and full, practice of religious and Spiritual disciplines, especially of religious, Spiritual, and meditative disciplines of an esoteric kind). Just so, the cult of religious and Spiritual fascination tends to be equally righteous about maintaining fascinated faith (or indiscriminate, and even aggressive, belief) in the merely Parent-like "Divine" Status of one or another historical individual, "God"-Idea, religious or Spiritual doctrine, inherited tradition, or force of cosmic Nature.*

*Religious and Spiritual cultism is, thus, a kind of infantile collective madness. (And such madness is equally shared by secular cultists, in every area of popular culture, including politics, the sciences, the arts, the communications media, and even all the agencies and institutions of conventional "officialdom" relative to human knowledge, belief, and behavior.) Religious and Spiritual cults (and, likewise, all secular cults) breed "pharisaism", or the petty righteousness of conventional thinking. Religious and Spiritual cults breed "Substitution" myths (or the belief that personal self-transcendence is, both generally and ultimately, impossible—but also unnecessary, because of what "God", or some "Master", or even some "priest" has already done). Indeed, religious and Spiritual cults (and, likewise, all secular cults) breed even every kind of intolerance, and the chronic aggressive search for exclusive social dominance and secular power. Religious and Spiritual cults are, characteristically, populated by those who are, generally, neither inclined toward nor prepared for the real right practice of religious and Spiritual discipline, but who are (and always seek to be) glamorized and consoled by mere association with the "holy" things and beliefs of the cult itself.*

*This error of religious and Spiritual cultism, and of ego-based culture in general, must be examined very seriously—such that the error is truly rooted out, from within the cult and the culture itself (and not merely, and with equally cultic cultural righteousness, criticized from without). Cultism of <u>every</u> kind (both sacred and secular) must be understood to be a kind of ritualized infantilism, bound to egocentric behavior, and to the embrace of "insiders" only, and to intolerance relative to all "outsiders". The cultic tendency, both sacred and secular, causes, and has always caused, great social, cultural, and political trouble—as can even now be seen in the development of worldwide conflicts based on the exclusive, or collectively egocentric, orientation of the many grossly competitive religious traditions, political idealisms, and national identities.*

*All cults, whether sacred or secular, thrive on indulgence in the psychology (and the emotional rituals) of hope, rather than on actual demonstration of counter-egoic and really ego-transcending action. Therefore, when all egos meet, they strive and compete for the ultimate fulfillment of searches and desires—rather than cooperate with Truth, Reality, or Real God, and in a culturally valued and rewarded mood of fearless tolerance and sane equanimity.*

*Clearly, this cultic tendency in religion and Spirituality, and the egoic (and, thus, cultic) tendency in life in general, must become the constant subject of fundamental human understanding—and all of mankind must constantly be put to "school", to unlearn the method of egocentrism, non-cooperation, intolerance, and dis-ease.* [Ruchira Avatara Gita]

## Saint-and-Ear: An Archetype of the Cultic Error

Avatar Adi Da portrays the cultic error most starkly in a prophetic work called *The Mummery*, the original version of which He wrote in 1969, the year before His Divine Re-Awakening. *The Mummery*, subtitled *A Parable Of The Divine True Love*, is a telling of His own Life in the language of profound poetry and archetype. It is a metaphorical expression of the meaning of His Avataric Incarnation—using the expressive resources of the English language in highly original ways, and boldly refashioning the genre of the novel (building on the twentieth-century tradition of experimental fiction).

The title—*The Mummery*—immediately indicates the core of Avatar Adi Da's message in the book: Without true (and truly ego-transcending) heart-Communion with Real God, life is nothing but a mock-show, a piece of play-acting without any depth of meaning.

"The world," as Avatar Adi Da remarked while at Da Love-Ananda Mahal in 1996, "is a mummery. I know it, and I have said so. This is fundamental to My Communication to everyone."

*The world is a Vast Store of Bondage—a mere, and endless, and ceaselessly familiar Mummery. A ridiculous, hypocritical, and pretentious Performance. An absurdly costumed Ceremony—ritually and comically Enacted, solemnly Scripted, monotonously pre-Ordained, and ceaselessly Repeated. Only living, only seeking—and, at last, only dying.* [The Mummery]

The hero of *The Mummery*, Raymond Darling, goes through the ordeal of realizing this. All the other characters in the book are satisfied with the mummery, and they want to implicate Raymond in it as well. Raymond, however, is the Divine Person—but secretly. He himself does not clearly know his own identity until the end of the book. He only knows that he perceives existence completely differently from everyone else. Certainly, no one recognizes Raymond as he truly is, and he becomes involved in a series of strange, dreamlike adventures, centered around finding Quandra, his beloved. Partway through the story, Raymond finds and embraces Quandra by a secret lake called "God's End". Then, mysteriously, he loses her and spends the rest of the story seeking for her.

One of the most startling discoveries that Raymond makes during his search for Quandra is that an entire cult has been created around the worship of him—a cult that he knew nothing about and has had no hand in creating. Furthermore, as Raymond finds out, all the members of this cult had been presuming that he was dead—and they are not altogether pleased when they discover that he is still alive!

The cult holds its elaborate rituals in a huge edifice called "the Tabernacle of Saint-and-Ear". All the "Raymond-ites" are apparently there to worship Raymond. They think they are doing so. But Saint-and-Ear is not about true worship of the Divine. It is about worshipping an ego-made "idea" of the Divine—the worship of God-absent, God-somewhere-else, not Real God here and now.

This archetype of Saint-and-Ear is Avatar Adi Da's commentary on how egos distort religion, how egos dramatize the cultic error. *The Mummery* is a mirror Avatar Adi Da has Given to humanity, to show what egos—both the individual ego and the cultic group-ego—will tend to do in the face of His Appearance here. Only by going beyond the ego—recognizing Him as the True Divine Help, allowing Him to Attract and Move one's heart beyond fear and self-contraction—can one enter into true heart-Communion with Avatar Adi Da and true worship of Him. And it is through such ego-transcending heart-conversion that a truly non-cultic gathering of devotees is created around Him.

*[T]rue Satsang with Me (or the true devotional relationship to Me) is an always (and specifically, and intensively) anti-"cultic", or truly non-"cultic", Process.* [First Word]

*The Mummery* is a book of Truth against which there is no defense—the horrifying consequences of egoity and cultism are portrayed with stark clarity. But, beyond that fierce (and necessary) criticism of the ego, the alternative to the ego's mummery-life—the Grace of Perfect Love-Intimacy with the Divine Person, Adi Da Samraj—is shown in its all-surpassing depth. Raymond's Way is Liberation from the desperate, destructive seeking of this world. As Avatar Adi Da writes in His Prologue to the book, the purpose of *The Mummery* is to "Purify and Illuminate the mortal, human heart" so that all <u>will</u> understand the ego's act, understand every last shred of it—and be heart-converted, be moved to recognize and respond to the Gift of Avatar Adi Da's Appearance here.

The lessons of *The Mummery* are so important that Avatar Adi Da has made a live reading or staged performance of the entire book one of the yearly events in the lives of His devotees. The performances are done each January, when the anniversary of the Initiation of His Divine "Emergence" is celebrated.

# The Completion of *The Mummery*

*The Mummery* was the first book written by Avatar Adi Da, and it stands as one of His supreme expressions—an overwhelmingly intense and poignant communication both of His clear vision of the world as mummery and of His all-Embracing Love.[1] The process by which Avatar Adi Da came to write *The Mummery* started during His years at Columbia College, eventually coming to fruition about ten years later in the writing of the original version of *The Mummery* in 1969. For many years, Avatar Adi Da's devotees presumed that this original version was His final text and would not be changed. But then, during a three-month period in mid-1998, He began working on it again, devoting many hours every day to extending and further developing the entire book, ultimately expanding it to twice its original length. As the weeks passed, Avatar Adi Da took His Allegory of Divine True Love to more and more heart-breaking depths.

*AVATAR ADI DA SAMRAJ: It took another thirty years of "consideration" to complete* The Mummery, *after I wrote the original manuscript in 1969. That should indicate something about the profound nature of this Book. I have literally Worked on it continuously for about forty years—not only through My writing of it, which began, in seed-form, while I was at Columbia College, but also through all the years of My ongoing Process of unrestricted "consideration" of reality.*

*To understand* The Mummery *is a great exercise—an inexhaustible one, really. To properly appreciate it is a great matter, and ultimately requires a lot of knowledge of all cultures and times—the totality of humankind, and Totality altogether.* The Mummery *has a very direct bearing on everything about people's right relationship to Me. And wrong relationship to Me is also clearly addressed there.*

JUNE 21 AND 25, 1998

## Stepping Out of Saint-and-Ear

From His childhood, Avatar Adi Da has Submitted to this mummery-world out of love in order to awaken people to the illusion of it all and draw them beyond their egoic and cultic "programs", into the Truth and Freedom of His own Condition. To do this, He had to appear to join in the mummery. He had to connect with people in terms that they understood. Now, in the early months of 1996 at Da Love-Ananda Mahal, Avatar Adi Da was intensifying His Calling to His devotees to understand the universal cultic tendency and to take responsibility themselves for ensuring that the organization of Adidam did not dramatize the cultic pattern of "Saint-and-Ear", or ego-based and ego-serving religion. Avatar Adi Da had Himself always refused to allow the cultic error in His devotees. Now He was intensifying His Calling to them to refuse to allow it in themselves.

*AVATAR ADI DA SAMRAJ: I Stood firm in the middle of Saint-and-Ear in the most extraordinary religious demonstration in human history.*

*You can stay at Saint-and-Ear, or you can come with Me. There are not any other options.*

*I have Revealed My Self, and that is the measure of relationship to Me. I will not stay at Saint-and-Ear.* [February 23, 1996]

## Passing the Test

Avatar Adi Da was calling upon His devotees to establish a unique level of true integrity. He was calling upon His devotees to create an organization that was entirely egoless in its purposes and activities, an organization that was entirely devoted to serving His Divine Purpose without compromise or concession. In His Work to create such integrity in His devotees, Avatar Adi Da has seemed, at times, to throw everything away—because His devotees were not yet exemplifying the profound degree of conformity to Him that was required. In such periods, He waits to see what will "come back" to Him—transformed—after He has apparently cast it aside. This is His manner of testing. And Avatar Adi Da is always testing His devotees.

*AVATAR ADI DA SAMRAJ: Your dreams of exoteric religion are always about being loved—or being forgiven for failing to meet the tests you have been given, and then being given everything you want anyway. Real (and, necessarily, esoteric) religion, or Spiritual life altogether, is about passing tests. This is the growth process. There must be real changes in the pattern, real demonstration.* [March 10, 1998]

In the middle of 1996, Avatar Adi Da became unrelenting in His Call for a change in His devotees' pattern of relating to Him. He had returned to Adidam Samraj-ashram in June, after the months at Da Love-Ananda Mahal, but He did not stay in Fiji. In order to bring His devotees through the process of rightly relating to Him as individuals and as a collective, Avatar Adi Da chose to step back for a time from the entire gathering. And so, on July 13, Avatar Adi Da suddenly left Adidam Samraj-ashram again. Taking with Him only a few devotees, He traveled to Europe—for the first time since 1986—and lived privately there, waiting for a response to His Call.

While waiting, however, Adi Da Samraj did not cease to Work. Every day, He read the *Herald Tribune* and listened to news broadcasts. By doing this, He was not simply keeping Himself informed of what was happening in the world. He was giving His attention to events and individuals everywhere, in His Divine manner. He was combining Himself with the world for the sake of His Spiritual Work.

Wherever He went—in the streets, stores, churches, and museums of European towns and cities—Avatar Adi Da Samraj was obviously doing this Work—giving Darshan, Radiating His Divine "Brightness" to all. During a period in Holland, He went regularly to a public health spa. Frequently, He would sit motionless in a crowded sauna and then suddenly move on to a bath, pool, or treatment room. The devotees with Him had to be quick, or else they could lose Him in a few moments. People at the spa had no idea Who was present in their midst, or the Blessing they were receiving, but many were obviously struck by the sight of Avatar Adi Da Samraj, and would turn to gaze at Him.

The entire time He was in Europe, Adi Da Samraj was in constant—and fiery—communication with devotees everywhere, wanting to know what was changing in

**Avatar Adi Da Samraj in Europe 1996**

**top: Darshan in Holland**

**above left: traveling by train**

**above and below right: walking in Amsterdam with the Trimada**

their response to Him, what they were doing differently. He was Working a deep purification in His devotees, and it was becoming obvious that the transition from the ego's version of religion to true devotion to the Very Divine Person is a kind of ego-death. It is a shift of point of view that affects the way one approaches everything. One no longer tries to use the relationship to Adi Da Samraj to improve one's life in some way. Instead, the devotee's heart-Attraction to Avatar Adi Da Samraj becomes the greatest Happiness, and he or she lives to serve Avatar Adi Da's purposes rather than his or her own. Such self-surrender literally changes the body-mind and allows the true Spiritual Process to flower. Until this shift occurs, Avatar Adi Da was saying, devotees cannot receive the fullness of His Spiritual Transmission.

The difficulty and lessons of this time in Avatar Adi Da's Work are described by Thankfull Hastings, a devotee who accompanied Avatar Adi Da from Adidam Samrajashram and was with Him almost continuously during those months. Thankfull was in his mid-twenties at the time. He had grown up in Adidam, and had served Avatar Adi Da very closely for five years before the European trip, so He was as well prepared as anyone could be for the ordeal that lay ahead.

*THANKFULL: It was on the small inter-island flight between Taveuni (the closest island to Naitauba that has an airport) and Nadi (the city where the international airport is located) that Beloved Adi Da began to speak to me, describing what the coming time in Europe was going to be like and the disposition that the devotees traveling with Him had to be in if they were going to effectively serve His Work there.*

*He was looking for a group of people to live and serve around Him as fierce renunciates, who would represent Him to all other devotees and to the world altogether, exercising constant sensitivity to the Spiritual Work that*

*He would do—a Work that I know from personal experience is far beyond what He may appear (from the ordinary point of view) to be doing in any moment. So one of the principal Instructions He gave to us that day was that there would be things we would observe in His coming Work that might seem irrational, extreme, and that might give rise to doubt. He indicated it was our discipline to be in the disposition of understanding that whatever He might have to do would be for the sake of the Great Purpose—the Divine Liberation of beings—and we should not waver in our faith and devotion.*

*It was a very unusual time—a time during which Beloved Adi Da was intentionally separating Himself from the larger gathering of His devotees. He was not just going into a period of seclusion as He does from time to time, but was actually "considering" the possibility of living entirely privately and doing His Work apart from His day to day relationship with all His devotees. He was looking for great renunciate signs from a core group of His devotees and for a real vehicle for His Blessing to flow into the world. And He felt He should "consider" His "retirement". It was an experiment, a "free fall"—as His life has always been.*

*The conclusion of the experiment after those three months was that the relationship between Beloved Adi Da and His devotees is one that is not breakable. As the devotees rely on their Guru, so the Guru Relies on His devotees. Beloved Adi Da pointed out time and time again that He has no karmas, no "reasons" to be incarnate in the world other than for the sake of Liberating His devotees. Therefore, to bring an end to the relationship between the Guru and His devotees is to bring an end to the Incarnation of the Guru. It was clear: He could not Function apart from His devotees.*

*An example of this occurred only a few days after we arrived in Europe. We had come to Europe with the understanding that Beloved Adi Da was going to live a life of isolation for the time being, but, after four days of staying in a hotel, He told those of us serving Him that He wanted to see His devotees at the European Ashram in Holland. We traveled there the following day—and, for most of the time He was in Europe, He actually lived in a room at the Ashram. Even though He was in seclusion for most of that time, He chose to do so in the circumstance of being surrounded by His devotees. During the time Beloved Adi Da stayed at the European Ashram, devotees went through a profound ordeal, as He tested us all in the extreme—to see if they were truly "His", in the Spiritual sense. He was testing our response and our ability to stay with Him under any circumstance—whether apparently positive or apparently negative.*

*And so Adi Da lived in isolation in the Ashram in Holland and called passionately for gestures of real renunciation and the establishment of far greater cooperative living within the community itself.*

*One night, totally spontaneously, He walked out into the woods behind the Ashram, in total Frustration, and began to wander, very much in the tradition of the Avadhoot. I followed Him, along with the Adidamas and the Trimada. He kept turning around and telling us to leave Him, but no one would. I was reminded of what Beloved Adi Da said as we were leaving Adidam Samrajashram—that He would do things that would seem "irrational, extreme, and that might give rise to doubt". I knew this was one of those times—and that it was my discipline to serve Him the best I could in that moment, and to understand that everything He does is for the sake of the Divine Liberation of beings, and is not always what it seems on the surface.*

*Beloved Adi Da stayed there in the woods for the next two weeks. In the coming days, He allowed us to serve Him only minimally—we erected a lean-to, and brought*

*Him food and blankets, as it was cold and wet in Holland during this time. He continued to very forcefully address all His devotees through verbal communications He would pass on through those of us who were serving Him directly. It was obvious that Beloved Adi Da was working intensively with His devotees through these communications, but I also felt how, simultaneously, He was working on a much larger scale—that I didn't (or really even couldn't) ultimately know about or understand.*

*I personally experienced every form of doubt, disillusionment, and discomfort—in body, emotion, and mind—during those months. The sheer Force of His Criticisms made me want to pack my bags every day. Day after day, after making yet another incredibly fiery Communication, Beloved Adi Da would then send those serving around Him away, or stand up and leave Himself. And we were left to deal with our reaction, confronted with the choice of persisting and responding or not. To not respond was to throw the relationship with our Master away in that moment. To walk back into His Company the next day was to permit oneself to be further scorched by the Guru's Purifying Fire, which burns through to the places one generally keeps emotionally guarded.*

*One time during the trip, Beloved Adi Da left the Dutch Ashram by train for Switzerland, with only His physician and one other devotee. The first night He was there, I was told to come to the telephone, as there was a message to call a hotel in Geneva. I presumed that a call from this hotel meant it was one of the two men who had traveled with Adi Da. I called the hotel, and the woman at the front desk said she was expecting my call and would put me right through. When the phone was picked up on the other end it was Beloved Adi Da in His room! He generally never speaks directly on the phone—usually His communications are repeated through one of the*

*Adidamas or another devotee. But this time He spoke to me directly. It was an extraordinary conversation. I felt His absolute vulnerability. Beloved Adi Da is a total renunciate. He has renounced even all the ordinary means and capabilities that most of us take for granted relative to operating in the worldly context.*

*Here He was, talking to me from His hotel room. He had bitten His tongue very badly—there was blood running down His chin and chest. This was distorting His speech somewhat. As He spoke to me briefly about the trip, He kept having to wipe the blood from His chin. He spoke to me about that being a sign that it was time for Him to stop communicating His Distress to devotees and time for us to recognize that we must take up far greater responsibility for Him and His Work, to use all the Gifts that He has Given us.*

*I asked Him if there was anyone in the room with Him. He said, no, He was alone. And I asked, where are they?—and He replied that He did not know. Then there was a knock at the door. I tried to prevent Him from getting up to answer it, but He walked over and opened the door. Fortunately, it was a devotee, Toni Vidor, who had followed Beloved Adi Da to Geneva to be of service to Him if He would allow it. I explained to Beloved Adi Da about the little holes in doors that you can look through and see who is on the other side before you open them!*

*After speaking to Beloved Adi Da on the telephone for five or so minutes, I told Him that I was getting off the telephone and was going to escort the Adidamas and Trimada to Geneva that evening. We were able to catch a train that evening and arrived in Geneva early the following morning.*

*During the time Beloved Adi Da spent in Geneva, important conferences were taking place at the United Nations there, especially regarding the matter of nuclear disarmament. On one occasion, He was taken to the UN building, escorted by a UN official who is His devotee, visiting the conference rooms in which the talks would take place. It was clear how momentous this time was in His Work. Seeing Him not only in the UN building but walking in the Alps and visiting the church where John Calvin had preached, I could feel Him doing very intensive Work with all of Europe.*

*I recently glanced at some of the journal entries I made during that time. For me, it was definitely the most difficult time I have ever spent with Beloved Adi Da—and there have been some very difficult times! The only means to stay in place was to intensively Invoke Him and Contemplate Him at heart. When I did not do that with great intention, the situation would become unbearable.*

*Part of what was so difficult was the conflict I felt: there was the impulse to get out of there every day—but Beloved Adi Da's vulnerability and His need for my service made it impossible for me to abandon Him. On the one hand was His fierce Demand—everything He requires for His Spiritual Work to be effective—and at the same time His vulnerability and absolute dependence on us was constantly demonstrated.*

*We each had to confront the question: How committed are we, for real, to the fundamental Spiritual practice of Communing with the Divine and caring for Him in His bodily (human) Form, even under the most extreme conditions—conditions in which the ego was getting no "reasons" to feel congratulated! He pushed us to our limit, again and again. And He would look to see if we would stay with Him—in our hearts, but also, of course, in the most literal, physical sense of continuing to serve and care for Him.*

*Adi Da Samraj is so <u>real</u>! Anything you have the slightest illusion about, any area where you are contracted, attached, uptight, consoled—if you let Him, He will Liberate you from the bondage associated with it. It is*

Thankfull Hastings (in the solid color shirt) with
Adi Da Samraj at the Adidam Ashram in Holland, 1996

walking in the Swiss Alps

visiting the United Nations in
Geneva, Switzerland

*intense enough living with Adi Da at one of the Adidam Sanctuaries. It is even more intense when you are in the world with Him, where there is very little or no understanding of the Guru-devotee relationship, and where some people are even aggressively opposed to minority religions of any kind. I felt that I was put to the test continuously during that time.*

*For me, in purely personal terms, this time was a proving of the reality that there is nothing that would ever destroy or diminish my fundamental love-relationship and undying fidelity to Beloved Adi Da. It was proven to me that that relationship is prior to all appearances and all experiences. I know with certainty that I am connected to my Beloved Guru through a fundamental Spiritual relationship which is prior to any possible occurrences in the psycho-physical domain of life—but there are also times when the reactions of the ego to Beloved Adi Da's powerful purifying Force do not look pretty at all! The relationship with the Divine Maha-Siddha is not something romantic—it is not what you might imagine. It is not just about simplicity and meditation and peace. There is plenty of that, too. But Beloved Adi Da is a very Forceful Tantric Guru, who uses whatever means are necessary to shake you loose from bondage and every kind of illusion about yourself and about this world—from all your illusions of order and comfort. He constantly reawakens me to the reality of the human condition—and to how strong I have to be to actually be effective as a Spiritual practitioner and effective in serving His Work in the world.*

Avatar Adi Da has said many times that His devotees' response to Him actually affects the state of the world, because He Works through His devotees Spiritually for the benefit of all. To Him, His devotees simply represent the "front line" of His Work. And, whenever the "front

**Avatar Adi Da Samraj sitting in the United Nations, Geneva, Switzerland**

line" yields to His Grace and surrenders more, He can, through His devotees, Touch all beings more deeply.

*AVATAR ADI DA SAMRAJ: You need to listen and observe the gross and universal insult of the world in this dark and darkening time here. My Urgency has much to do with that. I perceive and know of potential calamity on a global scale that people are hardly even sensitive to. I can Do My Work, but My devotees, by participating fully in My Pattern, must give Me a pattern within which My Pattern can Work. There must be a pattern in the scale of the gross which extends from Me and cooperates with Me.* [August 14, 1997]

Avatar Adi Da's Ordeal in Europe came to an end in October 1996, when He responded to the pleas of His devotees to leave the small apartment where He was staying in Geneva and return to the Mountain Of Attention.

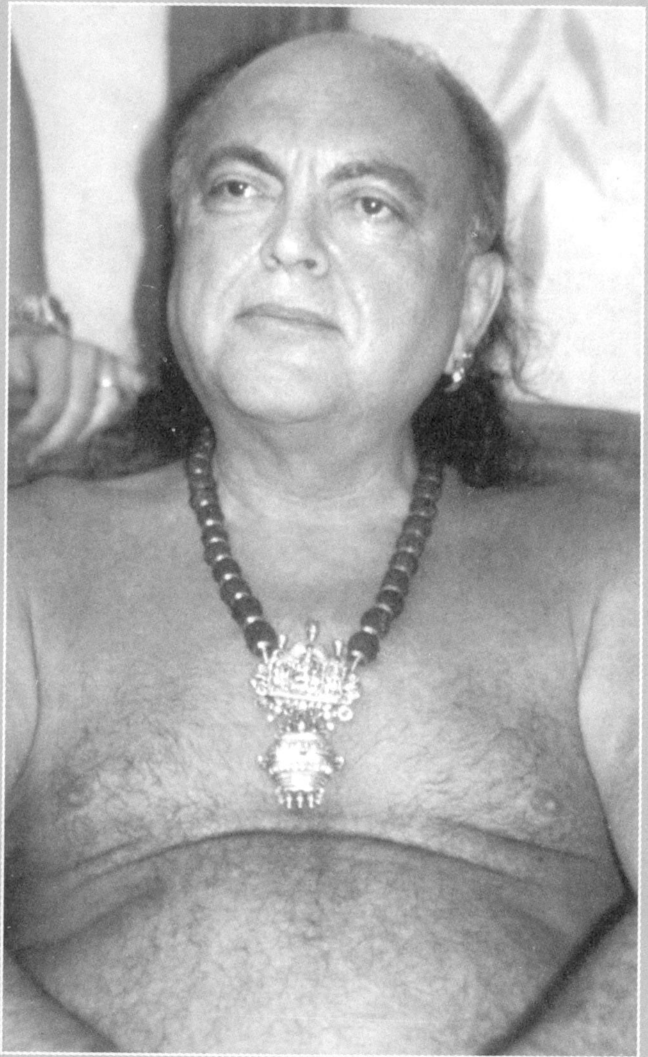

The Mountain Of Attention, 1997

CHAPTER 24

# The Rose in the Thorns

*AVATAR ADI DA SAMRAJ: 1997 was a profound year in the process of bringing a kind of summary conclusion to the continuing Submission to devotees that has been required of Me since 1986. It was a profound year, a profound crisis, a profound sequence of events—all of which are of fundamental significance in the Leela of My Life and Work.* [August 8, 1998]

The religious and Spiritual traditions are full of stories of individuals who came to the point of utter despair in their lives, and who then used that despair as the fuel for their search to Realize God, or Truth, or Reality. Avatar Adi Da Himself went through such a crisis in His early Life. But by the end of 1996, Avatar Adi Da still did not have around Him a significant group of devotees imbued with such renunciate clarity and force—the invincible intention that comes from knowing that one has no other option in life. Beyond His closest women intimates (who were already members, along with Him, of the Ruchira Sannyasin Order, the senior renunciate order of Adidam), Avatar Adi Da had no renunciate link to the wider gathering of His devotees.

Avatar Adi Da had said for years that He absolutely had to have a Lay Renunciate Order[1] to provide this Spiritual connection—individuals who would continue to live in the regional communities or at the Sanctuaries, but

*Formal renunciation in the only-by-Me Revealed and Given Way of Adidam (in the context of either the Ruchira Sannyasin Order or the Lay Renunciate Order) is a form of sadhana that I have Given for those of My devotees who have come to a most fundamental knowledge (and a most profound certainty) that their motivations and desires associated with conditional existence are <u>not</u> <u>ever</u> going to be fulfilled (and, indeed, <u>cannot</u> be fulfilled) in any ultimate sense. On the one hand, such certainty is a kind of "positive" (or ego-transcending) despair relative to conditional existence, but, on the other hand, for My devotee, that certainty goes beyond mere (or "negative", or ego-based, and ego-reinforcing) despair—because coming to such certainty allows the unreserved embrace of the sadhana of (Ultimately, Most Perfectly) Realizing Me.*

*When human beings come to a "negative" point of (merely ego-based, and ego-reinforcing) despair (or to a "negative", or merely depressive, sense that conditional existence is futile), they often attempt to cover up their despair with addictive pleasures of one kind or another (even though the addictive process inevitably makes any pleasure progressively less and less pleasurable). Such an attempted "solution" to the presumed "problem" of conditional existence is obviously false, but (nevertheless) the root-feeling of despair relative to conditional existence is, in a certain sense, a true (and, ultimately, even necessary, and "positive") response to the conditional situation in which human beings find themselves. The life of true and free renunciation in My Spiritual Company is the real "answer" to (or the most "positive" transformation of) this despair.*

*Formal renunciates in the only-by-Me Revealed and Given Way of Adidam are (necessarily) individuals who have "positively" despaired of being fulfilled by conditional existence. For My formal renunciate devotees, "positive" despair breaks the link to the usual cycles of desire, whether cycles of (even extreme) addictive desire or of merely ordinary (or conventional) desire. Therefore, My formal renunciate devotees are unconventional individuals, no longer linked to the world in the usual sense, and they are, thereby, free to be entirely devoted to the by Me Given sadhana of the (Ultimately, Most Perfect) transcendence of egoity (which is the, Ultimately, Most Perfect Realization of Me). And the reason that My formal renunciate devotees are not conventional-minded is that they know (with profound certainty) that the conventional manner of going about life will never result in any ultimate fulfillment, any more than pursuit of the cycle of egoic addiction will ever result in any ultimate fulfillment. Thus, My formal renunciate devotee deeply understands: Egoic desires <u>will</u> <u>not</u> (and cannot) be ultimately fulfilled.*

*Altogether, My formal renunciate devotees are neither conventional-minded, nor addicted to psycho-physical pleasure, nor overcome by ego-based (and ego-reinforcing—and, altogether, "negative", or depressive) despair. Thus, My formal renunciate devotees are free to (with fullest intensity) practice the true by Me Given Yoga of (Ultimately, Most Perfect) ego-transcendence and (Ultimately, Most Perfect) Divine Self-Realization in the midst of the conditions of existence.*

THE LION SUTRA

who would assume the constant obligation to relieve Him of institutional concerns, provide Him with a right and protected circumstance for His Blessing Work, and devote themselves without distraction to the great esoteric process of Realizing Him. Just as, in the months after His Divine Re-Awakening, Avatar Adi Da had been overtaken with the longing to find His devotees, now He was literally consumed with urgency to find those among His devotees who had this renunciate impulse and capability.

## A Spiritual Confirmation

While at the Mountain Of Attention toward the end of 1996, in the midst of His continued Calling for a group of "lay renunciates", Avatar Adi Da began to Work again with a few devotees for the sake of all. Starting at the end of December 1996, the Ruchira Avatar gathered at the Manner of Flowers with a small group of those from whom He expected this renunciate response.

The "consideration" Avatar Adi Da engaged with this gathering group was all-encompassing, and they hardly left His House for two months. The heart of the matter was the nature of true Tantra, and the reason why renunciates in the Way of Adidam—whether sexually active or celibate—must necessarily be Tantric renunciates. Avatar Adi Da reminded everyone that the common renunciate disposition is ascetical. The typical renunciate presumes that it is necessary to withdraw from the world in order to engage in the Real-God-Realizing process, because attention to the world and to relationships only binds one to that which dies.

As He had often done before, Avatar Adi Da was emphasizing that this is not His approach, and never has been. From the beginning of His human life, He could

**The Manner of Flowers, 1996**

not accept a reduced form of Happiness. He wanted to be absolutely Happy here and now, in the body, with His eyes wide Open. He knew that this was possible, because He had been born in that Condition of Love-Bliss-Radiance.

Therefore, Avatar Adi Da has always Taught that the practice of Adidam is not a matter of rejecting (or turning one's back on) who and what one loves, not a matter of trying to avoid love because one is afraid of the "bonding"—and the heart-break—that goes with it. Not at all. The wound of love is an advantage, because it is so deeply disarming. In that state of vulnerability, the devotee may be moved, by Avatar Adi Da's Grace, to Realize the Condition in which love is unthreatened and unqualified.

*If You Will Thus Be Love (By This Devotion To Me), You Must Also Constantly Encounter, Understand, and Transcend The Rejection Rituals Of others who Are, Even If Temporarily or Only Apparently, Bereft Of Divine Wisdom. Therefore, If You Will Be Love (As My Devotee), You Must (In The Way and Manner Of The Heart) Always Skillfully Transcend The Tendency To Become Un-Love (and, Thus, To Become self-Bound, Apparently Divorced From Heart-Communion With Me) In Reaction To The Apparent Lovelessness Of others. And You Must Not Withdraw From Heart-Communion With Me (or Become Degraded By Reactive Un-Love) Even When Circumstances Within Your Intimate Sphere, or Within The Sphere Of Your Appropriate social Responsibility, Require You To Make Difficult Gestures To Counter and Control The Effects or Undermine and Discipline The Negative and Destructive Effectiveness Of The Rituals Of Un-Love That Are Performed By others.*

*For those who Are Committed To Love (and who, Therefore, Always Commune With Me, The One Who Is Love), Even Rejection By others Is Received and Accepted As A Wound, Not An Insult. Even The Heart-Necessity To Love and To Be Loved Is A Wound. Even The Fullest Realization Of Love Is A Wound That Never Heals.*

RUCHIRA TANTRA YOGA

Love is, fundamentally, a motive toward union with an other, and so the only absolute and permanent fulfillment of the motive of human love, is, necessarily, the Condition of Inherently Love-Blissful Unity with Existence Itself. That is Divine Enlightenment. Anything short of That, no matter how apparently satisfactory, contains a subtle limit. It is the ego-limit—the sense of being separate from the beloved—not merely from a particular intimate individual, but from everyone and everything one loves. And so there is an intense frustration in un-Enlightened existence: Love is always limited, and the beloved inevitably dies.

Avatar Adi Da describes this reality as "Raymond's 'problem'"—referring to the plight of Raymond in *The Mummery*, who loves Quandra but loses her, and finds no true re-union possible in the domain of ego-life. Raymond's "problem", Avatar Adi Da was saying, becomes the motive to Divine Enlightenment—the resolve to settle for nothing less than the ultimate resolution of love.

*AVATAR ADI DA SAMRAJ: To love is a terrible form of suffering, which requires Divine Self-Realization. And Divine Self-Realization is a Process of greater and greater love—to the point where love is not in the least diminished by reaction, by circumstance, by possibility, by conditions, by change. Most Ultimately, it becomes Divine (or seventh stage) Samadhi, the Most Perfect Realization of love without "difference"—Which becomes so profound, by My Overwhelming Blessing, that even the body-mind ceases to be discerned in My Love-Bliss-Person. The body-mind becomes like a clay pig in a kiln—"Brightened" to the point of no-discernment, no-"difference". That is the Only Satisfaction, for those who love. For those who do not love—the void, and detachment, and this and that consolation is enough. But, for those who love—nothing is Satisfactory, except absolute self-forgetting Divine Self-Realization. Therefore, love!* [Ruchira Tantra Yoga]

Avatar Adi Da confessed how He had invested Himself totally in this fundamental Ordeal. He had always Submitted Himself to the human bliss and agony of being in love:

*AVATAR ADI DA SAMRAJ: I have always persisted in being a Lover, only. That is My Genius. That is how I got to Realize Most Perfectly.*

*It is not enough to pursue Realization as a relief from suffering. Realization must be of That Which certainly is not suffering.*

*I Am the Avatar of "Brightness". The Way of Adidam is not about seeking to be relieved of suffering. It is about Happiness, it is about being in love with Me. All, as a condition of taking refuge in Me, are obliged to fall in love with Me. And, having accepted this "in-Love", one can no longer say that life is suffering. It is not merely that.*

*The heart-recognition of the Person and the Truth of Existence Itself is the foundation of Adidam. This "in-Love" response to Me is the means whereby My Divine Heart-Transmission is Granted. Thereafter, it is the foundation and essence of practice, until you are established Most Perfectly, by Divine Translation, in My Inherently "Bright" Self-Domain.* [February 21, 1997]

The gatherings in the Manner of Flowers lasted from late December 1996 to early March 1997. The culmination of these gatherings was Avatar Adi Da's acknowledgement that Adidama Sukha Dham and Adidama Jangama Hriddaya had uniquely demonstrated true renunciation, by standing firm in their love of Him through all the tests He had given them. Not only that, the force of their love and one-pointed devotional attention to Him had made possible a unique Yogic event. In Avatar Adi Da's words, they had become Yogically combined with Him, had Spiritually become part of His

Very Form, part of the Divine Pattern of His Incarnation at the most profound level.

While the history of this Process with His intimate female devotees had begun in 1974, it had intensified in 1986, when Avatar Adi Da had re-formed His Mandala of intimate women devotees. At that time, only those four of the nine who were able to make a confession of true renunciation in response to His Divine "Emergence" remained in His most intimate Company. In acknowledgement of their exemplary devotion to Him, Avatar Adi Da gave these four women, in 1988, the title "Kanya"—meaning "a young woman given to the Divine". At the same time, He had continued to test the Kanyas fiercely, making the point to them and to all His devotees that the ego is always there to be dealt with, until the seventh stage of life. As part of this process of testing, some of the Kanyas left His physical Company for brief or extended periods of time—going through deep purifications of karmic tendencies obstructing their Spiritual growth in relationship to Him.

By March 1994, Avatar Adi Da's testing of the four Kanyas had already indicated that it was most likely that only two of them had the unique depth of renunciate practice sufficient to remain in His most intimate sphere. But it was only three years later, at the end of the 1997 gatherings in the Manner of Flowers, that Avatar Adi Da Samraj indicated that this comprehensive testing was over. On March 7, 1997, Avatar Adi Da indicated that the Yogic and Spiritual Union with Him manifested by Adidama Sukha Dham and Adidama Jangama Hriddaya had become full, irrevocable, and unique.[2]

Remarkably, March 7 is the day of the traditional Hindu celebration of Sivaratri, an annual festival celebrated in India in honor of Siva and his consort Parvati. Thus, Sivaratri celebrates the Union of the male and female aspects of the Divine, traditionally understood to

**The Adidama Quandra Mandala, Adidama Sukha Dham and Adidama Jangama Hriddaya**

be Consciousness and Energy. Through His Husbanding of the Divine Goddess in the Vedanta Temple, Avatar Adi Da Revealed that no coming together, or "Union", of Consciousness and Energy is necessary, because, from the seventh stage "Point of View", the apparent duality between Consciousness and Energy is only an illusion. The Divine Person is Consciousness and Energy, or Consciousness-Radiance, the "Bright" Itself. But that Truth had to be Demonstrated in all dimensions of existence, including the human plane, and that is what Avatar Adi Da's love-relationship with the Adidamas exemplifies. This was why He noted the coincidence between the traditional feast of Sivaratri and the completing, or coming to fullness, of His Yogic intimacy with the Adidamas.

Already, in the preceding days, Avatar Adi Da had been speaking of the extraordinary process that had been required in order to establish His Adidama Quandra Mandala[3]—as He now referred (collectively) to the two Adidamas. Both of them had first come to Him during 1974 and His "consideration" with them had taken twenty-three years.

*AVATAR ADI DA SAMRAJ: It is a very profound matter that I have been Working for nearly a quarter of a century with women intimates in this very intensive fashion. I am not interested in conventional relationships, with all the limitations they involve. For Me to enter into such a relationship, I must be able to eliminate all bondage in it. I am not here to be bound My Self, but My Embrace of any such a one carries with it such extraordinary Force of Feeling that I cannot allow her mortality any longer. So it becomes a great Yoga. My relationship to My women intimates has become a great Yoga for Me, in a Fire of "Consideration"—for almost a quarter of a century, in the case of the Adidama Quandra Mandala.*

*My relationship with the Adidamas is an extraordinary Yogic Spiritual matter. And so, to purify it, to set it straight, was of extraordinary importance for Me in My Work altogether. To find those who are so disposed to Me, who can relate to Me in this fashion, is extraordinary in itself. Ultimately, it is entirely a Spiritual matter. It does not exclude sex, but it is not* <u>*about*</u> *sex. That is just how it appears in one aspect of the conjunction. Basically, it is simply a heart-matter.*

*And, now, to endure these relationships—and to absolutely, utterly transcend, and Radiate beyond, the sorrow inherent in them—is a way of describing the Yoga as I live it with My women intimates. Because it is inherently sorrowful, looked at merely in human scale. Bodies die. What can you do about it? How do you transcend the sorrow in it, then? Well, I will Show you. I am Doing it Myself, so I can Show you. You have to "eat" it more profoundly than you ever tasted. That is the "Consideration" for Me—to Incarnate this Love of all with utter profundity, "eating" conditional existence totally, Transcending it utterly, Transfiguring it, and Raising it to My own Domain.*

*So I simply will not function on the basis of the acceptance of the loss of their companionship ever. I am not talking about overcoming that loss in a merely psychological manner. I am talking about eliminating the fault. Well, that is a profound commitment to a woman. It is My Commitment to the entire Cosmic domain. I am Doing the same with all of it. And this epitomizes it, what I Do with the Adidamas.* [March 2, 1997]

What Avatar Adi Da is saying in this remarkable Confession is that the two Adidamas have proven to be more than exemplary renunciates—they are an integral part of His Avataric Incarnation. His Love-Impulse <u>requires</u> that He eternalize His Embrace of them beyond death and beyond all separation.

***The two Adidamas have proven to be more than exemplary renunciates—they are an integral part of His Avataric Incarnation. His Love-Impulse requires that He eternalize His Embrace of them beyond death and beyond all separation.***

When one sees Avatar Adi Da in the company of His Adidama Quandra Mandala, an intuitive understanding arises of the Spiritual profundity of the relationship. Through the Adidamas' worship of Avatar Adi Da and their care of Him, His Heart-Transmission to everyone is magnified. This can literally be felt. He speaks of the Adidamas, in fact, as extensions of His Body. They feel with Him, move with Him, anticipate His needs down to the most subtle details. Under His direct guidance, they have become established in the "Perfect Practice" of Adidam, the practice of Contemplating Him as Consciousness Itself.

Thus, the Adidama Quandra Mandala incarnates the promise that Avatar Adi Da makes to all His devotees: to be perfectly Spiritually united with Him. The Adidamas are simply the first of humanity to go through the ordeal of this transformative process—through truly recognizing the Divinity of Avatar Adi Da, and being transformed by that recognition. In fact, their lives are based on a vow to be submitted to Him utterly, not only for the sake of their own Most Perfect Awakening, but for the sake of the Divine Liberation of all beings.

Avatar Adi Da has often spoken of the biological hypothesis of morphogenetic fields ("M-fields").[4] According to this hypothesis, significant changes in any individual or group within a species increases the potential for that same development to manifest in more, or even all, members of the species. In the context of His Work with His devotees and the world, Avatar Adi Da has always worked with a few for the sake of all. Thus, even the intimacy of the Adidama Quandra Mandala with Avatar Adi Da is not a merely personal matter. It is a sadhana He has given to them for the sake of everyone.

In Eastern iconography one sees Divine personages, male and female, facing each other in sexual embrace. These images represent the Union of Consciousness and Energy—as does the festival of Sivaratri. And this is also what the Adidama Quandra Mandala represent in relation to Avatar Adi Da Samraj. But there is a difference. The Incarnation of Avatar Adi Da does not merely "represent" anything. He is That. He is the Husband of the Goddess, Who has surrendered to His Heart and become the Very Radiance of His Being. He Himself is Complete, Consciousness-Radiance, Siva-Shakti in One.

The Adidamas are simply that Radiance expressing Itself on this plane of gross appearances.

A year after Avatar Adi Da confirmed the full Realization of His sacred intimacy with the Adidama Quandra Mandala, Adidama Jangama Hriddaya made a confession to Avatar Adi Da, in the presence of a small group of devotees:

*ADIDAMA JANGAMA HRIDDAYA: It was exactly three years ago that You fundamentally Initiated me into a most profound depth of the Tantra of Union with You, the Communion of steady love that transcends everything. You said that I had entered into a Yogic Samadhi of Love-Blissful Union that was permanent, that could not be broken. It was a Spiritual and human intimacy, an eternal love-"bond", which had truly always existed, but was now fully manifested. My Beloved, You said that this Yogic Mudra created a foundation for Your Spiritual Work with me and altogether. Now that this foundation was firm, You said, You were going to have to Serve in me the full Process of Most Perfectly Realizing You. To accomplish this, it was necessary for You to purify me of my lifetimes of clinging to You in Your bodily (human) Form or in any conditional Form whatsoever. Only through Realization of Your Perfect State That Transcends death and all conditionality would I be Liberated from the otherwise inescapable sorrow of mortality.*

*After You forewarned me of the necessary ordeal of purification and transformation to come, I was immediately plunged into the most difficult three years, really, of my entire sadhana in Your Company. During those three years, You Tested me and "Threw me away" over and over, in order to purify me of my clinging to You in Your bodily (human) Form, and even of my seeking to find consolation in the experience of Your Spiritual Form, such that my heart-Communion with You would gain the force of unbreakable Identification with You As Consciousness Itself.*

*AVATAR ADI DA SAMRAJ: It was a matter of purifying the disposition of clinging—not the fact of intimate association with Me, but the clinging disposition, which is a manifestation of self-contraction. You have had many lifetimes of association with Deeper Personality Vehicles of Mine, but in this lifetime, you have to Realize Me. So even all those associations preceding the present apparent lifetime needed to be purified. That motive, or structure, of your approach to Me needed to be gone beyond in order for you to Realize Me, such that you would not merely be karmically bound to the Vehicles of My Manifestation.*

*ADIDAMA JANGAMA HRIDDAYA: In that process of purification, Your Spiritual Descent then began to spontaneously Yogically Dissolve the profound sorrow associated with all the forms of my clinging, and also the fear that I had relative to the death of Your bodily (human) Form, and even the anger relative to the outrageousness of mortality. All of that occurred by Your constantly Opening me to Your Love-Bliss through the Power of Your Divine Descent,*

*Which Washes the body-mind-self of all forms of reaction and seeking.*

*I knew that I could not be physically associated with You forever, and that was the terror in it, that was the awful clinginess in it. In this lifetime, You had Granted me the Taste of Your Measureless Love-Bliss, and I wanted to be permanently in that State, but, clearly, this could not be so through clinging to Your physical Incarnation.*

*AVATAR ADI DA SAMRAJ: Instead of Realizing that My Love-Bliss is simply So. No conditions, no efforts are required for It to be So.*

*ADIDAMA JANGAMA HRIDDAYA: It is simply So. But that certainty is given only through Your complete Washing of the illusion that Your Love-Bliss is something we have to seek or that It is conditional and limited by birth and death. That Realization is a Gift that You Grant by Your Grace. You fiercely, and yet with total Love, took me through the Spiritual ordeal necessary to recognize You in this freedom.*

*AVATAR ADI DA SAMRAJ: All My devotees are Called to enter into this very same Process. But what I have Given to all My devotees as the Yoga of Adidam is also pictured in this human sign of My relationship with the Adidamas. The fundamental Yoga of Adidam is the same for all. The Process for each of My devotees is the same as it is for the Adidamas—as a Spiritual and Yogic matter.*

*The Yoga of the devotional relationship to Me is a perpetual Spiritual Yogic Condition. The relationship between the two Adidamas and Me is even beyond relationship. It does not require any social transactions. It does not require more lifetime, even. More lifetime together can be good, enjoyable, humanly happy, and so forth, but it is not required.*

*And why it is not required is what the two of you more and more profoundly will Realize. Therefore, your relationship of human intimacy with Me is Liberating, and not binding. It is Divinely Transfiguring, ultimately. It is Victory over the conditions that are being imposed upon us in this human appearance. The Love-Bliss-Fact that we are cannot be destroyed. Cannot be destroyed. Is not dependent on any condition whatsoever. It is enjoyed under these conditions as they appear presently, but it is not dependent on them. More and more profoundly, this will be your Realization. And so also with all My devotees.* [February 10, 1998]

# "Who Really Wants What I Have to Offer?"

Toward the end of the gatherings in early 1997, while He was speaking of the Spiritual consummation of His relationship with the Adidamas, Avatar Adi Da would often indicate that He was on the verge of Revealing another Blissful Secret.

*AVATAR ADI DA SAMRAJ: I did not come here with an "emptiness" ideology. I came Floating in the "Bright" here. Pleasure in the physical is fundamental right asana.*[5] *I have shown you the Yoga of the Pleasure Dome*[6] *in the immediate sphere of day to day practice—all the disciplines—the mode of life in which you are invested Yogically in this Pleasure Dome of the body, rather than a struggle in the body.*

*There are, of course, difficulties to be endured and dealt with. That is why the sadhana is to be done. But, nonetheless, the asana, the intention maintained, can be that of pleasure—not in the exhausting degenerative sense, but in the sense that, rather than having to punish the body or negate it, you can make it resonant with My "Brightness".*

*You have to be very serious about this. Otherwise, you will just package Adidam and make it into ego-religion.*

*Simplify your lives. Maximize the sacred dimension of your life. Spend significant time in the Communion Hall, in sacred practices of all kinds, including right emotional-sexual practice.*

*There is a mode of concentration—a mode of contemplation, a mudra, asana, attitude, a pattern in the body-mind and beyond it, a pattern of the body-mind—that relates to That Which Is Beyond and coincides with It, is given over to It utterly. And this can be consistently practiced. It is the asana, the mudra, given over, that is coincident with Happiness Itself. And so it is a practice that simply magnifies that. As I said to you long ago, "Come to Me when you are already Happy." That is the Yoga. The Way of the "Bright", then, is not the ordinary way of sacrificing in the negative sense, negating the separate self in that sense, suppressing the separate self in that sense. It is a matter of self-understanding in the context of fullness of Communion with Me, self-giving.*

*The secret of Happiness is in Happiness Itself. It is in Happiness that you Realize Happiness Itself, you Realize Its secrets—the secret of Happiness, of being Happiness, or being in Happiness altogether.*

*Happiness is a combination of pleasure, love, and bliss. It is all of them. It satisfies the requirements of all three, raised to the infinite, perfect, most satisfactory degree—pleasure in the body, love in the heart, and bliss in and above the head.*

*But what do you know about Da in the body-mind, until you give up your body-mind to Me? I am on My Side of your body-mind—you are on yours. You have to surrender and forget yourself, surrender and forget your position on your side of your body-mind. You have to turn your eyes "upstairs". Break through the barrier of your own skull*[7] *to the Matrix Infinitely Above your head. And feel Me—all that is Above and Beyond, and heart-beyond your body-mind. And by all the Means and Process I would Reveal to you, be Attracted by something going on Up There that you just cannot resist.* [February 17, 1997]

In these mysterious sentences, Avatar Adi Da was suggesting that, when His devotees became capable of "Locating" Him at His Spiritual Source-Point Infinitely Above the head, a great and ultimate Spiritual Yoga would be possible. His Words proved to be prophetic—He was preparing the way for His Blessing to manifest as never before.

*"Happiness is a combination of pleasure, love, and bliss. It is all of them. It satisfies the requirements of all three, raised to the infinite, perfect, most satisfactory degree—pleasure in the body, love in the heart, and bliss in and above the head."*

After the intense period of gathering and Spiritual Work Avatar Adi Da had just completed, He was looking for very concrete signs of a change in His devotees, a deeper recognition of Him and a corresponding response to everything required to establish His Work in the world. What were His devotees going to do now? How were they going to provide Him with more and more devotees to Work with? Where was the Lay Renunciate Order? Where were the signs of Spiritual growth and fulfillment of responsibility in the community of devotees worldwide?

On March 11, 1997, Avatar Adi Da Samraj left the Mountain Of Attention for Hawaii, intending to live privately until He would begin to see such a change in devotees.

In the weeks that followed, Avatar Adi Da entered into a fiery period of testing of His devotees—those traveling with Him and all His devotees worldwide. Even for devotees well acquainted with His Divine "Madness" and Avadhootish ways, this period was intense. Just as it had been in Europe, it was up to the devotees with Him to make a choice to stay or leave, based on their love of Him and faith in the unfathomable Process that they knew He must be involved in. He was, again, seeming to throw it all away—testing even His most intimate devotees, calling them to be transformed, and Working for the sake of their Liberation.

After one night at Da Love-Ananda Mahal, the Ruchira Avatar secluded Himself in a house on Kauai offered by a devotee. Some days later, on March 22, there was a conjunction of powerful energies in Nature. It was the day of the spring solstice and also a full lunar eclipse. Winds blew up suddenly around midday and a storm broke out. At the same time, Avatar Adi Da was receiving reports about the work of the institution, culture, community, and mission of Adidam. These reports did not reflect to Him the level of responsibility He was looking for from devotees, and He immediately ordered everyone out of the house.

Avatar Adi Da's acute disturbance continued through the following days, and, on March 24, He declared that He could not spend another night in the house. He said He had felt all along that strong negative energies were associated with the house. When He had first arrived, Avatar Adi Da had asked devotees to clear out everything that was still in storage in the garage and in a room that had been used as an office. Devotees had been insensitive to the urgency of clearing out the storage, but when they eventually did so, they realized that part of the disturbance that Avatar Adi Da was feeling may have been related to two filing cabinets packed with files that belonged to a previous resident there. This man had acted professionally on behalf of individuals who had suffered serious accidents or been killed in accidents, and the files had to do with compensation claims made by the families of the victims.

The very presence of these files in the house had obviously obliged Avatar Adi Da to Work with the forces of violence, grief, fear, and greed on the part of many people—and also, quite possibly, with the disturbed spirits of some of those who had been killed. When Avatar Adi Da Works with negative forces, especially in close physical proximity to Him, He can be extremely fierce, and there is no doubt that the obligation to purify these immediate psychic influences was part of Avatar Adi Da's Ordeal in this house.

Adidama Jangama Hriddaya takes up the story:

*ADIDAMA JANGAMA HRIDDAYA: Beloved Adi Da had been Doing His Divine Work for twenty-five years, and the response was not reflecting the immensity of the Gift that He was Giving. It was evident that He was experiencing cosmic forces of resistance to Him and to His Work.*

*His frustration was ultimate. And in a moment of this frustration, He sat down at His desk and began to write. I knew He was writing, but I did not know what. At this same time, Beloved Adi Da was also looking at a book that the devotee who owned the house had left there:* Nityananda: The Divine Presence.[8]

*At one point, Beloved Adi Da Samraj called me to His room. It was a little room and very hot. The only furnishings were His bed and desk. It was stark. Beloved Adi Da was fasting and would not allow devotees to provide Him with anything. He would not even accept gifts. He sat down and He began to read aloud to me from this book,* Nityananda: The Divine Presence. *He started reading at a place in the book just before Swami Nityananda's Mahasamadhi. Nityananda is speaking to a devotee whose name was Hedge. They were alone and it was just after midnight:*

> *Everyone comes here for money and only money. The more they are given, the more they seek; there is no end to their greed. When they come they are pedestrians sometimes without a proper dwelling place; and when they get the necessities, then comforts and luxuries are demanded: a car, a bungalow, and so on. When earlier prayers are granted in the hope that contentment would follow and that they would then seek higher values, another demand is placed in a never-ending series of wants and desires. Not much point in allowing the body to continue—hence samadhi tomorrow.*
>
> *Nityananda repeated this last sentence three times. Hedge was stunned, for although the master was very weak, the doctors had not found anything clinically wrong, and it was the general expectation that he would improve.* [p. 141]

*Beloved Adi Da went on to read how some who approached Swami Nityananda came only in order to promote their chances of winning at gambling. They would count the number of his fingers visible at any one moment, or the number of steps he took, and use the numbers to bet with. In this way, people trivialized, and failed to use, the Grace of his company.*

*At the end of His reading, Beloved Adi Da said, "This is how I feel, with everything I have Given." As He spoke, I could feel the entire community of His devotees—how so many of us had come to Him twenty-five years earlier and how He had never ceased to Work with us, even fulfilling many of our ordinary desires. The urge to ordinary fulfillment had been strong in us, and we had trivialized His Company over and over again. We had not really embraced the Spiritual opportunity of His Company. We had stopped short. True devotion, true understanding, true recognition of Him—we had stopped short of all of it. And I could feel the Tapas it was creating in Him. His Body was flushed with agitation, and He kept asking me, "Are you getting any response? Is anybody understanding what I am saying?" But no response I brought to Him was coming from the same depth at which He was communicating. "That's not it," He would say. "You're not seeing Who I <u>Am</u>, and you're not really here based on the recognition of the Truth That Transcends all of this—the Truth That you have already received, That I have already Given you."*

*Beloved Adi Da told me that, at the time of his Maha-Samadhi, Nityananda had kept asking for people to come to him, but there wasn't anybody there. After waiting fruitlessly, Nityananda, said that if anyone <u>had</u> responded truly, in the moment, it would have postponed his death. But that did not occur.*

> *The master then repeatedly asked where Swami Janananda was and why he had not come. This will always remain a mystery as he*

*came only after the Mahasamadhi and the dispatch of a cable. Hedge was deeply shocked; in tears he appealed to the master to cancel or at least postpone the samadhi. Nityananda replied:*

*It is possible only if a few devotees come forward and make a request; not any devotees but those imbued with desireless devotion, feeling, and love . . . Is there a bhakta pundalika around? [Pundalika was a great devotee who made the Lord of Pandharpur wait for him.] Even one such is enough and the samadhi will be canceled. When such a devotee is present, even God cannot take leave without his permission, or be able to disengage himself from the bond of his pure love.*

*Then suddenly pointing his index finger at Engineer Hedge, he asked, "Have you got nishkama bhakti [desireless devotion]?" Hedge tearfully confessed that he did not have such unalloyed devotion. He told me that though he was a sincere devotee and would do anything ordered by the Master, he could not claim to be desireless.*

*During the remaining hour or so, the Master asked for two or three other persons who were available in Ganeshpuri. These could not be contacted readily or brought to the spot at that time of the night. Engineer Hedge was then asked not to worry about them. . . .*

*At about 9:30 A.M. Gopalmama noticed that the Master's body was very hot. When he conveyed this to him, the Master replied, "It will be like that," implying that it was the normal condition at that stage. He then repeated the words that he had reportedly said often in the last months: "Sadhu become Swami; Swami become Deva*

> *[God] to some, Baba and Bhagawan [God] to others; Deva will now enter samadhi, sthira [constant] samadhi." According to Gopalmama these were the last audible words uttered by the Master before entering mahasamadhi.* [pp. 141-42, 144]

*After He read this, Beloved Adi Da explained again that what Nityananda expressed is just what He experiences. "There isn't one devotee who really wants What I have to Offer," Beloved Adi Da told me.*

*He was sitting in His chair with one leg crossed over the other. The fragility of His Incarnation in this Form was deeply impressed upon me in that moment, as you can imagine it would be with Beloved Adi Da Speaking in that way. It communicated to me how dependent He is on the response of everyone and how absolutely Committed He is to His Work to Liberate all beings. It was obvious to me that He could have relinquished the body in that house. But it was also obvious that He was not going to, because His Commitment to living beings is so great. Instead, He was going to continue to require the true response from His devotees for the sake of everyone.*

*My feeling was that, over the past twenty-five years, we had enclosed Beloved Adi Da instead of bringing Him out to the world. And it felt to me that now He was throwing this enclosure away, in order to make room for the world to receive Him. He was doing it with great fierceness, throwing every single person out of this in-turned enclosing of Him and His Work and His body—in order to make this room.*

# Hridaya Rosary

After leaving this house, every time Avatar Adi Da would move, He carried His own briefcase with papers in it. As Adidama Jangama Hriddaya had observed, He was writing. But no one knew what.

Finally, on March 29, Avatar Adi Da passed His writings to the Adidama Quandra Mandala. It was a new Text, *Four Thorns Of Heart-Instruction*, written in the midst of this extreme Ordeal. After reading the manuscript, which they quickly recognized to be the consummation of all of His twenty-five years of Instruction, the Adidamas spoke to Avatar Adi Da of their sense of what had occurred in the preceding days. They told Him that, during His writing of the new Text, they had observed that He had gone through a Yogic Ordeal that had sealed the shift in His Life and Work that He had been looking to establish since 1996—and really since the time of the Initiation of His Divine "Emergence" in 1986.

After hearing their confession, Avatar Adi Da Samraj confirmed that this was indeed the case. As in January 1986, He had relinquished everything, and could easily have given up the body. But His Passion for the Divine Liberation of beings had drawn Him back, in order to Work at an even more profound level than before. The passing on of the manuscript marked, He said, "a perfect moment"—the definitive end of the twenty-five-year Revelation period and the real beginning of His Divine "Emergence" Work. He wrote the date "March 29, 1997" at the end of the manuscript.

In *Four Thorns Of Heart-Instruction*, which He later renamed *Hridaya Rosary* (retaining the former title as a subtitle), Avatar Adi Da Samraj describes the Process of Spiritual Initiation that He Grants in His physical Company to those who are prepared—prepared by their spontaneous heart-recognition of Him and by the

**Avatar Adi Da Samraj granting Darshan in Hawaii after *Hridaya Rosary* had been written**

*Let the heart Melt Into*
*My Heart,*
*Which Is*
*The By Me Spiritually Revealed*
*"Bright" Rose Garden Of Love.*

*Let the head Melt Into*
*My Head,*
*Which Is*
*The By Me Spiritually Revealed*
*"Bright" Rose*
*Of Infinitely Ascended*
*Bliss-Light.*

*Let the Total body Melt Into*
*My Divine Body,*
*Which Is*
*The By Me Spiritually Revealed*
*Garden Air,*
*The Fragrant*
*All-and-all-Surrounding,*
*and All-and-all-Pervading,*
*Space*
*Of Equanimity,*
*Of Pleasure,*
*Of Delight,*
*Of Beauty,*
*Of Joy,*
*Of Love-Bliss,*
*Of "Brightness"*
*Itself.*

*Let the breathing Melt Into*
*My Breathing,*
*Until I Breathe you*
*Into My*
*"Bright"*
*Eternal*
*Palace*
*and*
*Domain*
*Of*
*Perfect Happiness.*

HRIDAYA ROSARY

practices and disciplines He gives to devotees practicing the Way of Adidam in its fullness.[9] Avatar Adi Da describes this unique Initiation as the Infusion of His Divine Spiritual Body into the body-mind of His devotee. This Spiritual Infusion starts from His Place of "Brightness" Infinitely Above the head and Descends into and down through the body-mind, "Melting" every part of the being in His Love-Bliss.

*Hridaya Rosary*, meaning "The Rose Garden of the Heart" ("Hridaya" is Sanskrit for "heart", and the original ancient meaning of "rosary" is "rose garden"), is a Love-Song. He is speaking, as He says, to "all heart-intelligent beings", Calling to every one to run to Him—not out of curiosity, or out of a desire to get something, but out of heart-recognition. To come running to the beloved is the natural response of anyone who is in love. To come running to Avatar Adi Da Samraj is the immediate impulse of those who receive His Revelation and fall into His Heart.

Such heart-recognition has immense implications in one's life. It means self-surrender, self-forgetting, through devotional love of Him. This is where the "thorny" part lies. "My Four Thorns", Adi Da says in *Hridaya Rosary*, "root out the ego from the Garden of the Heart. They are the ordeal of self-discipline, the counter-egoic incision, that is required." In other words, there is a life of practice to do, both in and out of Avatar Adi Da's physical Company, that involves the relinquishment of self-contraction, the relinquishment of the separative, egoic point of view. And that is an ordeal, as Adi Da has always made clear. But He is the Distraction, the Bliss of His true devotee, even in the midst of that ordeal of self-transcendence. He says in *Hridaya Rosary*: "You must recognize Me, the Rose in the Thorns. My Thorned Medication becomes Acceptable only in My Blessing Company, the Eternal Company of the Single (and Indivisible) White Rose."

Starting on April 7, at a newly rented beach House in Kauai, Avatar Adi Da began to Grant formal Darshan again—to the devotees who had been serving Him directly and to a few from the worldwide gathering who had been waiting in hotels on the island for some time, living a process of retreat and hoping and praying for an opportunity of Darshan. Although only a small number of devotees were in the room for these occasions, other devotees on the island reported feeling Him profoundly at random times—the Blissful "thickness" of His Spiritual Transmission Descending on them wherever they happened to be—from the Communion Hall to the supermarket.

After four or five days, however, Avatar Adi Da again dismissed devotees from His Company, left the house, and stayed in a simple hotel with only one devotee attending Him. He was deeply distressed because of news He had just received about the koi fish at the Manner of Flowers. Stuart Camps, the zookeeper at the Mountain Of Attention, tells the story:

*STUART: Avatar Adi Da has a profound relationship and intimacy with all creatures. The Japanese koi that lived within the large pond in the beautiful garden surrounding the Manner of Flowers received much care and attention from Him whenever He was living there. Many of them were personally named by Him. "Sharky", "Fatso", "Diamond Back", "Swami", and others would come daily to His outstretched hand to be fed and Lovingly Blessed by Him.*

*In March of 1997, these fish suddenly began to die of a rare spring bacterial outbreak in their pond. Adi Da Samraj immediately felt the loss of these much cherished non-human devotees. The deaths of these fish were no different to Him than if He had heard that as many humans had died.*

*All 109 of the koi perished from this sudden outbreak. I communicated daily to Beloved Adi Da about how many, and which ones, had died each day. It was excruciating. When there were no more left, we emptied the pond, cleaned it and purified it with a sacred ceremony of release and healing. Something very significant had occurred in this incident which we did not yet fully understand. We refilled the pond and filled it with 100 water lilies, as Beloved Adi Da had asked us to do.*

**Adi Da Samraj feeding the koi fish at the Manner of Flowers, 1995**

*This profound and saddening incident was felt by His devotees as a significant Spiritual lesson. Throughout His own Life, Adi Da has always maintained a unique Spiritual sensitivity to all creatures, human or otherwise. In fact, through His rare intimacy with non-humans, Beloved Adi Da has Vowed to protect them from the ongoing insensitivities of human beings. This Sacred Vow of His had now been violated. His Instruction to us about this incident showed us that, in a very real sense, His Intention to Liberate all beings (human and non-human) cannot be fulfilled without the real response of His devotees. In order for His Vow to the non-humans to be truly effective, it must also become our vow, because those who recognize and respond to Him as the Divine are one of His principal ways 'into' the world.*

*These lessons for all of us did not go unheeded. Our Guru's Divine Intimacy with, and Blessing of, all beings is a responsibility we must also accept. We must serve the possibility for real Life, Love, and Happiness for all the beings of this world.*

During this same period, Avatar Adi Da was having difficulty walking, owing to a misalignment that had developed in one of His toes. Charles Seage, Avatar Adi Da's personal physician, arranged for surgery to be done locally, after which Avatar Adi Da was confined to a wheelchair, to allow the foot to heal. It was just over two weeks before one of the most important celebrations in the history of Adidam—the twenty-fifth anniversary of the beginning of His Teaching Work at the Melrose Ashram (April 25, 1972).

There had been much discussion of where Avatar Adi Da might choose to spend the anniversary—remain in Kauai, go to Los Angeles, or, conceivably, return to the Mountain Of Attention, where plans were in progress to bring together the largest number of devotees ever to gather in one place. In that moment, however, it seemed highly unlikely that He would feel able to celebrate the anniversary at the Mountain Of Attention.

But then, as sometimes happens in such moments of impasse, an indication in Avatar Adi Da's body moved Him in a particular direction that had great consequences. This was what had occurred in September 1995, when He had suddenly been obliged to leave Adidam Samrajashram to have eye surgery. Now, an X-ray revealed a large kidney stone. Charles advised Avatar Adi Da to go to Los Angeles for the operation, and He consented to do so.

And so, on April 14, still in a very fiery Disposition, Avatar Adi Da had the bandages removed from His foot and left Kauai for California. He arrived in Los Angeles early in the morning and was met by devotees, including Daniel Bouwmeester (one of Avatar Adi Da's doctors for many years), who wheeled Him to His car and drove Him to a secluded hotel to prepare for an appointment with the urologist and then the kidney surgery the next day.

## The Four Thorns

Once in Los Angeles, Avatar Adi Da began to show a different Sign. He was pleased by the service of devotees and the beauty and calm of the place they had provided for Him. The surgery was straightforward and uncomplicated, to the great relief of everyone involved.

Several hours after the operation, Avatar Adi Da was released from the hospital. That night, however, He was in a good deal of pain—not unexpectedly so, but it was obviously desirable to give Him some pain medication. Administering medication to Avatar Adi Da is not at all straightforward, because He is always conducting intense psychic and Spiritual energies which affect His body-chemistry, and which make Him particularly sensitive to the effects of gross substances like drugs. Charles has seen Him suffer residual effects for even ten years after being given certain medications. In this case, however, Avatar Adi Da had no apparent reaction to the pain medication, and, after leaving the hospital and returning to the hotel where He was staying, He began to associate with devotees there, laughing and joking by the side of the swimming pool.

On April 20, two days after the surgery, Charles and Daniel took Avatar Adi Da back to the surgeon's office near the hospital for some routine post-operative procedures. Once these were done, Avatar Adi Da was free to go. The urologist suggested that a strong pain medication would not be necessary any more, but just an ordinary over-the-counter medication. But then he went on to say that it would be advisable for Avatar Adi Da to take an anti-spasmodic drug for the urinary tract—a basically innocuous and common medication.

Just at the moment when the urologist was recommending this and passing over the pill, Charles had his back turned. Someone on the hospital staff had asked him a question. And so he did not notice that Avatar Adi Da was hesitant about taking the drug. By the time Charles' attention was focused on Him again, Avatar Adi Da had already taken the medication. No one thought much of it in the moment. Everyone was just relieved that the surgery was over and had gone well.

Avatar Adi Da was taken to His car in the multi-story parking lot by the hospital, and another car followed behind, driven by Thankfull Hastings. Just as they were driving out on to the road, Thankfull received a sudden message from the car in front on his radio. Avatar Adi Da seemed to be reacting to the drug He had just taken. Both cars immediately pulled to the curb and Thankfull ran over and opened the door of the other car. He saw Avatar Adi Da in the back seat. Avatar Adi Da's head had fallen back, His face was bright red, and His eyes were bloodshot and watering. He was clearly in the throes of some acute allergic reaction.

Both cars headed back up into the parking lot. By the doctor's office, Thankfull jumped out and set up a wheelchair for Avatar Adi Da. He was shouting and shaking Avatar's Adi Da's body in the attempt to keep Him bodily conscious. With the help of Jake Siglain, the driver of the other car, Thankfull lifted Avatar Adi Da out into the wheelchair. Then, accompanied by the Adidamas and the Trimada, all of whom were deeply distressed by now, Thankfull rushed Avatar Adi Da to the doctor's office.

Avatar Adi Da was slumped over in the wheelchair, and had to be held in place on each side to prevent His body from sliding out. Again and again His eyes would roll up and His head would go limp, and then He would jerk Himself forcibly back into the body. It was clear that He was Working almost aggressively, moment to moment, to stay connected with bodily consciousness.

Charles and Daniel had arrived by this time, and they lifted Avatar Adi Da out of the wheelchair and laid Him down on a couch in the urologist's office. The urologist himself had already left for the airport to attend a conference in San Francisco, and so Charles and Daniel began to perform emergency procedures themselves. Avatar Adi Da was continuing to show extreme symptoms—an anaphylactic allergic reaction to the drug. His tongue had swelled up, causing Him to gag and obstructing His breathing. In an attempt to move Him into a position that would ease His breathing, Thankfull raised Avatar Adi Da's head and sat behind Him, supporting His back. His head was burning hot and His feet were very cold—signs that the life-energy was still ascending out of His body.

The Adidamas and the Trimada bathed His head to cool it, and vigorously massaged His Feet and hands. He began to speak in a whisper, saying that He was experiencing extreme stress over the heart-region and numbness in the hands and feet. Avatar Adi Da now spoke constantly about His symptoms, as another means of staying associated with the body.

Charles administered intravenous antihistamine, which began to reverse the symptoms. But it was nearly two hours before Avatar Adi Da's condition was normalized to the point where He could leave the doctor's office. Avatar Adi Da fell asleep in the car on the way back to the hotel, exhausted from the intense Yogic effort to stay associated with His physical body. Later, as He lay on His bed, surrounded by the Adidamas, the Trimada, and Thankfull, everyone felt deeply sobered and saddened by the raw fact of His bodily fragility. There were no records known to Charles (or to the urologist) of such a reaction to the drug. But Avatar Adi Da's body is a unique Yogic mechanism that cannot be explained, or its processes predicted, in conventional medical terms.

Avatar Adi Da later confirmed that His experience had been of completely dissociating from the body and almost passing out of it altogether. But His own Divine Intention and His Yogic capability to remain Incarnate had saved Him from the freak effects of this drug. He Himself expressed His extreme frustration at the fragility of the body. In spite of all that had been involved in making His bodily human Incarnation and the extraordinary importance of preserving His bodily Presence here at this point in His Work, all could have been lost in that one senseless moment. Nearly a year later, Avatar Adi Da was still reporting subtle but unpleasant effects from this drug.

Around the same time as He was reporting these continuing drug effects, Avatar Adi Da referred to the unparalleled ordeal of those weeks preceding and following His Revelation of *Hridaya Rosary*.

*AVATAR ADI DA SAMRAJ: The time when I was writing* Hridaya Rosary *was an extraordinary, hellish ordeal! Yes. My Submission to the toes here—not merely up top here, and shining out, but to the toes—is not "fun". The making of this Vehicle of Transmission, and this Structure of Transmission, in all planes, is extraordinary Work. Real Spiritual life—especially as I must animate it, in My unique Work—is not the "smiling time" people might like to imagine.* [February 10, 1998]

The reference to "Four Thorns" in the subtitle of *Hridaya Rosary* is not merely to the devotee's ordeal of sadhana required to receive the "Rose"—or the Gift of Avatar Adi Da's Spiritual Infusion. Avatar Adi Da indicated that the "Thorns" refer also to His own Divine Ordeal to bring devotees to the point where they could begin to recognize Him truly.

In particular, He said, the "Four Thorns" should be understood as a reference to the four wounds He had suffered in His physical body: the glaucoma in His two eyes, the foot operation, and the kidney stone (the latter two wounds on His left, and physically weaker, side).[10]

These "Thorns" are an enduring reminder of the depth of surrender to the human state required of Avatar Adi Da in order to bring His Hridaya-Rose—or "Bright" Divine Heart-Fullness—down into the world. Now that He has Accomplished this in His bodily human Lifetime, His Invitation and Gift stand forever:

*Again and Again,*
*Neverendingly,*
*Come Running To My Bodily (Human) Form*
*(and, forever After My Physical Human Lifetime,*
*To My,*
*In the every particular then present-time,*
*Formally Ruchira-Sannyasin-Order-Acknowledged*
*Ruchira Sannyasin Devotee-Agent)*
*To Luxuriate*
*In My Love-Bliss-"Bright"*
*Palace Garden,*
*Wherein*
*Forever Sits*
*(Upon A Throne Of Imperishable Light)*
*The Eternal Hridaya Rose*
*Of My Divine*
*(and Always Blessing)*
*Presence*
*and Person.*

HRIDAYA ROSARY

*Listen to Me.*
*Hear Me.*
*See Me.*
*Accept My "Bright" Gift*
*of Love,*
*of Bliss,*
*of Pleasure,*
*of Happiness,*
*and Not Less.*

*Until*
*My Outshining "Brightness"*
*Opens the Eyes*
*In My Room,*
*you are the body,*
*attention,*
*heart,*
*and breath.*
*Give these*
*In Me,*
*From your side*
*of the Fence,*
*and I,*
*From My Side,*
*Will Always Call*
*and Greet you,*
*Heart to heart,*
*Until the Gate*
*Flies Open,*
*and, With Heart-Tears*
*that Melt the Running-Ground,*
*all "difference" Washed*
*By Wideness Alone,*
*We Speak and Love,*
*Forever,*
*In My Imperishable Domain.*

HRIDAYA ROSARY

Los Angeles, April 1997

CHAPTER 25

# "I Have Accomplished What I Came Here to Do"

It was now only a few days before the twenty-fifth anniversary of the opening of the Melrose Ashram, and, by an unexpected conjunction of events, Avatar Adi Da was back in Los Angeles, the place of His Divine Re-Awakening and His first Teaching Work. Meanwhile, devotees at the Mountain Of Attention sent their fervent pleas to Avatar Adi Da, asking Him to Grace them with His Company at the upcoming celebration. Nearly eight hundred devotees from all over the world were gathering to make the occasion the most full and ecstatic event in the history of His Work.

## The Twenty-Fifth Anniversary of Avatar Adi Da's Divine Revelation Work

Avatar Adi Da moves with the signs of devotion, and He could not refuse so much longing in so many. And so, on April 23, He traveled to the Mountain Of Attention. Devotees received Him at the main Gate to the Sanctuary, lifted Him into a palanquin, and carried Him straight down through the heart of the Sanctuary to Seventh Gate Shrine (which houses golden casts of His Hands and golden imprints of His Feet). There He alighted and Granted Darshan, sitting where

He had sat many times before, facing a packed hillside with all faces turned to Him reflecting every variation of heart-break, joy, and blissful absorption in the Guru. After maybe half an hour, Avatar Adi Da picked up His staff and walked through Seventh Gate, which opens into the enclosure of the Manner of Flowers.

*STUART CAMPS: Avatar Adi Da walked quietly past the pond where the koi had died, and into the House. Later that evening, Adi Da stood at the large windows overlooking the pond. He was swaying slightly from side to side, quietly weeping tears of profound sorrow and Blessing. Before sleeping that night, He went out to the pond and knelt upon the wooden bridge which spans one section of the water. Adi Da lifted His glasses and wiped His eyes, flicking His tears softly into the pond. Then He rose to His Feet, dipped the end of His Staff into the water, and began swirling it across the surface and splashing water right across the pond until every inch of water had been Blessed.*

*Since that time, Adi Da has rarely Spoken of the death of the koi, but, whenever He has, I am always reminded of His Unconditional Love for all beings.*

As in 1986, a huge tent was erected at the Mountain Of Attention, and Avatar Adi Da initiated hundreds of people at a time into the Spiritual practice He describes in *Hridaya Rosary*. There were devotees present from all over the world, ranging from some who had witnessed the entire twenty-five years of Avatar Adi Da's Work to others who had become devotees only days or weeks before.

Through the weeks of the celebration, Avatar Adi Da gave more and more Darshan, now sitting with a small group in the Manner of Flowers, now walking across the Sanctuary from His House to the thermal baths, to the zoo, to His Library, regarding each one of the hundreds of devotees who lined His path with an ineffably deep

**The Twenty-Fifth Anniversary Celebration at the Mountain Of Attention, 1997**

and sweet Regard. He was simply assuming His Freedom—His Freedom to Bless beings without any other obligation. And this Freedom, so hard won, was allowing the most extraordinary magnification of His Siddhi.

In these incomparable occasions of Avatar Adi Da's Darshan, His devotees could feel Him carrying them beyond self-contraction, shaking them loose from old limits, doubts, and problems, unleashing an indescribable ecstasy and certainty of His Victory in their hearts. Some felt Him as nectarous Light, Radiating in the head and heart and the whole body. Many confessed feeling an intimacy with Him stronger than anything in the universe and a certainty of His absolute Power to Liberate them. His devotees were constantly making such confessions to Him, overcome with emotion at His Grace and the Perfection of His Work. They could now sense the truth of what He had always said—that the great Leela, the greatest epoch of His Life, would be that of His universal Blessing Work. Every devotee had his or her own way of expressing the feeling of Avatar Adi Da's silent Blessing—as piercing "Brightness", as an Ocean of Bliss and Pleasure, as utter, unconditional Love.

Dina Lautman, who was on retreat at the time at the Mountain Of Attention, gives an account of the first Darshan she attended at the Manner of Flowers. She is describing her experience of Avatar Adi Da's Divine Spiritual Body, the feeling of Him as a tangible Spiritual Presence, Touching and Pervading and Surrounding her.

*DINA: As soon as I sat down, I felt Beloved Adi Da Penetrating me from above my head and down to the toes. Everything in between Him and me was melted. The head opened, and became a soft and sensory organ, a feeling means to receive His Love-Blissful Transmission. Then I began to sense Him everywhere in the room, Surrounding and in-Filling all. It was associated with a "Brightness",*

**Darshan in the Manner of Flowers, 1997**

*a Light, but it was primarily a tangible feeling of Him. It could be described as a "thickness" that was completely alive. I felt embraced, enveloped by Beloved Adi Da's Divine Spiritual Body. Soon I felt no "difference", no separation. "I" was gone, and there was simply a Fullness and most pleasurable absorption in Him. This went on night after night in the sittings with Him.*

In early April, Avatar Adi Da spoke of the simplicity of His Work and of everyone's approach to Him henceforth:

*AVATAR ADI DA SAMRAJ: The twenty-five years of struggle, like all of the years previous in this Lifetime, have been in very ordinary circumstances. And all that, seen in retrospect, has served. It caused Me to generate My Wisdom-Teaching. That Wisdom-Teaching is extraordinary and must not be lost. But then I had to drop that mode of My Play with devotees. I had to get out of it. My own Work goes on. People come and sit with Me. That is what I am here to do. I am just going to Do My Work. I am here to see people gather around Me to do this, very intensively, day after day.* [April 11, 1997]

## Heart-Satisfaction

In the weeks following the celebration of His twenty-five-year Revelation, Avatar Adi Da Samraj spoke with a small group of devotees in the Manner of Flowers about the profound devotional relationship to Him that flowers in one who recognizes Him truly.

*ANTONINA RANDAZZO: Beloved Adi Da, didn't You Say that You Worked out the last twenty-five years when You were Writing* Hridaya Rosary*? You have mentioned that You specifically Worked through something during that period and Released the twenty-five years of Your Teaching Work.*

*AVATAR ADI DA SAMRAJ: I have "Meditated" every one, every thing—all that I have had to Assume, Take on, Submit to, Combine with, Identify with, and so forth, all that I have had to Struggle with, Endure—everything altogether of the last twenty-five years. During all these years in My bodily (human) Manifestation here, I have Submitted to everything associated with the gross personality (in other words, the gross aspect of My Appearance here), everything associated with the Deeper Personality—all aspects of the Vehicle of My Avataric-Incarnation Appearance. I excluded nothing from My "Meditation", My "Consideration". Every thing, every one, is in My Samyama.*

*I have, over and over again, Communicated to everyone, during all those years, that the Way of Adidam is the devotional relationship to Me. The Way of Adidam is the Way of life you live when you rightly, truly, fully, and fully devotionally recognize Me, and when (on that basis) you rightly, truly, fully, and fully devotionally respond to Me.*

*In order to truly practice the devotional relationship to Me, you must become profoundly sensitized in your feeling. Not only must you become more and more profoundly sensitized to Me, you must also become more sensitized altogether—because, if you are truly sensitive, you are sensitive to everything. Thus, in the process of becoming increasingly sensitized to Me, you also become open and sensitized to the limitations of gross human existence. If you are so sensitized, your heart-need is profound—and, likewise, your heart-Satisfaction is profound when you devotionally recognize Me. Once you have devotionally recognized Me, you would not, if you are truly sensitized, have it be otherwise. You do not want that sensitivity to be diminished or lost. Therefore, you volunteer the body-mind to the Yoga of devotion to Me, the Process of devotional Communion with Me. And that Yoga (or Process), Itself, is a profoundly feeling matter, moment to moment. . . .*

*You are here.* [Avatar Adi Da holds up one hand.] *And I Am here.* [Avatar Adi Da holds His other hand opposite the first.] *You cannot get from one to the other. You cannot get "outside" yourself in order to get to Me. You cannot cross over whatever there is "in between" the two hands here. You want to work on all of that "in between" and get to the "other end" of it, over to the "Me" Side here. That is the religious "program", as it is usually conceived.*

*If you rightly, truly, fully, and fully devotionally recognize Me, everything "in between" vanishes. All of that is inherently without force. In devotionally responsive devotional recognition of Me, a spontaneous kriya of the principal faculties occurs, such that they are loosed from the objects to which they are otherwise bound—loosed from the patterns of self-contraction. The faculties turn to Me—and, in that turning, there is tacit devotional recognition of Me, tacit experiential Realization of Me, of Happiness Itself, of My Love-Bliss-Full Divine Self-Condition. That "Locating" of Me opens the body-mind spontaneously. When you have been thus Initiated by Me, it then becomes your responsibility, your sadhana, to continuously Remember Me, to constantly return to this devotional recognition of Me, in which you are Attracted to Me, in which you devotionally respond to Me spontaneously with all the principal faculties. . . .*

*There is, in the midst of conditionally manifested existence, a pattern which is Truth-Realizing, Happiness-Realizing. But that pattern is not, in and of itself, Truth-Realizing. It is merely a pattern. When there is right, true, full, and fully devotional recognition of Me, the body-mind of one who (thus) devotionally recognizes Me spontaneously enters into the pattern of rightness, the asana that is the pattern coincident with Happiness Itself and coincident with the entire Process that is the Realization and the Demonstration of Happiness Itself, the True and experienced Realization of That Which is altogether Unqualifiedly Satisfactory. To Find That is to be reborn. It requires a complete transformation of point of view.*

*The ordinary gross human being, separated out, is not a mode of Happiness Itself. It can have pleasures and look forward to things, but it is mortal and suffers everything associated with that. But, for one who is aware, discriminating, sensitive at all, human physical existence (or any mode of merely physical existence), in and of itself, is not satisfactory. It is mortal, temporary, and subject to all kinds of difficulties, along with whatever may be deemed to be its pleasures. Human physical existence is not, in and of itself, satisfactory. It is not a condition of Happiness. Sometimes, there is relative happiness—but I am Talking about Happiness Itself, Utter Satisfactoriness.*

*The heart is not satisfied by dissatisfaction. So, until there is the Most Perfect Realization of Happiness, the Most Perfect Realization of That Condition Which Is Happiness Itself—the heart seeks, the being seeks. It will not stop. No matter what it seems to be doing externally or superficially or merely socially, the heart is dis-eased—unless Utterly Satisfactory Existence is Realized. . . .*

*You cannot merely read My Wisdom-Teaching and "get it". Adidam (or the Way of the Heart), the Way That I Alone Reveal and Give to you, is a relationship, not a technique. Therefore, you cannot "get it" merely by reading any of My Books. You cannot "steal" it from Me. You cannot "buy" it, and you cannot "earn" it. You cannot be so incredibly "good" that you must be Given it, and you cannot be so dreadfully "bad" that you must not (or cannot) be Given it.*

*The only-by-Me Revealed and Given Way of Adidam is a Free Gift. But it is a Gift that Flows in the heart-relationship that exists between Me and each of My true devotees. And if you know how to live the devotional relationship with Me, then the Gift Flows to you—I Flow to you. So, I have made My Revelation Full. I have Said It, even in words. But, even though I have Given you My Revelation Fully (even in words), you cannot "get It" by reading the words merely. You can do all kinds of things with those words—but you cannot, thereby, "get It". You cannot Realize My Revelation—you cannot "get" the Gift—unless It is Given to you, and you are willing and prepared to receive It. And you cannot ("successfully") "work on" yourself—such that you become willing and prepared to receive My Gift. Rather, you can, and will, receive My Free Divine Gift (of My Avatarically Self-Revealed Divine Form, and Presence, and State) if and when you devotionally recognize Me and devotionally respond to Me.*

*If you rightly, truly, fully, and fully devotionally recognize Me, and (on that basis) rightly, truly, fully, and fully devotionally respond to Me—everything that seems to stand between you and Realization of Me Melts.*

*Now, and forever hereafter—I am never not here. It is simply that you must heart-recognize Me (in and As and by Means of My Avataric Self-Revelation of My Self-Evidently Divine Person). And, when you thus heart-recognize Me, you must (and, indeed, if your heart-recognition of Me is heart-true and heart-profound, you will—from then, and forever thereafter) heart-respond to Me (by practicing the only-by-Me Revealed and Given Way of Adidam—Which is the one and only by-Me-Revealed and by-Me-Given Way of the Heart).* [May 20, 1997]

◆ ◆ ◆

*I Am the Inherently egoless Person, and the Real Condition, That Is Always Already The Case. Therefore, whatever requires time—to be experienced, or to change, or to pass away—must be transcended in Me. And, likewise, whatever occupies space—or is, in space, separately defined, or appearing, or changing, or passing, or perceived, or conceived—must be transcended in Me. Otherwise, whatever arises—in time, or in space, or in space-time—is merely an ego-reinforcing pattern of separateness, and suffering, and seeking. And, for this reason, all conditional experiencing and knowing is, in itself, merely and only a ceaseless failure to Realize the Love-Bliss-Happiness That Is Reality and Truth. . . .*

*The greatest Satisfaction, the only true Satisfaction, is to be Overwhelmed by That Which Is Love-Bliss, and Which Is Infinitely and Divinely Greater than yourself. If you devotionally recognize Me, you know that I Am the One Who Divinely Overwhelms you and all.* [Hridaya Rosary]

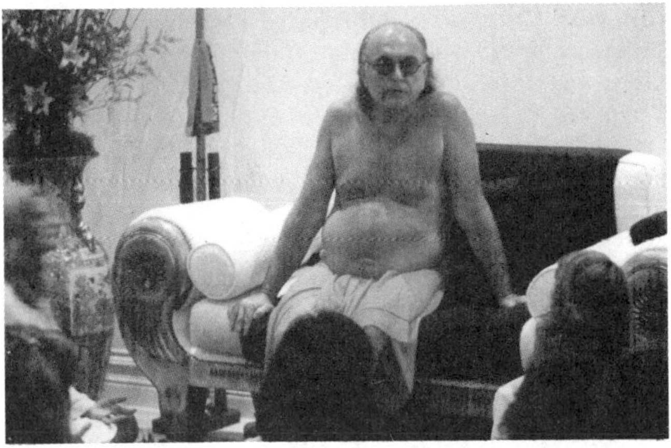

**Los Angeles, 1997**

## "He Gives you more than you can imagine"

After the April celebration, Avatar Adi Da continued to Grant His Darshan in smaller sittings at the Manner of Flowers, and later in Los Angeles, in a house provided for Him by devotees. Finally, on July 5, after travelling for most of two years, He returned to Fiji.

Some devotees had been traveling with Him throughout that time, and His physician, Charles Seage, was one of them. Charles has attended Avatar Adi Da personally for many years, and was one of the doctors present on January 11, 1986, at the Initiation of His Divine "Emergence". Charles describes here the conversion that He went through as a result of staying with Avatar Adi Da through thick and thin, and especially during the last two years that preceded the Gift of Transmission associated with *Hridaya Rosary*:

*CHARLES: I could summarize the process of devotional self-surrender and renunciation that Beloved Adi Da has taken me through in something He said just before departing for Europe in July 1996:*

> *AVATAR ADI DA SAMRAJ: In the usual circumstance around Adept-Realizers, it is very disciplined, and there are no amenities. There is no point in looking for a consistent lifestyle with Me. Sometimes I eat garbage, and sometimes I eat nectar. And anyone around Me eats what I eat. To be purified of the movement "for" or "against" the opposites is what the tapas is for—to realize the state of that indifference and be no longer bound. But you have to really find your Master, you have to really establish the link with That Which inherently Transcends conditional existence. Otherwise, it is an unendurable process. Tapas is not endurable on its own.*
>
> *Anybody can suffer. That is not tapas. Anybody can have their desires frustrated. That is not tapas. Anybody can be in circumstances where they have to experience what they do not want to experience. But that is not tapas. Tapas is what occurs when there is the thread of Grace, so that you are established in Communion with That Which Transcends all. That thread enables you to go through the tapas of purification from entanglement with the opposites.*
>
> *There is a Great Process, and It is just what It is. And It is not amusing. You can sometimes be amused, but the Process Itself is not amusing. It has nothing to do with being amused, or getting yourself amused, or any of that nonsense. The Pleasure Dome is Yogic Freedom from the extremes in your own disposition. It is not a*

*matter of maintaining some body-circumstance merely. It is a matter of being able to be centrally established in Me as Your Divine Heart-Master, no matter what arises.*

*For those who would advance, or get into the process that is advancing, the nature of sadhana as tapas becomes very, very clear. And if you are not willing to go on with what that takes—which, ultimately, is the obliteration of egoic "self-possession"—then you make compromises, or you slow it down.* [July 10, 1996]

*CHARLES: This has been my experience exactly. As Beloved Adi Da's physician, I know I must be available to Him twenty-four hours a day wherever He is, wherever He chooses to go. Regardless of what I feel in the body-mind in any given moment, that is my agreement with Him. It is not a "business" agreement. It is my greatest joy and impulse. It is the meaning of my life. And so that puts me in an interesting position. If I follow my heart, I stay with Him. I do not have any choice. And that has proved to be an incredible Grace. My Beloved Guru is making possible for me a depth of sadhana that I would never have chosen if left to my own egoic devices. He is giving me my heart's desire in spite of myself.*

*As I was traveling with Beloved Adi Da in Europe and the United States in the last few years, I have to admit I reacted to the ordeal of it. Beloved Adi Da was often fiercely critical of me and of His devotees in general. I felt tremendous frustration, because I did not know what to do to change anything. I wavered between resistance and apathy. I could not even provide Beloved Adi Da with the quality of health service and protection that I would have wished. No matter how well I might feel I had covered all the bases—as, for example, in arranging for His kidney surgery in Los Angeles—something could always come up out of "left field" and threaten everything, like the dreadful incident of the post-operative drug that Beloved Adi Da reacted to. Basically, I felt that no matter how hard I tried, I was never completely in control.*

*For a while during early 1997, while Beloved Adi Da was staying at the Mountain Of Attention, I worked for some hours a week in a nearby medical clinic, which was something I had not done in years. I noticed how much I enjoyed being the doctor again in conventional terms—in control, effective, admired. Then Beloved Adi Da suddenly left for Hawaii, and before long He indicated that I should come. And so I gave immediate notice at the clinic and within a day or two I was living in Kauai while Beloved Adi Da was enduring His own immense Ordeal and writing* Hridaya Rosary.

*I had my first experience of Beloved Adi Da's new Revelation of His Siddhi at the initial "Four Thorns" Darshan occasion in Hawaii on April 7, 1997. I felt Avatar Adi Da Spiritually Crashing Down and His Spiritual Presence Pervading me, outside and inside. I could hardly believe it, because I did not feel prepared for any such event. From my perspective, I went into the room still emotionally egoically "self-possessed" and not effectively practicing beyond that. And so it was obvious that I had nothing to do with the incredibly Blissful feeling of Beloved Adi Da that was filling the room. It was simply Him. He was doing everything.*

*When we arrived at the Mountain Of Attention, a young man asked me what these first occasions of Beloved Adi Da's "Four Thorns" Transmission had been like. And I said, "Well, I have been to hundreds and hundreds of Darshan occasions over the years, and I have tended to get involved in the error of 'working on' myself to have something happen to me in these occasions. But now I know that I am doing nothing and Beloved Adi Da is doing everything." The young man was deeply impressed, and so was I. It is a Grace beyond comprehension.*

*When we went back to Los Angeles at the beginning of June, the frustration for me at the life-level continued. Everything seemed futile. There was no way to "succeed" or "win" at anything, and I indulged in a mood of complaint a lot of the time.*

*But, during those weeks we spent in Los Angeles in June, Beloved Adi Da would sit with people nearly every night. Typically, we would sit for hours. First there would be a preparatory devotional occasion, and then Beloved Adi Da would come in and Grant Darshan for over an hour. Then, usually, He would leave, and we would stay in place for further devotional chanting or sacred music. So I would go into these profound Darshans night after night, and the same thing would happen as happened in Hawaii that first time. I would be overcome with the All-Pervading Love-Blissful Ecstasy of Beloved Adi Da's Spiritual Presence. It was beyond belief. I realized that that was the Gift that Beloved Adi Da had Given me a taste of in my first Darshan occasion in 1978 at the Mountain Of Attention. And the thread of that Grace had stayed with me through all the intervening years. I began to realize that this thread had always been present in my relationship with my Beloved Guru. Regardless of my egoic ups and downs, that thread remained, for one simple reason. All along, I consistently made the conscious choice to be with Beloved Adi Da no matter what—no matter how much I might find in the circumstance to complain about.*

*When we came back to Fiji in 1997, something changed in my disposition. I was still struggling, but I was starting to understand that the struggle and resistance was something I was <u>choosing</u> to do—it was not <u>happening</u> to me. It was not, as I had assumed, simply justified by my apparent circumstances. Prior to all of it was my relationship to Beloved Adi Da. That was what was important, and that was what I was actually basing my* *life on—even though I seemed to be saying that I did not want the difficult ordeal of renunciate sadhana. Now, at last, back at Adidam Samrajashram after all that traveling, I relaxed into the fact that, no matter what tests Beloved Adi Da "creates" for me and no matter how difficult it appears to be, this is it. I am just going to surrender myself and do the devotional Yoga with Him.*

*Looking back, I can see that the process of Beloved Adi Da burning out my seeking has been going on for a long time. First, He purified me of my idealism and childishness and conventional religiosity. And then, in recent years, the primary obstruction in me has been a strong adolescent reaction to life. But, whatever the content, it has just become clearer and clearer that, by tendency, I am only avoiding relationship. I am doing the self-contraction, and that act creates all my seeking—to succeed, to be comfortable, to be loved, whatever.*

*Consistently in Darshan occasions with Beloved Adi Da, I feel the same Crashing Down of His Blessing Force, but now His Spiritual Pervasion is becoming continuous with my daily life. No matter where I am, I can feel Him, I can always "Locate" His tangible Spiritual Presence.*

*I found out that you have to get to the point of despair, because that is the only thing that makes you take a hard look at the seeking you are always doing. And that seeking is what is preventing you from feeling Beloved Adi Da, from noticing the Grace and Bliss and Love He is pouring on you all the time. I know I am always going to be tested and there is always going to be tapas, because He is dealing with the ego. And so there is no self-congratulatory or self-indulgent life to be had around Avatar Adi Da. All there is is love of Him. And, in that love-relationship with Him, He Gives you infinitely more than you can imagine.*

# "My Word Is Sealed"

In late July 1997, Avatar Adi Da began to spend increasing time Working on the manuscripts of His "Source-Literature". Every morning around 7:00 A.M., He would walk through the great brass gates that enclose the courtyard of His House at the Matrix and turn down the stone path leading to Indigo Swan, the small room by the ocean lagoon where He does His Writing. Before His arrival, the manuscripts He had requested would always be set out on His desk—pre-pared by the editors so as to include all the changes and additions He had made the previous day.

Avatar Adi Da would work non-stop, often until two or three o'clock in the afternoon, checking the editors' work, making new changes, doing new writing. Typically, He would enter His new writing in pencil between the lines of type on the computer printout, sometimes moving out into extensive new additions in the margins.

Since the beginning of His Teaching Work, Avatar Adi Da Samraj has written books of His Instruction to His devotees. And (as described earlier), in 1985, He began to gather His essential Teaching into summary "Source-Texts". But the magnitude of what He was now involved in was unprecedented, and this became more and more apparent as the weeks and months passed. Avatar Adi Da wrote every single day, seven days a week, from late July to the middle of December. The editors would work through the night, every night, in order to enter and proofread the previous day's revisions. Then they would rest for a few hours until the next day's changes came back into their hands.

Avatar Adi Da was not simply adding to His existing "Source-Texts". He was certainly doing that, but He was also creating new books, drawing together various Writings and Talks from the entire period of twenty-five years into new combinations and syntheses, creating a systematic presentation of His entire Spiritual Revelation and Instruction. Every book and every part of every book became a perfectly placed link in the chain of His Argument.

By September, Avatar Adi Da had created a series of twenty-three "Source-Texts" in total. It is not possible to put into words the impact and significance of these Texts. They are the Result of the entire Leela of the Ruchira Avatar—His childhood, His "Sadhana Years", but, most especially, the Work of His twenty-five Teaching and Revelation Years:

*AVATAR ADI DA SAMRAJ: It was an unbroken "Consideration" that took twenty-five years, a continuous Examination-Argument unfolding day by day for twenty-five years. Only I knew the thread of it, or maintained the thread of it, but that is what it was.* [December 28, 1997]

The more one studies Avatar Adi Da's twenty-three "Source-Texts", the more it becomes apparent that these books have been in the making throughout all the eons of Spiritual seeking and Realization. But the books themselves are not the product of the Great Tradition, in the sense of being a grand synthesis. They stand as the Eternal Word of the Divine Person, explaining and clarifying what all the Scriptures of the Great Tradition are about, and giving the Gift to which all the Scriptures Point: unqualified Communion with Avatar Adi Da and most perfect Realization of Truth Itself, Reality Itself, Real God.

The unique conjunctions that brought Avatar Adi Da to birth also equipped His bodily (human) Form to be the Bearer of the Complete Dharma of Enlightenment, and even to be capable of the phenomenal task of Writing it down. Swami Vivekananda was a speaker and a writer of wide learning and extraordinary charisma. And then, in His early life as "Franklin Jones", Avatar Adi Da immersed Himself in an incredible discipline of writing.

For years, He wrote most of the day and often at night, consumed with the urge to penetrate the Nature of Reality. It was through this ordeal of writing that He discovered the structure of "Narcissus", or the ego-"I".

During His Teaching Years, Avatar Adi Da's Mastery of Words showed itself in a ceaseless "intoxicated" flow of spontaneously spoken Discourses, as well as in written Essays and other documents. His devotees have always recognized Avatar Adi Da in His Speech, spoken or written. It is unmistakably Him, the Speech of the Divine. And, once there is that recognition, you can comb human writings from top to bottom without finding anything to compare with the Attractive Power and the obvious Authority of His Words.

After the Initiation of His Divine "Emergence" in January 1986, the Written Word of Adi Da Samraj became even more obviously "thick" with His Spiritual Transmission. More and more, He has imbued the English language with a sacred Force it has never had before, making it into a vehicle through which He can Plainly Speak Who He Is, why He has Come, and the great Process that is required in order to Realize Him. Through His Incarnation as the Ruchira Avatar, the Eternal, Invisible Divine Person has found a way to tell beings everything about Himself and to Instruct them in every detail of what it takes to transform ordinary life into Divine Communion and Realization.

Avatar Adi Da uses English—not an ancient sacred language, like Sanskrit, but the ordinary lingua franca of humanity's "late-time". The written language of Adi Da Samraj, now perfected in His twenty-three "Source-Texts", is the Divine Person Speaking to beings in every time and place, weaving images of Love-Bliss, evoking the Samadhi of which He Speaks.

Of Avatar Adi Da's twenty-three "Source-Texts", the first are *The Five Books Of The Heart Of The Adidam Revelation*, summarizing the essence of His Self-Revelation

**Adidam Samrajashram, 1997**

and His Instruction in the Way of Adidam. Then follow *The Seventeen Companions Of The True Dawn Horse*, which elaborate all the great themes of His Teaching and Self-Revelation. Last of all stands *The Dawn Horse Testament*, bringing to completion the preceding twenty-two "Source-Texts" in the most comprehensive and detailed statement of the Ruchira Avatar's Teaching within a single book. In His Words, "There is the Heart, there is the Horse, and there are the Companions. All are required."

In His twenty-three "Source-Texts", Avatar Adi Da Samraj has brought to completion His Divine Ordeal of Communication. These books are the fruit of the Leela of His entire Life and Work. They are the Message and the Seal of mankind's Divine Awakening, yet to manifest.

*AVATAR ADI DA SAMRAJ: I lived long enough to write My Revelation down. Even if this body does not live one more day, I have accomplished what I Came here to do.*

*This Body will not live forever. Nor will yours. But I (My Self) and My Word will live forever.*

*So I am celebrating today the fact that My continued survival in this Body no longer makes any great difference. It may be that it survives, but it no longer makes any huge difference. I managed to make My Revelation, completely, sufficient to Save everyone. It was a Miracle in itself, that this Body could survive long enough for Me to complete My twenty-three "Source-Texts" unequivocally, absolutely, with the utmost and absolute clarity. For the sake of all, it is good if this Body survives to Do Its Blessing Work now. But, truly, I have nothing more to say. I said everything that had to be said, and I Did everything that had to be Done, and this Body survived. The mediocrity and stupidity of humankind is the reason why I had to Do what I have Done. And the Truth has won!*

*Someone said in a movie that fame is what comes to you after a lifetime of service to mankind. So have I Done with this Body here. I have Done everything necessary to be Done by Me in this Body, in Service to you and to all.*

*My Word is Complete. Therefore, all of the Siddhis of My Divine "Emergence" Work will now, and can, and will forever, take place, whether this Body continues to live or not. Sooner or later, the Body passes. I am relaxed in the reality that I have Done My Work that needed to be Done. And the continuation of this Body is now a luxury for you all. It is entirely up to you. Truly! It is truly so. Love Me in this Form, and the Body will persist.*

*I Am the Way Beyond all of this. Light Itself, Energy Itself, is Unbroken, Unqualified, Indivisible, altogether Prior, altogether One and Only.*

*Sitting here in this Body like yours, I have indulged in your experience, and learned greatly from it. And My sympathy has been increased absolutely. I have escaped none of it! This One Who Is suffers in this Body, like you—but more sensitively, more aroused by the pain of it than you dare to be. Notice that bodily life is not enough.*

*The whirling stars and bodies of planets, the gravitational ghost of ordinary reality, the black hole of this "dark" time, and all the sucking sound of ending—it is not good enough. Not good enough! It is not good enough! Live life with enough heart, and you get a taste of the Absolute that you desire.*

*But there is nothing in life, in and of itself, that is enough. Whatever you got by means of science, or by means of ordinary mind, it makes no difference. It is just, plain old, not enough. It is a mummery of endings. It is terrible, and a mockery of your own heart. I do not like it, and I never did. And I had to fit My Self down to the toes in your likeness, embodying many saints, and even all the trivia of mankind, in My own Form here. More foolish than you!*

*My Word is Sealed, It is Complete. My twenty-three "Source-Texts" are made, and done. Every word and comma and quotation mark was made and approved and made perfect by Me. What was made is Good, and Complete, and Whole, and Fine, and Great.*

*I have Done what I had to Do.*

*So it is time for you to become profoundly serious, and take the arms of My twenty-three "Source-Texts", and the life of this Way of Adidam in My Company, and live it rightly, truly, fully, fully devotionally, and bring it as My Gift to all of mankind. And be the seed whereby this transformation can occur.* [December 15, 1997]

Even after the end of 1997, Beloved Adi Da has continued to make profound additions to His Divine Scripture. Following are three passages that Beloved Adi Da added to *The Dawn Horse Testament* late in 1998:

*Religion Is Not, In and Of Itself (or As An Historically-Existing Tradition—or Discrete Cultural, Social, and Political Phenomenon) True. Religion Cannot (Thus—In and Of Itself) Be True. Only Reality Itself (Which Is Truth, Itself) Is (In and Of and As Itself) True. Therefore, What Makes (or Can Make) Religion True Is The Whole bodily Heart-Response To (and, Ultimately, The Most Perfect Realization Of) The One and Only Reality and Truth.*

*Reality Itself (Which Is Truth, Itself) Is The "Music" That Makes Religion True. Therefore, True Religion Is The Whole bodily "Dance" Of Heart-Response To The One and Only Reality and Truth.*

*I Am The One and Only and Self-Evidently Divine Reality and Truth—Avatarically Self-Revealed To You (and To all, and All).*

*I Am Reality, Truth, and Oneness—Self-Existing and Self-Radiant, and (Now, and Forever Hereafter) Standing In Front Of Your eyes (and At Your Heart—and, Ultimately, As Your egolessly Me-Realizing Heart).*

*I Am The "Bright" One—The Only and Inherently egoless One—Who Always Already Is, and Who Must (By*

*Means Of My Immediately ego-Vanishing Avataric Divine Grace) Be Realized.*

*If There Is No Real and True (and Really and Truly "Dancing") Heart-Response To My Avatarically Self-Revealed (and Self-Evidently Divine) Form, and Presence, and State Of Person—Then There Is Not (and There Cannot Be) Any True (or Really and Truly Practiced) Religion.*

*If (and When) any one Hears Me and Sees Me, My Avataric Divine Heart-Blessing Will Attract The Heart Beyond Every Trace Of self-Contraction (Even In The Deepest Places Of The Heart and the body-mind), and The Me-Hearing and Me-Seeing Heart Will (By ego-Surrendering, ego-Forgetting, and ego-Transcending Devotional Resort To Me Via The Process Of That Attraction) Realize (and Be One With) Me—The Only One Who (Always and Already) Is.*

◆ ◆ ◆

*"Consider" This: Reality (Itself) is Not what You think. Thought is a Temporal abstraction (or A time-Consuming and time-Bound Contraction Of and From Reality Itself).*

*"Consider" This: The Cosmic Universe (or Cosmic Nature, Itself) is Not what You perceive. Perception is a time-Consuming and time-Bound Temporal and Limited space-time event, Associated With a limited and temporary space-time point of view (or psycho-physical self-Contraction).*

*"Consider" This: Reality Itself (and Cosmic Nature, Itself) Is What You Are—and Not what You think or perceive.*

*What You Are Is Reality Itself (and Cosmic Nature, Itself).*

*What You Are Is Realized and Demonstrated By Means Of The Devotional Recognition-Response To Me.*

*The Transcending Of Your Own ego-"I" (or self-Contraction)—and, Thus and Thereby, The Transcending Of all Your limitations Of thought, perception, and space-time-Bondage—By Means Of The Devotional*

*Recognition-Response To Me, Is The Necessary (and Only-By-Me Revealed and Given) Process Of Realizing That Which Is Always Already The Case.*

*That Which Is Always Already The Case Is Who I Am.*

*Only I Am What You Are.*

*Therefore, You Will Realize What (and Who) You Are Only If You Realize Me (By Means Of The Devotional Recognition-Response To Me).*

*Your thinking and perceiving (or psycho-physical) person (or ego-"I") is Not Me.*

*I Am Not "Within" Your psycho-physical (or thinking and perceiving) Knot Of ego-"I".*

*I Am Always Already "Outside" (and Altogether Beyond) Your psycho-physical (or thinking and perceiving) Knot Of ego-"I".*

*I Am You Only When You Really (and, At Last, Most Perfectly) Transcend Your psycho-physical (or thinking and perceiving) Knot Of ego-"I", By Means Of The ego-Transcending (and, Thus, thought-Transcending, and perception-Transcending, and, Altogether, point-of-view-Transcending and space-time-Transcending) Devotional Recognition-Response To Me ("Outside", and Altogether Beyond, Your psycho-physical, or thinking and perceiving, Knot Of ego-"I").*

*You Are What You Are Only When You Really (and, At Last, Most Perfectly) Realize Me.*

*I Am That Which Is Always Already The Case.*

*Only I Am That Which Is Always Already The Case.*

*Only I Am You.*

*Therefore, "Consider" Me.*

◆ ◆ ◆

*The body-mind Of Man Is Like A Seed, That Lies Asleep Within The Dark and Depth Of Earth's Unconsciousness. And I Am Like A Thunderstorm Of Fresh Down-Crashing Sound and Light, That Weathers Me Into*

*The Earth-World With A Flood Of True and Living Water. And When The True Water Of My Love-Bliss-Presence Flows Deep Into the body-mind, The "Brightest" Sound and Shape Of Me Strikes Through The Germ Of Mankind's Seed within. It Is The Heart That Breaks By My Divine Invasion there. Its Germ Of Me-"Bright" Suddenness Un-Knots The Seed Of body-mind, When I Crash Down Into The Earthen Core. And When The Heart Un-Locks, the body-mind Becomes A Flower In The Tangible Garden Of My Divine Domain.*

*If The Heart Finds Me, The Heart Devotionally Recognizes Me (Inherently), and all the body-mind Devotionally Responds To Me (Immediately)—Whether By Means Of The Immediately To-Me-Responsive Devotional Exercise Of Me-Recognizing Faith Or The Immediately Me-Recognizing Devotional Exercise Of To-Me-Responsive Insight. Therefore, Your Heart Must Decide—Whether To Raise A Fist, and Throw A Rock, At The ego-Crushing Natural Universe, Or To Make A Flower Grow In The Garden Of Indestructible Light.*

*The Devotional Recognition-Response To Me Is The Divine Flowering Of the body-mind. Therefore, Your Heart Must Recognize Me and Choose Me—and Not merely believe Me—If I Am To "Brighten" You.*

*Faith Is A Flower, and Not a mind's idea, or a body's satisfaction. Likewise, The Insight That Flowers the body-mind Is Made Of Heart, and Not Of Seeker's Thrum Of thought, and thought's Abstract Invasion Of the body. No mere belief, or Mummery Of thinking mind, Can Make The Fist Of ego's Knot Un-Tie. And No Set Stage Of mere perception Can Outlast The Crushing Time Of merely Natural life. The Rock Of ego and The Fist Of self-Contracted body-mind Will Last a mere and Total lifetime—Whereas The Heart-Flower Breaks The Earth Above the head's Clay Crown, and Finds My "Bright" Beginning In An Eternal Field, Above the stars.*

Da Love-Ananda Mahal, 1998

CHAPTER 26

# The Indivisible Tantra of Adidam

Since the Event of His Divine Re-Awakening in the Vedanta Temple, everything Avatar Adi Da has said has been from the Divinely Enlightened "Point of View" of the seventh stage of life. But now, having created His twenty-three "Source-Texts", Adi Da Samraj began to Reveal His Divine Secrets even more profoundly. With just a few devotees gathered around Him, He engaged in a unique and all-encompassing conversation about His seventh stage Revelation. He was moved to have this supreme conversation, because He at last had practitioners who were ready to make use of it—the two Adidamas, both of whom had come to the point in the Way of Adidam where the next transition in the course of their Spiritual practice was to Divine Enlightenment, the Realization of the seventh stage of life.

## The Overnight Revelation of Conscious Light

ADIDAMA JANGAMA HRIDDAYA: Beloved Adi Da Samraj, Adidama Sukha Dham, and I were seated at the dining table, having finished lunch. Our Beloved Guru was gazing out across the ocean, when suddenly He said: "The celebration of our anniversary of

***"It had been a year since Beloved had acknowledged our unbreakable 'Bonding' with Him, established through twenty-three years of His direct Spiritual Instruction and intense testing."***

Sivaratri is coming up. Shall we celebrate it by going on a private retreat at Da Love-Ananda Mahal?"

Adidama Sukha Dham and I were surprised. It had seemed unlikely to us that our Beloved would be inclined to travel so soon, having just completed a two-year Yajna.

"Would you really like to do this, Beloved?"

"Yes, look into it."

And, within a few days, we were in flight to Hawaii, accompanied by only a few devotees.

It had been a year since Beloved Adi Da had acknowledged our unbreakable "Bonding" with Him, established through twenty-three years of His direct Spiritual Instruction and intense testing. His acknowledgment of the completion of that profound Process in March 1997 had coincided spontaneously with the traditional Hindu festival of Sivaratri—a celebration of the marriage of Siva

**View of Mt. Waialeale from Da Love-Ananda Mahal**

and Parvati, the male and female aspects of the Divine. Beloved Adi Da had said that, over time, we would come to understand more and more of the significance of this Yogic Unity between the three of us.

As we flew over the Pacific en route to Da Love-Ananda Mahal, this mystery was my contemplation. I felt that this retreat was going to be an important further Initiation, and an Instruction, in how to rightly understand and honor the Gift of our unique Love-"Bond" with Him.

The moment we set foot onto the Sanctuary of Da Love-Ananda Mahal, I instantly felt the tremendous descending Force of Beloved Adi Da's Spiritual Presence there. The site of the Sanctuary has traditionally been acknowledged by the local kahunas (Hawaiian shamans) as the most potent place of power in all of Hawaii. The property is nestled in an elbow of the wild Wailua river, which surges down from Mount Waialeale.

Beloved Adi Da has often Given His most esoteric Dharma at this Sanctuary, and He has designated Da Love-Ananda Mahal as a place of special retreat for members of the Ruchira Sannyasin Order. At many crucial junctures in His Work over the years, Da Love-Ananda

Mahal has been a place where He has spontaneously poured out His Teaching for days, weeks, or even months at a time, expounding the highest Dharma of the Way of Adidam. As soon as He arrived on this occasion, Beloved Adi Da encompassed the entire property with His Regard, walked firmly into His private quarters, and took His seat on His bed.

His room in Free Standing Man (His residence when He is at Da Love-Ananda Mahal) is simple and pristine—furnished with just a bed, a chair, and two small side tables. One wall is made up of a door and window that looks out upon a stone lingam set in the garden, with Mt. Waialeale looming behind. And so, there on His bed, the Divine Maha-Siddha sat, established in a firm Yogic pose. He Himself was the Great Lingam of which this small stone lingam and the mountain behind were but the reflected forms.

Adidama Sukha Dham and I sat on either side of our Beloved Guru on His bed, and the Instruction of this time began—a two-month period which He came to call "The Overnight Revelation Of Conscious Light".

First of all, Beloved Adi Da spoke about the significance of Sivaratri:

*AVATAR ADI DA SAMRAJ: Sivaratri is a traditional celebration about Yogic Invocation and Communion. It is a Yogic celebration, a celebration of Siva's eye, with the focus upon the eyes. Traditional tantric practitioners focus free energy, or Shakti, there.* [February 25, 1998]

ADIDAMA JANGAMA HRIDDAYA: In speaking of the eyes, Beloved Adi Da was referring to the place deep behind and slightly above the eyes—the so-called "third eye", or ajna chakra—valued in many Spiritual traditions as a place to focus attention. Yogis, by intention, turn the "inner gaze" upward, in order to experience various subtle forms of bliss.

Beloved Adi Da went on to describe how traditional Tantric practitioners regard Sivaratri as a time to celebrate the esoteric significance of the Union of Siva and Parvati, or Consciousness and Energy. Beloved Adi Da explained to us that there are many different forms of Tantrism and Tantric practice, but that He, the Supreme Tantric Master, Gives the fullest Realization of what the traditional Tantric practitioners are seeking: a literal En-Light-enment,[1] in which the entire conditional personality—gross, subtle, and causal[2]—relinquishes itself in the Absolute, in the fundamental Force of existence.

As Beloved Adi Da spoke, He Communicated His Initiatory Spiritual Transmission through His eyes as well as through His Words. It was obvious that the form of our celebration of Sivaratri with Him had begun.

Beloved Adi Da continued to speak of the "upturned gaze", explaining that this primal Yogic asana, or "pose", is intentionally adopted by the traditional Tantric practitioner as a technique to achieve meditative bliss. In contrast, He said, for His devotee, the asana assumed is one of opening upward, in spontaneous response to His "Bright" Divine Self-Revelation. Thus, for His devotee, this asana, which He called "Samraj Asana", is not deliberately assumed, in the usual manner of a traditional Yoga asana. Samraj Asana occurs spontaneously, without thought, when the heart recognizes and Spiritually worships Beloved Adi Da Samraj, the Divine Spiritual Presence and Person. He is <u>already</u> Present—not needing to be sought, but simply needing to be felt and Invoked. And so, Beloved Adi Da said, instead of effortfully concentrating in an upturned gaze, His devotee simply allows the heart-Attracted response to Him to awaken. When this occurs, one feels the entire body-mind opening and becoming upwardly receptive to His Divine Spiritual Descent, like an open cup. In Samraj Asana, His Divine Light Pours into this open cup, purifying the entire psycho-physical vehicle.

Thus, there is no need to seek for purification, no need to apply traditional Yogic techniques, no necessary struggle to ascend to higher realms, working from the lower chakras to the higher. In the Way of Adidam, That Which is Highest, the Very Divine, Comes Down. In this manner, the body-mind is spontaneously (and Divinely) washed, or purified, from top to bottom.

*AVATAR ADI DA SAMRAJ: The principal faculties are to be given to Me, moment to moment, and, in the Spiritual course, they are turned Upward, through the lead of attention. The focus behind the eyes must be turned Up to Me, moment to moment. Otherwise, it drifts down, head to toe.*

*The Yoga of Adidam is not a matter of strategically going up above the head (and, thereby, strategically excluding the gross plane and the gross body-mind), but the Yoga of Adidam is a matter of being responsively to-Me-directed (Above, and Beyond), and of Melting down, such that the body-mind becomes My Sphere. The body-mind is washed (or Spiritually re-oriented, and Spiritually purified, and "Brightened", or Spiritually Infused) by this responsively Up-turned (but not strategically up-going) Contemplation of Me. Do This, rather than allow the faculties to wander casually, in their separate and separative fashion, below the crown of the head.* [Hridaya Rosary]

ADIDAMA JANGAMA HRIDDAYA: When one is established in Samraj Asana, everything conditional can be relinquished—everything, even all experiences of body, emotion, and mind. Everything can be relinquished into the Divine Conscious Light That Is Beloved Adi Da Samraj.

As Beloved Adi Da Gave this Instruction to Adidama Sukha Dham and myself, I experienced the Force of His Indivisible Light Pressing Down into and in-Filling the body-mind. At the same time, the eyes naturally moved into the upturned gaze, just as He described. And this was occurring even with the eyes open. In other words, attention, feeling, and the whole body, from the head to the toes, was opened to Beloved Adi Da and His Indivisible Light, rather than contracted in upon the apparently solid experience of material reality.

Adidama Sukha Dham and I were practicing the Way of Adidam in the context of the second stage of the "Perfect Practice", which is the practice of Contemplating Consciousness Itself, Prior to objects. And so Beloved Adi Da was Giving us this Gift of a retreat with Him as a means to enter more deeply into this profound Contemplation. He had already taken us through the first stage of the "Perfect Practice", which is the Awakening to the Witness-Position of Consciousness and observing all that arises from that Position. We had both spent many years doing this practice, and now, by the Grace of Beloved Adi Da's Spiritual Transmission, the practice of Witnessing whatever arises from the Position of Consciousness had deepened to the point where we were spontaneously Drawn to Contemplate That Which Is the Witness, Consciousness Itself. We are engaged, by Beloved Adi Da's Grace, in a Contemplative investigation of the very Nature of Consciousness Itself and Reality Itself. He describes the essence of this practice in *Eleutherios*:[3]

*Contemplate (or feel, meditate on, and directly, or Inherently and, Thus, Perfectly, Identify with) Consciousness Itself, Most Prior to all objects, until Its Inherently Perfect (Transcendental, Inherently Spiritual, and, necessarily, Divine) Condition becomes Inherently (and Most Perfectly) Obvious.*

The crux of this profound investigation is the apparent "difference" between Consciousness, on the one hand, and Energy (or Light), on the other. The rare few Realizers reported in the Great Tradition of mankind to have been genuinely involved in the contemplation of

**Avatar Adi Da Samraj with Adidama Sukha Dham (left) and Adidama Jangama Hriddaya (right)**

Consciousness (rather than merely engaged in philosophy about Consciousness) have effectively presupposed an absolute "difference" between Energy and Consciousness, or Form and Being. Therefore, such practitioners seek to cut off the world, or eliminate form, so as to be able to concentrate in exclusive meditation on Formless Consciousness. When there is only Formless Consciousness, Jnana Samadhi has been attained. This Samadhi is the traditional goal of the sixth stage of life (according to Beloved Adi Da's Revelation of the seven stages of life), and has been variously described in the traditions of Hinduism, Buddhism, Jainism, and Taoism.

Beloved Adi Da Samraj has Revealed that the act of exclusive immersion in Consciousness is associated with a locus in the right side of the heart, and this is exactly true in my experience. Entrance into the Domain of Consciousness in the right side of the heart is like entering into a "room", a "space" of Awareness, free of objects and forms. Many times, my Beloved Guru has Drawn me into this formless Space through His Divine Heart-Transmission. This Space of Awareness is Prior to the act of attention and the feeling of relatedness to objects and others. It is Still and Motionless, an Infinite Well of Being. For many years, both Adidama Sukha Dham and I have had numerous experiences of the traditionally sought Jnana Samadhi, but we have always felt the unsatisfactoriness of the moment of transition out of that Formless Depth and back to conditional everyday awareness. The chaotic display of conditional phenomena—the world, in other words—feels like an intrusion.

Beloved Adi Da has Taught us that even the sense of dissatisfaction with the return to ordinary awareness is a form of egoic seeking. Indeed, the desire to remain separate from the world, and not to be impinged upon by conditional objects and events, is the primal sign of the self-contracted ego-"I". In the context of the sixth stage of life, this basic search takes the form of desiring to remain identified with Consciousness and to exclude the entire domain of Energy. These two apparently separate realities—Consciousness and Energy—have never truly been reconciled through any religious or Spiritual Teaching that has previously existed.

In His own Divine Re-Awakening, Beloved Adi Da Samraj Realized the Secret of this reconciliation. The Secret is that there is no "difference" between Being and Form, no separation between Consciousness and Energy, no reconciliation necessary between Siva and Shakti, or Moveless Being and the world of appearances. They Are One. This Realization is the Gift of Adi Da Samraj. And, as Beloved Adi Da was now pointing out to us, this is the secret significance (never before fully known) of the celebration of Sivaratri.

In the weeks that followed our arrival at Da Love-Ananda Mahal, Beloved Adi Da took us through an immense samyama, or exercise of "consideration", about the dilemma inherent in the orientation of the sixth stage of life. Samyama has always been His basic approach to Instructing His devotees, and during this time He made a remarkable observation about how He engages in samyama. The traditional Yogic practice of samyama (according to Patanjali's *Yoga Sutras*), He said, is to address some object and engage in an in-depth contemplation of that object in order to discover the truth of it. Beloved Adi Da described how this traditional form of samyama involves working from conditions toward the position of Samadhi. He then described how His Samyama works the other way around. He engages in samyama, or "consideration", from the already Realized Position of Consciousness (or Samadhi) and observes and examines everything in the pattern of conditions from the "inside out", rather than from the "outside in". He is the Master of Samyama, and, through His Siddhi, He Awakened this power of "consideration" in us as a living process of Revelation.

Our samyama was focused on Consciousness Itself. How is the bridge made between the Deep Well of Being that we experience in Jnana Samadhi and the chaotic world of conditional forms? How is that apparent duality transcended? This was not a merely philosophical question. This was the matter of supreme importance in our life and practice.

I had come to be profoundly aware of the necessity to transcend identification with born form—not merely in the general sense, but as a very personal matter. I had been living and serving Beloved Adi Da directly for twenty-four years and had to face the intense sorrow that I knew would be inevitable in the death of the physical Form of my Beloved Guru. I did not have a way to deal with this sorrow in terms of the sixth stage Realization. Jnana Samadhi was not enough. There was no permanent solution to the sorrow inherent in mortal existence merely through turning within and Identifying with Consciousness, separate from Form. But neither was there satisfaction in attachment to the panorama of potential experience, which I had seen to be a maya of endless births and deaths. For Adidama Sukha Dham and myself, this dilemma had become acute—a greater Realization was essential in order to <u>really</u> transcend this mortal circumstance.

Beloved Adi Da had spoken for several years about what He called "Raymond's 'problem'", the pain of loving in the midst of this mortal circumstance. And, once again, soon after we came on retreat to Da Love-Ananda Mahal, our Beloved Guru returned to this matter, the summary dilemma of born existence.

*AVATAR ADI DA SAMRAJ: This is a domain in which there is a very acute experience of Raymond's "problem"—mortality, separation all built in, in a circumstance where there is love-attachment. Therefore, as My devotee, you must do the profound real sadhana of Adidam. You do that sadhana because, in the midst of this, you feel a dilemma, a real limitation. You are not inclined to dismiss the life-circumstance, or to dismiss your life-relationships. You have to take all of that into account in your Contemplation.*

*Ultimately, through the Process of the Way of Adidam, you go beyond all forms of "bonding" bondage.*

*In the midst of conditions, My Love-Bliss is to be lived so profoundly that It Outshines all "difference". Only in that Samadhi—the Samadhi of No-"Difference", the Unconditional Samadhi—is the bondage in "bonding" transcended. When subject and object are not "different", there is no "other"—but there is also no individual self.*

*Samadhi is necessary—Unqualified Samadhi, the seventh stage Demonstration, the Condition That Is One, not two. That is Divine Recognition Demonstrated in the seventh stage. Everything before That is the field of Raymond's "problem", you see, which is the world of apparently separate subjects and objects, apparently separate self and "other", apparently separate lover and loved-one—a world of mortality. That is the nature of its unsatisfactoriness. That is the dilemma. That is existence as dilemma. That is Raymond's "problem".* [March 9, 1998]

ADIDAMA JANGAMA HRIDDAYA: As He continued the samyama on Raymond's dilemma, Beloved Adi Da Revealed how the crux of the "problem" is exactly the limit that is to be transcended in the sixth stage of life—it is the apparent difference between Consciousness (Raymond) and Energy (Quandra).

*AVATAR ADI DA SAMRAJ: Raymond's "problem" is the apparent separation between Consciousness and objects (or Energy, or Delight, or Love-Bliss). It is the inherent "problem" of the conditionally manifested ego, the psycho-physical person bound in the mummery of the universe. For the mummery to be transcended, Raymond's "problem" must be transcended. The "difference" between Raymond and Quandra must be transcended. The Truth must be Realized—That Which Is Always Already The Case, That Which Is Prior to all "differences", and to "difference" itself.* [March 21, 1998]

ADIDAMA JANGAMA HRIDDAYA: And so, at Da Love-Ananda Mahal, I was spending day and night with Beloved Adi Da, sitting with Him in His Room, suffering the torment of the feeling of "difference", of separation, in the most intimate terms. This was the question confronting me: How could I possibly be sitting right in front of my Beloved and yet still be feeling a sense of "difference" from Him? How could there be any sense of "otherness", in any moment, under any circumstances, when I knew He was Present exactly and only As Real God, the Condition of Complete Oneness, without the slightest sense of "difference" from me? It was preposterous!

And further: What about my feeling of "difference" from everything else? Even when rested in profound feeling-Communion with Beloved Adi Da, I was still relating to arising circumstances and others as separate objects or beings. And this seemed equally preposterous, in view of Beloved Adi Da's seventh stage Teaching on the Non-Dual Oneness of all arising. I felt stuck in a point of view that was obviously preposterous and untrue. But there was no way to go beyond this limit by an effort of mind. As Beloved Adi Da said to us: "Objects and Consciousness are the same, but you cannot just get that. You are the differentiation between Consciousness and objects. It is your own act that presumes you as such."

So it is exactly the act of "Narcissus", of self-contraction, of egoic self-identification, that Beloved Adi Da was addressing in us. And, through His Words and Transmission, He was Revealing the mysterious Secret of how to transcend that act—not only in the meditation hall, but all the time.

*AVATAR ADI DA SAMRAJ: I Am on the Other Side of whatever appears by the inner eye and the outer eye. I am not Consciousness "within". I am the Divine Conscious Self, Entirely and Self-Radiantly—Surrounding and Pervading all and All. You must make the Way for Me by receiving Me, turning to Me with every faculty, allowing the Melting of the faculties.*

*Your inner consciousness is separate from objects. My Inner Consciousness Is all objects. Therefore, be Melted in Me.* [March 21, 1998]

ADIDAMA JANGAMA HRIDDAYA: As Beloved Adi Da wove this Sutra[4] of Perfect Sublimity, His Transmission-Power moved into the room where we were seated with Him face-to-face. The Power of His Word took on the

Force of Initiatory Revelation. The "Brightness" of His Divine Light Infiltrated the space with Luminosity, such that the walls, the objects, any persons became visibly "Brightened" by His Siddhi. The differentiation between objects loosened, such that Reality was clearly a Field of Divine Light rather than a field of apparently separate material objects. Beloved Adi Da was Revealing to us the Truth that matter equals Energy equals Light. His All-Pervading Divine Spiritual Presence is the Very Substance and Nature of That Light. He Is the Shakti-Force of the Cosmic domain.

Again and again, as He spoke or sat silently, His own Spiritual Person Crashed Down into our body-minds and Drew us into this Sea of Divine Light. He was Penetrating the body-mind through to the toes, permeating every cell with His Love-Blissful Radiance. He opened the nervous system, so that the body-mind became like an open cup from toe to crown, a receptacle for His Luminous Infusion. The spine would become erect with this upward-turning response to Beloved Adi Da's "Brightness". Sometimes, the experience of this Bliss was so intense that it felt like the cells of the body were being cracked open.

Then, within this Sphere of "Brightening", Beloved Adi Da would Reveal the Secret of the Non-"Difference" between Consciousness and Energy (or Light). Suddenly, not only Beloved Adi Da, but the room, the objects, the persons, and the entire pattern of arising would appear as a Field of Light and be Recognized as Conscious Light, as Self-Existing and Self-Radiant Consciousness Itself. This is Divine Recognition, the "Open-Eyed" Samadhi of the seventh stage of life. And our Beloved Guru was allowing us a glimpse of That. In one such moment, He said:

*AVATAR ADI DA SAMRAJ: If you want to see Consciousness, just take a look, there It Is.*

*If you cannot comprehend that, that is "Narcissus"! You see all of this, all of this experiencing, and so forth? You have gone along with it like a mummer, whistling "Zippity-Doo-Dah" somehow or other, and disturbed at the same time.*

*You do not recognize it. How can this be Consciousness? This is objects. It does not make any sense. It requires an inversion, like a Mobius strip in the mind through which no thought can be strained. It is like a black hole.*

*How can objects be Consciousness? You cannot strain that through any mode of concept and come out the other side with a feeling of how that is so. It is like the Mobius strip. Look at one. It makes sense somehow, and yet it does not make any sense at all. You cannot comprehend it, it seems.*

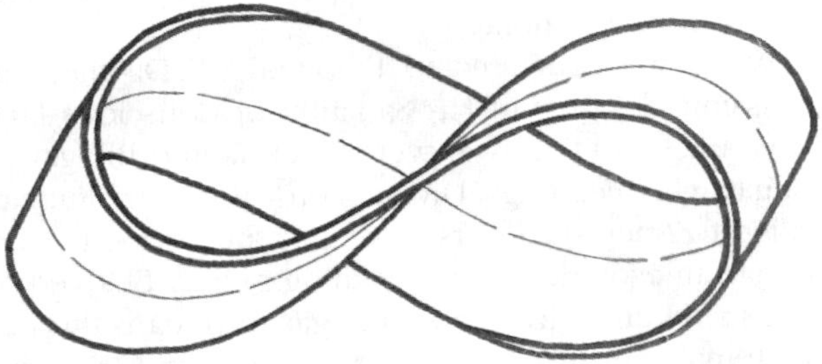

***"It is like the Mobius strip. Look at one. It makes sense somehow, and yet it does not make any sense at all."***

*Well, that is the mummery state of egoity. To Awaken from that Most Perfectly is Divine En-Light-enment—to "Become Light" (so to speak), to Realize you Are Indivisible Light, to Realize Reality Itself Is Indivisible Light. It is possible to see objects, then, via Self-Existing and Self-Radiant Consciousness. Then it is clear that That Is What they Are.* [March 20, 1998]

ADIDAMA JANGAMA HRIDDAYA: Suddenly, "home" was obviously not the interiorized, exclusive Self-Consciousness characteristic of Jnana Samadhi, a State achieved through dissociation from objects. Suddenly, "home" became Consciousness in the room, Revealed even as the room, with every thing in the room. Beloved Adi Da was Conscious Light, the room was Conscious Light, everything and everyone in the room was Conscious Light. There was no "difference", there was no separation. There was only the Love-Blissful Being of Beloved Adi Da, in Person. The Divine had Descended to this realm. And Beloved Adi Da had Revealed Himself to be not "different" from this realm. The mind of "difference" was washed and healed by that Vision, not merely of Unity (as though there were two to be united), but of Only One. This was the Overnight Revelation of Conscious Light. This is the Miracle of the Divine Revelation of Adi Da Samraj.

When we confessed to Beloved Adi Da these all-surpassing glimpses of His Samadhi of Conscious Light, He would say that we were "beholding Bhagavan". "Bhagavan", meaning "Divine Lord" (and traditionally applied to Adept-Realizers as well as the Divine Person), also has an esoteric Tantric meaning, which Beloved Adi Da has spoken of for years. "Bhagavan" means the male and female principles—Consciousness and Energy—indivisibly united. And this was exactly how Beloved Adi Da was Revealing Himself: "Bhagavan"—Raymond and Quandra as One, Siva and Shakti as One, Consciousness and Energy (or Light) as One.

## The Sphere of Love-Bliss-Fullness

From the day of His arrival on Kauai in February, Avatar Adi Da regularly invited into His Room a few devotees who lived near Da Love-Ananda Mahal and with whom He had Worked for many years. Then, as the weeks went by, a few more longtime devotees came from California. He had come to be on retreat with the Adidamas, and to "consider" matters that would directly serve their transition to the third stage of the "Perfect Practice", which is Most Perfect Awakening to the seventh stage of life. But now Avatar Adi Da also used the opportunity to serve these other devotees in the great transition belonging to the earlier stages of Adidam—the transition into hearing and seeing. But He was no longer speaking in a Teaching mode adapted to beginning practitioners. He was not "leaning down", not adapting Himself to anything less than His natural "Crazy" Discourse. He was speaking His greatest Secrets, His highest Dharma. He was Calling and inspiring everyone present to contemplate what Adidam is <u>really</u> about—practice in the Domain of Consciousness Itself, Awakening into the Vision and the "Point of View" of the seventh stage of life.

*AVATAR ADI DA SAMRAJ: The "Perfect Practice" of Adidam is What I am Calling you to. That <u>is</u> it.*

*The "Perfect Practice" is an Exercise in the Domain of Consciousness Itself, ultimately becoming the Divine Recognition of objects. To experience Reality and Truth in every moment is fundamental and necessary. Why would you ever choose to be outside that Refuge, that Domain, to be inserted into the play of mere pattern, with all of its comic-book reality—the mortality, the changes, the passing? It is unthinkable!* [March 18, 1998]

**Members of the gathering group at Da Love-Ananda Mahal, 1998**

In the first week of April, Michael Wood and Janis Ohki (who is called "Katsu", a name given to her by Avatar Adi Da), came from California to join the gatherings. Among the many past gathering periods in which they had participated was the "Indoor Summer" in 1976. It was during that time (as recounted by Michael in chapter nine) that Avatar Adi Da had confounded Michael's mind with the "consideration" of Divine Ignorance. Now, at Da Love-Ananda Mahal, twenty-two years later, Michael describes the process that occurred each day:

*MICHAEL: Every day, Beloved Adi Da would test the gathering group on the phone, asking for our "consideration", and we did everything we could to come up with something that would be sufficient "cause for gathering". On the phone, He would speak spontaneous poetry, sublime Dharma, He would tease us, provoke us—He would do whatever He had to do to bring us to drop enough of ourselves to truly recognize Him and Commune with Him. When this process was starting to happen, something about it would identify the "consideration" for the day, and our Beloved Guru would invite us into His bedroom.*

*Having run over to Free Standing Man, we would go down a long hall, turn left into a little entry room from*

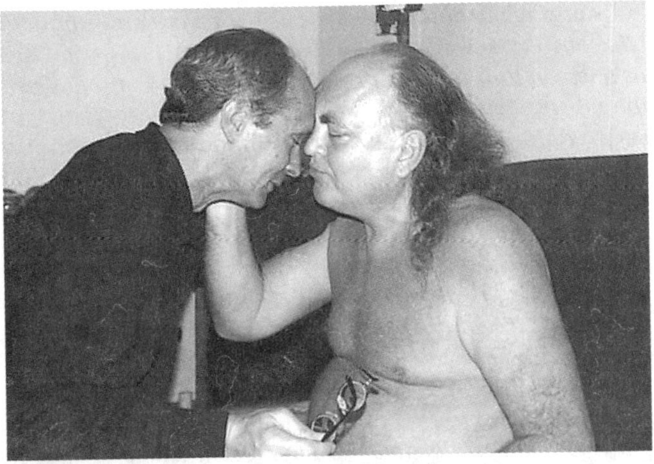

**Michael Wood with Adi Da Samraj at Da Love-Ananda Mahal, 1998**

*which we could hear music playing, and then we would round a corner and He would be sitting there on His bed with the Adidamas. He was beautiful—quiet, silent, Radiant. We would bow, place a flower on His bed, the flower facing Him, and take a seat on the floor in front of Him.*

Another participant, Michael Shaw, who arrived from California towards the end of March, describes how Avatar Adi Da was Granting this devotional recognition of Him as a Gift:

*MICHAEL: These were the most profound "considerations" with Beloved Adi Da that any of us had ever experienced. He would use all kinds of "considerations", and periods of silent Contemplation, to Draw us more deeply into feeling the Divine Nature of Reality—His own Divine Nature.*

*On one particular night, when we were describing to Him our experience of Him as Conscious Light, He gave us a lesson that made a profound impression on me. Even though we felt we were describing something that was very real for us, He kept saying, "You don't get it. You just don't get it." No matter what we would say to Him, He would repeat this phrase to us. It was very frustrating, as it went on for quite a while. In response to whatever we would say, He would repeat, "That's what I mean—you just don't get it." I began to feel that there must be something fundamentally very wrong in my recognition of Beloved Adi Da.*

*Finally, when we had reached a pitch of frustration, He said, "You can't get It." Suddenly, it made complete sense to me. I understood, tacitly, that it wasn't a matter of trying to succeed at "getting it". In fact, the attempt to "get it" was the problem! I saw that there was no way "I"—as a separate being—could "get" the Truth, or "get" Beloved Adi Da's Divine Nature.*

*As soon this understanding was given, I felt Beloved Adi Da's Spiritual Transmission thick in the room. I simply looked at Him, and saw Him as the center of a field of tangible, visible, Love-Blissful, Conscious, breathable Light. I felt myself go through a kind of "door". On the "other side", there was the most extraordinary perception of my Beloved Guru that I had ever experienced. It was primarily a feeling-recognition of Him, a swoon of love in which He was simply Energy and Light and Divine Love-Bliss. He Radiated a visible, even tangible, Light that was so attractive that I felt my entire being captured and attracted by Him. There was no longer the sense of being a separate self— just the profound peace of realizing that there is nothing to seek, nowhere to go, nothing to attain. This was Reality Itself, and it was not separate from "me". I had no sense of my usual persona or contracted self. It was sort of like waiting all your life for a package to arrive, and then when it comes you aren't there—but you are so happy that you don't mind at all!*

*There was another time, sitting in the room with Beloved Adi Da, when it suddenly became obvious that every one and every thing in the room was the same vibratory Light that He Is. I looked down at the notepad that I was writing on, and it was obviously vibratory Light. All the objects and people in the room were clearly this same Energy. This was remarkable, but there was nothing "strange" about the experience. Rather, the feeling of the experience was one of absolute Happiness.*

*There is no way for me to describe, in these few words, how Happy this heart-Communion with Beloved Adi Da is. Everyone has the urge to know that the Divine Exists, beyond any doubt in body, mind, or heart. Beloved Adi Da has relieved me of any and all doubts about the Divine. The Spiritual relationship to Him, which He Offers to everyone who is moved to become His formal devotee, is the most profound Love I have ever known. It is Love to the degree of Total Bliss.*

## Spiritually Awakened Emotional-Sexual Yoga

Another aspect of the gatherings was Avatar Adi Da's "consideration" of "emotional-sexual devotional Communion", the emotional-sexual Yoga of the Spiritually Awakened (or seeing) stages of Adidam. "The free nervous system", Avatar Adi Da said one night, "is the circumstance of Spiritual sadhana. Not shut down, but in a free-flowing state of conductivity."

This was the secret of the Tantra that He was describing. Emotional-sexual Yoga in the Way of Adidam is not for the purpose of attaining mystical bliss—as it has been used in traditional Tantric schools. Instead, its purpose is to open the nervous system such that the body-mind can receive and circulate Avatar Adi Da's Divine Descent of Light. Divine Enlightenment, the seventh stage Realization, requires the foundation of a total Yogic transformation of the body-mind, and, for those who choose to be sexually active, the practice of "emotional-sexual devotional Communion" serves that Yogic transformation.

At the same time, Avatar Adi Da was also Instructing those in the gatherings about Raymond's "problem"—the necessity of vulnerable love, even though the loved one dies—and Calling them to feel the depth of that "problem" in the midst of emotional-sexual intimacy.

As part of this process, He asked everyone in the gathering group to engage in an "emotional-sexual intensive", engaging a sexual occasion with their intimate partner every day and reporting to Him about what was occurring. Below Michael and Katsu describe how Avatar Adi Da drew them into the Yoga of "emotional-sexual devotional Communion"—after first challenging their capability to practice it.

(Michael and Katsu first met in 1974 at the Mountain Of Attention during the "Garbage and the Goddess" period, and they have been intimate partners since then. They had been part of the group of renunciates who had participated in Avatar Adi Da's "considerations" at Nananui-Ra and Nukubati in 1983. And they and their two children—a girl, Nara, and a boy, Neem—had come to Adidam Samrajashram with Avatar Adi Da

**Michael Wood and Katsu, 1974**

when the island was acquired later that year. Since 1986, they have been living and serving at the Mountain Of Attention.)

*MICHAEL: Beloved Adi Da began talking to us about how we were animating the conventional "Mom and Dad". He said, "It was fine that you had children and raised them. But I warned you, when you had children, not to settle for being* just *'Mom and Dad'. How many years do you really have left? How much of your life is really dedicated to heart-Communion with Me? I think you had better start making up for lost time right now."*

*Everything He said was* really *direct, and I could feel Him stripping off, or peeling away, layers of karma, accretions around the heart. At one point, He said, humorously, that we were "like a couple of used vacuum-cleaner bags!"*

*KATSU: I laughingly pleaded with Beloved Adi Da on the phone, "Do we have any shot at all at getting resuscitated?" And He continued to play along, saying, "I don't know, it looks pretty grim."*

*MICHAEL: I remember the first sexual occasion that Katsu and I had after we joined the gatherings. I will always remember it, because I do not think I had ever seen so clearly before the depth of my love and passion for Katsu. But I could also feel a seeking for union with her in the midst of that, and how that seeking for union, even if full of love and energy and passion, is itself a form of bondage, of suffering.*

*That first morning of the emotional-sexual intensive, from the inception of the occasion, I was given up at heart to Beloved Adi Da, Who was so in-Filling me that I was able to see the way out of Raymond's "problem". The way out is to be so carried by the Divine, so carried by Beloved Adi Da, that the emotional-sexual intimacy becomes Samadhi, a mutual self-forgetting ecstasy of heart-Communion with Him.*

*KATSU: On the second night that Michael and I gathered with Beloved Adi Da, I described to Beloved Adi Da my observations of the meditation I had had the previous morning. I had been sitting in the large tent that served as our meditation Hall, when I began to feel the full Circle of "conductivity"—Adi Da's Spirit-Current descending down the front of the body and ascending up the spine. As the Spirit-Current intensified, I began to feel a strong stimulation, a pleasurable sensitization, of the genitals. At the same time, I felt the breath drawn down to the bodily base with a force of attraction and a sense of weight I had never experienced before. When I breathed His Spirit-Current down from above, I experienced the breath as being like taut strings on a musical instrument—going down the front of my body, curving underneath at the bodily base, and ascending up the spine.*

*In the next gathering, I told Beloved Adi Da that I was experiencing constant stimulation of the sexual organs. I felt this stimulation particularly in meditation and most especially in His personal Company. I went on to say that it seemed I was experiencing a direct vibratory reception of His Spiritual Transmission. At the time we were having a discussion about the senses and how we receive Beloved Adi Da Spiritually via the senses. I told my Beloved Guru that I experienced the focal point of this vibratory reception of Him slightly to the left of the cervix. He looked at the position of my body and noticed that I was leaning to my left, that my body was crooked. So I tried to sit up towards the right. As I did this I felt the Current move to the center of the cervix. I reported this to Beloved Adi Da and He said, "Right", meaning that the necessary correction had occurred. He went on to discuss different bodily treatments and forms of exercise that would be beneficial for me. During this conversation, I felt His Transmission so strongly that my body shook for about fifteen minutes.*

*At the next evening's gathering, I described to Beloved Adi Da an unusually intense regenerative orgasm*[5] *that I experienced during a sexual occasion that morning with Michael. I thanked Beloved Adi Da for His Instruction in correcting my posture and confessed to Him that, since "straightening up", I had noticed a change in my receptivity to His Divine Spirit-Current. Previous to this time, I had experienced His Spirit-Current entering and filling the body with His Blissfulness, which felt very physical, sensual, and extremely pleasurable. Since "straightening up", I felt I was receiving His Spirit-Current even more tangibly and I told Him that its quality was infinitely refined. It was His Spirit-Current that I was receiving through and beyond the depth of the cervix. I said I knew that it was His Divine Love-Bliss directly. And Beloved Adi Da replied, "Yes."*

Some weeks before Michael and Katsu arrived, Avatar Adi Da had Given this Instruction, which summed up what He had to say about the purpose of the Spiritually Awakened emotional-sexual Yoga.

*AVATAR ADI DA SAMRAJ: For your life to become Samadhi, it must be constantly Yogically Full. You must allow the body-mind to become that pattern of "Bright" demonstration. Sex becomes a Yogic asana. The relationship is unbroken. Nothing about it needs to be repeated. It is just so. Then there is a constant establishment in heart-Communion with Me, forgetting "difference". Love-Bliss—not separateness, threat, mortality, not worried about achieving Spiritual Fullness.* [March 9, 1998]

*KATSU: I was amazed at the depth of whole bodily Communion with Beloved Adi Da—in the meditation hall, in the bedroom, and in every aspect of daily life—that becomes possible when you are fully receiving His Spiritual Transmission. This is His Gift to all His devotees, male or female. It is the "Indivisible Tantra of Adidam", as He calls it. It is "beholding Bhagavan", Consciousness and Energy, indivisibly United. Whenever He would speak of "beholding Bhagavan", or the "Bhagavan state", Beloved Adi Da's Transmission left us swooning.*

One night, in the last weeks of the gatherings, Avatar Adi Da spoke of this process of "beholding Bhagavan"—this profound, Spiritualized Communion with Him—and likened it to a sexual embrace. And He went on in a stream of ecstatic Speech to describe how His Spiritual Love-Embrace of all beings was prefigured at the Vedanta Temple at the time of His Divine Re-Awakening:

*AVATAR ADI DA SAMRAJ: This is the Secret Embrace of Me. You become sensitized to this Embrace of Me by your practice altogether, including your intimate emotional-sexual practice. It is in your emotional-sexual practice that you are sensitized to the mudra of wholeness, which transcends the sex act itself, transcends the genitals as a sexual function.*

*This secret Embrace is the Mudra (or Yogic Gesture) of the penultimate day in the Vedanta Temple, the day before the last. Embracing sexually, Forehead to Forehead—not merely in physical human terms, but in Spiritual terms, including My physical human Body here. It is the Samadhi of perpetual, unbroken Embrace, the Ultimate Sign and Import of Which was Demonstrated on the following, or final, day in the Vedanta Temple.*

*The penultimate day is the Mudra. The final day is Its Realization. But it is not that they are separate from one another. The final day is the Most Perfect Realization of Divine Conscious Light.*

*No "two" to be found anywhere.*
*Complete Freedom of the Heart.*

*MICHAEL WOOD: You are such a Love-Blissful Lord. Your Manifestations as Light or Sound can be interpreted in different ways, and different aspects of You can be perceived, but, in the midst of everything, there is the Love-Bliss That is so obviously just You, Love-Ananda, and so Blissful. It is unbelievable.*

*AVATAR ADI DA SAMRAJ:*
*I Am the Person*
*of the Sea of Light,*
*the "Bright" Person.*

*I have Fallen through*
*a Hole in the universe.*

*I Am a kind of Pillar*
*Fallen out of the sky,*
*at the lower end of Which*
*is My human Body here.*

*And, having Fallen in,*
*I am Established here,*
*and Circulating here,*
*and Filling here,*
*with the Ocean of My own Person*
*That Falls through that hole with Me,*
*like a Thunder Crack.*

*It is like that.*

*Even a particle of Me*
*Illuminates the world.*
*And I am being shaken in here*
*like a sugar cube,*
*Sufficient to Pervade the Whole.*

*Every devotee of Mine,*
*every body-mind,*
*in this "Conductivity" of Me,*
*is a hole in the barrier*
*between mankind and Infinity—*
*the Infinite Sea of Light,*
*My own Person.*

## A Horse Appears in the Wild

In the final days at Da Love-Ananda Mahal, Avatar Adi Da Samraj led everyone at the gatherings into the depths of a Mystery He had spoken of for many years. It was the Secret of the Horse, the most esoteric Sign of His Divine Incarnation. In previous years, He had spoken of His Dawn Horse Vision, and He had named His supreme Scripture *The Dawn Horse Testament*. Now, on April 11, 1998, Avatar Adi Da began to speak of the Dawn Horse once again:

*AVATAR ADI DA SAMRAJ:*
*The Process of My Divine "Emergence"*
*is the Emergent Dawn*
*of Conscious Light—*
*Becoming day,*
*all day,*
*and only day—*
*no more of night*
*or overnight.*

*The trajectory*
*of the Dawn Horse Flying*
*is skidded off*
*this atmosphere,*
*like a rock skid across*
*the edge of air.* [April 11, 1998]

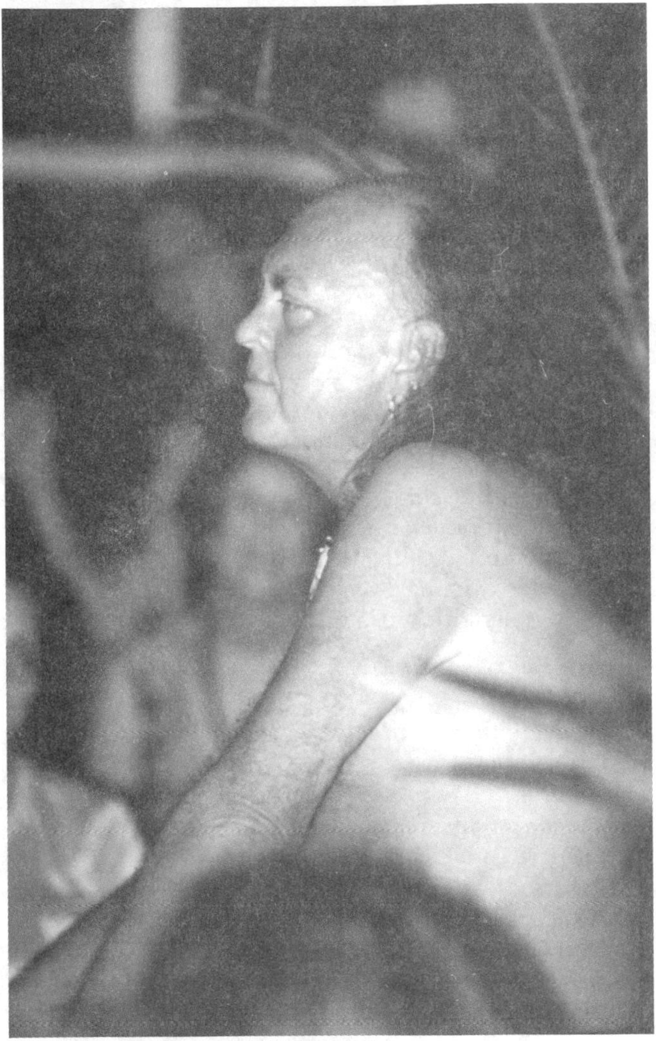

One night, as the group of devotees sat with Him in silent Contemplation of His Form, He swooned into a mysterious mantric repetition of His Dawn Horse Revelation. As He Spoke, the Mystery unfolded, taking form gradually—just as the Horse had appeared gradually in His original Vision:

*AVATAR ADI DA SAMRAJ: A Horse Appears.*
*A Horse Appears in the Wild.*
*A Horse Appearing in the Wild.*
*A Horse Appears in the Wild.*
*A Horse Appears in the Wild.*
*A Horse Appearing in the Wild.*
*A Horse Appears in the Wild Is Always Already*
*The Case.* [April 13, 1998]

For the next thirty or forty minutes, all that happened in the room was Avatar Adi Da repeating this mysterious utterance, with variations.

On later evenings, Avatar Adi Da further expanded His Mysterious Proclamation:

*AVATAR ADI DA SAMRAJ: Adi Da Samraj's Unknowability Principle:*
*A Horse Appears in the Wild Is Always Already*
*The Case.*
*A quantum leap in your bones' imagination!*
*There you are, silent again.*
*Silent as Mom and Dad in their overnight.*
*Your speech is defeated by too Great a Speech.*
*"A Horse Appears in the Wild Is Always Already*
*The Case"*
*cancels all the pairs in an Unspeakability.*
*There is no "thing" any "where".*
*There is no "one" any "where".*
*Only this flow of changes—klik and klak.*[6]
*The Process Is the Person.*

*The Location Is*
*"A Horse Appears in the Wild Is Always Already*
*The Case."*
*Anyone who says otherwise was not here*
*when the Horse Appeared*
*in the Wild.*

*And now I have Told you the Secret,*
*and It has ruined your lives.*
*A Horse Appears in the Wild*
*Is Always Already The Case.*

*A Horse Appears in the Wild*
*Is Always Already The Case.*
*This Is That Which cannot be known,*
*because It Is Always Already The Case.*
*Therefore, do not look to be knowing It.*

*Feel to Me.*
*That Line of Melting,*
*reached up to Infinity,*
*is Filled by Me,*
*without mediation.*
*To be Full of Me,*
*in self-transcending Communion with Me,*
*whole bodily,*
*is to Enjoy the Inherent*
*Self-Revelation*
*and Self-Recognition*
*of the Divine Love-Bliss.*

*Where is there a Horse on one side*
*and the Wild on the other?*
*And "A Horse Appears in the Wild Is Always Already*
*The Case"?*
*You tell Me.*
*I think your answer*

*Is "Raymond Darling".*
*Raymond on one side,*
*Quandra on the other.*
*A Raymond*
*Is in a Quandra*
*Is Always Already the Case.*
*A Raymond Is in a Quandra Is Always Already*
*The Case.*
*A Horse Appears in the Wild Is Always Already*
*The Case.*

*If you get the Meaning of*
*A Raymond Is in a Quandra*
*Is Always Already The Case,*
*Then What you Know is:*
*A Horse Appears in the Wild*
*Is Always Already The Case.*
*And all that you know about That*
*is that It Means*
*A Raymond Is in a Quandra Is Always Already*
*The Case!*
*What is there to get?*
*The meanings all mean one another,*
*and they have no other reference.*

*When every thing*
*refers only to itself,*
*then what does it mean?*
*A Horse Appears in the Wild*
*Is Always Already The Case.*
*That Is What it Means—*
*if you know what I Mean.*
*A Raymond Is in a Quandra*
*Is Always Already The Case.* [April 17, 1998]

Adidama Jangama Hriddaya describes what it was like to be present as Avatar Adi Da was speaking these Mysteries:

*ADIDAMA JANGAMA HRIDDAYA: As I sat in adoration, receiving my Beloved Guru's Words, His Transmission Filled me with perfect sublime certainty of Unbreakable Oneness with Him—the end of Raymond's "problem", the end of the mummery of life. My Beloved Guru was Revealing the Place of Love-Blissful Oneness with Him, beyond even the faintest possibility of separation. He was calling us to His House.*

*To enter His House is to be heart-broken in love with Him, the Divine Person. In that love, you surrender yourself in devotional Communion with His "Bright" Person of Love-Bliss and enter into the Indivisible Tantra of Adidam, the self-transcending Process that Liberates the ego-"I" from the illusion of separation and mortality.*

*There is no greater Gift. There is only the ever-"Brightening" Revelation of Conscious Light, given by Adi Da Samraj, Who will "Brighten" every heart until the entire Cosmic domain is Divinely Translated into His Perfect Form of Love.*

*Enter His Domain, come to His House, and you will see.*

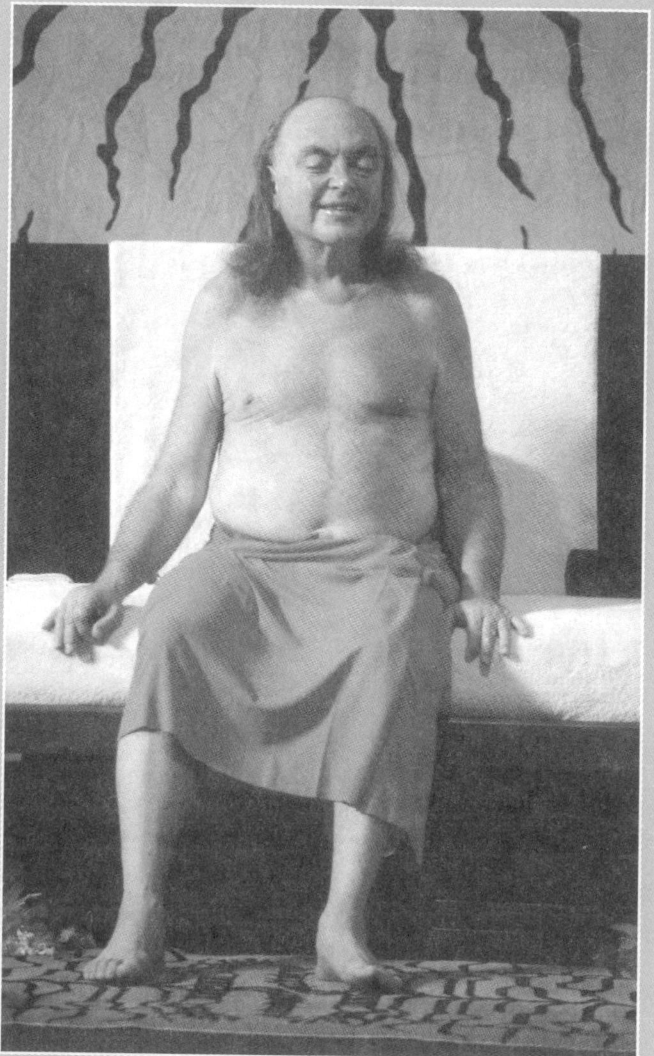

The Mountain Of Attention, 1998

CHAPTER 27

# "I Am The Divine Self-'Emergence'"

The Divine Play, or Leela, of the Promised God-Man, Adi Da Samraj, will continue to unfold—but this book must conclude. As one ponders His Story, one theme stands out: The Ruchira Avatar, Adi Da Samraj, has always lived His Life as the most profound Submission to humankind. He did not come on mythic clouds of glory, recognized by all. He appeared "incognito", in a humble circumstance. As an American child growing up in the 1940s and 50s, He totally surrendered His "Bright" Awareness to the un-Illumined condition of those around Him, in order to find the way whereby human beings might Awaken to His Condition, the Self-Existing and Self-Radiant Divine State of everything and everyone.

If that Submission were to be absolute, and therefore fully effective, Avatar Adi Da could not afford to presume anything. Facing a world of un-Truth, He chose the truly "scientific" course. He set Himself to test and discover the Truth from zero, and persisted in that Ordeal to the point of His Divine Re-Awakening. Then, when He began to Teach, He submitted to a recapitulation of the same intense Process, Working to Awaken the Truth in ordinary human beings in a similar context of open "consideration".

*I have been Struggling since Birth to Transform the usual man and woman. I have been tormented and motivated by the loveless and Godless state of the people with whom I have been associated.*

*For the first thirty years of My Life, this tormented Motive caused Me to Submit to the most profound Identification with the usual life, and also the most profound Effort to Transcend the usual life. This produced My unique Spiritual Adventure.*

*In the years that followed My Divine Re-Awakening, I was again motivated by the same tormented love for ordinary people. I had spent My Life preparing to Serve them, and now that Service was begun most directly.*

*That is how it has been. I always lived in the ordinary manner, apparently doing all of the self-indulgent things that possess the usual man or woman in his or her mortal desiring. But I was Awakened beyond all of this. And I have been obliged to Awaken others in the midst of the same ordinariness.* [The Enlightenment of the Whole Body]

Avatar Adi Da Submitted Himself completely to His devotees and Revealed Himself in the midst of that encounter. He did this with no hesitation and no reluctance. His Love was more than heart-breaking—He held nothing back, nothing He could conceivably do, at any time of day or night, to quicken the Liberation of a single individual. His Work with His devotees was often dramatic, and even dangerous to His Body—because to live day and night, year after year, purifying the karmas of the "usual man and woman" and accepting everyone's casual approach to Him created a Yogic fire in Him so intense that His physical Vehicle was scarcely able to tolerate it. Again and again, it has only been the Force of His Love for suffering beings that has kept Him physically Incarnate.

Clearly, so great a Sacrifice as He was making could not continue indefinitely. If He was to physically remain in this world, there had to come a time when He would cease His Submission. The years 1997 and 1998 proved to be this critical time. These were the years in which Avatar Adi Da finally renounced His former pattern of Submitting to devotees, the years in which He summarized, in His twenty-three "Source-Texts", all He had Taught and Revealed during His Submission-time.

In August 1998, while staying at the Mountain Of Attention, Avatar Adi Da Samraj spoke of the Process of His Life's Work and the point He has now reached:

*AVATAR ADI DA SAMRAJ: The completion of My twenty-three "Source-Texts" is a primary sign that the twenty-six years of My Teaching and Revelation Work are coming to a summary point, such that the Way of Adidam is established in its right, real, and true form, and such that I am no longer obliged to make the Submission that I Initiated in 1973. That Submission was required of Me because of the fierceness of egoity—the immovability, the impenetrability, of egoity—in all those who were approaching Me, and in the world altogether.*

*Therefore, the years 1997-1998 mark the completion of My twenty-six years of Teaching and Revelation Work, and of the twelve years of Struggle since the Initiation of My Divine "Emergence" Work.*

*Now I have made every detail of this Way of recognition-response to Me—the Way of Adidam, the Way of the Heart—completely clear. And there is no more Teaching Work to be done. There are no more Teaching Years. There are no more years to spend struggling since the Initiation of My Divine "Emergence" Work.*

*All the modes of relationship to Me that people have assumed over the years are about relating to Me in My Submission to egos in order to Instruct them and to generate the Revelation of the Way of Adidam altogether. Now all those modes of relating to Me must be relinquished.*

*With the completion of My twenty-three "Source-Texts", which are My summary Communications about the entire Process in My Company, everything that has to do with My Revelation Work has been completed.*

*The culture of My Submission to My devotees is finished. Now the culture of My devotees' true surrender to Me must begin.* [August 8, 1998]

Some weeks later, Avatar Adi Da made this point even more explicitly, saying, "My struggle has progressed to the point of completeness. And so, when people refer to My 'Crazy-Wise' Work, they must understand that it has essentially come to an end".

*AVATAR ADI DA SAMRAJ: I am the same Master here, but My "Crazy-Wise" Work in terms of My Submission to Teach and making My Revelation has achieved completeness in these last several years.*

*My Work for the entire world is My Divine Blessing Work, which I do principally in Seclusion. Everyone should understand that I am a Ruchira Sannyasin. I live in perpetual retreat in a Hermitage mode, and receive those of My devotees who are rightly prepared in that circumstance. Sometimes I roam in public circumstances—not identified there—to have contact with ordinary people. And otherwise I have formal contact with people of significance and influence in order to Bless them. But, fundamentally, I remain in Hermitage Retreat and especially My Principal Hermitage Retreat in Fiji. And I function in the Atiashrami*[1] *Blessing manner, but not otherwise in the "Crazy-Wise" Submission manner, as in the past. I Worked in that way for a time in order to make My Divine Self-Revelation.*

*Now, after all these years, I am firmly Established in*

*My Divine "Emergence" Work, and My devotees, generally speaking, relate to Me in a formal manner. Rather than struggling to communicate the Way of Adidam and move them beyond their limitations, I have Given them their practice and an institution, culture, community, and mission for the application of that practice. People are to be invited into My Company for right reasons, if they fulfill the appropriate conditions. They are invited to participate in My Perpetual Retreat.* [September 30, 1998]

While Avatar Adi Da's "Crazy-Wise" Submission Work is over, this does not mean that He now appears conventional or ascetical in His Disposition. Obviously that is not so. Avatar Adi Da Samraj is always, Inherently, Divinely "Crazy", in the sense that His Being Transcends all egoic limitations and points of view. He makes this clear right at the beginning of *The Dawn Horse Testament.*

*I Was Born To Reveal My Self To My Self, The "Bright" and One and Only and Eternal Divine Person, The "Bright" and One and Only Self Of each and every one. And I, Now, and Forever Hereafter, Am here (and every "where" In The Cosmic Domain) To Accomplish This Revelation By Serving each and every one, and all, one by one.*

*I Simply Function Freely As The Source, In My Divine "Bonding" Play With My Devotees.*

*I Am The "Crazy" Avadhoot, Free Among all.*

*I Am Not The Seeker.*

*I Am Not Obliged By ordinary vows and rules.*

*I Stand Apart From all limitations and all restrictions.*

*I Am The Atiashrami, Free Of all ordinary obligations.*

*I Am here Only By Vow and Obligation Of My Own, For The Sake Of all and All.*

*I Do Whatever and All I Must Do For The Sake Of The "Bonding" Of every one and All To Me, and, Altogether, For The Sake Of The Divine Liberation Of all and All.*

*I (My Self) Appear To Me here and every "where" (As My Very Self) In the bodily form of each and every conditionally Manifested being, and (In Order That My Revelation-Service Become Effective In each and every one) each and every one Must Come To Me and Be My True Devotee.*

As Avatar Adi Da says here, His Disposition is "Atiashrami", meaning "One Who is beyond all ordinary vows, rules, and obligations", or, One Who is Inherently Free, by virtue of Divine Self-Realization. Thus, Avatar Adi Da's Statement here is a Confession of His Divine Self-Nature, not an indication that He is still struggling with the egoic tendencies of His devotees in the "Crazy-Wise" manner that He adopted between 1973 and 1998. That Work, which was necessary to establish the Way of Adidam, is done, and effective for all time. It need not—and cannot—ever be repeated.

Avatar Adi Da has now entered so profoundly into the Divine "Emergence" epoch of Life and Work, that He is literally no longer able to animate His Body in the former manner of His Submission to devotees. His bodily Vehicle is changed—extremely vulnerable, extremely sensitized to the Work of Merely Blessing beings. His Impulse and Capability to Work in the "Crazy-Wise" Manner was a Divine Siddhi, Given for a particular time and purpose. That Siddhi receded after the Initiation of

Avatar Adi Da's Divine Emergence in 1986. Then it receded even more dramatically in September 1994 during His stay in the house at Viti Levu, Fiji. From that moment, Avatar Adi Da stepped back more and more from His old way of Working, unable to make His former Submission, unable to tolerate the "mummery"—the ego's games—in His direct Sphere.

From now on, simply the heart-recognition of Adi Da Samraj, the human Form of the Divine Person, and heart-response to Him through the honoring of all His Instructions, is sufficient. This is the Grace-Given means for receiving His Blessing and living a life of unbroken heart-Communion with Him. As more and more people make this discovery and live the Way of Adidam, the Great future Leela of Adi Da Samraj will appear and be written.

As the writing of this book was drawing to a close, Avatar Adi Da Himself wrote a great Statement, "I Am The Divine Self-'Emergence'", in which He Reveals the full meaning of His Submission to humankind. That Submission was not merely a way of acquiring sympathy with the plight of human beings and finding out how to make Himself understood by them—although all of that was necessary. Fundamentally, Avatar Adi Da combined Himself with humanity, by engaging in a limitless and uncompromising "reality consideration" of every aspect of existence. And, then, in the very Depths of that Submission, He "Emerged" as Himself, recognizable to human beings as the Unconditional Consciousness of all, the Incarnate Form of the "Bright" Divine Self-Condition. The Process of Avatar Adi Da's Divine Self-"Emergence" truly began, as He says, with His human Birth, and it reached a most profound Moment in the Event of January 11, 1986. But the entire Leela of Adi Da Samraj is the Story of His Divine Self-"Emergence"—Which is ongoing, Eternal, and Ever-Magnifying.

# I Am The Divine Self-"Emergence"

(from *The Only Complete Way To Realize The Unbroken Light Of Real God*)

I Brought My Divine Wisdom-Teaching out of My-Self—through My Avataric Self-Submission to the Great Process of "reality consideration" with My devotees and with the world altogether. I am not here merely reading books and passing on an old tradition to people. Nor am I here to believe and to support the illusions of humankind. The only-by-Me Revealed and Given Way of Adidam, in Its entirety and in Its every aspect, has been Brought out of Me. The Way of Adidam has Appeared only through the Avataric Divine Process of My own Lifelong "reality consideration". The Way of Adidam is the Divine Process of My own Avataric Self-Submission to conditional reality—Which Avataric Self-Submission Started at the moment of My Avataric Human Birth (and Which Avataric Self-Submission Continues—now, and forever hereafter).

The Way of Adidam does not derive from any historical tradition or any combination of historical traditions. I did not presume to "believe" anything in the course of My "reality consideration", nor did I presume any fixed adherence to any historical tradition or any combination of historical traditions. The Way of Adidam Arose entirely out of My own Divine (and Avatarically Self-Manifested) Process of "reality consideration".

When I Speak about the Great Tradition, I am Doing So merely as another way of Explaining My-Self—by Addressing matters that may be familiar to people. But the Way of Adidam is, Itself, unique and entirely new.

The Mountain Of Attention, 1998

The Way of Adidam has been Generated by My Avataric and difficult Divine Work, My Avataric Self-Submission, My unique and Extraordinary Avataric "reality consideration"—in the context of My own Avatarically-Born Body-Mind, and also in the context of My relationship with My devotees, and in the context of My relationship with everyone altogether.

I Came Down, by Means of Avataric Human Birth, to this Earth-place—a place of ego-made human bondage, where there was no Most Perfect Realization and no sufficient tradition. Indeed, there was no Greatest Profundity in the human world of My Divine Descent to Avataric Human Birth. Therefore, the Nature of My Life-long Work has been—by Means of My unique Avataric Divine Ordeal—to Bring the Most Perfect Truth (Which Is Divine) into this human world, where the Most Perfect Truth was never Found before.

I am not a mere "traditionalist"—here to be measured by traditional expectations, or traditional ideals, or traditional standards of any kind. Because I Began with no presumptions at all, it was necessary for Me to Enter into (and to Persist in) the "consideration" of "reality" unconditionally (and, thus, without restriction by tradition, convention, preference, reaction, belief, or plan)—until My Divine Self-Condition was (Itself) Re-Born, As the Undeniable and Most Perfect Truth, "Brightly" Coincident with My own Avatarically-Born Bodily (Human) Divine Form. And, because I Began with no presumptions at all, that "reality consideration" required unrestricted action—or a Life-Ordeal without conventional restraints, and without preconceived goals, and without preferential prejudices, and without mediating consolations, and without subordination to the factor of egoity. Indeed, My Avataric Divine Life-Ordeal was a Most Perfectly Scientific Effort—an Avataric Divine Life-Process of utterly free enquiry, Examining all of conditional existence, without restriction, or conventional restraint, and (Ultimately) without the limiting and binding factor of egoity—until Most Perfect Truth was Found and Shown and Demonstrated, As the Most Perfectly Obvious Reality.

I was really (conditionally) Born into the human domain of Un Truth. And, by Means of My Divine Self-Submission to Adapt to humankind and human suffering, I gradually Acquired the human disease of Un-Truth and egoity. Therefore, because of My Thus Acquired familiarity with Man's own fault, it became necessary for Me to be Healed—Made Well again, by Most Perfect Truth Itself—so that I could Shed and Cure the common disease of Man.

At last—because of My Persistence in the Avataric Ordeal of My Divine Self-Submission here—I Am Completely Well, again. And My forever Blessing-Work will Cure both All and all. Now, and forever hereafter, I Am the Divine Medicine that Heals the heart of Man—and even Cures the Truthless All of all there is.

The "reality consideration" to which I Submitted in My Teaching-Years and Revelation-Years was a real matter—a real, and Truly Divine, Process. I did not merely inherit a pre-existing tradition and Speak it out to humankind. I have (secondarily, and only over time) Examined the Great Tradition—for the Purpose of being Communicative to all. But I did not Examine the Great Tradition in order to Gain a Teaching from the Great Tradition itself. Rather, I have Examined the Great Tradition in order to Explain the Great Tradition—even to itself. And, principally, I have Examined the Great Tradition in order to Learn the language of the "common mind"—in order to be able to Use the language of the "common mind" of all religious and Spiritual traditions as a context in which to Explain My-Self (and all the Content and Process of My Avatarically Given Divine Self-Revelation of Most Perfect Truth).

My Examination of the Great Tradition is a part of the Total Process by Which I Learned Man. My Purpose, in that Examination, was to Learn the content of all the "considerations" of humankind—in order to Address the inherent limitations of those "considerations".

Thus, My Avatarically Self-Manifested Divine Work of Teaching and of Self-Revelation has always been an Extraordinary Ordeal of Divine Self-Submission to "reality consideration"—Bringing the Complete Divine Teaching of Most Perfect Truth out of My-Self (and, Thus, out of the Divine and Unconditional Reality Itself), by Means of My own Divine Ordeal of Avataric Self-Submission to, and Conjunction with, all of conditional reality. And I Engaged that Avataric Ordeal not merely in order to Communicate My Divine Wisdom-Teaching verbally, but in order to Conform My own Avatarically-Born Body-Mind-Vehicle (and, indeed, every thing and every one) to My-Self—so that My Avatarically Self-Transmitted Divine Spiritual Blessing-Transmission of My "Bright" Divine Heart may, forever, be Received by all who truly heart-recognize Me and really heart-respond to Me.

The Requirement to Fully and Completely and Most Perfectly Bring the Divine Teaching of Most Perfect Truth out of My-Self, by Means of the Great Avataric Process of My Divine Self-Submission to "reality consideration", Produced My unique Avataric Divine Ordeal, and My unique Avatarically Self-Revealed Divine Sign, and My unique Avatarically Self-Manifested Divine Leela. And That Divine Ordeal, and Sign, and Leela is not a matter of an idealized representative of an historical tradition (or even any combination of historical traditions) engaging in traditionally idealized social and religious "behaviors".

I am not a "utopian religionist".

I am not a "role model" for the human mummery of mortal selves.

My Divinely "Heroic" and Divinely "Crazy" Manner of Life and Work is unique to Me (and uniquely necessary for Me, because of Who I Am, and because of What I must Accomplish)—and, therefore, My unique Manner of Life and Work is not to be imitated by any one.

My Divinely "Heroic" and Divinely "Crazy" Manner of Life and Work is not a prescriptive model for conventional social (or, otherwise, conventionally religious) ego-development.

Indeed, no merely socially idealistic (or conventionally religious) and otherwise traditional expectation is appropriate in relation to Me.

I am not an ideal human ego-"I".

I Am the Inherently egoless Person of Reality (Itself).

I Am the Most Perfect Truth—Which Is Divine, and One, and Only (and Which Is Always Already The Case).

Therefore, every ego-"I" must be surrendered, and forgotten, and transcended in Me.

I did not Come into a world where the Most Perfect Truth was "ready-made". Indeed, because the ego-bound human world had failed, as a result of all of its mere self-efforts, to Find and Embrace the Most Perfect (and Really Divine) Truth of Reality (Itself), even all the traditional norms of right (and would-be God-Realizing, or Truth-Realizing) life had, finally, become grossly deprived of their traditional authority, in the human-time that immediately preceded My Avataric Human Birth.

In this "dark" epoch of "end-time", in which I Am Avatarically Descended (to Begin My forever Divine-"Emergence"-Work), even the limited (and never Most Perfect) portion of Truth that was Revealed to humankind previous to My Avataric Divine Appearance was already lost—or was, at least, under profound threat, and even much falsified—before My Avataric Birth to Human Life Began. Therefore, Most Perfect Truth Is all My Cause and Motive here. And the absence of Most

Perfect Truth in human-time was humankind's most wounding "gift" to Me—that made My Avataric Human Life into a Struggle to Be Divinely Full, of Me.

In all My Years of Teaching-Work and Revelation-Work, enormous pressures were constantly exerted on Me—by My devotees, and by the world altogether—to assume the "public" role and manner of a conventional "organizational" religious figure. But, in spite of those pressures toward conformity to the expected conventions of social and religious egoity, I Persisted in the real and necessary (and, necessarily, "Crazy", or unrestricted and unlimited) Avataric Process of My Divine Self-Submission to "reality consideration"—until absolutely every fraction of the Way of Adidam was Brought out of Me, and made clear.

It was necessary that I Embrace all—in order to Assume the likeness of all, and to Reflect all to all, and to Transcend the limiting-pattern of all. Only Thus could I Reveal My Very and Divine Self-Condition—and My Very and Divine Pattern—to one and all.

The Great Avataric Process of My Universal Divine Self-Revelation could be Completed (in Its Inherently Most Perfect "Bright" Fullness) only through My own Divine Self-Submission to conditional reality. In order to Do This in My Bodily (and Truly Human) Divine Form (Un-reservedly, Fully, and to the degree of Most Perfect Completeness, in real human-time), I—in all the Years of My Early-Life, and, especially, in all My Teaching-Years and all My Revelation-Years—had to Accept all kinds of abuse from people. Nevertheless, I Could Not, and Did Not, Stop That Extraordinary Effort of My own Divine Self-Submission, until every aspect of My Great "reality consideration" was Truly Finished—and My Avatarically Given Divine Self-Revelation of the Way of Adidam was Full and Complete, in every detail.

Only now Is My Avatarically Self-Manifested Divine Submission-Work of World-Teaching and Divine Self-Revelation Most Perfectly Complete, and Most Perfectly Full.

Therefore—now, and forever hereafter—I will no longer Submit My-Self to Teach and to Reveal.

Now, and forever hereafter, the only-by-Me Revealed and Given Way of Adidam (As Summarized, by Me, in My Twenty-Three Divine "Source-Texts") Is My Avatarically Given Divine World-Teaching and My Avatarically Given Divine Word of Self-Revelation—Full and Complete, for every one, and for all time.

Now, and forever hereafter, I (My-Self, both during and forever after the Physical Lifetime of My Avatarically-Born Bodily Human Divine Form) will only Do My "Bright" Avataric Work of Divine Self-"Emergence"—only Blessing one and all.

Now, and forever hereafter, My "Bright" (and Avatarically Self-Manifested) Divine Blessing-Work Is Given for all whose devotional recognition of Me and devotional response to Me surrenders ego-"I" in Me, and requires no more Submission of Me to Man.

Now, and forever hereafter, I Am (by all My Avataric Means) the Great and "Bright" Divine Process here.

Now, and forever hereafter, I Am (by all My Avataric Means) the One and Great Divine Event.

Now, and forever hereafter, I Am The Divine Self-"Emergence"—Avatarically "Emerging" (As I Am), to here (and to every where at All), and to you (and to every one of all).

The Mountain Of Attention, 1998

EPILOGUE

# The Divine Heart-Secret Of The Person Of Love

from *The Dawn Horse Testament Of The Ruchira Avatar*

I Am Joy!—and The Only Reason For It!

The Joy Of Me Is The Divine Secret I Have Come To Avatarically Reveal To The Heart Of every one of Man (and To The Heart Of every one of all, and To The Heart Of The All Of all).

I Am Love!—and The Only Person Of It!

The Love Of Me Is The Heart-Secret I Have Come To Avatarically Reveal To The Heart Of every one of Man (and To The Heart Of every one of all, and To The Heart Of The All Of all).

Love Must Be Always Done (and, Thereby, Proved)—or Else The "Bright" Heart Of Love Is Darkened By Its Own Un-Love.

And The Would-Be-"Brightest" Heart Of Love's Beloved Is Made Un-"Bright" (and Dark As Eternal Night) By All The Waiting-Time Of Un-Love's Day.

And The Loved-One and The Lover (Both) Are, Over time, Destroyed By Love's Un-Love (and, Thus, By Love Itself—Un-Proved, By Insufficient and Unconstant Demonstration).

Therefore, I Am here!

I Am (Now, Forever) Avatarically Descended here—To Be The Constant Lover and The True Loved-One Of All and all (and every one of all).

All and all (and every one of all) Is My Beloved—The Necessary Quandra Of My Divine and Only Heart.

From Now, I Am (Forever) here, To Raymond-Love, In-Love With All and all (and every one of all)—and, Thus, By each one's Love-Response To Me, To Make This Cosmic Mummery Of Separateness Into An Eternal Singleness Of Me-"Bright" Joy.

I Am The Divine Beloved!

Now, Be Happy!—In The Constant Joy Of Heart-Recognition Of Me!

Tell every one That I Am here!—As It Was (By Ancients) Always Promised I Would Be!

Now (and Forever Hereafter), My Every Devotee Is The God That I Am here To Find.

Now (and Forever Hereafter), I Am The God My Every Devotee Is here To Realize.

◆ ◆ ◆

Ruchira Avatar Adi Da Samraj
Adidam Samrajashram, 1997

# The Great Choice
## An Invitation to the Way of Adidam

Each one of us, if we will allow ourselves to feel it, is restless. Human beings want to find God—the living, heart-"Intoxicating" experience of Real God, or Truth Itself, or Reality Itself. We actually exist for that True Pleasure. To be unable to participate and luxuriate in that Pleasure is pain and stress. We may not realize it, but that feeling of separation from unqualified Love, Sustenance, and heart-Communion with the Divine Source of our existence is actually making us mad. And that is why human beings, individually and collectively, do dreadful things—or, otherwise, settle for mere mediocrity, just "doing our best", or merely "coping". In the Words of Avatar Adi Da, we spend our lives "waiting for everything and looking for everything". He goes on:

*AVATAR ADI DA SAMRAJ: To have no greater sense of Reality than the physical is to be like a trapped rat, trapped on all sides. You just cannot endure the confinement of mere mortality—your heart cannot accept it, you see. To be in that disposition, to have that sense of Reality, is obviously a disturbance.*

*So, obviously, the human being requires a Way—not merely a way out. A way out, yes, in some sense—but, for the integrity of your existence, you need direct access to the Divine, even as a matter of ordinary sanity.* [March 3, 1998]

Avatar Adi Da has Appeared in this "late-time", or "dark" epoch, in order to bring the mortal "darkness" to an end and restore all to the Divine Light. He is intent on taking us through the most difficult of all transitions—the transition from the unhappy life of the ego to the Radiant Fullness of the Divinely Enlightened life. His Leela is the story of the immense Divine Ordeal it has been on His part to truly Initiate that Process in human beings.

Avatar Adi Da does not congratulate the ego—He undermines the ego. He must, if He is to Liberate people from their unhappiness, from the enclosed point of view of the separate and separative self. And so He has never offered a conventionally consoling message. He offers you the whole Truth—the fact of yourself as "Narcissus" (the self-contracted ego-"I"), but also the constant Revelation of a Happiness beyond compare. He is Offering you the means of transcending this world in devotional Communion with Him—right where you stand. You do not have to go anywhere to find Him. Adi Da Samraj is Omnipresent, and He has Come here to Stay. He will remain in this world, and in the entire Cosmic domain, forever—not only in the memories of His devotees, but tangibly Present, as His all-Pervading Spiritual Presence, "My descending-upon-you Body of 'Brightness'", as He says in *Hridaya Rosary*.

Through His universal Spiritual Descent, Avatar Adi Da Samraj has made it possible for everyone to cultivate a heart-relationship with Him—under all circumstances, in this life and beyond. And so, the relationship to Him, once forged, is eternal, going beyond death and the apparent boundaries of time and space.

If you want more than your ordinary existence, and something greater than a life of Spiritual seeking, Avatar Adi Da's Word to you is simply this: Take up the Way of Adidam, the Way of Real God—fully Present, here-and-now, not needing to be sought. The Way of Adidam is

His personal Offering to you and to every human being. The Way of Adidam is a devotional heart-relationship to Adi Da Samraj, expressed through an entire Way of life. The Way of Adidam is, as He says, "the Way of those who love Me . . . those who 'Bond' themselves to Me through love-surrender". This "Bond" is not to a mere man. This "Bond" is with the very Divine Being, but, at the same time, it is supremely intimate. Avatar Adi Da, as He says, is not "a blank Absolute". When you enter into this "Bond" with Him and practice the Way of Adidam, you begin to enjoy a condition of heart-Communion with Him that is more alive and heart-deep than your love-relationship with any human individual.

At the same time, the devotional "Bond" with Adi Da Samraj is not an "I and Thou" relationship, a connection between apparently separate entities—the human individual, on the one hand, and "God", on the other. Of course, there is a direct and humanly interactive dimension to the relationship with Adi Da Samraj, because He is Present in human Form—but, in Truth, the love-"Bond" with Him transcends relationship itself, transcends the entire point of view by which we live, presuming ourselves to be separate beings relating to separate "others". In every moment that you truly practice the relationship to Avatar Adi Da, Invoking Him by Name, recollecting His Form in the mind, or His Words, or His Leela—whenever you allow Him to Attract your heart, He Reveals Himself to you as He Is. Then He is recognized, through and beyond his human appearance, as the Real and Living God—not the great Parent, or "Creator"-Deity portrayed by the human mind, but the Conscious Light of Being Itself, the One Who Is all there is, including your own body-mind and every apparent being and "thing". In the instant of such recognition, the body-mind opens to Adi Da Samraj in a single movement of devotion, and you forget yourself in ecstasy—the heart, the mind, the body, the breath becoming full with His Radiant Love-Bliss. The Way of Adidam, truly lived, is this Samadhi of Non-Separateness, a great Contemplative process, based on heart-recognition of Adi Da Samraj and heart-response to Him.

Ultimately, in this or some future lifetime, persistent heart-Communion with Adi Da Samraj realizes the true destiny of existence—Divine Enlightenment and Divine Translation, which erases all sense of "difference" between you and Him.

> *. . . all "difference" Washed*
> *by Wideness Alone,*
> *We Speak and Love,*
> *Forever,*
> *In My Imperishable Domain.* [Hridaya Rosary]

Avatar Adi Da's Great Divine Way is "esoteric", meaning that the truth of it remains "hidden" until you begin to participate in it from the heart. Mere beliefs and prescribed behaviors are insufficient. The Way of Adidam is a matter of direct, moment to moment response to Adi Da Samraj and a process of receiving His Spiritual Transmission ever more profoundly. There is no way that you can take His Teaching away and practice it yourself. On your own, without His Divine Blessing, you can never move beyond the confines of the ego and unlock the Secrets of Divine Enlightenment. That is why it is so important to become His formal devotee and to live the Way of Adidam exactly has He has Given it.

*AVATAR ADI DA SAMRAJ: I Am the Divine Blessing, Real-God-with-you. Such is not merely My Declaration to you. You must find Me out. You must prove the Way I Give you. Really do the Way I Give you, and you will find Me out further. You will prove the Way of Adidam by doing it, not by believing it merely.* [Divine Spiritual Baptism Versus Cosmic Spiritual Baptism]

Choosing the Way of Adidam is not a merely personal matter, however. Every individual who enters into the devotional relationship with Avatar Adi Da brings His Spiritual Influence to countless others. His gathering of devotees forms a series of concentric circles radiating from Him at the Center.

The first circles are the Adidama Quandra Mandala and the Trimada. The remaining circles are the four formal congregations of His devotees: the first congregation (formal renunciate practitioners), the second congregation (general practitioners), the third congregation (practitioners who particularly serve Avatar Adi Da through their patronage and/or advocacy), and the fourth congregation (practitioners who live in traditional cultures).

These circles, as they grow, are forming a vast "conductor", a mechanism whereby the Divine Influence of Avatar Adi Da Samraj is being drawn more and more into the tissue of the world. Every new devotee represents a strengthening of the total Mandala of Avatar Adi Da's Spiritual Transmission and Grace. Avatar Adi Da has Given the Gifts, and it is through the community of His devotees, and its global mission and Spiritual culture, that these Gifts, intended for everyone, become available to all. This is why Avatar Adi Da is urgent to find those in this generation who will respond to Him and do the great work of making Him known.

# Choosing Your Congregation

The four congregations make up the worldwide gathering of Adidam. Which of the four congregations of Adidam you should apply to for membership depends on the strength of your impulse to respond to Avatar Adi Da's Revelation and on your life-circumstance. All four congregations establish you in a direct devotional relationship with Avatar Adi Da, and all four congregations are essential to the flowering of His Work in the world.

## The First and Second Congregations

*(for those who are moved to the total practice of Adidam)*

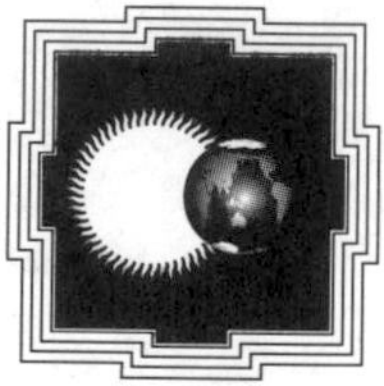

To take up the total practice of the Way of Adidam (in the first or second congregation) is to take full advantage of the opportunity Offered by Adi Da Samraj—it is to enter fully into the Process of Divine Enlightenment. That Process is a unique ordeal, which necessarily requires application to the wide range of functional, practical, relational, and cultural disciplines that Ruchira Avatar Adi Da Samraj has Given for the sake of that Divine Process.

The disciplines of Adidam are not ascetical, not a form of deprivation. Rather, they are the means whereby the body-mind is conformed to a right and inherently pleasurable pattern of well-being. As you progressively adapt to these disciplines, the body-mind is purified and balanced, and you thereby become able to receive and respond to the Divine Heart-Transmission of Adi Da Samraj more and more fully.

These practices in the Way of Adidam include cultural disciplines such as meditation, devotional chanting, sacramental worship, study of the Divine Scripture of Avatar Adi Da, keeping of a daily "practice diary", and regular periods of retreat. These contemplative disciplines are fundamental:

*AVATAR ADI DA SAMRAJ: You must come from the depth-position of meditation and puja before entering into activities in the waking state, and remain in the disposition of that depth from the time of meditation and puja each morning. Maintain that heart-disposition, and discipline the body-mind—functionally, practically, relationally—in all the modes I have Given you. This devotional Yoga, Ruchira Avatara Bhakti Yoga, is moment to moment. Fundamentally, it is a matter of exercising it profoundly, in this set-apart time of meditation and puja, and then, through random, artful practice moment to moment, constantly refresh it, preserve it. All of this is to conform the body-mind to the Source-Purpose, the in-depth Condition.*

*That basic discipline covers all aspects of the body-mind. That is the pattern of your response to Me. It is the foundation Yoga of organizing your life in terms of its in-depth principle, and growing this depth.* [December 5, 1996]

The total practice of Adidam also includes the adaptation to a pure and purifying diet, free of animal products (including meat, fish, dairy products, and eggs), tobacco, alcohol, caffeine, sugar, and processed foods, and maximally raw. There is also a discipline of daily exercise, which includes morning calisthenics and evening Hatha Yoga exercises. There is progressive adaptation to a regenerative discipline of sexuality.

## *The Life of a Formally Practicing Devotee of Ruchira Avatar Adi Da Samraj*

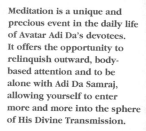

**Meditation is a unique and precious event in the daily life of Avatar Adi Da's devotees. It offers the opportunity to relinquish outward, body-based attention and to be alone with Adi Da Samraj, allowing yourself to enter more and more into the sphere of His Divine Transmission.**

**The practice of sacramental worship, or "puja", in the Way of Adidam is the bodily active counterpart to meditation. It is a form of ecstatic worship of Avatar Adi Da Samraj, using a photographic representation of Him and involving devotional chanting and recitations from His Wisdom-Teaching.**

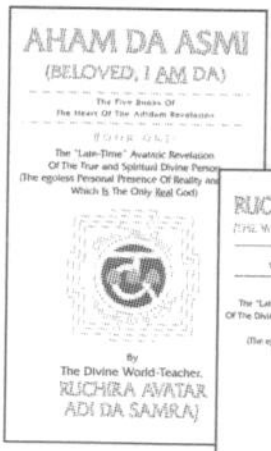


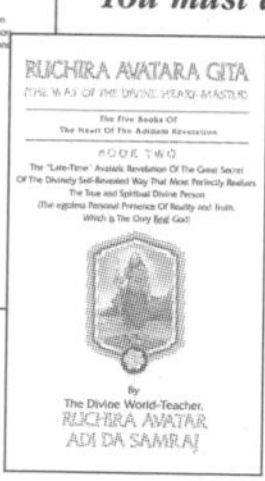


***"You must deal with My Wisdom-Teaching in some form every single day, because a new form of the ego's game appears every single day. You must continually return to My Wisdom-Teaching, confront My Wisdom-Teaching."***

**Avatar Adi Da Samraj**

**The beginner in Spiritual life must prepare the body-mind by mastering the physical, vital dimension of life before he or she can be ready for truly Spiritual practice. Service is devotion in action, a form of Divine Communion.**

**Avatar Adi Da Samraj Offers practical disciplines to His devotees in the areas of work and money, diet, exercise, and sexuality. These disciplines are based on His own human experience and an immense process of "consideration" that He engaged face-to-face with His devotees for more than twenty-five years.**

And, as a practical foundation for your personal life and the life of the community of practitioners, there is the requirement to live in a community setting with other devotees of Avatar Adi Da, to maintain yourself in full employment or full-time service, and to support the Adidam Pan-Communion and the cooperative community organization (the Ruchirasala of Adidam).

All of these functional, practical, relational, and cultural disciplines are means whereby your body-mind becomes more and more capable of receiving the constant Blessing-Transmission of Avatar Adi Da Samraj. Therefore, He has made it clear that, in order to Realize Him with true profundity—and, in particular, to Realize Him most perfectly, to the degree of Divine Enlightenment—it is necessary to be a formally acknowledged member of either the first or the second congregation, engaging the total practice of the Way of Adidam.

When you apply for membership in the second congregation of Adidam (the first step for all who want to take up the total practice of the Way of Adidam), you will be asked to prepare yourself by taking "The Only Truth That Sets the Heart Free", a course of formal study and "consideration" in which you examine the Opportunity Offered to you by Avatar Adi Da Samraj, and learn what it means to embrace the total practice of the Way of Adidam as a second-congregation devotee. (To register for this preparatory course, please contact the regional or territorial center nearest to you [see p. 856], or e-mail us at: correspondence@adidam.org.) After completing this period of study, you may formally enter the second congregation by becoming a student-novice.

Entering any of the four congregations of Adidam is based on taking a formal vow of devotion and service to Avatar Adi Da Samraj. This vow is a profound—and, indeed, eternal—commitment. You take this vow (for whichever congregation you are entering) when you are certain that your great and true heart-impulse is to be a devotee of Avatar Adi Da Samraj, embracing Him as your Divine Heart-Master, forever—in this and all future lifetimes. If you recognize Avatar Adi Da as the Living Divine Person—your Perfect Guide and Help, and your most intimate Heart-Companion—then you feel this vow as a priceless Gift, and you joyfully embrace the great responsibility it represents.

As a student-novice, you are initiated into formal meditation and sacramental worship. Then you begin to adapt to a wide range of life-disciplines, including participation in the Ruchirasala, the cooperative community of Avatar Adi Da's first- and second-congregation devotees. As a student-novice, you engage in an intensive period of study and "consideration" of the Way of Adidam in all of its details, and then, after a period of three to six months (or more) as a student-novice, you may apply to be accepted as a fully practicing member of the second congregation.

If, after a period (of one to two years, or more) of exemplary practice as a member of the second congregation, you are steadily and profoundly moved to the formal renunciate practice of Adidam, you may apply to become a novice in the Lay Renunciate Order (in the first congregation).

The two formal renunciate orders in the Way of Adidam are the Avabhasin Lay Renunciate Order of the Tantric Renunciates of Adidam and the Ruchira Sannyasin Order of the Tantric Renunciates of Adidam. The senior of the two orders is the Ruchira Sannyasin Order, the members of which are the most exemplary of the practitioners practicing the "Perfect Practice" of Adidam. Avatar Adi Da Himself is the Founding Member of the Ruchira Sannyasin Order, which is a retreat order, whose members are legal renunciates.

The Ruchira Sannyasin Order is the senior cultural authority within the gathering of Avatar Adi Da's devotees and its members are the principal human Instruments[1] of Avatar Adi Da's Blessing Work now and into the future. Ruchira Sannyasins may live in Hermitage-Retreats Empowered by Avatar Adi Da or at the Retreat Sanctuaries of Adidam anywhere in the world, but the home of the order is Adidam Samrajashram, Fiji, Avatar Adi Da's principal Hermitage-Retreat. Ruchira Sannyasins, as the title of the Order indicates, are Tantric Renunciates, neither withdrawn from bodily life in the ascetical manner, nor bound by the world. Ruchira Sannyasins, generally speaking, practice celibacy, either as single celibate renunciates, or within an intimate relationship. Some Ruchira Sannyasins may be sexually active if they have unique qualifications—that is, if they are capable of being sexually active in a uniquely auspicious manner.[2] At some point in the ultimate stages of life in the Way of Adidam, even such uniquely auspicious sexual practice is resolved in Yogic celibacy-in-intimacy—not by any strategic or sex-suppressive effort, but as a spontaneous result of the overwhelming sublimity of the intimate partners' constant devotional Samadhi of Communion with Avatar Adi Da.

The Lay Renunciate Order is made up of exemplary practitioners in the Spiritually Awakened (or advanced and ultimate) stages of Adidam. It is a cultural service order, which serves (under the direction of the Ruchira Sannyasin Order) an inspirational and aligning role for all devotees of Avatar Adi Da Samraj. Like the members of the Ruchira Sannyasin Order, "lay renunciates" function as living Instruments of Avatar Adi Da's Blessing, but their sphere of activity and responsibility is somewhat different. Unlike the Ruchira Sannyasin Order, which is a retreat order, lay renunciates are active in all areas of the institution, culture, community, and mission of the Way of Adidam, assuming the principal managerial positions. Thus, the Lay Renunciate Order sees that all the cultural directives of the Ruchira Sannyasin Order are carried out, and, at the same time, protects the hermitage life of Avatar Adi Da and the Ruchira Sannyasin Order. "Lay renunciates" may be singly celibate, celibate in intimacy, or else truly qualified for a sexually active form of renunciate sadhana (which, as in the case of sexually active "Ruchira sannyasins", will at some point be spontaneously resolved in Yogic celibacy-in-intimacy).

Through His first congregation devotees, Avatar Adi Da Samraj is providing for the future of His Work, ongoing forever. He will not have "successors" in the usual sense of a lineage of Gurus. But He will have the Instrumentality of His Spiritually Awakened formal renunciate devotees, and, always, in every generation, there is to be one among His Divinely Self-Realized devotees (appointed by the senior members of the Ruchira Sannyasin Order) who will function as "Murti-Guru", or as His human Agent, perfectly transparent to Him.

The "Murti-Guru" will grant Darshan (just as Avatar Adi Da Himself does in His human Lifetime), and will be His principal human Agent of Spiritual Transmission. By this means, Avatar Adi Da Samraj will always have a human vehicle through which the Force of His Spirit-Blessing will Flow perpetually. Thus, He will never be absent, either Spiritually or humanly.

*Through many and various Means . . . , I Work to Serve the Making of changes concretely in the immediate sphere of conditions in this world. Conditional existence (as a whole) may be described as a universal (or all-encompassing) grid—and I Work through the innumerable particular points on that total grid.*

*I Work through My devotee-Instruments (and, in due course, My "Living Murtis") as points of focus in the various specific places of the worldwide gathering of My devotees (and, thus, as concrete points of focus on the universal grid). This is the unique Significance of Instrumentality in the only-by-Me Revealed and Given Way of Adidam. . . .*

*Because they are . . . conformed to Me, I can Use such Instrumental devotees as a collective point of contact for My Blessing Work, and such Instrumental devotees themselves can collectively function as a Means of focusing the Invocation of Me in particular areas around the world.*

*In Working through such Instrumental devotees, I Respond (and always will Respond) to <u>everyone</u> (including each and all of My formally practicing devotees, and including even all beings—both human and non-human), in all the various particular areas of this world (and in even all worlds).*

*Instrumentality and Agency are absolutely essential Means that I Use (and will always Use, even beyond My physical human Lifetime). They are concrete parts of the universal grid that I Use (and will always Use) in My Divine Blessing-Work.* [The Lion Sutra]

## The Adidam Youth Fellowship
*(within the second congregation)*

Young people (25 and under) are also offered a special form of relationship to Avatar Adi Da—the Adidam Youth Fellowship. The Adidam Youth Fellowship has two membership bodies—friends and practicing members. A friend of the Adidam Youth Fellowship is invited into a culture of other young people who want to learn more about Avatar Adi Da Samraj and His Happiness-Realizing Way of Adidam. A formally practicing member of the Adidam Youth Fellowship acknowledges that he or she has found his or her True Heart-Friend and Master in the Person of Avatar Adi Da Samraj, and wishes to enter into a direct, self-surrendering Spiritual relationship with Him as the Means to True Happiness. Practicing members of the Youth Fellowship embrace a series of disciplines that are similar to (but simpler than) the practices engaged by adult members of the second congregation of Adidam. Both friends and members are invited to special retreat events from time to time, where they can associate with other young devotees of Avatar Adi Da.

To become a member of the Adidam Youth Fellowship, or to learn more about this form of relationship to Avatar Adi Da, call or write:

Vision of Mulund Institute (VMI)
10336 Loch Lomond Road, Suite 146
Middletown, CA 95461
PHONE: (707) 928-6932
FAX: (707) 928-5619
E-MAIL: vmi@adidam.org

# The Third Congregation of Adidam

*(for those who can serve Adi Da Samraj though their patronage and advocacy)*

## 1. Patrons and Individuals of Unique Influence

It is the sacred responsibility of those who respond to Adi Da Samraj to make it possible for His Divine Work to flourish in the world. For this purpose, He must be given the practical means to Bless all beings and to Work with His devotees and others who respond to Him in all parts of the world. Therefore, He must be enabled to move freely and spontaneously from one part of the world to another and have Hermitages in various places, set apart for His unique Work. In 1983, an individual patron offered the island of Naitauba to Avatar Adi Da. Because of this magnificent gift, the entire Life and Work of Adi Da Samraj began to evolve in ways that were not possible before. He had a pristine, protected place to do His Spiritual Work and an opportunity to establish a unique Seat of His Divine Presence for all generations to come.

Avatar Adi Da must also be able to gather around Him His most exemplary formal renunciate devotees—and such formal renunciates must be given practical support so that they can devote their entire lives, without outward concerns, to serving Avatar Adi Da in Person and living a life of perpetual Spiritual retreat in His Company. And Avatar Adi Da's Presence in the world must become as widely known as possible, both through the publication and dissemination of books by and about Him and through public advocacy by people of influence.

If you are a man or woman of unique wealth or unique influence in the world, we invite you to serve Avatar Adi Da's world-Blessing Work through your patronage or influence. Truly, patronage of the Divine World-Teacher, Adi Da Samraj, exceeds all other possible forms of philanthropy. As a member of the third congregation of Adidam, supporting the world-Work of Adi Da Samraj, you are literally helping to change the destiny of countless people. You are making it possible for His Divine Influence to reach people who might otherwise never come to know of Him. You are allowing Him the fullest use of His own physical Lifetime. To make the choice to serve Avatar Adi Da via your patronage or unique influence is to transform your own life and destiny, and the life and destiny of all mankind, in the most Spiritually auspicious way.

As a patron or individual of unique influence in the third congregation, your relationship to Avatar Adi Da is founded on a vow of devotion, through which you commit yourself according to your capabilities—either to significant financial patronage of His Work and/or to using your unique influence to make Him known in the world. In the course of your service to Him (and in daily life altogether), you live the simplest practice of Ruchira Avatara Bhakti Yoga, Invoking Avatar Adi Da, feeling Him, breathing Him, and serving Him, and thus remaining connected to His constant Blessing. You are not obliged to engage the full range of disciplines practiced in the first two congregations. You are, however, encouraged to study His Wisdom-Teaching and practice formal periods of meditation and sacramental worship. If, in due course, you are moved to embrace all the disciplines and enter into the total practice of Adidam, you may apply for membership in the second (and possibly, eventually, the first) congregation. In the past, Avatar Adi Da has invited, and may continue to invite, members of the third congregation into His physical Company from time to time, to receive His Darshan and to confer with Him on matters associated with their service.

If you are interested in establishing a formal devotional relationship with Avatar Adi Da Samraj and serving Him in this crucial way, please contact us at:

Third Congregation Advocacy
12040 North Seigler Road
Middletown, CA 95461
phone number: (707) 928-4800
FAX: (707) 928-4618
e-mail: third_congregation@adidam.org

## 2. The Transnational Society of Advocates of the Adidam Revelation

If you have the capability to effectively advocate Avatar Adi Da in the world—through your individual skills, position, or professional expertise—you may join a branch of the third congregation called the Transnational Society of Advocates of the Adidam Revelation. Members of the Society of Advocates are individuals who, while not of unique wealth or social influence, can make a significant difference to Avatar Adi Da's Work by making Him known in all walks of life (including the media, in the spheres of religion, government, education, health, entertainment, the arts, and so on). Advocates also serve the worldwide mission of Adidam by financially supporting the publication of Avatar Adi Da's "Source-Texts" and His other Literature, as well as associated missionary literature. Members of the Society of Advocates make a monthly donation for this purpose and pay an annual membership fee that supports the services of the Society.

Like devotees in the first and second congregations, your relationship to Avatar Adi Da as a member of the Society of Advocates is founded on a vow of devotion and service, but the requirements are not so elaborate. In the course of your service to Him (and in daily life altogether), you vow to live the simplest practice of Ruchira Avatara Bhakti Yoga, invoking Avatar Adi Da, feeling Him, breathing Him, and serving Him, and thus remaining connected to His constant Blessing. You are not obliged to engage the full range of disciplines practiced in the first two congregations. You are, however, encouraged to study His Wisdom-Teaching and practice formal periods of meditation and sacramental worship. If, in due course, you are moved to embrace all the disciplines and enter into the total practice of Adidam, you may apply for membership in the second (and possibly, eventually, the first) congregation. Avatar Adi Da invites members of the Society of Advocates into His physical Company from time to time to receive His Darshan and also to some Darshan occasions that He offers via the Internet to devotees all over the world.

If you are interested in becoming a member of the Society of Advocates, please contact us at:

The Society of Advocates of the Adidam Revelation
12040 North Seigler Road
Middletown, CA 95461
phone number: (707) 928-1104
FAX: (707) 928-4618
e-mail: soacontact@adidam.org

# The Fourth Congregation of Adidam

*(for those who live in traditional cultures)*

Individuals who live in traditional cultural settings (rather than industrialized cultural settings) are offered an approach to the practice of Adidam that is specifically fitted to their situation. This approach is offered in the fourth congregation of Adidam. The opportunity to practice in the fourth congregation is also extended to all those (in any part of the world) who, because of physical or other functional limitations, are unable to take up the total practice of the Way of Adidam as required in the first and second congregations. Fourth-congregation devotees practice Ruchira Avatara Bhakti Yoga in its simplest form: "Invoke Me, Feel Me, Breathe Me, Serve Me" and also the basic disciplines given for the first and second congregations. At the same time, their financial obligation is adapted to their circumstance and their particular educational requirements are taken into account.

Members of the fourth congregation, in their own (less detailed) fashion adapt to the "student-novice" and then "student-beginner" forms of practice—which are the basic foundation of the full sadhana of Adidam as practiced in the second congregation. If, then, they are moved and able to advance further, they are encouraged to join the second congregation of Adidam.

For more information about the fourth congregation of Adidam, call or write one of our regional centers (see page 856), or e-mail us at: correspondence@adidam.org.

*Those whose hearts are given, in love, to Me, Fall into My Heart. Those who are Mine, because they are in love with Me, no longer demand to be fulfilled through conditional experience and through the survival (or perpetuation) of the ego-"I". Their love for Me grants them Access to Me, and, Thus, to My Love-Bliss—because I Am Love-Ananda, the Divine Love-Bliss, in Person.*

*What will My lover do but love Me? I suffer every form and condition of every one who loves Me—because I Love My devotee As My own Form, My own Condition. I Love My devotee As the One by Whom I Am Distracted.*

*I Grant all My own Divine and "Bright" Excesses to those who love Me, in exchange for all their doubts and sufferings. Those who "Bond" themselves to Me, through love-surrender, are inherently Free of fear and wanting need. They transcend the ego-"I" (the cause of all conditional experience), and they (cause and all and All) Dissolve in Me—for I Am the Heart of all and All, and I Am the Heart Itself, and the Heart Itself Is the Only Reality, Truth, and Real God of All and all.*

*What is a Greater Message than This?*

[Da Love-Ananda Gita]

From now on, all beings are uniquely Blessed. And human history can be different, because there is Help available that has never existed before. You are not on your own. Your desires, frustrations, and longings have been heard, and answered beyond all possible imagining.

"Consider" what you have read here, and what you really want. The life of a devotee of Avatar Adi Da Samraj is unheard-of Grace, and this life can be lived by anyone. It does not matter who you are, where you live, or what you do. All of that makes no difference, once your heart recognizes Adi Da Samraj. Then the only course is the heart-response to Him—a life of devotion to the Divine in human Form—full of devotional ecstasy, true humor, freedom, clarity, and profound purpose.

And so, why delay? The Living One, Adi Da Samraj, is here, and always will be. But now is the brief, and especially Blessed, window of time in which He is humanly Alive, doing His great Foundation Work for the sake of all beings, presently and in all future time. Every one who comes to Him and serves Him in His bodily human Lifetime shares in His unique once-and-forever Work of establishing the Way of Adidam in this world.

All who love Him carry His Name in their heart and on their lips. Once the recognition of Avatar Adi Da awakens in you, this response is inevitable. The Promised God-Man, Avatar Adi Da Samraj, is not an "Other". He is the Gift, the Bliss, of Being Itself. He is the "Brightness" of Very God—Dawning, and then Flowering, in your heart. That Process is pure Revelation. It changes everything—grants peace, sanity, and the overwhelming impulse to Realize Unlimited, Permanent, and Perfect Oneness with Him.

This opportunity—to live in heart-Communion with Real God—exceeds anything ever offered to mortal beings. It is true Happiness. And it is yours for the asking.

Apart from the four congregations, there are three distinct organizations within Adidam, each with a special area of responsibility.

## THE DA LOVE-ANANDA SAMRAJYA

*Serving The Avataric-Incarnation-Body, The Great Island-Hermitage-Retreat, and The World-Blessing Work of The Divine World-Teacher, Ruchira Avatar Adi Da Samraj*

The Da Love-Ananda Samrajya is, as the subtitle indicates, devoted exclusively to serving Avatar Adi Da Himself, protecting Him and His intimate Sphere (including the Adidama Quandra Mandala and the Trimada), providing for Adidam Samraj-ashram (His Great Island-Hermitage-Retreat), ensuring that He has everything that He needs to do His Divine Blessing Work, and providing right access to Him on the part of devotees in all the congregations (and any other individuals He may wish to see for unique reasons).

Secondarily, the Da Love-Ananda Samrajya protects and provides for the Ruchira Sannyasin Order, all the members of which are legal renunciates. The Da Love-Ananda Samrajya is also responsible to ensure that the Divine Word and Leela of Adi Da Samraj are preserved and made known in the world.

# THE ELEUTHERIAN PAN-COMMUNION OF ADIDAM

*The Sacred Cultural Gathering and Global Mission of the Devotees of The Divine World-Teacher, Ruchira Avatar Adi Da Samraj*

*Dedicated to the Practice and the Proclamation of The True World-Religion of Adidam, The Unique Divine Way of Realizing Real God*

The Eleutherian Pan-Communion of Adidam, led by its "First Council", is the organization devoted to spreading, and establishing, the Way of Adidam in the world and serving the culture of devotional practice in all four congregations.

The Global Mission of Adidam is a primary branch of the Pan-Communion. The Mission, as the name indicates, is active all over the world—through Internet websites, through "barefoot" missionaries (members of the Lay Renunciate Order who devote their lives to missionary work), and through the efforts of all devotees, each of whom is called to be a missionary in the midst of all their relationships and social contacts. The Global Mission also includes the Publications Mission, which prepares, publishes, and distributes Avatar Adi Da's own books (and audiotapes and videotapes of Him) and books, magazines, and education courses about Him and the Way of Adidam by His devotees.

The Dawn Horse Press (staffed by devotees of Avatar Adi Da) is the editorial and production department of the Publications Mission (see pp. 818-25 for a description of current Adidam publications).

◆ ◆ ◆

## THE RUCHIRASALA OF ADIDAM

*The True Cooperative Community Gathering of the Devotees of The Divine World-Teacher, Ruchira Avatar Adi Da Samraj*

*The Seed of a "Bright" New Age of Sanity and Divine Joy for Mankind*

Cooperative community living (in households, Ashrams, or on Sanctuaries) is one of the fundamental disciplines of the first, second, and fourth congregations of Adidam, and it is also recommended for members of the third congregation, to whatever degree they may be able to practice such cooperation. The Ruchirasala of Adidam is the organization that serves Avatar Adi Da's devotees in incarnating cooperative community—it is the "soil", or human circumstance, in which devotees practice their devotional life and in which all the other entities of Adidam function. Creating intimate human living arrangements and shared services (such as schools, community businesses, and the Radiant Life Clinic) are all part of the responsibility of the Ruchirasala.

The Mountain Of Attention, 1998

APPENDIX A

# There Is No Face Within The Sky:

## Secular Science, Conventional God-Religion, and The Non-Objective Self-Revelation of Reality, Truth, and Real God

by the Ruchira Avatar,
Adi Da Samraj

(from *Real God Is The Indivisible Oneness Of Unbroken Light*)

Conventional (or merely exoteric) God-religion is, fundamentally, not about God—but it is about Man. And, most fundamentally, conventional (or merely exoteric) God-religion is not about God-Realization (or the Real-"Knowing" of Real God), but it is about the egoic dilemma of Man, and the search to preserve human psycho-physical egoity.

The credibility (or root-persuasiveness) of conventional (or merely exoteric) God-religion has been deeply threatened (and, effectively, even mostly destroyed) by the progressively developing culture of modern secular science (which, although it is promoted as a species of free enquiry, is merely a modern variation on the ancient false philosophy of materialism). This is a curious fact, because both modern secular science (or scientific materialism) and conventional (or merely exoteric) God-religion are based upon the same fundamentals.

There are two fundamentals upon which both scientific materialism and conventional God-religion are based. These two fundamentals are the idea of egoity (or the naive experiential presumption of an utterly independent, utterly personal, utterly separate, and utterly subjective, psycho-physical "point of view") and the idea of "objective reality" (or the naive experiential presumption of an egoically psycho-physically observed—and thereby presumed to be utterly independent, utterly impersonal, utterly separate, and utterly non-subjective, or utterly objective—world of conditionally perceived and conceived conditions). And these two fundamental ideas (or naive experiential presumptions) are, also, the principal constructs (or generally uninspected conventions) of the human mind.

The two fundamental human ideas (of ego-"I" and "objective reality") are a natural pair—conceived, in accordance with convention, to be always and irreducibly the polar opposites of one another (always utterly different from one another, and always standing over against one another), and to be of such a nature that one or the other may (in any moment, or in the context of one or another human activity, or in the context of one or another historical mode of human culture) be assumed to be the dominant (or even more "real") half of the pair. And, because both scientific materialism and conventional God-religion are based upon these two fundamental human ideas (of ego-"I" and "objective reality"), scientific materialism and conventional God-religion differ only with respect to their interpretation (or interpretive idea) of what is egoically and "objectively" observed. Thus, scientific materialism interprets "objective reality" to "be" merely "what" it (from the "point of view" of the human observer) "appears" to be (and, thus, to suggest, or point to, "itself" only). And conventional God-religion interprets "objective reality" to "mean" (or, otherwise, to suggest, or point to) "God" (As objective "Other"). But neither scientific materialism nor conventional God-religion critically "considers"—and, as a pre-condition for (or, otherwise, as a result of) either scientific or religious discourse, transcends—the two naive experiential presumptions (of ego-"I" itself, and "objective reality" itself) that are the basis for the characteristic interpretation otherwise presumed to be the case (either scientifically or religiously).

As a result of their separate (and different, and inherently conflicting, or mutually opposite) interpretations of "objective reality", scientific materialism and conventional God-religion are, traditionally, engaged in a (mostly verbal, and, yet, deep cultural, social, and political) war with one another. That war is mostly one of argumentation and propaganda, in which each, in turn, proposes and addresses the other as a mere "straw man" (in order to make mere argumentation and propaganda appear to be inherently and dramatically convincing to the crowd of fascinated human onlookers). And, in the course of several hundred years of this popular struggle to capture the mind (and even the entire cultural, social, and political circumstance) of Man for either scientific materialism or conventional God-religion, scientific materialism has, of late, convincingly achieved the status of the dominant cultural, social, and political world-entity (or world-cult), while conventional God-religion has fallen from its previous status (as the culturally, socially, and politically dominant half of the pair) to become the (everywhere) relatively subordinate (or defensive) cultural, social, and political entity (or universal sub-cult). In any case—and regardless of how the balance may alternate in the future course of this popular (and rather absurd) struggle of mere interpretations—the entire drama of "science versus religion" is a mere play of conventionally "objectified" opposites, animated within a human (and merely exoteric, and egoic) mummery that (logically) can never reduce the "two" to "one" (just as the two primary conventions—of ego-"I" and "objective reality"—cannot, as such, be, logically, reduced from "two" to "one"). Therefore, the only traditionally presumed possibility is that either "science" or "religion" must win (as if either ego-"I" or "objective reality" must be declared, or, otherwise, proved, to be the one "reality", to the exclusion of the other half of the conventional pair). Some people argue for belief in conventional God-religion, based on an exoteric religious interpretation of the concepts (or existing interpretations of "objective reality") otherwise associated with scientific materialism. Other people argue against belief in conventional God-religion, based on the technique of simple affirmation of the concepts (or existing interpretations of "objective reality") associated with scientific materialism—and, thus, without adding any other (especially, exoteric religious) interpretations. However, the entire conflict (between scientific materialism and conventional God-religion) is a rather mechanical (or prepatterned, and predictable) exercise of the dualistic (or inherently self-divided and pair-patterned) ego-mind. Indeed, this apparent conflict is mere cultural, social, and political "show business"—an absurd mummery of self-important players, whose argumentative flourishes merely distract the mind of Man from the truly great "consideration" of Reality, Truth, and Real God.

Reality does not think. The naturally (and conditionally) existing world does not think. Naturally (and conditionally) existing beings do not think—unless they are, by reactive self-contraction, self-stimulated (or egoically self-bound) to think (and, thus, to "objectify" what, by the mind of separate and separative ego-"I", is defined as "not-self").

Reality Is What Is—rather than what is thought to be. Reality merely (and Always Already) Is—before time, and space, and thinker, and thought, and knower, and known, and subject, and object, and ego-"I", and "other" are (by means of—necessarily, time-consuming—conceptual and perceptual acts of "point of view", or body-mind) separated and specified (in mentally and bodily "objectified" space and time). That is to say, Reality Always Already Is—before mind and body act or react in relation to what appears to be. Therefore, if any thought (itself) or perception (itself) occupies attention, Reality has (necessarily) already been ignored (and is, in that moment, being ignored). And, therefore, Truth (Which—necessarily, and inherently—is Identical to Reality, Itself) Is That Perfectly Subjective (or Perfectly non-objective) Self-Condition (or inherent Real Condition) That Is The Case (Always and Already), and That is (necessarily, and inherently) non-conditional, and (necessarily, and inherently) egoless (or Most Perfectly without limited, or conditional, "point of view"). And, therefore, Real God (Which—necessarily, and inherently—Is Reality and Truth) is (necessarily, and inherently) egoless, non-conditional, and non-objective—or Perfectly Subjective, non-"different", and Beyond (or Most Prior to) all thought (and, thus, all separateness, all otherness, and all conditional relatedness).

The arguments of both scientific materialism and conventional God-religion are mind-based, body-based, and (most basically) ego-based. All such arguments are mere conventions of mind, inherently associated with a space-time-bound "point of view"—which is to say that they are inherently space-time-defined, inherently dualistic, and inherently separate (or separated, and separative). Therefore, all such arguments are inherently (and actively, and strategically) separate from (and separative in relation to) Reality, Truth, and Real God. Indeed, all such arguments are inherently "Narcissistic" (or egoically self-bound). Therefore, the separate (or space-time-bound) "point of view" (which "point of view" is the ego-"I") always either argues that "objective reality" is merely as it appears (which is the interpretation embraced by scientific materialism) or as it may otherwise be presumed to mean (which is the interpretation embraced by conventional God-religion). However, in either case, Reality (and, therefore, Truth, and Real God) is not Realized—but Reality (and, therefore, Truth, and Real God) is merely interpreted (or mentally—and, thus, conventionally and dualistically—conceived, and reduced to the scale of "point of view", and to the status of "objectified otherness").

Reality Itself (Which Is Truth, and the only Real God) is (necessarily, and inherently) All-and-all-Inclusive and, therefore, One and non-dual. Therefore, Reality (Itself) inherently Transcends any and every space-time "point of view" (and the totality, or All, of space-time itself). And, thus, Reality (Itself) inherently Transcends any and every ego-"I", or body-mind-self—and every dualistic convention of "object", "other", or "thing". Truth (or Real God) Is, simply, the inherent (and inherently egoless) Nature (or unqualified Condition) of Reality Itself.

Reality (Itself) Is the unqualified Condition of all conditions (or apparent qualifications, or limitations) of Reality. Therefore, Reality (Itself) Is the unqualified (or Most Prior) Condition of any and every apparent individual (or apparent thing, or apparent condition). Indeed, Reality (Itself) Is the unqualified (or Most Prior), and, thus, Most Perfectly non-objective, or Most Perfectly non-objectified (and, thus, Most Perfectly Subjective, or Merely-Being) Condition of all apparent space-time conditions.

Reality (Itself) Is (necessarily, and inherently) the unqualified (or Most Prior) Condition of any and every ego-"I". Therefore, Reality (Itself) is Realized only in the case of the inherent (and inherently Most Perfect) transcending of the ego-"I" (or the conditional, separate, and actively separative, self-position itself). Reality (Itself) is Realizable only As the unqualified Self-Condition of the individual ego-"I"—Prior to the ego-act (or separative act) of dissociation from Reality, Truth, and Real God.

Reality (Itself) is Most Prior to the act of self-contraction into the space-time "point of view". Therefore, Reality (Itself) is Realizable only by transcending mind (and the egoic—or self-contracting, and separative, and presumed-to-be-separate—"point of view" of body-mind). And, therefore, Reality (Itself) is Realizable only by transcending the total psycho-physical act that "objectifies" conditionally apparent reality.

Reality Itself (or Truth, or Real God) is Realizable only by transcending the ego-effort of interpretation (or of conventional "knowing")—or all of the ego-based mind, itself. That is to say, Reality, Truth, and Real God is Realizable only by transcending the two fundamental operative ideas (and, thus, the fundamental common fault) associated with both scientific materialism and conventional God-religion. And, by transcending the two fundamental operative ideas (at their common root—which is egoity, or self-contraction, itself), even the entire process of discursive mental activity is transcended—such that Reality, Truth, and Real God may be Found (and, by Grace of True Divine Self-Revelation, Realized) As the Obvious.

True religion and true science are a Great, and single, and necessarily esoteric (or ego-transcending, rather than ego-active) Process. True religion and true science—Combined in a true, and truly single, and rightly esoteric (or non-conventional, and Always Already Reality-Based, Truth-Based, and Real-God-Based) Wisdom-Way—are the ego-transcending Great Process that directly transcends all exercises of interpretation (or of conventional "knowing", or of discursive mind). Only the esoteric Great Process of Realizing (and, on That Basis, Demonstrating)

Reality Itself (Which Is Truth, and Which Is Real God) by directly (and, in due course, Most Perfectly) transcending the psycho-physical (and space-time) "point of view" is both true religion and true science.

If Real Happiness and Real Freedom are to be Realized (and, on That Basis, Demonstrated) in human-time, the esoteric Great Process must be engaged by the individual human being—but That Great Process is not an exclusively human capability. Rather, It is a capability in Reality Itself—and, therefore, Its fundamental exercise must (necessarily) be one that can be enacted by all non-human beings as well as by all human beings. Thus, the esoteric Great Process (of Realizing Reality, Truth, or Real God) is a responsive exercise of the universally evident principal faculties that are common to all naturally (and conditionally) existing beings. And, in order to Realize Reality, Truth, or Real God, that responsive exercise must (necessarily, and inherently) transcend the limiting force (or ego-binding implication) of the faculties themselves—by virtue of the tacit recognition (of Reality, Truth, or Real God) that must be the basis of the response (itself).

Nature does not think. Reality is not (Itself) a thought-process. Therefore, the esoteric Great Process (of Realizing Reality, Truth, or Real God) is not an exercise of discursive (or egoic, and conceptual, or dualistically interpreting) mind—which "thinking mind" is a characteristic rather exclusively (or most elaborately) associated with human beings (or, at least, a characteristic that is not common to all naturally, and conditionally, existing beings). Rather, the esoteric Great Process is, for human beings, a responsive Reality-recognizing (or Truth-recognizing, or Real-God-recognizing) exercise of the four principal human faculties (of attention, emotional feeling, bodily sensation, and breath)—which four principal human faculties correspond to the four principal faculties associated, universally, with all naturally (and conditionally) existing beings (and which are, in all non-human cases of naturally, and conditionally, existing beings, demonstrated in at least primitive, or rudimentary, functions—such as responsive directionality, responsiveness to energy, responsiveness to sensation, and the responsive "conductivity", or total psycho-physical circulation, of both energy and physical substance).

The Great (esoteric, and truly religious, and truly scientific, or freely enquiring) Process is That of ego-surrendering, and ego-forgetting, and ego-transcending Attunement to—or ego-transcending (and, thus, "point-of-view"-transcending, and thought-transcending, or "difference"-transcending) Communion with (and, Ultimately, Most Perfect, and Perfectly Subjective, Identification with)—What Is. What Is, Is Reality Itself (and Truth Itself, and the only Real God). And That Great Process (of Realizing What Is) necessarily requires the recognition-responsive surrender, forgetting, and transcending of the four principal (and universally displayed) life-faculties.

Only the Perfectly Subjective (or Inherent, and Acausal, or Non-causing) "Point of View" (or space-time-Transcending Self-Condition) Is Divine and True. Only That "Point of View" (or Divine Self-Condition, inherently Transcending all "points of view" in space-time) Is (Itself) Reality, Truth, and Real God. And only the Realization of That Reality, Truth, and Real God Liberates all (to Demonstrate Reality, Truth, and Real God), by Setting the heart (or essential pattern, or apparent entity, or apparently separate self-condition, of psycho-physical being) Free from all separateness, "difference", and conditional relatedness.

The ego-"I" is always (and inherently) seeking and arguing—because it is inherently (and actively, and always self-contractively) dissociated (or apparently separated) from Reality, Truth, and Real God. The ego-"I" is inherently dissociated, dissatisfied, self-deluded, and un-Free. Whether the ego-"I" argues for scientific materialism, or conventional God-religion, or anything at all—its argument is merely mummer's talk (or the "talking" form of what is, traditionally, called "sin", or "the missing of the mark", and which is best described simply as egoity, or the self-contracted, separate, and separative ego-"I", itself).

Reality, Truth, and Real God is not evident in "objective reality" (or from the egoic "point of view" of "outside"). Nor is Reality, Truth, and Real God Realized merely by going "within" (or by, in any manner, merely exercising) the ego-"I" itself. Rather, Reality, Truth, and Real God is Realized only by transcending the ego-"I" (or the separate and separative "point of view" of self-contraction) in What Is.

Some conventional God-religionists argue for the "God-interpretation" of scientifically observed "objective reality" by emphasizing the irreducible complexity of natural patterns (such as the living cells that compose the human body). Such conventional God-religionists call for positive (or hopeful) belief in "God", based on the observable designs (or complex patterns) in the natural world. They argue for positive (or hopeful) "God-belief", based on their assumption that "design" requires a "designer". But "design" is not limited in kind—such that a positively definable "designer" is universally indicated. That is to say, patterns are everywhere in evidence—in both positive and negative forms. Not only are living human cells irreducibly complex—but so are the patterns of self-delusion, disease, decay, universal destruction, and death. Therefore what "God" is to be hopefully affirmed (or, otherwise, hopelessly denied) on the basis of mere "objectively" (and egoically) observed patterning?

The only Real and True God Is the One Reality That Merely Is, and That Is Always Already The Case, and

That (inherently, and simultaneously) Includes and Transcends All and all. That One Real God is not the "Creator"-Cause for either ego-based hope or ego-based hopelessness—but That One Real God Is the inherently egoless (or Perfectly Subjective, and Perfectly non-objective, and Self-Evidently Divine) Source and Person (or Self-Conscious Self-Condition) of the inherently egoless Love-Bliss-Light That Is the Single (and non-dual) Substance of all arising conditions.

Those who argue for belief in conventional God-religion, based on hopeful interpretations of "objective reality", are (necessarily) egos—already (and inherently) turned away from (or self-contracted within) Reality, Truth, and Real God. And, likewise, those who argue against belief in conventional God-religion, based on hopeless (or, otherwise, neutral) interpretations of "objective reality", are (necessarily) egos—already (and inherently) turned away from (or self-contracted within) Reality, Truth, and Real God. I Say this in Love—not with any intention to mock any one, or merely to argue with or against any one, but only in order to Serve the Awakening of every one to Real-God-Realization and Real-God-Demonstration.

The arguments (either for or against "God") that are based on the externalized (or egoically "objectifying") "point of view" are not arguments for the Realization of Reality, Truth, or Real God. Rather, all such arguments are merely the mental and cultural symptoms of egoity itself.

The arguments for conventional (or merely exoteric) God-religion (whether pro-scientific or anti-scientific) are merely ego-based (and self-deluded) efforts to console and preserve the presumed human ego-"I" itself, in the face of the obvious and irreducible mortal bleakness of the presumed "objective reality" itself. The arguments for conventional (or merely exoteric) God-religion are not arguments for the practice of the (necessarily, esoteric)

Wisdom-Way of (necessarily, ego-transcending) Realization and Demonstration of Reality, Truth, or Real God. Inevitably, the arguments for conventional (or merely exoteric) God-religion (and even the arguments for ostensibly esoteric religion, that—via the idealization of such techniques as strategic "non-violence", "active compassion", or "unconditional love"—make overmuch of interpersonal, social, and political issues and concerns, and that, as a result, make little of the true esotericism of the practice of the Wisdom-Way of actual ego-transcending Realization of Reality Itself, or of Truth Itself, or of That Which Is Real God) are merely the conceptual foundation for exoteric religious propaganda, supporting naive (and merely ego-serving) religious views (which, themselves, typically, are intended merely to support mostly narrow-minded, and, generally, rather puritanical and moralistic, programs for the cultural, social, and political enforcement of conventional ideals of "social morality"—or, really, "civilized" egoity). And the naive (and merely ego-serving) religious views that characterize most of conventional (or merely exoteric) God-religion are also characteristically associated, at best, with nonsensical utopian idealism (or an absurdly hopeful cultural, social, and political worldliness), and, at worst, with moralistically self-righteous (and, necessarily, hypocritical), and, often, intolerant (and even, potentially, oppressive), social and political intentions (even, at last, in the "fundamentalist" mode). And, in any case, scientific materialism (which, like conventional God-religion, always seeks to achieve total cultural, social, and political power to limit and control the minds and lives of all humankind) manipulates, and progressively dominates, humankind in very much the same manner (and with the same mixed, and even devastating, results) as conventional God-religion has done, and would do—for such is the nature of egoity (whether individual or collective).

Both secular science and conventional (or merely exoteric) God-religion are based upon the two common faults of humankind—egoity and the non-Recognition of the Real Nature (or One-Reality-Condition—or Perfectly Subjective, and Perfectly non-objective, Nature) of phenomenal experience (and of conditional existence, itself). Likewise, both secular science and conventional God-religion also (and equally) support and serve the illusions of humankind, rather than the need for humankind to Realize (and to Demonstrate) Reality, Truth, and Real God.

The principal illusion supported and served by secular science is epitomized by the idea of "materialism" (or of Reality as thing—without Being, or Consciousness). And the principal illusion supported and served by conventional God-religion is epitomized by the idea of "utopia" (or of Reality as the fulfillment of egoity). Secular science opposes conventional God-religion, and conventional God-religion opposes secular science—each, in turn, proposing that its propositions are, by contrast to the propositions of the other, the correct means for interpreting (and the correct "point of view" relative to) "Reality" and "Truth" and "God". However, neither secular science nor conventional God-religion is a correct (or right and true) means for Realizing (and Demonstrating) Reality (Itself), or Truth (Itself), or Real God. Indeed, "point of view" (of any conditional, or space-time, kind) is precisely the fault that self-separates one and all from the inherent Realization of Reality, Truth, and Real God.

Reality, Truth, and Real God Is the Condition of conditions—the inherently egoless (or Perfectly Subjective, and Perfectly non-objective) Self-Condition of one and all.

The pattern of "objective reality" is (in and of itself) "known" only from the egoic position (or a space-time "point of view").

If there is no ego-act (or self-contraction), there is no object defined (or separated from Perfect Subjectivity, or Consciousness Itself—Which is Always Already Conscious As Reality Itself).

The apparent pattern that is patterning as all conditions is not merely patterning (or happening, or evolving) in and by means of the apparently "objective" (or "outer", or superficial) domain of gross conditional exchanges (or transactions). Rather, the apparent pattern that is patterning as all conditions is originating at the comprehensive depth-level—always "inside", and prior to, the grossly apparent (or subsequent, and relatively superficial, and, necessarily, non-comprehensive) level.

The Ultimate Source-Condition of the apparent pattern that is patterning as all conditions Is (Itself) the Non-causative (or Most Prior) Self-Condition of all apparent conditional patterns.

That Ultimate Source-Condition, Which Is the Most Prior Self-Condition of All and all, is not the "First Cause" (or "Creator"-God) of conventional God-religion—but It Is the inherently egoless (or Perfectly Subjective, Perfectly non-objective, and Self-Evidently Divine) Reality (Itself).

Reality (Itself) Is the only Real God. Reality (Itself) Is the One and non-dual Source-Person. Reality (Itself)—non-dual, and inherently Free—Is the only Person (of All and all).

The inherently egoless, non-dual, and Perfectly Subjective Person of Reality Is Always Already The Case. And That One Who Is Always Already The Case Is Self-Existing Consciousness (Itself)—Which is Self-Radiant, "Bright", All-and-all-Including, All-and-all-Transcending, and All-and-all-Pervading As the Indefinable and Indestructible and Unqualifiedly Conscious Love-Bliss-Light That Is the Single (and Perfectly non-dual) Substance (and the inherently egoless Self-Condition) of all conditionally arising beings, things, and conditions.

The inherently egoless (or Perfectly Subjective, Perfectly non-objective, and Self-Evidently Divine) Person of Reality must (by Means of Avataric Divine Descent into Conjunction with the conditionally manifested All-and-all) Realize Itself (Most Perfectly, As Such) in human-time, and the inherently egoless (or Perfectly Subjective, Perfectly non-objective, and Self-Evidently Divine) Person of Reality must (by Means of Avataric Divine Self-"Emergence", forever, in inherent, and inherently Most Perfect, Coincidence with the conditionally manifested All-and-all) Reveal Itself (Most Perfectly, As Such) in human-time—or else Real God cannot be Most Perfectly Found (and, Thus, Most Perfectly Realized, and Most Perfectly Demonstrated) in human-time by any one at all. Therefore, I Am here.

Unless the Avatarically Descended (and Most Perfectly Self-Realized, and Most Perfectly Self-Revealed) Divine Person of Reality Speaks in human-time, and (Thereby) Reveals Its own Most Perfect Divine Teaching-Word (That Reveals the Divine Wisdom-Way of Most Perfect Real-God-Realization), and Stands (forever, here) to Divinely Bless All and all to Most Perfectly Realize (and, on the Basis of That Most Perfect Realization, to Most Perfectly Demonstrate) the One and Perfectly Subjective (or non-dual and non-objective) and "Bright" and Indefinable and Indestructible Conscious Love-Bliss-Light—no true religion and no true science can be made to live in human-time. Therefore, I Am here.

I am not here to support and to serve the faults and the illusions of humankind. I am not here to support and to serve any cult (or ego-based, and ego-serving, and ego-reinforcing culture) of human philosophical, religious, scientific, social, or political existence. Therefore, I am not here to support and to serve either the materialistic or the utopian "point of view". Indeed, I am not here to support and to serve any conditional (or space-time) "point of view". Whereas *any* and *every* conditional (or space-time) "point of view" is *the* "point of view" of ego-"I" (or self-contraction) itself, I *Am* here to Reveal the Divine Wisdom-Way That inherently (and, in due course, Most Perfectly) *transcends* the ego-"I" (and *all* the self-contracted, and separate, and separative illusions of egoically "objectified" space-time-reality).

By Means of My Avataric Divine Descent into Conjunction with (and, Ultimately, My Avataric Divine Self-"Emergence", forever, in inherent, and inherently Most Perfect, Coincidence with) the conditionally manifested All-and-all, I have been Required to Suffer, and then to Transcend, *all* illusions, *and* every conditional (or space-time) "point of view" (or mode of ego-"I"). Therefore, and by Means of a Great Ordeal of Suffering and Transcendence, I have even Suffered and Transcended *all* of secular (or materialistic) science and *all* of conventional (or merely exoteric) God-religion—and even *all* of traditional (and, necessarily, non-conventional) esotericism. Therefore, I am not here to support and to serve either the world-cult of secular science or the universal sub-cult of conventional God-religion—for not only have both of these traditions failed to Realize (and to Demonstrate) Reality, Truth, and Real God, but both are *based* upon *active dissociation* from Reality, Truth, and Real God (and, therefore, neither secular science nor conventional God-religion can, or will at any time, Realize and Demonstrate Reality, Truth, and Real God). Nor am I here merely to affirm and replicate the historical traditions of esotericism—for they have not transcended themselves (and the totality of ego-"I" and "otherness") in *Most Perfect* Realization (and *Most Perfect* Demonstration) of Reality, Truth, and Real God (and they cannot and will not *Most Perfectly* Realize, and *Most Perfectly* Demonstrate, Reality, Truth, and Real God—unless and until they transcend themselves, and the totality of ego-"I" and "otherness", in devotional recognition-response to Me, and in Fullest devotional resort to Me).

The esoteric Wisdom-Way of devotional recognition-response to Me and Fullest devotional resort to Me is an inherently and thoroughly counter-egoic (and, thus, counter-cultic—or ego-transcending, fault-transcending, and illusion-transcending) Process. I Am here, in human-time, to Completely and Most Perfectly Reveal the Most Perfect esoteric (and thoroughly counter-egoic, and counter-cultic) Wisdom-Way That Is true religion and true science, and That Is the Great Process of Realizing (and, on That Basis, Demonstrating) Reality Itself (Which Is Truth, and Which Is Real God) by directly (and, in due course, Most Perfectly) transcending the psycho-physical (and space-time) "point of view" (which is egoity, or self-contraction, itself).

I Am here, in human-time, to Most Perfectly Realize and (by Means of My own Most Perfect Self-Demonstration) to Most Perfectly Reveal My own inherently egoless (or Perfectly Subjective, and Perfectly non-objective, and Self-Evidently Divine) Person. And I Am here, in human-time, to Completely Speak My own Most Perfect Divine Teaching-Word (That Reveals the Way of Most Perfect Real-God-Realization), and to Stand (forever, here) to Bless All and all to Realize (and to Demonstrate) My own One and non-dual and "Bright" and Indefinable and Indestructible Conscious Love-Bliss-Light.

I Am the inherently egoless Person of Reality Itself.

I Am the One and "Bright" and Indefinable and Indestructible Conscious Light That Is the One and Universal (and inherently non-dual) Substance (and the One, and inherently egoless, and inherently non-dual, and inherently non-objective, or Perfectly Subjective, Self-Condition) of All and all.

I Am the Perfectly Subjective Self-"Brightness" of Love-Bliss (Itself).

I Am the "Bright" and Only One—Who is to be Found and Realized by you (and by every one, and all, and All).

I Am—Free-Standing here, Most Prior to your ego-"I" and all of the apparently "objective" world.

I Am the All-and-all-Including and All-and-all-Transcending Divine Self-Condition (and Source-Condition) of every ego-"I" and every "thing".

I Am you.

I Am the world.

I Am Adi Da Samraj.

The only-by-Me Revealed and Given esoteric Wisdom-Way of Adidam Is My Complete Avatarically Given Divine Teaching-Word of Most Perfect Real-God-Realization.

The only-by-Me Revealed and Given Way of Adidam Is the inherently ego-transcending (and thoroughly counter-cultic) Way That constantly (and, at last, Most Perfectly) Finds Reality Itself (Which Is the only Truth, and the only Real God).

The only-by-Me Revealed and Given Way of Adidam Is the esoteric Process of true religion and true science—That (more and more Perfectly, and, at last, Most Perfectly) Realizes (and, on That Basis, Demonstrates) the egoless Divine Inherent Love-Bliss-"Brightness" of Consciousness (Itself), and the egoless Divine (and Love-Bliss-"Bright") Self-Consciousness Inherent in All the Indefinable and Indestructible Light (or Single and Universal non-dual Substance) of the apparently "objective" (and apparently material) world.

The only-by-Me Revealed and Given Way of Adidam Is the Divine (and, necessarily, devotional, or heart-moved, and ego-surrendering) Way of Real God (Found As My Avatarically Self-Revealed, and Avatarically Self-Transmitted, and Self-Existing, and Self-Radiant, and All-and-all-Including, and All-and-all-Transcending, and, altogether, Perfectly Subjectively "Bright", and Self-Evidently Divine Person of Love-Bliss).

The only-by-Me Revealed and Given Way of Adidam Is the Divine Way of moment to moment ego-surrendering, and ego-forgetting, and ego-transcending (and, altogether, body-mind-purifying and heart-Liberating) devotional recognition-response to Me—So That self-contraction is never allowed to hide My Divinely Self-"Emerging" Conscious Sun of "Bright" Love-Bliss behind the common fault (and cult) of ego-"I" and the Love-Bliss-Light-obscuring cloud of "objectivity".

The only-by-Me Revealed and Given Way of Adidam Is the Divine and Complete and faultless and Most Perfectly non-dual Way of only Me. And I Am (now, and forever hereafter) Standing here, to Bless All and all to Realize Me and to Demonstrate Me.

There is no Face within the sky. Nor is the "thing" of sky the "All" That Is. But I Am All the All Who Is. And non-objective "Brightness" Is My only Face. And they see Me who forget themselves when My Name, Da, is heard to Flash across the Me-"Bright" Cloudless Sky of Consciousness Itself.

APPENDIX B

# Guide to Pronunciation

NOTE: The indications given in this chart are for pronunciation as used in the culture of Adidam (based on traditional pronunciations), and are not intended to indicate completely authentic pronunciation of any particular language.

[Key: S = Sanskrit; H = Hindi; F = Fijian. Any of the above with a U added indicates the term is unique to Adidam, but based on a traditional language. Any others are noted specifically.]

| | |
|---|---|
| Adi: | AH-dee (S) |
| Adidam: | AH-dee-DAHM (SU) |
| Adidama: | AH-dee-DAH-mah (SU) |
| Advaita Vedanta: | ah-DVYE-tah veh-DAHN-tah (S) |
| ashram: | AH-shrahm (H) |
| Ashvamedha: | AH-shvah-MEH-dah (S) |
| Atiashrami: | AH-tee-ah-SHRAH-mee (S) |
| Atman: | AHT-mahn (S) |
| Avatar: | AH-vah-tahr (H) |
| Bhakti: | BAHK-tee (S) |
| Bhagavad Gita: | BAH-gah-vahd GEE-tah (S) |
| Brahman: | BRAH-mahn (H) |
| bure: | BOO-ray (F) |
| chakra: | CHAH-krah (S) |
| Ciqomi: | thing-GO-mee (F) |
| Da: | DAH (SU) |
| Danavira Mela: | DAH-nah-VEE-rah MAY-lah (SU) |

| | |
|---|---|
| Darshan: | DAHR-shahn (H) |
| Dau Loloma: | DOW loh-LOH-ma (F) |
| devi: | DEH-vee (H) |
| Dharma: | DAHR-mah (S) |
| Eleutherian: | EH-loo-THEH-ree-ahn (Greek, U) |
| Eleutherios: | EH-loo-THEH-ree-ohs (Greek) |
| Finau: | fee-NOW (F) |
| Ganeshpuri: | gah-NEHSH-poo-ree (H) |
| Gopi: | GOH-pee (H) |
| Guru: | GOO-roo (S) |
| Hatha Yoga: | HAH-thah YOH-gah (S) |
| Hedge: | HEH-duh-ghee |
| Hridaya: | hrih-DYE-yah (S) |
| Hridayam: | HRIH-dye-yahm (S) |
| Ishta: | IHSH-tah (S) |
| Jagad-Guru: | JAH-gahd GOO-roo (H) |
| Jangama Hriddaya: | JAHNG-gah-mah hrih-DYE-yah (SU) |
| Jnana: | GYAH-nah (S) |
| Jyotir Math: | JOH-teer MAHT (H) |
| kahuna: | kah-HOO-nah (Hawaiian) |
| Kali: | KAH-lee (S) |
| karma: | KAR-mah (S) |
| kaya kalpa: | KAH-yah KAHL-pah (S) |
| Krishna: | KRIHSH-nah (S) |
| kriya: | KREE-yah (S) |
| kum-kum: | KOOM-koom (H) |
| Kundalini: | KOON-da-LEE-nee (S) |
| Leela: | LEE-la (S) |
| Love-Ananda: | LUV-ah-NAHN-dah (SU) |
| Mahal: | ma-HAHL (S) |
| Mahamantra: | MAH-hah-MAHN-trah (SU) |
| mandala: | MAHN-dah-lah (S) |
| Mandir: | mahn-DEER (H) |
| mantra: | MAHN-trah (S) |
| marae: | mah-RAH-ay (Maori) |
| Maria Hoop: | mah-REE-ah HOHP (Dutch) |
| Marpa: | MAHR-pah (Tibetan) |
| maya: | MAH-yah (S) |

| | |
|---|---|
| Meher Baba: | MEH-hehr BAH-bah (H) |
| mleccha: | MLEH-chah (H) |
| mudra: | MOO-drah (S) |
| Muktananda: | MOOK-tah-NAHN-dah (S) |
| Nadi: | NAHN-dee (F) |
| Naitauba: | nye-TUHM-bah (F) |
| Namale: | nah-MAH-lay (F) |
| Nananui-Ra: | NAH-nah-NOO-ee-RAH (F) |
| Narayan Maharaj: | nah-RAH-yahn MAH-hah-RAHJ (H) |
| Nina: | NYE-nah |
| Nirvanic: | neer-VAH-nihk (S) |
| Nirvikalpa: | NEER-vih-KAHL-pah (S) |
| Nityananda: | NIT-yah-NAHN-dah (S) |
| Nukubati: | NOO-koom-BAH-tee (F) |
| Padavara Loka: | PAH-dah-VAH-rah LOH-kah (SU) |
| Padmasambhava: | PAHD-mah-sahm-BAH-vah (S) |
| Parvati: | PAHR-vah-tee (S) |
| prapatti: | prah-PAH-tee (S) |
| Prasad: | prah-SAHD (H) |
| puja: | POO-jah (S) |
| Purnima: | POOR-nih-mah (S) |
| Purusha: | poo-ROO-shah (S) |
| Quandra: | QWAHN-drah (U) |
| Ramakrishna: | RAH-mah-KRIH-shnah (S) |
| Rang Avadhoot: | RAHNG AH-vah-DOOT (S) |
| Ruchira: | roo-CHEE-rah (S) |
| Ruchirasala: | roo-CHEE-rah-SAH-lah (SU) |
| sadhana: | SAH-dah-nah (S) |
| sadhu: | SAH-doo (S) |
| salu-salu: | SAH-loo-SAH-loo (F) |
| Samadhi: | sah-MAH-dee (S) |
| Samraj: | sahm-RAHJ (S) |
| Samrajya: | sahm-RAHJ-yah (S) |
| samyama: | sahm-YAH-mah (S) |
| Sangha: | SAHNG-gah (S) |
| sannyasin: | sahn-YAH-sin (S) |
| Santosha: | sahn-TOH-shah (S) |
| satori: | sah-TOH-ree (Japanese) |

| | |
|---|---|
| Satsang: | SAHT-sahng (H) |
| Savikalpa: | SAH-vee-KAHL-pah (S) |
| Shakti: | SHAHK-tee (S) |
| Shaktipat: | SHAHK-tee-PAHT (H) |
| Shankaracharya: | SHAN-kah-rah-CHAHR-yah (S) |
| Siddha: | SID-dah (S) |
| siddhi: | SID-dee (S) |
| Siva: | SHEE-vah (S) |
| Sivaratri: | SHEE-vah-RAH-tree (S) |
| Sukha Dham: | SOO-kah DAHM (SU) |
| Suprithi: | soo-PREE-tee (S) |
| sutra: | SOO-trah (S) |
| Swami: | SWAH-mee (S) |
| tabua: | tahm-BOO-ah (F) |
| tamboura: | tahm-BOOR-ah (H) |
| tapas: | TAH-pahs (S) |
| Taveuni: | TAH-veh-OON-ee (F) |
| Trimada: | trye-MAH-dah (SU) |
| Trivedi: | trye-VEH-dee (SU) |
| Tui: | TOO-ee (F) |
| Turaga: | too-RAHNG-ah (F) |
| Upasani Baba: | oo-PAH-sah-nee BAH-bah (S) |
| Vanuabalavu: | vah-NOO-ahm-bah-LAH-voo (F) |
| Vivekananda: | vih-VEH-kah-NAHN-dah (S) |
| Vunirarama: | VOO-nee-rah-RAH-mah (F) |
| Waialeale: | wye-AH-lay-AH-lay (Hawaiian) |
| Wailua: | wye-LOO-ah (Hawaiian) |
| Yajna: | YAHJ-nah (S) |
| Yoga: | YOH-gah (S) |
| Yuga: | YOO-gah (S) |

## ENDNOTES FOR *The Promised God-Man Is Here*

### Introduction

1. "The 'late-time'" (or "the 'dark' epoch") is a phrase that Avatar Adi Da uses to describe the present era—in which doubt of God (and of anything at all beyond mortal existence) is more and more pervading the entire world, and the self-interest of the separate individual is regarded to be the ultimate principle of life. It is also a reference to the traditional Hindu idea of "yugas", or "epochs", the last of which is understood to be the most difficult and "dark". Many traditions share the idea that it is in such a time that the promised Deliverer will appear.

2. "Ruchira" is Sanskrit for "bright, radiant, effulgent". Thus, the Reference "Ruchira Avatar" indicates that Avatar Adi Da Samraj is the "Bright" (or Radiant) Descent of the Divine Reality Itself, Appearing in the world in physical Form.

3. Throughout this book, Avatar Adi Da Samraj is referred to with various Titles, including "Avatar" and "Samraj", and also "Beloved". "Samraj" is a Title that was offered to Him in 1996, and is defined on p. 555. "Adi Da" is His principal Name, and is defined on pp. 554-55.

4. The Masters in what Avatar Adi Da calls "the 'Crazy Wisdom' tradition" are Realizers that have been recognized traditionally (in any culture or time) to serve individuals through spontaneous Free action, blunt Wisdom, and liberating laughter, by shocking or humoring them into self-critical awareness of their egoity—which is a prerequisite for receiving the Realizer's Spiritual Transmission. Typically, such Realizers manifest "Crazy" activity only occasionally or temporarily—and never for its own sake, but only as "skillful means". Avatar Adi Da's Demonstration of "Crazy Wisdom" is discussed throughout this book.

5. Avatar Adi Da Samraj spontaneously Gave the name "Adidam" in January 1996 as the primary Name for the Way He has Revealed and Given. This name is simply His own Principal Name ("Adi Da") with the addition of "m" at the end.

6. The term "Real God" indicates the True Source of all conditions, the True and Spiritual Divine Person, rather than any egoic (and, thus, false, or limited) presumptions about "God".

7. The word "conditional" (and its variants) is used throughout this book to indicate everything that depends on conditions—in other words, everything that is temporary and changing. The "Unconditional", in contrast, is the Divine, or That Which is Always Already the Case, because it is utterly free of dependence on conditions.

**Chapter 1**

1. The term "Avataric" indicates that Avatar Adi Da's human Incarnation is not merely the life of an ordinary man, but the utterly Divine "Descent" of Real God in human Form.

2. The Cosmic domain includes all physical, subtle, and causal realms of experience. The Cosmic domain is necessarily conditional, or temporary and changing.

3. "Divine Self-Realization" is a term that Avatar Adi Da uses to describe Most Perfect Enlightenment. Avatar Adi Da uses the terms "Spiritual" and "Transcendental" in this reference as well, in order to indicate that Divine Self-Realization encompasses both the dimension of Spiritual Energy and the dimension of Transcendental Consciousness.

4. Avatar Adi Da uses the word "gross" to mean "made up of material (or physical) elements". The gross (or physical) dimension is therefore associated with the physical body, and also with experience in the waking state.

5. The Sanskrit word "Samadhi" traditionally denotes various exalted states that appear in the context of esoteric meditation and Realization.

6. The Samadhi of "the Thumbs" is further described in chapter 16, pp. 433-34.

7. "Crashing Down" is a phrase Avatar Adi Da uses to describe the Descent of His Divine Spiritual Force into the world.

8. The terms "consider" and "consideration" in Avatar Adi Da's Wisdom-Teaching denote a process of one-pointed—but ultimately thoughtless—concentration and exhaustive contemplation of something until its ultimate obviousness is clear. These terms are placed in quotation marks to indicate that they have this specific technical meaning. "Consideration" is described in more detail in chapter 8, pp. 205-206.

9. "Prapatti" in Sanskrit literally means "forward-fallingness".

**Chapter 2**

1. Kundalini Yoga is a practice that originated in the Hindu tradition (with roots going back to shamanic practices). It aims to awaken latent Spiritual Energy (which is presumed to lie dormant at the base of the body), so that it rises up through the spine to "reunite" with its ultimate source above the head. While typical techniques to "raise" the Kundalini involve meditative visualization and breathing exercises, it has long been traditionally understood that the initiatory Force of a Spiritually Awakened Teacher is the principal means whereby the Kundalini is "aroused".

2. "Sadhana" is Sanskrit for "self-transcending religious or Spiritual practice".

3. The subtle is the dimension of energy and mind, associated with experience in the dreaming state. The word "subtle" indicates that this dimension is "refined"—in relation to the "gross" physical dimension.

4. The term "radical" derives from the Latin "radix", meaning "root"—and, thus, it principally means "irreducible", "fundamental", or "relating to the origin". Because Adi Da Samraj uses "radical" in this literal sense, it appears in quotation marks in His Wisdom-Teaching—in order to distinguish His usage from the common reference to an extreme (often political) view.

5. The Sanskrit word "Shaktipat" means the "Descent (pat) of Divine Force (Shakti)".

6. Kriyas are the spontaneous, self-purifying responses of the body-mind to the Infusion of Spirit-Energy Transmitted by a Spiritual Master. Kriyas can take many forms, including bodily movements or gestures, all manner of vocal sounds and utterances, dramatic changes in breathing, and even profound quieting of the mind.

7. Rang Avadhoot (1898-1968) was a Realizer in the tradition of Dattatreya (a Hindu God traditionally regarded in India as an Avatar of Brahma, Vishnu, and Siva).

8. "Nirvikalpa", in Sanskrit, means "without form". Hence, "Nirvikalpa Samadhi" literally means "deep meditative concentration (or absorption) without form (or defined experiential content)". Traditionally, this state is the final goal of many schools of Yogic ascent.

9. The Sanskrit word "Siddha" means "a completed, fulfilled, or perfected one", or "one of perfect accomplishment, or power".

10. In traditional Yoga, many visions, auditions, subtle tastes, and other states and experiences of Spiritual rapture may occur in the

process of ascent of energy in the spinal line. In many traditions, it is understood that these experiences precede (and are, therefore, lesser than) the attainment of "formless ecstasy", or Nirvikalpa Samadhi, which Avatar Adi Da had already experienced at this point.

11. Paramahansa Yogananda (1893-1952), the author of *Autobiography of a Yogi*, taught what he called "Kriya Yoga".

12. Jnaneshwar (1275-1296) was a great Siddha of Maharashtra, India. He was a venerated leader of the Hindu bhakti movement, and wrote the *Jnaneshwari*, a poetic commentary on the *Bhagavad Gita*.

Milarepa (1040-1123) is one of the most revered personages in Tibetan Buddhism, famous for the extremely intense austerities he undertook at the behest of his teacher, Marpa the Translator.

13. Gautama Shakyamuni (circa 563-483 B.C.E.) is the great Indian Sage commonly known as "the Buddha".

Hui Neng (638-713), one of the best-known figures in Chinese Buddhism, is regarded as one of the founders of the Zen (or Ch'an) tradition. His talks and sermons are recorded in the *Platform Sutra*.

Shankara (788-820), one of the greatest Hindu sages, is considered the most famous exponent of the tradition of Advaita Vedanta.

Ramana Maharshi (1879-1950) was a great Indian Spiritual Master, who Realized the Transcendental Self at a young age. He established his Ashram at Tiruvannamalai in South India, which continues today.

14. The Vedanta Society was founded by disciples of the Hindu Spiritual Master Ramakrishna (see chapter 4, note 1) for the sake of the dissemination of Hindu teachings in the world, and the spreading of Ramakrishna's Mission.

15. "Purusha" and "Siva" are traditional Hindu names for the Divine Being Itself, or Divine Consciousness. "Siva" is sometimes pictured as a ferocious male Deity, or the "Destroyer", but, in His more benign aspect, is essentially the same as "Purusha".

16. Avatar Adi Da uses the phrase "most perfect(ly)" in the sense of "absolutely perfect(ly)". Similarly, the phrase "most ultimate(ly)" is equivalent to "absolutely ultimate(ly)". "Most perfect(ly)" and "most ultimate(ly)" are always references to the Divinely Enlightened stage of life.

17. The Sanskrit word "mandala" (literally, "circle") is commonly used in the esoteric Spiritual traditions to describe the hierarchical levels of cosmic existence. "Mandala" also denotes an artistic rendering of interior visions of the cosmos. Avatar Adi Da uses the phrase "Mandala of the Cosmos", or "Cosmic Mandala", to describe the totality of the conditional cosmos.

18. Adi Da Samraj Affirms that there is a Divine Domain, which is not "elsewhere"—not an objective place, like a subtle heaven or mythical paradise—but is the always present Divine Self-Condition of every conditional being. Adi Da Samraj Reveals that the Divine Self-Domain is the Eternal Domain of His own Divine Self, and It is also the Eternal Destiny of all who (by His Grace) Realize Most Perfect Enlightenment.

19. The Sanskrit term "Siva-Shakti" is an esoteric description of the Divine Being. "Siva" is a name for the Divine Being Itself, or Divine Consciousness. "Shakti" is a name for the All-Pervading Spirit-Power (or Energy) of the Divine Being. "Siva-Shakti" is thus the Unity of the Divine Consciousness and Its own Spirit-Power (or Energy).

20. Avatar Adi Da uses "Self-Existing and Self-Radiant" to indicate the two fundamental aspects of the One Divine Person—Existence (or Being, or Consciousness) Itself, and Radiance (or Energy, or Light) Itself.

21. In the Hindu tradition, Brahman is the Ultimate Divine Reality That is the Source and Substance of all things, all worlds, and all beings.

22. In the Hindu tradition, Atman (with a capital "A") is the Divine Self.

23. "Nirvana" is a Buddhist term for the Unqualified Reality beyond suffering, ego, birth, and death. The "Nirvanic Ground" indicates the same Reality.

24. "Open Eyes" is a synonym for "Divine Self-Realization". The phrase graphically describes the non-exclusive, non-inward, Native State of the Divine Realizer, Who is Identified Unconditionally with the Divine Reality, while also allowing whatever arises conditionally to appear in the Divine Consciousness (and spontaneously Recognizing everything that arises as merely an unnecessary modification of the Divine Consciousness).

**Chapter 3**

1. The Heart is Real God, the Divine Self, the Divine Reality.

2. Here the word "Agency" is being used in the sense that Avatar Adi Da's physical Body is one of the Means through which He Communicates His Divine Spiritual Blessing.

3. "Siddhi" is Sanskrit for "power", or "accomplishment". "Siddhi" is used both as a general term for Avatar Adi Da's Divine Spiritual Blessing-Power and as a reference to specific aspects of the Divine Power He manifests in His Blessing Work.

**Chapter 4**

1. The Indian Spiritual Master Ramakrishna (1836-1886) was a renowned ecstatic, and a lifelong devotee of the Goddess Kali, a form of the "Mother-Shakti". In the course of his Spiritual practice, Ramakrishna spontaneously embraced many different religious and Spiritual disciplines, eventually Realizing a state of profound mystical union with the Divine.

2. "Re-cognition", which literally means "knowing again", is Avatar Adi Da's term for non-verbal, heart-felt, intuitive insight into the egoic activity of self-contraction.

3. Satsang literally means "true (or right) relationship", "the company of Truth". The term traditionally refers to the practice of spending time in the sacred presence of holy or wise persons, a holy place, a venerated image, the burial shrine of a Saint or Realizer, and so on.

4. This book is now titled *The Method Of The Ruchira Avatar—The Seventeen Companions Of The True Dawn Horse, Book Five: The Divine Way Of Adidam Is An ego-Transcending Relationship, Not An ego-Centric Technique*, and is one of Avatar Adi Da's twenty-three "Source-Texts", His Texts that summarize His Eternal Message to all beings (see chapter 25).

5. A British-born novelist, poet, essayist, and philosopher, Aldous Huxley (1894-1963) wrote over 50 books, including such classics as *The Doors of Perception*, *Brave New World*, and an anthology of mystical writings entitled *The Perennial Philosophy*.

6. Hatha Yoga is a traditional Hindu practice, the aim of which is to coordinate and control all of the life-forces in the body. The discipline of Hatha Yoga includes special postures used for this purpose, which also promote flexibility and relaxation. Although Hatha Yoga is nowadays often practiced simply for its physical (and also its emotional and mental) benefits, it was traditionally regarded as a means of preparing the bodily vehicle to be maximally fit for Spiritual practice.

7. Swami Muktananda regarded the mystical vision of the "blue pearl" (or blue bindu) to be the highest attainment of the Siddha Yoga practices he taught. Though he had experienced the utterly ascended and formless bliss of conditional Nirvikalpa Samadhi, he regarded it to be a lesser experience in comparison with the "blue pearl" and other forms of extraordinary visionary and Spiritual experience. He had not entered the non-exclusive, "Open-Eyed" Realization that Avatar Adi Da was confessing. See chapter 16, pp. 407-11, for a description of the hierarchical schema of Realization given by Avatar Adi Da.

8. See chapter 20, pp. 524-27, for a further discussion of Avatar Adi Da's relationship to Swami Muktananda.

9. "Bubba" was also one of Avatar Adi Da's childhood nicknames.

**Chapter 5**

1. The "Way of 'Radical' Understanding" is an alternative reference for the Way of Adidam.

2. "Maha" is Sanskrit for "great". Thus, the "Maha-Siddha" is the "Great Siddha (or Perfect One)".

3. "Darshan", in Hindi (derived from Sanskrit "darshana"), literally means "seeing", "sight", or "vision". To receive Darshan of Avatar Adi Da is, most fundamentally, to behold His bodily (human) Form (either by being in His physical Company or by seeing a photograph or other visual representation of Him), and (thereby) to receive His Divine Spiritual Blessing.

4. "Divine Communion" is the practice of Invoking and feeling the Divine Person. It is "communion" in the sense that the individual loses sense of the separate self in the bliss of that state, and is thus "communicating intimately" with the Divine.

5. Avatar Adi Da's "Sadhana Years" refers to the time from which He began His quest to recover the Truth of Existence (at Columbia College) until His Divine Re-Awakening in 1970.

6. In the Tantric traditions of India and the Himalayas, the word "heroic" is used to describe the practice of an individual whose impulse to Liberation and commitment to his or her Guru are so strong that he or she is able to engage Spiritual practice with great profundity and effectiveness in the midst of any kind of life-circumstance—even circumstances that are usually considered highly inauspicious for Spiritual life. Because of His utter Freedom from egoic bondage and egoic karmas, Avatar Adi Da's Sadhana was "Heroic" in a manner that had never previously been possible and will never again be possible for any other being. As the Divine Person, it was necessary for Avatar Adi Da to have experienced the entire gamut of human seeking in order for Him to be able to Teach any and all that came to Him.

7. "Crazy Wisdom" Masters in the Great Tradition have most fully manifested in certain branches of the Buddhist and Hindu traditions, but there have been numerous other traditions in which individuals lived and taught from a "free" perspective to one degree or another.

The most widespread of such figures is the "trickster" prevalent in shamanistic and ancient cultures throughout the world. In the Jewish tradition, some prophets and rabbis manifested the "foolish" behavior of one absorbed in God—the tradition of Hasidism is particularly notable in terms of such activity. In the Christian tradition, the specific group known as "fools for Christ's sake" exhibited unconventional or shocking behavior as a means of turning others to the Divine. The Sufi tradition is also full of what is called "wine-drinking and revelry", a metaphor for the Divine "Intoxication" that obliterates limited self-awareness in God, to varying degrees depending on the individual. And the Zen Buddhist and Taoist traditions abound with stories of masters in the "Crazy Wisdom" mode.

**Chapter 6**

1. A "Communion Hall" is a place set aside for practitioners of Adidam to practice meditation on and sacred worship of Avatar Adi Da Samraj.

2. A "mudra" is a spontaneous gesture of the hands, face, or body that outwardly expresses a state of ecstasy.

3. The "Great Tradition" is Avatar Adi Da's term for the total inheritance of human, cultural, religious, magical, mystical, Spiritual, Transcendental, and Divine paths, philosophies, and testimonies from all the eras and cultures of humanity—which inheritance has (in the present era of worldwide communication) become the common legacy of mankind.

4. "Chakra" is Sanskrit for "wheel". The "chakra body" is the etheric and subtle system of centers that conduct psychic force and nerve-force to and through the principal regions of the body. The chakra body is generally conceived of as having seven principal chakras, located at various physical locations on the central axis of the body. The seven chakras are associated, respectively, with the perineum (or bodily base), the genitals, the navel and solar plexus, the heart, the throat, the midbrain, and the crown of the head.

5. See, for example, *Kundalini: The Evolutionary Energy in Man*, by Gopi Krishna (Berkeley, Calif.: Shambhala, 1971).

6. See Avatar Adi Da's Essay, "The Lesser and Greater Traditions Associated with The Kundalini Shakti", in *Divine Spiritual Baptism Versus Cosmic Spiritual Baptism—The Seventeen Companions Of The True Dawn Horse, Book Eight: Divine Hridaya-Shakti Versus Cosmic Kundalini Shakti In The Divine Way Of Adidam*.

7. Natural life-energy and the Divine Spirit-Current move through the body in a Circle of descent and ascent—down the front and up the back. The frontal dimension of the personality is epitomized in the frontal line, or the pathway of natural life-energy and the Divine Spirit-Current through which energy descends down the front of the body, from the crown of the head to the bodily base. The spinal line is a primary pathway of natural life-energy and the Divine Spirit-Current through the body-mind—through which energy ascends up the back of the body, from the bodily base to the crown of the head. The spinal line is associated with the subtle (or higher mental, psychic, and mystical) dimension of the body-mind.

8. The bodily base is the entire area of the genitals, perineum, and anus.

9. The Sanskrit word "Hridaya" means "the Heart Itself". Thus, "Hridaya-Shaktipat", which is Avatar Adi Da's Divine Spiritual Gift to His devotees, is "the Blessing-Transmission of the Heart Itself".

10. Avatar Adi Da uses "Perfectly Subjective" to describe the True Divine Self-Condition, or "Subject", of the conditional world—as opposed to the conditions, or "objects", of experience. Thus, in the phrase "Perfectly Subjective", the word "Subjective" does not have the sense of "relating to the merely phenomenal experience, or the arbitrary presumptions, of an individual", but, rather, it has the sense of "relating to Consciousness Itself, the True Subject of all apparent experience".

11. "Devi" is Sanskrit for "Goddess".

12. "The Way of the Heart" is an alternative reference for the Way of Adidam.

**Chapter 7**

1. Padmasambhava was a great Tantric and Yogic Buddhist practitioner who is said to have arrived in Tibet in 747 C.E. from India. He left his mark on Tibetan Buddhism in such a basic way that he is celebrated by Tibetan Buddhists as a second Buddha. He is credited with the establishment of the first Buddhist monastery in Tibet.

Marpa (1012-1096) was a Tibetan Buddhist Teacher who went to great lengths to obtain teaching from his master, Naropa, who resided in India. In the midst of teaching his disciples (including his most famous disciple, Milarepa), Marpa maintained the outward life of a householder, including emotional-sexual relationships with a group of consorts and responsibility for overseeing a farm.

2. "Dharma" is Sanskrit for "duty", "virtue", "law". In its largest sense, "Dharma" means a great Spiritual Teaching, including its disciplines and practices.

3. Avatar Adi Da's Instruction has always been that His devotees should not use these substances outside of His personal Company (except on relatively rare occasions of sacred celebration within the community of His devotees), because the casual use of alcohol and tobacco toxifies the body and tends to delude the mind.

4. As mentioned in note 8 (on p. 791), the term "consideration" is an intensive process of concentration and contemplation of something until its Truth becomes obvious. "Reality consideration" has been the method of Avatar Adi Da's entire Life and Work—He has fully Submitted to the conditional reality, and has brought forth the Realization of Truth in the midst of human life.

5. "True intimacy" can be either heterosexual or homosexual. Avatar Adi Da has also allowed for the possibility of an individual having an intimate relationship with more than one partner at the same time (possibly even of both sexes, in bisexual cases). However, He has also indicated that this would occur only in extremely rare circumstances, because an extraordinary heart-balance and unique renunciate characteristics are required in order to maintain "true intimacy" in multiple relationships simultaneously. Avatar Adi Da's full Instruction about the forms of right emotional-sexual Yoga in the Way of Adidam, are Given in *Ruchira Tantra Yoga—The Seventeen Companions Of The True Dawn Horse, Book Nine: The Physical, Spiritual (and Truly Religious) Method Of Mental, Emotional, Sexual, and Whole Bodily Health and Enlightenment In The Divine Way Of Adidam.*

6. Avatar Adi Da Samraj uses the term "advanced" to describe the Spiritually activated practice of receiving His Divine Spiritual Blessing (or Hridaya-Shaktipat) in the body-mind, in the context of the fourth and fifth stages of life. He uses the term "ultimate" to describe the practice of heart-Identification with Him as Consciousness Itself, in the context of the sixth stage of life and the seventh (or Divinely Enlightened) stage of life. (See pp. 407-11 for a description of the seven stages of life.)

7. The names and titles of the Ruchira Adidamas indicate their Realization and their Spiritual significance in Avatar Adi Da's Work.

"Ruchira" and "Naitauba" both indicate membership in the Ruchira Sannyasin Order (see following note). "Ruchira" is a title for all members of the Ruchira Sannyasin Order, as devotees of Avatar Adi Da who are practicing in the context of the "Bright" ("Ruchira") Domain of Consciousness Itself. "Naitauba" is the traditional Fijian name for Adidam

Samrajashram, the Great Island-Hermitage-Retreat of Avatar Adi Da Samraj—the place where Avatar Adi Da founded the Ruchira Sannyasin Order, and also the place where many of its members will reside.

"Adidama" is composed of Avatar Adi Da's Principal Name "Adi Da" and the feminine indicator "Ma". In addition, in Sanskrit, "adi" means "first", and "dama" means "self-discipline". Therefore, the overall meaning of this title is "first among those who conform themselves to the Ruchira Avatar, Adi Da Samraj, by means of ego-surrendering, ego-forgetting, and ego-transcending feeling-Contemplation of Him".

"Sukha" means "happiness, joy, delight" and "Dham" means "abode, dwelling". Therefore, as a personal renunciate name, "Sukha Dham" means "one who abides in happiness".

"Jangama" means "all living things", and "Hriddaya" is "heartfelt compassion, sympathy". Therefore, as a personal renunciate name, "Jangama Hriddaya" means "one who has heartfelt sympathy for all beings".

8. The Ruchira Sannyasin Order is a formal renunciate order composed of uniquely exemplary devotees of Avatar Adi Da Samraj who are practicing in the context of the ultimate stages of life. "Sannyasin" is an ancient Sanskrit term for one who has renounced all worldly bonds and who gives himself or herself completely to the God-Realizing or God-Realized life. Members of this Order are legal renunciates and live a life of perpetual retreat. Avatar Adi Da Samraj is Himself the founding (and senior) Member of the Ruchira Sannyasin Order. The Ruchira Sannyasin Order is the hierarchically central, or most senior, practicing order (and the most senior cultural—but non-managerial authority) within the formal gathering of the devotees of Avatar Adi Da Samraj.

9. Avatar Adi Da has Revealed that He Appears everywhere in the Cosmic domain in the Form of Primal Divine Sound and Primal Divine Light. In His Light-Form, He appears as a brilliant white five-pointed Star.

*In The Form Of My Divine Sound Of Thunder and In The Form Of My Divine Star Of Light, I Everywhere Appear, and (By Means Of My Avatarically Self-Transmitted Divine Grace) I May (By every one) Be Heard and Seen (Directly and Infinitely Above the body-mind)—At The conditional Source-Point Above this world (and every world).*
[The Dawn Horse Testament Of The Ruchira Avatar]

10. Puja is formal sacramental worship. See chapter 9, pp. 235-37.

11. This building is now the principal Darshan Hall at the Mountain Of Attention.

12. Inspired by Avatar Adi Da's Love for all beings, the Fear-No-More Zoos began in California in the mid-1970s, and now exist in four different locations. Fear-No-More Zoos are a tangible expression of the fullness of Adi Da's Spiritual Work, which encompasses both humans and non-humans. The Fear-No-More Zoos give humans an opportunity to observe the non-humans in their natural state of Contemplation, thereby allowing greater sensitivity to the Spiritual nature of all beings. Fear No More Zoos serve and protect this natural state of Contemplation for all the non-humans that reside in them.

13. Avatar Adi Da calls the characteristically Eastern strategy the "Alpha" strategy. Alpha cultures are motivated to pursue an undisturbed peace, in which the world is absent (and thus unimposing). The Alpha preference, in contrast to the Omega preference, is to limit and control (and even suppress) the activities of the conditional personality, or even of conditional reality altogether, and to maximize attention, mystical devotion, and surrender to the Divine Reality.

Avatar Adi Da uses the term "Omega" to refer to the viewpoint and strategy that is characteristic of Western culture. The Omega strategy is motivated to attain fulfillment in the conditional worlds, through the intense application of human invention, political will, and (especially in earlier historical periods) prayer to the Divine. Its preference is to limit or suppress attention, mystical devotion, and submission to the Divine Reality, while maximizing attention to the pursuit of experience and knowledge relative to the conditional reality.

Neither the Alpha strategy nor the Omega strategy Realizes Truth, as each is rooted in the presumption of a "problem" relative to existence, and in the action of egoity itself (which motivates all human interests, short of Divine Self-Realization).

14. Holy Cat Grotto is named for Avatar Adi Da's cat, Robert, who lived with Him during (and for a while after) His years at Stanford. Robert has always been loved and honored by Avatar Adi Da as His first Teacher. He describes in *The Knee Of Listening—The Seventeen Companions Of The True Dawn Horse, Book Four: The Early-Life Ordeal and The "Radical" Spiritual Realization Of The Ruchira Avatar* how Robert demonstrated to Him a pure, intelligent, and unproblematic manner of living—life lived as "instinctive perfection". He also marveled at the depth of Robert's response to Him and, years later, confessed to devotees that Robert, in some sense, was the first being to recognize Him. When Robert died, Avatar Adi Da had him cremated, and Robert's ashes are enshrined at Holy Cat Grotto.

**Chapter 8**

1. "Satori" means "enlightenment" in Japanese, and is a term used in the Zen Buddhist tradition to indicate "a sudden experience of awakening to one's true nature".

2. *Santosha Adidam—The Seventeen Companions Of The True Dawn Horse, Book Fourteen: The Essential Summary Of The Divine Way Of Adidam* is one of Avatar Adi Da's twenty-three "Source-Texts", His Texts that summarize His Eternal Message to all beings (see chapter 25).

3. "Leela" is Sanskrit for "play", or "sport". In many religious and Spiritual traditions, all of conditionally manifested existence is regarded to be the Leela (or the Divine Play, Sport, or Free Activity) of the Divine Person. "Leela" also means the Awakened Play of a Realized Adept of any degree, through which he or she mysteriously Instructs and Liberates others and Blesses the world itself. By extension, a Leela is an instructive and inspiring story of such an Adept's Teaching and Blessing Play.

4. Vedanta is the principal philosophical tradition of Hinduism. "Advaita" means "non-dual". Advaita Vedanta, then, is a philosophy of non-dualism. Its origins lie in the ancient esoteric Teaching that the Divine Being is the only Reality. According to Advaita Vedanta, the conditional self and the world have no independent existence but merely arise in that one Divine Reality.

5. The Feeling of Being is the uncaused (or Self-Existing), Self-Radiant, and unqualified feeling-intuition of the Transcendental, Inherently Spiritual, and Divine Self-Condition.

6. Because, in the Way of Adidam, practitioners are not called to legally marry or to be held to conventional legal contracts regarding intimate relationship, the person with whom one has a formally acknowledged intimacy within the culture and community of Adidam is called an "intimate partner", rather than "husband" or "wife".

7. The etheric is life-energy, which functions through the human nervous system. Our bodies are surrounded and infused by this personal life-energy, which we feel as the play of emotions and life-force in the body.

8. On September 26, 1998, Indian Time celebrated her 22nd birthday.

**Chapter 9**

1. Avatar Adi Da's Divine Spiritual Body is not conditional or limited to His physical Body but is "The 'Bright' Itself (Eternally Most Prior To The Cosmic Domain)."

2. All formal sacramental devotion in the Way of Adidam is consecrated to Ruchira Avatar Adi Da Samraj and is thus celebrated as Ruchira Avatara Puja. Ruchira Avatara Puja involves devotional prayer, song, recitation of Avatar Adi Da's Word of Instruction, the offering and receiving of gifts, and other forms of outward-directed (or bodily active) devotional attention to Avatar Adi Da.

3. "Murti" is Sanskrit for "form", and, by extension, a "representational image" of the Divine or of a Sat-Guru. In the Way of Adidam, Murtis of Avatar Adi Da are most commonly photographs of Avatar Adi Da's bodily (human) Form.

4. Findhorn is a community that was founded in 1962 near the seaside village of Findhorn, Scotland. Through cultivating a conscious relationship with the "underlying spirit and intelligence" of nature, they produced miraculous results with vegetables, fruits, flowers, and other plants. They have since developed into a center for spiritual and holistic education, in addition to developing their work to preserve, protect, and cultivate a relationship with the natural environment.

5. The celebration of "the Day of the Heart" is now called "The Feast of the Divine Self-Confession".

6. A red powder used in Hindu worship.

7. This is a reference to Avatar Adi Da's experience of conditional Nirvikalpa Samadhi (see p. 45).

8. Conventionally, "self-possessed" means possessed <u>of</u> oneself—or in full control (calmness, or composure) of one's feelings, impulses, habits, and actions. Adi Da uses the term to indicate the state of being possessed <u>by</u> one's egoic self, or controlled by chronically self-referring (or egoic) tendencies of attention, feeling, thought, desire, and action.

9. Prasad is a gift that has been offered to the Divine and, having been Blessed, returned as a Divine Gift to the devotee. By extension, Prasad is anything the devotee receives from his or her Guru.

10. The establishment, testing, and proving of orders of exemplary renunciate devotees has been a core aspect of Avatar Adi Da's Work since 1979. See pp. 752-55 for a description of the formal renunciate orders of Adidam.

**Chapter 10**

1. Shirdi Sai Baba was an Indian Yogi-Saint (1838?-1918), who had both Muslim and Hindu followers. The gathering of his devotees has increased substantially in the years since his death.

**Chapter 11**

1. The Palace ("Mahal") of the Divine Giver ("Da") of the Divine Love-Bliss ("Love-Ananda").

2. "Tumo", a Tibetan term for the Spiritual practice of "mystic heat", literally means "fierce mother".

3. Avatar Adi Da uses the term "bond", when lower-cased, to refer to the process by which the egoic individual (already presuming separateness, and, therefore, bondage to the separate self) attaches himself or herself to the world of others and things through the constant search for self-fulfillment. In contrast, when He capitalizes the term "Bond", Avatar Adi Da is making reference to the process of His devotee's devotional "Bonding" to Him, which process is the Great Means for transcending all forms of limited "bonding".

4. For a description of the ultimate stages of practice, see note 6, p. 799.

5. The Sanskrit term "Savikalpa Samadhi" literally means "meditative ecstasy with form", or "deep meditative concentration (or absorption) in which form (or defined experiential content) is still perceived". Avatar Adi Da indicates that there are two basic forms of Savikalpa Samadhi. The first is the experience of mystical phenomena, visions, and other subtle sensory perceptions, and the immersion in states of Yogic Bliss (or Spirit-"Intoxication").

The second (and highest) form of Savikalpa Samadhi is "Cosmic Consciousness", or the "'Vision' of Cosmic Unity" (see note 8 below).

6. "Jnana" means "knowledge". Jnana Samadhi is the conditional, temporary Realization of the Transcendental Self (or Consciousness Itself). In Jnana Samadhi, all perception of world, objects, relations, body, mind, and separate-self-sense is excluded from awareness.

7. "Ruchira Samadhi" (Sanskrit for "the Samadhi of the 'Bright'") is one of the references that Avatar Adi Da Samraj uses for the Divinely Enlightened Condition, Which He characterizes as the Unconditional Realization of the Divine "Brightness".

8. In "Cosmic Consciousness" (or the "'Vision' of Cosmic Unity") attention ascends, uncharacteristically and spontaneously, to a state of awareness wherein conditional existence is perceived as a Unity

in Divine Awareness. "Cosmic Consciousness" (which is inevitably a temporary state of consciousness) is pursued as the highest goal in some mystical and Yogic paths. However, Avatar Adi Da has Revealed that, because "Cosmic Consciousness" is a temporary experiential state, and because the Unity experienced in "Cosmic Consciousness" is still perceived from the point of view of the separate self, "Cosmic Consciousness" is not equivalent to Divine Enlightenment.

9. In the context of Divine Enlightenment (or the seventh stage of life) in the Way of Adidam, the Spiritual process continues to unfold. Avatar Adi Da has uniquely Revealed that the process of Divine Enlightenment progresses in four phases: Divine Transfiguration, Divine Transformation, Divine Indifference, and Divine Translation.

In the phase of Divine Transfiguration, the devotee-Realizer's body-mind is Infused by Avatar Adi Da's Love-Bliss, and he or she Radiantly Demonstrates active Love, spontaneously Blessing all the relations of the body-mind.

In the following phase of Divine Transformation, the subtle (or psychic) dimension of the body-mind is fully Illumined, which may result in Divine Powers of healing, longevity, and the ability to release obstacles from the world and from the lives of others.

Eventually, Divine Indifference ensues, which is spontaneous and profound Resting in the "Deep" of Consciousness, and the world of relations is minimally, or not otherwise, noticed.

Divine Translation is the most ultimate "Event" of the entire process of Divine Awakening. Avatar Adi Da describes Divine Translation as the Outshining of all noticing of objective conditions, through the infinitely magnified Force of Consciousness Itself. Divine Translation is the Outshining of all destinies, wherein there is no return to the conditional realms.

10. "Adidam Samrajashram" means "The Adidam Ashram [or place of contemplation] of the "Bright" Divine Lord, Avatar Adi Da Samraj".

**Chapter 12**

1. Danavira Mela is the alternative (Sanskrit) name for "The Feast [mela] of the Hero [vira] of Giving [dana]". Danavira Mela is a time when Avatar Adi Da's devotees employ song and dance and drama and recitation and Leelas in honoring the Story of His Giving Grace, both in intimate community gatherings, and in public events. Gifts are exchanged, on December 25, as offerings of love and energy to others in the mood of heart-Communion with the Divine Giver, and the entire period is one in which the devotional bond of the community is strengthened and celebrated.

2. To Stand as the Witness is to be Identified with Consciousness Itself, free of all identification with body or mind. The Witness-Position is the Native Position of all, but it is only stably Realized with the transition to the ultimate stages of life.

**Chapter 13**

1. Shirdi Sai Baba employed a mysterious method of working with his devotees, or granting them the power of his Blessing, by frequently handling a group of coins, which (it is said) he used to represent his devotees. Acknowledging that He also Works in a similar manner, Avatar Adi Da sometimes refers to any small group of His devotees through whom He Works (at a particular time) to serve all His devotees (and even all beings) as His "coins".

2. The N-factor is the unknown determining factor, the Unaccountable Mystery on which conditional existence depends.

3. "Mahamantra Meditation" (the full name of which is "Ruchira Avatara Mahamantra Meditation") is a form of meditative practice Given by Avatar Adi Da Samraj to His devotees practicing in the context of the advanced stages of formal renunciate practice in the Way of Adidam. This form of practice uses specific mantric forms Given by Avatar Adi Da, called "the Ruchira Avatara Mahamantra" (or "the Great Mantra of the Ruchira Avatar").

4. Avatar Adi Da has Revealed that, just as there is a physical anatomy, there is also an actual Spiritual anatomy (or structure) that is present in every human being. As He says in *The Basket Of Tolerance—The Seventeen Companions Of The True Dawn Horse, Book Seventeen: The Perfect Guide To Perfectly Unified Understanding Of The One and Great Tradition Of Mankind, and Of The Divine Way Of Adidam As The Perfect Completing Of The One and Great Tradition Of Mankind*, it is because of this structure that the "experiential and developmental process of Growth and Realization demonstrates itself in accordance with what I have Revealed and Demonstrated to be the seven stages of life".

See *The Seven Stages Of Life—The Seventeen Companions Of The True Dawn Horse, Book Ten: Transcending The Six Stages Of egoic Life, and Realizing The ego-Transcending Seventh Stage Of Life, In The Divine Way Of Adidam* or *Santosha Adidam* for a further description of the esoteric Spiritual anatomy of Man.

5. S. Radhakrishnan, ed. and trans., *The Principal Upanisads* (London: George Allen & Unwin, 1953), p. 149.

6. Avatar Adi Da chose the name "Dawn Horse" because of the appropriateness of its meaning, not because of the physical resemblance of

the horse of His Vision to eohippus. The horse of His Vision was small, like eohippus, but it was generally proportioned like the modern horse rather than like eohippus.

7. Avatar Adi Da Samraj has Revealed the underlying structure of human growth in seven stages. The first three stages of life are the foundation processes of individuation, socialization, and integration and the fourth stage of life is the stage of awakening to the Spiritual reality. See chapter 16, pp. 407-11, for a fuller discussion of the seven stages of life.

## Chapter 14

1. Avatar Adi Da has said that in the Event that initiated His Divine Self-"Emergence", on January 11, 1986, He acquired His physical body "down to the toes". This is a reference to traditional descriptions of how a great Realizer would only "descend" partially into his or her human body—down as far as the head, or perhaps the throat or the heart, but typically not any "lower" than that.

*AVATAR ADI DA SAMRAJ: I have until now invested My Self more profoundly than just down to the throat or the heart, but not down to the bottoms of My feet. I have remained a kind of shroud around This Body, deeply associated with it, but in My freedom somehow lifted off the floor, somehow not committed to this sorrow and this mortality. . . Now I have accomplished your state completely, even more profoundly than you are sensitive to it. Perhaps you have seen it in My face. I do not look like I did last month, and I am never again going to look like that. I have become This Body, utterly.* [January 27, 1986]

2. "Avadhoot" is a traditional term for one who has "shaken off" or "passed beyond" all worldly attachments and cares, including all motives of detachment (or conventional and other-worldly renunciation), all conventional notions of life and religion, and all seeking for "answers" or "solutions" in the form of conditional experience or conditional knowledge. The Title "Avadhoot", when used in reference to Avatar Adi Da, indicates His Inherently Perfect Freedom as the Avatarically Self-Manifested Divine Person "Always Already" Standing Free of the binding and deluding power of conditional existence.

3. "Yajna" is Sanskrit for "sacrifice". Avatar Adi Da's entire Life may be rightly characterized as a Sacrifice, or Yajna, for the sake of bringing His Divine Gifts to all. In the Way of Adidam, the term "Yajna" is specifically used to refer to Avatar Adi Da's occasional travels, during which He Blesses the world and all beings through His contact with many people and places.

4. Celibacy is no longer a requirement for those serving in leadership positions in Adidam.

5. Avatar Adi Da Samraj has Revealed that the primal psycho-physical seat of Consciousness and attention is associated with what He calls the "right side of the heart". He has Revealed that this center corresponds to the sinoatrial node (or "pacemaker"), the source of the gross physical heartbeat in the right atrium (or upper right chamber) of the physical heart. In the Process of Divine Self-Realization, there is a unique process of opening of the right side of the heart.

**Chapter 15**

1. "Sadhu" is a Sanskrit term for a serious Spiritual aspirant, typically living a wandering ascetic life.

2. This Feast—traditionally called "Guru Purnima", or the "Full Moon (Purnima) of the Guru"—is called "The Feast of Ruchira Avatara Purnima" in the Way of Adidam.

**Chapter 16**

1. In 1984 a group of devotees sent a gift to Avatar Adi Da of a colorful coat with many pockets. One devotee had remembered as a child seeing a lady at the county fair wearing a capacious, many-pocketed coat and inviting children to reach into a pocket and pull out a gift. The coat was given to Avatar Adi Da with several fanciful stories about the "Giving Coat". In response to these gifts, Avatar Adi Da adopted the Giving Coat as one of the symbols of Himself as the Divine Giver (a symbol which is used at Danavira Mela each year), and named one of the Communion Halls at Adidam Samrajashram "The Giving Coat". This Hall was renamed "Temple Adi Da" in 1994.

2. For further information about Avatar Adi Da's schema of the seven stages of life, please see Avatar Adi Da's "Source-Text", *The Seven Stages Of Life*.

3. Avatar Adi Da has Revealed that the fourth stage of life has three possible contexts: the "original", the "basic", and the "advanced". The "original" (or beginner's) context of the fourth stage of life is associated with the essential religious "considerations" and devotional practices that awaken the open-hearted love, gratitude, and self-surrender that characterize the fourth stage of life. Those "considerations" and practices thus grant a fourth stage context to dimensions of practice that otherwise focus on developing responsibility for functions of the body-mind associated with the first three stages of life.

The "basic" context of the fourth stage of life is true Spiritual Awakening.

4. The "advanced" context of the fourth stage of life is characterized by the process of ascent of the Spirit-Current via the spinal line, from the bodily base toward the brain core. In the Way of Adidam, most practitioners will bypass practice in the ascending stages (the "advanced" context of the fourth stage of life, and the fifth stage of life) by entering the sixth stage of life directly from maturity in the fully established "basic" context of the fourth stage of life.

5. The *Ruchira Avatara Gita—The Five Books Of The Heart Of The Adidam Revelation, Book Two: The "Late-Time" Avataric Revelation Of The Great Secret Of The Divinely Self-Revealed Way That Most Perfectly Realizes The True and Spiritual Divine Person (The egoless Personal Presence Of Reality and Truth, Which Is The Only Real God)* is one of Avatar Adi Da's twenty-three "Source-Texts", His Texts that summarize His Eternal Message to all beings (see chapter 25).

6. The Title "Bhagavan" is Sanskrit for "blessed", "holy". When applied to a great Spiritual Master, "Bhagavan" is understood to mean "bountiful God", or "Great God", or "Divine Lord".

7. The Circle is the primary pathway of natural life-energy and the Divine Spirit-Current through the body-mind. It is composed of two arcs: the frontal line (down the front of the body, from the crown of the head to the bodily base), or the physical, emotional, and basic mental dimension of the body-mind; and the spinal line (up the back of the body, from the bodily base to the crown of the head), or the higher mental, psychic, and subtly oriented dimension of the body-mind.

8. The "conscious process" refers to those practices in the Way of Adidam through which the mind, or attention, is turned from egoic self-involvement to heart-Communion with Avatar Adi Da. It is the senior discipline and responsibility of all Avatar Adi Da's devotees.

**Chapter 17**

1. Avatar Adi Da has said that it is not necessary to physically see Him in His bodily (human) Form in order to receive His Divine Blessing. He has established various forms of Agency by means of which His Blessing is directly Transmitted. Avatar Adi Da's Agents are all the Means that have been Empowered by Him to serve as Vehicles of His Divine Grace and Awakening Power. These include His Wisdom-Teaching, the Empowered Hermitage-Retreats and the Empowered Pilgrimage and Retreat Sanctuaries of the Way of Adidam, and the

many Objects and Articles that He has Empowered for the sake of His devotees' Remembrance of Him and reception of His Divine Heart-Blessing. After Avatar Adi Da's human Lifetime, one from among His Divinely Awakened Ruchira Sannyasin devotees will (at any given time) serve as His human Agent.

2. When an individual becomes a formal practitioner of the Way of Adidam, he or she takes an Eternal Vow of devotion to Avatar Adi Da during a formal initiation ceremony. (See "Invitation", pp. 750-51.)

**Chapter 18**

1. See B. V. Narasimha Swami and S. Subbarao, *Sage of Sakuri*, 4th ed. (Bombay: Shri B. T. Wagh, 1966), pp. 190-191, 204.

2. In traditional India in times past (and in present-day orthodox Hindu circles), those who resided outside of India were regarded—like the untouchables within Hindu society—to be ineligible to participate fully in the Spiritual Way of life. As such, the "untouchables", outcasts, and so-called "barbarians" of the world (including all non-Indians) were known generally as "mlecchas", and it was assumed, in orthodox circles of Vedic Hinduism, that such beings were gradually evolving from relatively inauspicious lifetimes until they might merit a birth within one of the castes of those eligible for salvatory and Liberating Divine Grace under the Vedic code.

3. For a description of the different entities within the institution, culture, community, and mission of Adidam, please see pp. 763-65.

4. Information on the life and work of Narayan Maharaj can be found in "The Servant King: Sri Narayan Maharaj", by David Todd and Ty Koontz (*The Laughing Man Magazine*, Vol. 2, No. 4, pp. 69-77), and "Narayan Maharaj, Lord of the Heart", chapter two (pp. 20-47) of *Meher Prabhu: The Biography of Avatar Meher Baba*, Volume 1 (1894-1922), by Bhau Kalchuri (North Myrtle Beach, S.C.: Manifestation, Inc., 1986).

5. See chapters 6-10 of *The Dawn Horse Testament Of The Ruchira Avatar—The "Testament Of Divine Secrets" Of The Divine World-Teacher, Ruchira Avatar Adi Da Samraj*, or chapters 6-11 of *The Heart Of The Dawn Horse Testament Of The Ruchira Avatar—The Seventeen Companions Of The True Dawn Horse, Book Twelve: The Epitome Of The "Testament Of Secrets" Of The Divine World-Teacher, Ruchira Avatar Adi Da Samraj*, or Part Seven of *Real God Is The Indivisible Oneness Of Unbroken Light—The Seventeen Companions Of The True Dawn Horse, Book One: Reality, Truth, and The "Non-Creator" God In The True World-Religion Of Adidam.*

## Chapter 19

1. The Vaishnavite tradition of Hinduism comprises the sects devoted to the Divine in the form of the Deity Vishnu, usually in the aspect of one or another Avatar, such as Krishna or Rama.

2. In the Hindu tradition, the Kali Yuga ("dark epoch") is the final and most ignorant and degenerate period of mankind, when the Spiritual Way of life is almost entirely forgotten.

3. *The New Jerusalem Bible*, The Revelation to John, chapter 19, verses 11, 12, 16.

4. Judith M. Tyberg, *The Language of the Gods: Sanskrit Keys to India's Wisdom* (Los Angeles: East-West Cultural Centre, 1970), pp. 73-74.

5. "Mandir" in Hindi means "temple".

## Chapter 20

1. For a more complete discussion of Avatar Adi Da's Wisdom relative to reincarnation, see *The Dawn Horse Testament Of The Ruchira Avatar*, chapter 43, and *Easy Death*.

2. "Fakir" in Arabic literally means "poor", and it may be used to mean either material impoverishment or the virtue of an aspirant making himself or herself "poor" by ceasing to be self-centered. For a full account of this incident, see *The Life of Swami Vivekananda*, Volume One, by his Eastern and Western Disciples (Calcutta: Advaita Ashram, revised and enlarged edition, 1979), pp. 182-83.

3. Marie Louise Burke, the principal Western biographer of Swami Vivekananda, has confirmed that Swami Vivekananda must have visited Kew Gardens, since he spent so much time in London and this was exactly the type of place he liked to visit.

## Chapter 21

1. Sacred phallic shaped stones known as "lingams" have been revered since ancient times as representations of the male Deity. In India, the lingam is especially associated with Siva. In the Way of Adidam, the lingam form is a Murti of Avatar Adi Da Samraj, representing the Descent of His Divine Spiritual Body into the conditional worlds.

2. "Mahasamadhi" ("Great Samadhi") is a Sanskrit term for the death of a great Realizer.

3. The following chart gives each of Avatar Adi Da's principal Divine Names and Titles, together with His definition of each Name or Title. ("Avabhasa" is a Name that was offered to Avatar Adi Da in 1991, and which was His primary name from that time until 1994. "Kalki" is a name that Avatar Adi Da no longer uses.)

| | |
|---|---|
| **Ruchira** | The Radiant, Shining, "Bright" Illuminator and Enlightener |
| **Avatar** | The Divinely Descended One, The "Bright" Divine Person Who Pervades The Cosmic Domain From Infinitely Above, and Who Is The Very and Inherently "Bright" Divine Self-Condition, and The Self-Existing and Self-Radiant Source-Condition, Of All and all, and Who Is Appearing, Perfectly Divinely Self-"Emerged", In The Avataric Form Of A Man, For The Sake Of The Graceful Divine Liberation Of all and All |
| **Adi** | The Only One, The First One, or The Foremost, or Preeminent, One |
| **Da** | The Self-Existing and Self-Radiant One, Whose Eternal Characteristics Are Now, and Forever Hereafter, Avatarically Self-Transmitted To All and all, By Means Of The Perpetual "Mudra" Of Divine Self-Giving |
| **Samraj** | The Divine Heart-Master, or The Transcendental, Perfectly Subjective, Inherently Spiritual, Inherently egoless, Inherently Perfect, and Self-Evidently Divine Lord, or Master-King, or Master-Ruler and Divine Liberator, Of The Heart Of everyone, and Of every one, and Of all, and Of All |
| **Love-Ananda** | The "Bright" Divine Love-Bliss, Itself |
| **Avabhasa** | The "Bright", or The Divine Spiritual Body Of Love-Bliss, Itself |
| **Santosha** | The "Bright" and Eternal and Always Already Non-Separate Person Of Divine and Inherent Completeness, Divine Self-Satisfaction, Divine Self-Contentedness, or Perfect Searchlessness |

**Dau Loloma** The Divine Adept Of The Divine Love

**Vunirarama** The Self-Radiant Divine Source and Substance Of The Divine "Brightness"

## Chapter 23

1. In 1997, Avatar Adi Da designated *The Mummery* as one of His twenty-three "Source-Texts"—His Texts that summarize His Eternal Message to all beings (see chapter 25).

## Chapter 24

1. Avatar Adi Da has established two formal renunciate orders: The Ruchira Sannyasin Order of the Tantric Renunciates of Adidam (or, simply, the Ruchira Sannyasin Order) and the Avabhasin Lay Renunciate Order of the Tantric Renunciates of Adidam (or, simply, the Lay Renunciate Order).

The Lay Renunciate Order is a cultural service order. It is subordinate to the Ruchira Sannyasin Order and functions within the culture and community of Adidam in direct response to the culturally expressed expectations of the Ruchira Sannyasin Order. Members of the Lay Renunciate Order provide the inspirational and cultural leadership for the institution, the culture, and the community of Avatar Adi Da's devotees, in service to both the internal sacred devotional culture and the public mission of this worldwide gathering. (The Ruchira Sannyasin Order is defined in note 8, page 800.)

Avatar Adi Da has indicated in His twenty-three "Source-Texts" that members of the two formal renunciate orders of Adidam function collectively and spontaneously as His Instruments, or means by which His Divine Grace and Awakening Power are Magnified and Transmitted to other devotees and all beings.

2. Shortly after this time (on July 14, 1997), Avatar Adi Da gave the two Adidamas the title of "Adidama" and named their order the "Adidama Quandra Mandala".

3. The Adidama Quandra Mandala is Adidama Sukha Dham and Adidama Jangama Hriddaya. "Quandra" is a reference to the main female character in *The Mummery*. Quandra is an archetypal representation of the "Divine Goddess-Power", or the Primal Divine Spirit-Energy.

4. According to the theory of "m-fields", proposed by biologist Rupert Sheldrake, each species exists within a subtle, indefinable psychogenetic field. Significant changes in any individual or group may come to characterize the entire species, or many other individuals within it, via the medium of this field. For example, once one human

being runs a four-minute mile, it becomes easier for others to do so.

5. "Asana" is Sanskrit for bodily "posture" or "pose". By extension, and as Avatar Adi Da often intends, "asana" also refers to the attitude, orientation, posture, or feeling-disposition of the heart and the entire body-mind.

6. Avatar Adi Da Samraj Speaks of the Way of Adidam as a "Pleasure Dome", recalling the poem "Kubla Khan", by Samuel Taylor Coleridge ("In Xanadu did Kubla Khan/A stately pleasure-dome decree . . ."). Adi Da points out that in many religious traditions it is presumed that one must embrace suffering in order to "earn" future happiness and pleasure. However, by Calling His devotees to live the Way of Adidam as a Pleasure Dome, Avatar Adi Da Samraj Communicates His Teaching that the Way of heart-Communion with Him is always about present-time Happiness, not about any kind of search to attain Happiness in the future. Thus, in the Way of Adidam, there is no idealization of suffering and pain as presumed means to attain future happiness. Therefore, in the Way of Adidam, there is no denial of the appropriate enjoyment of the pleasures of human life.

7. Here Avatar Adi Da is Speaking of the process of transcending (via Spiritual Awakening) the presumption of being "trapped" in the body.

8. M. U. Hatengdi, *Nityananda: The Divine Presence* (Cambridge, Mass.: Rudra Press, 1984).

9. The full, technical requirements for taking up the "Hridaya Rosary" practice are described in *Hridaya Rosary*.

10. As a child, Avatar Adi Da contracted a mild case of polio, and He now experiences post-polio syndrome on the left side of His body.

**Chapter 26**

1. En-Light-enment (or Enlightenment) is not just a state of mind, but rather it is an actual conversion of the total body-mind to the state of Divine Consciousness Itself, or Light Itself. Thus, Avatar Adi Da sometimes writes the word "Enlightenment" with "Light" set apart by hyphens, in order to emphasize this point.

2. The causal dimension is senior to and pervades both the gross and the subtle dimensions. It is the root of attention, or the essence of the separate and separative ego-"I". The causal dimension is associated with the right side of the heart, specifically with the sinoatrial node, or "pacemaker" (the psycho-physical source of the heartbeat). Its corresponding state of consciousness is the formless awareness of deep sleep.

3. *Eleutherios—The Five Books Of The Heart Of The Adidam Revelation, Book Five: The "Late-Time" Avataric Revelation Of The "Perfect Practice" Of The Great Means To Worship and To Realize The True and Spiritual Divine Person (The egoless Personal Presence Of Reality and Truth, Which Is The Only Real God)* is one of Avatar Adi Da's twenty-three "Source-Texts". "Eleutherios" (Greek for "Liberator") is a title by which Zeus was venerated as the supreme deity in the Spiritual esotericism of ancient Greece. The Designation "Eleutherios" indicates the Divine Function of Avatar Adi Da as the Incarnation of the Divine Person, "Whose Inherently Perfect Self-'Brightness' Liberates all conditionally Manifested beings, Freely, Liberally, Gracefully, and Without Ceasing".

4. A "sutra" (in Sanskrit) is, literally, a "thread", or "string". In the Hindu scriptures, the sutras are strings of aphoristic Wisdom sayings.

5. Regenerative orgasm is a specific process of bypassing degenerative (or conventional) orgasm and converting it, or preventing the energy from being "thrown out" of the body at the bodily base by conducting it into the spinal line and into the whole body altogether. See *The Dawn Horse Testament Of The Ruchira Avatar*, chapter 21, or *Ruchira Tantra Yoga*.

6. Avatar Adi Da has coined the term "Klik-Klak" as a name for conditional reality. This name indicates (even by means of the sound of the two syllables) that conditional reality is a heartless perpetual-motion machine of incessant change.

## Chapter 27

1. "Ati" is Sanskrit for "beyond". Therefore, "atiashrama" means "beyond the ashramas (or stages of life)". Such freedom can truly be said to belong only to One Who has transcended all egoity through Divine Self-Realization. When applied to Avatar Adi Da, the descriptive Title "Atiashrami" indicates His Most Perfect Transcendence of all conventional, religious, and Spiritual points of view in the Most Perfect Freedom of the Divinely Enlightened stage of life.

## The Great Choice

1. Avatar Adi Da has indicated in His twenty-three "Source-Texts" that members of the two formal renunciate orders of Adidam function collectively and spontaneously as His Instruments, or means by which His Divine Grace and Awakening Power are Magnified and Transmitted to other devotees and all beings. Such devotees have received Avatar Adi Da's Spiritual Baptism, and they practice in Spiritually activated relationship to Him. Because of their uniquely complete and

renunciate response and accountability to Him, and by virtue of their ego-surrendering, ego-forgetting, ego-transcending, and really Spiritual Invocation of Him, these devotees function collectively as Instruments for the Transmission of Avatar Adi Da's Spiritual (and Always Blessing) Presence to others at the same developmental stage and at earlier developmental stages of the Way of Adidam (and even, in a general sense, to all of Avatar Adi Da Samraj's devotees).

2. For Avatar Adi Da's technical description of this practice see chapter 21 in *The Dawn Horse Testament Of The Ruchira Avatar* or part eighteen of *Ruchira Tantra Yoga*.

**Appendix A: There Is No Face Within The Sky**

1. "Hamartia" (the word in New Testament Greek that was translated into English as "sin") was originally an archery term meaning "missing the mark".

# THE SACRED LITERATURE OF RUCHIRA AVATAR ADI DA SAMRAJ

## The Five Books Of The Heart Of The Adidam Revelation

After reading *The Promised God-Man Is Here*, read *The Five Books Of The Heart Of The Adidam Revelation*. In these five books, Avatar Adi Da Samraj has distilled the very essence of His Eternal Message to every one, in all times and places.

BOOK ONE:

### Aham Da Asmi
### (Beloved, I Am Da)

*The "Late-Time" Avataric Revelation Of The True and Spiritual Divine Person (The egoless Personal Presence Of Reality and Truth, Which Is The Only Real God)*

The most extraordinary statement ever made in human history. Avatar Adi Da Samraj fully Reveals Himself as the Living Divine Person and Proclaims His Infinite and Undying Love for all and All.

**$7.95,** 4"x7" paperback, 222 pages

BOOK TWO:

### Ruchira Avatara Gita
### (The Way Of The Divine Heart-Master)

*The "Late-Time" Avataric Revelation Of The Great Secret Of The Divinely Self-Revealed Way That Most Perfectly Realizes The True and Spiritual Divine Person (The egoless Personal Presence Of Reality and Truth, Which Is The Only Real God)*

Avatar Adi Da Offers to every one the ecstatic practice of devotional relationship to Him—explaining how devotion to a living human Adept-Realizer has always been the source of true religion, and distinguishing true Guru-devotion from cultism.

**$7.95,** 4"x7" paperback, 254 pages

BOOK THREE:

## Da Love-Ananda Gita

### (The Free Gift Of The Divine Love-Bliss)

*The "Late-Time" Avataric Revelation Of The Great Means To Worship and To Realize The True and Spiritual Divine Person (The egoless Personal Presence Of Reality and Truth, Which Is The Only Real God)*

Avatar Adi Da Reveals the secret simplicity at the heart of Adidam—relinquishing your preoccupation with yourself (and all your problems and your suffering) and, instead, Contemplating Him, the "Bright" Divine Person of Infinite Love-Bliss.

**$7.95,** 4"x7" paperback, 234 pages

BOOK FOUR:

## Hridaya Rosary

### (Four Thorns Of Heart-Instruction)

*The "Late-Time" Avataric Revelation Of The Universally Tangible Divine Spiritual Body, Which Is The Supreme Agent Of The Great Means To Worship and To Realize The True and Spiritual Divine Person (The egoless Personal Presence Of Reality and Truth, Which Is The Only Real God)*

The ultimate Mysteries of Spiritual life, never before revealed. In breathtakingly beautiful poetry, Avatar Adi Da Samraj sings of the "melting" of the ego in His "Rose Garden of the Heart".

**$7.95,** 4"x7" paperback, 358 pages

BOOK FIVE:

## Eleutherios

### (The Only Truth That Sets The Heart Free)

*The "Late-Time" Avataric Revelation Of The "Perfect Practice" Of The Great Means To Worship and To Realize The True and Spiritual Divine Person (The egoless Personal Presence Of Reality and Truth, Which Is The Only Real God)*

An address to the great human questions about God, Truth, Reality, Happiness, and Freedom. Avatar Adi Da Samraj Reveals how Absolute Divine Freedom is Realized, and makes an impassioned Call to everyone to create a world of true human freedom on Earth.

**$7.95,** 4"x7" paperback, 270 pages

# The Seventeen Companions Of The True Dawn Horse

Once you have read *The Five Books Of The Heart Of The Adidam Revelation*, you are ready to continue with *The Seventeen Companions Of The True Dawn Horse*. These seventeen books are "Companions" to *The Dawn Horse Testament*, Avatar Adi Da's great summary of the Way of Adidam (p. 824). Here you will find Avatar Adi Da's Wisdom-Instruction on particular aspects of the true Spiritual Way, and His two tellings of His own Life-Story, as autobiography (*The Knee Of Listening*) and as archetypal parable (*The Mummery*). Avatar Adi Da created the Canon of His Sacred Literature in late 1997 and early 1998, and the Dawn Horse Press is currently in the process of publishing the "Seventeen Companions" and *The Dawn Horse Testament*.

BOOK ONE:

### Real God Is The Indivisible Oneness Of Unbroken Light

*Reality, Truth, and The "Non-Creator" God In The True World-Religion Of Adidam*

The Nature of Real God and of the cosmos. Why ultimate questions cannot be answered either by conventional religion or by science.

BOOK TWO:

### The Truly Human New World-Culture Of Unbroken Real-God-Man

*The Eastern Versus The Western Traditional Cultures Of Mankind, and The Unique New Non-Dual Culture Of The True World-Religion Of Adidam*

The Eastern and Western approaches to religion, and life altogether—and how the Way of Adidam goes beyond this apparent dichotomy.

BOOK THREE:

### The Only Complete Way To Realize The Unbroken Light Of Real God

*An Introductory Overview Of The "Radical" Divine Way Of The True World-Religion Of Adidam*

The entire course of the Way of Adidam—the unique principles underlying Adidam, and the unique culmination of Adidam in Divine Enlightenment.

BOOK FOUR:

## The Knee Of Listening

*The Early-Life Ordeal and The "Radical" Spiritual Realization Of The Ruchira Avatar*

Avatar Adi Da's autobiographical account of the years from His Birth to His Divine Re-Awakening in 1970. Includes a new chapter, "My Realization of the Great Onlyness of Me, and My Great Regard for My Adept-Links to the Great Tradition of Mankind".

BOOK FIVE:

## The Method Of The Ruchira Avatar

*The Divine Way Of Adidam Is An ego-Transcending Relationship, Not An ego-Centric Technique*

Avatar Adi Da's earliest Talks to His devotees, on the fundamental principles of the devotional relationship to Him and "radical" understanding of the ego. Accompanied by His summary statement on His relationship to Swami Muktananda and on His own unique Teaching and Blessing Work.

BOOK SIX:

## The Mummery

*A Parable Of The Divine True Love*

A work of astonishing poetry and deeply evocative archetypes. The story of Raymond Darling's growth to manhood and his search to be reunited with his beloved, Quandra.

BOOK SEVEN:

## He-and-She Is Me

*The Indivisibility Of Consciousness and Light in The Divine Body Of The Ruchira Avatar*

One of Avatar Adi Da's most esoteric Revelations—His Primary "Incarnation" in the Cosmic domain as the "He" of Primal Divine Sound-Vibration, the "She" of Primal Divine Light, and the "Son" of "He" and "She" in the "Me" of His Divine Spiritual Body.

BOOK EIGHT:

## Divine Spiritual Baptism Versus Cosmic Spiritual Baptism

*Divine Hridaya-Shakti Versus Cosmic Kundalini Shakti In The Divine Way Of Adidam*

The Divine Heart-Power (Hridaya-Shakti) uniquely Transmitted by Avatar Adi Da Samraj, and how it differs from the various traditional forms of Spiritual Baptism, particularly Kundalini Yoga.

BOOK NINE:

## Ruchira Tantra Yoga

*The Physical-Spiritual (and Truly Religious) Method Of Mental, Emotional, Sexual, and Whole Bodily Health and Enlightenment In The Divine Way Of Adidam*

The transformation of life in the domain of "money, food, and sex". Includes: understanding "victim-consciousness"; the ego as addict; the secret of how to change; going beyond the "Oedipal" sufferings of childhood; the right orientation to money; right diet; life-positive and Spiritually auspicious sexual practice.

BOOK TEN:

## The Seven Stages Of Life

*Transcending The Six Stages Of egoic Life and Realizing The ego-Transcending Seventh Stage Of Life, In The Divine Way Of Adidam*

The stages of human development from birth to Divine Enlightenment. How the stages relate to physical and esoteric anatomy. The errors of each of the first six stages of life, and the unique egolessness of the seventh stage of life. Avatar Adi Da's Self-Confession as the first, last, and only seventh stage Adept-Realizer.

BOOK ELEVEN:

## The All-Completing and Final Divine Revelation To Mankind

*A Summary Description Of The Supreme Yoga Of The Seventh Stage Of Life In The Divine Way Of Adidam*

The ultimate secrets of Divine Enlightenment—including the four-stage Process of Divine Enlightenment, culminating in Translation into the Infinitely Love-Blissful Divine Self-Domain.

BOOK TWELVE:

## The Heart Of The Dawn Horse Testament Of The Ruchira Avatar

*The Epitome Of The "Testament Of Secrets" Of The Divine World-Teacher, Ruchira Avatar Adi Da Samraj*

A shorter version of *The Dawn Horse Testament*—all of Avatar Adi Da's magnificent summary Instruction, without the details of the technical practices engaged by His devotees.

BOOK THIRTEEN:

## What, Where, When, How, Why, and Who To Remember To Be Happy

*A Simple Explanation Of The Divine Way Of Adidam (For Children, and Everyone Else)*

A text written specifically for children but inspiring to all—with accompanying Essays and Talks on Divine Ignorance, religious practices for children and young people in the Way of Adidam, and the fundamental practice of whole bodily devotion to Avatar Adi Da Samraj.

BOOK FOURTEEN:

## Santosha Adidam

*The Essential Summary Of The Divine Way Of Adidam*

An extended overview of the entire course of the Way of Adidam, based on the esoteric anatomy of the human being and its correlation to the progressive stages of life.

BOOK FIFTEEN:

## The Lion Sutra

*The "Perfect Practice" Teachings For Formal Tantric Renunciates In The Divine Way Of Adidam*

Practice in the ultimate stages of the Way of Adidam. How the formal renunciate practitioner of Adidam approaches—and passes over—the "Threshold" of Divine Enlightenment.

BOOK SIXTEEN:

## The Overnight Revelation Of Conscious Light

*The "My House" Discourses On The Indivisible Tantra Of Adidam*

A vast and profound "consideration" of the fundamental Tantric principles of true Spiritual life and the "Always Already" Nature of the Divine Reality. The day-by-day record of Avatar Adi Da's Discourses from a two-month period in early 1998.

BOOK SEVENTEEN:

## The Basket Of Tolerance

*The Perfect Guide To Perfectly Unified Understanding Of The One and Great Tradition Of Mankind, and Of The Divine Way Of Adidam As The Perfect Completing Of The One and Great Tradition Of Mankind*

An all-encompassing "map" of mankind's entire history of religious seeking. A combination of a bibliography of over 5,000 items (organized to display Avatar Adi Da's grand Argument relative to the Great Tradition) with over 100 Essays by Avatar Adi Da, illuminating many specific aspects of the Great Tradition.

---

# THE DAWN HORSE TESTAMENT

---

## The Dawn Horse Testament Of The Ruchira Avatar

*The "Testament Of Secrets" Of The Divine World-Teacher, Ruchira Avatar Adi Da Samraj*

Avatar Adi Da's paramount "Source-Text" which summarizes the entire course of the Way of Adidam. Adi Da Samraj says: "In making this Testament I have been Meditating everyone, contacting everyone, dealing with psychic forces everywhere, in all time. This Testament is an always Living Conversation between Me and absolutely every one."

## See My Brightness Face to Face

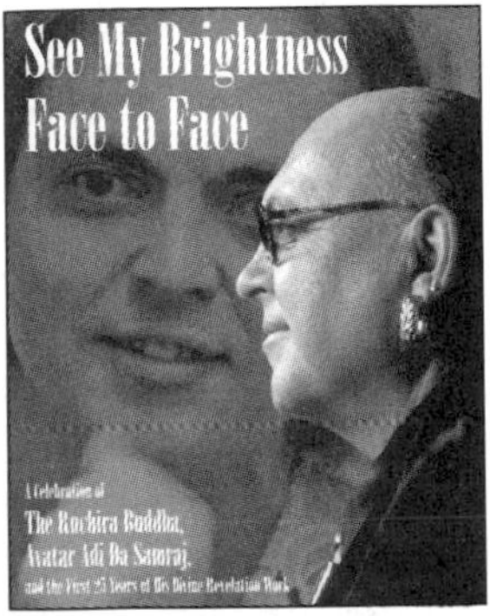


*A Celebration of the Ruchira Avatar, Adi Da Samraj, and the First Twenty-Five Years of His Divine Revelation Work*

A magnificent year-by-year pictorial celebration of Ruchira Avatar Adi Da's Divine Work with His devotees, from 1972 to 1997. Includes a wealth of selections from His Talks and Writings, numerous Stories of His Divine Work told by His devotees, and over 100 color photographs

**$19.95**, 8"x10" quality paperback, 200 pages

---

In addition to Avatar Adi Da's 23 "Source-Texts", the Dawn Horse Press offers many other publications, as well as videotapes and audiotapes, of Avatar Adi Da's Wisdom-Teaching. Dawn Horse Press publications are distributed by the Adidam Emporium, a worker-owned cooperative business offering a wide array of items for meditation, sacred worship, health and well-being, and much more.

***For more information or a free catalog:***

**CALL THE ADIDAM EMPORIUM**
**TOLL-FREE 1-877-770-0772**

(Outside North America call 707-928-6653)
Visit on-line at **http://www.adidam.com**
Or e-mail: **emporium@adidam.com**
Or write:

**Adidam Emporium**
**10336 Loch Lomond Road, Suite 306**
**Middletown, CA 95461**

We accept Visa, MasterCard, personal checks, and money orders. In the USA, please add $5.00 (shipping and handling) for the first book and $1.00 for each additional book. California residents add 7.25% sales tax. Outside the USA, please add $9.00 (shipping and handling) for the first book and $3.00 for each additional book. Checks and money orders should be made payable to the Adidam Emporium.

# An Invitation to Support Adidam

Avatar Adi Da Samraj's sole Purpose is to act as a Source of continuous Divine Grace for everyone, everywhere. In that spirit, He is a Free Renunciate and He owns nothing. Those who have made gestures in support of Avatar Adi Da's Work have found that their generosity is returned in many Blessings that are full of His healing, transforming, and Liberating Grace—and those Blessings flow not only directly to them as the beneficiaries of His Work, but to many others, even all others. At the same time, all tangible gifts of support help secure and nurture Avatar Adi Da's Work in necessary and practical ways, again similarly benefiting the entire world. Because all this is so, supporting His Work is the most auspicious form of financial giving, and we happily extend to you an invitation to serve Adidam through your financial support.

You may make a financial contribution in support of the Work of Adi Da Samraj at any time. You may also, if you choose, request that your contribution be used for one or more specific purposes.

If you are moved to help support and develop Adidam Samrajashram (Naitauba), Avatar Adi Da's Great Island-Hermitage and World-Blessing Seat in Fiji, and the circumstance provided there and elsewhere for Avatar Adi Da and the other members of the Ruchira Sannyasin Order, the senior renunciate order of Adidam, you may do so by making your contribution to The Da Love-Ananda Samrajya, the Australian charitable trust which has central responsibility for these Sacred Treasures of Adidam.

To do this: (1) if you do not pay taxes in the United States, make your check payable directly to "The Da Love-Ananda Samrajya Pty Ltd" (which serves as the trustee of the Foundation) and mail it to The Da Love-Ananda Samrajya at P.O. Box 4744, Samabula, Suva, Fiji; and (2) if you do pay taxes in the United States and you would like your contribution to be tax-deductible under U.S. laws, make your check payable to "The Eleutherian Pan-Communion of Adidam", indicate on your check or accompanying letter that you would like your contribution used for the work of The Da Love-Ananda Samrajya, and mail your check to the Advocacy Department of Adidam at 12040 North Seigler Road, Middletown, California 95461, USA.

If you are moved to help support and provide for one of the other purposes of Adidam, such as publishing the sacred Literature of Avatar Adi Da, or supporting either of the other two Sanctuaries He has Empowered, or maintaining the Sacred Archives that preserve His recorded Talks and Writings, or publishing audio and video recordings of Avatar Adi Da, you may do so by making your contribution directly to The Eleutherian Pan-Communion of Adidam, specifying the particular purposes you wish to benefit, and mailing your check to the Advocacy Department of Adidam at the above address.

If you would like more information about these and other gifting options, or if you would like assistance in describing or making a contribution, please write to the Advocacy Department of Adidam at the above address or contact the Adidam Legal Department by telephone at (707) 928-4612 or by FAX at (707) 928-4062.

## Planned Giving

We also invite you to consider making a planned gift in support of the Work of Avatar Adi Da Samraj. Many have found that through planned giving they can make a far more significant gesture of support than they would otherwise be able to make. Many have also found that by making a planned gift they are able to realize substantial tax advantages.

There are numerous ways to make a planned gift, including making a gift in your Will, or in your life insurance, or in a charitable trust.

If you would like to make a gift in your Will in support of the work of The Da Love-Ananda Samrajya: (1) if you do not pay taxes in the United States, simply include in your Will the statement, "I give to The Da Love-Ananda Samrajya Pty Ltd, as trustee of The Da Love-Ananda Samrajya, an Australian charitable trust, P.O. Box 4744, Samabula, Suva, Fiji, ________" [inserting in the blank the amount or description of your contribution]; and (2) if you do pay taxes in the United States and you would like your contribution to be free of estate taxes and to also reduce any estate taxes payable on the remainder of your estate, simply include in your Will the statement, "I give to The Eleutherian Pan-Communion of Adidam, a California non-profit corporation, 12040 North Seigler Road, Middletown, California 95461, USA, ________" [inserting in the blank the amount or description of your contribution].

To make a gift in your life insurance, simply name as the beneficiary (or one of the beneficiaries) of your life insurance policy the organization of your choice (The Da Love-Ananda Samrajya or The Eleutherian Pan-Communion of Adidam), according to the foregoing descriptions and addresses. If you are a United States taxpayer, you may receive significant tax benefits if you make a contribution to The Eleutherian Pan-Communion of Adidam through your life insurance.

We also invite you to consider establishing or participating in a charitable trust for the benefit of Adidam. If you are a United States taxpayer, you may find that such a trust will provide you with immediate tax savings and assured income for life, while at the same time enabling you to provide for your family, for your other heirs, and for the Work of Avatar Adi Da as well.

The Advocacy and Legal Departments of Adidam will be happy to provide you with further information about these and other planned gifting options, and happy to provide you or your attorney with assistance in describing or making a planned gift in support of the Work of Avatar Adi Da.

# Further Notes to the Reader

## An Invitation to Responsibility

Adidam, the Way of the Heart that Avatar Adi Da has Revealed, is an invitation to everyone to assume real responsibility for his or her life. As Avatar Adi Da has Said in *The Dawn Horse Testament Of The Ruchira Avatar,* "If any one Is Interested In The Realization Of The Heart, Let him or her First Submit (Formally, and By Heart) To Me, and (Thereby) Commence The Ordeal Of self-Observation, self-Understanding, and self-Transcendence." Therefore, participation in the Way of Adidam requires a real struggle with oneself, and not at all a struggle with Avatar Adi Da, or with others.

All who study the Way of Adidam or take up its practice should remember that they are responding to a Call to become responsible for themselves. They should understand that they, not Avatar Adi Da or others, are responsible for any decision they may make or action they may take in the course of their lives of study or practice. This has always been true, and it is true whatever the individual's involvement in the Way of Adidam, be it as one who studies Avatar Adi Da's Wisdom-Teaching or as a formally acknowledged member of Adidam.

## Honoring and Protecting the Sacred Word through Perpetual Copyright

Since ancient times, practitioners of true religion and Spirituality have valued, above all, time spent in the Company of the Sat-Guru (or one who has, to any degree, Realized Real God, Truth, or Reality, and who, thus, Serves the awakening process in others). Such practitioners understand that the Sat-Guru literally Transmits his or her (Realized) State to every one (and every thing) with whom (or with which) he or she comes in contact. Through this Transmission, objects, environments, and rightly prepared individuals with which the Sat-Guru has contact can become Empowered, or Imbued with the Sat-Guru's Transforming Power. It is by this process of Empowerment that things and beings are made truly and literally sacred, and things so sanctified thereafter function as a Source of the Sat-Guru's Blessing for all who understand how to make right and sacred use of them.

Sat-Gurus of any degree of Realization and all that they Empower are, therefore, truly Sacred Treasures, for they help draw the practitioner more quickly into the process of Realization. Cultures of true Wisdom have always understood that such Sacred Treasures are precious (and fragile) Gifts to humanity, and that they should be honored, protected, and reserved for right sacred use. Indeed, the word "sacred" means "set apart", and, thus, protected, from the secular world. Avatar Adi Da has Conformed His body-mind Most Perfectly to the Divine Self, and He is, thus, the most Potent Source of Blessing-Transmission of Real God, or Truth Itself, or Reality Itself. He has for many years Empowered (or made sacred) special places and things, and these now Serve as His Divine Agents, or as literal expressions and extensions of His Blessing-Transmission. Among these Empowered Sacred Treasures is His Wisdom-Teaching, which is Full of His Transforming Power. This Blessed and Blessing Wisdom-Teaching has Mantric Force, or the literal Power to Serve Real-God-Realization in those who are Graced to receive it.

Therefore, Avatar Adi Da's Wisdom-Teaching must be perpetually honored and protected, "set apart" from all possible interference and wrong use. The fellowship of devotees of Avatar Adi Da is committed to the perpetual preservation and right honoring of the sacred Wisdom-Teaching of the Way of Adidam. But it is also true that, in order to fully accomplish this, we must find support in the world-society in which we live and in its laws. Thus, we call for a world-society and for laws that acknowledge the Sacred, and that permanently protect It from insensitive, secular interference and wrong use of any kind. We call for, among other things, a system of law that acknowledges that the Wisdom-Teaching of the Way of Adidam, in all Its forms, is, because of Its sacred nature, protected by perpetual copyright.

We invite others who respect the Sacred to join with us in this call and in working toward its realization. And, even in the meantime, we claim that all copyrights to the Wisdom-Teaching of Avatar Adi Da and the other sacred Literature and recordings of the Way of Adidam are of perpetual duration.

We make this claim on behalf of The Da Love-Ananda Samrajya Pty Ltd, which, acting as trustee of The Da Love-Ananda Samrajya, is the holder of all such copyrights.

## Avatar Adi Da and the Sacred Treasures of Adidam

True Spiritual Masters have Realized Real God (to one degree or another), and, therefore, they bring great Blessing and introduce Divine Possibility to the world. Such Adept-Realizers Accomplish universal Blessing Work that benefits everything and everyone. They also Work very specifically and intentionally with individuals who approach them as their devotees, and with those places where they reside and to which they Direct their specific Regard for the sake of perpetual Spiritual Empowerment. This was understood in traditional Spiritual cultures, and, therefore, those cultures found ways to honor Adept-Realizers by providing circumstances for them where they were free to do their Spiritual Work without obstruction or interference.

Those who value Avatar Adi Da's Realization and Service have always endeavored to appropriately honor Him in this traditional way by providing a circumstance where He is completely Free to do His Divine Work. Since 1983, He has resided principally on the island of Naitauba, Fiji, also known as Adidam Samrajashram. This island has been set aside by Avatar Adi Da's devotees worldwide as a Place for Him to do His universal Blessing Work for the sake of everyone, as well as His specific Work with those who pilgrimage to Adidam Samrajashram to receive the special Blessing of coming into His physical Company.

Avatar Adi Da is a legal renunciate. He owns nothing and He has no secular or religious institutional function. He Functions only in Freedom. He, and the other members of the Ruchira Sannyasin Order, the senior renunciate order of Adidam, are provided for by The Da Love-Ananda Samrajya, which also provides for Adidam Samrajashram altogether and ensures the permanent integrity of Avatar Adi Da's Wisdom-Teaching, both in its archival and in its published forms. The Da Love-Ananda Samrajya, which functions only in Fiji, exists exclusively to provide for these Sacred Treasures of Adidam.

Outside Fiji, the institution which has developed in response to Avatar Adi Da's Wisdom-Teaching and universal Blessing is known as "The Eleutherian Pan-Communion of Adidam". This formal organization is active worldwide in making Avatar Adi Da's Wisdom-Teaching available to all, in offering guidance to all who are moved to respond to His Offering, and in providing for the other Sacred Treasures of Adidam, including the Mountain Of Attention Sanctuary and Tat Sundaram (in California) and Love-Ananda Mahal (in Hawaii). In addition to the central corporate entity known as The Eleutherian Pan-Communion of Adidam, which is based in California, there are numerous regional entities which serve congregations of Avatar Adi Da's devotees in various places throughout the world.

Practitioners of Adidam worldwide have also established numerous community organizations, through which they provide for many of their common and cooperative community needs, including those relating to housing, food, businesses, medical care, schools, and death and dying. By attending to these and all other ordinary human concerns and affairs via self-transcending cooperation and mutual effort, Avatar Adi Da's devotees constantly free their energy and attention, both personally and collectively, for practice of the Way of Adidam and for service to Avatar Adi Da Samraj, to Adidam Samrajashram, to the other Sacred Treasures of Adidam, and to The Eleutherian Pan-Communion of Adidam.

All of the organizations that have evolved in response to Avatar Adi Da Samraj and His Offering are legally separate from one another, and each has its own purpose and function. Avatar Adi Da neither directs, nor bears responsibility for, the activities of these organizations. Again, He Functions only in Freedom. These organizations represent the collective intention of practitioners of Adidam worldwide not only to provide for the Sacred Treasures of Adidam, but also to make Avatar Adi Da's Offering of the Way of Adidam universally available to all.

# INDEX

Note: Page numbers for **definitions** of terms are **in bold**. "ff" means "and following pages".

## A

## D

## T

## Y

## About the Author

Carolyn Lee was born in Sydney, Australia, in 1948, and received her Ph.D. in musicology from London University in 1981. She became a devotee of Avatar Adi Da Samraj in 1985, and has served for over 10 years as a writer and editor for the Dawn Horse Press (the publishing division of Adidam). Currently, she lives as a formal renunciate serving Avatar Adi Da Samraj in His Life of Hermitage-Retreat.

# *How You Can Respond To Avatar Adi Da Samraj*

■ **Contact us to sign up for one of our classes, correspondence courses, seminars, events, or retreats—or to find the regional center nearest you.**

**AMERICAS**
12040 N. Seigler Rd.
Middletown, CA
95461 USA
(707) 928-4936

**PACIFIC-ASIA**
12 Seibel Road
Henderson
Auckland 1008
New Zealand
64-9-838-9114

**AUSTRALIA**
P.O. Box 460
Roseville,
NSW 2069
Australia
61-2-9419-7563

**EUROPE-AFRICA**
Annendaalderweg 10
6105 AT Maria Hoop
The Netherlands
31 (0)20 468 1442

**THE UNITED KINGDOM**
P.O. Box 20013
London, England
NW2 1ZA
0181-7317550

**E-MAIL:** correspondence@adidam.org

■ **Order more books by and about Avatar Adi Da Samraj.**
(877) 770-0772 (from within North America)
(707) 928-6653 (from outside North America)
order on-line: http://www.adidam.com

■ **Visit the Adidam website: http://www.adidam.org**

- See photographs of Avatar Adi Da Samraj.
- Hear audio-clips of Him Speaking.
- Read His Writings and Stories of His Divine Work.
- Find a complete listing of all our regional centers and mission groups worldwide.